# Texts and Studies in Ancient Judaism

## Texte und Studien zum Antiken Judentum

Edited by

Peter Schäfer (Princeton, NJ)
Annette Y. Reed (Philadelphia, PA)
Seth Schwartz (New York, NY)
Azzan Yadin (New Brunswick, NJ)

123

# Antiquity in Antiquity

## Jewish and Christian Pasts in the Greco-Roman World

Edited by

Gregg Gardner and Kevin L. Osterloh

Mohr Siebeck

*Gregg Gardner*, born 1976; MA in History of the Jewish People from the Hebrew University of Jerusalem, and MA in Religion from Princeton University; is finishing a doctorate in Religion at Princeton University.

*Kevin L. Osterloh*, born 1969, is an Assistant Professor of Ancient History at Miami University.



ISBN 978-3-16-149411-6
ISSN 0721-8753 (Texts and Studies in Ancient Judaism)

Die Deutsche Nationalbibliothek lists this publication in the Deutsche Nationalbibliographie; detailed bibliographic data is available in the Internet at *http://dnb.d-nb.de.*



The book was printed by Gulde-Druck in Tübingen on non-aging paper and bound by Buchbinderei Spinner in Ottersweier.

Printed in Germany.

# Preface

From January 22–24, 2006, the editors of this volume together with Peter Schäfer held a colloquium entitled "Antiquity in Antiquity: Jewish and Christian Pasts in the Greco-Roman World" at Princeton University. The papers explored how collective memory and group history played roles in identity formation, political propaganda, social relations, artistic expression, religious belief and practice, and the establishment of official corpora of ancestral traditions for Jews, Christians, and their pagan neighbors in the ancient Mediterranean and Near Eastern world from the second century B.C.E. to the seventh century C.E. In short, the participants examined how people living in antiquity viewed their *own* antiquity. The contributions collected in this volume stem from the colloquium presentations. All abbreviations are according to Patrick H. Alexander, et. al. (eds.), *The SBL Handbook of Style: For Ancient Near Eastern, Biblical, and Early Christian Studies* (Peabody, Mass.: Hendrickson, 1999).

The *Antiquity in Antiquity* colloquium was sponsored by Princeton University's Dean of the Graduate School, the Department of Religion, and the Program in Judaic Studies. We would like to thank Marcie Citron, Lorraine Fuhrmann, and Baru Saul for making the conference a reality, as well as Eric Gregory, Martha Himmelfarb, Adam Jackson, Lance Jenott, Daniel L. Schwartz, and Holger M. Zellentin for serving as session chairs. We would also like to thank our predecessors in the late antique religions conference-publication projects, Adam H. Becker, Ra'anan S. Boustan, Eduard Iricinschi, Annette Yoshiko Reed, and Holger M. Zellentin, all of whom provided invaluable help along the way. At Mohr Siebeck, Ilse König and Henning Ziebritzki guided this volume to its completion. We would also like to thank Carey A. Brown, Laura G. Fisher, Rena Lauer, and Paul Westermeyer for their support. We owe a special debt of gratitude to Peter Schäfer, whose direction and confidence in us made this project possible. This book is dedicated with love to our families, the Browns, Gardners, and Osterlohs.

September 14, 2008
14th of Elul 5768

Gregg Gardner
*Princeton University*

Kevin L. Osterloh
*Miami University*

# Table of Contents

# The Significance of Antiquity in Antiquity

## An Introduction

GREGG GARDNER and KEVIN L. OSTERLOH

## I. The Nature of This Volume

Societies share a need to enshrine the present within the legitimating realm of the past.[1] This necessity leads successive generations to reshape "yesterday" – their received traditions, beliefs and customs – into line with their perceptions of "today" – contemporary reality. Indeed, the establishment and proper interpretation of tradition and "collective memory" was as important in the ancient world as it is in modernity.[2] In common with twenty-first century moderns and the many generations in between, the

---

[1] We would like to thank Wietse de Boer, Harriet Flower, Adam Gregerman, Martha Himmelfarb, Daniel Prior, and Peter Schäfer for their helpful feedback on this essay.

[2] In his posthumous *La mémoire collective* (1950), the sociologist Maurice Halbwachs (1877–1945) helped establish the socially constructed nature of "collective memory" while dispelling the notion of its separate existence as a quasi-metaphysical "group mind." Collective memory indicates, rather, the way socially embedded individuals recall and recreate the symbolic package – e.g. the sets of memories inscribed in monuments and literature – which evokes "the group." In his earlier *La topographie légendaire des évangiles en terre sainte*: *Etude de mémoire collective* (1941), Halbwachs emphasizes the outcome of perpetual recall and recreation in the present, by demonstrating how each generation reinvests the collective past with new symbolic value. This insight has been labeled by some as the "presentist" approach, an emphasis on rupture over continuity, which can lead to the "presentist flaw" – all is rupture and change, there is no continuity with the past. In this view, present historical reconstructions do not represent plausible pictures of the past, but only images of present concerns; the rupture with the past and its meaning is total (see Lewis A. Coser, "Introduction: Maurice Halbwachs 1877–1945," in Maurice Halbwachs, *On Collective Memory* [ed., trans., and introduced by L. A. Coser; Chicago: University of Chicago Press, 1992], 1–34). However, as Amos Funkenstein notes (*Perceptions of Jewish History* [Berkeley: University of California Press, 1993], 10–24; see also below), it is a mistake to associate Halbwachs entirely with the "presentist" view, as Halbwachs holds that modern "objective" scholars are indeed capable of reconstructing distinct periods of the ancient past (e.g. Halbwachs' reconstruction of the Holy Land according to the Gospels in *La topographie légendaire*), even while our ancient objects of inquiry apparently were not!

ancients were often compelled to demonstrate continuity with – and the discontinuity of rivals from – a shared past through an ongoing interpretation of communal tradition.

The need for perceived continuity serves many purposes, such as the promotion of communal prestige and an individual sense of self. Down through the ages, established group histories and collective memories have continued to play decisive roles in the processes of communal identity construction, political advancement, religious legitimization and the enhancement of social status. These objectives are realized when elite powerbrokers and shapers of public imagination inscribe their own status and that of their perceived ancestors – i.e. their collective identity – into the symbolic literary and material package that is presented as "collective memory".[3] Of course, "elite society" is never monolithic. Competing claims to status, views of the past, collective memories, and accepted traditions often survive from the same time and place. Whether or not we are tuned into the nature of the competition, the past, *per se*, is a contested legacy for us all.

Ancient efforts to retrieve and reinterpret the past have left an indelible mark on the literary and material record of the Greco-Roman world. Such historical artifacts enable contemporary scholars of the ancient Mediterranean and Near East to study these reconstructions of the even more distant past. Indeed, the study of collective memory and identity in the ancient world has gained increasing prominence in scholarly circles in recent years.[4] Yet, the use of antiquity by the ancient peoples themselves is a

---

[3] In this sense, "collective memory" is shorthand for "the perpetually reinvented traditional view of the past." Funkenstein offers a helpful model for understanding the individual recall, and thus reinvention, of "collective memory" by reusing Ferdinand de Saussure's notion of *langue* (language) and *parole* (speech). *Langue* equals the symbolic package that evokes "the group", e.g. "signs, symbols, and practices: memorial dates, names of places, monuments and victory arches, museums and texts, customs and manners, stereotype images (incorporated, for instance, in manners of expression), and even language itself (in de Saussure's terms)." *Parole*, on the other hand, indicates the speech act of the individual as s/he is acted upon by inherited *langue*, and in turn acts upon *langue* through the reinvestment of contemporary meaning into inherited symbols, i.e. the reinvention of communal memory, tradition and identity, etc. Funkenstein relates *langue* to the biblical Hebrew terms *zekher/zikaron* ("memory") and *parole* to the verb *zakhar* ("memory as a mental act"), in order to show that this concept of collective memory existed already in proto-theory in ancient Israel. The imperative *zakhor* was a biblical call "to remember" the collective past, which in its perpetual recall by historically embedded individuals was consequently reinvented, as biblical and post-biblical intertextual references show. See Funkenstein, *Perceptions of Jewish History*, 6–10.

[4] For example, on ancient Jewish society and Judaism see Shaye J. D. Cohen, *The Beginnings of Jewishness: Boundaries, Varieties, Uncertainties* (Berkeley: University of

broad topic that could conceivably cover many different aspects of the entire panoply of our ancient objects' already ancient legacy. So what do we mean to convey by *Antiquity in Antiquity*?

First, to which period(s) of antiquity, and to which specific places and peoples are we referring by the second part of the phrase *in Antiquity*? The answer is somewhat arbitrary, but nonetheless succinct. The timeframe, geographic *loci*, and social exemplars examined in this volume are restricted by the intellectual interests of its editors and contributors. Nearly all of the authors herein deal with aspects of Jewish and Christian communal history within the greater "pagan," or polytheistic, Greco-Roman world. They address the period immediately before the consolidation of the Roman Empire in the Mediterranean basin, through the years of the Empire's height, and finally the period of the decline of western Roman political power and the reconsolidation of Rome in the East, also known as the early Byzantine period. In other words, the studies in this volume cover slightly less than 1000 years of ancient history, or c. 200 B.C.E.–c.700 C.E.

Second, to what are we referring in the first half of the phrase, i.e. that which was already considered *Antiquity*, or ancient, *in Antiquity*? Generally speaking, our goal is to address the particular set of relationships which the ancient objects of our inquiries cultivated with their own past(s). This raises yet another question: What is distinctive about the approach of our ancient objects toward their own past(s) that makes its study relevant to the contemporary world? Indeed, many periods of ancient, medieval and modern history are replete with accounts of individuals, families, communities, and (later) nations that reinvent their past in the process of reinventing themselves. Furthermore, many themes of this volume – e.g. the nature of tradition, contested legacies, socially constructed identities and memories – are applicable to the study of any human society, ancient, medieval or modern, regardless of geography. But relevance is gained from similarity as well as difference. Thus, the ubiquity of these issues across space and time can only add to the present value of this volume, as it grants our

---

California Press, 1999), and David Goodblatt, *Elements of Ancient Jewish Nationalism* (New York: Cambridge University Press, 2006); on ancient Greece and Rome see Simon Goldhill, ed., *Being Greek Under Rome*: *Cultural Identity, The Second Sophistic and the Development of Empire* (Cambridge, U.K.: Cambridge University Press, 2001), and Emma Dench, *Romulus' Asylum: Roman Identities from the Age of Alexander to the Age of Hadrian* (Oxford: Oxford University Press, 2005); and, on early Christians and Christianity, see Denise Kimber Buell, *Why This New Race*: *Ethnic Reasoning in Early Christianity* (New York: Columbia University Press, 2005), and Aaron P. Johnson, *Ethnicity and Argument in Eusebius' Praeparatio Evangelica* (Oxford: Oxford University Press, 2006).

ancient objects of inquiry contemporary, twenty-first century relevance. The ancients, in many ways, were not so different from ourselves.

On the other hand, the ancients do exhibit a certain approach to their own past that, while not entirely unique to them, does mark them as particularly interesting objects for contemporary reflection. In short, what the term *Antiquity in Antiquity* conveys most succinctly is an ongoing preoccupation with the reinterpretation of the past by our ancient objects themselves who are distinguished by an emphatically classicizing stance with respect to their own antiquity.[5] Their communal identity, memory, and tradition is often viewed as the continuation of an earlier glorious age, upon which they perpetually focused as the lens through which they understood themselves. This volume of articles, appropriately titled *Antiquity in Antiquity*, seeks in turn to use ancient literary and material artifacts for the twenty-first century reconstruction of the social history of three successive classicizing ages. These sequential epochs include the Hellenistic/Second Temple period, the Greco-Roman/Imperial period, and the Late Antique/Byzantine period,[6] during which the potential inherited legacy is perpetually augmented by syncretizing new traditions from old sources,

[5] Seth Schwartz, "Language, Power and Identity in Ancient Palestine," *Past and Present* 148 (1995): 3–47, speaks of the literary classicism of such Judean works as Jubilees, Ben Sira, and the Temple Scroll, which are the product of "the tendency to emulate a more or less discrete body of writing which has come to be thought uniquely valuable and significant. The self-consciousness which classicism implies is, in fact, a novel and defining characteristic of Judaean literature from the third century B.C.E. onwards," (ibid., 30). Schwartz offers a view of a classicizing process which is primarily an act of imitation, while holding that the "detailed study, explication and commentary" on the ancient biblical corpus, i.e. its creative expansion, is best described as "scholasticism" (ibid., 31). For the purposes of the present essay, we mean to identify all such acts of self-reflection – imitation, creative expansion, reinvention, etc. – that take the inherited past into account as classicizing acts, thus we refer to the periods in question as "classicizing ages."

[6] We recognize that periodization is an exercise in the arbitrary. This is captured, for instance, in the Hellenistic/Second Temple period, since the Hellenistic Period is often viewed as ending in 31 B.C.E (the battle of Actium), while the Second Temple Period does not end till a century later in 70 C.E. In the subsection headings that divide this volume, we have altered this (due to the range of our contributions) to the Late Hellenistic-Early Imperial Period. Our point is not that each period is distinctly unique, but rather that each designated period represents a particular, sequential stage of ancient societies dealing with their own antiquity. As each period segues into the next (i.e. there is no "real" division between them) the antiquity in play for the ancient objects of our inquiry is continually compounded. At the same time, as a number of the contributions demonstrate, the interconnection between originally distinct antiquities – Jewish, Greco-Roman/Pagan, and Christian – often becomes stronger and deeper.

while the creative intellectual impulse remains focused on reinterpreting this "new" past.

It remains then to distinguish the particular approaches of our twenty-first century contributors. Generally speaking, the studies contained in this volume emphasize the analysis of communal over individual history, with implications primarily for affairs in the temporal domain.[7] Of major importance to this analysis is the process of communal identity construction (and/or reinvention) within the context of contested legacies, by which members of elite groups seek to form discursive group-border lines and associated claims of difference.[8] Equally important is the nature of tradition, and collective memory as inscribed in both literature and material remains, and as (re)interpreted by members of rival elite groups. Such reinterpretations are undertaken so as to remake individual and social-group identity in order to strengthen discursive borders between in-group and out-group and to establish group continuity with (and the discontinuity of rival groups from) the common ancestral legacy.[9]

Nearly all of the social groups examined in this volume define themselves and/or rival groups in light of a perceived set of shared pasts, or

---

[7] While the identity claims of the social groups analyzed in this volume occasionally impinge upon their, and their rivals', perceived standing in the heavenly realm, this volume's primary foci are the reinvented traditions, memories, and identities that affected our ancient objects of inquiry in the temporal domain. Of course, ancient Near Eastern and Mediterranean societies were also greatly concerned with the implications of earthly actions on heavenly reality and vice versa, and the indelible interconnection between the divine and the temporal, see Ra'anan S. Boustan and Annette Yoshiko Reed, eds., *Heavenly Realms and Earthly Realities in Late Antique Religions* (Cambridge, U.K.: Cambridge University Press, 2004).

[8] Discursive boundary formation, i.e. the declared emphasis on Insider versus Outsider, serves to obfuscate the actual complexity of social interactions which are, ironically, central to the very same processes of identity formation. On digital (a dichotomous, "us versus them", 1:1 approach) and analogue (identity expressed as an accepted range of individual and communal practices) paradigms of identity formation in ancient Greece, see Jonathan M. Hall, *Hellenicity: Between Ethnicity and Culture* (Chicago: University of Chicago Press, 2002), 179, 220–26. On the discourse of boundary formation between ancient Judaism and Christianity, see Adam H. Becker and Annette Yoshiko Reed, eds., *The Ways that Never Parted: Jews and Christians in Late Antiquity and the Early Middle Ages* (Texts and Studies in Ancient Judaism 95; Tübingen: Mohr Siebeck, 2003; repr. Minneapolis: Fortress Press, 2007).

[9] For the rivalry between sects of ancient Jews, Christians, Pagans and the many groups in between these socially constructed, discursive categories, and the concurrent application of "heresy, heresies, heretical" to perceived outsiders and its impact on questions of ancient identity, see Eduard Iricinschi and Holger M. Zellentin, eds., *Heresy and Identity in Late Antiquity* (Texts and Studies in Ancient Judaism 119; Tübingen: Mohr Siebeck, 2008).

legacies, of ancient Greece, early Rome, or the ancient Near Eastern world of ancient Israel, Egypt, Assyria and Babylonia. Indeed, the further along the timeline we move – from the Hellenistic to the Byzantine period – the more the trajectories of initially distinct shared pasts are perceived as a single Greco-Roman-Jewish/Biblical past. It is by reinterpreting this particular conglomerate past that certain Late Antique groups as well as some of our own twenty-first century contemporaries define themselves. In fact, the modern (or at least modern scholarly) obsession with reconstructing the ancient past began with our ancient objects of inquiry. As scholars have observed, while the ancients tended to blur the separate contexts for historical *data*, they were nonetheless imbued with a sense of historical consciousness.[10] That is, many of the ancients acknowledged and assiduously sought out the sources of their inherited legacy – if perhaps only to control

[10] See Peter Schäfer, "Zur Geschichtsauffassung des rabbinischen Judentums," *Journal for the Study of* Judaism 6 (1975): 167–88; repr. in *Studien zur Geschichte und Theologie des rabbinischen Judentums* (ed. P. Schäfer; Arbeiten zur Geschichte des antiken Judentums und des Urchristentums 15; Leiden: Brill, 1978), 23–44. See also Funkenstein, *Perceptions of Jewish History*, where he takes issue with both Halbwachs' view of premoderns' supposedly uncritical reception of the past before the Enlightenment and the founding of the modern academy. In particular, Funkenstein challenges Yosef Hayim Yerushalmi, who (in his *Zakhor*: *Jewish History and Jewish Memory* [Seattle: University of Washington Press, 1982]) reapplies Halbwachs' theory to the whole of the Jewish past from the first-century C.E. – the time of the last ancient Jewish historiographer, Josephus – until the rise of nineteenth-century *Wissenschaft des Judentums*. Funkenstein notes, "Yerushalmi, like Halbwachs before him, inevitably polarizes the contrast between historical narrative and "collective memory"; while modern scholars compose "objective" historiography, premoderns were supposedly caught up merely in a perpetual cycle of unreflective modifications of communal memory over time," (Funkenstein, *Perceptions of Jewish History*, 10–11).

Funkenstein (ibid., 10–21) confronts this view as follows. First, while allowing that modern academics often apply self-consciously reflective methods to their studies of the past, he questions their "objectivity" – since, however self-aware they may be, they are still historically embedded individuals whose historiographic products also answer present needs. Second, he claims that even though the ancients, in this case the ancient Jewish objects of his inquiry, did not apply modern historical-critical methods to their examination of the past, they still approached their own past in a reflective manner. Indeed, they often occupied a taxonomic middle ground between the modern academic posture and the Halbwachs-Yerushalmi foil position: viz. un-selfconscious re-creators of tradition. As such, they often took part in self-reflective processes of creative reinvention of communal memory, tradition, and identity. More precisely, they were intimately aware of the common sources of their communal past, and were often ready to offer up novel reinterpretations of this past in order to defend contested, present interests and points of view. In other words, they possessed an "historical consciousness" (Funkenstein's taxonomic middle ground).

its interpretation and govern the application of its "new" meaning in the present.

## II. Three Classicizing Ages: Contextualizing the Contributions

The Hellenistic Age (323–31 B.C.E.), ushered in by the conquests of Alexander the Great and the wars of the Diadochi, marks the immediate prehistory and beginnings of the first classicizing period of this volume: the Late Hellenistic to the early Imperial period (c. 200 B.C.E.–100 C.E.). The earlier glorious time of fifth-century Hellas during the Persian Wars and subsequent Athenian *Pentakontaetia*, and the even earlier Homeric heroic period, were idealized in the Hellenistic Age, as copyists and commentators collated the classical Greek heritage in centers of learning at Alexandria, Athens, Pergamum, and elsewhere.[11]

The coming of the Hellenistic Age marks a major turning point in the Second Temple period of Jewish History (539 B.C.E.–70 C.E.). Long before Alexander's conquests, the exiles of Judah had reestablished themselves and rebuilt their Temple in Jerusalem. As the self-proclaimed "remnant" of biblical Israel,[12] they had also begun to edit and augment their ancient literary and cultural heritage. The cultural interaction between the Jewish and Hellenic worlds – both already fixated on the past – amplified

[11] Arrian (*Anabasis* 1.11–12) tells how, before crossing the Hellespont, Alexander sacrificed upon the tomb of Protesilaus (the first of Agamemnon's expedition to reach Asia). After crossing the Hellespont, he set out directly for Troy (Ilium) and once there sacrificed to Athena. Plutarch adds (*Life of Alexander* 15.4–5) that, while at Troy, Alexander anointed the tombstone of Achilles, ran a race naked with his companions while anointed with oil in honor of the hero, and then crowned the tombstone with garlands. There he declared Achilles blessed, for in life he had had a faithful friend (Patroclus), and in death a great herald of his fame (Homer). Also, after the victorious Battle of Granicus in 334, Plutarch writes (*Life of Alexander*, 16.8) that Alexander sent 300 Persian shields (Arrian: 300 suits of armor, *Anabasis* 1.17) to the Athenians, an act surely meant to gain their good graces by commemorating both their symbolic leading role in the present "panhellenic campaign" against Persia, and their historic defense of Hellas against the Persians 150 years before. On the ancient library of Alexandria and other libraries of the Greco-Roman world, see Roy Macleod, ed., *The Library of Alexandria: Centre of Learning in the Ancient World* (New York: I. B. Tauris, 2000); and Lionel Casson, *Libraries in the Ancient World* (New Haven: Yale University Press, 2001).

[12] On Judeans as the "remnant" of biblical Israel, see Isaiah 46:3 – כל-שארית בית ישראל, and centuries later the Damascus Document 3.12–13 which labels the sectarians – ובמחזיקים במצות אל אשר נותרו מהם הקים אל את בריתו לישראל עד עולם "Those who hold fast to the commandments of God, who remained from them (i.e. all previous Israelite generations), with whom God made firm his Covenant with Israel forever."

this classicizing sensibility, due to the ensuing context of cultural competition between various Jewish groups and between Jews and non-Jews within the broader Hellenistic world.

With stereotypical *interpretatio Graeca*, Hecataeus of Abdera in the decades after Alexander's death bequeathed Judeans an honorable foundation under their enlightened lawgiver Moses, and a valorous and principled way of life. Judeans, in Hecataeus' words, maintained a disciplined and egalitarian lifestyle; they were a Near Eastern version of the Spartans. His contemporary Clearchus of Soli accorded Judeans a noble genealogy: descent from philosophers of India. According to this same Clearchus, Aristotle's Judean interlocutor not only spoke Greek, but was indeed a Greek himself in *psychê*.[13]

The Hellenistic-Jewish fragments found in Eusebius' *Praeparatio Evangelica* (via Polyhistor) illustrate this new creative tension from the Jewish perspective, where the ancient past is recreated to benefit the prestige of contemporary Jewish society in its new Hellenistic setting, most likely Alexandria of Egypt. Ezekiel the Tragedian's second-century B.C.E. *Exagoge* retells the Exodus as a Greek tragedy, in which the hubris of Pharaoh and the Egyptians is punished by the Jewish deity who is thus linked to Greek ideas of Fortune, Fate, and Nemesis. The work is perfuse with Greek tragedy's stereotypical dramatic reversal, benefiting none other than Moses and the Israelites.[14] Likewise, in the history of Artapanus, the Jewish ancestors Abraham, Joseph, and Moses are re-imagined as culture-heroes who bequeath the benefits of civilization to the Egyptians, and correlative riches of cultural capital to the Jews living among the second-century B.C.E. descendants of their Egyptian beneficiaries. Indeed, as Holger Zellentin's article in this volume, "The End of Jewish Egypt: Artapanus and the Second Exodus," shows, such depictions of Judean ancestral heroes, especially Joseph as vizier and Moses as military commander, would have appealed to the Jewish military elite of Egypt, in particular those associated with the Oniad cleruchy at Leontopolis.

---

[13] For Clearchus of Soli's *On Sleep*, see Josephus, *Contra Apionem* 1.176–82. Even leaving aside the potentially problematic citations of Hecataeus in Josephus (*Contra Apionem* 1.183–204), we are still left with Hecataeus' quite complimentary depiction of the Judeans (however inaccurate) from the fragments (of his *Aegyptiaca*?) found in Diodorus Siculus (40.3). On the skepticism of modern scholars regarding the authenticity of the Hecataeus fragments in Josephus, Bickerman (*The Jews in the Greek Age* [Cambridge, Mass.: Harvard University Press, 1988], 18) astutely remarks, "Nobody...has ever explained why a Greek author who admired Egyptian wisdom could not have admired Jewish wisdom as well."

[14] See the excellent treatment by Erich S. Gruen, *Heritage and Hellenism: The Reinvention of Jewish Tradition* (Berkeley: University of California Press, 1998), 128–35.

Circumstances in Hellenistic Egypt, of course, could turn against the Jews. It is just such a context – the anti-Jewish agitation of Ptolemy VIII in 118 B.C.E. – where Zellentin locates Artapanus' account which constitutes, *inter alia*, a renewed call for the Jews to flee Egypt. Long before, Greek elites had already come to know of native Egyptian animosity toward the Jews, which Ptolemy VIII might easily call upon in pursuit of his own policies. In the first decades of Macedonian rule, when Hecataeus and Clearchus composed their generous albeit Greco-centric accounts, the Egyptian hellenophile Manetho composed his "counter history" of the Jewish people. Fragments of this account in Josephus' later *Contra Apionem* confirm Amos Funkenstein's sense of the concept: Manetho's "counter history" of the Jewish people inverts the biblical account of the Exodus in an explicit attempt to discredit the Jews, by delegitimizing their origins and association with ancient, and thus also present-day (i.e. early third century B.C.E.) Egypt.[15]

In Hellenistic-period Palestine, we witness Judeans before and after the Hasmonean rebellion engaged in ongoing discourse with their ancient Israelite past within a broader Hellenistic context. Ben Sira, c. 180 B.C.E., locates the source of Wisdom in the Law of the Most High God (Sir 24:23). But, when he – as a devotee of the Law – describes the dialectical process of attaining Wisdom, the reader is told to seek it through the insights of all the ancients, regardless of origin. That is, to be a student of the Law, or Torah, and truly discern its meaning one must do as Ben-Sira did: serve among the great, appear before rulers, travel in foreign lands (of other *ethnê*), and learn the nature of good and evil among all humans (Sir 39:1–4).[16] Surely, it is a mistake to view Ben-Sira as an anti-Hellenistic reactionary[17] – a view predicated on an unrealistic, dichotomous view of

---

[15] Funkenstein applies the concept of "counter history" directly to Manetho among other scurrilous accounts of the other, such as the later medieval *Toledot Yeshu*; see *Perceptions of Jewish History*, 36–40.

[16] Πλὴν τοῦ ἐπιδιδόντος τὴν ψυχὴν αὐτοῦ καὶ διανοουμένου ἐν νόμῳ ὑψίστου, σοφίαν πάντων ἀρχαίων ἐκζητήσει...ἀνὰ μέσον μεγιστάνων ὑπηρετήσει καὶ ἔναντι ἡγουμένων ὀφθήσεται· ἐν γῇ ἀλλοτρίων ἐθνῶν διελεύσεται, ἀγαθὰ γὰρ καὶ κακὰ ἐν ἀνθρώποις ἐπείρασεν.

[17] See Victor Tcherikover, *Hellenistic Civilization and the Jews* (Philadelphia: Jewish Publication Society, 1959; repr. Peabody, Mass.: Hendrickson, 1999), 142–51: "Ben Sira opposes the spirit of free Hellenism" (143); and "The new spirit [of Hellenism] noticeable in Ben Sira crept into his book without the author's intending that it should" (149–50). While Martin Hengel (*Judaism and Hellenism*: *Studies in their Encounter in Palestine during the Early Hellenistic Period* [trans. J. Bowden; Philadelphia: Fortress Press, 1974]) provides a more thorough account of Ben Sira's reliance on common tenets of Hellenistic "philosophical" thought, he ultimately maintains Tcherikover's conclusions: "We must...assign him to that conservative, nationalist-Jewish movement...[later]

identity and the all too easy dismissal of such passages as these, which inundate his discourse on Wisdom, i.e. on the meaning of the Torah itself.[18]

From the first, the Hasmoneans followed a similar course. From the diplomacy of Judah, Jonathan, Simon, and John Hyrcanus I, to the depiction of the Judean community in 1 and 2 Maccabees, we witness the interactive process whereby Judean elites sought to remain loyal to ancestral tradition by redefining it within a broader Hellenistic culture. The decree of gratitude offered up by the Judeans in 1 Macc 14 follows the form and function of a common Hellenistic benefaction decree.[19] Since the last days of Judah Maccabee, the Judeans had gained the goodwill of new friends and allies – the Romans – who provided them with a successful model of socio-cultural interaction within the Hellenistic world worthy of emulation. Judea's successful diplomatic overtures with Sparta, Pergamum and Athens from the time of Jonathan to John Hyrcanus I cannot be adequately explained outside of a newly triangulated relationship between Judeans, Greeks, and Romans.[20]

Already by the early third century B.C.E., members of the Roman elite had begun to reinterpret the nature of their own collective identity and ancestral traditions (the *mos maiorum*) within a Hellenistic world. From the 160s B.C.E. onward, they continued to do so within the dynamic context of a city-state republic transitioning to imperial rule over this same

---

represented by the Hasmoneans," (153), a movement Hengel subsequently describes in the context of the "repudiation of Hellenism" (247–54).

[18] As far as we know, the link in Ben Sira between the consensus view that Wisdom, *per se*, is equal to Torah (lit. the Law of the Most High God), on the one hand (as based on Sir 24), and the insight, on the other hand, that Torah must then be equal to the Wisdom Ben Sira acquires from all mankind on his travels (as Sir 39 describes the proper pursuit of Wisdom) has not appeared elsewhere. And neither, as far as we know, has the correlative conclusion that what Ben Sira has thus produced in his book is in fact Torah, i.e. Wisdom which he has acquired, in part, on his journeys to the lands of non-Judean, *ethnê*. Yet, to assume otherwise is to ignore the plain meaning of Sir 39:1–4 as understood with Sir 24. In other words, Ben Sira links Wisdom directly with the Pentateuch in Sir 24, while the interpretive lens of these Laws (as well as the accompanying customs and stories of the collective Judean past) is the great stock of ancient Wisdom available at cultural centers throughout the Hellenistic-period Mediterranean and Near East.

[19] See Gregg Gardner, "Jewish Leadership and Hellenistic Civic Benefaction in the Second Century B.C.E.," *Journal of Biblical Literature* 126 (2007): 327–43.

[20] See Kevin Lee Osterloh, "Judea, Rome and the Hellenistic *Oikoumenê*: Emulation and the Reinvention of Communal Identity," in *Heresy and Identity in Late Antiquity* (ed. E. Iricinschi and H. M. Zellentin; Texts and Studies in Ancient Judaism 119; Tübingen: Mohr Siebeck, 2008), 168–206.

Greek-speaking *Oikoumenê*.[21] In Harriet Flower's "Remembering and Forgetting Temple Destruction: The Destruction of the Temple of Jupiter Optimus Maximus in 83 BC," she utilizes the various episodes of the Capitoline Temple's destruction by fire (83 B.C.E., 69 and 80 C.E.) and the building of three successive temples on the ashes of the previous sanctuaries to explore how Romans dealt with the strife which brought on the end of the Republic and the loss of ancestral values. For the Romans, she writes, "To rebuild the Temple was to rebuild society." Yet, she continues, "Those who remembered the destruction later were always aware of themselves as inhabiting another age, as survivors looking back after the Fall."

The destruction and repair of the Temple in Jerusalem possessed a similar hold on contemporaneous Jewish imagination. For the Hasmoneans, the cleansing of the Temple (25 Kislev, 164 B.C.E.) by Judah Maccabee and his men, marked a new age, celebrated by Hanukkah. This Judean spin on Hellenistic festivals of liberation, propagated at home and in the Diaspora – as the festal letters prefaced to 2 Maccabees show – incorporated Hasmonean glory within the celebration of the Temple's liberation by their hands.[22] Later, when Herod lavishly rebuilt this Temple on a grandiose scale, it was told that rain fell only at night so that the builders, protected from above, could speed their work to its completion – a day heralded as coinciding with Herod's accession.[23] For other Judeans, Hasmonean high-priesthood meant not redemption but defilement. The Qumran sectarians, led by Zadokite priests ousted by Hasmonean usurpers, responded by rebuilding the Temple within themselves, and elevating their daily life to a consummate level of sanctity. This Temple-restoration *in corpore communitatis* signaled a new age for their sect: "A New Covenant in the Land of Damascus"; just as it signaled the beginning of the End Time for all humanity.[24]

---

[21] Kevin Lee Osterloh, "Empire and the Reinvention of Collective Identity: The Rise of Roman Hegemony in a Hellenistic World," *Studies in Ethnicity and Nationalism, Special Issue*: *Nation and Empire* (2005): 103–25.

[22] See Jan Willem van Henten, "2 Maccabees as a History of Liberation," in *Jews and Gentiles in the Holy Land in the Days of the Second Temple, the Mishnah and the Talmud* (ed. M. Mor, et al.; Jerusalem: Yad Ben-Zvi, 2003), 63–86.

[23] King, Temple, God and People are thus united in Herod's self-aggrandizement as *Basileus Ioudaiôn*; see *Antiquitates Judaicae* 15.421–25; the tale of the cessation of rain in daytime appears also in the Bavli, *Ta'anit* 23a.

[24] See the introductory comments of Geza Vermes, *The Complete Dead Scrolls in English* (rev. ed.; London: Penguin Books, 2004), 1–90, and his notes on the Damascus Document, 127–45. In his comments on the literary corpus of the Qumran sect/Essenes (*Complete Dead Scrolls in English*, 24–25), Vermes emphasizes the classicizing nature of the age: "The laws and rules, hymns and other liturgical works as well as the Bible commentaries of the Qumran community...add substance and depth to the historical

The Romans brought an end to the Qumran sect in 68 C.E. and two years later to the Temple in Jerusalem, causing yet another rupture in Jewish time, another point of intense reflection, and communal reinvention.[25] While the authors of 4 Ezra and 2 Baruch dealt with this catastrophe by going back to the days of the first destruction in 586 B.C.E., the Judean historian Josephus – now a Roman citizen living in Rome – reflected on his involvement and that of his elite peers in the recent catastrophe. Steve Mason in "The Greeks and the Distant Past in Josephus's *Judaean War*," describes, among other issues, how Josephus draws upon images of proper elite leadership vis-à-vis the unruly masses among former and current Greek writers. Josephus remakes himself and Agrippa II into loyal Judean leaders who had sought to moderate the passions of the Judean mob destined to bring ruin upon themselves, their community, and the Temple.

All these attempts to selectively remember, forget, and reinterpret the past, explains Doron Mendels in his essay, "How Was Antiquity Treated in Societies with a Hellenistic Heritage? And Why Did the Rabbis Avoid Writing History?", leave us with a fragmented, disjointed picture of antiquity in antiquity. This view of the past, Mendels writes, is a product of the fact that the writing of "linear history" was the exception, not the rule. The past for the ancients was useful primarily for the present, and not as an object of study in its own right. Ancient historians employed a utilitarian editing process – e.g. Josephus' minimization of prior, successful Judean militancy (per Mason's description) – which led to further fragmentation of the past, by helping to create multiple versions of select, preserved events. This is true for all the classicizing ages of this volume, as we see upon moving from the Hellenistic-Early Imperial to the Greco-Roman period (c. 100–450 C.E.).

In the early third-century C.E. Mishnah, the rabbis, mesmerized by the temporal break of the Temple's destruction in 70 C.E., ironically mask their obsession through deafening silence. On the one hand, they pretend that it had not been destroyed at all. On the other, they write themselves into the pre-destruction narrative they preserved as part of their own communal reinvention. Tractate *Yoma* offers an example of the latter process; here we encounter an imbecile high-priest in the Temple on the Day of Atonement, and a class of sages (חכמים), the supposed early rabbis, who "naturally" instruct him in his duties, effectively running the show. Peter

---

period in which Jewish Christianity and rabbinic Judaism originated. They reveal one facet of the spiritual ferment at work among the various Palestinian religious parties at that time, a ferment which culminated in a thorough reexamination and reinterpretation of the fundamentals of the Jewish faith."

[25] Vermes, Complete Dead Sea Scrolls in English, 49–66.

Schäfer, in his essay "Rabbis and Priests, or: How to Do Away with the Glorious Past of the Sons of Aaron," demonstrates how rabbinic self-aggrandizement led to the *ex-post-facto* replacement of the priestly caste by the sages in the earlier Second Temple Age throughout the rabbinic corpus. An aspect best exemplified, explains Schäfer, by their foundation document, Mishnah *Avot* 1:1 – where the chain of transmission proceeds from Sinai to Moses, Joshua, Elders, Prophets, the Great Assembly, and on to the Sages. Here, the Rabbis are the rightful heirs of ancestral tradition, the legitimate interpreters of the Sinai revelation and the Covenant between God and Israel. The Aaronide priests are nowhere to be found.

The Temple's destruction in 70, and the later suppression of the Bar Kokhba Revolt in 135, are part of a set of decisive turning points for both subjects and rulers of Rome regarding the identity of the Empire as a coherent sociopolitical unit. In fact, it is not until the reign of Vespasian (69–79) that Romans reconciled themselves completely to the concept of absolute rule by an Emperor, the *Imperator* of the *lex de imperio Vespasiani*.[26] For the Flavians, the capture of the symbols of Judean Antiquity vindicated their rule over the empire, as proclaimed by *Judaea Capta* coinage, the Temple of Peace housing the Jerusalem Temple treasures, and the arch of Titus which immortalized the transference of Judean Antiquity to the imperial city.[27]

As the Senate in 69 C.E. looked back in *lex de imperio Vespasiani* to Augustus as precedent for the permanence of imperatorial rule, the emperor Hadrian (117–138) looked to the antiquity of Greece and Egypt[28] in

---

[26] Colin Wells, *The Roman Empire* (2d ed.; Cambridge, Mass.: Harvard University Press, 1992), 7: "only with the Emperor Vespasian...does *imperator*, whence 'emperor', become the usual title by which the emperor is known. ...although it is convenient to refer to Augustus and his immediate successors as 'emperor', it is, strictly speaking, anachronistic. Augustus preferred *princeps*, roughly equivalent to 'first citizen'." Wells (ibid., 41) adds, "Vespasian's coin types hark back to those of Augustus; we remember that the *lex de imperio Vespasiani* keeps referring to Augustus's powers as a suitable precedent for those conferred on Vespasian." While Wells correctly downplays the actual change in *de-facto* political reality (ibid., 158–59, "It is wrong to see in this law any new departure, nor is the Senate...asserting its own *auctoritas*"), as his earlier analysis makes plain, this *lex* does mark a significant conceptual turning point. For the prior Augustan Age is now officially enshrined as the touchstone for imperial rectitude, while the importance of the republican formulae – which Augustus once prized – is greatly diminished.

[27] See Wells, *Roman Empire*, 160; and, in this volume, Ra'anan S. Boustan, "The Spoils of the Jerusalem Temple at Rome and Constantinople: Jewish Counter-Geography in a Christianizing Empire," 327–72.

[28] Hadrian embraced these particular eastern cultures of his empire while disavowing another cultural product of the East: Judean custom and antiquity. At least, such is the implication of Hadrian's imperial policy before, during and after the Bar Kokhba Revolt

order to make sense of imperial unity under Rome. His villa at Tivoli functioned, in part, as a map of the Empire, housing an amalgam of symbols expressing a cultural unity. Here he built his own *Poicile*, recalling Athens' famous Painted Stoa, and three structures named after Athens' Lyceum, Academy, and Prytaneum respectively. A majestic pool was constructed on the grounds, likely labeled after the Egyptian Nile-Delta town of Canopus, and ringed by Athenian-style Caryatids, and representations of the Nile and the Egyptian divinities Isis and Ptah, among other statuary.[29] The villa is more than monumental bricabrac for the Empire's most famous tourist, it is the reflection of Hadrian's attempt to craft in his person and in his empire a unifying Greco-Romanness.

Hadrian's coins declare a *saeculum aureum* (a "golden age") a claim connected not only to *Pax Romana*, but also to cultural rebirth; imperial elites had woken up to the cultural fact of Empire and its Greco-Roman identity.[30] Hadrian's older contemporary Plutarch (46–120), whose life and

---

(132–135), e.g. the re-founding of Jerusalem as *Aelia Capitolina*, the establishment of a temple to Jupiter on the ruins of the Temple, outlawing any Jewish presence in the city, changing the name of the province of Iudaea to Syria Palaestina, and by apparently outlawing circumcision, etc. On the Bar Kokhba Revolt see Peter Schäfer, *Der Bar Kokhba-Aufstand: Studien zum zweiten jüdischen Krieg gegen Rom* (Texte und Studien zum antiken Judentum 1; Tübingen: J. C. B. Mohr, 1981). For a recent collection of scholarly articles on a variety of issues related to the revolt see Peter Schäfer, ed., *The Bar Kokhba War Reconsidered: New Perspectives on the Second Jewish Revolt Against Rome* (Texts and Studies in Ancient Judaism 100; Tübingen: Mohr Siebeck, 2003).

[29] Our primary source is the admittedly problematic *Historia Augusta* 26.5, where we read that Hadrian constructed the site in a manner that would allow him to inscribe upon it the names of the provinces and other famous places, such as those listed above, as well as the Vale of Tempe in Thessaly, and even Hades (*Tiburtam Villam mire exaedificavit, ita ut in ea et provinciarum et locorum celeberrima nomina inscriberet, velut Lyceum, Academian, Prytaneum, Canopum, Poicilen, Tempe vocaret. Et, ut nihil praetermitteret, etiam inferos finxit*). However, the remains of the site itself seem to bear out the veracity of the *HA*'s description; see William L. MacDonald and John A. Pinto, *Hadrian's Villa and Its Legacy* (New Haven: Yale University Press, 1995). While MacDonald and Pinto are skeptical of the common scholarly identification of the excavated pool with the Canopus of *HA* (*Hadrian's Villa and Its Legacy*, 108–11), their comments on the meaning of the discovered sculpture within the context of the excavated Villa are revealing: "The wide range of sculptural styles and subjects at the Villa…is rooted above all in the eclectic nature of High Empire culture, the result in turn of the Romans' well-developed historical consciousness, a condition indispensable to eclectic thought and preferences. In this sense the Villa is very much an empire creation, a place where non-Roman images mix handily with Roman ones, some of them, in architecture particularly, unseen elsewhere… Villa sculpture did not comprise a collection or a museum so much as it expressed the historical awareness of the times and thus much of the scaffolding of contemporary civilization and education" (ibid., 141).

[30] See Colin Wells, *Roman Empire*, 203–7.

work parallel the beginning of the classicizing Second Sophistic, is at the forefront of the creation of Greco-Romanness from the Hellenic side. Whatever distinctiveness he may have ascribed to Greek culture, the direct comparison between Greeks and Romans in his *Parallel Lives* points to a perceived cultural continuity between ancient Hellas and Rome that continued in his own time. Indeed, Plutarch himself attained both Roman citizenship and, under Hadrian, the office of procurator of Achaea, if only in a ceremonial capacity. Plutarch's deep interest in the Egyptian deities Osiris and Isis, coterminous with his ongoing role as High Priest at Delphi, expose the merging multiple realms of antiquity from which the Greco-Roman elite drew inspiration.[31]

The Greco-Roman elite, of course, included Christian intellectuals, such as the North African Tertullian (c. 160–225). From his *De Anima*, 30.3 we read:

> The World is every day better known, better cultivated and more civilized... Everywhere roads are traced, every district is known, every country opened to commerce. Smiling fields have invaded the forests, flocks and herds have routed the wild beasts, the very sands are sown, the rocks are broken up, the marshes drained...Wherever there is a trace of life, there are houses, human habitations and well-ordered governments.[32]

Here we find a fitting description of Hadrian's *saeculum aureum* extended into the days of the Severids. Yet this idyllic depiction stems from an advocate of Christian martyrdom before Roman authority who exhorts potential martyrs to emulate the discipline and bravery of famous ancient Roman, Greek, and even Carthaginian heroes.[33] Again, Tertullian asks

---

[31] On Plutarch's public life and literary career see, R. H. Barrow, *Plutarch and His Times* (Bloomington: Indiana University Press, 1967); C. P. Jones, *Plutarch and Rome* (Oxford: Clarendon Press, 1971); D. A. Russell, *Plutarch* (London: Duckworth, 1973); and also the more recent introduction by Robert Lamberton, *Plutarch* (New Haven: Yale University Press, 2001). On aspects of ancient history and Plutarch's *Parallel Lives*, see Philip A. Stadter, ed., *Plutarch and the Historical Tradition* (London: Routledge, 1992); and Christopher Pelling, *Plutarch and History* (London: Classical Press of Wales, 2002).

[32] The translation is by Colin Wells, Roman Empire, 220; (Latin: *Certe quidem ipse orbis in promptu est cultior de die et instructior pristino. Omnia iam pervia, omnia nota, omnia negotiosa, solitudines famosas retro fundi amoenissimi obliteraverunt, silvas arva domuerunt, feras pecora fugaverunt, arenae seruntur, saxa panguntur, paludes eliquantur, tantae urbes iam quantae non casae quondam. Iam nec insulae horrent nec scopuli terrent; ubique domus, ubique populus, ubique respublica, ubique vita*).

[33] See in particular Tertullian's *Ad Martyras* 4, and *De Fuga in Persecutione*; for parallel lists of ancient heroes see his *Ad Nationes* 1.18, and *Apologeticum* 50. On Tertullian and the Roman social context for early Christian martyrdom, see in particular Timothy D. Barnes, *Tertullian: A Historical and Literary Study* (Oxford: Clarendon Press, 1971), and G. W. Bowersock, *Martyrdom and Rome* (Cambridge, U.K.: Cambridge

"What has Athens to do with Jerusalem?"[34] Such binaries serve to demarcate communal boundaries while obscuring the complexity of Tertullian's social context and personality. A master of the rhetorical and literary crafts of the Second Sophistic, Tertullian sought not to destroy but co-opt the Greco-Roman past and wed it to his Christian "Jerusalem" – the beneficiary of Judaism's ancient heritage, from which contemporary Jews were conveniently excluded. Tertullian's writings abound with proof-texts and encouraging exempla from Greco-Roman and Jewish antiquity, a process of appropriation and reinvention born out of a necessity for proximity with the vitality of antiquity, which makes his move to Montanism understandable.[35]

The Montanist movement, with its call to return to the immediacy of direct revelation,[36] anticipates the enshrinement of a new period of antiquity, namely the Apostolic Age of the first disciples who had known Jesus in the flesh. Annette Yoshiko Reed in her essay, "'Jewish Christianity' as Counterhistory? The Apostolic Past in Eusebius' *Ecclesiastical History* and the Pseudo-Clementine *Homilies*," demonstrates the responsibility of Eusebius of Caesarea (263–339) for this novel periodization in his early fourth-century *Ecclesiastical History*. In her essay she presents an insightful analysis of the "Jewish Christianity" of the contemporaneous Pseudo-Clementine *Homilies* as a "counter history" of Christian communal identity and apostolic succession, which was constructed in direct competition with Eusebius' view of a Christian Church divorced from its moribund Jewish roots.

For Eusebius, all realms of antiquity in antiquity studied in this volume were grist for the exegetical mill. He turned to Josephus and Philo to refute Judaism, domesticating them into witnesses for Christianity. Plato was coopted but subordinated to ancient Hebrew "philosophy," while the Hebrews were divested of any connection with the Jews, and remade as the first Christians, which gave Christianity a venerable, ancient pedigree. Greek paganism was shown to be derivative from astral religions of Egypt

University Press, 1995); cf. Daniel Boyarin, *Dying for God: Martyrdom and the Making of Christianity and Judaism* (Stanford: Stanford University Press, 1999).

[34] *De Praescriptione Haereticorum*, 7.9; the parallelism of Jerusalem with the Christian *ekklêsia* is confirmed by Tertullian's subsequent two questions: "Or what has the Academy in common with the Church?, or heretics with Christians?" (Latin: *Quid ergo Athenis et Hierosolymis? Quid academiae et ecclesiae? Quid haereticis et christianis?*).

[35] See Barnes, *Tertullian: A Historical and Literary Study*, 130–42; and the more recent David Rankin, *Tertullian and the Church* (Cambridge, U.K.: Cambridge University Press, 1995), 41–51.

[36] Michael J. St. Clair, *Millenarian Movements in Historical Context* (New York: Garland, 1992), 75–94.

and Phoenicia, and in its present forms controlled by demons.[37] Eusebius pursued this course not only against real and imagined heretical and Jewish competitors but also against the very real rivalry of learned pagan intellectuals such as the Neoplatonist Porphyry (233–309), who considered Christians "apostates, both from Greco-Roman religion and culture and from Jewish religion and culture,"[38] and who thus posed a direct threat to Eusebius.

For Neoplatonists such as Porphyry, Christianity's special dispensation held no meaning; no one religion was to be privileged, and certainly not Christianity which lacked antiquity. For Porphyry, Greek philosophy and religious revelation were in harmony; divine truth was revealed by all religions with an ancient pedigree. Neoplatonists, furthermore, tended toward a competing concept of the One, a single deity to which all other divine emanations are subordinate.[39]

This philosophical approach was part of a general monotheizing trend in pagan thought and practice, which also gains expression in the artwork of the time. In her "Tradition and Transmission: Hermes Kourotrophos in Nea Paphos, Cyprus," Elizabeth Kessler-Dimin describes the symbols of a monotheizing cult of Dionysus in Cypriot mosaics of the early fourth-century C.E., which preserve indications of Pagan and Christian competition over a common antiquity for the sake of contemporary legitimacy. Dionysus' ancient Hellenic legacy is here re-inscribed for singular devotion at the dawn of imperial sanction of Christianity, while the depiction of infant Dionysus on Hermes' lap indicates that the parallel image of the Christ child on Mary's lap owes much to iconic rivalry between Christians and pagans.

Jews were not unaffected by these common cultural and artistic trends. At the necropolis of Beit She'arim in Palestine, with third to fourth century burials, Jews were interred in sarcophagi which evoke contemporary Ro-

---

[37] As established in his *Praeparatio* and *Demonstratio Evangelica*; see also Timothy D. Barnes, *Constantine and Eusebius* (Cambridge, Mass.: Harvard University Press, 1981), 179–86.

[38] Timothy D. Barnes, *Constantine and Eusebius*, 178.

[39] On Porphyry's views on Christianity (and other religions), see Barnes, *Constantine and Eusebius*, 174–79. For a general introduction to Plotinus, Porphyry and Neoplatonism, see R. T. Wallis, *Neoplatonism* (London: Duckworth, 1972). For more on the Neoplatonic concept of the One, see J. M. Rist, *Plotinus*: *The Road to Reality* (Cambridge, U.K.: Cambridge University Press, 1967); and, more recently (in a study of the commonalities between concepts of the divine in Neoplatonist and Gnostic thought), Curtis L. Hancock, "Negative Theology in Gnosticism and Neoplatonism," in *Neoplatonism and Gnosticism* (ed. R. T. Wallis; Albany, N.Y.: State University of New York Press, 1992), 167–86.

man models, "decorated, for example, with a bucranium-and-acanthus design, with eagles, shells, or simplified hunt scenes."[40] One sarcophagus – displaying an image of Hercules on one side, Leda and the Swan on another – likely housed the remains of a local commemorated by a standard Greek epigram for a young aristocrat taken too soon. On a lintel in catacomb 19, a Dionysiac mask is displayed, while on a number of walls Jewish *menorot* are carved in crude graffito fashion.[41] While a few inscriptions are in Aramaic, most are in Hebrew or Greek. Two centuries of activity in this Jewish city of the dead point to the multiple antiquities with which Jews of the time associated, an image reflected – if the Babylonian Talmud can be relied upon – in the earlier, daily activities of the court of Gamaliel II, where 1000 youths pursued two curricular lines: 500 in Hellenic studies, 500 in Hebraic learning.[42]

This trend in Jewish artwork continues in the later synagogues of Sephoris, Beit Alfa and elsewhere, where fifth- and sixth-century mosaic floors reveal Greco-Roman images of the Zodiac, replete with anthropomorphic symbols for the seasons, all centered on a depiction of Helios. These images rest comfortably next to adjoining panels displaying Jewish symbols: the shofar, lulav, and incense shovel; and biblical scenes like the Sacrifice of Isaac.[43] As Lee Levine shows in his essay, "Jewish Collective Memory in Late Antiquity: Challenges in the Interpretation of Jewish Art," the Biblical Age gained renewed meaning in the artwork of fourth-seventh century Palestinian synagogues. Retrieval of these images strengthened Jewish association with the Bible and Israelite history and thus bolstered Jewish communal identity in the face of competition with and hostility from Christian neighbors and rulers in the Byzantine Age.

With Levine's contribution, spanning the fourth-seventh centuries C.E., we move from the Greco-Roman to our final classicizing period: Late Antiquity. This span of time coincides with one of the more creative pe-

---

[40] Seth Schwartz, *Imperialism and Jewish Society* (Princeton: Princeton University Press, 2001), 157.

[41] Ibid., 153–58.

[42] Bavli, *Bava Qama* 83a. Here Yehudah ha-Nasi says that Shemuel attributed this statement to R. Shim'on ben Gamaliel II regarding the House of his Father, Gamaliel II (c. 100 C.E.); cf. Saul Lieberman, *Hellenism in Jewish Palestine* (New York: Jewish Theological Seminary of America, 1950), 104, and more generally on the study of Homer (or Greek wisdom) in rabbinic society, 100–14.

[43] For astrology and its juxtaposition with biblical themes, with references to the archaeological finds, see Gregg Gardner, "Astrology in the Talmud: An Analysis of Bavli Shabbat 156," in *Heresy and Identity in Late Antiquity* (ed. E. Iricinschi and H. M. Zellentin; Texts and Studies in Ancient Judaism 119; Tübingen: Mohr Siebeck, 2008), 314–38.

riods in the Jewish reclamation of Biblical as well as Second Temple (and Tannaitic) antiquity, and the consequent reinvention of Jewish collective identity, as evidenced by the gradual compilation and editing of the two *talmudim*: the Yerushalmi and the Bavli. Among other significant themes, Moulie Vidas' contribution, "The Bavli's Discussion of Genealogy in *Qiddushin* IV," tackles the issue of Babylonian rabbinic views on the precedence of geography and genealogy with respect to Jewish authenticity. In this particular conversation, the Bavli questions the legacy of the biblical hero Ezra who, in the fifth century B.C.E., spearheaded a return from Babylon to the Land of Israel predicated upon genealogical purity. Thus, the Babylonian Talmud problematizes the spatial and ethnic boundaries of the Jewish community in an age of the rise of Babylonia as the major center of Jewish life and learning under Sassanid-Persian rule, and the decline of Palestinian Judaism under Byzantium.

The reign of the Byzantine Emperor Justinian (527–565) provides an exemplar for the merging realms of retrievable antiquity in Late Antiquity. By committing his armies to the re conquest of the "lost" western provinces (533–552), Justinian asserted the identity of his empire as true inheritor of Rome's legacy. But this was only one side of a much broader project of collective and imperial reinvention, which rested upon a re-association with the most potent symbols of Byzantium's composite heritage. The same emperor who commissioned the codification of Roman law redacted in the Latin of Old Rome, the *Corpus Juris Civilis*, lavishly rebuilt the Hagia Sophia on an immense scale, in part to recall and outdistance – if the apocryphal account holds truth – the Israelite Temple in Jerusalem: "Solomon, I have outdone thee!"[44] While claiming ownership over the Christian-Roman-Israelite past, Justinian subverted the role of potential competitors; he formally ended the Pagan-Hellenic curriculum at the

[44] On the source of Justinian's apocryphal self-proclaimed rivalry with Solomon, John W. Barker (*Justinian and the Later Roman Empire* [Madison: University of Wisconsin Press, 1966], 183, n. 12) adds "This exclamation ["Glory be to God Who considered me worthy of this task! O Solomon, I have outdone thee!"] is...probably apocryphal. It appears only in a source of a much later period, the Greek title of which translates as *On the Structure of the Temple of the Holy Wisdom*, known also by the Latin title of *Narratio de aedifictione templi Sanctae Sophiae,* formerly ascribed to the fourteenth-century Byzantine writer Georgios Kodinos, but now held to be an earlier work of perhaps the eleventh or twelfth century." For more on this eleventh-twelfth century text, see also, as Barker cites (ibid.), *Scriptores originum Constantinopolitanarum* (ed. T. Preger; Teubner Series; Leipzig, 1901), I:105.

Academy of Athens in 529, and placed restrictions on Jewish communal life and liturgy.[45]

Whatever their reality, the apocryphal sentiments attributed to Justinian reflect a prevailing Byzantine discourse on antiquity and identity. Yannis Papadoyannakis' "A Debate about the Rebuilding of the Temple in Sixth-Century Byzantium," reveals the depth of Byzantine Christian anxiety over Jewish associations with the sacred geography of Palestine in Justinian's day. The *Erotapokriseis* of pseudo-Kaisarios, explains Papadoyannakis, offers a counter-attack to antiquity-based claims of Jewish ownership of Jerusalem and the Temple. The work extends a series of "divinely-ordained" defeats of the Jewish people – from scriptural and post-scriptural prooftexts – into the Byzantine present to justify current Jewish suffering and alienation from their former sacred center. Regardless of the reality of sixth-century Jewish claims to their ancestral homeland, such exegetical practices reveal the problematic implications of Christianity's foundational basis in the expropriation of Jewish antiquity.

Yet, contemporaneous Jewish thinkers understood the nature of the challenge to their posterity and offered competing versions to Byzantine Christian ownership over the antiquity of both Rome and Israel. Ra'anan Boustan in "The Spoils of the Jerusalem Temple at Rome and Constantinople: Jewish Counter-Geography in a Christianizing Empire," explores Byzantine claims to have regained the spoils of Solomon's Temple in their wars of re-conquest. These claims were countered, Boustan reveals, by early Byzantine Jewish compositions that subverted both their ownership of these relics and the function of the latter in Christian supersessionist narratives. Such Jewish counter-narratives mark the eschatological re-appropriation by Jews of their most sacred relics. They work not only to reverse the victory of the Flavians 500 years before, but also to undermine Christian supercessionist notions of spiritual progression from Jerusalem to Rome.

Late Antique eschatology brings us to the Christian Kingdom of Ethiopia, c. 350–650. The ruling elites of this kingdom provide us with a striking example of communal reinvention predicated on the inheritance of a fully merged Greco-Roman-Christian-Jewish Antiquity, within a dynamic context of direct competition and/or co-operation with rival claimants to

[45] For a brief overview of Justinian's reign see George Ostrogorsky, *History of the Byzantine State* (rev. ed.; New Brunswick, N.J.: Rutgers University Press, 1969), 68–86. For a more detailed examination, see Barker, *Justinian and the Later Roman Empire*; and Robert Browning, *Justinian and Theodora* (London: Weidenfeld and Nicolson, 1971). For the relationship between Justinian and the Jews, see Andrew Scharf, *Byzantine Jewry: From Justinian to the Fourth Crusade* (New York: Schocken, 1971), 19–41.

all or part of this same conglomerate past. Christianized c. 350 C.E., the rulers of Aksum rooted their origins in the son of Solomon and the Queen of Sheba, Menelik. After Chalcedon (451),[46] monophysite Ethiopian kings reinvented themselves as defenders of Orthodoxy, the true inheritors of Rome's legacy versus the heretic emperors of Constantinople.

Yet this did not hinder an expedient, sixth-century alliance between them against a common enemy, the Jewish kingdom of Ḥimyar. With emperor Justin I (r. 518–527) as their ally, the Ethiopian forces of Kaleb Ellah Esbaha crossed the straits to Yemen where they fought a successful campaign against the army of the Jewish king of Ḥimyar, Yusuf Dhu Nuwas who was himself recently occupied by a war against the Christians of Najran. The defeat of Dhu Nuwas spawned apocryphal accounts of him riding his steed off the cliffs into the sea.[47] The epigraphic record provides us with Kaleb's celebration of this same victory over Jewish Ḥimyar in a monument he placed in Marib in Yemen which recalls, and thus associates the Ethiopian ruling house with, the Glory of King David.

A number of these aforementioned details are addressed in G. W. Bowersock's essay, "Helena's Bridle and the Chariot of Ethiopia."[48] According to Bowersock, monophysite mythmakers and propagandists – both Syriac Christians and Ethiopians – transformed the Ethiopian Kingdom from peripheral player into eschatological superpower by monopolizing both Urzeit and Endzeit. Through creative genealogy, an early king of Ethiopia was reinvented as the forefather of Buz (Byzantium), whose daughter married Romulus, making Ethiopia the forebear of both Old and New Rome. While at the End Time, when the apocalyptic horse is harnessed by Helena's Bridle, the Ethiopian "King of the Greeks" will return triumphant to Jerusalem with the Ark of the Covenant, the sacred relic of Ethiopia.

Turning to late antique Syriac Christianity brings us to the final contribution to our volume, which also returns us to our own day. Adam Becker's "The Ancient Near East in the Late Antique Near East: Syriac

---

[46] On the Council of Chalcedon, See Timothy Gregory, *Vox Populi: Popular Opinion and Violence in the Religious Controversies of the Fifth Century A.D.* (Columbus: Ohio State University Press, 1979), 163–201.

[47] On Dhu Nuwas and the Jewish Kingdom of Ḥimyar, see Salo Baron, *A Social and Religious History of the Jews* (New York: Columbia University Press, 1957), 3:63–69, 257–60; Irfan Shahîd, "Pre-Islamic Arabia," in *The Cambridge History of Islam* (Cambridge, U.K.: Cambridge University Press, 1970), 1:3–29; and Alessandro de Maigret, *Arabia Felix* (trans. R. Thompson; London: Stacey International, 2002), 108–9, 227–56.

[48] Bowersock's essay is our source for Kaleb's monument, the origin-myths of Ethiopian kings, their espousal of monophysitism after Chalcedon, as well as all of the topics raised in the present paragraph.

Christian Appropriation of the Biblical East" tells the story of twenty-first century "Assyrians" who ascribe their own origins to the ancient Near Eastern Assyrians, antagonists *par excellence* of ancient Israel, whom they recast as generous city-builders and pious Christians. Eschewing both contemporary Assyrians' primordialist claim linking their ethnicity to ancient Assyria, and the skepticism of modern scholars who impute their origins to the creativity of nineteenth-century Christian missionaries, Becker locates their origins rather among Syriac Christian communities of Sassanid Mesopotamia in the sixth-century C.E. The late antique ethnogenesis of the Assyrians, a specific people tied to a specific land within a broader Syriac Christian culture, sheds new light on the categories of ethnicity and religion in a premodern setting. Such a scenario problematizes the conclusions of modernist/presentist scholarship – which privileges rupture over continuity between the modern and the premodern periods not to mention the ancient – while it opens up new possibilities for fertile cross-disciplinary exchange between scholars of the contemporary world and those of antiquity.[49]

[49] For a modernist/presentist approach in ethnicity and nationalism studies, see Ernest Gellner, *Nations and Nationalism* (Ithaca, N.Y.: Cornell University Press, 1983); Benedict Anderson, *Imagined Communities: Reflections on the Origin and Spread of Nationalism* (London: Verso Press, 1983); and Eric Hobsbawm, *Nations and Nationalism since 1780, Programme, Myth, Reality* (Cambridge, U.K.: Cambridge University Press, 1990). Hobsbawm's research, in particular, follows a modernist line, divorcing the modern nation from its pre-1789 (pre-French Revolution) foundations. For a critique of this position, see Adrian Hastings, *The Construction of Nationhood: Ethnicity, Religion and Nationalism* (Cambridge, U.K.: Cambridge University Press, 1997), who views religion as a foundational element of many modern nation-states whose roots are thus also found in a much earlier medieval context if not earlier; and also Anthony W. Marx, *Faith in Nation: Exclusionary Origins of Nationalism* (Oxford: Oxford University Press, 2003), who demonstrates the rise of modern Spain in the fifteenth-sixteenth centuries on a "religio-cultural" basis, through galvanization of the Catholic population against heretics and Jews; see also Funkenstein on the modernist/presentist approach of Halbwachs and Yerushalmi (see above nn. 2, 3, and 10). Anthony D. Smith, *The Ethnic Origins of Nations* (Oxford: Blackwell, 1986), has done much to bridge the gap between modern and ancient studies by emphasizing the common ethnic basis for communal identity in both premodern and modern periods. For a survey of modernist/presentist, primordialist, and other approaches in the study of ethnicity and nationalism, see Anthony D. Smith, *The Nation in History: Historiographical Debates about Ethnicity and Nationalism* (Hanover, N. H.: University Press of New England, 2000).

## III. Conclusion

From the emic, or insider's, perspective of modern-day Assyrians, the antiquity of antiquity is clearly a matter of immediate twenty-first century relevance. From the etic perspective of the scholar-outsider, the case of the Assyrians and numerous other modern-day exemplars allow us to grasp the ongoing relevance of Greco-Roman, Jewish and Christian antiquity not only for antiquity but for modernity as well.

Indeed, the broad perspective of the ancient historian allows for a necessary corrective to the modern intellectual tendency to ignore continuity with the ancient past at the expense of rupture. When we place the supposed premodern-modern rupture posited by the modernist/presentist camp against the backdrop of the ancient classicizing periods of this volume, it appears as simply one more stage in an ongoing discourse on continuity and rupture that has obtained from the days of antiquity through the present. In the wake of each classicizing age in this volume, former disparate antiquities are merged into a common legacy, ready and available for reinterpretation and re-appropriation. Within each new context the inheritance of the past is refashioned to meet present needs. But this legacy also helps determine present concepts, actions, and identities. While reinvention is perpetual, so too is the conversation on the past which allows for it; no mere artifacts have the ancients given us, but a set of discourses as well.

Our ancient heritage is malleable, just as it is undeniable. The body of articles presented in this volume establish the impact of antiquity in antiquity both in its own right and as an essential step for grasping the legacy of antiquity in modernity. To escape the ancient past is as impossible as escaping the present, it is always already there. Yet one must be wary of the primordialist urge (present reality has always been thus), on the one hand, and the modernist/presentist fallacy (rupture trumps continuity), on the other. Rather, by coming to grips with the significance of antiquity in antiquity, we become more aware of the possibilities offered by our contemporary intellectual context and our common ancient heritage. What follows in this volume are the results of interdisciplinary conversations in the aligned fields of twenty-first century ancient studies, the latest stage in a long, evolving conversation on the meaning of the ancient past, which began with the ancients themselves.

Part One

# Jewish and Pagan Antiquities from the Late Hellenistic to the Early Imperial Period

# The End of Jewish Egypt

## Artapanus and the Second Exodus

HOLGER M. ZELLENTIN

"And 'mid this tumult Kubla heard from far
Ancestral voices prophesying war!"

– Samuel Taylor Coleridge, *Kubla Khan. Or: A Vision in a Dream. A Fragment.*

Artapanus's writings come to us third hand: Eusebius, in his *Preparatio Evangelica*, presents materials from Alexander Polyhistor, a Greek, taken to Rome by Sulla, who taught and wrote in Rome until his sudden death in 35 B.C.E.[1] Among Polyhistor's material are two short passages and one extended passage attributed to a certain "Artapanus."[2] In these writings, Artapanus re-imagines, in a thoroughly Hellenistic way, the lives of three biblical figures in which Egypt figures prominently: Abraham, Joseph, and Moses. These patriarchs become founders of Egyptian civilization and the

I would like to express my sincere gratitude to David Frankfurter and Erich Gruen for reading earlier drafts of this article, and to the editors of this volume for their thorough suggestions. I dedicate this article to my teacher Martha Himmelfarb, whose inspiration and critical eye have carried this project through many unexpected turns.

[1] All dates in the study, unless otherwise noted, are B.C.E. Alexander Polyhistor was born in Miletus and taken captive to Rome during the Mithradatic wars.

[2] Eusebius of Caesarea, *Praeparatio evangelica*, IX. 1.1, cited from Édouard des Places, *Eusèbe de Césarée, La Préparation Évangélique, Livres VIII–IX–X* (Paris: Les Éditions du Cerf, 1991), 239–41, 263–65, and 271–81. All subsequent citations of this work are from the same edition (herein after *Praep. ev.*). All translations are my own. The only other ancient source that mentions Artapanus is Clement of Alexandria, *Stromata* I. 154, 2–3. In addition, Josephus used a source akin to Artapanus in his account of Moses in the *Antiquities*; see Donna Runnalls, "Moses's Ethiopian Campaign," *Journal for the Study of Judaism in the Persian, Hellenistic and Roman Periods* 14 (1983): 135–56; Tessa Rajak, "Moses in Ethiopia: Legend and Literature, *Journal of Jewish Studies* 39 (1978): 111–22; Avigdor Shinan, "Moses and the Ethiopian Woman: Sources of a Story in the Chronicle of Moses," *Scripta Hierosolymitana* 27 (1978): 66–78; Isidore Lévy, "Moïse en Ethiopie," *Revue des études juives* 53 (1907): 201–11; and Solomon Rappaport, *Agada und Exegese bei Flavius Josephus* (Vienna: Alexander Kohut Memorial Foundation, 1930).

heroes of his epic, surviving numerous dangers and acts of treachery. The tale comes to a dramatic end when the Egyptian king, jealous of the fame Moses had attained as his general, seeks to have him killed. As a result, the Jews leave Egypt and much of Egyptian civilization is destroyed during the Exodus.[3]

Neither Polyhistor nor Eusebius specify Artapanus's provenance or ethnicity. Nevertheless, almost all scholars have understood him to be a Jew from Egypt. If we accept this, then we must understand Artapanus against the background of growing tensions between people classified as "native" Egyptians and those who laid claim to be Hellenes – a hallmark of Ptolemaic Egyptian society.[4] Among the latter class, at least by their own understanding, figured the Greek-speaking Jews of Egypt.[5] Yet Howard Jacobson's recent article points to the fact that it is premature to assume Jewish authorship of the Artapanus text solely based on its pro-Jewish attitude.[6] In line with this viewpoint, I will consider the text's implied audience – the audience inscribed in and recoverable from the text – and will only then turn to the more speculative question of the identities of the historical audience and author. One cannot simply assume that the text is Egyptian just because it deals with Egyptian subject matter, one of the most popular topics of Late Antique historiography. Rather, I suggest that an examination of Artapanus's perspective on Egyptian politics will allow us to situate him socially and chronologically in the following (indeed, Egyptian) context.

The Persian provenance of the name "Artapanus" reflects the author's choice not to cast himself as a clearly identifiable Jew.[7] Instead, I suggest

---

[3] For a more extensive summary, see the table below.

[4] See Per Bilde, ed., *Ethnicity in Hellenistic Egypt* (Aarhus: Aarhus University Press, 1992); and Koen Goudriaan, *Ethnicity in Ptolemaic Egypt* (Amsterdam: J. Gieben, 1988).

[5] Much to the dismay of native Egyptians like Manetho, there is little evidence of Greco-Egyptian anti-Judaism prior to the second century. See Aryeh Kasher, *The Jews in Hellenistic and Roman Egypt: The Struggle for Equal Rights* (Tübingen: Mohr Siebeck, 1985). Erkki Koskenniemi also seeks to construct a conflict between Greeks and Jews in Artapanus's time, though he does not provide historical evidence (ibid., "Greeks, Egyptians, and Jews in the Fragments of Artapanus," *Journal for the Study of the Pseudepigrapha* 13 [2002]: 17–31). On the relationship between Artapanus and Manetho, see footnote 35.

[6] Howard Jacobson, "Artapanus Judaeus," *Journal of Jewish Studies* 57 (2006): 210–21. The suggestion that Artapanus might have been of mixed descent had been made earlier by Peter Marshall Fraser in *Ptolemaic Alexandria* (Oxford: Clarendon Press, 1972), I:706, II:985 n. 199.

[7] We cannot know for certain whether Artapanus is only a pen name, or the author's real name; my observation is independent of this question. Indeed, Fraser has shown that Jews in Egypt occasionally had Persian names. A Persian name, therefore, would not be

that he chooses a name that allows for maximum ambiguity, in line with the ambiguity he creates for the Jewish patriarchs who also become Egyptian Hellenistic heroes. Artapanus uses the narrative of the biblical Exodus and Greek sources on the heroes of Egypt (which were also used by Diodorus Siculus) in order to recast the Jewish patriarchs in the tradition of the Osiris, Sesoosis (= Sesostris), and Dionysus myths.

In my view, Artapanus creates his own version of the biblical Exodus narrative in order to encourage his audience to flee Egypt towards "Syria," which denotes Palestine in Ptolemaic geography. His account focuses on the partially joint fate of the Greco-Egyptian Jews and that of ethnic Egyptian land laborers and soldiers, whom he contrasts with Egyptian kings and priests. He discusses the evolution of Egyptian agriculture, technology, warfare, and religion from the point of view that I here call "euhemeristic philanthropy." It is euhemeristic because the Egyptians allegedly deified the Jewish patriarchs who bestowed upon them a continuum of social and technological innovations that benefited mankind.[8] It is philanthropic in as far as Artapanus expects his audience to identify with the Jewish patriarchs' vain pursuit of the welfare of contemporary Egypt.[9]

I argue that Artapanus's implied audience is to be found among Greco-Egyptian Jewish military officers and governors. The text can be dated towards the end of the second reign of Ptolemy VIII ("Physcon") and his two wives Cleopatra II and III (145–116), which saw a radical emancipation of native Egyptian culture.[10] I further argue that Artapanus's work is a

an effective way to either disguise or emphasize one's Jewishness. See Fraser, *Ptolemaic Alexandria*, I:706, 2:985 n 199. Intriguingly, the town "Artapatou" is attested near Oxyrhyncus.

[8] The term "euhemeristic" derives from the fourth century scholar of religion Euhemeros, who tended to rationalize myths by tracing them to historical events. See Jan Dochhorn, "Zur Entstehungsgeschichte der Religion bei Euhemeros – mit einem Ausblick auf Philo von Byblos," *Zeitschrift für Religions- und Geistesgeschichte* 53 (2001): 289–301; Albert Baumgarten, "Euhemerus' Eternal Gods: or, how not to be embarrassed by Greek Mythology," in *Classical Studies in Honor of David Sohlberg* (ed. R. Katzoff; Ramat Gan, Israel: Bar-Ilan University Press, 1996), 91–103; Carsten Colpe, "Utopie und Atheismus in der Euhemeros-Tradition," in *Panchaia. Festschrift für Klaus Thraede* (ed. M. Wacht; Münster: Aschendorff, 1995), 32–44. On Artapanus's Euhemerism, see Collins, *Between Athens and Jerusalem*, 42.

[9] I view Artapanus within the context of the much broader Greco-Roman custom of publicly displaying the donation of goods or services to a city. See Paul Veyne, *Le Pain et le cirque: sociologie historique d'un pluralisme politique* (Paris: Ed. du Seuil, 1995).

[10] Throughout this paper, I will make use of the phrase "native Egyptian," as opposed to "Greco-Egyptian," in a strictly rhetorical sense. I suggest understanding Ptolemy VIII's return to "authentic" Egyptian religion, and his program of advancing the case of his native subjects, in the same Hellenistic framework as the parallel intentions of his

response to Ptolemy's *philantropa* decree of 118, which sought to alleviate agricultural hardship by granting substantial relief to the small farmers, especially to the Egyptian veterans of the army. This decree also reprimanded corrupt officers and *dioiketes*, confirmed the rights of the priests to their land, and financed the (substantial) burial for the *Apis* bull.

In my view, Artapanus uses the memory of the Jewish patriarchs in order to create a Greco-Jewish contrast to the pro-native-Egyptian turn of Ptolemy VIII. *Pace* Ptolemy VIII, he conflates the interests of native Egyptian soldiers and the Greek elite. Artapanus associates Ptolemy VIII with native Egyptians by associating him with the rebel Pharao Chenephres (who had defied the rule of Ptolemy V), and insists that anything good in Egyptian culture was actually instituted by Abraham, Joseph, and Moses. He makes Joseph a *dioiketes* and Moses the hero of the Egyptian soldiers and officers. Moreover, he travesties Ptolemy's payment for the sacred bull's burial as the king's effort to bury the sacred animals alive. Artapanus portrays the Jewish patriarchs as militarily apt and as fertilizing the Egyptian soil and intellect. I propose to look for his audience among the Jewish military aristocracy of Ptolemaic Egypt. Most of all, Artapanus uses the antique story of the Exodus to promote his clear message to his contemporary audience: leave Egypt for "Syria;" this land is doomed.

Before presenting my argument, a word on Eusebius, our source for Artapanus, may be helpful in considering our primary uncertainty about Artapanus: his fragmentary nature. Given Eusebius's encyclopedic approach, we have little reason to suspect him of ideologically motivated distortion or deletion of any of his sources.[11] Eusebius came across Polyhistor's citations of Artapanus during his elaborate effort to collect evidence for his claim that "the most distinguished Hellenes seemed not to have been ignoring the issues of the Hebrews."[12] After providing general and ethnographic information on the Hebrews, his claimed intellectual and

---

Maccabean contemporaries. See Martha Himmelfarb, "Judaism and Hellenism in 2 Maccabees," *Poetics Today* 19 (1998): 19–40.

[11] In the second part of Eusebius's presentation of the evidence (Chapter IX.10.7–42.4), he determines the sequence of the individual excerpts by the appearance of authors in one of his sources, namely Josephus (and probably also in Polyhistor). Alternatively, Eusebius at times arranges his sources thematically. Eusebius's and Polyhistor's wide range of topics – some of them (pro-)Jewish, some of them anti-Jewish – suggests their personal disengagement as well as their moderate care for detail. It also becomes clear, however, that Eusebius was unsuspecting of the political and ethnic context of Artapanus which I propose, leaving me with the text as we have it as the sole basis of inquiry. On Eusebius's ethnic politics, see Aaron Johnson, *Ethnicity and Argument in Eusebius'* Praeparatio Evangelica (Oxford: Oxford University Press, 2006).

[12] *Praep. ev.* IX. 1.1.

spiritual ancestors, Eusebius introduces the second part of his book IX, Chapters 10.7–42.4, with the words, "Concerning the history of patriarchs, look how many agree!" In this part of *Prep. ev.*, citations from Josephus and Alexander Polyhistor provide the main sources.[13] In Eusebius's long list of mostly gentile Greek authors (who are as diverse in their background as they are polyphonic in their respective accounts), Artapanus appears in three separate sections: the story of Abraham in Chapter 18, of Joseph in Chapter 23, and of Moses in Chapter 27.[14] Since Eusebius's cumulative argument depends upon the number of sources that he presents, it is possible that he might have shortened his text – yet we should not assume that he withheld any topic discussed by Artapanus. In most of this article, therefore, I will treat our fragments of Artapanus as fragments; however, I will later attempt to show that the inner coherence and literary structure of Artapanus's three textual units actually allows for a surprisingly coherent literary reading. Just as in the case of Coleridge's "fragment," we may not lack much of his work after all.

## Artapanus's Sources

In order to evaluate Artapanus's text, it is important to understand both the sources he used and whether he would have presumed his audience's familiarity with these sources. Would Artapanus have selected Moses as the hero if he had targeted a contemporary audience entirely ignorant of the Exodus story? Erich Gruen's reading of Artapanus as employing humor becomes helpful when recast as follows: Artapanus expected that his audience would appreciate his intent to portray Moses as incongruent with the Moses of any other ancient text.[15] Indeed, the text's meaning changes

[13] Eusebius quotes Josephus mainly from *Jewish Antiquities*, Book I. Eusebius also cites parts of *Against Apion* in Chapter VIII and the end of chapter IX of the *Praep. Ev.*

[14] More precisely, Artapanus's first passage is preceded by the Jew Eupolemos, truncated by accounts from Molon and the Jew Philo the Elder, by Josephus, Demetrius, Aristeas, by a certain Theodotus of uncertain ethnicity, and by the Jewish Ezekiel the Tragedian. For a more detailed discussion, see Jeffrey S. Siker, "Abraham in Graeco-Roman Paganism," *Journal for the Study of Judaism in the Persian, Hellenistic and Roman Period* 18 (1987): 188–208; and Geza Vermes, "A Summary of the Law by Flavius Josephus," *Novum Testamentum* 24 (1982): 289–303.

[15] Gruen has drawn out humorous aspects of Artapanus in his *Heritage and Hellenism: The Reinvention of Jewish Tradition* (Berkeley: University of California Press, 1998), 158, and more recently in *Diaspora: Jews among Greeks and Romans* (Cambridge, Mass.: Harvard University Press, 2002), 201–12 and 331–34. The wholesale criticism against Gruen's suggestions (such as for example by Gideon Bohak, "Recent

dramatically when we assume that Artapanus's intended audience knew the established versions of patriarchal and heroic traditions. I contend that we can only fully comprehend Artapanus by assuming that his audience was familiar with the biblical account of the Exodus, Greek historiographical traditions about Osiris/Dionysus, Sesoosis, and possibly with the political situation following the amnesty granted by Ptolemy VIII (to which I will return later in this article).

### *1. The Bible*

Artapanus's relationship with the Septuagint is not as clear-cut as most modern scholars have posited.[16] In fact, a close, synoptic reading of Artapanus and the Septuagint reveals that the supposed connection is far more problematic than previously realized. Lexical "dependence" of individual words can indeed be established for the entire work, as well as "dependence" of a cluster of words for one short section – Artapanus's narrative on the ten plagues.[17] That said, it is of course possible that Artapanus

---

Trends in the Study of Greco-Roman Jews," *The Classical Journal* 99 [2003]: 195–202) should be re-assessed in light of the present article.

[16] See, e.g., Jacob Freudenthal, *Hellenistische Studien I-II, Alexander Polyhistor und die von ihm erhaltenen Reste jüdischer und samaritanischer Geschichtswerke* (Jahresbericht des jüdisch-theologischen Seminars; Breslau: H. Skutsch, 1875), 216 and John J. Collins, *Between Athens and Jerusalem: Jewish Identity in the Hellenistic Diaspora* (Grand Rapids: Eerdmans, 2000), 38. For a different view and bibliography see also Gregory E. Sterling, *Historiography and Self-Definition, Josephos, Luke-Acts and Apologetic Historiograph*y (Leiden; Brill 1992), 174f. and Pieter Willem van der Horst, "Schriftgebruik bij drie vroege joods-hellenistische historici: Demetrius, Artapanus, Eupolemus," *Amsterdamse Cahiers voor Exegese en Bijbelse Theologie* 6 (1985): 144-161.

[17] A few examples illustrate this form of textual "dependence." In Exod 1:12, Israel becomes numerous (πλείους) in Egypt, Artapanus describes his Syrians as πλεονάσαι in 23.3, using the same root. The bricks are called πλινθεία in Exod 1:14, Artapanus uses the same term in 27.11 (πλίνθου). Pharaoh's intention to kill Moses is expressed with the verb ἀνελεῖν in Exod 2:15 as well as in Artapanus 27.7. There are only two clusters of words in the Septuagint and Artapanus that I could identify as akin to one another. First, Moses's staff, the snake into which it transforms and the striking of the ground/water are described in terms of ῥάβδος, δράκοντα (LXX and Artapanus 27.30, but 27.27 has ὄφιν for Moses's snake!) and πατάξαν quite consistently. Second, the plagues themselves are called by very similar names in both accounts. In Exod 7:20 ἐπώζεσεν ὁ ποταμός, the water turns foul, the same term Artapanus uses in 27.28 (ἐποζέσαι). The same applies for the frogs (βάτραχον, Exod 7.26–29, Artapanus 27.32), the grasshopper (ἀκρὶς Exod 10, passim, Artapanus 27.32), the flies (σκνῖφες, Exod 8:12, Artapanus 27.32) and the hail (χάλαζαν Exod 9:26, Artapanus 27.22). But how decisive are these examples? The words in question are not particularly known to have endless synonyms in Greek. Even if the cumulative evidence of lexical proximity points to the Septuagint, it remains intri-

utilized a written, instead of an oral, version of the Bible that circulated during his lifetime. As such, it would be reasonable to posit that he knew a text of Genesis and Exodus that was closer to the Septuagint than any other Greek version that has reached us today. The lexical correspondences between Artapanus and the Bible, however, suggests that the former represents a reworking of the latter from the memory of a literate person – a point to which I will return.[18]

The more important issue seems to be *how* he treated this biblical text, and what he expected his audience to make of the discrepancies between the biblical narrative and his own account. Rather than following Eusebius and recent scholarship in attributing to Artapanus a more or less ignorant embellishment of a distorted biblical text, I believe that Artapanus indeed expected his audience to notice the differences between the Bible and his own work, and to generate meaning precisely through the implied audience's tacit approval of the ensuing ethical and historical incongruities. I argue below that Artapanus followed an intelligible pattern of imitation and distortion of the Bible, as well as of other historical sources, which can be illustrated by the example of Hellenistic historiographic material preserved by Diodorus Siculus.

## 2. *Diodorus*

In 1907, Isidore Levy argued that the work of Hecateaus of Abdera, possibly a prominent source of Diodorus Siculus, was important for the study of Artapanus.[19] Many scholars, from Freudenthal onward, have realized the importance of the materials preserved in Diodorus.[20] Some years later, Tiede argued convincingly that most of Artapanus's depictions of Moses were based on the Egyptian prototypical hero *Sesoosis* (known elsewhere as *Sesostris*).[21] Tiede draws most of his information about Sesoosis from

---

guing that neither Freudenthal nor his successors were able to prove a single, unambiguous textual relationship between Artapanus and the Septuagint. This topic, I believe, needs to be reassessed. The Exodus as described in Psalms 78, 105, or 106 is not any closer to Artapanus than the version in biblical Book of Exodus.

[18] Given our uncertainty about the exact chronology of the Septuagint's writing, I henceforth use the term "biblical" fully aware of the term's possible ambiguity. On the Septuagint, see most recently Anneli Aejmelaeus's collection of essays, *On the Trail of the Septuagint Translators* (revised and expanded ed.; Leuven and Dudley, Mass.: Peeters, 2007).

[19] Isidore Lévy, "Moïse en Ethiopie," *Revue des études juives* 53 (1907): 201–11

[20] See Jacob Freudenthal, *Hellenistische Studien*, 216 and John J. Collins, *Between Athens and Jerusalem*, 38.

[21] David Lenz Tiede, *The Charismatic Figure as Miracle Worker* (Society of Biblical Literature Dissertation Series 1; Missoula: Scholar's Press, 1972), 153–55.

Diodorus and the latter's source, Herodotus. Ignorant of Levy, Tiede did not pursue the possibility that Artapanus might have used the material preserved in Diodorus in a more substantial way. Just as in the case with Artapanus's biblical source, the close literary familiarity with Diodorus does not necessarily point towards the author's precise adaptation of an extant written source.[22] I will cautiously use Diodorus's testimony as representative of some of the commonly accepted stories about Sesoosis, Dionysus/Osiris and Hermes, which Artapanus expected his audience to recognize as the garb in which he clothed Moses.[23] Furthermore, Artapanus's indiscriminate appropriation of these heroes' attributes for the patriarchs reflects the Diodoran practice of cross-identifying them. Likewise, and more importantly, Artapanus adopts the aforementioned model of "euhemeristic philanthropy" of which Diodorus presents various prominent examples, as well as a program to Hellenize the Egyptian cultural heritage comparable to that of Diodorus.[24] In doing so, Artapanus deviates from the agenda shared with Diodorus in order to establish the moral and technical superiority of the Jewish patriarchs even over the Greek heroes on whose model he had constructed their characters.

I present my analysis first in the form of a table and then in the form of a discussion of representative examples from this table. I suggest that, far more often than previously acknowledged, Artapanus's story is in direct dialogue with the Bible, or with the sources shared with Diodorus – and often with both simultaneously. My approach assumes that Artapanus follows one literary technique throughout his entire narrative, that of simultaneously imitating and subverting all of his sources. For the historian, the uncertainties of combining an analysis of textual imitation with that of textual subversion increase the possible margin of error when assessing literary dependencies. The same two modes of imitation and subversion of earlier texts are firmly joined in literary concepts of textual adaptation such as "travesty."[25] For an audience to decode the message created

[22] On Diodorus's relationship to his sources see below, note 38.

[23] Of these heroes, Artapanus names Hermes explicitly in *Praep. ev.* IX 27.6, see below.

[24] Diodorus mentions Euhemerus in VI.1.9–10.

[25] The term "travesty," i.e. dressing a sacred text in the clothing of exaggerated imitation, seems an appropriately loose description of Artapanus's project. Travesty is not necessarily comical; and the intention of the author need not be critical, hence the term leaves open these two fundamental aspects of Artapanus which I shall discuss below (on Artapanus's possibly humorous intentions, see footnote 15). See Gérard Genette, *Palmipsestes: La littérature au second degré* (Paris: Seuil, 1982); Wolfgang Karrer, *Parodie, Travestie, Pastiche* (München: W. Fink, 1977). Needless to say, this basic literary technique is demonstrable from the time of Aristophanes to our own.

through narrative subversion, the identity of the imitated text must be clear enough to allow the audience to recognize the connection. Here, I will present evidence suggesting that Artapanus created his version of Exodus by combining and "travestying" two sets of texts: a version of the biblical narrative and stories about Egyptian heroes. While the travesty of the Bible and of the Hellenistic stories certainly reflected Artapanus's worldview of euhemeristic philanthropy, his criticism of the Bible and of Greek culture is that of an insider for insiders. His primary target was the anti-Hellenistic and pro-Egyptian political sentiment that had come to the fore during the rule of Ptolemy VIII.

### *3. Table*

The following table provides a summary of Artapanus's account (*Praep. ev.* IX) in the left column. In the right column, I list the passages that Artapanus possibly shared with Diodorus (paraphrased or cited from the Loeb edition). In the center column, I reference pertinent material from the Septuagint (using paraphrases or modified quotes from the New Revised Standard Version) and, as indicated *ad loc.*, occasionally additional material presented separately by Diodorus that Artapanus combined in his adaption. The italicized and Greek words can be used as a guide to the manifold shared elements that the constraints of an article do not allow me to discuss here.

| | Artapanus | Septuagint & Additional Sources | Diodorus Siculus, *Library* |
|---|---|---|---|
| 1. | Abraham teaches astrology, first *to* the Phoenicians, then *to* Pharaoh in Egypt (18.2). Abraham returns to Syria (18.1). | Abraham leaves Haran (Gen 12), passes Canaan on his way to the Negev, then flees to Egypt and returns to the Negev (Gen 12.10–13.1). | "And according to [the Egyptians] the Chaldeans of Babylon, being colonists from Egypt, enjoy the fame which they have for their astrology, because they learned that science *from* the priests in Egypt" (I.81.6). |
| 2. | Abraham is the offspring of Israel, and the (fore)father of Isaac. The kings of Arabia are the brothers of Isaac. Jacob [of a later generation] is the father of Joseph. (23.1). | Abraham raises Isaac and Ishmael, Isaac raises Jacob/Israel, Jacob raises Joseph (Gen 20:18–35). | Osiris is Dionysus. The latter was born in Arabia (I.15.6). According to some, Dionysus/Osiris is buried in Arabia (I.27.3). |
| 3. | Joseph exceeds (διενεγκόντα) his brothers in wisdom (συνέσει) and under- | Joseph's dreams (Gen 37). | Orpheus exceeds (διενεγκόντα) all other men in nature and learning (III.65.6). |

| | Artapanus | Septuagint & Additional Sources | Diodorus Siculus, *Library* |
|---|---|---|---|
| | standing (φρονήσει, 23.1). | | Hermes is deified for his wisdom (σύνεσιν) and philanthropy (I.13.1). His understanding (φρονήσει) exceeds that of Osiris's other friends (I.17.3). |
| 4. | Joseph's brothers are jealous and conspire (ἐπιβουλευθῆναι) against him. Joseph predicts (προϊδόμενον) this and asks the Arabs to bring him to Egypt. He becomes governor *immediately* (23.2). | The brothers plot (ἐπονηρεύοντο) against Joseph because of his superiority, they predict (προεῖδον) his arrival (Gen 37.18) and sell him to the Arabs. Joseph is imprisoned but *later* becomes governor (Gen 37–41). | Typhon is the conspirator (ἐπιβουλεύσαντα) against Osiris (I.88.4). |
| 5. | Egyptian agriculture is in disorder (ἀτάκτως), the region is undivided and the strong inflict suffering upon the weak (23.2). | During the famine, Joseph enslaves all the Egyptians for Pharaoh, taking their land and cattle (Gen 47). | The court of Isis and Osiris makes implements to work the soil (I.15.5).<br>Osiris is a friend of agriculture (φιλογέωργον, I.15.6). |
| 6. | Joseph reorganizes the land, re-cultivates barren land and gives land to the priests (23.2). He invents measurements (23.3). | Joseph only spares the priests and their land (Gen 47:20). | Isis gives a third of the land (χώρας) to the priests (I.21.7). |
| 7. | Joseph is loved by the Egyptians. He marries Aseneth, the daughter of the priest of Heliopolis (23.3). Joseph had stocked (παραθέσθαι) the grain of seven years and had become the master of Egypt (23.4). | Joseph marries Aseneth, the daughter of the priest of On (i.e. Heliopolis) (Gen 41:44).<br>Joseph gathers grain in the seven abundant years (41.35, 49) | Dionysus instructs on storing (παραθέσεως) fruit (II.38.5, cf. III.73.5, V.75.4). Sesoosis wins the goodwill of all the Egyptians by euergetism, amnesty, and elaborate gifts of money, debt-release, and land (I.54.2). |
| 8. | The Jews settle in Sais and *Heliopolis* (23.3). | Jacob's family settles in the "City of the Heroes in the Land of Ramses" (Gen 46:28–29); or in the (Arabian) Goshen (Gen 46:34; 47:27).[26] | |

[26] At this point, the Septuagint and Artapanus are clearly at odds in their geography. The Septuagint situates Goshen in Arabia and equates it with the "City of the Heroes," the present day Suez (cf. Strabo XVII, Pliny, *Natural History* VI, and Diodorus IV.12).

| | Artapanus | Septuagint & Additional Sources | Diodorus Siculus, *Library* |
|---|---|---|---|
| 9. | After the death of Abraham, the new king of the northern part of Egypt, Palmanoth, dislikes the Jews and therefore builds temples at Sais and *Heliopolis* (27.2). | The new king makes the Israelites build Pithom and Ramses, and On, which is *Heliopolis*. They have to bake bricks and labor in the fields (Exod 1:11–14). | Sesoosis makes his captives build temples. Unable to endure the hardship, the Babylonian captives revolt against the Egyptians and ravage the neighboring territories. After accepting amnesty, they settle in Egypt (I.56.3f.). |
| 10. | Palmanoth has a daughter called Merris (Μέρριν) whom he marries to Chenephres, king of lower Egypt (south of Memphis). She adopts Moses, *called* Mousaios by the Greeks, the teacher of Orpheus. (27.3f.). | The daughter of Pharaoh adopts Moses (Exod 2). | Orpheus visits Egypt and is initiated into the cult of Dionysus (I.23.2 and 92.3). The priests of Egypt say that they were *visited by* Orpheus and Mousaios (I.96.2). |
| 11. | Moses invents many useful machines (εὔχρηστα παραδοῦναι), among them boats and machines to handle water (καὶ τὰ ὄργανα τὰ ὑδρευτικὰ, 27.4). | *Diodorus:* "The one most highly honoured by him [i.e. Osiris/ Dionysus] was Hermes, who was endowed with unusual ingenuity for devising things capable of improving the social life of man" (I.15.9). | Dionysus invents many things useful for life (τὸν βίον χρησίμων παραδοῦναι, II.38.5, cf. III.70.8). Sesoosis is the first to use large trunks for building boats (I.55.2). The Egyptian king Moiris builds a lake at Memphis, remarkable for its utility (εὐχρηστίᾳ), for irrigation (I.51.5). His canal opens and closes by a skillful device (κλειομένου φιλοτέχνως, I.52.2). |
| 12. | Moses divides (διελεῖν) the *polis* into thirty-six *nomes* (νομοὺς), instructing each *nome* how to venerate God (ἑκάστῳ τῶν νομῶν ἀποτάξαι τὸν θεὸν σεφθήσεσθαι), ordering the priests to have hieroglyphs, cats, dogs and ibises. He also | *Diodorus's third reason for Egyptian animal worship*: the animals have a use (τὴν χρείαν). The bull ploughs the earth (τὴν ἐλαφρὰν τῆς γῆς ἀροῦν), the dog is useful for hunting and protection, the cat is useful against asps and other reptiles, the ibis is | Orpheus institutes many changes in religious rites (III.65.6). Sesoosis divides (διελὼν) the land into thirty-six nomes (νομούς) and appoints a *nomarch* over each of them, who is charged with tax collection and administration (I.54.3). Hermes prescribes |

Artapanus, by having the Jews settle in the Nile Delta, places them much closer to the probable location of the biblical Goshen.

| | Artapanus | Septuagint & Additional Sources | Diodorus Siculus, *Library* |
|---|---|---|---|
| | assigns certain land (χώραν) to the priests (27.4). | useful as a protector against snakes, the locusts, and caterpillars (I.87.1f.). *Bible*: Moses gives land to the Levites (Num 35:1ff.). | (διαταχθῆναι) honors (τιμὰς) and sacrifices for the gods (I.16.4). Sesoosis builds a temple in each city for the god it honors the most (I.56.2). On the gift of land, see #6 and #13 in this table. |
| 13. | Moses's reforms aim to defend the monarchy of Chenephres from the disorderly (ἀδιατάκτους) crowds that sometimes chased the king away, and sometimes instituted a new one – often the same king as before, but sometimes a new one (27.5). | *Diodorus's second reason for animal worship*: The Egyptian army had lost because it was in disorder (ἀταξίαν). The Egyptians used animals as standards to organize the army. The animals, therefore, became sacred (86.4). | *Diodorus's fourth reason for animal worship:* "Since under the early kings the multitude were often revolting and conspiring against their rulers, one of the kings who was especially wise divided the land into a number of parts and commanded the inhabitants of each to revere a certain animal or else not to eat a certain food, his thought being that, with each group of people revering (σεβομένων) what was honored among themselves but despising what was sacred to all the rest, all the inhabitants of Egypt would never be able to be of one mind" (I.89.6f.). |
| 14. | Because he organized the country, Moses is loved by the crowds (ὑπὸ τῶν ὄχλων) and receives divine honors (ἰσοθέου τιμῆς) from the priests. He is called Hermes because he *interpreted* the sacred letters (διὰ τὴν τῶν ἱερῶν γραμμάτων ἑρμηνείαν, 27.6).[27] | | The masses (τοὺς ὄχλους) accord divine honors (τιμὰς ἰσοθέους) to Dionysus (III.64.2, see IV.81.3 and I.20.5f.). Hermes invents the alphabet (τήν τε εὕρεσιν τῶν γραμμάτων γενέσθαι, I.16.1). He taught hermeneutics (ἑρμηνείαν) to the Greeks, therefore he is called Hermes. He was the sacred scribe |

[27] Note also that the Jews are called *hermiouth* (18.1) and that Moses founds *hermopolis* (27.8, 9) – both of which probably play on the same root.

| | Artapanus | Septuagint & Additional Sources | Diodorus Siculus, *Library* |
|---|---|---|---|
| | | | (ἱερογραματέα) of Osiris (I.16.2).[28] |
| 15. | The king is jealous of Moses's virtue (τὴν ἀρετὴν) (27.6). | | Sesoosis humiliates the kings he has overpowered by using them to pull his chariot since they cannot compete with Sesoosis for the prize of virtue (ἀρετῆς, I.58.2). |
| 16. | The jealous king wants to have Moses killed in war and sends him to fight off the invading Ethiopians with an army (δύναμιν) of land-laborers, hoping they would be killed. Moses prevails as the war lasts ten years (27.7f.). | Moses marries an Ethiopian woman (Num 12:1). | Dionysus had not been able to subdue Ethiopia (III.3.1). Sesoosis first marches against Ethiopia with the most able of men and appoints as commanders men inured (ἐνηθληκότας) to warfare (I.54.5). He prepared his army (δύναμιν) and conquered most of the known East; his campaign lasts nine years (I.55.1–10). |
| 17. | Because of the size of the expedition (μέγεθος τῆς στρατιᾶς), Moses founds (κτίσαι) a city in Hermopolis of the same name, and consecrates it to the ibis because it kills the animals that are a nuisance to man (27.9). | | Hermes founds (ἐκτισμένας) a city. The ibis is useful as a protector against snakes, locusts, and caterpillars (I.87.1f.). |
| 18. | The Ethiopians and all of the Egyptian priests learn circumcision (τὴν περιτομὴν) from Moses (27.10). | | Some of the Egyptians found the nation of the Colchi, the proof of their Egyptian descent being that they practice circumcision (περιτέμνεσθαι), as the Jews do (I.55.5). |
| 19. | After the war, Chenephres conspires (ἐπιβουλεύειν) against Moses unsuccessfully (27.11). | | After the war, Sesoosis returns to Egypt and his brother conspires (ἐπιβουλὴν) against him unsuccessfully (I.57.6). On the conspiracy, see #25. |

[28] See also Pseudo-Eupolemos in *Praep. ev.* 9.26.

| | Artapanus | Septuagint & Additional Sources | Diodorus Siculus, *Library* |
|---|---|---|---|
| 20. | Chenephres sends Moses to Diospolis together with Nacherot, who has come with him to Memphis, in order to destroy the temple built of baked bricks and replace it with one of stone (27.11). | On bricks, see #9. | Osiris builds a temple in Thebes (= Diospolis) which is famous for its size and expense.<br>Isis and Osiris are buried in Memphis (I.22.2). |
| 21. | Moses then consecrates the cow (βοῶν) for its utility (εὔχρηστον), as it can plough the earth (διὰ τὸ τὴν γῆν ἀπὸ τούτων ἀροῦσθαι, 27.12). | *Diodorus:* "The consecration to Osiris, however, of the sacred bull, which are given the names Apis and Mnevis, and the worship of them as gods were introduced generally among all the Egyptians, since these animals had, more than any others, rendered aid to those who discovered the fruit of the grain [i.e. Isis and Osiris], in connection with both the sowing of the seed and with every agricultural labour from which mankind profits" (I.21.10f.). | *Diodorus's second reason for animal worship* (see #12 and #13) is the animals' utility, the cow (βοῦν) ploughs the earth (τὴν ἐλαφρὰν τῆς γῆς ἀροῦν, I.87.2).<br>Dionysus is the first man to yoke cows to the plough (βοῦς ὑπ' ἄροτρον)" (III.64.1, cf. IV. 4.2). |
| 22. | Chenephres calls the bull (ταῦρον) Apis, he orders the masses to construct a temple to bury it (θάπτειν). The king is banned as a result (27.12). | Sin of the Golden Calf (Exod 32). | *Diodorus's first reason for animal worship:* The gods took on the form of animals in order to be protected from mankind. After they became rulers, they made sacred (ἀφιερῶσαι) those kinds of animals whose form they had assumed, and instruct man to maintain them while they are alive and to bury them (θάπτειν) at their death (I.86.3–4).[29] |

[29] One of Dionysus's signs, according to Euripides, is the wild bull (*Bachae* 762, 1130–34, 1261, 1439, 1469).

| | Artapanus | Septuagint & Additional Sources | Diodorus Siculus, *Library* |
|---|---|---|---|
| | | | After the sacred bull (ἱερὸν ταῦρον) died, it is buried (ταφῇ) and taken to a sanctuary in Memphis (I.85.1ff.). |
| 23. | Moses names another city and river Meroe (Μερόην), after his deceased stepmother, whom he laid in a tomb (θάψαι) (27.15f.). | | Cambsys founds Meroe (Μερόης) for his mother (I.33.1). Dionysus leads his army to a place called Meros (Μερόν, II.38.4).[30] |
| 24. | Meroe honored no less than Isis (27.16). | | The Ethiopians at Meroe honor Isis (III.9.1f.). |
| 25. | Chenephres again conspires (ἐπιβουλὴν) to kill Moses (ἀναιρήσοντας). Aaron reveals the conspiracy and advises Moses to flee to Arabia. Moses does so and crosses the Nile at the height of Memphis. An assassin sent by Chenephres tries to kill him. Moses anticipates the attack and kills the Egyptian (27.13-18). | Moses kills an Egyptian who mistreats a Hebrew. Pharaoh hears about it and plans to kill Moses, who then flees to Midian (Exod 2:11–15). | Typhon is the conspirator (ἐπιβουλεύσαντα) against Osiris (I.88.4). Typhon kills (ἀναιρεθῆναι) Osiris (I.21.3). On conspiracy, see #9. |
| 26. | Moses flees to Arabia and to its ruler (ἄρχοντι), Raguel. He marries his daughter and Raguel encourages him to wage war against Egypt in order to secure a dynasty (δυναστείαν) for his daughter. Moses dissuades him and the Arabs from waging war (στρατεύειν) with Egypt (27.19). | Moses marries the daughter of the "priest of Midian" Jethro/Raguel (Exod 2:11–2) | Sesoosis's father sends him with an army to Arabia where he conquers and enslaves the entire nation. After he becomes king himself, his daughter urges him to acquire a dynasty (δυναστείαν) (I.53.8). |

[30] In Euripides, Dionysus honors his mother, Semele, in a sanctuary made for her (*Bacchae* 13).

| | Artapanus | Septuagint & Additional Sources | Diodorus Siculus, *Library* |
|---|---|---|---|
| 27. | Chenephres is the first man to die of Elephantiasas (27.20). | "After a long time, the king of Egypt died. The Israelites groaned under their slavery, and cried out…God looked upon the Israelites, and took notice of them" (Exod 2:23ff.). | Dionysus is the first man to celebrate a campaign seated on an Elephant (IV.2.3, cf. III. 65.8). |
| 28. | The king's death is a result of forcing the Jews to wear linen (σινδόνας), but not woolen cloths, in order to identify and punish them (27.20). | The Seleucid king forces the Jews, "when a festival of Dionysus was celebrated... to wear wreaths of ivy and to walk in the procession in honor of Dionysus (2 Macc 6:7).[31] | Upon the death of the king, the Egyptians wrap themselves in linen (σινδόνας) cloth (I.72.2). |
| 29. | Moses prays to God (εὔχεσθαι τῷ θεῷ) to end the suffering of his people. During his supplication, a fire suddenly comes from the earth without anything to consume it. Moses wants to flee, but a divine voice tells him to fight (στρατεύειν) Egypt and to save the Jews (27.21f.). | "The angel of the Lord appeared to him in a flame of fire out of a bush; he looked, and the bush was blazing, yet it was not consumed." Moses turns towards the bush to examine it. God sends him to Pharaoh to bring the Israelites out of Egypt, Moses tries to refuse, and God reveals his name (Exod 3:2–16). | Sesoosis's brother tries to burn him at night. Sesoosis raises his hands and prays to the gods (τοῖς θεοῖς εὐξάμενος) for his salvation. He manages, together with most of his family, to run through the flames unhurt (57.6). |
| 30. | In Arabia, Moses decides to send his fighting forces (δύναμιν πολεμίαν) against Egypt (τοῖς Αἰγυπτίοις). But first (πρῶτον) he meets his brother Aaron (27.22). | Moses meets Aaron on his way to Egypt (Exod 4:27). | Dionysus grows up in Arabia and fights against Egypt (πρῶτον ἐπὶ τὴν Αἴγυπτον στρατεῦσαι, III.73.4). First (πρῶτον) Sesoosis is sent by his father from Egypt to conquer Arabia with his forces (μετὰ δυνάμεως εἰς τὴν Ἀραβίαν, I. 53.5, cf. I.55.1). |
| 31. | The king of Egypt asks Moses about his plans, Moses responds that the "ruler of the world" (τὸν τῆς οἰκουμένης | "Afterward Moses and Aaron went to Pharaoh and said, "Thus says the Lord, the God of Israel, 'Let my people go, so | |

[31] The King of Egypt, according to a later text, has the Jews marked with an ivy leaf, the sign of Dionysus (3 Macc 2:29; see footnotes 39 and 59 below).

| | Artapanus | Septuagint & Additional Sources | Diodorus Siculus, *Library* |
|---|---|---|---|
| | δεσπότην) told him to deliver the Jews (27.23). | that they may celebrate a festival to me in the wilderness'" (Exod 5:1). Pharaoh responds by hardening the labors of the Israelites (Exod 5). | |
| 32. | The king puts Moses in prison, a "door-miracle" allows him to go to Pharaoh again (27.23f.).[32] Pharaoh asks for the name of the god that has sent him (27.24). | On the divine name, see #29. | |
| 33. | Moses whispers the divine name into Pharaoh's ear, the latter faints, speechless (ἄφωνον). Moses writes the name on a tablet. The priests, who think badly of the holy name, die with convulsions (27.26). | | |
| 34. | The king tells Moses to perform a sign (σημεῖόν), Moses throws his rod (ῥάβδον), it becomes a snake. Moses takes it by its tail, kills it and it reverts back into a rod (27.27). Moses then hits the Nile with his rod and the river floods (κατακλύζειν) the entire country. Pharaoh promises to let the Jews go if Moses makes the waters recede. The king convokes the priests | "The Lord said to Moses and Aaron, "When Pharaoh says to you, 'Perform a sign (σημεῖόν),' then you shall say to Aaron: 'Take your staff (ῥάβδον) and throw it down before Pharaoh, and it will become a snake'.... Then Pharaoh summoned the wise men and the sorcerers; and they also, the magicians of Egypt, did the same by their secret arts.... but Aaron's staff swallowed theirs." (Exod | The Egyptians are able to predict the pestilences that attack men and beast, they have prior knowledge of earthquakes and floods (σεισμούς τε καὶ κατακλυσμοὺς, I.81.5). |

32 This passage is also transmitted, almost *verbatim*, by Clement of Alexandria, *Stromata* I. 154, 2–3, where the prison doors are opened by the will of God (in Eusebius, the doors open by themselves). On this "door-miracle" in broader context and especially in the Dionysus traditions, see below and O. Weinreich, "Gebet und Wunder II: Türöffnung im Wunder-, Prodigien- und Zauberglauben der Antike, des Judentums und Christentums" in *Genethliakon* (ed. W. Schmidt; Stuttgart: Kohlhammer, 1929): 200–452.

| | Artapanus | Septuagint & Additional Sources | Diodorus Siculus, *Library* |
|---|---|---|---|
| | from south of Memphis and threatens to kill them and tear down their temples if they cannot do likewise. Because they succeeded in creating a snake and coloring the water, he punishes the Jews (27.27–31). | 7:8–12) Moses then strikes the Nile which turns into blood, the Egyptians can do the same (Exod 7). | |
| 35. | Moses performs more signs: By striking the earth, Isis, with his rod, Moses makes a winged animal (ζῷόν τι πτηνὸν) that molests the Egyptians; ulcers form on their skin, which cannot be healed by doctors. Moses creates frogs (βάτραχον), locusts (ἀκρίδας) and gnats (σκνίφας, 27.31). In each temple, the Egyptians venerate a rod and Isis, who, as the earth, performed the miracles (τὰ τέρατα ἀνεῖναι, 27.33). | Moses sends frogs (βατράχους, Exod 8:3) gnats (σκνίφας, 8.13 *sic*), flies (8.21) and "festering boils" (9.9). "The magicians could not stand before Moses because of the boils, for the boils afflicted the magicians as well as all the Egyptians" (Exod 9:11). Moses also sends locusts (ἀκρις, Exod 10). | |
| 36. | During the night, Moses produces hail (χαλάζης) and an earthquake (σεισμοὺς) which kills all of the Egyptians. All the houses, and most of the temples, collapse (27.33). | After a warning, "the hail (χαλάζα) struck down everything that was in the open field… both human and animal" (Exod 9:25). During the death of the firstborn, God "passed over the houses of the Israelites, when he struck down the Egyptians but spared our houses" (Exod 12:27). | On prediction, see # 34. |
| 37. | Pharaoh liberates the Jews. They take "a large number of cups, not few clothes (ἱματισμὸν) and a lot of other goods (παμπληθῆ γάζαν)," (27.34). | After the death of the firstborn, Pharaoh urges Moses to leave. "The Israelites… had asked the Egyptians for jewelry of silver and gold, and for clothing (ἱματισμὸν)… | |

| | Artapanus | Septuagint & Additional Sources | Diodorus Siculus, *Library* |
|---|---|---|---|
| | | and so they plundered the Egyptians" (Exod 12.22). | |
| 38. | They cross the rivers (ποταμοὺς) of Arabia. They arrive at the Red Sea (τὴν Ἐρυθρὰν … Θάλασσαν, 27.34). | "So God led the people by the roundabout way of the wilderness towards the Red Sea (τὴν Ἐρυθρὰν Θάλασσαν)" (Exod 13:18). | After curbing the rivers (ποταμὸν) of Ethiopia, Osiris continues his march through Arabia along the shore of the Red Sea (Ἐρυθρὰν Θάλατταν, I.19.6). |
| 39. | According to the Memphites, Moses, observed the low tide of the land and therefore made the people cross on dry land (διὰ ξηρᾶς, 27.35). | "But the Israelites walked on dry ground (ξηρᾶς) through the sea" (Exod 14:29). | |
| 40. | According to the Heliopolitans, the king pursued them with a great force and the sacred animals, since the Jews had taken goods from the Egyptians. Moses splits the sea, the Jews pass, the Egyptians are barred from advancing by a great fire and all perish by the fire and the flood (27.35–37). | "At the morning watch the Lord in the pillar of fire and cloud looked down on the Egyptian army, and threw the Egyptian army into panic. He clogged their chariot wheels, so that they turned with difficulty…The Lord tossed the Egyptians into the sea" (Exod 14:26). | |
| 41. | The Jews spend forty years in the desert and eat honey-dew flour which is the color of snow (27.37). | The forty years in the desert. "In the morning there was a layer of dew around the camp. When the layer of dew lifted, there on the surface of the wilderness was a fine flaky substance, as fine as frost on the ground" (Exod 16:13). | |
| 42. | Moses was tall (μακρόν), red (πυρρακῆ), and around eighty-nine years old at this time (27.37). | "Moses was eighty years old and Aaron eighty-three when they spoke to Pharaoh" (Exod 7:7). "Moses was one hundred twenty years old when he died; *his sight was unimpaired* and his vigor not abated" (Deut 34:7). | Sesoosis is four cubits and four palms (about seven feet) tall (I.55.9). The only bulls that are sacrificed are the red (πυρροὺς) ones, since this is the color of Typhon (I.88.4). "And after a reign of thirty-three years, he [Sesoosis] deliberately took his own |

| | Artapanus | Septuagint & Additional Sources | Diodorus Siculus, *Library* |
|---|---|---|---|
| | | | life, *his eyesight having failed him*" (I.58.3). |

## The Bible in Artapanus

The above comparison shows that the structure of Artapanus's narrative follows the Exodus story as it is recorded in the Bible. Yet, Artapanus uses the Exodus merely as a starting point for a skilled literary endeavor in which he uses the Bible as a quarry, exploiting it without much interest in the integrity of the work as we know it. The changes he introduces are systematic and point to an intentional distortion rather than to a deviant source. As Droge has shown, the most obvious change Artapanus introduces to the narrative is to make Moses a communicator of culture rather than a lawgiver.[33] Other than circumcision, there are no obligations or restrictions attached to "Mosaic culture;" rather, the account exclusively focuses on the well-being of mankind.

Accusations of Jewish misanthropy – quite common in later times, but also attested early on in the writings of the third century native Egyptian priest Manetho – have led some scholars to argue that Artapanus wrote to refute such claims, countering misanthropy with philanthropy. While it is of course impossible to falsify the general cultural antagonism of the two writers, Tiede had already dismissed such speculation based on his close reading of Artapanus:

> The account of appropriation of Egyptian goods and the Memphite rationalized version of the crossing of the Red Sea may suggest further that if Artapanus was aware of the charges of the literary polemicists, he was not concerned to respond apologetically to them.[34]

There is no evidence that Artapanus knew of, or was interested in, any anti-Jewish text. Instead, every element of the anti-Jewish narratives that Artapanus allegedly counters can be traced to the stories also preserved by Diodorus, which Artapanus appropriates without any concern for other

[33] Arthur J. Droge, *Homer or Moses? Early Christian Interpretations of the History of Culture* (Tübingen: Mohr Siebeck, 1989), 29. Diodorus refers to both Moses and Sesoosis explicitly as lawgivers (I.95.2 and 4). None of this appears in Artapanus's Moses, and I do not see any particular reason why either Alexander Polyhistor or Eusebius would suppress such information. Artapanus does not in any way refer to Pseudo-Hecataeus's account of the Jews, which has been preserved in Diodorus. Here, Moses is a priest, warlord, and lawgiver, as well as an unfriendly figure.

[34] Tiede, *Charismatic Figure*, 175.

literature.[35] If the general tendency of Artapanus's version of the Exodus contradicts that of the anti-Jewish versions, it is perhaps more likely due to his reliance upon the biblical narrative which the polemicists sought to counter in the first place.

Artapanus's treatment of the Bible does not cast him as an apologist for the Jews. He not only changed, he also contradicted the biblical account when it came to the question of the patriarchs' euhemeristic philanthropy. Given the scope of a full discussion of Artapanus's hermeneutics (both

---

[35] The idea that Artapanus refutes Manetho was first proposed by Freudenthal (*Hellenistische Studien*, 161), subsequently elaborated by P. M. Fraser (*Ptolamaic Alexandria*, I:706) and finally treated by Collins (*Between Athens and Jerusalem*, 40). If Artapanus is understood as an adaptation of the source he shares with Diodorus, none of the proposed "refutations" of Manetho holds true. Five examples shall suffice. First, Freudenthal pointed to the fact that Manetho claimed that the Jews were driven out of Egypt because of their leprosy, whereas Chenephres dies of "leprosy" (Freudenthal, *Hellenistische Studien*, 161). The disease, however, is not leprosy, but "Elephantiasis," and there are many other possibilities as to why Artapanus might have chosen this disease. In Diodorus, for example, Dionysus was the *first man* to celebrate his victory on an Elephant. To have Chenephres be the *first man* to die of Elephantiasis travesties this tradition at the expense of the Egyptian king (see #27 in the table above). Second, Fraser pointed to the role of Ethiopia in Manetho's account, which is clearly dominant in Artapanus as well. However, Ethiopia is likewise a major focus of the Egyptian royal stories in Diodorus's sources (Fraser, *Ptolemaic Alexandria*, 1:705–6). Third, Collins specifies that "Manetho... alleged that Moses forbade his people to worship the gods or abstain from the flesh of the sacred animals... Artapanus claimed that it was Moses who established these cults" (Collins, *Between Athens and Jerusalem*, 40). When Artapanus portrays his Moses as consecrating various animals, he follows closely the rationale given in Diodorus's four possible rationalizations of animal worship (see #12, 13, and 21 in the table above). It should also be noted that in Artapanus, the animals all sank in tumult to a lifeless ocean – which would be a rather disingenuous refutation of Manetho. Fourth, Collins argues that "Manetho alleged that Moses had invaded Egypt... Artapanus claimed that Moses restrained Raguel and the Arabs from invading" (ibid). Why, then, does Moses go on to destroy Egypt and unleash "his military forces" onto Egypt if Artapanus seeks to refute Manetho? Even if one were to object that Moses at first restrains Raguel from invading Egypt, and only invades Egypt after having received a divine command to do so, it seems unlikely to me that a hostile audience would appreciate such a subtle theological defense against Manetho's charge. Similarly, it is unlikely that Artapanus's dramatic exaggerations of the Exodus's carnage (see #36 in the table above) would gain sympathy for Jewish concerns in Egypt. Cf. also John J. Collins, "Reinventing Exodus" Exegesis and Legend in Hellenistic Egypt," in *For a Later Generation, The Transformation of Tradition in Israel, Early Judaism, and Early Christianity* (ed. R. A. Argall et al.; Harrisburg, Pa.: Trinity Press, 2000), 52–62; Holladay, *Fragments from Hellenistic Jewish Authors*, I:213; Sterling, *Historiography and Self-Definition*, 182–83; and Albert-Marie Denise, "Le portrait de Moïse par l'antisémite Manéthon (III s. av. J.-C.) et la réfutation juive de l'historien Artapan," *Le Muséon* 100 (1987): 49–65.

here and in the following section), three representative examples shall suffice (the numerals in the following refer to the table above):

First, the biblical Joseph does his best to enslave all of Egypt and to collect everyone's land for Pharaoh, sparing only the priests (#5). In Artapanus, Joseph seeks to stop the strong peasants from oppressing the weak ones, and gives land to the priests – a partial travesty of the biblical account. Second, the biblical Moses is best-known for his Deuteronomistic stringency with respect to monotheism and iconoclasm, as well as for his laws. Artapanus's Moses, however, freely attributes the symbols of the Egyptian cult to the priests (#12, 17 and 21), and Isis's rule is mentioned as well (#35).[36] Even though the text assumes the practice of circumcision (#18), Moses nowhere legislates any laws. Third, in contradistinction to his rosy image of Moses as euhemeristic philanthropist, Artapanus describes God's retribution for the Egyptian king's viciousness in much harsher terms than in the Bible. The biblical Exodus account is quite explicit in limiting the damage done to Egypt; the people are even warned before the hail comes down. Artapanus, however, adds (#36) an earthquake to the lethal hail and maximizes Egyptian casualties to nearly 100 percent. Artapanus's Egyptians are hit unprepared. And he not only travesties the biblical story, but also contradicts Diodorus's claim that the Egyptians can predict earthquakes – which leads us to consider how Artapanus treats Diodorus's sources.

## Diodorus Siculus and Artapanus

Diodorus visited Egypt between 60 and 56, where he began to work on his *Bibliotheque* (*Library*).[37] Artapanus therefore considerably predates Diodorus. Given the numerous similarities between Artapanus's story of Moses and Diodorus's stories of Osiris/Dionysus and Sesoosis, as indicated above, it appears that Diodorus and Artapanus learned similar stories about these heroes, and that they both learned them in Egypt. These similarities, in my view, are so far reaching that we can tentatively use Diodorus's text

[36] Interestingly, Isis was taught by Hermes, whose role Moses assumes in Artapanus. See Diodorus 1.17.3, 1.27.4, and Tiede, *Charismatic Figure*, 155.

[37] Diodorus then moved to Rome and completed his work by 30. He composed his first three books before the deification of Julius Caesar around 41. See Gerhard Wirth, *Diodor und das Ende des Hellenismus* (Vienna: Verlag der Österreichischen Akademie der Wissenschaften, 1993); Kenneth S. Sacks, *Diodorus Siculus and the First Century* (Princeton: Princeton University Press, 1990); Anne Burton, *Diodorus Siculus, Book I: A Commentary* (Leiden: Brill, 1972).

as an approximate substitute for Artapanus's own putative sources. The cumulative evidence resulting from this attempt allows us to take the next step of evaluating the effects of Artapanus's reworking of his proto-Diodoran sources.[38]

From a narrative point of view, Artapanus had excellent reason to identify Moses with Diodorus's heroes, namely the manifold coincidental similarities between the Bible and the source shared with Diodorus. Some examples include the conspiracies of Joseph's and Osiris's brothers (#4), Joseph's and Isis's giving land to priests (#6), the stocking of grain (#6), Moses's and Sesoosis's dealings with Arabia and Ethiopia, or their leadership in religion and culture throughout the narrative, and the narrative's emphasis on their eyesight (#42). Another established discourse Artapanus might have integrated into his work is the association of Moses, or the Jews, with Dionysus.[39]

We do not know what Artapanus thought of these similarities, yet we can say that he treated the material shared with Diodorus in the same way

---

[38] It is not impossible that the congruencies between Diodorus and Artapanus are due to shared literary sources, such as Herodotus or Hecateaus of Abdera. A comparison of the material shared by Artapanus and Diodorus with that shared by Herodotus and Artapanus, however, shows that Artapanus alludes to nothing from Herodotus that Diodorus did not appropriate himself. Diodorus, however, presents much to which Artapanus responds that is absent from Herodotus (this is true for both the Sesoosis and the Dionysus material). The situation concerning Hecataeus's lost work is more complicated. While Hecateaus certainly was an important source for Diodorus's first book, Diodorus mentions him only twice in his first book, and that in a group with other historians (see Diodorus I. 37.3, I.46.9). Kenneth Sacks points out that Diodorus was more creative in the usage of sources than has long been held, and Anne Burton convincingly argues that "it is impossible to attribute to [Hecataeus] the major part of [Diodorus's] book [I].... It is too easy to attribute to an author, the major part of whose work has been lost, passages for which an alternative source is not immediately apparent." Burton, *Diodorus Siculus, Book I,* 34; Sacks, *Diodorus Siculus and the First Century*, esp. chs. 1-3. While I follow Burton's view that it is "too easy" to posit a single (lost) written source that Diodorus used, the generic affinity between the two euhemeristic writings and the lexical similarities of Diodorus and of Artapanus remain intriguing.

[39] Carl Holladay suggested that Moses's miraculous escape from prison is a reference to Dionysus's escape from prison (#32, Holladay, *Fragments from Hellenistic Jewish Authors*, I:205–9). Furthermore, the association of Jews with the Dionysus cult may be implicit in 2 and 3 Maccabees (#28). Even if most authors date the current version of 3 Maccabees to more than a century after Artapanus, the stories that it reflects may be indicative of those that circulated earlier about the Ptolemies and their treatment of the Jews. Yet again, Artapanus's motif seems foremost to travesty the depiction transmitted in Diodorus of Egyptian mourning rituals: in Diodorus, Egyptians wear linen after the Egyptian king dies, while Artapanus's Egyptian king dies after forcing the Jews to wear linen. Cf. the suggestions in Lucien Cerfaux, *Receuil Lucien Cerfaux, études d'exégèse et d'histoire religieuse* (Gembloux: Duculot, 1954), I:81–85.

that he approached the biblical material. Rather than parodying the Hellenistic stories as such, he transfers – while amplifying – the deeds of the ancient heroes to the patriarchs. In addition, he denigrates the few moments of romanticized native Egyptian culture he finds in his sources. For example, Artapanus retells the Exodus story by inverting the claim, transmitted by Diodorus, that Egyptians had mantic powers: whereas they are specifically warned about hail in the Bible and claim to predict earthquakes in Diodorus, they do not anticipate the deadly hail and earthquake in Artapanus (#36).

At crucial points, Artapanus changes the deeds of proto-Diodorus's mythical figures and sets them against his version of Mosaic philanthropy. The most interesting examples have already been treated by Tiede, without the larger framework I now present. For example, in #16 and #26 in the above table, Sesoosis attacks first Arabia and then conquers Ethiopia with his best men – a task impossible even for Dionysus. In Artapanus, it is Moses who wins this battle against Ethiopia, and he does so not with skilled warriors but with earth-workers.[40] In another example argued by Tiede (#15), Sesoosis demonstrates his virtue (ἀρετὴν) by tormenting subdued leaders, while Artapanus's Moses displays his virtue by advancing culture and technology (#15).[41] The contrast between the ideals of Artapanus and those of (proto-)Diodorus concerning "virtue" is as stark as that between Artapanus's Joseph and the Joseph of the Exodus narrative concerning slavery – yet both are understandable only to a discerning audience that knows both sets of Artapanus's sources.

Most interestingly is the division of Egypt into thirty-six nomes by both Sesoosis and Moses (#12 and 13).[42] Sesoosis divides the land to collect taxes. Artapanus contrasts this to Moses, who divides the land in order to establish worship of the divine –in line with (proto-)Diodorus's portrait of Hermes as establishing proper worship.[43] Moses furthermore assigns sa-

---

[40] Tiede, *Charismatic Figure*, 158.

[41] Tiede, *Charismatic Figure*, 159.

[42] This was first proposed by Lévy, "Moïse en Ethiopie," 207.

[43] The Greek has been read creatively by some scholars. In Artapanus, Moses ἑκάστῳ τῶν νομῶν ἀποτάξαι τὸν θεὸν σεφθήσεσθαι. Freudenthal suggested to read ἑκάστῳ in a distributive way and to connect it to τὸν θεὸν (Freudenthal, *Hellenistische Studien*, 147). Many scholars followed him uncritically and understood Moses to assign an animal to be venerated as god in each nome. The text, however, simply states that "Moses prescribed to each nome to venerate god," without specifying which god is intended, let alone that the animals *were* gods. The simplest reading of this line would, in fact, identify this god to be Moses's god, the ruler of the universe. The line between Artapanus's monolatry and Egyptian polytheism – which he condemns – is illustrated through his polemic against the construction of a temple and the burial of the Apis bull (see below).

cred letters, animals, and land to the priests – just as Isis gave land to the priests according to (proto-)Diodorus. Nowhere is Artapanus's creative synthesis of the Bible and (proto-)Diodorus more impressive than it is here. In the Bible, Moses organizes (Israelite) worship and assigns land to the priests. Diodorus states that an unnamed king divided the country and assigned different objects of veneration to each nome, including animals, in order to appease the country. Elsewhere, he states that cats, dogs and ibises are deified because of their utility. Artapanus combines the biblical with the (proto-)Diodoran elements and states that Moses divided the country, told the people how to venerate god (through the use of animals), and at the same time attributed land, sacred letters and the aforementioned animals to the priests. He thereby appeases the country. Artapanus formulates his own euhemeristic form of a Mosaic Hellenism based on whatever is useful for mankind. The Bible, for him, is a source as welcome as the ones shared with Diodorus, and he imitates and travesties both sets of texts alike.

Consequently, Artapanus makes a threefold move. He recasts the bibli cal Abraham, Joseph and Moses as the most benevolent and egalitarian leaders and purges from their characters (especially Joseph), any form of injustice, as well as any affinity with Jewish law (other than circumcision). He, moreover, augments their fame by transferring the cultural and social innovations of Osiris/Dionysus, Hermes, Orpheus and Sesoosis to them: astrology, letters, boats, etc. Finally, he changes all of the features of Diodorus's heroes that he dislikes: Moses's virtue is euergetism, not subduing foreign leaders; he excels as military leader, but with the weakest rather than with the strongest of men, and so on. With Artapanus's treatment of his literary sources in mind, we can now turn to the historical situation of his implied audience.

---

Indeed, Artapanus does not deviate from the monolatry that appears time and again in his work, although he allows for sacred objects and mythological beings besides the "God of the *Oikoumene*" whom he names later. Many scholars have argued about Artapanus's theology: see John M. G. Barclay, *Jews in the Mediterranean Diaspora from Alexander to Trajan (323 BCE–117 CE)* (Edinburgh: T&T Clark, 1996), 132; Tiede, *Charismatic Figure*, 166–74; cf. Rob Kugler, "Hearing the Story of Moses in Ptolemaic Egypt: Artapanus Accommodates the Tradition," in *The Wisdom of Egypt: Jewish, Early Christian, and Gnostic Essays in Honour of Gerard P. Luttikhuizen* (ed. A. Hilhors and G. H. van Kooten; Leiden: Brill, 2005), 74–77. Collins, however, rightly stresses that "Artapanus's theology is an offshoot of his politics" (*Between Athens and Jerusalem*, 45). Collins earlier described him as henotheistic (ibid., 42 n. 68) – i.e. believing in a central God that is superior to all other deities. This seems correct to me, although the text itself does not provide certainty.

## The Historical Context

John Collins correctly states that "the date of Artapanus is far from certain. Since he is dependent on the Septuagint and was used by Polyhistor, he must have written somewhere between 250 and 60 B.C.E."[44] While I agree that Artapanus's dating is problematic, I would like to challenge the premises of both ends of Collins's suggested range and propose a much more precise dating.[45]

To establish a *terminus ante quem*, I first note that Alexander Polyhistor died abruptly in 35.[46] We do not know at what point Polyhistor authored his writings on the Jews and there is no reason to exclude such a late date a priori. Nor can one posit that Polyhistor stopped integrating new materials twenty-five years before his death. That is, we cannot rule out 35 as an extreme, yet plausible *terminus ante quem* for his Jewish writings.

The establishment of a *terminus post quem*, however, is more delicate. Rather than using the fuzzy publication dates of the Septuagint, I suggest turning to more concrete historical data. Artapanus mentions that Moses fought a war against Ethiopia in which he defeated "about a hundred thousand (περὶ δέκα μυριάδας) land-laborers." Fraser has already suggested

---

[44] On the use of Artapanus's dependence on the Septuagint to indicate a date after 250, see footnotes 16 and 17.

[45] In his recent article, Rob Kugler writes that "it is... generally agreed that [Artapanus] was likely in circulation among the Jews of Egypt by around the middle of the second century BCE" (Kugler, "Hearing the Story of Moses in Ptolemaic Egypt," 69). True, some authors have speculated about placing Artapanus in the middle of the second century, yet such a "general agreement" is not reflected in the scholarly literature known to me, and Kugler oddly references Collins's aforementioned summary to support his view, which dates Artapanus between 250 and 60. Kugler also claims that a "handful of other indicators have assured most observers that the work was completed before the last third of the second century BCE." (Kugler, "Hearing the Story," 69 n. 6). However, he does not provide details about the "handful of indicators;" instead he merely refers to Collins to support his claim. Finally, Kugler writes "that [Artapanus's] work comes not from Alexandria, but from the *chora*, as is in any case widely accepted; see, for example, Collins [*Between Athens and Jerusalem*], 39." (Kugler, "Hearing the Story," 69 n. 4). However, Collins (*ad loc.*) writes that when placing Artapanus in Egypt, "we need not necessarily think of Alexandria. Artapanus has little in common with the known Jewish literature of Alexandria and may well have lived in another settlement." This marks the third instance in which Kugler misinterprets Collins's careful and tentative suggestions – in order to promote a date which should become the *communis opinio* if my findings will be confirmed!

[46] Elizabeth Rawson, *Intellectual Life in the Late Roman Republic* (Baltimore: Johns Hopkins University Press, 1985), and L. Troiani, "Sull'opera di Cornelio Alessandro soprannominato Polistore," in Idem, *Due studi di storiografia e religione antiche* (Como: Biblioteca di Athenaeum 10, 1988), 7–39.

that this emphasis on native Egyptians enlisted in the army recalls the battle of Raphia in 217 B.C.E, in which Ptolemy IV Philopator defeated the Seleucids with the help of about 20,000 native Egyptian soldiers. This marked the first time in which a Ptolemaic king enlisted native Egyptians.[47] Fraser's observation yields a valuable point of reference. Native Egyptian soldiers continued to play an important role in Egyptian politics for subsequent centuries.

The inclusion of the name of the king of Upper Egypt allows me to date Artapanus a bit more precisely. I do not agree with Wacholder that it is "otiose to speculate on what basis Artapanus made up" the names of his Egyptian heroes. Indeed, the main antagonist of Moses bears a historical name. Artapanus writes that Moses is adopted by the sterile Merris, daughter of the king of lower Egypt, and her husband Chenephres (Χενεφρῇ), who "reigned over the region above Memphis, since there were, then, many kings in Egypt" (27.3).[48]

I suggest understanding Artapanus's use of the name Chenphres as evoking the memory of a native Egyptian ruler based in Memphis. As mentioned before, the native Egyptian soldiers became a permanent institution after the battle of Raphia, and continued to play an important role in the battle's aftermath. After the battle, they returned to the impoverished countryside and were directly affected by the king's oppression of the peasants. A revolt broke out in 206, in which the native soldiers seem to have played a leading role.[49] Under two successive indigenous kings, Upper Egypt prospered for about twenty years, from 206 to 186 – the year when Ptolemy V Epiphanes regained power.[50] The Greek name of the second of these rebel kings, who styled himself as Pharaoh, was

[47] See Günther Hölbl, *A History of the Ptolemaic Empire* (London: Routledge, 2001), 131–34 and Werner Huß, *Ägypten in hellenistischer Zeit, 332–30 v. Chr.* (Munich: Beck, 2001), 286–403.

[48] Yehoshua Gutman first pointed out that Manetho's list of the Pharaohs attests to the enthronement name of King Sobekhotep IV – the ninth ruler of the Thirteenth Dynasty in the eighteenth century – as Χενεφρὴς (a transcription of *Ĥ'-nfr-R'*). The Thirteenth Dynasty, however, was based in – not above – Memphis and did not share power in Egypt with other rulers. The name of Chenephres, therefore, is certainly not invented (as I will argue more fully below), yet Manetho's list does not help in dating Artapanus beyond the latter's own time; see Gutman's *The Beginnings of Jewish-Hellenistic Literature* (Jerusalem: Mossad Bialik, 1958; in Hebrew), 135. See also K. Müller, *Fragmenta historicorum Graecorum (FHG)* (Paris: Didot, 1848), 2:526–616.

[49] Polybius V. 107.1–3, see Koen Goudriaan, *Ethnicity in Ptolemaic Egypt*, 124.

[50] See Hölbl, *History of the Ptolemaic Empire*, 153–59 and Huß, *Ägypten in hellenistischer Zeit*, 506–13. It is noteworthy that one of the fragments of Diodorus Siculus' later books (XXXI.17a) reports about such a revolt in the Thebaid under Ptolemy IV.

Χαοννώφριος.[51] The consonants of Chaonophris's name resemble those of Chenephres's. The geography of his kingdom – based in Thebes, above Memphis – was also similar to the realm of Artapanus's Chenephres. Hence, if it is from this king that Artapanus drew inspiration for his own hero, I suggest he would have written after the turn of the second century B.C.E, at a time when this name would still be remembered.

A much later date, however, can be derived from Artapanus's geography. Artapanus's Joseph, loved by the people, brings his father and his brothers (whom he calls "Syrians"), and makes them settle in Heliopolis and the nearby Sais (#8). This fits well with the fact that Ptolemy VI allowed Onias IV, the son of the high priest Onias III, to settle in Egypt with a considerable following and to build a temple to the Jewish God in Leontopolis, in the nome of Heliopolis.[52] The romance between Joseph and Aseneth strengthens the association between Joseph and Heliopolis; likewise, the Septuagint, in Exod 1:11, adds Heliopolis to the list of temples that the Jews had built (#9).[53] Yet, whereas the Septuagint locates the settlement of the Jews, the biblical Goshen, in present-day Suez (see #8), Artapanus refers to Jewish settlements in Heliopolis as a well-established fact. Thus, we can date him after 162 at the earliest, when the temple seems to have been established.[54] Martin Hengel, furthermore, has suggested that Artapanus "könnte auf Grund ihrer politischen Ansprüche und ihrer synkretistischen Tendenz aus der Militärkolonie um den

---

[51] In 1978, Karl-Theodor Zauzich had suggested a new transliteration for the second of the two kings, who ruled in Thebes in the second century: *'nĥ-wn-nfr*. Based on this transliteration, Willy Clarysse published a Greek manuscript which attests to the Greek transliteration of this rebel king as Χαοννώφριος. See Karl-Theodor Zauzich, "Neue Namen für die Könige Harmachis and Anchmachis," *Göttinger Miszellen: Beiträge zur ägyptologischen Diskussion* 29 (1978): 157–58; and Willy Clarysse, "Hurganaphor et Chaonnophris, les derniers pharaons indigenes," *Chronique d'Egypte* 53: 106 (1978): 243–53.

[52] *Jewish Antiquities* 12.387; 13.65–71; 14.131; *Jewish War* 1.190; 7.427–30, *Against Apion* II.49. In ancient Egypt, the nome in which Leontopolis was situated was also called Leontopolis, rather than Heliopolis; yet Josephus's usage seems to reflect the geography of the Ptolemaic period.

[53] See *Joseph and Aseneth*, 1.3. Gideon Bohak convincingly argues that the romance justifies Onias's temple. See Gideon Bohak, *Joseph and Aseneth and the Jewish Temple in Heliopolis* (Atlanta: Scholars Press, 1996).

[54] See also Peter Schäfer, "From Jerusalem the Great to Alexandria the Small," in *The Talmud Yerushalmi and Graeco-Roman Culture* (ed. P. Schäfer; Texts and Studies in Ancient Judaism 71; Tübingen: Mohr Siebeck 1998), I:136. Schäfer suggests that the temple in Leontopolis was erected between 167 and 164. We do not have any evidence of a Jewish settlement preceding the temple in Leontopolis.

jüdischen Tempel von Leontopolis stammen."[55] I will return to Hengel's suggestion in more detail below.

Likewise, Sara Johnson noted that "the behavior of the mob here [in Artapanus] strikingly recalls the tumultuous years of civil war between Ptolemy VI and Ptolemy VIII in the mid-second century..., in which the whims of the Alexandrian mob played a significant role."[56] I would like to make an argument for dating Artapanus to a period only shortly after that suggested by Johnson, based on a hitherto overlooked detail of Moses's actions, which would indicate a later date for Artapanus. The idea of the Egyptians being an unruly people who conspire against their kings is not uncommon, and indeed equally attested also in Diodorus (#13). Artapanus, however, adds yet another detail:

> Moses did all this [i.e. religious and political reforms] in order to preserve the monarchy of Chenephres, since earlier (πρότερον), the crowds were disorderly, and at times (ποτὲ μὲν) chased kings away, at other times (ποτὲ δὲ) instituted them, often (πολλάκις) the same ones, some times (ἐνιάκις) others (*Praep. ev.* 27.5, #13).

While several of the Ptolemies suffered violent deaths, the startling piece of information Artapanus gives here is that the Egyptians are said to "often," or "repeatedly" (πολλάκις) reinstate the same king. In all of Hellenistic history, the reinstitution of an Egyptian king occurred only towards the end of the Ptolemaic Empire: namely, the two enthronements of Ptolemy VI Philometor (who ruled 180–164 and 163–145) and those of Ptolemy VIII (who ruled 164–163, 144–132, and 126–116). A short reconstruction of the main events and some noteworthy details will help situate Artapanus.

### *Chenephres and Ptolemy VIII*

From 180 on, Ptolemy VI shared power with his wife Cleopatra II until his brother Ptolemy VIII Euergetes II "Physcon" ousted him in 164. Ptolemy VI sought (and received) the help and the recognition of the Roman senate (especially that of Cato), but it was the Alexandrians who recalled Ptolemy VI in 163.[57] He ruled until he died in 145. The Alexandrians again recalled

---

[55] Martin Hengel, "Anonymität, Pseudepigraphie und 'literarische Fälschung' in der jüdisch-hellenistischen Literatur," in *Pseudepigrapha 1: Pseudopythagorica. Lettres de Platon. Litterature pseudépigraphique juive* (ed. K. Von Fritz; Entretiens sur l'Antiquité Classique 18; Geneva: Vandoeuvres, 1973), 239.

[56] Sara Johnson, *Historical Fictions and Hellenistic Jewish Identity: Third Maccabees in its Cultural Context* (Berkeley: University of California Press, 2004), 105.

[57] See Hölbl, *History of the Ptolemaic Empire*, 183–84. On the role of the Romans in the ascent to power of Ptolemy VIII see Anssi Lampela, *Rome and the Ptolemies of*

Ptolemy VIII, marking the second return to power of an Egyptian king.[58] If Josephus's account is accurate, Cleopatra II, the sister and widow of Ptolemy VI and the sister of Ptolemy VIII, tried to secure the crown for her own son, opposing her brother. Josephus tells us that Onias IV, the Jewish priest of Leontopolis, and a certain Jew named Dositheus sided with Cleopatra, marching with an army against Alexandria. He relates that Ptolemy VIII then captured the Jewish population of Alexandria and attempted to kill them with the help of intoxicated elephants.[59] Apparently, Ptolemy VIII prevailed, married his sister, killed the young son of Cleopatra II and Ptolemy VI and sent many Greek intellectuals into exile.[60]

In 144, Cleopatra II bore a son, Memphites. In 140, however, Ptolemy VIII married a second wife, the daughter of Cleopatra II, and instituted her as Queen Cleopatra III. In 132, a civil war broke out between the party of Cleopatra II and that of Ptolemy VIII. Ptolemy VIII murdered his own son, and the war devastated much of the country. During the war, Cleopatra II ruled in Alexandria with the support of the Greek population.[61] Ptolemy VIII continued to rule Upper Egypt, which he placed under the rule of his officer Paos, the first native Egyptian to hold such a high office (I will discuss the importance of native Egyptian culture for Ptolemy VIII below).[62]

---

*Egypt: The Development of their Political Relations 273–80 B.C.* (Helsinki: Societas Scientiarum Fennica, 1998), 196–215. Interestingly, Diodorus's report on this incident shares a peculiar Greek phrase with Artapanus: μέγεθος τῆς στρατιᾶς appears in Artapanus (#17, 27.9), where it describes the enormous size of Moses's army during his expedition to Ethiopia. To my knowledge, in the entirety of Greek literature recorded by the *Thesaurus Linguae Graece*, the term only appears once more: in the fragments of Diodorus XXXI.33 it describes the army of Ptolemy VI, who wins his war against the revolting Ptolemy VIII because of the size of his army. If this is no coincidence, the matter further fruitfully complicates the relationship between Artapanus and (Proto-) Diodorus. Further investigation into this matter is a desideratum.

[58] On Ptolemy VIII see Hölbl, *History of the Ptolemaic Empire*, 194–203; Madelaine Della Monica, *Les dernier pharaons* (Paris: Maisonneuve et Larose, 1993), 88–95 and Huß, *Ägypten in hellenistischer Zeit*, 537–625.

[59] *Against Apion* 2.50–52. Part of this report, such as the presence of the Roman ambassador Thermus, is verifiable. The report of the elephants trampling the allies of Ptolemy, which, according to 3 Maccabees occurred under Ptolemy IV, might have been inspired by the panic among the military elephants during the battle of Raphia, where such an incident did occur. On Thermus see Lampela, *Roma and the Ptolemies*, 199–200 and Erich Gruen, *The Hellenistic World and the Coming of Rome* (Berkeley: University of California Press, 1984), 714.

[60] See Hölbl, *History of the Ptolemaic Empire*, 194–95.

[61] On the role of Onias's sons, see below.

[62] See Hölbl, *History of the Ptolemaic Empire*, 197–204.

At this point, for the first time in Egyptian history, we have a political constellation that Artapanus's audience might have recognized: a king who was reinstituted by the Egyptians multiple times, namely Ptolemy VIII in 164 and 145 (and once more in 126). Even more precisely, readers could have identified the agonistic regimes of Ptolemy VIII and Cleopatra II during the civil war from 131 to 126, upon reading Artapanus's description of the simultaneous rule of multiple kings.

If we take Artapanus seriously, the matter allows for an even more precise localization. In 126, Ptolemy VIII prevailed over Cleopatra II. While he included his sister next to his step-daughter during the last part of his rule – at least formally so – he again took revenge on the Greek supporters of Cleopatra II, killing many Greeks in Alexandria.[63] We do not know the role and fate of the Jews at this moment. Because they had shared the fate of Greek intellectuals of Alexandria in 145, the Egyptian Jews may have had every reason to be concerned about their fate in 126. Indeed, in my view, the period just after the civil war allows us to contextualize Artapanus. I suggest that he was mainly concerned with the Jewish population of Egypt after the second return to power of Ptolemy VIII. My argument is based on the general historical situation just described, the two rulers' respective attitudes towards the Egyptian Greeks and Jews, and the decree of amnesty of 118. The cumulative force of such a dense contextualization outweighs my own suspicion against attributing too narrow a suggested timeframe. I suggest that Artapanus meant his audience to understand some of the figures in the following way:

- Ptolemy VI Philometor (the brother and predecessor of Ptolemy VIII and Cleopatra II) had been favorable to the Jews, as he allowed Onias IV to settle in Leontopolis. When Artapanus speaks about the benevolent king of Joseph's time, during which the Jews settled in "Sais and Heliopolis" (9.23.3) – i.e. in the immediate vicinity of Leontopolis – he might expect his audience to understand this as an allusion to Ptolemy VI.
- The son of Ptolemy VI was called Memphites ("of Memphis"); the son of the benevolent king in Artapanus is called Mempsasthenoth (Μεμψασθενώθ, 27.1).[64] The Egyptian-sounding ending [ώθ] (cf. the deity Toth, Θώθ) only thinly veils the fact that this name is, unlike Chenephres, not based on any known historical model.[65] Rather, the

[63] See Hölbl, *History of the Ptolemaic Empire*, 200–1.

[64] Artapanus's text at this point is difficult: it is unclear whether Mempsasthenoth is the name of Abraham's son, that of the king of Egypt, or that of the king's son.

[65] It is unclear how playful Artapanus's names are. Two more of them contain the Pseudo-Egyptian ending *-oth*: Palmanoth (#9 and 10), and Χανεθώθην (P.E. 27.14). If

second part of this bizarre compound, [ασθεν], means "weak" or "irrelevant." What educated Greco-Egyptian could have avoided dissecting such a name? In this process, it becomes clear that the first part of this name, [μεμψ-] can either be read as "blame," "censure," "complaint" (μεμψις), or as a compound containing "Memphis."[66] Hence, Artapanus's audience may easily have associated the dead Mempsasthenoth with the son of Ptolemy VI, the "irrelevant Memphites," whom Ptolemy VIII had killed.

- Through his auxiliary native Egyptian officer Paos, Ptolemy VIII had ruled the region above Memphis for several years during the civil war. As mentioned earlier, the same region had, under the rule of Ptolemy VIII's father five decades before, been ruled by the last native Egyptian Pharaoh Chaonophris. Based on the geography, Artapanus could have expected his audience to understand his figure of the Egyptian "king of Upper Egypt," bearing the native Egyptian name Chenephres, as a reference to the rule of Ptolemy VIII (through Paos). And even though we do not have any information as to how well Chaonophris was remembered, the general Egyptian emphasis on royal history, combined with the epigraphic attestation of Chaonophris's name, would have allowed Artapanus's audience to appreciate the homophony of names, as well as the congruence of territories.
- Furthermore, Ptolemy VIII persecuted the Jews after regaining power in 145 and probably also in 126. Artapanus's villain, who plans to destroy the Jews, is the Egyptian king Chenephres. If one dates Artapanus to the second half of the second century, his audience would have understood Chenephres's persecutions as a second reference to the country's current administration.

---

one were to understand χανε as the imperative of χασκω ("to yawn," or "to gape"), then the name would roughly mean: "Thoth, yawn!" Equally, the figure Ναχέρωτα (#20) may recall the Αχέρων, the river in the underworld (*Odyssey* 10.513). Although these suggestions are speculative, they may help shed some light on Artapanus's playfulness in general.

[66] Kugler suggests that Artapanus's "intense interest in Egyptian religious tradition suggests an origin in the Memphite region…" (Kugler, "Hearing the Story," 69). He does not support this conjecture, which seems to imply that an interest in religious traditions would be less likely in other regions of Egypt. As Kugler rightly points out, Memphis was a religious center of Egypt, yet his conclusion seems forced. We should note, however, that Memphis and the Memphite priests figure prominently in Artapanus's account (*Praep. ev.* IX 27.3 [#10], 27.30 [#34], 27.35 [#39]), which might imply that Artapanus had a bone to pick with the place or its establishment. Equally, the Apis cult had its center in Memphis, a cult which Artapanus criticizes from his own euhemeristic perspective (see Dorothy J. Thompson, *Memphis under the Ptolemies* [Princeton: Princeton University Press, 1988], 190–212).

- The wife of Ptolemy VIII, Cleopatra II, was well-disposed towards the Jews. Artapanus portrays Chenephres's wife as adopting (the later general) Moses. While Artapanus generally chose to ignore the powerful rule of female Egyptian royals, Cleopatra II's use of Jewish generals might also have resonated in the ears of his audience, who had heard of Moses's adoption through the wife of an anti-Jewish Egyptian king (I will return to this point below).

The similarities between the historical figures and those employed by Artapanus are suggestive: while I suggest that the implied audience would have been fully able to map the story onto the historical situation of its time, the story's chronological alienation by Artapanus also leaves enough leeway for his playful travesties of stories and events. For example, Artapanus's Palmanoth, the king of Lower Egypt (and the father-in-law of Chenephres), does not have any known Ptolemaic counterpart. Yet his actions correspond to those of the Pharaoh whom Artapanus carried over from the biblical Exodus: he is the one who suffers from the plagues and drowns in the Red Sea. If Artapanus expected his audience to know this narrative, as I argue he did, he may equally have expected it to be able to differentiate between literary artifact and the contemporary king of Egypt. The economic situation after 118 provides an additional reason to believe that this was indeed Artapanus's intention.

*The Decree of Amnesty of 118*

In 118, after the reconciliation between a victorious Ptolemy VIII and Cleopatra II, his acquiescing sister/wife, the royal couple sought to reestablish its power after a devastating civil war. They issued a decree of amnesty and adopted a large number of measures to establish order in the land and to advance native Egyptian religious institutions. The decree was of major importance and has been found in several copies, which allows us to assume that it became widely known in Egypt. If so, it might allow us to reconstruct with some precision the economic and cultural situation of the time to which Artapanus might have reacted. I will summarize the decree's main points:[67]

[67] The following summary points include references in parentheses to line numbers of the most complete papyrus of the decree, found in *Umm el-Baragat*, in the Egyptian Fayoum region (53), complemented by a fragment found in the *Souchos* sanctuary in *Tebtynis* (55). Both cited from the edition of Marie-Thérèse Lenger, *Corpus des ordonnances des Ptolémées* (Bruxelles: Palais des académies, 1980), 133–42 and 167–68.

(a) The most important provision addressed unjust land ownership among soldiers who had been compensated with land for their services and had become peasants (κεκληρουχημένηνους), as well as the tenants of consecrated land (τὴν ἱερὰν γῆν). The decree instructs the tenants of these groups who occupy too much land to officially declare this excess. Upon payment of a fine, they will then be granted amnesty; yet the native Egyptian former soldiers (μαχίμους) and the former native Egyptian members of the navy (ναύκληρομαχίμους) are confirmed in their tenant rights (lines 53:36–48).

(b) Consecrated land held by temples and other temple revenues are to remain untouched, with the priests left to administer their own affairs (53:50–61). Overdue tax revenue from temples, high-priests, priests, clergy, prophets and scribes is remitted. Those in charge of chapels consecrated to Isis, sacred ibises, hawks, and Anubis have the same privileges (53:62–67).

(c) The Pharaoh takes over the burial costs for the sacred bulls Apis and Mnevis, as well as other sacred animals (53:77–79).

(d) The Pharaoh reinstitutes measures (μέτροις) and threatens the death penalty to those who forge them (53:85–92).

(e) Farmers (γεω[ργοῦντας]) who plant on dried up (ἀμπελῖτιν) or flooded land (παραδείσους) are exempted from taxes.

(f) Houses and temples that were destroyed can be rebuilt (53:134–138, 147–154).

(g) Military officers (στρατηγοὺς) are greatly limited in their power. They are prohibited from forcing peasants to labor and from forcing them to feed military animals (53:231–247). Moreover, they are not allowed to exercise power because of personal hatred (55:10–20).

(h) Houses, livestock, and agricultural tools cannot be confiscated from the royal farmers and producers of linen (53:231–247). They should produce clothing for the king and other divinities (55:4–6).

This decree makes the dire situation of the Egyptian population readily apparent. Lenger emphasizes the great extent of the country's disorganization prior to the decree, throughout the troubled reign of Ptolemy VIII.[68] In the words of Hölbl,

> The senseless civil war and the military intervention in Syria resulted in a new age of decline for Egypt. After a period of progress in the last years of Ptolemy VI's reign, the condition of the lower classes must have deteriorated significantly once again.… [T]the phenomenon of anachoresis was once again on the rise.[69]

---

[68] Lenger, *Corpus des ordonnances des Ptolémées*, 128–31.

[69] Hölbl, *History of the Ptolemaic Empire*, 201.

Reading Artapanus against this background, as suggested by the identification of Chenephres with Ptolemy VIII, makes it possible to establish his message. Through a comparison with Artapanus's sources, I reconstruct his call for philanthropy and a euhemeristic Hellenized version of Egyptian worship. Based on this message, I argue that Artapanus appropriates for the Jewish patriarchs those actions of the Ptolemaic decree that line up with his own agenda. Those aspects of the decree that favor native Egyptian over Greco-Egyptian interests and those aspects of Egyptian worship with which he disagrees, however, Artapanus once more travesties, attributing them to Chenephres. In other words, Artapanus is not anti-Egyptian as long as the definition of Egyptian cult and culture remains in his own hands, with the elite status of the Greeks remaining untouched.

### *Land Reforms*

In Artapanus, Joseph becomes "*dioiketes* of the entire country" (διοικητὴν τῆς ὅλης ... χώρας, 23.2, #4). The title of *dioiketes*, steward of the land, is attested in Egypt from at least the third century.[70] Artapanus writes that Egyptian agriculture is in disorder (ἀτάκτως), the region is undivided, and the weak suffer at the hands of the strong. Joseph reorganizes the land, indicates its limits, re-cultivates barren land, and gives land to the priests (#6). He also invents standards of measure. If Artapanus implies that his audience knows of the Ptolemaic decree of 118, he would expect them to understand that he confers on Joseph responsibility for the same philanthropic acts performed by Ptolemy VIII:

- Just as Ptolemy VIII had done in the events described in item (a) of the previous section, Artapanus imagines Joseph to have reorganized the land, taking land from owners who held too much land ("the strong ones"), and protecting the ones who had too little (see #5).[71]
- Artapanus's motif of protecting the weak also reflects Ptolemy VIII's attempt to curtail the despotism of the military officers in (g).
- In addition, Joseph's alleged attempts to make fertile the barren land (#6) corresponds exactly to the tax-exemption granted to the farmers of hitherto dried up or flooded land by the Ptolemies in (e).
- Ptolemy VIII's reinstitution of the measures in (d) is reflected in Joseph's invention of them (#6).

[70] In Greek generally, *'dioiketes'* describes the manager of a private estate. In Egyptian Greek, however, it implies the manager of a large area.

[71] On the legal implications of forcing a *kleruch* to leave the land belonging to a Temple, see Tycho Quririnus Mrsich, *Rechtsgeschichtliches zur Ackerverpachtung auf Tempelland nach Demotischem Formular* (Vienna: Verlag der Österreichischen Akademie der Wissenschaften, 2003), 45–47.

– Artapanus's Joseph, in turn, gives land to the priests (#6, just as Moses in #12), reflecting the Ptolemaic decree's intensive protection of temple land in (a) and (b).

*Soldiers*

Section (g) of the Ptolemaic decree seeks chiefly to curtail the despotism of the military officers, the majority of whom were Greco-Egyptian, against the predominantly native Egyptian soldiers. As such, the decree reflects Ptolemy VIII's favoring of native Egyptian concerns over those of the Greek upper-class – which he portrays (perhaps justifiably so) as oppressing the masses. Artapanus, however, makes his Greco-Egyptian Moses go to war with native Egyptian land-laborers, with his king hoping that Moses will be killed in the process (#16). Needless to say, he implies that Chenephres would have sent the native Egyptian soldiers to certain death together with their Greco-Egyptian general. Artapanus gives the military officers (στρατηγοὺς) the important task of winning the war, together with Moses and the native Egyptian soldiers. Hence, Artapanus assures his audience, *pace* Ptolemy VIII, that the collaboration between the Greco-Egyptian elite and the native Egyptian masses is essential for the survival of both parts of society.

*Religion*

Ptolemy VIII, in (b), reduces taxes for the temple of the ibis and thereby favors an important aspect of the native Egyptian cult. Artapanus reminds his audience that Moses consecrates the ibis on account of its usefulness (#17), thereby relegating Egyptian religion to his own framework of Hellenistic euhemerism. Artapanus's polemic against the religious reforms of Ptolemy VIII becomes explicit when he portrays Chenephres as trying to build a temple to bury the bull whom he calls Apis, where Moses by contrast wants to use the bulls to work the land (#21). Interestingly, an Apis bull was buried in Memphis in 119, just a year before my suggested chronology for Artapanus.[72] Artapanus criticizes the waste of means of production for religious purposes in light of the manifest crisis of the population. In light of the Ptolemaic attempt to take over the burial costs for Apis in (c), Artapanus's criticism seems to travesty this very action. The king of Egypt, as Artapanus contends, should invest in the living rather than in the dead.

---

[72] While we do not know to what extent this burial was state-sponsored, the prominence of the ritual makes royal engagement on some level almost a certainty. See Thompson, *Memphis under the Ptolemies*, 292.

The temple-building efforts of Chenephres can be placed in the same discourse. Ptolemy VIII protects the privileges of the priests and the temples in (b) by guaranteeing their land rights, and in (f) by making efforts to have destroyed temples and houses rebuilt. Artapanus tells us, on the other hand, that these structures are all destroyed during the Exodus (#36), as his attitude near the end of his narrative towards the Egyptian priests (from south of Memphis!) turns sour (#33, 34). Finally, during the Exodus, Moses strikes the earth, Isis, with his (phallic) rod (#35). The imagery suggests that Artapanus trumps the timid measure of Ptolemy VIII (who merely exempted the temples of Isis from taxes), yet at the same time aggressively establishes Greco-Jewish (male) dominance over the effeminate country of Egypt and its chief Goddess (the imagery of "male" Jewish fertility vis-à-vis Egyptian "female" barrenness, both of the queen and of the land, will be discussed below).

We can see that Artapanus sides with those whom the Ptolemaic decree reprimands, namely the (Greek) military officers. Simultaneously, he opposes the new elite whom the decree favors, the Egyptian priests, representative of the native-Egyptian variety of Egyptian culture that Artapanus rejects. Both parties, Ptolemy VIII and Artapanus, seek to ensure for themselves the favor of the *kleruchs*, the rising caste of the time.

The forgoing discussion demonstrates that we can read Artapanus's message as a response to Ptolemy's decree of 118. While many of the decree's themes were relevant throughout the second century (e.g. desertion of fields, suppression of peasants, anti-(Greek)-colonial struggles), we can contextualize much of Artapanus's narrative only in light of Ptolemy VIII's radical turn to native-Egyptian economic, social, and religious concerns. Both Ptolemy VIII and Cleopatra II died in 116 and the decree ultimately failed in its attempt to reestablish native Egyptians as the dominant element of society.[73] Its effects, then, would have only been palpable immediately after its issuance. Hence, I suggest dating Artapanus's text between 118 and 116, which leads me back to Hengel's aforementioned association of Artapanus with the Greco-Egyptian Jewish military elite.[74]

## Artapanus and the Oniads

Interestingly, Artapanus portrays Moses as acting to save Chenephres's monarchy. This brings to mind Kugler's speculation that, after 124, the Jews would have sought "the stability and prosperity of ... [the] kingdom

[73] See Lenger, *Corpus des ordonnances des Ptolémées*, 128–31.

[74] See above.

[of Ptolemy VIII] lest he hold Onias's mistaken allegiance against him.[75] And indeed, I would like to revisit Hengel's suggestion that we should place Artapanus, if not in the vicinity of Leontopolis, then at least in the historical context of the Greco-Egyptian Jewish elite of the second century. If we can situate Artapanus after 118, the following speculations about Artapanus's Joseph, Moses and Aaron, and their relationship to the historical Onias IV, Ananias, and Chelkias could be appended to the suggested historical contextualization. Since our information on these historical figures derives mostly from Josephus, I wish to emphasize that one can evaluate the following suggestions separately from the previous discussion, which relies on less problematic sources.

In all likelihood, Onias IV fled Jerusalem after 162 and relocated to Leontopolis in Egypt, where he was allowed to construct a temple.[76] According to Josephus, Onias IV and his follower Dositheus became the chief generals of Ptolemy VI Philometor and Cleopatra II.[77] After the period in question, Onias IV's sons, Ananias and Chelkias, served under Cleopatra III in her war against her son, Ptolemy IX.[78] We have no information on the activities of Onias IV and his two sons during the period of 118–116.

While Josephus's accounts are colored by religious apologetics, they can nevertheless be used cautiously, since he must have expected his own audience to find his claims credible. They would have been verifiable for part of his audience, making it unlikely that he would have invented them entirely. Furthermore, the historicity of Onias IV and of a Jewish temple in Leontopolis is beyond doubt and the name Chelkias is attested as a military officer (στρατηγὸς) in Egypt.[79] We can, therefore, assume that there were Jewish military or political officials favored by Cleopatra II and Cleopatra III. Josephus reports Ptolemy VIII to be extremely anti-Jewish. Hence, it seems reasonable that Cleopatra II's enemy's enemies would be her friends and Josephus reports that Cleopatra III used Jewish generals for a period

[75] Kugler, "Hearing the Story of Moses in Ptolemaic Egypt," 70.

[76] Collins, *Between Athens and Jerusalem*, 69–76.

[77] Kugler claims that, after the return to power of Ptolemy VIII, "[o]nly because Physcon had the wisdom to marry Cleopatra [II], his brother's widow, did the crisis end and were the parties to it spared further punishment, the Jews under Onias's command included" (Kugler, "Hearing the Story of Moses in Ptolemaic Egypt," 69). Kugler's depiction of Ptolemy VIII's "wisdom" does not sufficiently reflect our complete ignorance of the Ptolemaic royal policies of the time, and especially about the roles of the Jews. Kugler does not give any evidence for this claim, and does not discuss Josephus.

[78] *Jewish Antiquities* 13.10.4 §§284–87. Ptolemy IX defeated Alexander Jannaeus in Palestine ("Syria"), and only Cleopatra III's victory against her son saved the Jewish kingdom (*Jewish Antiquities* 13.13.2 §354).

[79] Collins, *Between Athens and Jerusalem*, 76.

after the death of Ptolemy VIII. We can therefore expect continuity of Jewish military service under Cleopatras II and III, and finding Onias's two sons in this service indicates a prominent role for Jews in the Egyptian military throughout the second century. During the short joint reign of Ptolemy VIII and Cleopatra II and III, when Ptolemy instituted severe measures against the Greeks, the situation of the Greco-Egyptian Jewish elite must have been equally precarious, to say the least.

Therefore, we may use Josephus to imagine at least one of the possible historical audiences that Artapanus addressed. The reign of Ptolemy VIII saw the ascendance of native Egyptians in politics and religion, as well as the decisive decline of Greek culture in Alexandria.[80] Onias IV and his sons, as well as other high-ranking Jews, were part of the foreign element in Egypt, that of Greeks and Jews. Some of these Jews, inside or outside of Onias's family, may have served in the army of Cleopatra II (as they later did in that of Cleopatra III). They received land for their services, and were deeply concerned about the disorderly state of Egyptian agriculture and politics. The reconciliation between Cleopatra II and Ptolemy VIII in 126 dramatically challenged the status of the Jews: Ptolemy VIII again began to murder the Greek elite of Alexandria, these measures naturally extending towards the Jews, and Josephus insists that the Jews had been hit especially hard in 145. In this situation, someone intimately acquainted with the Greek legends about Dionysus and Sesoosis, and with some superficial knowledge of the narrative of the Exodus, sought to address the Jewish generals of Cleopatra II, who were left without adequate protection against Ptolemy VIII. This person chose, or happened to have, a Persian name, which gave his account a sense of objectifying distance as he turned the Exodus into a tale of contemporary relevance. His story glorifies Joseph, a Jewish *dioiketes*, and Moses, a Jewish military officer. Artapanus insists that Moses strives to assure the reign of the Pharaoh.

After the reconciliation between Ptolemy VIII and Cleopatra II, any Jewish general having served under Cleopatra II would likely have tried to convince the Egyptian royals that the Jews always sought to support the monarchy, as Kugler suggests. Yet Ptolemy VIII took revenge against his Greek and Jewish enemies and his policy to strengthen native Egyptians (especially native Egyptian priests and temples) would have led Artapanus to realize that the glory of Greek and Jewish Egypt had passed. He casts Joseph and Moses, respectively, as a conveyer of culture and civilization and as the ideal ruler of Egypt in the model of Sesoosis – yet he simultaneously predicts the reversal of all that has been achieved. Such an account would have flattered any Jewish military officer in the country – especially

[80] See Hölbl, *History of the Ptolemaic Empire*, 182.

one with a father who had already figured prominently in Egyptian politics. Any member of the Oniad family, and especially Onias IV's priestly sons, would easily have compared Onias IV with Joseph and themselves with Moses and Aaron, whose ancestors also came from Palestine to Egypt. Artapanus's amplification of the Exodus narrative and his insistence on treachery and conspiracy would have made his message clear to Jewish military leaders: leave the country, an assassination attempt is imminent, there is no shame in fleeing. The patriarchs had likewise all fled – and were justified in doing so.

My suggestions leave open an important question: why did Artapanus choose the figures of Joseph and Moses to respond to the decree of Ptolemy VIII? I would like to address three possible reasons: censorship, rhetoric, and art.

- First, if Artapanus wrote between 118 and 116, or even shortly thereafter, explicit criticism of the ruling king might have invited danger. The Exodus narrative, however, provides sufficient cover for implicitly criticizing Ptolemy VIII without arousing attention. Thus, using the figures of Joseph and Moses would have been an effective way to communicate to the Jewish elite beneath the radar of Ptolemaic eavesdroppers.
- Secondly, perhaps more importantly, Artapanus seeks to convince his Jewish audience that despite the previous Jewish prosperity in Egypt, the situation is now quite dangerous. Joseph and Moses provide easily identifiable, venerated figures – offering both flattering and instructive models for a Jewish elite that is perhaps unwilling to come to terms with the fact that they have placed their bets on the wrong royal, Cleopatra II.
- Third, despite the bleak picture, the educated author may have thought it suitable to comfort herself with the fact that, even if the present situation is terrible, it is not unprecedented, and that the Jewish people have a good record in surviving attempted genocides. The literary playfulness of the piece would have worked well if presented to an educated Greco-Egyptian Jewish audience. It is not unlikely that Artapanus would have allowed his audience to derive comic pleasure from his bold, playful, and lucid Exodus narrative, as Gruen has suggested.

If I were to take my best guess as to who "Artapanus" is, I would picture the text as the result of an afternoon's hastily drafted political satire, perhaps a prototype of a Passover Haggadah by an officer's friend, an educated slave like Polyhistor, or an Abyssinian maid in the entourage of the Oniads. Rather than adding to the manifold attempts to prematurely classify Artapanus, though, I propose deferring any judgment on the more nuanced points of his agenda or identity so as to focus on one last aspect of the text's obvious literary structure: the coherent repetition of themes throughout the three fragments.

## Reading Artapanus

In the following, I will supplement my historical analysis by approaching Artapanus's narrative and message from an intra-textual perspective. As mentioned above, the text is transmitted in the form of three separate sections, the story of Abraham in Chapter 18; of Joseph, in Chapter 23; and of Moses in Chapter 27. This tripartite structure may not be entirely due to the preservation methods of Polyhistor or Eusebius, as I have suggested reasons that neither author omitted entire sections or artificially broke up the text.[81] Now, the basic technique for my analysis will be to examine the text's structure, imagery, and vocabulary. Both the strength and the weakness of my proposal lies in suspending the fragmented nature of the text as we now have it; I will even bracket my historical and Hellenistic literary contextualization and return to it only in the conclusion. This allows for scrutiny and interpretation based on "hard" evidence. True, the many distortions and possible lacunae or additions by Eusebius and Polyhistor, and especially their potential preference for some Greek terms over others, create a certain level of uncertainty in the following. Yet the evidence of Artapanus consistently connecting all of his three fragments in a number of interwoven discourses minimizes the impact of this risk.

The primary recurring motif concerning our three patriarchal heroes is that of imminent lethal danger and the resultant flight to avoid it. This migration then leads to the agricultural, intellectual, architectural, martial and biological fertilization of Egypt. As Moses and his people finally leave Egypt, most of the blessings bestowed upon the Egyptians are effaced through the plagues and at the Red Sea with water and fire.

Again, a few examples of Artapanus's literary techniques must suffice. He creates part of his narrative frame through his use of location. For instance, the story of Abraham moves from the east to Egypt, then back to "Syria" in a well-balanced, continuous movement.[82] Then, we can see that

---

[81] Indeed, by placing "Israel" before Abraham and before "Jacob", and by placing Moses in the generation directly after Joseph, Artapanus shows his ignorance of, or disinterest in, biblical genealogy, see Gen 15:13f., Exod 12:40f.

[82] The Jews, as noted above, are called "Syrians." Joseph's story begins at the same place as that of Abraham (in Syria) with the words that, "Abraham had Joseph as offspring, the son of Jacob" (*Praep. ev.* 23.1), thereby directly connecting the narratives of Abraham and Joseph. Joseph then moves back from the east to Egypt. Moses's story

Artapanus's basic story line consists of recurring plots to commit – and flights to avoid – homicide. These two themes recur at various points and are both connected with the repeated usage of three Greek roots: [επιβουλ] for conspiring, [φυγ] or [φευγ] for fleeing, and [αναιρ], for killing.[83] Artapanus, therefore, prominently repeats a similar motif, using the same Greek roots, as was common in Hellenistic literature.[84] In the present case, the repetitions seem to have multiple effects. First, the similarity of theme and root connects the narratives of Joseph and Moses.[85] Second, the futile attempt of the Egyptians to flee and the manifold ways in which they are killed serves to emphasize even further the Jews' respective flights in a counter-point technique: the flight of the Egyptians is the only escape in the narrative that does not succeed, as it brings death. When Artapanus juxtaposes the collective flight of the Jews at the Red Sea with that of the Egyptians who perish, he produces a mutually polarizing dramatic effect. This elaborate composition connects the misfortune of Hebrews and Egyptians and conveys a keen awareness of the reciprocity of each people's suffering. The Jews are on the road to ever-improving divine favor. Yet the Egyptians, when they decide to expel the Jews, find themselves on an

---

begins in Egypt with the death of Abraham and his son (i.e., Joseph), providing a smooth narrative that leads from Egypt back and forth to Arabia and Ethiopia, and concludes with the Exodus to the east, providing a literary frame enclosed by localities.

[83] Abraham's son Joseph predicts his brothers' plotting (ἐπιβουλευθῆναι, 23.1) against him and flees with the help of Arab kings. In Egypt, Moses flees to an Arab king and the Egyptians try in vain to flee: After Chenephres, Moses's Egyptian stepfather, plots (ἐπιβουλεύειν, 27.11, ἐπιβουλήν, 27.13) with his friends and encourages Chanethoth to kill Moses (ἀναιρήσοντας, 27.14; ἀναιρεθήσεσθαι, 27.15f.) on the way to the burial of Moses's stepmother. However, both Moses and his brother Aaron hear of the plot (ἐπιβουλήν, 27.16 and 17), in which Aaron advises his brother to flee (φυγεῖν, 27.17, φυγήν, 27.18) from Egypt to Arabia. When Moses views the flames of the fire (without the bush) he wishes to flee (φεύγειν, 27.21) from the epiphany, but is told to stay. After Moses performs miracles in front of Pharaoh, Pharaoh in turn threatens to kill (ἀναιρήσειν, 27.30) the priests of Memphis (and to overturn their temples) if they do not produce similar miracles. During one of the plagues, the Egyptians that escape (φεύγοντας, 27.33) from the earthquake without being killed (ἀναιρεῖσθαι, 27.33) die from the rebounding hail. Finally, the Jews flee (διαφυγόντας, 27.37) from the danger of flood and fire in the Red Sea in which the Egyptians die. The use of the term does not seem to be governed by lexical constraint; see the usage of the verb [ανελ-] in 27.7 (Pharaoh wants to kill [ἀνελεῖν] Moses) and 27.27 (Moses kills [ἀνελέσθαι] the snake).

[84] This technique is best documented for Greek novels. See Shadi Bartsch, *Decoding the Ancient Novel: The Reader and the Role of Description in Heliodorus and Achilles Tatius* (Princeton: Princeton University Press, 1998).

[85] In addition, Artapanus connects Abraham and Moses by repeating the verb [απαλλαγ-] when Abraham left (ἀπαλλαγῆναι) back to Syria (18.1) and Moses leaves (ἀπαλλάσσεσθαι) to Arabia (27.1).

increasingly brutal path of inflicting, and suffering from, violence that leads to divine genocide through earthquake, hail, water and fire.

The theme of danger and destruction, however, is only one aspect of Artapanus's story. He repeatedly and consistently combines the fruits of intellectual intercourse with those of physical intercourse between the patriarchs and "Egypt." Again, he structures his narrative around the three Jewish patriarchs in the same tripartite framework given above, with Abraham presented as having forged the beginning of prosperity, Joseph reinforcing it, and Moses bringing the greatest bliss – with the Exodus destroying most of what has been achieved.[86] I suggest placing Artapanus's combined imagery of intellectual, physical and agricultural fertility in the context of his use of gender. His central metaphor is that of the "female" earth, the Land of Egypt along with its effeminate and boorish inhabitants, which needs the "male" activity of Jews in order to become fertile. The earth, as Artapanus explains explicitly in the middle of the climactic Exodus episode, is actually the goddess Isis (τὴν γῆν εἶναι Ἶσιν, 27.32).[87] Aside from Moses's suggested "plowing" of the earth with the

---

[86] Abraham begins the intellectual fertilization of Egypt by teaching astrology to its king (18.1). Joseph goes a step further, managing to reorganize a disorderly (ἀτάκτως, 23.2) Egyptian agricultural system. Artapanus first alludes to the connection between agricultural and sexual fertility in the imagery of Joseph making plots of land usable that had been described as χερσευομένην (23.2) – a term that denotes both agricultural and feminine infertility. These plots of land are then allotted to the Egyptian priests who, together with the royal class, seem to be the primary beneficiaries of Jewish fertilization. In the next sentence, Joseph marries the daughter of the priest of Heliopolis, who bears children for Joseph. Joseph also invents "measures" (μέτρα, 23.3) – such intellectual activity connects him with both Abraham and Moses. Moses is introduced to the story as a Jewish child whom the king's daughter adopts because of her infertility (στεῖραν, 27.3) – thus emphasizing Jewish fertility over Egyptian impotence. Moses amplifies the intellectual heritage of Abraham by inventing philosophy, he also reinvents Joseph's projects on a much larger scale by dividing not only fields (as Joseph), but the entire country, while restructuring its worship (see above). Moses's major intellectual achievement, however, is the innovation of sacred letters for the priests, grounds on which the latter see him as divine. Both Joseph and Moses are beloved (ἀγαπηθῆναι, 23.3, 27.6) by the Egyptian crowds, another element common to the patriarchs and a fact that triggers the king's (and eventually the priest's) discomfort with Moses. Artapanus stresses that all of Moses's efforts were aimed merely to protect the king's legacy against Egyptian disorderly (ἀδιατάκτους, 27.5) behavior, just as Joseph fought against the disorderly (ἀτάκτως, 23.2) agricultural system. Also in this latter case, the usage of the same Greek root [τακτ] twice is by no means coincidental, but instead connects the patriarchs' efforts to fertilize both agriculture and culture.

[87] Artapanus prepares his "revelation" that the earth is a female Isis in need of fertilization in several steps throughout the narrative, again employing repetitive terminology. As soon as Joseph takes control of the Egyptian land (χώρας, 23.2) he organizes it (γῆν,

help of the bull, the epitome of the Egyptian fertility cult, the phallic imagery of Moses's striking of the earth with his rod is perhaps the most explicit depiction of Artapanus's cultural policies. Throughout the narrative, male Jews, along with their male God, dominate and fertilize the barren land of Egypt, including the land's supreme Goddess, in every conceivable way.[88]

One more aspect of Jewish intellectual fertilization is Artapanus's view of the rise and fall of the Egyptian cult enacted in the narrative about Jewish and Egyptian building activity. Again, he carefully sets up the account throughout the three sections of his narrative (that of Abraham, Joseph, and Moses) by repeatedly using Greek roots: [σκευαζ] and [οικ]. He seems

---

idem) in the wake of Egyptian agronomic disorder (τὴν χώραν ἀδιαίρετον εἶναι, idem), making the ground fertile again (γεωργήσιμον, 23.2f.). When Moses enters the scene, he likewise contributes land (χώρας, 27.4). After having won the Ethiopian battle with help of his "earth-laborers" and his intimate knowledge of the land, he "invents" the bull – the epitome of male procreative power – as an aid to plough the earth (διὰ τὸ τὴν γῆν ... ἀροῦσθαι, 27.12). His impotent stepfather reacts by seeking to bury (θάπτειν) the bull and naming (προσαγορεύσαντα, 27.12) it Apis. Moses, as if in response, buries (θάψαι, 27.15 and 16) his deceased barren stepmother Merris and, in a complete parallelism, names (προσαγορεῦσαι, 27.16) the adjacent river and village after her. At this point Isis, the goddess of the land (ἐγχωρίων, 27.17) who also is known to have a burial place in the same region, is mentioned for the first time when we learn that Merris is no less honored then Isis. But only in 27.32 does Isis herself enter the scene.

[88] In my view, we can evaluate Artapanus's portrait of the relationship between Isis and God (τῷ θεῷ in 27.21) only in light of the equation of Moses and Isis's husband, Osiris. While Osiris is generally the main deity of Egypt throughout Artapanus's text, Artapanus mainly works with the (Proto-)Diodoran material on Osiris – which I have set aside for the present discussion. Yet even without Diodorus, we can place his theology into the henotheistic framework that Collins had suggested (see footnote 43). The fire in which God reveals himself consists of a fire (πῦρ) that suddenly appears ἐκ τῆς γῆς, "from the earth" (27.21) – i.e. the realm of Isis. God's audible command brings Moses to battle against the Egyptians. Then God disappears from the stage. Artapanus states, or repeats the (ignorant?) Egyptian opinion, that the miracles (τῶν τεράτων, 27.29) performed by Moses through striking the earth were actually performed by Isis (τὰ τέρατα, 27.33, while the Memphite priests only manage to present τερατουργήσωσί, "miracle-works" 27.30 of rare device which were not divinely authored). Either way, Isis seems to be dominated by the male Jewish God. Artapanus, furthermore, might imply that the water-related miracles, such as the rising of the Nile and the splitting of the Red Sea, might not have been authored by the goddess. The divine voice (φωνὴν... θείαν, 27.21) that ordered Moses to attack Egypt reappears at exactly the point of the story in which the very same voice (φωνὴν θείαν, 27.36) invites him to strike the sea with his staff. If God appears then to have direct control over the water and indirect control over Isis and her earth, Artapanus would appear to have taken over the Greco-Egyptian attributes generally associated with the deity of the sacred river, Osiris.

to differentiate between secular buildings and Egyptian temples.[89] Artapanus contrasts the Mosaic building activities with Egyptian temple building: the Jews found cities, not temples. The anticipated result of the attitude of the anti-Jewish and pro-native-Egyptian king is the destruction of the Egyptian houses and temples at the very moment that the Israelites leave. During the Exodus, all the houses and most of the temples collapse, and the consecrated animals, carried with the Egyptians on their pursuit through the Red Sea, drown with them.

It is clear, then, that the Jews are Artapanus's protagonist. Who, then, are the antagonists? The Egyptian masses seem to love Moses, and the priests deify him at first. The priests, however, already singled out through their thematic and linguistic association with the problematic temples, are portrayed negatively later in the story: the ones who think badly of the holy name die with convulsions, just as the king who thought badly of the Jews dies from disease (both times using the root [φαυλ]). The priests do not act by themselves. Only when the king threatens to kill them and to destroy their temples do the Memphite priests begin to employ their cheap tricks. In this way, Artapanus portrays the king as the enemy of the Jewish people, of the supreme deity, and even of the native Egyptians because he buries useful animals and sends them to their death on the battle field. Once more, Artapanus also juxtaposes Moses and the king through a number of roots that he employs.[90]

---

[89] In the first part, Abraham moves to Egypt with his entire household (πανοικίᾳ, 18.1). In the second part, Joseph, after bringing his family to Egypt, settles them in Sais and Heliopolis (κατοικισθῆναι, 23.3). The third section begins with the new king's evil intentions toward the Jews. Seemingly because of this negative attitude, he founds (οἰκοδομῆσαι) Sais, "installs" (καθιδρύσασθαι) its adjacent sanctuary and commissions (κατασκευάσαι, 27.2) the temple in Heliopolis. By connecting the king's bad intentions with his construction of temples and with the aforementioned Jewish settlements, Artapanus leaves little doubt that he perceived temple construction as a fitting means by which to intimidate, punish, or at least upset the Jews. Moses, by contrast, after his successful campaign against Ethiopia, founds (κτίσαι) Hermopolis and consecrates it (καθιερῶσαι, 27.9) to the ibis. Moses's stepfather reacts to his building of the city on even terms. First he has the temple of Diospolis (i.e. Thebes) rebuilt (οἰκοδομίας, 27.11), then he orders a sanctuary to be built (καθιδρύσασθαι) in order to bury the bulls which Moses had consecrated (καθιερωθέντα, 27.12). Just as Artapanus presents the temple constructions in Sais and Heliopolis as anti-Jewish reactions to Joseph's settling his family there, so too he seems to want his audience to understand this temple construction as a reaction – measure for measure – to Moses's founding of Hermopolis and his consecration of the ibis and the bull.

[90] When the king hears (ἀκούσαντα) God's name and faints ἄφωνον, "speechless" (27.26), the Greek roots used, [φων] and [ακου], create a juxtaposition of the king and Moses who heard the voice (φωνὴν) of God in the desert and at the sea, where he "obeys" (ἀκούσαντα, 27.36) God. Artapanus portrays the Egyptian king as an unworthy

Repetition, in addition to being a key feature of Hellenistic literature, is also a basic didactic device. As such, Artapanus's audience would have understood the themes which he stresses by repetition – fertility, building, and royal viciousness – as highlighting the role of Moses. Artapanus depicts Moses in contrast to the king, and he employs the entire Exodus narrative in order to portray him as the ideal political and military leader. In this case, Artapanus combines the repetition of the root [στρατ-] with terms for the land and its workers.[91] These land workers epitomize how Moses transforms the weak Egyptians, as he leads them to victory over Ethiopia, unleashing the full potential of the fertile connection between hyper-male Jews and effeminate Egyptians.

## Conclusion

The preceding tentative literary analysis dovetails with, and complements, my suggested historical contextualization. Through repetition of roots and motifs, Artapanus emphasizes the necessity for fertilizing the Egyptian soil and for social reforms in favor of the native Egyptian agricultural working class – under the auspices of benevolent Greco-Egyptian Jewish military and political leaders. True, the disorderly state of agriculture was a constant factor during the entire reign of Ptolemy VIII. Yet Artapanus's strong emphasis on the land workers, which he highlights through narrative and lexical repetition, especially recalls the royal measures to restart the pro-

opponent for Moses. Even the king's friends refuse to "obey" him (ὑπακούσαντος, 27.14) when he orders them to kill Moses, using the same Greek root for the third time. This weakness is an indication that the denigration of the Egyptian kings is one of the main literary efforts of the story. And Artapanus's audience would certainly have appreciated the severe but exact punishment of the sins of Chenephres, king of Upper Egypt who wanted to punish the Jews (κολάζωνται, 27.20) but died of a disease. Similarly, Palmanoth, the king of Lower Egypt, who also wanted to punish the Jews (κολάσει, 27.31), was killed following the Exodus.

[91] In 27.7, the Ethiopians fight together (ἐπιστρατευσαμένων) against Egypt and Moses becomes chief of the army (στρατηγόν). The weakness of the earth-working (γεωργῶν, 27.7) soldiers (στρατιωτῶν) should endanger Moses's life, but Moses sends out army chiefs (στρατηγοὺς) to observe the region (27.8) and is victorious. Moses founds Hermopolis and consecrates it to the ibis on behalf of the greatness of the military expedition (μέγεθος τῆς στρατιᾶς, 27.9). In 27.19 Ragouel wants to march (στρατεύειν) against Egypt, but Moses dissuades him from doing so (στρατεύειν). Finally, in 27.21 God tells Moses to march (στρατεύειν) against Egypt. Moses schemes to organize the field workers through observation of the land (χώρας, 27.8). This is the very same procedure that he, according to the Memphite priests, used to lead the Jews through the Red Sea when he first inspected the land (τῆς χώρας, 27.35).

duction of grain after the amnesty decree of 118. The same holds true for Ptolemy VIII's advancement of native Egyptian religion at the expense of the Hellenistic, euhemeristic interpretation that Artapanus favors. The literary devices portray the mutual interest of the native Egyptian workers and of the military and political elite. In line with Artapanus's general hermeneutics, he appropriates part of the royal reforms for himself, yet fully counters the ones of which he disapproves. Hence, reading Artapanus in dialogue with (Proto-)Diodorus, or on his own, both point to 118–116.

Finally, Artapanus's emphasis on Moses's military role – which I have sought to portray separately through the narrative, the (Proto-) Diodoran background, and the literary technique – strongly suggests that we can indeed imagine his audience among the Greco-Egyptian Jewish military elite. This audience would have known some version of the Exodus account, they certainly would have been familiar with the Egyptian myths of legendary generals like Dionysus/Osiris and Sesostris, and they would have enjoyed the flattering picture of a Jewish general in the Egyptian army. Through Josephus, we can be certain that such an elite existed. In light of the fate of the Jewish population of Egypt in the subsequent centuries, I cannot help but wish that they had heeded Artapanus's poetic exhortation for a second Exodus.

# Remembering and Forgetting Temple Destruction

## The Destruction of the Temple of Jupiter Optimus Maximus in 83 BC

Harriet I. Flower

> Sic Capitolium clausis foribus indefensum et indireptum conflagravit.
>
> Tacitus Historiae 3.71

> Sed nihil aeque quam incendium Capitolii, ut finem imperio adesse crederent, impulerat. Captam olim a Gallis urbem, sed integra Iovis sede mansisse imperium: fatali nunc igne signum caelestis irae datum et possessionem rerum humanarum Transalpinis gentibus portendi superstitione vana Druidae canebant.
>
> Tacitus Historiae 4.54

On the sixth of July 83 BC the Temple of Jupiter Optimus Maximus on the Capitol, Rome's most important archaic temple, was completely destroyed by a devastating fire whose exact cause never appears to have been securely established, at least according to the historian Appian.[1] This seems to have been the first major damage to the temple, which by this time was over 400 years old. It took the Romans many years to rebuild, despite the central role played by Jupiter's principal shrine in their religious life, both in the secular calendar and especially in the military sphere. The Capitoline Temple was the destination of every triumphal procession and sacrifice in thanksgiving for major victory abroad and thus became the symbol of Rome's world empire.[2] Unlike colleagues in religious studies, ancient historians have not been much concerned with temple destruction, with the result that neither this first destruction, nor even the subsequent and better attested burning of the Second Capitoline Temple in AD 69, have received the attention they deserve.[3] This paper will consider first the significance

---

[1] *BC* 1.83 (discussed below) and 86. Other references to the fire: Cic. *Cat.* 3.4.9; Sall. *Cat.* 47.2; DH 4.62.5, Ovid *Fast.* 1.201; Pliny *NH* 33.5.16; Plut. *Publ.* 15; *Sulla* 27.6; *de Is. et Os.* 71; Tac. *Hist.* 3.72; Obs. 57; Cass. *Chron.* 132.486M.

[2] See now A. Thein, "The Capitolium and Roman World Rule," *American Journal of Ancient History* 6 (2007), forthcoming.

[3] See, for example, F. Kolb, *Rom. Geschichte der Stadt in der Antike* (2d. ed.; Munich: Beck, 2002), 254–55 who confuses the two destructions and describes the fire of 83

of the destruction of 83 BC in its own cultural and religious context, and next the various ways in which Roman writers looked back to remember the loss in later ages. My contention is that the accidental burning of their most significant temple was experienced as a traumatic portent that overshadowed the time of Sulla's dictatorship in Rome, as well as the next generation, commonly referred to as the last generation of the Roman Republic. The complex rhetoric of ancient authors as they tried to come to terms with loss, devastation, and the wrath of the gods reveals ever new layers of reinterpretation and remembering of the past, whether in the immediate aftermath of the destruction or for its significance in the eyes of later Romans.

The Capitoline Temple was an archaic Tuscan style temple that housed three main deities, Jupiter (called Optimus Maximus in this shrine), Juno and Minerva.[4] Jupiter's great seated statue could be found in the larger central cella, while smaller shrines on either side were designed for Juno and Minerva. Some other deities, who were earlier inhabitants of the Capitol, also lived here, notably Terminus, the god of boundaries, and Juventas, the patron goddess of young men.[5] Both of these had been worshipped here before the building of the great archaic temple and had refused to make way, even when other gods did, for the new Capitoline triad. The whole Capitoline area also housed other temples nearby, although its topography has not so far been clarified in any detail by archaeological discoveries.[6] The design and construction of the archaic temple, which clearly changed the nature of this part of the hill even at the cost of trespassing on ground that had already been consecrated for other deities, is attributed by ancient sources to the two Tarquins, Etruscan kings who ruled in Rome.[7] However,

---

BC as the result of a battle between Marians and Sullans, although Sulla and his army did not arrive in Rome until the following year.

[4] For the Capitoline Temple, see *Paulys Realencyclopädie der classischen Altertumswissenschaft*, s.v. Iuppiter (Thulin, 1917); G. Tagliamonte (the temple until 83 BC) and S. De Angeli (the late republican and imperial temple) in *Lexicon Topographicum Urbis Romae*, vol. 3 (ed. E. M. Steinby; Rome: Quasar, 1996), *ad loc.*

[5] For Terminus, see Ovid *Fast.* 2.50, 641–84. For Iuventas (goddess of the *iuvenes*, the men of military age), see DH 3.69–70; Livy 5.54.7. For the dedication of the Capitoline Temple, see Cato fr. 24P = Fest. 160L; Livy 1.55; Gell. 12.6.2; Aug. *CD* 4.21, 23.

[6] Other gods who are recorded as having temples or shrines on the Capitol include Jupiter Feretrius, Fides, Mens, Ops, Venus Erucina, Jupiter Tonans, Jupiter Custos, Veiovis, and Juno Moneta on the *arx*. For discussion and bibliography, see C. Reusser (s.v. Area Capitolina, Capitolium) in *Lexicon Topographicum Urbis Romae*, vol. 1 (ed. E. M. Steinby; Rome: Quasar, 1993); F. Coarelli, *Roma* (Bari: Laterza, 1997), 37–51; and A. Claridge, *Rome: An Oxford Archaeological Guide* (Oxford: Oxford University Press, 1998), 229–41.

[7] For the founding of the temple, see especially DH 4.59–61 and Tac. *Hist.* 3.72.

tradition has it that the dedication actually fell after the expulsion of the last king, Tarquin the Proud, in the very early Republic and perhaps even in its first year and by one of its first consuls, Marcus Horatius Pulvillus. Every year a nail was hammered into the wall of the temple in a system that was used for dating and that closely associated the temple's era with that of the Roman Republic itself.[8] Regardless of the historical accuracy of this traditional chronology, it is notable that despite its regal and Etruscan aspects, the Capitoline Temple became most closely identified with Rome as a city and with her characteristic republican culture, as it was to develop over the subsequent centuries.

It would be difficult to overstate the importance and prominence of the Capitoline Temple, which loomed over the republican city on its acropolis-style hill, and which faced the river and market places that brought so many visitors to Rome, as the city came to be a crossroads between north and south, the sea and the hinterland. Every year the consuls performed their first New Year's sacrifice here. The senate met here for its first meeting, as well as for others, eventually using the temple as a kind of archive.[9] The great games celebrated in honor of Jupiter every September, known as the *Ludi Maximi* or *Ludi Romani*, were the first and most splendid in Rome.[10] The temple was also the home of the Sibylline Books, a collection of prophetic wisdom and religious advice that was consulted in response to requests from the senate by special Roman priests devoted only to this task. According to tradition, these books had also been acquired by one of the Tarquins and became associated with the (manifest) destiny of the city of Rome.[11]

Departing generals took their auspices and made sacrifice here as they set out for war, just as they hoped to return in triumph to process up the hill and sacrifice to Jupiter at the end of a victorious campaign.[12] The

---

[8] For the Capitoline era, see Livy 7.5–9 with D. Feeney, *Caesar's Calendar: Ancient Time and the Beginnings of History* (Berkeley: University of California Press, 2007), 141–42, 176.

[9] The New Year on the Capitol: Livy 22.1.6; 41.14.7; Ovid *Fast.* 1.75, 79; *ex Pont.* 4.4; senate meetings on the Capitol: Cic. *Leg. Agr.* 1.18; *Dom.* 14; *Sest.* 129; Livy 23. 31.1; 26.1.1; 30.27.1; App. *BC* 3.50; Ser. *Aen.* 3.134; 4.201; Lyd. *Mens.* 4.3. For the senate's archives on the Capitol in the imperial period, see Suet. *Dom.* 8.9.

[10] For the *ludi Romani*, see Kolb, *Rom*, 194 and F. H. Bernstein, *Ludi Publici. Untersuchungen zur Entstehung und Entwicklung der öffentlichen Spiele im republikanischen Rom* (Stuttgart: Steiner, 1998), 35–78, 119–29.

[11] DH 4.62.5.

[12] The senate's declaration of war on the Capitol: Livy 33.25.7; App. *BC* 7.5; the generals depart for their provinces after sacrificing on the Capitol: Livy 21.63.9; 42.49.1; the triumphal vows are fulfilled here: Livy 38.48.16; 45.39.11.

general who had been voted a triumph by his peers in the senate would ride into the city and up the hill in a chariot dressed in the garb of Jupiter Optimus Maximus and with his face colored red in imitation of the archaic terracotta statue of the god. Despite the many new deities who received thanks and new temples in Rome as a result of vows made by generals on the battlefield, the ultimate accolade of thanksgiving and celebration always belonged to Jupiter Optimus Maximus. Similarly, the honor of celebrating a triumph was the highest achievement a Roman politician could aim at, more prestigious than any elected office or other honor.[13] Hence Rome's office-holding élite enjoyed a special association with Jupiter on the Capitol, cultivated by every generation until Rome's first emperor Augustus ensured that no one outside the imperial family would ever celebrate a triumph again.[14] Consequently, it is clear that the Capitoline Temple, and especially its central cult of Jupiter Optimus Maximus, had a preeminent place in Roman political and religious culture, closely linked to Rome's pretensions to leadership in Italy and beyond, that was not affected by the ever increasing number of temples in the city during the Republic or by the rich varieties of religious experience enjoyed by Romans.[15]

The Capitol saw four successive temples to its three gods built on the same footprint and fulfilling a similar cultic role.[16] The original archaic temple, evidence of whose podium has recently been further excavated below the Palazzo Caffarelli, was built in the sixth century BC and burned in 83 BC. It was replaced by a Second Temple, dedicated in 69 BC but still essentially under construction throughout the 60s and perhaps even beyond. It was this Second Temple that burned on 19th December AD 69, in the course of a battle between supporters of the rival emperors Vitellius and Vespasian, at the end of the so-called Year of the Four Emperors. The

[13] For the triumph as the highest honor in the context of other honors and ritual celebrations, see H. I. Flower, "Spectacle and Political Culture in the Roman Republic," in *The Cambridge Companion to the Roman Republic* (ed. H. I. Flower; Cambridge, U.K.: Cambridge University Press, 2004), 322–43. For the republican triumph in general, see now T. Itgenshorst, *Tota illa pompa: der Triumph in der römischen Republik* (Göttingen: Vandenhoeck and Ruprecht, 2005) and M. Beard, *The Roman Triumph* (Cambridge, Mass.: Harvard University Press, 2007).

[14] For Augustus and the triumph, see F. Hickson, "Augustus *triumphator*: Manipulation of the Triumphal Theme in the Political Program of Augustus," *Latomus* 50 (1991): 124–38.

[15] For temple building in Rome during the Republic, see A. Ziolkowski, *The Temples of Mid-republican Rome and their Historical and Topographical Context* (Rome: Bretschneider 1992); M. Aberson, *Temples votifs et butin de guerre dans la Rome républicaine* (Rome: Institut Suisse de Rome, 1994); E. Orlin, *Temples, Religion and Politics in the Roman Republic* (Leiden: Brill, 1997).

[16] Plut. *Publ.* 14–15.

Third Temple was built rapidly by the victorious new emperor Vespasian, with all due respect for republican precedent, during the early 70s AD. This Flavian temple burned in the great fire of AD 80, which devastated large areas of the city while Titus was emperor. The last rebuilding of the temple came during the early 80s under Domitian, the younger son of Vespasian. Domitian's magnificent temple, all sheathed in white Pentelic marble from Greece, stood on the Capitol to the end of antiquity as an enduring symbol of Rome and of her empire.[17] Fragments of Pentelic marble attest to the fine workmanship of the Fourth Temple. Otherwise, there are few archaeological remains to document the temple's various phases in any detail, which can only be suggested on the basis of literary evidence, artistic representations, and images on coins.

The size and grandeur of the original archaic temple have been a matter for dispute amongst scholars for generations, but it seems that recent excavations of much more of the podium than was laid bare in the 1930s, should settle the basic issue of contention.[18] How big was the original temple? Was it really a huge structure that dwarfed others in Italy and in the Greek world of the same date, as is also suggested by Jupiter's cult title Optimus Maximus (Best [and] Greatest)? The new excavations have revealed enough to suggest that the temple did indeed have the expansive dimensions described by Dionysius of Halicarnassus, who was living in Rome at the time of Augustus.[19] This massive size in itself indicates the kind of ambitions developed for Rome by political leaders and kings in the sixth century BC, as well as the resources and manpower at their disposal in carrying out a building project that seems to have taken several decades to complete. Moreover, there is no parallel for a design that would have placed a small archaic temple on top of such a huge podium, especially at this early date.[20] The rebuilding of 69 BC included an effort to make the temple look higher by adding steps, although it proved impossible to exca-

[17] See Amm. Marc. 16.10.14, 22.16.12; Ausonius 11.19.14–17. The temple was intact when plundered by Stilicho (Zos. 5.38.5) at the end of the fourth century AD.

[18] A. Mura Sommella, "Le recenti scoperti sul Campidoglio e la fondazione del Tempio di Giove Capitolino," *Rendiconti della Pontifica Academia Romana di Archeologia* 70 (1997–8): 57–79 and "'La grande Roma dei Tarquini': alterne vicende di una felice intuizione," *Bullettino della Commissione Archeologica Comunale di Roma* 101 (2000): 7–26.

[19] DH 4.61–2, cf. Vitr. 4.7.1–2, 3.3.5.

[20] For an alternative reconstruction, which tries to challenge the recent archaeological findings, see J. Stamper, "The Temple of Capitoline Jupiter in Rome: A New Reconstruction," *Hephaistos* 16/17 (1998–1999): 107–38 and *The Architecture of Roman Temples: The Republic to the Middle Empire* (Cambridge, U.K.: Cambridge Universtiy Press, 2005), 19–33.

vate the surrounding area because of many pits (*favissae*) used for ritual burial of old votives and other material sacred to the deities but no longer displayed in the temple.[21] If the earlier temple had already been reached by a series of steps, the design issues debated during the 70s BC would not have arisen.

Another question raised by the history of Rome's Republic is whether the original temple was destroyed by the Gallic Sack of Rome in 390 or 387 BC. Scholars who have posited such a destruction, have argued for a small archaic temple, replaced after the sack by a much larger, monumental temple in the fourth century BC, once Rome was indeed emerging as the dominant power in Italy.[22] Again, the new excavations appear to rule out this reconstruction, which also relies on a repression in the ancient sources of what would have been a devastating loss. Archaeological evidence has, therefore, recently (re)confirmed the ancient tradition that the Capitol was not burned by the Gauls.

The logical result of these considerations is that the massive archaic temple, which had stood on the Capitol since the beginning of the Republic, burned on the sixth of July 83 BC, causing the loss of the most significant old building in the city and almost all of its contents. The temple treasure (coined money and bullion) had been removed to Praeneste by the consul C. Marius, but everything else was destroyed by the conflagration and there is no evidence of any attempt either to put the fire out or to rescue items of value.[23] It is no longer possible to make a detailed inventory of the losses but they included the archaic cult statue of Jupiter, all the votives and art objects currently in the building, and even the Sibylline books, which were kept in a special chest in an underground room.[24] Need-

---

[21] For Catulus's new temple, see Cic. *Verr.* 2.4.69; Livy *Per.* 98; Val. Max. 2.4.6; 6.9.5; Mart. 5.10; Plut. *Publ.* 15.1; Pliny *NH* 19.23; 33.57; Tac. *Hist.* 3.72.5; Amm. Marc. 14.6.25. For the design of the new podium, see Gell. 2.10 (Varro); Festus 78L; cf. Vitr. 3.3.5. For Catulus's prophetic dreams after the dedication, see Suet. *DJ* 15.1; *DA* 94.8. Catulus himself dedicated a statue of Athena by Euphranor (Pliny *NH* 34.77).

[22] For the argument in favor of a large temple first built in the fourth century BC, see Kolb, *Rom*, 91–97. There is no archaeological evidence for a small, archaic temple on the Capitol.

[23] Pliny *NH* 33.16 claims that temple treasure taken by Marius to Praeneste and subsequently paraded in Sulla's triumph of 81 BC amounted to 14,000 pounds of gold and 6000 pounds of silver. This treasure was from the Capitol but also from elsewhere.

[24] For the cult statue of Jupiter and its loss, see Pliny *NH* 35.45.157 (Varro); Plut. *Mor.* 379D; Aug. *CD* 4.31. For the Sibylline books, see DH 4.62.5–6; Tac. *Ann.* 6.12.4; Lact. *Inst.* 1.6.14. For votives in the temple before the fire, see Livy 2.22.6; 6.4.3 (three golden bowls dedicated by Camillus, possibly with an inscription); Pliny *NH* 35.69 (a painting of Theseus by Parrasius); Livy 25.39.17 (Valerius Antias F 23P, the clipeus of

less to say, these items were essentially irreplaceable and represented memorials of generations of Romans. The temple had been further adorned by many leading Romans during the time of Rome's imperial expansion in the second century BC, both as regards its fabric and its votives.[25] Consequently, the structure and items that burned also reflected the more recent wealth of empire and the competitive culture of Rome's office-holding élite during the middle Republic. The only direct testimony as to why the temple burned is contained in a late corrupt passage of Julius Obsequens:

*** aeditui Capitolium una nocte conflagravit. ("fraude" add. Rossbach / "culpa" add. Scaliger). Blame is, therefore, attached to a temple guardian (*aedituus*) but the lacuna in the text makes it unclear whether negligence or arson was directly ascribed to him or whether he was punished.

The political context of the fire provides the essential background to interpreting its meaning for contemporaries, who surely saw it as a terrible portent of both disaster and the end of an era. As Tacitus attests, the burning of the Second Temple in AD 69 was interpreted by some of her enemies as a sign of Rome's impending fall.[26] Moreover, at the time of the fire in 83 BC, there was no *flamen Dialis* (the principal priest of Jupiter) in office, because four years previously the last incumbent, L. Cornelius Merula, had committed suicide in the sanctuary, spilling his own blood on the altar and calling down curses on Cinna and Rome's government.[27] This terrible event, which had been the result of the prosecution of Merula in a rigged trial, had clearly resonated in Rome. No other priest of Jupiter had been inaugurated by Merula's enemies in the intervening years and Merula's curses, which had called on Jupiter to exact vengeance, were surely

---

Marcius with a portrait of Hasdrubal, captured in Spain in 211 BC); Livy 33.36.13 (Valerius Antias F 34P, spoils of Marcellus from 196 BC).

[25] Second century BC changes to the temple include the following: in 193 BC the aediles decorated the temple with golden shields (Livy 35.10.11); in 179 BC the censors restored and embellished the temple (Livy 41.10); in 149 BC the *cellae* were paved with *opus sutulatum* (Pliny *NH* 36.61.185, Livy 40. 51.3); in 142 BC the ceilings were covered with gilded bronze plates (Pliny *NH* 33.18.57).

[26] Tac. *Hist.* 4.54 (see epigraph above).

[27] L. Cornelius Merula (cos. suff. 87 BC, *Paulys Realencyclopädie der classischen Altertumswissenschaft*, s.v. Cornelius number 272): Val. Max. 9.12.5; Vell. Pat. 2.22.2; Appian BC 1.74. Tac. *Ann.* 3.58 and Dio 54.36 record a hiatus of 75 years before another *flamen Dialis* was appointed, under Augustus. On Merula, see also E. S. Gruen, *Roman Politics and the Criminal Courts 149–78 BC* (Cambridge, Mass.: Harvard University Press, 1968), 231–33 and F. M. Simón, *Flamen Dialis. El sacerdote de Júpiter en la religion romana* (Madrid: Ediciones Clásicas 1996), 205–6. The young Julius Caesar seems to have been nominated as *flamen Dialis* before his uncle Marius died on 13th January 86, but was never inaugurated (Vell. Pat. 2.43.1; Suet. *DJ* 1.2).

remembered by Romans in July 83 when they saw the great Capitoline Temple in ruins.

The year 83 BC was the time of the final clash between the surviving partisans of Marius and Cinna, notably the consuls Cn. Papirius Carbo and C. Marius, son of Sulla's old enemy, and Sulla, who had returned to Italy that Spring with most of Rome's soldiers from the East.[28] Sulla was now fighting his way through the peninsula and approaching the city of Rome, which he had already taken once with a Roman army in 88 BC. Now he had vowed revenge on his enemies and the city had already seen partisan violence and sectarian killings. This renewed civil war was to culminate on the first of November 82 BC in the Battle of the Colline Gate, as Sulla captured Rome by storm and put his enemies to the sword, either immediately or through proscriptions and prices on the heads of those now labeled as enemies of the state (*hostes*). Within Rome's system of portents and divine signs, nothing could have been more fearful than the complete destruction of its main temple, so closely identified with the Republic itself, and its books of prophecies, so often the ultimate resort in previous times of crisis. Such a portent could only have acquired deeper significance in light of immediately subsequent events, the capture of the city, the deaths of thousands in Rome and throughout Italy, the widespread redistribution of goods and land amongst the invaders (fellow Romans who would now stop at nothing), the collapse of the constitution, and the institution of a dictatorship. Contemporary Romans expected that such a change would surely have been predicted, even as it was allowed to happen, by the will of the gods who had made Rome great over the centuries.

Echoes of contemporary fears and efforts to formulate an explanation for the unthinkable can be found in a passage of Appian (*BC* 1.83), who was writing in Greek in Alexandria in the mid-second century AD.[29]

> It seemed to them also that the gods foretold the results of the war in the following ways. For irrational terrors came upon many throughout Italy, both individually and in groups. Ancient, frightening oracles were recalled. Many unnatural things happened. A mule foaled, and a woman gave birth to a snake instead of a child. The god caused severe earthquakes and some of the temples in Rome were thrown down. The Romans took such events very seriously. The Capitol, which had been built by the kings 400 years before, was burned down, and nobody found out the

---

[28] For the age of Marius and Sulla, see R. Seager, "Sulla," in *The Cambridge Ancient History* 9 (ed. J. A. Crook, A. Lintott, and E. Rawson; 2d ed.; Cambridge, U.K.: Cambridge University Press, 1994), 165–207; K. Christ, *Sulla. Eine römische Karriere* (Munich: Beck, 2002); B. Linke, *Die römische Republik von den Gracchen bis Sulla* (Darmstadt: Wissenschaftliche Buchgesellschaft, 2005).

[29] Plut. *Sulla* 7 records prophecies of a new age for the year 88 BC, the first time that Sulla marched on Rome.

cause. All things seemed to indicate the large number of violent deaths, the conquest of Italy, and as regards the Romans themselves, the capture of their city and political revolution.

Despite this explicit testimony there are relatively few ancient texts or modern discussions that have engaged directly with what surely was a devastating loss for the Romans, psychologically and materially. The premise of the discussion that follows is that Appian was essentially right to draw attention to the temple's destruction as an event that represented a terrible portent in the political and religious context of the times. The rest of this paper will look at five attempts to recall and to define the meaning of the temple's destruction in 83 BC. They range from Sulla, Rome's dictator and the designer of her New Republic in the immediate aftermath of the fire, to Cicero the young lawyer pleading one of his first cases in 80 BC, to reactions on the anniversaries of 63 BC (twenty years) and 43 BC (forty years), to conclude with commentary by the senator and historian Tacitus, writing around AD 110, a generation after the temple had suffered two more destructions and been rebuilt twice, at ever greater expense.

Sulla himself certainly appears as the most striking contemporary witness, even as he was the most powerful opinion-maker in the years immediately after 83 BC. As Appian suggests, this fire looked like a bad omen for Sulla, casting him in the role of an invading enemy who would capture the city and perhaps even put an end to an era, in a way even more destructive than the Gallic Sack. It is fortuitous, although perhaps not surprising, that Plutarch has preserved for us Sulla's own interpretation of the omen, as recorded in the expansive memoirs he wrote in self-justification during his brief retirement from public life, before his death in 78 BC:

> He (Sulla) says that at Silvium a household slave of Pontius met him, a messenger from the gods, saying that he announced to him success in war and victory from Bellona. But that if he did not hurry, the Capitol would be burned; and this actually happened on the very day which the man foretold, namely, the sixth day (one day before the nones) of Quintilis, which we now call July. (*Sulla* 27.12)

It is fascinating to see Sulla, whose writings confirm the picture of heightened religious sensibility and fear that Appian records for this period, deflect and reshape a portent that must have been much discussed throughout Italy. He makes three claims: that the gods (and one of his own favorites, Bellona) had given him a precise warning before the fire; that his presence would have saved the temple; and consequently that the portent is somehow associated with his victory. A premise of his writing is that the temple must have burned because the gods ordained that it would, even on that very day. This strategy of religious redirection does not actually offer a direct explanation of the portent in the way that Appian's narrative provides. Indeed it avoids any explicit interpretation but without actually denying the importance of the fire. Sulla represented himself as the savior of Rome and hence claims that he could have saved the temple. Meanwhile, his superior foreknowledge and special relationship with the gods marks him out. Because he knew the temple would burn on that day, his very knowledge is used to suggest that the situation is somehow under control and would have been worse without him. It is evident that he has taken refuge in his own particular religious interpretation of events.

By way of contrast with Sulla's reading, Cicero makes explicit mention of the powers of Jupiter Optimus Maximus in a famous passage from the *Pro Roscio Amerino*, a speech he delivered in 80 BC during Sulla's second consulship.

> Etenim si Iuppiter Optimus Maximus cuius nutu et arbitrio caelum terra mariaque reguntur saepe ventis vehementioribus aut immoderatis tempestatibus aut nimio calore aut intolerabili frigore hominibus nocuit, urbis delevit, fruges perdidit, quorum nihil pernicii causa divino consilio sed vi ipsa et magnitudine rerum factum putamus, at contra commoda quibus utimus lucemque qua fruimur spiritumque quem ducimus ab eo nobis dari atque impertiri videmus, quid miramur, iudices, L. Sullam cum solus rem publicam regeret orbemque terrarum gubernaret imperique maiestatem quam armis receperat iam legibus confirmaret, aliqua animadvertere non potuisse?

> Moreover, if Jupiter Optimus Maximus, at whose nod and command the sky, earth, and seas are ruled, has often hurt mortals with gales or hurricanes or excessive heat or unbearable cold, if he has destroyed cities and ruined crops, we do not think that any of these calamities are the result of a divine plan to cause harm but rather a consequence of the forces and magnitude of nature. Conversely, we see that the good things we make use of, the light we enjoy, the life we have are also gifts bestowed by him. Why then should we be surprised, men of the jury, if it was possible for Lucius Sulla to have overlooked something, at the time when he alone ruled the state and governed the whole world and he was even then establishing laws for the majesty of the empire that he had taken over by force of arms? (*Pro Rosc.* 131)

In this passage Cicero is claiming that just as Jupiter is not responsible for every natural disaster that befalls humankind, so too Sulla should not be blamed for every crime or death that happened during his dictatorship. It is unusual that Cicero here gives Jupiter his specifically Capitoline cult title. He could certainly have made the same general point without using that title. In other words, he seems to evoke Jupiter on the Capitol at a time when the temple was in ruins or just beginning to be rebuilt. Even more unexpected is the assertion that most Romans, or at least the senators on the jury, would not see extraordinary natural phenomena or the destruction of whole cities as a sign of divine anger. It is hard to see how anyone in Rome, however much of a rationalist, would have posited such a position as the majority view. Cicero seems to be reacting deliberately against religious interpretations, especially with regard to portents, of the kind that

Sulla himself espoused. It is not easy to know what the jury would have made of such a statement, which seems to refer to the temple but without explicitly mentioning it. Depending on where the case was being heard, the ruins of the temple may even have been visible to the jury as Cicero was speaking.

In this context it is emblematic of Sulla's whole approach that he used the ruined temple as the backdrop for many important events during his time of dominance in Rome from late 82 to the end of 80 BC. The year 81 saw three triumphs, starting with Sulla's over Mithridates in January, followed by those of his two associates Licinius Murena and Valerius Flaccus.[30] Each of these must have ended with a huge sacrifice in front of the ruins. Sulla seems to have taken the *cognomen* Felix at his triumphal address to the people in this same setting.[31] His *Ludi Victoriae* on the first of November were to recall his battle for Rome in triumphal terms every year. Sulla was the first Roman since the regal period to extend the city's ceremonial religious boundary (*pomerium*) and to establish a new constitution. Despite the loss of the Sibylline books, which were to be replaced only slowly and through a painstaking process of collecting and editing other Sibylline prophecies from Greek cities in the East, Sulla increased the number of priests responsible for the books from ten to fifteen. Sulla's announcement of a new age centered on triumphal imagery and on Rome as the capital of a world empire.[32] Both these aspects of his self-presentation were linked to the temple itself, an icon representing Rome, and apparently still present and vividly evoked in people's imaginations as an expression of their hopes for a renewed Republic.

Sulla's one regret, according to Pliny, was the fact that he realized that he would not live to rededicate the new temple with his name on the front,

---

[30] There had been no triumphs in the time of Cinna (87–84 BC). The triumphs of 81 BC were celebrated by Sulla over Mithridates in January, by L. Licinius Murena over Mithridates, and by C. Valerius Flaccus over Celtiberians and Gauls. Pompey's triumph over Africa can probably be dated to 79 BC, followed by Dollabella's over Macedonia in 78 BC. In the 70s there were only seven more triumphs of which four were celebrated in 71 BC. There was no flood of triumphs in the 60s once the new temple was dedicated: only five more were celebrated before Caesar crossed the Rubicon. See now the list in T. Itgenshorst, *Tota illa pompa*, 269–70.

[31] Plut. *Sulla* 24.

[32] For Sulla's self-presentation, see H. Behr, *Die Selbstdarstellung Sullas. Ein aristokratischer Politiker zwischen persönlichem Führungsanspruch und Standessolidarität* (Frankfurt: Lang 1993); C. S. Mackay, "Sulla and the Monuments: Studies in his Public Persona," *Historia* 49.2 (2000): 161–210; and especially A. Thein, *Sulla's Public Image and the Politics of Civic Renewal* (Ph.D. diss. University of Pennsylvania, 2002). For his annual victory games, see Bernstein, *Ludi publici*, 314–27.

in place of that of the Republic's first consul.[33] At the very end of his life, he was still busy collecting money to finance the rebuilding. Instead the temple was officially rededicated in 69 BC by Sulla's supporter Q. Lutatius Catulus, who on this occasion was the first to use temporary awnings to provide shade for the crowds gathered to watch the grand ceremonies.[34] However, the new cult statue was not installed until 65 BC and questions about "finishing" the restoration were voiced throughout the 60s.[35] This slow rebuilding, over about twenty years, contrasts completely with the rapid restorations achieved by the Flavians, who seem to have held ceremonies of rededication in AD 75 and again before AD 85.[36] The Late Republican struggle to rebuild is indicative of the divisive political climate, echoed in insistent criticisms of Catulus's design and of his honesty in administering the funds for the new temple.[37] Other Romans, notably Pompey and Caesar, could and sometimes apparently did imagine their names on the front of the magnificent new temple. Meanwhile, it is evident that even the money and spoils Sulla had brought back from his expedition to the East did not cover the cost of rebuilding quickly in a city that had suffered so much other civil war damage.

In the increasingly tense political climate of the 60s BC it is not surprising to see that the twentieth anniversary of the temple fire in 63 was apparently evoked by Catiline's fellow conspirators, who were accused of planning to set fire to the city and to overthrow its traditional government, in alliance with some Gauls. Cicero alleges that the conspirators, and especially P. Cornelius Lentulus Sura, were inspired by prophecies of revolution and one-man rule connected with the anniversary of the great fire.

> Lentulum autem sibi confirmasse ex fatis Sibyllinis haruspiciumque responsis se esse tertium illum Cornelium ad quem regnum huius urbis atque imperium pervenire esset necesse: Cinnam ante se et Sullam fuisse. Eundemque dixisse fatalem

---

[33] Pliny *NH* 7.138, cf. Tac. *Hist.* 3.72.3.

[34] For the inauguration of Catulus's temple in 69 BC, see Cic. *Verr.* 2.4.69, Livy *Per.* 98, Val. Max. 6.9.5, Mart. 5.10.6, Plut. *Publ.* 15.1, Plin. *NH* 7.138; 19.1.3; Tac. *Hist.* 3.72.3, Suet. *DJ* 15.1, *DA* 94.8, Gell. 2.10 (Varro). Catulus's temple is represented on a cup from Boscoreale, see A. Kuttner, *Dynasty and Empire in the Age of Augustus: The Case of the Boscoreale Cups* (Berkeley: University of California Press, 1995).

[35] For Jupiter's cult statue on the Capitol, attributed to Apollonios, see Cic. *Div.* 2.46; Livy 5.50.6; Jos. *Ant.* 19.1.2; Pliny *NH* 33.14; Dio 54.25.4; 59.28.7.

[36] For the Flavian rebuilding of the temple, see R. H. Darwall-Smith, *Emperors and Architecture: A Study of Flavian Rome* (Brussels: Latomus, 1996), 41–47 (Vespasian's temple), 105–110 (Domitian's temple). Domitian's temple is represented on the *exstispicium* relief from the Louvre and a relief of Marcus Aurelius dating to AD 176 (See D. Kleiner, *Roman Sculpture*, New Haven: Yale University Press, 1992, figs. 187 and 262).

[37] For criticisms of Catulus, see Suet. *DJ* 15 and Dio 37.44.1–2.

> hunc annum esse ad interitum huius urbis atque imperi qui esset annus decimus post virginum absolutionem, post Capitoli autem incensionem vicesimus.
>
> Lentulus, however, affirmed that he had been assured by Sibylline oracles and the responses of the *haruspices* that he would be that third Cornelius to whom rule over the city of Rome and supreme power was destined to come: Cinna and Sulla had come before him. He also said that this was the fated year in which the city and empire would be destroyed, because it was the tenth year since the acquittal of the (Vestal) virgins, and the twentieth since the burning of the Capitol. (Cicero *In Cat.* 3.9)

The *haruspices* (Etruscan seers) could presumably have been consulted for a fee but it would be interesting to know how Lentulus claimed to have access to the Sibylline books, which had always been so closely connected with the temple. Did he have his own record of one of the original prophecies that had been burned in 83 or was his text from some other source of Sibylline wisdom? On the other hand, some might doubt the accuracy of Cicero's account of the private conversations of the conspirators – especially in a version of a speech published in self-justification after they had been executed without a trial. Nevertheless, Cicero's evidence strongly suggests that this kind of thing was being said about the anniversary of the fire of 83. If these men did not say this, others probably did.[38]

Meanwhile, we are not well informed about the trial and acquittal of the Vestals in 73 BC on the tenth anniversary of the fire. Such trials were often connected with military defeats and other pressures that aroused religious dread: the year 73 BC had seen the outbreak of a serious slave revolt led by Spartacus.[39] Sallust also mentions similar prophecies, although it is unclear whether he had any sources independent of Cicero. His text suggests specific predictions of renewed civil war connected with memories of the temple's destruction.

> ... ex libris Sibyllinis regnum Romae tribus Corneliis portendi; Cinnam atque Sullam antea, se tertium esse quoi fatum foret urbis potiri; praeterea ab incenso Capitolio illum esse uigesumum annum, quem saepe ex prodigiis haruspices respondissent bello civili cruentum fore.
>
> (He said that)... The Sibylline books foretold a kingship in Rome for three Cornelii. Cinna and Sulla had come before, and he himself was the third whose fate it was to rule the city. Besides it was the twentieth year since the Capitol had been burned, which the *haruspices* had often foretold on the basis of prodigies would be a year bloody with civil war. (Sallust *BC* 47.2)

---

[38] For prophecy in the late Republic, see T. P. Wiseman, "Lucretius, Catiline, and the Survival of Prophecy," in *Historiography and Imagination: Eight Essays on Roman Culture* (ed. T. P. Wiseman; Exeter: Exeter University Press, 1994), 49–67.

[39] See B. D. Shaw, *Spartacus and the Slave Wars: A Brief History with Documents* (Boston: Bedford, 2001).

The splendid Second Temple on the Capitol had apparently not allayed the fears and emotions of Romans who tended to dread the anniversaries of destructions or defeats.[40] Ten years later, in 53 BC, the thirtieth anniversary of the fire coincided with the disastrous defeat of the Romans at Carrhae in Syria and the ignominious death of their general Crassus, as well as with political instability in Rome.[41]

We should not be so surprised, therefore, to see the temple appear on a silver *denarius* in 43 BC, minted by Petillius Capitolinus.[42] The temple on this coin surely provides more than a simple reference to the *cognomen* of the moneyer. Rather the imagery recalls the temple fire and its subsequent rebuilding on the fortieth anniversary of its destruction. Moreover, the year 43 was marked by the establishment of the (second) Triumvirate, a takeover of the Roman government by three men, Antony, Octavian and Lepidus, which was to last for ten years and to end in the civil war between Octavian and Antony. The argument has been made that the new political scene after the assassination of the dictator Caesar on the Ides of March 44 BC marked the real end of the Roman Republic.[43] The year had certainly seen a renewal of civil war, resulting in the deaths of both consuls, and new proscriptions of political opponents that recalled the age of Sulla. The image of the Capitoline Temple on the coin recalled the Republic and may have expressed the hopes of many that Rome had more to look forward to than renewed autocracy and more civil bloodshed. However, no politician now followed Sulla's example in reestablishing a republican constitution.

To sum up the argument made so far: the destruction of 83 BC was a pivotal event for the Romans, both for those who witnessed the fire and its immediate aftermath, and for those who came afterwards. The loss of their most important temple, with all its contents accumulated throughout the Republic, seemed very much a sign of the times, when things were not the same as they had been before and the future of their community looked increasingly uncertain. The ruin of the temple portended divine disfavor

---

[40] See U. Walter, Memoria *und* res publica. *Zur Geschichtskultur im republikanischen Rom* (Frankfurt: Verlag Antike 2004), 204–7.

[41] For Carrhae and the death of Crassus in 53 BC, see Plut. *Crass*. 28.2–32.3, Dio 40.26–7 with T. P. Wiseman, "Caesar, Pompey and Rome, 59–50 BC," in *Cambridge Ancient History* 9, 402–3. According to the chronology of Varro, the year 53 was the 700th birthday of the city of Rome.

[42] M. Crawford, *Roman Republican Coinage* (Cambridge, U.K.: Cambridge University Press, 1974), no. 487.1–2, figs. 58.6–7, *denarii* of 43 BC.

[43] See U. Gotter, *Der Diktator ist Tot! Politik im Rom zwischen den Iden des März und der Begründung des Zweiten Triumvirats* (Stuttgart: Steiner, 1996) 233–66 and J. Osgood, *Caesar's Legacy: Civil War and the Emergence of the Roman Empire* (Cambridge, U.K.: Cambridge University Press, 2006).

and a possible change in Rome's status as an imperial power, but was especially connected with the two closely associated evils of civil discord and political instability. For many generations the Roman Republic had been characterized by cooperation between citizens, an absence of political violence, and a system of government that relied on compromise and consensus on the basis of shared values and accepted precedents (*mos maiorum*).[44] Now Romans felt caught in a cycle of violence and instability, reflected in their religious anxieties as they looked for explanations of the past that would indicate the future.[45] Similar patterns of recalling the temple fire of 83 BC seem to have persisted throughout the last generation of the Republic, as continued instability and violence fed not unjustified fears that the Republic would fall apart and that traditional Roman political culture would be or perhaps already had been lost. There may even have been some who recalled the sixtieth anniversary of the fire in 23 BC when political uncertainty, the death of Marcellus, and Augustus's own serious illness, caused concern about the future.

Augustus moved many functions and items associated with the Capitoline Temple elsewhere to other temples, especially to his new Temple of Mars Ultor in the Forum Augustum.[46] Even the Sibylline books were now kept in Apollo's temple on the Palatine and were not consulted in the regular republican pattern anymore. Triumphal processions, although they still had the Capitoline Temple as their destination, became rare and only celebrated by the emperor or his close relatives. Yet later Romans still recalled the central symbolism of the Capitoline Temple for Rome, as is made clear by Tacitus who left an account of the burning of Catulus's Second Temple during a battle in the civil war of AD 69. The followers of Vespasian, including his brother Sabinus and son Domitian, had taken refuge on the Capitol and were under attack from the partisans of Vitellius when the temple caught fire. Inevitably, the second burning of the temple in the context of civil war and devastation in the city, had resonance with

---

[44] For the political culture of the Roman Republic, see especially B. Linke and M. Stemmler, eds., *Mos maiorum. Untersuchungen zu den Formen der Identitätsstiftung und Stabilisierung in der römischen Republik* (Stuttgart: Steiner, 2000) and K. J. Hölkeskamp, *Rekonstruktionen einer Republik. Die politische Kultur des antiken Rom und die Forschung der letzten Jahrzehnte* (Munich: Oldenbourg, 2004).

[45] For the general context of religious anxiety, see especially E. Rawson, "Religion and Politics in the Late Second Century BC," *Phoenix* 28 (1974): 149–68.

[46] For the Temple of Mars Ultor and the role assigned to it by Augustus, see M. Bonnefond, "Transferts de functions et mutation idéologique: le Capitale et le Forum d'Auguste," in *L'Urbs: espace urbain et histoire (1er siècle av. J.-C. - IIIe siècle ap. J.-C.)* (Rome: École française de Rome: 1987), 251–78. For the Sibylline Books at the Temple of Apollo on the Palatine after 12 BC, see Suet. *DA* 31.1; Serv. *Aen.* 6.36.72.

the events of 83. It also came at the end of a year marked by violent and bitter civil strife between Galba, Otho, Vitellius, and now Vespasian, for who would be the next emperor.[47]

In a famous passage written around AD 110, some 40 years after the events he is describing, Tacitus has the following to say.

> Sic Capitolium clausis foribus indefensum et indireptum conflagravit. (72) Id facinus post conditam urbem luctuosissimum foedissimumque rei publicae populi Romani accidit, nullo externo hoste, propitiis si per mores nostros liceret deis, sedem Iovis Optimi Maximi auspicato a maioribus pignus imperii conditam, quam non Porsenna dedita urbe neque Galli capta temerare potuissent, furore principum excindi. Arserat et ante Capitolium civili bello, sed fraude privata: nunc palam obsessum, palam incensum, quibus armorum causis? Quo tantae cladis pretio? Stetit dum pro patria bellavimus. Voverat Tarquinius Priscus rex bello Sabino, ieceratque fundamenta spe magis futurae magnitudinis quam quo modicae adhuc populi Romani res sufficerent. Mox Servius Tullius sociorum studio dein Tarquinius Superbus capta Suessa Pometia hostium spoliis exstruxere. Sed gloria operis libertati reservata: pulsis regibus Horatius Pulvillus iterum consul dedicavit ea magificentia quam immensae postea populi Romani opes ornarent potius quam augerent. Isdem rursus vestigiis situm est, postquam interiecto quadringentorum quindecim annorum spatio L. Scipione C. Norbano consulibus flagraverat. Curam victor Sulla suscepit neque tamen dedicavit: hoc solum felicitati eius negatum. Lutatii Catuli nomen inter tanta Caesarum opera usque ad Vitellium mansit. Ea tunc aedes cremabatur.

> In this way the Capitol burned, its doors closed, undefended and unplundered. That event was the saddest and foulest that happened to the Republic of the Roman people since the founding of the city. Without the presence of any foreign enemy, despite the fact that the gods would have been favorable if our way of life had allowed it, the seat of Iupiter Optimus Maximus, which had been founded and inaugurated by our ancestors as a pledge of empire, which neither Porsenna nor the Gauls had been able to harm when the city had been surrendered or captured, this temple was burned to the ground by the madness of Rome's leaders. The Capitol had indeed burned before during a civil war, but the responsibility lay with a private individual. Now it was openly under siege, openly burned, but for what cause? At what price such a calamity? The temple had stood while we fought on behalf of our country. King Tarquin the Elder had vowed it during the Sabine war, and had laid the foundations more in hope of future greatness than in proportion with the modest resources of the Roman people at the time. Soon the temple was built by Servius Tullius with enthusiastic allies, and then by Tarquin the Proud with enemy booty after the capture of Suessa Pometia. But the glory of the final construction was destined for a free state. After the expulsion of the kings Horatius Pulvillus dedicated that magnificent building in his second consulship. The huge wealth of the Roman people later decorated rather than expanded it. The temple was rebuilt on the same foundation, after an interval of 415 years, when it

[47] For the Year of the Four Emperors, see now G. Morgan, *69 AD: The Year of the Four Emperors* (Oxford: Oxford University Press, 2006).

> had burned in the consulship of L. Scipio and C. Norbanus. Sulla the victor undertook the task, but he did not dedicate it: this one thing was lacking from his good fortune. Amongst so many buildings erected by the Caesars the name of Lutatius Catulus remained until the time of Vitellius. That temple was burned down at that time. (*Hist.* 3.71–72)

This is a complex passage that reflects Tacitus's evocative and intricate writing style, as he recalls the fire of AD 69 in light of the temple's whole history. The passage functions like one of the obituary notices that Tacitus includes in his narrative when he records the death of a prominent Roman. In a similar way he gives his readers a vignette of past history with a view to recording the temple's significance and the meaning of its destruction, specifically in a context of civil conflict and political chaos. The use of ring composition gives this passage a self-contained and carefully crafted shape. Nineteenth century commentators noted the echoes of the burning of Troy as described by Virgil.[48]

The passage opens with the striking image of the undefended and unpillaged temple in flames. However, such a situation arose in 83 BC rather than in AD 69, when the fire was either an accidental or deliberate byproduct of the siege being prosecuted by the Vitellians (who were afterwards blamed by the Flavians for setting the fire deliberately). Surely Tacitus is here purposely conflating the two fires, even as he simultaneously evokes the absence of an enemy attacking the temple, specifically a Gallic enemy who might have sacked the temple in 390 BC, if given a chance. Now the temple burns despite the fact that the Romans have not lost their city to an invader, a fact that is the occasion for remorse and despair concerning the situation in Rome. Similarly, the statement that this was the worst and most mournful event for the Romans since the founding of the city seems to echo the voices of Sullan times and the first fire, although it is not easy to say exactly which republican sources Tacitus might have been reading.[49] Tacitus directly recalls the Republic in the phrase *res publicae populi Romani*. Then he quickly and briefly acknowledges the first fire for his readers: he knows that they have it in their minds by this point in his narrative. The image of the original archaic temple, together with its traditional early history, is powerful and vivid in the mind of Tacitus the new man (*novus homo*), that is to say someone whose ancestors had had no political

---

[48] For commentary on Tacitus's description of the temple fire of AD 69, see J. W. Mackail, *Latin Literature* (London: John Murray, 1895), 219ff.; R. Syme, *Tacitus*, vol. 1 (Oxford, Oxford University Press, 1958), 194; H. Heubner, *P. Cornelius Tacitus. Die Historien: Kommentar*, vol. 3 (Heidelberg: C. Winter, 1972), *ad loc*.

[49] There is a verbal echo here of Sallust's description (*BC* 18.8) of the terrible nature of the so-called First Catilinarian Conspiracy in 65 BC (... *eo die post conditam urbem Romam pessumum facinus patratum foret*).

office in the Rome of the Republic. His words are also designed to recall the tradition of republican historiography culminating with the monumental work of Livy. The shadow of Sulla and the limits of his felicity recall a different republican time from that of early Rome.

For Tacitus writing in the time of the emperor Trajan the Second Temple built by Catulus had become a symbol of the lost Republic in the Rome of the Caesars. By the end of the Julio-Claudian period Catulus's inscription was indeed one of the few prominent inscriptions left from preimperial times. Catulus had also been recalled in AD 68/69 by his descendent Galba, the first emperor to succeed Nero, but all these republican memorials were soon swept away, even as the aristocratic houses of the republican élite on the Palatine, with their trophies and memorials, had already been destroyed in the great fire of AD 64, five years before.[50] Ultimately, the temple fire of AD 69 caused Tacitus to display a marked nostalgia for a "republican past" that stretched back over seven hundred years. The pageant of early republican times is succeeded by a recollection of the times of Sulla and Catulus, now also distant and different. The message at the end is essentially two-fold: the terrible effect of the burning of Rome's most important temple, still so closely linked to her identity and heritage, is matched by the stark contrast between the civil strife of AD 69 and the lost republican past.

Tacitus, however, does not seek or see a message from the gods about an imminent revolution. Rather, for him the time of decline has already arrived and is marked by the loss of earlier virtues and the very purpose and seat of the Roman *imperium*. In fact, the gods are said to be propitious if only the Romans had retained their earlier way of life. Powerless gods faced with corrupted Romans present a rather different picture from a more traditional Rome, subject to manifest destiny and divine purpose. For Tacitus, the portent of the temple fire of AD 69 simultaneously fulfills its own prophecy. It is the Romans themselves who are now all equally guilty, regardless of partisan affiliation, for burning their own temple, in a state of madness that has made them forget their past history and the practices that built their community. Tacitus deliberately transcends the rhetoric of Flavian propaganda that sought to blame the Vitellians for the fire and to represent Jupiter as the protector of Domitian in his dramatic escape from the violence.[51] Similarly, he plays with ideas and images that equate or

---

[50] For the fire of AD 64, see Suet. *Nero* 38.2 and *Vesp.* 8.5. For Galba and his ancestor Catulus, see Suet. *Gal.* 2–3.

[51] For the Flavians and the temple fire of AD 69, see Jos. *BJ* 4.645–49; Pliny *NH* 34.38, Tac. *Hist.* 3.75 with T. P. Wiseman, "Flavians on the Capitol," *American Journal of Ancient History* 3 (1978): 163–78; K. Wellesley, "What happened on the Capitol in

conflate the fires of 83 BC and AD 69, while passing over completely the accidental fire of AD 80. Tacitus's Romans have changed so much from their ancestors that even the gods cannot help them now.

Finally, he chooses not to mention the magnificent Fourth Temple built by Domitian, with which his contemporary readers would have been most familiar. Tacitus, therefore, evokes temples that no longer exist, and the moments of their loss, as more powerful and meaningful markers than the splendid temple of his own day. This sense of tremendous waste and thoughtless destruction, closely associated with the violent loss of the republican past, is symbolized by the image of the burning temple, as it stands intact but alone and undefended.

In conclusion, a number of thoughts emerge from the ancient sources cited above. In ancient societies, the destruction of a major temple, whether accidental or deliberate, was a powerful portent that could be debated, pondered, and reinterpreted for generations to come.[52] In Rome of the late Republic it seems to have been associated in a specific way with civil war and constitutional change. In this sense, the Capitoline Temple represented Rome's relationship with her state gods, which was so closely linked to her republican political system and her world empire. In other words, the temple stood for identity and traditional heritage. Its destruction was hard either to explain or to dismiss, especially in a world full of divine signs that was governed by an equilibrium between the sphere of the gods and that of humans (*pax deorum*). Its destruction mirrored the Romans' deepest fears about the loss of the Republic and of their historical identity. By contrast, the rebuilding of the temple inevitably conjured up images of a New Age and a refounded republic, as Sulla (and Vespasian) was fully aware. To rebuild the temple was to rebuild society, a task that could not be lightly undertaken and that in itself was based on a recognition of an epochal break and a new beginning. Those who remembered the destruction later were always aware of themselves as inhabiting another age, as survivors looking back after the Fall.

---

December 69?" *American Journal of Ancient History* 6 (1981): 166–90; Darwall-Smith, *Emperors*, 41–43, and D. Wardle, "Vespasian, Helvidius Priscus and the Restoration of the Capitol," *Historia* 45 (1996): 208–22. For Domitian's temple of Jupiter Custos, see Darwall-Smith, *Emperors*, 110–15.

[52] For Greek temples that were burned under ominous circumstances, see Thuc. 4.133 for the accidental burning of the temple of Hera at Argos in 423 BC (cf. Paus. 2.17.7); Xen. *Hell.* 1.6.24–1.7.35 for the burning of Athena Polias in 406 BC before the battle of Arginousae; Plut. *Alex.* 2 for the destruction of the temple of Artemis at Ephesus in 356 BC as a portent of the birth of Alexander the Great.

# The Greeks and the Distant Past in Josephus's *Judaean War*

STEVE MASON

When we think of ancient authors who wrote about what was already for them the distant past, Flavius Josephus (37–100+? C.E.) must come immediately to mind. More than a third of his thirty-volume *oeuvre* is devoted to discussion of his people's ancient past (*archaiologia*), namely: *Antiquities* 1–11 and the two-volume *Against Apion*. Plainly, he considered antiquity an important component of his larger project, explicating Judaean culture in the city of Rome in the decades that followed Titus's destruction of Jerusalem in 70 C.E.

Josephus's biblical paraphrase itself has been the locus of vigorous research, anticipating by several decades – and providing important results for – the more recent surge of interest in his narratives as whole texts.[1] Yet this attentiveness to the biblical paraphrase has in large measure been an exercise in the external project of comparative "rewritten Bible," conducted against the background of other versions of the biblical text, the biblical scrolls from Qumran, apocrypha and pseudepigrapha, Philo, Pseudo-Philo, and rabbinic *halakha* and *haggada*. Scholars have most often focused upon Josephus's sources (e.g., the form of his biblical text) and his manipulations of them in this comparative context. They have not been much inclined to integrate this work into larger studies of the structures

[1] Important work on the biblical paraphrase began with such studies as Shlomo Rappaport, *Agada und Exegese bei Flavius Josephus* (Vienna: A. Kohut, 1930); Martin Braun, *Griechischer Roman und hellenistische Geschichtschreibung* (Frankfurt a. M.: Klostermann, 1934); and Horst R. Moehring, "Novelistic Elements in the Writings of Flavius Josephus" (Ph.D. diss., University of Chicago, 1957). More recent and systematic work on sequences of passages and themes has been done by Harold W. Attridge, *The Interpretation of Biblical History in the Antiquitates Judaicae of Flavius Josephus* (Missoula: Scholars Press, 1976); Christopher T. Begg, *Josephus' Account of the Early Divided Monarchy (AJ 8,212–420): Rewriting the Bible* (Leuven: Leuven University Press, 1993); idem, *Josephus' Story of the Later Monarchy* (Leuven: Leuven University Press, 2000); and Louis H. Feldman, *Josephus's Interpretation of the Bible* (Berkeley: University of California Press, 1998), synthesizing the results of decades of study; and idem, *Studies in Josephus' Rewritten Bible* (Leiden: Brill, 1998), which collects many of his dozens of articles.

and themes of the *Antiquities* as a whole, the work's total impact on a given audience, the ways in which Josephus's uses of antiquity served his general intellectual, literary, and rhetorical program, or his connections with contemporary authors.

The isolation of Josephus from both his contemporary "classical" environment and from the sorts of introductory questions we normally pose of classical (and biblical) texts has been a curious feature of the subdiscipline since it began. In the long history of study involving Josephus – ever since the church fathers – the compositional aspects of his writings have been mostly neglected in favor of referential questions. What he *refers to* (sites, people, and events, chiefly in Judea), or in modern study the sources he used for these questions, have mattered much more than what he actually *says:* his lexicon,[2] literary structures and themes, dramatic and rhetorical devices, interaction with expected audiences, efforts at irony, and so forth.[3] The completion of Rengstorf's *Complete Concordance* in 1983,[4] along with the subsequent development of digital tools,[5] has facilitated the latter kind of investigation, which is driving much of the current explosion of interest in this author.[6]

---

[2] This is not to say that no efforts were made – e.g. B. Brüne, *Flavius Josephus und seine Schriften in ihrem Verhältnis zum Judentume, zur griechisch-römischen Welt und zum Christentume* (Gütersloh: C. Bertelsmann, 1913), and Henry St. John Thackeray, *Lexicon to Josephus A–Δ* (Paris: Librairie Orientaliste P. Guethner [for the Jewish Institute of Religion], 1930) – but only that these projects (Thackeray's unfinished) did not succeed in shaping the direction of 20$^{th}$-century scholarship.

[3] A clear picture of the scholarly situation until the mid-1980s was given by Per Bilde, *Flavius Josephus between Jerusalem and Rome: His Life, His Works and Their Importance* (Sheffield: JSOT, 1988). In his summaries of modern scholarship to that point (e.g., pp. 71, 92, 102), Bilde was unable to find any significant research on these basic questions for Josephus's two major works.

[4] Karl Heinrich Rengstorf, et al., *A Complete Concordance to Flavius Josephus* (4 vols.; Leiden: E. J. Brill, 1973–1983).

[5] The digitized text of Josephus's Greek (with morphological analysis but without textual apparatus) is now widely available: in university-based online sites such as the Perseus Project (www.perseus.tufts.edu), the Thesaurus Linguae Graecae (www.tlg.uci), or the Project on Ancient Cultural Engagement (pace.cns.yorku.ca), and in commercial products for enhanced biblical study, from *inter alios* Oak Tree Software (Accordance), BibleWorks, and Logos Systems.

[6] The international colloquium of 1992 in San Miniato (proceedings in Fausto Parente and Joseph Sievers, eds., *Josephus and the History of the Greco-Roman Period* [Leiden: E. J. Brill, 1994]) turned out to be only the first of its kind, and a watershed. It has been followed by unprecedented numbers of dissertations, graduate seminars, volumes of collected essays, various international translation and commentary projects, and scholarly conferences devoted to Josephus – often two or more per year. The bibliography module at pace.cns.yorku.ca (for about 1995 onward) will illustrate.

Yet even this new direction has so far produced little on the structures and themes of the *Antiquities,* let alone on Josephus's relationship with his Greek literary environment. Louis Feldman has occasionally ventured in this direction, notably in a recent and illuminating essay comparing Josephus's Moses with Plutarch's Lycurgus.[7] The question is welcome and the evidence he adduces is telling, though his conclusions are still limited to the possible sources and literary influences shared by these authors: what lies behind the text's construction, rather than explicit discussion of Josephus's mental world or his transactions with his audiences (who lacked access to the comparative texts). In the field-defining work of Feldman and more recently Christopher Begg on the biblical paraphrase, Josephus's departures from the Bible and differences from other Jewish texts are typically categorized under the rubric of a "Hellenization" thought to be motivated by various communicative and apologetic constraints. Yet this seems to be more a categorization of certain textual phenomena than an analysis of Josephus's outlook.

The examination of Josephus's relationship to his Greek contemporaries together with his exploitation of antiquity is prompted by the circumstance that these other Greek authors living under Roman *imperium* were also turning to their cities' distant pasts in ways that had direct political relevance for the present. It is worth asking whether and to what extent Josephus shared their outlooks on this matter, as an instance of the larger problem of his participation in Greek culture.

The arrival of Rome in the early second century B.C.E. (culminating in the destruction of Corinth in 146 B.C.E.) and the depredations resulting from the Roman civil wars of the first century B.C.E. had, in their different ways, been devastating for old Greece and Asia Minor. But the rise of the Principate brought with it a new effort, shared by emperors and Greek elites,[8] to recover and strengthen Greek identity in harmony with the interests of Roman hegemony. The complex and contested process of reclaiming the Greek past can be seen locally in the restoration of ancient ceremonies and honors, in the gradual adoption of the Attic dialect as literary standard, in the use of old Greek names for places and persons as well as ancient measurements and dating systems, and in the choice of subjects for rhetorical exercises and declamation, which dealt overwhel-

[7] Louis H. Feldman, "Parallel Lives of Two Lawgivers: Josephus' Moses and Plutarch's Lycurgus," in *Flavius Josephus and Flavian Rome* (ed. J. Edmondson, S. Mason, and J. Rives; Oxford: Oxford University Press, 2005), 209–42.

[8] For the general concern with consensus, by no means limited to the handling of antiquity, see Clifford Ando, *Imperial Ideology and Provincial Loyalty in the Roman Empire* (Berkeley: University of California Press, 2000).

mingly with the glorious period before the death of Alexander.[9] The "philhellene" emperors – Nero, Trajan, and especially Hadrian – pushed forward this recovery process in dramatic ways, as one may see still today in the second-century ruins of Ephesus, Athens, and Sparta. The ancient past was an integral part of this renaissance, partly abetted by a Roman-Greek consensus in viewing Rome's persistent struggles with Parthia as a continuation of the Greek wars with Persia.[10] Rome presented itself as the current champion of this historic conflict, absorbing and reinforcing ingrained elements of Greek identity over against the exotic but always threatening easterners. Greeks could enjoy this Roman affirmation of their glorious past without necessarily accepting the Roman claim to ownership of it – keeping their distance from Rome and even using "figured speech" and irony in portraying their past to strengthen their own sense of identity at Rome's expense.[11]

This is all well known, but it is potentially important background for understanding Josephus, who did not live in a vacuum. He was composing the *Judaean War* in Rome just a few years after Nero's placement of the diadem on Tiridates as king of Armenia (66 C.E.) had sealed the rapprochement with Parthia; at the time that Plutarch was beginning his literary career and his visits to the capital, and when Dio Chrysostom was delivering his earliest orations in Prusa, Rhodes, and Alexandria;[12] and shortly before Scopelian of Smyrna, who was reportedly fascinated with the ancient Graeco-Persian wars, undertook his embassies to Rome. Josephus's debt to older Greek writers – Herodotus, Thucydides, Polybius, Diodorus, Dionysius, and Strabo – is much discussed in scholarship and analyzed ever more closely.[13] A recent dissertation has exposed his fami-

---

[9] Fundamental is Ewen L. Bowie, "The Greeks and their Past in the Second Sophistic," *Past and Present* 46 (1974): 3–41.

[10] See Antony Spawforth, "Symbol of Unity? The Persian-Wars Tradition in the Roman Empire," in *Greek Historiography* (ed. S. Hornblower; Oxford: Clarendon Press, 1994), 233–47.

[11] So, e.g., Simon Swain, *Hellenism and Empire: Language, Classicism, and Power in the Greek World, AD 50–250* (Oxford: Clarendon Press, 1996), 87–89; Tim Whitmarsh, *The Second Sophistic* (Oxford: Oxford University Press for the Classical Association, 2005), 66–70.

[12] Christopher P. Jones, *The Roman World of Dio Chrysostom* (Cambridge, Mass.: Harvard University Press, 1978), 19, 26, 36.

[13] For Thucydides (taking a long tradition of recognizing this influence to an extreme), Gottfried Mader, *Josephus and the Politics of Historiography: Apologetic and Impression Management in the Bellum Judaicum* (Leiden: Brill, 2000); for Polybius, e.g. Shaye J. D. Cohen, "Josephus, Jeremiah, and Polybius," *History and Theory* 21 (1982): 366–81; Arthur M. Eckstein, "Josephus and Polybius: A Reconsideration" *Classical Antiquity* 9 (1990): 175–208; for several others but focusing on Polybius and Strabo, see

liarity with classical tragedy,[14] and the prologue to the *Judaean War* must be reckoned among the fullest surviving examples of its type.[15] But still he has not often been included as a conversation partner with his Greek contemporaries, especially Plutarch and Dio Chrysostom.

Ewen Bowie's programmatic essay on the Greeks and their past (1974)[16] and the library of studies devoted to Greeks under Roman rule since that time[17] typically feature occupation with the distant past as a characteristic of the Greek revival.[18] Josephus is omitted from such discussion, however. Bowie set the tone: "The first century A.D. has left no contemporary history by a Greek until Plutarch's imperial biographies, although the existence of works on the civil wars of 69 is attested by Josephus (whom I exclude as a Jewish writer outside the main Greek tradition)."[19] It is odd that Bowie should single out one comment by Josephus

---

Yuval Shahar, *Josephus Geographicus: The Classical Context of Geography in Josephus* (Tübingen: Mohr Siebeck, 2004).

[14] Honora H. Chapman, "Spectacle and Theater in Josephus's *Bellum Judaicum*," (Ph.D. diss., Stanford University, 1998). It is available online at pace.cns.yorku.ca/dissertations.

[15] One way to see Josephus's illustrative value for ancient historiography, and not only in the prologue, is to peruse the indexed references to examples from his work in John Marincola, *Authority and Tradition in Ancient Historiography* (Cambridge, U.K.: Cambridge University Press, 1997) – one of the very few studies of Graeco-Roman literature to give significant space to Josephus.

[16] See Bowie, "Greeks."

[17] E.g., G. Anderson, *The Second Sophistic: A Cultural Phenomenon in the Roman Empire* (London: Routledge, 1993); John Moles, "Dio Chrysostom, Greece, and Rome," in *Ethics and Rhetoric: Classical Essays for Donald Russell on his Seventy-Fifth Birthday* (ed. D. Innes, H. Hine, and C. Pelling; Oxford: Clarendon Press, 1995), 177–92; Maude W. Gleason, *Making Men: Sophists and Self-presentation in Ancient Rome* (Princeton: Princeton University Press, 1995); Swain, *Hellenism*; idem, *Dio Chrysostom: Politics, Letters, and Philosophy* (Oxford: Oxford University Press, 2000); Simon Goldhill, *Being Greek under Rome: Cultural Identity, the Second Sophistic, and the Development of Empire* (Cambridge, U.K.: Cambridge University Press, 2001); Tim Whitmarsh, *Greek Literature and the Roman Empire: The Politics of Imitation* (Oxford: Oxford University Press, 2001); idem, *Sophistic*; Erik Nis Ostenfeld, *Greek Romans and Roman Greeks: Studies in Cultural Interaction* (Aarhus: Aarhus University Press, 2002); Lukas de Blois, ed., *The Statesman in Plutarch's Works: Proceedings of the Sixth International Conference of the International Plutarch Society, Nijmegen, Castle Hernen, May 1–5, 2002* (2 vols.; Leiden: Brill, 2004–2005). Although it did not integrate the Greek past into its analysis, an important herald of this wave of research on the Greek revival was Glen W. Bowersock, *Greek Sophists in the Roman Empire* (Oxford: Clarendon Press, 1969).

[18] E.g., Swain, *Hellenism*, 65–100; Whitmarsh, *Sophistic*, 66–70.

[19] Bowie, "Greeks," 180.

(*War* 4.496) on Roman affairs, for he not only says *much* more than this,[20] but he also wrote in the fashionable, renaissance-style Atticizing Greek and openly discussed current Greek literary trends (*War* 1.13–16, below). Bowie again: "No Greek seems to have been tempted to write a history of the Greek world (as a whole)..., nor even a treatment of the empire from the sole point of view of the Greek provinces."[21] But Judaea was a province in Josephus's adult years, and he wrote of the empire from precisely that provincial perspective. Lest one think that Bowie interprets "Greek provinces" narrowly, note that he also omits Josephus from his survey of *local* Greek histories, whereas he includes accounts of Levantine Byblos and Phoenicia.[22] Bowie and his successors, although they differ significantly in their assumptions and methods, mostly agree in neglecting what the prolific Greek writer Josephus might have had to say about both current Greek affairs and about antiquity – his and theirs.

This is all the more surprising because Josephus's thirty Greek volumes remain fully extant, reveal his thorough schooling in Graeco-Roman rhetoric and historiography, and often reach an impressive level of style. I wish to suggest that he is not so completely irrelevant to the world of Greek statesmen who tried to make sense of their place under Roman rule. Indeed, his widely recognized debts to Polybius tend to place him in the company of the many others who drew from the legacy of this programmatic historian, whose position as the first important Greek statesman to wrestle with the fact of Roman hegemony had generated both a lexicon and a moral-political framework for problems of Greek life under Rome.[23] Josephus must at least be included among Polybius's heirs, and may show himself surprisingly engaged with the same sort of problems as his contemporary Greek counterparts.

---

[20] See Steve Mason, "Of Audience and Meaning: Reading Josephus' *Bellum Judaicum* in the Context of a Flavian Audience," in *Josephus and Jewish History in Flavian Rome and Beyond* (ed. J. Sievers and G. Lembi; Leiden: Brill, 2005), 70–100; pp. 92–98 deal particularly with Roman affairs. On the extensive and detailed Roman material in *Antiquities*, see T. P. Wiseman, Death of an Emperor: Flavius Josephus (Exeter: University of Exeter Press, 1991) and Steve Mason, "Flavius Josephus and Flavian Rome: Reading on and Between the Lines," in *Flavian Rome: Image, Culture, Text* (ed. A. J. Boyle and W. J. Dominik; Leiden: Brill, 2003), 559–89.

[21] Bowie, "Greeks," 181.

[22] Bowie, "Greeks," 184–88.

[23] See especially Eckstein, *Moral Vision*, and Craige Champion, *Cultural Politics in Polybius' Histories* (Berkeley: University of California Press, 2005). Although scholars of the Greek renaissance under the Principate generally downplay its intellectual connections with Polybius (explicitly Swain, *Hellenism*, 160), this tendency may stem in part from an older view of Polybius, which Eckstein and Champion have successfully challenged.

In the present essay I deal with the ancient material in Josephus's earliest work, the *Judaean War*, which he wrote mainly under Vespasian's rule. The *War* may seem an odd choice, since it not only makes no claim to *archaiologia*, but actually seems to reject antiquity as a meaningful pursuit (*War* 1.13–16). Yet those prefatory remarks reveal much that merits investigation concerning the role of antiquity in Josephus's environment. He will later include an artful speech, given by his own character, concerning ancient Judaean history (5.375–400). Moreover, he devotes the first and longest of *War*'s seven volumes to what must count as the distant past: beginning 250 years before the war against Rome, with the Hasmonean revolt, then slowing to dwell on the reign of King Herod – still a century before the main war. By contrast, the sixty years between Herod's death and the outbreak of revolt are passed over at high speed in the first half of Book 2. This proportion already suggests that the era of Judaea's "greatest generations" furnished valuable *exempla* for our author.

In his own Polybius-influenced justification of his starting point (*War* 1.17), Josephus explains that the earlier periods have been written up accurately by others. But this is hardly an adequate criterion for beginning where he does, since the Hasmonean and Herodian periods too had produced plenty of literature, at least some of which was available to Josephus and his audience. We are justified in assuming that he chose his entry point because he had some new truth to extract from the ancestors. This assumption is put beyond doubt by the aforementioned speech of his character outside Jerusalem, which dramatically shapes the past so as to infer moral lessons from it.

Although we lack the space here to develop the required context, in all such investigations one must bear in mind the rhetorical bedrock of ancient elite values, the centrality of character (ἦθος) to rhetorical modes of thinking, the importance of origins and ancestry (γένος) to assessments of character – whether personal or ethnic-national, the ever-closer bond between rhetoric and historiography in the Hellenistic and Roman periods, which often resulted in history as serial biography, and the consequently widespread conception of history as a fund of moral exempla for the statesman.[24]

One advantage in our treating here Josephus's *War*, aside from the problem of sheer volume that attends any effort to discuss the *Antiquities*, is that there can be no question yet of his "Hellenizing" the biblical story

[24] Of the vast secondary literature on these questions, I mention only the classic by Anthony J. Woodman, *Rhetoric in Classical Historiography: Four Studies* (London: Croom Helm, 1988), and Christopher Pelling, *Literary Texts and the Greek Historian* (London: Routledge, 2000).

as a deliberate project. In the *War*, in which the ancient past is not yet central, we confront Josephus's earliest available analytical categories and language.

After briefly surveying his world of discourse in the *War*, by way of orientation, we shall move to the three examples mentioned above: a paragraph from the prologue, the antecedent history in Book 1, and Josephus's speech outside Jerusalem's walls.

## I. Josephus's World of Discourse in the *War*

In order to explore the relevant parts of the *War*, we need to keep one eye on the whole composition, though limited space precludes full discussion. The bane of older Josephus research was the quest for a simple caption or slogan that would cover the book's "agenda." Most often, the *War* has been considered a vehicle of Flavian propaganda, a statement to the world (especially the East) of what happens when nations challenge Rome and a celebration of Flavian fortune.[25] This widely accepted characterization married free speculation about the lost Aramaic precursor of the extant Greek *War* (cf. 1.3, 6–8) with jejune commentary on isolated fragments of the extant Greek work, wrenched out of context and assumed to reflect the Aramaic. Tessa Rajak effectively undermined crucial supports of this edifice.[26] From the rubble created by its collapse, another has attracted credibility: that Josephus wrote to absolve himself and his aristocratic peers from complicity in the recent conflict. According to this view, *War* clumsily overlays conflicting ideologies: the one that Josephus embraced while a committed rebel leader against Rome and the very different one he adopts after the fact, as narrator in Rome. One can then exploit the alleged points of conflict or contradiction to expose the truth about aristocratic support for the war.[27] Yet the first sentence of the prologue (1.1–3), in

---

[25] Richard Laqueur, *Der jüdische Historiker Flavius Josephus: ein biographischer Versuch auf neuer quellenkritischer Grundlage* (Darmstadt: Wissenschaftliche Buchgesellschaft, 1970 [1920]), 126–27; H. St. John Thackeray, *Josephus: The Man and the Historian* (New York: Ktav, 1967 [1929]), 27–28; Jacob Neusner, *A History of the Jews in Babylonia,* vol. 1: *The Parthian Period* (Leiden: E. J. Brill, 1969), 71; Cohen, "Jeremiah," 366; Seth Schwartz, *Josephus and Judaean Politics* (Leiden: E. J. Brill, 1990), 10.

[26] Tessa Rajak, *Josephus: The Man and His Society* (London: Duckworth, 1983).

[27] Heinrich Luther, *Josephus und Justus von Tiberias: ein Beitrag zur Geschichte des jüdischen Aufstandes* (Halle: Wischan & Burkhardt, 1910), 15; Martin D. Goodman, *The Ruling Class of Judaea: The Origins of the Jewish Revolt against Rome AD 66–70* (Cambridge, U.K.: Cambridge University Press, 1987), 20–21; Jonathan J. Price, *Jerusalem*

which Josephus proudly declares that he personally fought the Romans and only later found himself observing from their side "by necessity," along with the detailed account of his exploits as general, casts doubt on the suggestion that he hoped to conceal or minimize this participation. I have also yielded to the temptation of identifying *War*'s "thesis": that it was meant as a defense of Judaeans in general from post-war slander and reprisal.[28]

A few more years passed in close company with the text, however, have convinced me that this rich and multi-layered work cannot be adequately characterized in such lapidary terms. It is hard to see how the conveying of *any* simple ideas or propositions could be among its purposes. A rhetoricized mentality required compositions to reach their audiences at many levels – aesthetic and emotional as well as logical – and we see Josephus working at all these levels: taking care with his diction and sentence structure, his entertaining digressions, his construction of tragic scenes and battles. All these must be reckoned integrated parts of the story, even if they do not directly support an idea or theme. Moreover, the quest for simple propositions is thwarted by Josephus's habits of giving characters different and equally compelling views and of standing back as narrator and withholding directive moral judgment. His narrative even deliberately undermines the speeches of important characters, as we shall see, and this playfully ironic dimension of the work further frustrates any reader's desire to seek Josephus's ideology there – in the passages that come closest to sustained arguments.

His portrait of the chief priest Ananus, joint leader of the war preparations until his murder by Idumaeans and Zealots at the mid-point of the work, illustrates the problem of locating ideologies, for Ananus represents moral *values* rather than any single position. Josephus claims that, while preparing for war, Ananus's aim was gradually to bend the rebels toward a more beneficial course:

> In Jerusalem, Ananus the chief priest and those of the powerful men who were not sympathetic to the Romans were preparing the walls and many war machines. Throughout the whole city, projectiles and body armor were being forged.... Ananus, nonetheless, harbored the intention of bending to the more beneficial course (κάμψαι πρὸς τὸ συμφέρον) the insurgents and the recklessness of the so-called Zealots as he *gradually sidelined the preparations for war* (Ἀνάνῳ.... κατὰ μικρὸν ἀφισταμένῳ). But he succumbed to the violence. (*War* 2.648–51)

---

*Under Siege: The Collapse of the Jewish State, 66–70 C.E.* (Leiden: E. J. Brill, 1992), xi, 33, 186; Mader, *Politics*, 4, 10, 52.

[28] Steve Mason, *Flavius Josephus on the Pharisees* (Leiden: Brill, 1991), 54–80.

This description anticipates Plutarch's advice that the statesman must first understand the character and temper of his people, then seek to train their character, "nudging them gently towards the better course and handling them with mildness" (ἀτρέμα πρὸς τὸ βέλτιον ὑπάγοντα καὶ πράως μεταχειριζόμενον; *Praec.* [*Mor.*] 800a–b).

Josephus's later obituary on Ananus expands the same assessment. Notice the density of aristocratic virtues among his evaluative criteria:

> For he was indeed a man of dignity and unsurpassed justice in every area: along with the gravity resulting from his noble birth, status, and the honor he had achieved, he eagerly accorded equal honor to the humblest folk; unique in his love of freedom, and a partisan of democracy, he invariably placed the public advantage – and in every case making peace – above his private rewards. For he knew that what the Romans had was irresistible. But still he made careful preparations even for war, by necessity: so that if the Judeans should not be able to resolve the matter, they should distinguish themselves with skill. To say it briefly: with Ananus alive, they would certainly have resolved matters, for he was forceful in speaking and also in persuading the populace; he was already taking in hand those who were obstructing him. Or, in the case that war continued, they would have confronted the Romans with a long-protracted attrition under such a general. (*War* 4.319–21)

That characterization mirrors Josephus's handling of the same issues in his own career: although he too knew that war with Rome was futile, as a member of the governing elite he had to commit himself fully to this campaign – even at the peril of his life:

> For he could see to what a fall Judaean affairs were headed, and he knew that they had but one path of rescue: if they reversed course. Even though he himself could expect pardon from the Romans, he would have preferred to die many times over than to betray his homeland and the generalship that had been entrusted to him, to enjoy good fortune among those he had been sent to fight. Therefore, he decided to write to those in charge in Jerusalem, describing the situation with precision: neither distorting the strength of the enemy by increasing it, in which case he might be impugned for cowardice, nor reporting it to be inadequate – perhaps giving courage when they had already thought better of it. *So, if they were opting for treaty terms*, they should write back to this effect immediately; *if they had decided to continue fighting*, they should send him a force that was equal to combat against the Romans. (*War* 3.136–140)

In neither case can we detect anything as simple as pro- or anti-war (*bzw.* –Roman) *ideologies*. Rather, we see pragmatic statesmen who feel obligated to act in the best interests of their people's wellbeing, whatever course that might require (What they really felt is irrecoverable, of course; we are speaking of Josephus's narrative world). These men operate within what Eckstein, in his examination of Polybius's values, aptly calls the "restricted arc of political possibility."[29] With respect to the Third Punic War, Polybius claims that the Carthaginians could have gone in either of two *equally honorable* directions: *either* completely surrendering to Rome *or* fighting to the last man. Their culpable folly lay in first surrendering hostages and then dishonorably trying to fight – an emotional and reckless choice (36.7.3–5).[30] Compare Plutarch's prescriptions for the statesman, who must under no circumstances desert the ship of state – even if its problems are not of his creation – but must stand in solidarity with the populace, whose welfare is his reason for being (*Praec.* [*Mor.*] 815c–d). This Greek political discourse, like Josephus's, is about values and virtues rather than ideological programs.

Rather than trying to identify ideological propositions in the *War*, then, I would propose that amongst all of the rhetorical artifice, stylistic flourishes, speeches, digressions, and historiographical commonplaces we may identify a number of large thematic clusters that pervade the narrative, each of them signaled as important in the prologue. Different critics would count and link them differently, but for the sake of providing efficient background I might suggest four such clusters, having to do with character themes, tragic themes, *polis* themes, and cultic themes.

As for character themes: Josephus claims to write (*War* 1.2–3, 6–9) in response to a character problem for Judaeans after the year 70. A wide range of evidence confirms that the standard Roman and Flavian portraits of the recent conflict denigrated the defeated Judaeans in predictable ways: they appeared as an inherently rebellious people whose reckless aggression was not supported by true martial virtue. Their city was justly destroyed by the Flavian *genius*, the brilliance of the generals, and the legendary discipline of the legions. They appear on the CAPTA coins diminished, personified by a small woman or man and woman in a state of *aporia*, often contrasted with a tall and proud conquering Roman soldier. In other words, the Judaeans received the standard treatment,[31] except on a much larger scale because of the importance of the victory both in the legitimization of the Flavians and in their rebuilding of Rome: extinguishing Nero's memo-

[29] Eckstein, *Moral Vision*, 200.

[30] Cf. Eckstein, *Moral Vision*, 218.

[31] For the standard treatment and view of conquered enemies, see Adam Ziolkowski, "*Urbs Direpta*, or How the Romans Sacked Cities," in *War and Society in the Roman World* (ed. J. Rich and G. Shipley; London: Routledge, 1993), 69–91; Susan P. Mattern, *Rome and the Enemy: Imperial Strategy in the Principate* (Berkeley: University of California, 1999); I. M. Ferris, *Enemies of Rome: Barbarians through Roman Eyes* (Stroud: Sutton, 2000), 1–62.

ry with structures and monuments that would perpetuate the public's memory of the conquest.[32]

When Josephus complains, then, that the many accounts of the revolt already in circulation always disparage and diminish the Judaean side (καταβάλλουσιν δὲ ἀεὶ τὰ Ἰουδαίων καὶ ταπεινοῦσιν) in order to aggrandize the Romans (*War* 1.7), we have every reason to believe him. He promises that he will redress the balance (1.8–9). This redress means in the first instance that, from beginning to the end of the *War*, Josephus emphasizes the manly virtue of the Judaeans as a people. Knowing that the Spartans provide the benchmark of manly virtue, he presents the Judaeans very much in Spartan terms, without saying as much, emphasizing their manliness (ἀνδρεία/ἀνδρίζω/ἀνδραγαθία), steadfast endurance (καρτερία), rugged simplicity of life, orderliness and unity, and contempt for death (θανάτου καταφρονέω). Incidentally, this also seems to be the main reason (not the only one) why *War* includes the lengthy passage on the Essene "legion" (τάγμα) at 2.119–161: it has the highest concentration of "Spartan" themes in the entire work. This emphasis on Judaean virtue indirectly challenges both sides of the Flavian claim: that the conquered deserved harsh retribution and that the Roman legions under their illustrious commanders controlled the operation. Josephus goes far beyond the sort of enhancement of the Judaean side that might simply have increased Flavian glory (for having conquered such a tough adversary).[33]

A second thematic cluster, also announced in the prologue, has to do with tragic themes: suffering and high emotion, often pathetically conveyed by women and children; lamentation, wailing, and mourning evoking fear and pity; all this in response to fate, calamity, and catastrophic reversals of fortune. Though famously opposed to the writing of history as though it were tragedy, Polybius underscores the theme of fortune's reversals (τύχης μεταβολαί): for him, fortune is not merely capricious, but actually conspires to undo people just at the point of their apparent success (1.4.5, 35.2; 39.8.2 [40.12.19]).[34] The study of history, everyone agrees, is

[32] Cf. Fergus Millar, "Last Year in Jerusalem: Monuments of the Jewish War in Rome," in *Flavius Josephus and Flavian Rome* (ed. J. Edmondson, S. Mason, and J. Rives; Oxford: Oxford University Press, 2005), 101–128. The tone of Flavian self-congratulation on destroying Jerusalem and its temple is well captured by the dedicatory inscription from the Arch of Titus that used to stand in the Circus Maximus (*CIL* 6.944) and from Josephus's account of the triumph, which vividly represented the bloody devastation of both the city and its holy places.

[33] The impressiveness of Judaean valor as a challenge and spur to the faltering Romans is emphasized in passages such as 4.89–90; 5.315–16; 6.11–18, 42–44.

[34] F. W. Walbank, *Polybius* (Berkeley: University of California Press, 1972), 60–65; Eckstein, *Moral Vision*, 254–71.

the best remedy to fortune's turns (1.1.2): "indeed the most effective and only instructor for enabling one to bear nobly the reversals of fortune is the recollection of others' undoings" (ἐναργεστάτην δὲ καὶ μόνην διδάσκαλον τοῦ δύνασθαι τὰς τῆς τύχης μεταβολὰς γενναίως ὑποφέρειν τὴν τῶν ἀλλοτρίων περιπετειῶν ὑπόμνησιν). Such language is also common in Josephus's *War*, in crucial contexts. Already in the prologue Josephus introduces the powerful themes of pity and lament over the inexorable fate suffered by his people and his city: ἔλεος, ὀλόφυρσις, οἶκτος/οἰκτίζω/οἰκτείρω (*War* 1.12).[35] Not only that, but he draws heavily from the repertoire of classical tragedy in specific episodes. He has melded (consciously or unconsciously) Greek tragic themes with the Hebrew lament tradition associated with Jeremiah.[36] Against the background of Rome's constant upheavals (1.5, 23) come the reversals of fortune suffered by: Jerusalem, the greatest and happiest city now fallen to its nadir (1.11); various Roman, Seleucid, Hasmonean, and Herodian rulers (e.g., 1.95, 270, 282, 353; 2.113; further below); and Josephus himself as a now captured general (3.394–95). Josephus epitomizes the problem of dealing with fortune's turns through the "bad emperors" Gaius and Nero, offering the innovative assessment that they abused or outraged fortune (ἐξύβρισεν εἰς τὴν τύχην, 2.184, 250) – that is, they neglected Polybius's observations about the need to take special care while enjoying good fortune.

Third, *War* is replete with the kind of *polis* themes we find in Plutarch and Dio. Like them, Josephus draws a great deal from Polybius and partly from Thucydides. These themes concern both external politics, in relation to Rome, and the internal governance of Judaea. Prominent thematic situations include: the constant struggle between concord and against civil strife (ὁμόνοια/στάσις), trouble, disorder, or revolution (ταραχή, θόρυβος, νεωτερισμός); the efforts of the principal or powerful men (οἱ πρῶτοι, ἄριστοι, γνώριμοι, δυνατοί) to manage and guide the rabble (τὸ πλῆθος) so as to prevent them from acting out their reckless impulses; the enchanters and deceivers (γόητες, ἀπατεῶνες), who whip the rabble into a kind of frenzy or madness (μανία, ἀπόνοια) for their self-serving ends, aided by the predictable folly of the spirited young hot-heads (οἱ νέοι, θρασύτεροι, θερμότεροι); the dangers of a resulting tyranny (τυραννίς) under home-grown masters and of corresponding "slavery" (δουλεία) to them; the life-risking loyalty (πίστις) of the aristocracy – such as the chief priests Ananus and Jesus, Josephus himself, and colleagues – to prevent such an outcome; and hence, the true meaning of freedom and autonomy (ἐλευθερία/αὐτονομία). So large does the ironic interplay of freedom and

[35] The word groups mentioned occur some 115 times in *War* alone.

[36] Cf. Cohen, "Jeremiah."

slavery loom in Josephus's *War* that one might consider the entire work a meditation on this theme. We shall return to it below, along with the paradox that although the rebels claim to oppose oppressive foreigners (ἀλλόφυλοι), in fact the foreign power best protects the state against these dangerous native (ὁμόφυλοι) tyrants.

A final thematic cluster, which again cannot be rigidly separated from the others, has to do with the cult of Jerusalem's deity. In this domain we meet Josephus's recurring observations about the pollution (μιαίνω, μιαρός, μίασμα) of the holy precincts, including the shrine (ὁ ναός) and the sacred compound (τὸ ἱερόν), most often by the hot-headed rebels and their self-interested tyrant leaders, the slaughter or blood-letting (ἀποσφάζω, φόνος) of those who have come to offer innocent sacrifice along with their animal victims, especially at the great festival celebrating national "freedom" – Passover (e.g., 2.30, 224, 256; 4.402; 6.420–34),[37] and God's purging of his defiled sanctuary by the fire of war, which fire is constantly being "fanned" or "quenched."

## II. Josephus and Greek History in the *War*

That Josephus was entirely aware of current Greek trends in historical writing is clear from all of the language connected with these thematic clusters, and also from the opening sentences of *War*'s prologue (1.1–30). We have seen that this is among the fullest examples of the type. But the form and style are also striking. If we accept Niese's punctuation, the opening sentence of *War* contains 264 words, comprising half a dozen μὲν... δέ constructions, some of which include within them further contrasts signaled by other language. The prologue also contains a number of rare words (ἀτυχήματα, 1.12; ἐπηρεάζω, 1.13; προιστορέω 1.15; ἀρχαιολογέω, 1.17; διεξοδικός and προγενής, 1.18) and unusual formulations, especially the use of a neuter participle or adjective with article in place of a noun (τὸ νεωτερίζον, 1.4; τὸ κελτικόν, 1.5; τὰ στρατιωτικά, 1.5; τὸ ληστρικόν, 1.11) – usages that he will not repeat in the narrative itself, though he will often use the cognate verbs and adjectives. Moreover, Attic spelling (double-τ, double-ρ) is more prominent in the prologue and in Book 7 than in the rest, contributing to the work's concentric symmetry. Most intriguingly, Josephus often uses roots and compound forms that have sparse if any attestation before his time, but which then become fre-

---

[37] See Federico M. Colautti, *Passover in the Works of Josephus* (Leiden: Brill, 2002).

quent among his contemporary and later Greek authors.[38] He undertakes with scrupulous care to avoid the clashing of vowels (hiatus) in the prescribed Atticizing ways. Writing in the 70s, he turns out to be on the cutting edge of the old-new style. He is evidently striving to make an impression, to show that he can manipulate the Greek language at a high level.

Yet strangely, after carefully introducing his subject with all the canonical devices of the Greek prologue and thus flaunting his ability, Josephus suddenly turns on "the Greeks" in what seems a gratuitous attack:[39] he assails both Greek story-tellers (λόγιοι) who are preoccupied with the ancient glories of Hellas (while conceding their superior abilities in the language) and also those "sophists" (σοφισταί) who *have* written about the Judaean-Roman war – but incompetently.

> **13** And yet I myself might appropriately criticize the story-tellers among the Greeks (Καίτοι γε ἐπιτιμήσαιμ' ἂν αὐτὸς δικαίως τοῖς Ἑλλήνων λογίοις), who have positioned themselves as judges (κάθηνται κριταί) of these events of such moment, which have happened in their own times and which expose the ancient wars as paltry by comparison, while abusing those who rival them for honor (τοῖς φιλοτιμουμένοις ἐπηρεάζοντες) – in relation to whom, even if they prove superior in speech-craft, they are inferior in choice. They themselves write the history of the Assyrians and Medes (αὐτοὶ δὲ τὰ Ἀσσυρίων καὶ Μήδων συγγράφουσιν), as though these events had been less finely reported by the ancient historical writers. **14** And yet to the same degree that they are unequal to those men with respect to ability in writing, to that degree [they are also unequal] in judgment. For each of *those* men was keen to write of his own times [e.g., Thucydides, Xenophon], where indeed their presence at the events made the report vivid; lying, among those who were knowledgeable, was a shameful thing. **15** Certainly, at any rate, placing in memorial matters not previously treated histori-

[38] This is something I find repeatedly in translating *War* 2 and preparing its commentary. Details will appear in the published volume (Steve Mason, ed., *Flavius Josephus: Translation and Commentary*, Vol. 1b: *Judean War 2* [Leiden: Brill, expected 2008]).

[39] Gustav Hölscher ("Josephus," in *Paulys Realencyclopädie der classischen Altertumswissenschaft* 18 [1916]: 1948) proposed that λόγιοι was an inflated plural representing Josephus's major source for *War* 1, Nicolaus of Damascus. Helgo Lindner ("Eine offene Frage zur Auslegung des Bellum-Proömiums," in *Josephus-Studien: Untersuchungen zu Josephus, dem antiken Judentum und dem Neuen Testament* [ed. O. Betz, K. Haacker, and M. Hengel; Göttingen: Vandenhoeck & Ruprecht, 1974], 256–57), however, showed that the description does not suit Nicolaus. Rightly rejecting also the suggestion of Thackeray (*Josephus*, 105) that this is Josephus's thankless condemnation of his own literary assistants (cf. *Apion* 1.50), Lindner argues ("Frage," 258–59) that Josephus's anger must result from concrete legal actions against him, upon the publication of his *War*. All such proposals seem to me symptomatic of the isolation of Josephus from his Greek environment, described in the opening paragraphs above. Antony Spawforth ("Symbol," 244) is nearer the mark in reading part of this passage in light of the "Persian-wars 'mania'" among contemporary Greek writers.

> cally, and putting together the affairs of one's own times for those who come afterwards, is worthy of praise and acknowledgment. The industrious man is not the one who merely remodels another person's arrangement and order, but the one who, by speaking of recent things, also establishes the body of the history in a distinctive way. **16** For my part, it is through the greatest expenditures and exertions that I, *albeit a foreigner, present to Greeks and also Romans this memorial of achievements.* As for the natives [or 'genuine (Greeks)' – τοῖς δὲ γνησίοις]: when it comes to profits or lawsuits the mouth has immediately burst open and the tongue been let loose; but when it comes to history, where one must speak the truth and may only assemble the facts through much exertion, they stand muzzled, having allowed feebler men – and those who do not even know the deeds of the leaders [viz., the Flavians] – to write. Let the truth of history, then, be honored among us, since among the Greeks it has been neglected (τιμάσθω δὴ παρ' ἡμῖν τὸ τῆς ἱστορίας ἀληθές, ἐπεὶ παρ' Ἕλλησιν ἠμέληται). (*War* 1.13–16)

Note the *inclusio* created by forms of τιμάω at the beginning and end.

If the label "Greek" is itself notoriously problematic,[40] Josephus's position as a Greek-language writer who adopts all the contemporary standards while pointedly distancing himself from "the Greeks" makes things even more complicated. Writing in Greek for a Roman audience in the first instance, he conveniently latches on to Roman stereotypes of the Greeks as preening windbags.[41] He implies here a quintessentially elite-Roman distinction between admirable Greeks of yore and the currently living specimens.[42] By casting his contemporaries as preoccupied with their own ancient victories, Josephus cleverly questions their loyalty to the imperial family who have based so much of their image on the recent Judaean campaign. We need not see this as earnest support for the regime, because there is always an element of ironic playfulness in Josephus's resort to this *reductio ad gloriam Caesaris* (cf. *War* 1.8; 2.26–37). Here the strategy mainly serves to draw attention to himself and his great subject.

A few passages on the Greeks and antiquity from elsewhere in his writings will illustrate that Josephus defaults with some consistency to this quasi-Roman perspective on the older culture:

---

[40] E.g., Jonathan M. Hall, *Hellenicity: Between Ethnicity and Culture* (Chicago: University of Chicago Press, 2002).

[41] Roman critique of Greek oratory is commonly traced to Cato the Elder's assessment from his early encounter with the Athenian assembly (191 B.C.E.): "Among the Greeks, words issue from their lips; among the Romans, from their hearts" (Plutarch, *Cato Maj.* 12.5). Erich S. Gruen (*Cultural and National Identity in Republican Rome* [Ithaca: Cornell University Press, 1992], 52–83) attempts to interpret the Catonian anecdotes about the Greeks in a more positive way. For a sketch of the evidence and standard reading, see J. P. V. D. Balsdon, *Romans and Aliens* (Chapel Hill: University of North Carolina Press, 1979), 30–54.

[42] Cf. Ronald Syme on Tacitus and the Greeks in his *Tacitus* (2 vols.; Oxford: Clarendon Press, 1958), 2.511–12.

Some of the nations preserve the names given by their founders, but some changed them in order to make them appear more intelligible to their neighbors. *The Greeks are the ones responsible for this.* For when in later times they came to power *they made the glory of the past their own*, adorning the peoples with names intelligible to themselves and imposing upon them a political constitution *as if they were descended from themselves*. [In what follows,, Josephus makes a point of giving names in "our language," followed by a Greek translation.] (*Ant.* 1.121)

**263** For among my compatriots I am admitted to have an education in our country's customs that far surpasses theirs. And once I had consolidated my knowledge of Greek grammar, I worked very hard also to share in the learning of Greek letters and poetry, though my traditional habit has frustrated precision with respect to pronunciation. **264** Among us: they do not favor those who have mastered the accent of many nations and made their speech frilly with elegance of diction, because they consider such a pursuit to be common – not only among those who happen to be free citizens, but even among domestics if they desire it. They acknowledge wisdom only among those who clearly understand the legal system and who are able to bring out the force of the sacred literature. (*Ant.* 20.263)

By saying these things, he [Josephus's adversary Iustus of Tiberias] won over the mob. For he was rather good at manipulating the populace and overcoming the better arguments of disputants by craftiness and a kind of guile, which he achieved through words. In fact, he was well versed in the culture of the Greeks, on the basis of which he audaciously took it upon himself to record also the history of these events – as if he could overcome the truth itself by means of this speech-craft (ὡς τῷ λόγῳ τούτῳ περιεσόμενος τῆς ἀληθείας). **41** But concerning this man – how sordid his life became and how he was, with his brother, the cause of almost complete ruin – we shall explain as the story unfolds. (*Life* 40)

The first thing that occurs to me is utter astonishment at those who think one should pay attention only to Greeks on matters of great antiquity, expecting to learn the truth from them, while disbelieving us and the rest of humanity. For my part, I find the very opposite of this to be the case, if indeed one should not follow worthless opinions but derive a correct conclusion from the facts themselves. **7** For everything to do with the Greeks one would find to be new, so to speak "from yesterday or the day before" – I mean the founding of cities, and matters concerning the invention of arts and the recording of laws; and just about the most recent of all for them is care in relation to the writing of histories. (*Apion* 1.6–7)

Back in *War*'s prologue, then, several items confirm that Josephus is very much aware of current Greek debates. First, the opening phrase in 1.13: καίτοι γε ἐπιτιμήσαιμ' ἂν αὐτὸς δικαίως, takes over a common phrase from the orators (ἐπιτιμάω δικαίως), in contexts of epideictic rhetoric.[43] Given that Josephus is here attacking *wordy* authors or storytellers in particular, it is noteworthy that Diodorus Siculus opens his twentieth volume with the same phrase, in precisely such a context: "One might appropriate-

[43] Isocrates, *De pace* 8.4; *Panath.* 12.115; Aeschines, *Tim.* 1.38; Xenophon, *Mem.* 1.2.29.

ly censure (δικαίως ἄν τις ἐπιτιμήσειεν) those who insert too-wordy orations or make use of frequent speeches" (20.1.1). This appears to be, as Sacks argues,[44] an oblique accusation against the famous rhetorical historian Timaeus (c. 345–250 B.C.E.). Josephus has already assailed, in his prologue, the "sophist-like" reporting of the Judaean war (1.1), a charge easily connected with the memory of Timaeus, made famous by Polybius as *the* rhetorical historian. Timaeus was known by the nick-name Epitimaeus (Ἐπιτίμαιος), or "Critic," a pun on his relentless fault-finding (ἐπιτιμάω – the verb Josephus uses here; Diodorus Siculus 5.1.4; Athenaeus, *Deipn.* 6.103). Josephus knew Timaeus's reputation, since he mentions it in a later work (*Apion* 2.221). The paragraph we are presently considering, *War* 1.13 and following, attacks native Greek historians who rewrite Persian-era history merely for rhetorical improvement, to the neglect of important recent events, which is like the charge that Polybius levels against Timaeus (12.25a.5, 25b.4, 25d–e, 25g–h, 28a.4–10). It seems, therefore, that Josephus's use of ἐπιτιμάω here is carefully chosen, and intended ironically. He will paradoxically make himself a justifiable *epitimaios* in criticizing those Greek *Timaioi* who revel in their own pointless ancient history while not only ignoring the monumental Judaean campaign just completed, but also criticizing (as *epitimaioi* themselves) those engaged in such beneficial work (viz. Josephus).

Second, Josephus evokes the atmosphere of intense literary rivalry that characterized the Second Sophistic. Competition was intense and personal.[45] It focused largely on debates over the proper forms of Attic dialect, and generated a variety of competing lexica along with the petty sort of attacks captured in some of Lucian's satires.[46] Josephus reveals his involvement in this game when he indicates that he has been abused by Greek authors and again when he describes himself as their rival for honor (Greek τοῖς φιλοτιμουμένοις). According to the third-century C.E. Philostratus (*Vit. Soph.* 490–491), who charts the rise of the Greek revival, such rivalry (τὸ φιλότιμον) was particularly common among sophists. Josephus declines to explain either the nature of the abuse he has experienced or the reasons for it. But given the context, in which he concedes the superior speech-craft of his accusers, their criticism seems to have involved defects in his Greek style, perhaps including his accent. It appears that he has presented drafts of his material in public settings: the salon or the lecture hall. Note his remark at 1.22: "I am about *to speak* to those who know [my

---

[44] Kenneth S. Sacks, *Diodorus Siculus and the First Century* (Princeton: Princeton University Press, 1990), 93–96.

[45] See Bowersock, *Sophists*, 89–100.

[46] Swain, *Hellenism*, 17–64.

life story]," (μέλλων γε πρὸς εἰδότας ἐρεῖν). It may well have grated on Greek literary men seeking their main chance in the capital that this captured Judaean had achieved such a privileged position; they trained their guns with greater intensity on his deficiencies in the language.

Reaching for a tactic of proven effectiveness, however, Josephus tries to transform this defect in impressive speech into a virtue, by associating Greek rhetorical education with a lack of concern for truth: the Oriental and Judean (and genuine Roman!) concern for unadorned truth always trumps mere facility in language (see the passages above). He will later happily acknowledge that he needed collaborators "for the sake of the Greek sound [or language]," when he wrote the *War* (*Apion* 1.50). It is a badge of honor in Josephus's scheme of things that he should be lacking in Greek speech-craft (cf. *Apion* 1.73). Contrasting rhetoric with concern for simple truth had been a common and effective tactic at least since Thucydides,[47] and the contrast became part of the "laconic" Spartan and later Roman self-image. Whereas even Greek writers had rejected feckless rhetoric, however, Josephus maneuvers to characterize it as emblematic of Greek culture as a whole. Taking these comments together with such other observations as his notice about the despised emperor Gaius's facility in Greek (*Ant.* 19.208),[48] we may conclude that Josephus was attempting to tap established Roman sentiment about this corrupting culture.

A third striking phrase in this part of the prologue identifies *the Assyrians and Medes* as the subject of obscure Greek history. This is peculiar not only because these empires were so ancient, but also because they were not coeval: the Assyrian empire ended in 612 B.C.E. at the hands of the neo-Babylonians, who were in turn dislodged by the Medes and then the Persians, who conquered and absorbed them. It is surprising, therefore, that the Greeks' paradigmatically conquered foes, the Persians, are represented here by the Medes. What is going on?

As for the Assyrians: Representatives of the Greek renaissance, especially those who hailed from Syria, tended to call their region "Assyria," and the Syrian city of Hierapolis "Old Nineveh" (cf. Philostratus, *Vit. soph.* 20.512; 21.518; *Vit. Apoll.* 1.3, 19). So the term seems to have a contemporary though vague resonance in both identifying a once-glorious region and recalling ancient battles. As for the Medes: They were indeed a famous and important *element* of the Persian wars with Greece. Although the Persians had conquered them before crushing the Babylonians, Persian kings privileged Medes in their government, in part as a check against their

---

[47] Thucydides 1.21.1, 22.4; cf. Cicero, *Brut.* 70.247; Paul in 1 Cor 1:19–21; 2:4; Acts 4:13; Lucian, *Nigr.* 9–10.

[48] Comparable is Tacitus on Nero and the Greeks at *Ann.* 14.20.

own Persian nobility.[49] So, one of the two Persian commanders at Marathon in 493 B.C.E. was Datis the Mede,[50] and Medes constituted one of the prominent Persian contingents in Xerxes's fateful invasion of 480 B.C.E. Because of Media's earlier prominence, the euphonic "Medism" rather than "Persism" became the standard term also for alliance with Persia.

Still, why not mention the actual famous enemy: the Persians? According to Philostratus, a number of sophists from Josephus's time onward focused on the Medes in their speeches. Among these was Josephus's contemporary in Rome, Scopelian of Smyrna (*Vit. soph.* 519). One of Lucian's Greek characters, when given the opportunity to dream about what he would like to do with his life, opts to re-fight the wars with Persians and Medes (*Nav.* 25–39; "Medes" in 36). Lucian's treatise on history-writing shows that a large number of historians in the 160s C.E. were writing about Parthia (*Hist.* 28–33), though he attributes this trend to the recent campaigns under Lucius Verus (*Hist.* 2). Significantly, however, he observes that present-day Parthians are often equated in popular discourse with the Persians and Medes of old (*Hist.* 18, 30).

Although we do not know of other first-century Greek historians who treated "Assyrians and Medes" per se, it seems clear that Josephus was aware of such current interests and trends in language. I suggest that he chooses "Assyrians and Medes" quite pointedly, to emphasize the obscurity and irrelevance of the pursuits favored by his Greek critics. If he tries to position his work in relation to contemporary trends among Greek writers under Rome, we ought also to consider it from this perspective.

## III. Freedom and Autonomy, Foreign and Native Government

Let us turn now to Book 1, the longest of *War*'s seven volumes. It is an old and important question, why, after chiding his contemporaries for focusing on the ancient past, Josephus begins his own narrative some 250 years before the Judaean-Roman war, with the Hasmonean revolt against the Seleucids.

It seems to me that his reasons for including the distant past in *War* are broadly intelligible in light of contemporary Greek concerns with the uses and abuses of history. In the case of Judaea, the legacy of that past had been a significant element in the recent war and so it remained a contentious matter in need of resolution. For some Judaeans, apparently, the exploits of the Hasmoneans were a primary source of inspiration for all

[49] J. M. Cook, *The Persian Empire* (New York: Schocken, 1983), 52–53.
[50] Cook, *Persian*, 97–98.

later guerrilla campaigns against occupying powers. According to 1 Macc 2:24–26, the earlier revolt began when the Hasmonean patriarch Mattathias witnessed another Judaean about to sacrifice on a Greek altar, in violation of the ancestral laws: he ran forward and killed both him and the presiding official of Antiochus IV. In that passage, Mattathias's "burning with zeal" (twice mentioned) is favorably compared to the biblical example of Pinchas, son of Aaron the high priest, who ran through a prominent Israelite with his spear for taking a local Midianite woman as his wife. That episode (Num 25) receives authoritative divine support, and the theme of righteous, militant zeal for the law persevered as inspiration for the Hasmoneans. The Maccabees in their turn, as William R. Farmer and Martin Hengel[51] have argued in detail, furnished an ideological paradigm for Judaean resistance movements through the first century C.E. With interesting parallels to the Greek situation, old Hasmonean names (Mattathias, Judah, John, Simon, Hyrcanus) were extremely popular in the first century.[52]

Yet this is all background for Josephus's situation, as he is not speaking in the first instance to his Judean compatriots. Also, outside Judaea the legacy of the Hasmoneans was remembered, and this militant strain of biblical-Hasmonean tradition was often taken to exemplify a national trait of misanthropy. Hostile commentators claimed that Judaeans, under the direction of Moses' laws, had made unjust war on Egypt (Manetho, in *Apion* 1.73–91, 228–52). Centuries later, after winning their freedom from the Seleucids *by force of arms,* the Hasmoneans continually harassed their neighbors.[53] Tacitus makes similar points in the extant part of book 5 (e.g., *Hist.* 5.8), while introducing the character of the Judaean people *as background* for the fall of Jerusalem, which was described in the part of the book that is now lost. Albeit from quite different moral perspectives, then, both Judaean militants and some educated outsiders viewed the distant Judaean past as providing encouragement for armed confrontation.

This was by no means the only lesson to be learned from the Hasmonean revolt, however. Already in the book of Daniel, completed in about 164 B.C.E., we find an author stressing that God alone controls the rise

---

[51] William R. Farmer, "Judas, Simon and Athronges," *New Testament Studies* 4 (1958): 147–55; *Maccabees, Zealots, and Josephus: An Inquiry into Jewish Nationalism in the Greco-Roman Period* (Westport, Conn.: Greenwood Press, 1973 [1956]), e.g., 108; Martin Hengel, *The Zealots: Investigations into the Jewish Freedom Movement in the Period from Herod I until 70 A.D.* (trans. David Smith; Edinburgh: T. & T. Clark, 1989), 90–145.

[52] See Farmer's studies in the preceding note.

[53] Pompeius Trogus in Justin, *Epitome* 1.9; cf. 2.4; Menahem Stern, *Greek and Latin Authors on Jews and Judaism* (3 vols.; Jerusalem: Israel Academy of Sciences, 1974–1984), 1.334, 343.

and fall of kingdoms (2:21; 4:14, 22, 29, 44), and that he alone will install his kingdom (2:44; 6:17). Some famous passages (2:34, 45; 8:14, 25; 11:14, 34) criticize those who foolishly try to effect God's will with human hands. Whether or not some of these passages obliquely criticize the Hasmoneans, there is ample evidence here and in later texts (e.g., among Qumraners and the Jesus movement) for a quietist-pietist tradition that, although "apocalyptic," declined the Hasmonean call to arms and vigorously opposed the new priestly dynasty, preferring to leave the coming upheaval to God and the heavenly host. 1 Maccabees, written about 104 B.C.E., may already offer a friendly counter-reaction, appropriating the seer for its exaltation of the Hasmoneans (e.g., 2.61–68).[54]

What, then, is the *truth* about this older national past that Josephus wishes to establish? Himself a proud scion of the Hasmoneans (*Ant.* 16.187; *Life* 1–6), Josephus tries to reclaim the power of that past for his own political ends. His narrative is carefully tailored to feature values that fit closely with the *polis* themes current among his contemporary Greek statesmen. They had come to agree – Plutarch and Dio not yet lapsing into the sycophantic language of Aristides's *To Rome* – that in current circumstances the presence of Rome as external power, as a kind of political Oceanus around the *oikoumene*, was healthier and more liberating for the Greek cities than absolute native rule could possibly be. We shall consider some passages below.

Josephus takes over such themes with a vengeance, for the most part in a tone of cold *Realpolitik.* He insists, with abundant examples from the disastrous recent past, that the rebels' push for absolute freedom in Jerusalem only opened the door to local would-be tyrants, demagogues, and deceivers, who manipulated the masses for their own aggrandizement without caring how many people suffered in the process. Accepting the firm hand of Roman power, as God and fortune have decreed, paradoxically best guarantees the *freedom* of Jerusalem, which is to say: the freedom of the cultured native aristocracy to govern the people in peace. These are the points Josephus emphasizes in the Hasmonean-Herodian narrative. He gives so much attention to this period in the opening book of the *War* because he wants to reclaim that contested past from all those, whether compatriots or foreigners, who understand it as a paradigm for Judaean militancy.

In just the first ten Niese sections of *War*'s narrative (1.31–40), Josephus quickly introduces the main lines of his configuration, which set the

[54] See the discussion in Steve Mason, "Josephus, Daniel, and the Flavian House," in *Josephus and the History of the Greco-Roman Period* (ed. F. Parente and J. Sievers; Leiden: E. J. Brill, 1994), 161–91.

tone for the sequel. In close parallel to the pre-Augustan Roman civil wars, the story opens with members of the Judean elite short-sightedly competing with one another for supremacy (1.31): "Civil strife (στάσις) arose among the leaders of the Judaeans at the time when Antiochus surnamed Epiphanes had a quarrel with Ptolemy VI concerning all of Syria. Their ambitious rivalry concerned ultimate power, *since each person of rank could not tolerate submission to his peers*" (ἡ φιλοτιμία δ' ἦν αὐτοῖς περὶ δυναστείας ἑκάστου τῶν ἐν ἀξιώματι μὴ φέροντος τοῖς ὁμοίοις ὑποτετάχθαι). This prefigures the vain efforts of all future tyrants – Judaean and Roman – to gain sole supreme power. This initial *stasis* generates an alternative temple in Leontopolis (1.33), the Romans' destruction of which will close the *War* narrative in 7.420–436, completing a concentric symmetry.

This rivalry among Jerusalem's hereditary priests plays into the hands of a Syrian king who already harbors a deep hatred of the Judeans: Antiochus Epiphanes is unable to govern his passions (*War* 1.34: note the "Greek" analysis) and *that* is why he attempts to abolish the Judeans' ancestral customs. Everything Antiochus does violates the principle of moderation, his general Bacchides even torturing members of the Jerusalem aristocracy (1.35), as a Roman procurator and then Judaean tyrants would later do. In Josephus's narrative it is this abuse of the nobility – and not, as in 1 Maccabees (*War* 1.51–2.28), the abolition of *the laws*, with compulsion to sacrifice on pagan altars and eat forbidden food – that prompts the Hasmonean revolt. Mattathias and his sons face hopeless odds in attacking the Seleucid regime, but their extraordinary courage – another Leitmotif of the *War* – pay off when the oppressive foreigners are soon driven from the land.

Immediately after this charter episode, Josephus has the new leader Judas, as the *first act of his rule*, establish an alliance of friendship with the Romans (1.38). No explanation is needed for Josephus's Roman audience, and none is given, but it is a meaningful notice. With modern resources we can easily discover what Josephus's audience could not: that in 1 Maccabees, Judas's alliance with Rome came only at the end of his militant career, after he had won much glory in battle and shortly before his death (1 Macc 8:1; he dies at 9:18), whereas Josephus makes it the famous leader's first and most important action. This means that all his following exploits are achieved under the umbrella of a Roman alliance. It cannot be an accident that Judas's pact with Rome is brought forward in this way, for as soon as this ruler dies, his brother Jonathan renews the treaty (*War* 1.48), which again 1 Maccabees placed near the *end* of Jonathan's career (1 Macc 12:1–3; he dies at 12:48). And *this* means that political freedom for the Judaeans – even in the most glorious period of self-rule, for which the people pine again – was never absolute. It was always a matter of the elite making sound political judgments.

It is not only the Romans with whom the Hasmoneans make political treaties. Most shockingly, in spite of the life-and-death struggle between Judas and both Antiochus IV and his son Antiochus V, Josephus matter-of-factly reports that Jonathan also effected a truce with Antiochus V (*War* 1.48), which under his brother-successor Simon becomes an alliance against the would-be tyrant, Trypho (1.50). These alliances with particular Seleucid rulers never last long, but Josephus's Hasmonean princes keep making them. In doing so, they show themselves keenly aware of political realities. Such pacts are not made on the basis of ideological kinship; they are pragmatic in the highest degree. A pragmatic approach is not without moral values, however: the values in question concern the preservation of the Judean polity, ancestral laws, traditions, and customs, and the peace to cherish them under the leadership of stable priestly government.

This fancy political footwork paves the way for Josephus's elaborate story of King Herod. Unlike *Antiquities*, *War* cleanly divides its account of Herod's reign into two parts: the former concerning his political activities, the latter treating his domestic life, marriages, children, and palace intrigues. The political part is consumed to an extraordinary degree by the challenges Herod faced in dealing, in the footsteps of his father Antipater, with a steady rotation of Roman strongmen in the region during the civil wars. Father and son make agreements first with Pompey (*War* 1.127–131), then with Licinius Crassus (1.179), then with Pompey's enemy Julius Caesar (1.183), then with Caesar's assassin Cassius (1.218–220), then with Caesar's avenger Marc Antony, who arranged Herod's kingship (1.242), and finally with Antony's mortal enemy Octavian, who would nonetheless become Herod's *closest* friend (1.386, 400) to the benefit of Judaeans everywhere.

This ever-changing backdrop is integral to the story. It highlights at once the instability of Roman government in its own wrong-headed struggle[55] toward monarchy – a background theme throughout much of the *War* – and, without a hint of criticism, Hasmonean-Herodian political versatility. The great Judaean statesmen of the past constantly seek alliances with greater powers, but just as constantly change them: not out of ideological affiliation, in which case they might be morally culpable for abandoning principles, but out of a concern to ensure the stability of their own people and constitution. Like Plutarch's great helmsman (κυβερνήτης) Philopoe-

[55] See Steve Mason, "Figured Speech and Irony in T. Flavius Josephus," in *Flavius Josephus and Flavian Rome* (ed. J. Edmondson, S. Mason, and J. Rives; Oxford: Oxford University Press, 2005), 243–88.

men, they know when to steer, but also when to yield to forces that they cannot control, in order to maintain the ship of state (Plutarch, *Phil.* 17.3–4).

All this enhances the theme of Fortune's relentless undoing of people and events, mentioned above. Thus, although Antony was at the height of his powers when he persuaded the Senate to appoint Herod King of Judaea (1.282–285), and Herod had in turn been generous with his loyalty and military support for Antony (1.320), such that he would even have rushed to fight alongside Antony at Actium if he could have done so (1.388), the Judaean king immediately sees the need to seek Octavian's patronage after Actium. Josephus makes vivid the anxiety felt by Herod in this situation, and also his enormous relief when Octavian confirms him as king (1.387, 390, 393).

This portrait of skillful and devoted native leaders who manage foreign rulers for the nation's benefit frames a more basic issue that runs throughout the *War*, which concerns the true nature of freedom and slavery. The simplistic analysis of the demagogic tyrants and rebels could understand freedom only as absolute self-determination, and such men misled the people with promises impossible to fulfill. They excoriated other Judaeans and the aristocracy for accepting *slavery* to the Romans. Using a variety of tactics, however, Josephus consistently undermines this viewpoint, exposing it as both naïve and dangerous.

For example, when King Herod's will is being contested, his family members arrive in Rome to present their cases before Augustus. Josephus claims that the majority opposed Archelaus (*War* 2.22): "Each one was longing for self-government, preferably, *supervised by a Roman general* (καὶ προηγουμένως ἕκαστος αὐτονομίας ἐπεθύμει στρατηγῷ Ῥωμαίων διοικουμένης), but if this should fail, [each] wanted Antipas to be king." Later, a delegation of Judaean elders arrive to plead for the same arrangement, which would see a remote Roman overlord based in Syria cooperating with the local aristocracy in Jerusalem. Josephus's description reflects a carefully considered position:

> [they] had gone out as emissaries before the rebellion [of 4 B.C.E.], with Varus's indulgence, *with a view to the self-government of their nation* (περὶ τῆς τοῦ ἔθνους αὐτονομίας).... **90** They begged the Romans to have mercy on the remains of Judaea and not to toss away its remains to those who were savagely mauling it [viz., Herod's heirs], **91** *but after joining their region to Syria* to administer it by means of its own governors (δεῖσθαι δὲ Ῥωμαίων ἐλεῆσαι τά τε τῆς Ἰουδαίας λείψανα καὶ μὴ τὸ περισσὸν αὐτῆς ὑπορρῖψαι τοῖς ὠμῶς σπαράττουσιν, συνάψαντας δὲ τῇ Συρίᾳ τὴν χώραν αὐτῶν διοικεῖν ἐπ' ἰδίοις ἡγεμόσιν). For this would demonstrate that those now being maligned as insurgent and bellicose know how to tolerate mild governors. (*War* 2.80, 90–91)

In Josephus's narrative, this hoped-for arrangement, which will not be realized (and its absence may be a large factor in generating the revolt), would have marked a return to the pre-Herodian status quo created by the Roman proconsul of Syria, Gabinius:

> After these events [Aulus] Gabinius brought Hyrcanus back to Jerusalem, entrusted the custody of the temple to him, *and established the rest of the constitution under the primacy of the best men* (καθίστατο τὴν ἄλλην πολιτείαν ἐπὶ προστασίᾳ τῶν ἀρίστων). He divided the entire nation into five sectors. **170** One of them he attached to Jerusalem, another one to Gadara.... *Delighted at having been set free from the control of one person, they were administered by an aristocracy from then on* (ἀσμένως δὲ τῆς ἐξ ἑνὸς ἐπικρατείας ἐλευθερωθέντες τὸ λοιπὸν ἀριστοκρατίᾳ διῳκοῦντο). (*War* 1.169–170)

The underlying logic, which Josephus repeatedly brings to the fore, is that the greatest dangers to the body politic come not from foreigners but from natives who try to amass a personal following under the banner of a liberty naively conceived. Whenever they have the chance, these tyrants treat their own countrymen as slaves, *forcing* them to either comply with their "freedom" agenda – or die. Consider these passages from later in the work:

> For the enchanters and bandits came together and kept inciting many to defection, and cajoling them toward "freedom," threatening death to those who submitted to the Roman *imperium* and saying that they would forcibly eliminate *those who willingly chose "slavery"* (καὶ πρὸς βίαν ἀφαιρήσεσθαι λέγοντες τοὺς ἑκουσίως δουλεύειν προαιρουμένους). (*War* 2.264)

At *War* 4.177–78, the aristocratic leader Ananus, trying to wrest control of the city from local "tyrants," addresses the people:

> Yet there is now a war against Rome – I leave aside the question, whether it is profitable and advantageous or the opposite – but what is its pretext? Is it not "freedom"? (τίνα δ' οὖν ἔχει πρόφασιν; οὐ τὴν ἐλευθερίαν;) If, then, we are not tolerating even the masters of the inhabited earth [*sc.* the Romans], shall we put up with tyrants who are mere compatriots? (εἶτα τοὺς τῆς οἰκουμένης δεσπότας μὴ φέροντες τῶν ὁμοφύλων τυράννων ἀνεξόμεθα;) (*War* 4.177–178)

At *War* 7.255, Josephus narrates, the *sicarii* of Masada:

> banded together against those who *wished to submit to Rome* (ἐπὶ τοὺς ὑπακούειν Ῥωμαίων θέλοντας) and in every way regarded them as enemies: seizing their goods, rounding up their cattle, and setting fire to their homes; for, they asserted, they were in no way different from foreigners, who so ignobly forfeited the Judeans' hard-won *freedom* and openly *admitted that they chose slavery* under the Romans (οὐδὲν γὰρ ἀλλοφύλων αὐτοὺς ἔφασκον διαφέρειν οὕτως ἀγεννῶς τὴν περιμάχητον Ἰουδαίοις ἐλευθερίαν προεμένους καὶ δουλείαν αἱρεῖσθαι τὴν ὑπὸ Ῥωμαίοις ἀνωμολογηκότας). (*War* 7.255)

The tyrant of Masada, Eleazar, closes out this theme by calling for his comrades to forfeit their own lives before the besieging Roman forces arrived. This "free" decision, advocated as preferable to a life in slavery under the Romans (7.385–86), illustrates the literal dead end produced by the naïvely radical movement for national liberation. The final devastation of Jerusalem came about because of a contention for supremacy (*stasis*) among tyrants claiming to represent the people's welfare, exacerbated by a famine created by their stealing and hoarding of food. Again, the best remedy or prevention would have been the full incorporation of Judaea under remote Roman authority in Syria, which would have entrusted normal government to the local elite. Augustus's decision to impose a disastrous Herodian heir (Archelaus), followed by unworthy equestrian prefects and procurators – these were never the equal of the distinguished senators governing Syria – put the Judaean aristocracy in an untenable position: trying to manage local grievances constantly exacerbated by the all-too-visible governor and the power-seeking demagogues alike.

Although Josephus works out this view in the context of uniquely Judaean conditions, his cultured audience would immediately have recognized perspectives familiar from Polybius, Diodorus, Dionysius, Plutarch, and Dio, among others. These authors too made their peace with Rome not on the basis of ideological commitment to Roman supremacy but in the interest of preserving the constitutions and freedoms of their own cities. They too maintained that the best preserver of the city's autonomy, against the threat of local tyrants and demagogues, was a supreme outside power. As Christopher Jones has observed, the young Plutarch had the opportunity to witness an Achaea granted freedom by Nero; but liberty only nurtured a dangerous factionalism, and was abruptly ended by Vespasian.[56] The addressee of Plutarch's *Political Precepts* was living in Sardis, which had recently suffered from factional strife driven by contending citizens.[57] For Plutarch, it was better to embrace the Roman peace, with native elites providing collegial local government, than to suffer such endless internal struggles. He observed that, whereas cities, like human bodies, always need their healthy parts to remove the constantly threatening disease, "those cities that have fallen completely into turmoil are perfectly ruined [i.e., they have no healthy parts left], *unless* by encountering some constraint or discipline from outside, by the force of troubles they return to soundness of mind" (*Praec.* [*Mor.*] 824a, e).

Although Dio deals more in *stasis* between cities, he also recognizes the helpful role that an outside power can play (e.g., *Or.* 34.46; 38.5–29, 38). At least in the case of Alexandria, he asserts that the benign Romans

---

[56] Christopher P. Jones, *Plutarch and Rome* (Oxford: Clarendon Press, 1970), 17–19; cf. Pausanias 7.17.4.

[57] Jones, *Plutarch*, 117.

brought an end to civil strife (resulting in the ejection of Ptolemy XI in 58 B.C.E., who was recalled by the Romans); that even now the Romans maintain order patiently, being often more considerate than the locals themselves of the Alexandrians' welfare (*Or.* 32.69–72). Aristides would put the issue in flattering terms, claiming that the Romans were the first ones who knew how to govern: under their tutelage, he proposes, other nations have happily relinquished their former disputes, which had amounted to pointless shadowboxing (*Or.* 26.69).

Plutarch and Dio, however, did not understand the situation as either static or benign. They sounded ominous notes about the nature of the medicine that would be applied by the Romans to settle any internal strife. If the Roman governor had no reason to respect local leaders, those leaders were effectively giving him license to behave as a tyrant toward them (Dio, *Or.* 38.32–37). In his indignant speech following the bread riots in Prusa, Dio admonished that all such disturbances would come to the attention of the "greater governors" (i.e., the proconsuls), and so the citizens had better appoint magistrates to handle their own affairs (*Or.* 46.14). Although remote Roman governors were often considered the best functional guarantee of *polis* harmony, therefore, this reverse flow was also present: the need for constant vigilance in maintaining harmony, so as to keep the Roman masters at a distance.

The insight that outside powers might best secure internal harmony was most famously articulated in the designation of the second-century B.C.E. Roman general Titus Flamininus as "liberator of Greece" because he had brought an end to Greek struggles, especially over against the Macedonians but also by preventing the rise of new local tyrants, as long as he remained (the turbulent years after his departure proving the point). Plutarch's *Comparison of Philopoemen and Flamininus* emphasizes the paradox that a foreigner should contribute so much to Greek stability:

> Now as for the greatness of the benefits for the Greeks conferred by Titus [Flamininus], neither Philopoemen himself, nor any of the many better men than Philopoemen is worthy of comparison. For their wars involved Greeks against Greeks, whereas he, who was not even Greek, fought also for the benefit of Greeks. (*Comp. Phil. Flam.* 1.2)

Or again in the *Life of Flamininus*:

> Foreign men (ἀλλόφυλοι δ' ἄνδρες), who appear to have only the tiniest glimmers, or hardly any, commonalities of ancient ancestry, from whom it was amazing that Greece should gain anything useful in speech or thought, these men have through the greatest dangers and labors rescued Greece, liberating her from harsh despots and tyrants (οὗτοι τοῖς μεγίστοις κινδύνοις καὶ πόνοις ἐξελόμενοι τὴν Ἑλλάδα δεσποτῶν χαλεπῶν καὶ τυράννων ἐλευθεροῦσι). (*Life of Flamininus* 11.7)

From the perspectives of several contemporary statesmen, then, Roman overlords turn out to be the best guarantors of internal stability in Greek states, because – irrespective of their own motives – they serve to inhibit local strife and prevent incursions from predatory neighbors. This key ingredient of the consensus between Rome and the provincial elites[58] is a deep vein in Josephus's *War*. Yet in Josephus's hands, it has little sentimental worth; as with Plutarch and Dio, it is more a question of cold realism.

## IV. The Statesman as Orator: A Bowdlerized National History

Josephus's *War* contains a number of lengthy deliberative speeches. Two stand out as efforts by Judaean aristocrats to dissuade their countrymen from catastrophic opposition to Rome: the great speech of King Agrippa II in Book 2, then in Book 5 the speech of Josephus to Jerusalem's besieged rebels from outside the walls.

These two speeches have much in common, which may be encapsulated in the observation that the statesmen involved sound very much like their Greek counterparts. Both Agrippa and Josephus try to carve out a place for national dignity within the context of Roman rule, and both subject themselves to physical danger in doing so. Plutarch insists that, while taking the side of the people and understanding their grievances, the *politikos* must assume the role of a physician, curing any seditious disease on the spot so as to prevent the intrusion of medicine from the outside (*Praec.* [*Mor.*] 815c). He must employ frankness of speech (παρρησία) as a sacred anchor (ἄγκυραν ἱεράν) in the most severe storms (*Praec.* [*Mor.*] 815d). Important orations addressed to the masses must be free of affectation, genuinely high-minded, expressing the frankness and foresight of a father (802f–803a). They may include some pointed derision aimed at one's dangerous opponents (803c), and self-deprecation too (804b), but the essential ingredient is an authentic passion that will carry the audience (804a).

Plutarch's observation that even kings must rely on oratory to overcome the ferocity and violence of the rabble (*Praec.* [*Mor.*] 801e) is borne out by the great speech of Agrippa. The context is as important as the speech. When the king learns of the malfeasance of the equestrian governor Florus, he is enraged. When Florus accuses the Judaeans of agitation before the imperial legate Cestius Gallus in Syria, Agrippa's sister Berenice joins the Jerusalem elders in sending a counter-embassy and requesting Cestius's

58 Cf. Ando, *Ideology*, 54.

intervention against Florus. These royals thus understand the people's grievances and accept the mandate to represent them before the Romans. When Cestius dispatches an emissary to find out how things really stand, Agrippa personally meets him on the coast and escorts him to Jerusalem, to prove that the Judaean people are not in rebellion.

Notice Josephus's description of the moment at which Agrippa first hears about Florus's brutalities:

> At this, although Agrippa became indignant, he *strategically transferred his anger to those whom he really pitied, the Judaeans, wanting to bring down their high thoughts* (πρὸς ἣν ἠγανάκτει μὲν Ἀγρίππας, στρατηγικῶς δὲ τὴν ὀργὴν εἰς οὓς ἠλέει Ἰουδαίους μετέφερεν, ταπεινοῦν αὐτῶν βουλόμενος τὰ φρονήματα) and, by not *supposing* that they had suffered unjustly, to *turn them away from revenge*. And they, being distinguished men and in view of their holdings of property longing for peace, *shared the understanding that the king's reprimand was well-intentioned* (συνίεσαν εὐνοϊκὴν τὴν ἐπίπληξιν τοῦ βασιλέως). (*War* 2.337)

Here we have a classic double game. Agrippa finds himself in precisely the sort of predicament that Plutarch assumes the statesman will face: the populace demands an embassy to Nero, to denounce their governor; Agrippa fully sympathizes, and is all too aware that he cannot deny them this request and let the situation escalate; at the same time, he knows well that an embassy to Nero would make him a target for the accused governor. So he now attempts a no-holds-barred deliberative speech, again anticipating Plutarch's recipe for such occasions.

Space does not permit a full analysis, but the speech is a masterpiece worthy of closer attention.[59] Agrippa first appeals for a calm hearing, with the promise that those intent on rebellion may retain their feelings afterwards if still unpersuaded. This recalls a similar plea by Dio at the beginning of his *Or.* 46. Josephus's Agrippa begins by distinguishing the two cited pretexts (προφάσεις) for rebellion – the principle of political freedom from Rome and the behavior of Rome's governors – insisting that these motives are incompatible. This is like Dio's interrogation of the Nicomedians' reasons (αἰτίαι) for pursuing conflict with Nicaea (*Or.* 38.21). Agrippa replies that if freedom from Rome is the issue, then no governor should be tolerable, whereas if a governor's bad behavior is the problem, one should look for a replacement and not recklessly make war on Rome itself.

In addressing this enraged audience, tellingly, Agrippa does not try to put a pleasant face on Roman rule. He concedes immediately and repeated-

---

[59] Tessa Rajak, "Friends, Romans, Subjects: Agrippa II's Speech in Josephus's Jewish War," in *Images of Empire* (ed. L. Alexander; Sheffield: JSOT Press, 1991) provides the beginnings of a contextual analysis.

ly that Rome's procurators behave outrageously, and their regimes are *intolerably harsh* (*War* 2.348, 352). But what is the solution? Agrippa portrays the problem with apparent frankness, in the simple terms of raw power: the Romans rule the world now, as other nations have before them, *because they are stronger than anyone else*, and even the most famous armies of times past – the Athenians and Spartans, Gauls and Germans, Carthaginians and Parthians – have now bowed the knee to Rome. Whereas Aristides attributes the same conditions to the Romans' unique discovery of the principles of government, Agrippa is not nearly so sanguine. This is much more a Polybian and Plutarchan recognition of Rome's current fortune, as a fact of life that must be accommodated. Indeed, Agrippa's repeated reference to the *current* fortune of the Romans and the demise of their many predecessors in enjoying that fortune keeps open the prospect of Rome's ultimate fall, though that is beside the present point.

When he is finished, Agrippa bursts into tears along with his royal sister, and the emotional power of the speech moves the populace, as Plutarch would hope, to follow his advice and pay their overdue tribute to Rome (*War* 2.402–405). Like many performers, however, Agrippa does not know when to stop. When he tries to drive home his success in subsequent addenda, admonishing the people to tolerate this governor until a new one can be appointed, they become exasperated and proclaim his banishment from the city (2.406). The war is on.

Two features of Agrippa's speech merit emphasis. First, he frequently employs the dialectic of freedom and slavery, which as we have seen is a bedrock theme of the whole work; but to his credit Josephus as author does not bend Agrippa's treatment to the overall thrust – that true freedom comes in acceptance of Rome. Rather, Agrippa stipulates the rebel perspective that submission to Rome *is indeed slavery*. The Judaeans *have* lost their freedom (*War* 2.355). But so what? Instead of getting philosophical with them, he plainly tells the people *in their own terms* that if they ever had a chance for the sort of freedom they dream about, it was long ago under the Hasmoneans: they had a state of their own, and so they should have resisted the encroachment of Pompey in 63 B.C.E. But since they could not and did not do that, any talk of trying to reclaim that freedom now, when the Judaeans lack the resources of a kingdom and face overwhelming Roman power, is foolish (2.356–57).

A second striking feature is Agrippa's obvious manipulation of the facts. The king devotes most of the speech to a survey of foreign nations who now willingly submit to Rome, citing both their former glory as independent peoples and their current natural advantages, should they wish even now to rebel. And yet *they* would never dream of doing so. According to him, in spite of all their numbers and wealth, the Gauls are quite content to be a source of revenue for the Romans (2.373); the Britons, in spite of all natural advantages, are controlled by only four legions (2.378); and even the mighty Parthians bend before the Roman yoke (2.384). As if driving the point home, Agrippa ridicules the notion that the Adiabenians, in Parthian territory, would ever come to the Judaeans' aid if they rebelled (2.389).

Yet all of this must be, for Josephus's literary audience in Rome, ironic. That audience knows well about the ferocious revolt of Boudicca in 60–61 and the Germano-Gallic (Batavian) rebellion of 69; it seems that these regions were constantly seething with potential revolt. Indeed, the speeches of Dio reflect a degree of restiveness throughout the Greek world. But what seals the ironic intent are Josephus's clear statements elsewhere in the *War* that the Judaeans *did* enlist the aid of Adiabenian royalty; these distinguished young men from the East appear shortly after Agrippa's speech and remain as key instigators of the Judaean revolt until nearly the end (2.520; 4.568; 5.147, 253, 474). Josephus's Agrippa engages, then, in rhetorical mischief of a high order, but he does so for all the right reasons – under the statesman's burden of maintaining peace and the national welfare. Moral truth outweighs the mere facts of the case. Plutarch would presumably have admired this effort to lead the people, as he puts it, by their ears.

This brief survey of Agrippa's pivotal speech provides important context for the other one we are considering, which treats Judaean antiquity more directly: the last-ditch effort of the character Josephus before the walls of Jerusalem. Although this comes at a much later stage in the narrative than Agrippa's, shortly before the Romans' final assault on the city, the arguments – now for *surrender* – have a similar cast. Titus, understanding that "speech is often more effective than weapons" (πολλάκις γινώσκων ἀνυτικώτερον ὅπλων τὸν λόγον), orders Josephus to reason with his rebellious countrymen in their native language (presumably Aramaic). Perhaps, Titus reasons, they will listen to a ὁμόφυλος (5.361). Josephus's Titus thus understands well the role of the native statesman: this is an occasion for Josephus, like Agrippa, to interpose himself between the people and the Romans. Although Josephus presents this as a single coherent speech, he leaves a number of clues that it was distributed over several occasions,[60] seeming to flag an artificial construction. Like Agrippa, Josephus will close his speech by bursting into tears, insisting that he is ready to die if that will bring the rebels to their senses (5.419–20). Though he tries to stay out of missile range while making himself heard, he will

[60] E.g., πολλά at 5.362; cf. 5.375, 541.

subsequently be hit on the head by a rock, and taken for dead by the rebels (5.541–42).

The opening phase is much like Agrippa's early remarks. But first it dwells on the ὁμόφυλος/ἀλλόφυλος paradox underlying the *War*: here are the Romans eager to spare this *foreign* city and its holy shrine, while the *natives* who should be most concerned with its preservation are about to cause its destruction (5.362–64). Like Agrippa, Josephus then speaks of freedom and slavery, again not in the sophisticated way of the elite but in the simple terms of his immediate audience, reprising the claim that if the Judaeans could have preserved their freedom, they should have done so long ago, under more favorable circumstances (5.365–70). To promote rebellion *now* is the behavior not of freedom-lovers (φιλελευθέρων), as they would style themselves, but rather of those courting a miserable death (δυσθανατούντων) – one of those new Second-Sophistic words we find in Josephus.[61] Fidelity to Rome *does* mean a kind of slavery, he concedes, but in that sense it must simply be accepted.

Josephus reiterates two points from Agrippa's speech, though with yet greater vividness. First, he posits a harsh law of nature – the same for brute animals as for humans – that the weaker must yield to the stronger, and control belongs to those who have supremacy in weapons (5.368). This again obviates any sentimental attachment to Roman virtue, making Roman hegemony rather a fact that must be faced by all sane people. Second, whereas Agrippa's survey of fallen empires had *implied* that Fortune gives power in succession to different nations, the character Josephus drives this point home, saying: "Fortune had gone from all points over to them; and *the God who was bringing around the rule to each nation was now* over Italy" (5.367: μεταβῆναι γὰρ πρὸς αὐτοὺς πάντοθεν τὴν τύχην, καὶ κατὰ ἔθνος τὸν θεὸν ἐμπεριάγοντα τὴν ἀρχὴν νῦν ἐπὶ τῆς Ἰταλίας εἶναι). The image is very close to Plutarch's, in his *Life of Philopoemen* (*Phil.* 17.2):... their strength in all areas advanced mightily, with the aid of the divine spirit, and that end was near, which it was necessary for *the rotational movement of fortune* to reach" (ἡ δ' ἰσχὺς ἐπὶ πάντα πολλὴ μετὰ τοῦ δαίμονος ἐχώρει, καὶ τὸ τέλος ἐγγὺς ἦν εἰς ὃ τὴν τύχην ἔδει περιφερομένην ἐξικέσθαι). In keeping with Polybius's portrait of fortune's reversals and constant shifts, with the general disposition of contemporary Greek writers, and with Josephus's larger themes, this language makes

[61] This verb, δυσθανατάω (-εω), is rare before Josephus (in Euripides, 1 occurrence; Plato 1; Theophrastus 1; Philo 4; Chrysippus possibly 3, though only as reported in Plutarch). Josephus has it 6 times, only in *War* 4–6, and usage increases around his time: 10 occurrences in Plutarch, 2 in Galen, 1 each in Artemidorus and Philostratus, 7 in Cassius Dio.

Roman power provisional, no different in principle from that of the other empires, which Judaean statesmen such as the Hasmoneans and Herodians have always dealt with successfully.

When he cannot persuade the rebels with such considerations of *Realpoilitik* – which he labels "direct advice" (ὡς ταῖς φανεραῖς οὐκ ἔπειθε συμβουλίαις) – Josephus must tack in a different direction, and so decides to reflect on the nation's ancient history. Notice his language here, which stresses his bond with the people: he turned to their shared-compatriot history (μετέβαινεν ... ἐπὶ τὰς ὁμοφύλους ἱστορίας [5.375]). This part of his speech will provide a tour through the biblical past, but from a perspective that is decidedly different from the familiar one. Whereas the rebels took their inspiration from the zeal of both biblical heroes and the Hasmonean rebels, Josephus advances the argument that the Judaeans achieved all their historic victories *without arms*, depending exclusively upon God's favor, and indeed that *whenever* they resorted to arms they failed in their objective:

> To put it succinctly, it *never* happened that our fathers found success with arms, or failed without them when they entrusted matters to God. Whereas they were victorious when they remained where they were, as it pleased the Judge, when they fought they *always* stumbled. (*War* 5.390)

In a neatly balanced rhetorical construction, Josephus offers five examples of success without arms, then the summary statement just quoted, then four cases of disaster for the city when it took up arms, and a concluding observation to make the point again:

> Thus, *in no case have arms been granted* to our nation, and the waging of war is *certainly* attended by defeat. For it is necessary, I suppose, that those who are assigned sacred territory should entrust everything to the judgment of God and disdain the [use of] human hands, concentrating rather upon persuading the Magistrate above. (*War* 5.399)

In both statements Josephus attaches the will of God only to victory without arms; military action is categorically excluded.

Given the biblical narrative of Israel's conquest of Canaan and subsequent encounters with neighboring peoples, including the famous divine command to exterminate the Amalekites, this portrait comes as a great surprise. One need not know the Bible to feel the shock. Even a friendly observer such as Hecataeus *praised* Moses's reputation (albeit anachronistically) for training the nation's young men in martial virtues and leading armies against the neighboring peoples (in Diodorus Siculus 40.3.6–7); Hecataeus also claimed that Judaean units had fought with various foreign forces and he greatly admired a peerless Judaean archer who had served in the army of Alexander the Great (in *Apion* 1.200–204). Most importantly, we have seen that for Josephus himself martial skill was nothing to apologize for, but an essential feature of manly virtue. Throughout the *War*, he says a great deal about his training of an army and his compatriots' daring military exploits; similarly, his *Antiquities* enhances the martial achievements of the ancestors by, for example, adding the non-biblical story of Moses' leadership of Egyptian forces in the annihilation of the Ethiopians (*Ant.* 2.241–253). This Moses also directs Joshua, his successor, to obliterate the race of the Canaanites (4.300). And the biblical stories of conquest that follow are not diminished in Josephus's retelling; he emphasizes Joshua's policy of exterminating all living beings – men, women, and children, whether they resist or not (*Ant.* 5.25–29, 45–48, 59, 62). Joshua's understanding is said to be that God would always make the Israelite army superior to the weapons of the enemy (*Ant.* 5.39); there is no question here of simply allowing the deity to take care of the enemy without recourse to arms. It is precisely the Hebrews' remarkable success in battle that generates their reputation for manly virtue (περὶ τῆς τῶν Ἑβραίων ἀρετῆς; *Ant.* 5.63).

So this presentation of a nation that has never succeeded when it has taken up arms is obviously at variance with both the general tenor of Josephus's narratives and of Judaean history known to others. Why? The brief commentaries that we have[62] try to interpret the speech as earnest theology, focusing mainly on partial parallels to and sources for his divergences from the Bible, and citing a general "anti-Zealot" thrust,[63] while recognizing a few remaining "puzzles." The most thorough treatment of the passage I know comes in the 1990 monograph by Seth Schwartz, who cites it chiefly to argue that when Josephus wrote the *War* he did not know the Bible very well. Supposing that Josephus was implicitly responding to charges that he was unconcerned with Jewish tradition, Schwartz argues that (if Josephus had known the Bible) the stories he cites should have been "substantially identical with scripture, or at least conform to acceptable standards of exegesis."[64] Schwartz recognizes that Josephus has a rhetorical purpose, but still he finds it difficult to explain the many departures from the Bible (especially where he thinks that the original biblical story might have helped Josephus's position) if the ancient writer had known the text.

In my view, Josephus's radically pacifistic interpretation of the nation's ancient history in this speech before the walls of Jerusalem is, like Agrip-

[62] Otto Michel and Otto Bauernfeind, eds., *De Bello Judaico = der jüdische Krieg; Griechisch und Deutsch* (3 vols. in 4; Munich: Kösel Verlag, 1963), 2.1.266–67; André Pelletier, *Josèphe, Guerre des Juifs* (3 vols.; Paris: Belles Lettres, 1975), 3.262–65.

[63] Cf. Farmer, *Maccabees*, 97–110.

[64] Seth Schwartz, *Josephus and Judaean Politics* (Leiden: E. J. Brill, 1990), 28.

pa's earlier speech, offered to the literary audience quite deliberately as a statesman's *tour de force*, and is entirely conditioned by the present emergency, in which he is forced to use every rhetorical deceit for the greater good. As a statesman-orator, Josephus consciously bends Judaean history out of shape in order to sway the masses. I do not see how we might regard it as an earnest statement of his views; nor do I see how we can infer anything about his actual knowledge of the Bible from this oration. Even when he narrates his own career, the two accounts he gives in the *War* and the *Life* are completely different – in order of events, *dramatis personae* and their relations, and the specific content of episodes. Evidently he felt free to change his material as the occasion demanded.[65]

Just as Agrippa's speech included passionately made claims that the author and literary audience know to be false, so also in this case the speech is inconsistent with points that Josephus has already established. Whereas in *War* 1.34–69 he has made much of the Hasmoneans' courageous and just war of liberation against Antiochus and his successors, and in any case the Hasmonean victory was well known and remembered in Hanukkah, in this speech Josephus mentions the armed opposition to Antiochus only as an example of a failed attempt at military action (*War* 5.394).

It seems, then, that Josephus is advertising his ability, as both author and character in the story, to make whatever case the situation requires. He constructs this piece, which departs from what the literary audience knows or suspects to be the case, to illustrate the brilliant rhetoric of a statesman in crisis; he is determined to sway the mob from violence by disassociating the glorious national history from any tradition of military self-assertion. Dio and Plutarch knew that embracing the proud history of Greece was fraught with peril. It was all too easy for political leaders to rally popular support by summoning up old military achievements. Dio reveals that the Nicomedians of his time, at odds with Nicaea for primacy in Bithynia, were citing as a model the ancient conflict between Athens and Sparta (38.24–25). He saw clearly that this analogy was disastrous, for times had changed and things might easily get out of hand if the mobs became too excited by the past.

In Dio and Plutarch we see statesmen trying constantly to maintain a fine balance between restoring Greek dignity and keeping the masses quiescent. On this point, the famous remarks of Plutarch are worth citing again:

---

[65] For a revealing assessment of Plutarch's capacity for rewriting the same material according to rhetorical need, see Christopher Pelling, *Literary Texts and the Greek Historian* (London: Routledge, 2000), 44–60.

> When we see small children attempting to put their fathers' shoes on their own feet, or fasten on their laurels, we laugh at the childish behavior. But when leaders of the cities recklessly excite the masses, directing them to imitate the actions, ambitions, and achievements of their ancestors, which are out of keeping with the present times and conditions, although what they are doing is risible, they suffer something that is not to be laughed at. Certainly there are even now many things that one *can* point to, done by Greeks of former times, that conduce to character-formation and self-control: for example, with respect to Athens, recalling not deeds of war but .... By emulating these [ethical behaviors] it *is* possible even now to imitate the ancestors; but Marathon and Eurymedon and Plataea, and whatever other examples move the mobs to become puffed up and swagger about pointlessly, they should be consigned to the leisure activities of the sophists. (*Praec.* [*Mor.*] 814a–c)

Thus on this very particular occasion Josephus the author shows that he went to extreme lengths to present, as was his duty, a bowdlerized national history, sanitized of any bellicose traits.

## Conclusions

In much the same way as his learned Greek contemporaries, whose language he speaks and with whom he is in dialogue, Josephus has an intense interest in his people's past. Although only the compositions that he published from late in Domitian's reign explore this interest systematically, his earliest work already shows him wrestling with the power of *exempla* to influence present identity. The most important result of our investigation is that Josephus, though a product of local Jerusalem culture, breathes the same air as Plutarch and Dio. He too is a statesman (*politikos*) born and bred: he once threw himself into the turmoil that engulfed his people in their developing war with Rome, trying with all his resources (he says) to turn the tide, and now seeks to chart the causes and course of that conflict for the edification of his peers in Rome. In a sense he is even more "sophistic-ated" (pardon the pun) than his Greek contemporaries because, whereas they could only warn in speeches and brief essays of the *potential* dangers of mob impulse, reckless reaction, and demagoguery, Josephus's nation has recently and famously plunged into the abyss. He is now in a unique position to offer seven volumes of political analysis, exploring the many dimensions of such a real conflict in all its complexity.

Our study tends to diminish, then, the value of "Hellenization" as a category for explaining Josephus's literary art. In this work begun soon after his arrival in Rome, he reveals already a mature intellectual world in both concept and language. Even if he did enjoy help from more literary friends in Rome, it seems inconceivable that he acquired all this after docking in Puteoli. Whether we should call it a "Greek" outlook is unclear; it is doubtful that he would have done so. He is speaking in the common coin of the eastern-Mediterranean elites, which in his case draws also from long-refined meditation on authors from the Judaean canon such as Jeremiah and Daniel. At least, the prospect of a conscious attempt at putting a Greek overlay on essentially alien conceptions seems excluded by the depth and richness of his engagement with the larger culture. Incidentally, this analysis makes it increasingly difficult to imagine that whatever precursors of the *War* Josephus may have composed in Aramaic, for contacts across the Euphrates (cf. *War* 1.3, 6), matched the extant Greek narrative to any significant degree.

Whether Josephus should be included *among* the statesmen-authors of the Greek revival remains a thorny question. He normally presents the Greeks as Other, and betrays an instinct to mock them whenever the opportunity arises. Yet he also quietly recognizes their role as arbiters of culture; in the *Apion* he must show the worth of Judaean tradition by comparing it favorably with that of Athens and Sparta. We recall that he is writing in Rome, where he can usefully exploit old Roman stereotypes for persuasive advantage in the moment.

Perhaps the most important thing to remember here is the poisonous rivalry that characterized the Greek renaissance. From this vantage point, Josephus may indeed be considered a player, but one who imagines himself holding the ultimate trump card. While energetically "out-Greeking" the Greeks, as he almost puts it in the prologue – by doing *historia* better than they do (1.16) – and while flaunting the same traits that their fashionable work tries to exhibit, after all is said and done this confident ἀλλόφυλος can affect an utter contempt for the prize that loomed so large for a Favorinus or a Lucian: being accepted as a true Greek. And he can do this in the service of gaining a hearing for his own Judaean *ethnos* after 70.

# How Was Antiquity Treated in Societies with a Hellenistic Heritage?

## And Why Did the Rabbis Avoid Writing History?

Doron Mendels

A great deal has been written about a society's attitude towards its past as a measure of its social consciousness. But little has been said in the theoretical domain about the correlation between the image of a society and the modes it exploits to treat its own past. Referring briefly to what I call rationalistic historiography,[1] I will make an attempt to map perceptions of the past in societies of Antiquity (Greek and Roman, Jewish and Christian). The use of antiquity in Antiquity has so many facets that I will only be able to provide a few examples within the scope of this paper, which I hope will serve as an invitation for others to further elaborate on this issue in a more comprehensive manner. Two points serve to clarify my view:

1. Historiography of the Greco-Roman world, that is, the formal attempt to write down the events of the past in a given genre, was transmitted poorly in Antiquity. In other words, even those few who were interested in the genre and preserved the awareness of the past in certain societies were thus deprived of much historical knowledge.[2] Furthermore, it is also clear that ordinary citizens were not exposed to a wide range of historiography, which was available only to a few highly sophisticated societies at that time. In general, we can say that the broad majority of people still lived in

---

I wish to thank all those who offered helpful advice during the discussions following my lectures at Princeton University in the Winter of 2006, and at The Hebrew University of Jerusalem and the Society for Old Testament Studies conference in Durham, England, in the summer of 2006, where I presented the latest version as a keynote address. In particular, I had fruitful conversations with Ruth HaCohen, Donna Shalev, Diana Lipton and Eran Almagor.

[1] See D. Mendels, "'Creative History' in the Hellenistic Near East in the Third and Second Centuries BCE: The Jewish Case," in idem, *Identity, Religion and Historiography: Studies in Hellenistic History* (Sheffield: Sheffield Academic Press, 1998), 357–64.

[2] See my *Memory in Jewish, Pagan and Christian Societies of the Graeco-Roman World* (London and New York: T&T Clark and Continuum, 2004), chapter 1. This topic will be expanded in my *Hermeneia* commentary on 1 Maccabees, which will include the Jewish historical literature.

a largely oral society; only the minority elite classes were literate. This fact has significant implications regarding which perceptions of the past could even potentially be acquired.

2. What role did mythology play in ancient societies? Did people believe in their gods, as Paul Veyne once asked? I, of course, will not embark on this large question here, but I will make a brief comment bearing on my topic.[3] The use of antiquity in Antiquity indeed includes mythology because mythology permeated people's daily lives; they saw, heard and felt its presence all around them in paintings, inscriptions, temples and statues. Moreover, the depiction of people's beliefs in mythological figures by our ancient authors is quite complex.

On the one hand, Greek mythology was taken very seriously in the education process, as we see in Plato's *Republic*. That is to say, the narratives of the mythological gods could be very effective with respect to *paideia*, but this must be dissociated from questions of belief (Plato declares that a god is "not responsible for everything, but only for what is good" [380c]). Also, a god does not change: "god is certainly single in form and true, both in what he does and what he says. He does not change in himself, and he does not deceive others – waking or sleeping – either with apparitions, or with words, or by sending signs" (382e).

On the other hand, as is well known, belief in gods was not automatic in the Hellenistic era. The famous hymn, written for Demetrius Poliorketes in Athens in 290 B.C.E. shows this clearly: "the other gods are remote, or they have no ears, or they just do not exist. Or they do not listen to us, but you [Poliorketes] we see present, not in wood or stone, but real..." Such words are reminiscent of Hab 2:19–20, where it is said "see, it is gold and silver plated...But the Lord is in his holy temple; let all the earth keep silence for him."[4]

Indeed historians in Antiquity were keen to deal with the issue of belief in gods and heroes; it will suffice to cite one representative example, the geographer Strabo. Strabo distinguishes between mythology and history, but with him and many others the distinction remains theoretical, for mythology often had both a historical and sometimes even a practical political

[3] Paul Veyne, *Did the Greeks Believe in their Myths?* (Chicago: Chicago University Press, 1988).

[4] See also Ps 115:4–7, and the Letter of Jeremiah, verses 24–29 which refers to the "idols as being outwardly impressive...but they have no breath and cannot move or talk", and D. Mendels, "Jeremiah, Epistle of," in *The Anchor Bible Dictionary* (ed. D. N. Freedman; New York: Doubleday, 1992), 3:722.

use.[5] In fact, one of the most decisive statements about the "popular" historicity of mythology was pronounced by Strabo himself in his *Geography*: "there are many false beliefs current among the mass of mankind since they are ignorant of historical science and consider trustworthy whatever they have heard from childhood in choruses and tragedies" (I.III.2). This is, in effect, an answer to our question on how mythology was viewed, at least by the masses. Yet the issue is complex even for ancient historians; Diodorus Siculus narrates in his history of the world, the *Bibliotheke*, from the history of the mythological past down through the history of the Hellenistic period without drawing a clear line of demarcation between the two eras (this happens also in the Hebrew Bible, e.g. Genesis through 2 Kings).[6]

Against this background, and following my theoretical aim, to develop a model for treating the past, I will in the following essay deal with four themes: (I) the relationship of societies, groups and individuals to their past; (II) a provisional classification of the modes of using antiquity in Antiquity; (III) the temporal junctures during which people used the past in Antiquity; (IV) the agents who transmitted antiquity in Antiquity.

*Theme I: The relationship of societies, groups, and individuals to their past: A schematic approach.*

One can identify roughly three types of social responses in the ancient world with respect to a general attitude toward, and use of, the past:

First, we find that there are societies that are "stuck" so-to-speak in their past. Members of these societies, while leading their daily lives, are unable to depart from what has happened before. In other words, they are regularly putting antiquity – usually their "own" – to use. An example of this can be seen in the extraordinary case of Hellenistic Sparta. Both Agis IV and Cleomenes III in the second half of the third century B.C.E. thought it quite natural to retrieve the Lycurgan past in order to reform their manner of life in the present.[7] Also in Republican Rome at its height, people lived within the structure of the *mos maiorum* which had gradually evolved from the early days of the Republic. Cicero writes in *De Republica* II.2: "Cato used to say that our constitution was superior to those of other

---

[5] At one point Strabo says that mythology is impractical, and refers to it as pure entertainment, Strabo 1.1.19; according to Strabo, Homer is partly a historian since he bases his stories on facts, 1.2.9: *elaben oun para tes historias tas archas*.

[6] In general, for Diodorus Siculus see K. S. Sacks, *Diodorus Siculus and the First Century* (Princeton, N.J.: Princeton University Press, 1990).

[7] See P. Cartledge and A. Spawforth, *Hellenistic and Roman Sparta: A Tale of Two Cities* (London and New York: Routledge 1989), 38–58.

states on account of the fact that almost every one of these other commonwealths had been established by one man....On the other hand our own commonwealth was based upon the genius, not of one man, but of many; it was founded, not in one generation, but in a long period of several centuries and many ages of men" (*nostra autem res publica non unius esset ingenio, sed multorum, nec una hominis vita, sed aliquot constituta saeculis et aetatibus*). The Hellenistic period provides another salient example of this phenomenon in the native Egyptian population, which adhered to its old habits, associations and public memories of the past in the traditional Egyptian temples, as if nothing at all had changed after the Ptolemaic takeover.[8]

Second are those groups of people who constantly and consciously toy with the past and *manipulate* its memories. In this group we find Greek and native intellectuals, kings, and special reading and ideological communities. We can include here, among many others, authors such as Hecataeus of Abdera, Manetho, as well as the kings of Commagene who publicized themselves in lengthy syncretistic inscriptions.[9] To this group we could also add the circles from which the book of Jubilees emerged.[10]

Third are those people, groups and movements that look primarily forward, rather than backward. These groups and individuals try, at least ideologically, to start a new life with as little of their past hanging around as possible, although they usually cannot get rid of it altogether (in modern times, this can be likened to the Bolsheviks in Russia in the years following 1917, or the French Revolutionaries after 1789). Since it is, however, difficult to dispense with the past, there are always tensions between the suppressed past and the new ideas that are proposed in order to dissociate the society/group from its prior history. In Antiquity, and later, several "utopianists" proposed completely new paths (especially Iambulus and to a lesser degree Euhemerus[11]), whereas in the writings of other authors a tension is noticeable between the new beginning and memories of the past.

The author of the First Book of Maccabees is an example of the latter trend: the past is mentioned here and there but the overall approach tends toward a *new* beginning. As I wrote many years ago,[12] there were circles in the Hasmonean period that manipulated their past (for instance, the Book

[8] See my *Memory*, 69–80.

[9] For these inscriptions and art see R.R.R. Smith, *Hellenistic Sculpture* (London: Thames and Hudson, 1991), 226ff.

[10] For Jubilees see Doron Mendels, *The Land of Israel as a Political Concept in Hasmonean Literature* (Tübingen: J.C.B. Mohr [Paul Siebeck], 1987), 57–88.

[11] See J. Ferguson, *Utopias of the Classical World* (London: Thames and Hudson, 1975), 122–29.

[12] Mendels, *Land of Israel.*

of Jubilees, the *Vorlage* of the Testaments of the Twelve Patriarchs), but this approach to a new Hasmonean dynasty marks the presentation of something new (although David is mentioned twice in 1 Maccabees, the text provides no genealogy for the new dynasty, as one might have expected in this Judean culture that seeks such forms of legitimization, for instance as the authors of Luke and Matthew provided for Jesus [Matt 1:2–17; Luke 3:23–38]; and as the Chronicler, to some extent, provides in his work). First Maccabees can be seen, then, as an expression of a new beginning in Judaism and this trend is evident in the presentation of the issues that are the most symbolic of the new kingdom. This book, written during the reign of John Hyrcanus I, did not return to the territorial concepts of the Old Testament (or the notion of killing the seven peoples of the Land). The rulers of the Hasmonean kingdom are not depicted as kings (although later, in the time of Alexander Jannaeus, the Temple Scroll has a *peri basileias* document in Hebrew[13]); rather, the author, who belonged to Hasmonean circles, attempted to dissociate the ruler from the old Davidic kingdom of Israel. This applies also to rituals and ceremonies not mentioned in the Bible, such as the narration of Hanukkah as a commemoration of the cleansing of the Temple. We could also mention another novelty in the work: the end of prophecy and an almost complete lack of divine intervention (interestingly, most coins of the Hasmonean rulers are likewise not associated with past motifs[14]).

*Theme II: What were the modes for using the past in Antiquity?*

This discussion will give us a clue as to attitudes to the past in societies with a Hellenistic heritage. The following classification is based on different genres (from different periods) of Hellenistic literature and daily practice that refer to the past (except for historiography as such, which I shall deal with later).

A. *Wholesale acceptance of past material.* The recital of Homer in the Hellenistic period and beyond shows that intellectuals and readers took the corpus of Greek mythology very seriously. If Clement of Alexandria quotes classical sources in his *Stromateis* and does not make a point of changing them significantly, then we can say that he takes Antiquity in its inscribed form very seriously indeed (and, as we know, Homer was also viewed at this time partly as a historian). This also applies to the process of copying the biblical text at Qumran. The belief in an unchangeable past,

[13] See M. Hengel, J. H. Charlesworth and D. Mendels, "The Polemical Character of the 'On Kingship' in the Temple Scroll: An Attempt at Dating 11Q Temple," *Journal of Jewish Studies* 37 (1986): 28–38.

[14] Y. Meshorer, *Ancient Jewish Coinage* (New York: Amphora Books, 1982).

usually taken as a precedent for some contemporary matter, expresses a rationalistic approach to the past and to the need to preserve it in the present. Another example derives from a later historical event, which I have also analyzed in my most recent book.[15] The delegations from the cities of Asia Minor to Tiberius in 20 C.E., in order to convince him to erect temples in their cities, used local mythology to make their case, apparently with little attempt at modification. Tacitus writes: "The Ephesians were the first to appear. 'Apollo and Diana' they stated, 'were not, as commonly supposed, born at Delos' " (*Annales* 3.60ff). In this case we see, to use Strabo's formulation, that myth has become extremely practical (perhaps the geographer had such cases in mind). The aforementioned Spartan revolution provides another very good example of the wholesale application of antiquity to the "present" in Antiquity.

B. *Manipulation of past material and intentional modification.* How does the "manipulation" of the past occur and how is it expressed in its inscribed form? What do these processes teach us about the circles who initiate and accept such reinterpretations (different modes are often combined in the same text; while the inscribed form includes inscriptions referring to the past, such as from Commagene in Asia Minor)?

1) *"Frameworks" from the past (chronological, historical and cultural).* These frameworks are often filled with new data not necessarily taken from the same past; sometimes additional data are simply invented; at other times they have a factual basis but they might be taken from another cultural or historical context. For example, the journey of Sesostris, described by Hecataeus of Abdera (in Diodorus Siculus I.53–58), fits so-to-speak into a chronological framework (of the Twelfth Dynasty according to Egyptologists) and thus becomes part of a new hellenized national history of Egypt. This section of the *Aegyptiaca*, as well as others, constitutes a mixture of real history, geography, and many additional data taken from the two cultures, Greek and Egyptian (which can be analyzed against the background of the duplicate story, the journey of Osiris in Diodorus Siculus I. 17–22).[16]

2) *Manipulative use of historical figures.* Famous personalities were sometimes transformed into new personae, thus changing their traditional characters and roles in history (and myth) in the public (inscribed) memory. Hellenistic literature has many examples of this. Hermes loses his Greek character when he is seen as a mixture of Hermes and Thoth (yet he is called Hermes in Diodorus Siculus I.16). In the narrative of the Book of

---

[15] Mendels, *Memory*, 41–43.

[16] See D. Mendels, "The Polemical Character of Manetho's Aegyptiaca," in idem, *Identity*, 139–57.

Jubilees, Esau and Ishmael play roles quite different from their original roles in Genesis, and are even portrayed as friends of Isaac. Although Jubilees shows Ishmael as being removed from Judaism, as a result of an act of God (Jubilees 15:30–31), he nevertheless remained a close relative who celebrated the feast of *Shavuot* and even received a blessing together with his brother Isaac from their father Abraham (Gen 22:1). When Rebecca blesses Jacob and Esau, the latter declares: "I shall do everything which you have been saying to me...and Jacob, my brother, I shall love more than all flesh. And I have no brother in all the earth except him alone, etc."[17] In Artapanus' *Peri Ioudaion*, Moses plays a role quite different from his biblical depiction, becoming a foundation hero of a syncretistic Jewish society in Egypt that identifies itself through him with Hellenism on the one hand and Egyptian culture on the other.[18]

3) *The manipulative use of time*. Past and present are all mixed together. The finest example that comes to mind is the transfiguration scene in the Gospels (Matt 17.1–9; Mark 9:2–10; Luke 9.28–36) which forms part of a linear narrative of the life of Jesus, but brings in two figures from the past ("And behold, there appeared to them Moses and Elijah, talking with him" Matt 17:3). The narrative "awakens" the two from their traditional past and gives them a new role in the present. This text and its later interpretations, such as in proto-Renaissance art (e.g. the Duccio now in the National Gallery in London), managed to deeply imprint this scene upon Christian public memory.

Another interesting example is the appearance of Eli, in Eupolemus, many years after his death: "After reigning for forty years, David handed over the rule to Solomon, his son, who was twelve years old, in the presence of Eli the High Priest and the twelve rulers of the tribes." This, I believe, can be explained quite easily. Solomon receives his father's realm "in the presence of Eli, the High Priest, and the twelve heads of the tribes" (through the *Praep Evan* 9.30.8). Here Eupolemus follows the Chronicler who omits the revolution of Adoniah, but he (i.e. Eupolemus) does mention the twelve representatives. Eli, I would suggest, fits neatly into Eupolemus' picture. The omission of Adoniah would be in line with the author's tendency to ignore "uncomfortable" events in the biblical story. Secondly, Eli, according to biblical tradition, was a priest of Shilo (and we know that after his death the importance of this center began to fade). In line with Eupolemus' aim of showing the continuity between Shilo and Jerusalem, he brings Eli (whom, by the way, the Samaritans in their later

[17] See Mendels, *Land of Israel*, 57–88.

[18] For Artapanus, see C. R. Holladay, *Fragments from Hellenistic Jewish Authors* (Chico, Calif.: Scholars Press, 1983), 1:189–243.

theology despised) back into the historical scene, thus demonstrating the continuity of the priesthood between the two centers. We remember that in the Bible the house of Eli was demoted by Solomon, and the house of Zadok was installed in the High Priesthood in its stead (1 Chr 29:22; 1 Kgs 1–2, especially 2:26–27; 2:35). Thirdly, if Eupolemus' book *On the Kings of Judea* was written against the background of Onias IV's emigration to Egypt (or, as Josephus in *J.W.* 1.33 states, his escape), the change of names between Zadok, who in the Bible was present at Solomon's coronation and Eli, who was present according to Eupolemus, becomes even more significant.[19]

4) *Projection of a present ideology or condition (which exists on the ground) into the past.* The polemics on the issue of *patrios politeia* in Athens of the fifth and fourth centuries B.C.E. is an excellent example. It has been shown that *Athenaion Politeia* IV which describes the constitution of Draco, a celebrated lawgiver of the distant past (seventh century B.C.E.), is no more than the constitution of the moderate "party" of the fourth century B.C.E.[20] Aristotle here expresses an inscribed, fragmented memory of a certain political group more than two centuries after the alleged lawgiver lived. Another example is the projection of the polemics on the nature of the Mosaic Law in Hellenistic times into the narrative of Phineas by Josephus (for instance, the speech of Zambrias which mentions his "Greek" tyrannical traits, in *Ant.* 4.145).

5) *One past is projected onto another.* From the standpoint of Eusebius of Caesarea, Jesus is a figure of the past. Eusebius' projection of antiquity into Antiquity – and he was not alone in this – deserves special attention.[21] On the one hand he projects Christianity into the beginning of human history (according to him the universal ancestors were Christians since the "logos" was already active at the start of humankind: "Christians in fact, if not in name" *Hist. eccl.* I.4.6. The "logos" appeared to Abraham at the oak of Mamre, and to Jacob when he saw the ladder stretching to heaven[22]). On the other hand, he uses the Old Testament (one past) in order to claim that Jesus (another past, many centuries later) was already known in the bibli-

---

[19] *Land of Israel*, 40–41. For Eupolemus' fragments see Holladay, *Fragments*, 1:93–156.

[20] A. Fuks, *Studies in Politics and Society in Classical and Hellenistic Greece* (Jerusalem: Mossad Bialik, 1976), 87–96 (in Hebrew).

[21] For example, in Eusebius' *Demonstratio Evangelica*; and see G. F. Chesnut, *The First Christian Historians* (2d ed.; Macon, Ga.: Mercer University Press and Peeters, 1986), 65–96.

[22] See Eusebius, *Praeparatio Evangelica* 7.12.8 (321d), and *Demonstratio Evangelica* 1.5.10–18 (10d–11d), 5.19.4–5 (246d–247a).

cal past.[23] The earlier Book of Jubilees transfers the laws and festivals of the Jews to the beginnings of the nation and connects them to the first ancestors of Israel (against the canonical version of the Bible; Jubilees 32:25–29). In other instances, prophecies that should probably be seen as *vaticinia ex eventu* (using past memories or present occurrences) express a projection of the past into the future (e.g. the "Little Apocalypse" in Mark 13).

6) *Pure invention of past data.* It is difficult to assess whether the Spartan treaty with Judea during Jonathan's reign was a historical fact. But, the Jewish claim of "family ties" with the Spartans is one of those *topoi* where a common origin is invented. 1 Macc 12:1–23 imagines a common origin ("they are brothers," i.e. the Spartans and the Jews).[24] This invented "fact" became a part of the narrative of public memory in the Hasmonean period, when the insecurity of the national self prompted such connections with the larger gentile environment (this goes back to the notion that the ancestors of the Jews were actually "gentiles").

7) *Translations.* The Septuagint in its various layers and other translations of the Hebrew Bible into Latin and Aramaic, constitute a manipulation of the past. We do not need to go back to Saussure's view that different languages structure the world differently in order to grasp that the image of the past and its memories in the Greek-speaking Diaspora were different from that in the eastern Aramaic and Hebrew-speaking Diaspora.[25] Here we speak of occasional changes in the Hebrew text; but in the aggregate, they express a Diasporic view of the Old Testament. One of the more significant deviations occurs in the Book of Esther, where the LXX version includes a famous addition after 3:13ff. Leo Seeligmann, my

[23] In the *Demonstratio Evangelica*. For Eusebius' predecessors use of this method, see the survey of H. Schreckenberg, *Die christlichen Adversus-Judaeos-Texte und ihr literarisches und historisches Umfeld*, Bd 1; 1–11.Jh. (2d ed.; Frankfurt a. M.: Peter Lang, 1990), passim.

[24] On the common origin of the Persians and Athenians, see also Aeschylus, *Persians* vv. 176–202. Concerning the Jewish-Spartan relationship, see J. A. Goldstein, *1 Maccabees: A New Translation, With Introduction and Commentary* (Anchor Bible 41; Garden City, N.Y.: Doubleday, 1976), *ad loc*. For the invention of data, see in general my "'Creative History' in the Hellenistic Near East."

[25] F. Saussure, *Course in General Linguistics* (London: Peter Owen, 1960) (French original, 1916). See the very useful I. L. Seeligmann, *The Septuagint Version of Isaiah and Cognate Studies* (2d ed.; Tübingen: J.C.B. Mohr [Paul Siebeck], 2004), 124–294; R. Hanhart, *Studien zur Septuaginta und zur hellenistischen Judentum* (Tübingen: J. C. B. Mohr [Paul Siebeck], 1999) for the LXX as translation. For the split Diaspora in the Greco-Roman period, see A. Edrei and D. Mendels "A Split Jewish Diaspora: Its Dramatic Consequences," *Journal for the Study of the Pseudepigrapha* 16 (2007): 91–137; part two of this study is forthcoming in *JSP*.

teacher in Bible Studies at Hebrew University, showed that this addition is a reflection of all the anti-Jewish features ascribed by the gentiles to the Jews at that time: "a certain ill-disposed people...opposed in their laws to every other nation, and continually neglecting the commands of the kings...plotting to accomplish the worst of evils against our interests..."[26]

8) *One inscribed tradition of the past is contaminated by the "presence" of another.* A memory, tradition, or narrative of one event in the past can become contaminated because it is shaped according to another event from an earlier past. Sometimes the precedent itself is mentioned, as in the case of the description of Matthatias stabbing the Jew who goes to Modi'in to sacrifice to a pagan god (1 Macc 2:23–27), which is shaped according to the Phineas story in Num 25:8. Another example is Eusebius' description of the battle on the Milvian Bridge which is shaped in accordance with the story of the drowning of Pharaoh in the Red Sea: "As for example, in the days of Moses himself and the ancient and godly race of the Hebrews, 'Pharaoh's chariot and his host hath he cast into the sea...' in the same way also Maxentius and the armed soldiers and guards around him, went down into the depth like stone" (Eusebius, *Hist. eccl.* IX.IX). Sometimes the earlier event is not specifically mentioned. The immediate consequence is that the more recent memory (or for that matter, tradition) is contaminated by the use of an *exemplum.* This turns into a disaster for positivist historians working in line with von Ranke, since people who are looking for the "truth" have to deal here with contaminated memories that have become substitutes for "facts." Likewise, Peiro della Francesca's fresco in Arezzo imprinted a distorted image of the battle of the Milvian bridge onto his audience and later generations.

9) *Presenting the past as a linear sequence of carefully chosen key events.* In some cases, we see that certain historical events are carefully selected in order to demonstrate that the present is a natural continuation of the past. This not only serves to legitimize and quickly enshrine the present, but also further fragments the past.[27] This can be understood as a manipulation of a linear past.

---

[26] Seeligmann, *Septuagint Version,* 71. He writes that this passage "includes a justification of all the Hellenistic accusations against the Jews: separatism, misanthropy, and political infidelity – each of them is withdrawn in the second inserted letter of the king (after [Esther] 8:12), siding with the Jews against Haman."

[27] For instance, the epitomes of Israel's history in Acts 7, Jdt 5, 1 Macc 2, Apostolic Constitution 6, Sirach 44ff. for a selection of historical themes in early Renaissance art and its crucial impact on the creation of a (distorted) collective memory, see Doron Mendels, ed., *On Memory: An Interdisciplinary Approach* (Oxford and Vienna: Peter Lang, 2007), especially pages 9–18.

Interestingly, such presentations of the past (e.g. epitomes of biblical events) are usually set in the public sphere (which entails conveying one's distorted view of the past to others). See, for example, Deut 1:1, where Moses introduces his retelling of the past by speaking to *kol Yisrael* (all Israel), and 29:1 (again *el-kol Yisrael* [to all Israel]); in 31:30 he speaks *in the ears of Kehal Yisrael* (the community of Israel) in 32:44 he speaks *be'oznei ha'am* (in the ears of the people), and *el kol Yisrael* (to all Israel). Likewise, in Josh 24:1–2 Joshua assembles "all the tribes of Israel to Shechem, and [he] summoned the elders, the heads, the judges, and the officers of Israel; and they presented themselves before God. And Joshua said to all the people..." Here the past testifies to God's bond with his people – such testimony could only be given before a wide audience in the public sphere.

This public aspect is revealed also in the speech of Achior in Jdt 5:2 to the princes of Moab and the captains of Ammon and all the governors of the sea coast. Later in verse twenty-two, it is said that his audience was "all the people standing round about the tent." We see this also in Stephen's speech in Acts 7. Judas Maccabeus "heard" of the history of the Romans (which implies that it was common knowledge) and related, according to 1 Macc 8, a selection of events concerning the Roman Empire. This was done on the occasion of the conclusion of a treaty between Judea and Rome in 161 B.C.E., in order to show that the present pact was but a natural continuation of a long process of Roman imperialistic expansion.

The selectivity involved in creating a public memory that is while fragmented, also comprehensive and collective, oral and inscribed, has been discussed in my *Memory*. That any "serious" narrator has transmitted such a picture of the past to his audience, and that it successfully became a common genre, reveals something about the reading public. In this section we could also include genealogies, which essentially constitute carefully chosen lists of chosen events (Jesus's genealogy in Matt 1:1–17; Luke 3:23–38). Do such distorted, selective views of the past qualify as serious rationalistic views of history?

10) *A synoptic approach to the past.* Divided societies carry different versions of their past. Preserving such versions without making an attempt to harmonize them is yet another expression of the manipulation of a common past. A society as such may be insecure about its past but the different divisions of such a society may create a partisan sense of security in their own interpretations of the common past. Thus members of a society are obliged to internalize several traditions or memories about the same past. East and West Germany have had a synoptic view of history in relation to the Second World War. After the canonization of the Old Testament, the Jewish world was left with the Chronicler and the Books of

Kings, which appeared as a single volume, yet differed in many respects from each other. The same applies to the societies that had to cope with the image of Judas Maccabeus according to 1 Maccabees in contrast to that of 2 Maccabees. The case of the Synoptic Gospels and John is well known, as is the attempt in the second century to harmonize the four versions. Diodorus Siculus narrates four versions of the Dionysus myth and does not harmonize between them (Diodorus Siculus III.62.3–10; 63.1–66.1; 67.1–74.6; IV.2.1–5.4).[28]

The existence of different voices or interpretations of a past which have the "right" to exist side-by-side shows that the accurate reporting of past events was not necessarily on the agenda of societies and their authors in Antiquity. Leaving to readers the decision of what really happened tells us much about the nature of the societies we are dealing with (Polybius, who expresses a rationalistic approach to the past, knew how to tackle this by suggesting that history should be viewed as a *symploke*, [intertwining]; see his Book 12). With the canonization of the New Testament, early Christians were presented with four different versions of the life of Jesus. But Christianity internalized these four dimensions very easily into a "single narrative." Such a "synoptic approach" may be said to express an unrealistic view of history resulting from the perpetuation of a certain segmentation of society.

11) *Fragmentation of the past in the public sphere.* It is clear that in the living and working societies of the Hellenistic period there was a continuous process of fragmentation of the past in the public sphere (and even of the historical knowledge found in serious historians), as the public domain lacked anything comparable to modern mass media. This is evident in many aspects of lived reality. Taking the frequent use of the *exemplum* in public debates (for instance, in the Roman Senate[29]) together with works of art relating to the past (such as the columns of Trajan and Marcus Aurelius that narrated limited events to a limited audience[30]), one can deduce

---

[28] See the discussion in Iris Sulimani, "Journeys of Gods and Culture Heroes in the Bibliotheke of Diodorus Siculus" (Ph.D. diss., The Hebrew University of Jerusalem, 2004), 212–25 (in Hebrew).

[29] For instance, Sallust, *The War with Catiline* XVII, 5: *Bello Macedonico, quid cum rege Perse gessimus, Rhodiorum civitas magna atque magnifica, quod populi Romani opibus creverat, infida atque advorsa nobis fuit. Sed postquam bello, confecto de Thodiis consultum est, maiores nostri, ne quis divitiarum magis quam iniuriae causa bellum inceptum diceret, impunitos eos dimisere.*

[30] See Niels Hannestad, *Roman Art and Imperial Policy* (Aarhus: Aarhus University Press, 1986), chapter V; and in general P. J. Holliday, *The Origins of Roman Historical Commemoration in the Visual Arts* (Cambridge, U.K.: Cambridge University Press,

that people lived their daily lives with fragments of selected events from their pasts. Strabo alludes to these uses of the past, "what is noble and great, and what contains the practically useful, or memorable or entertaining," (Strabo 1.1.23). This is what matters. Rituals and ceremonies, such as the *pompe* in the Ptolemaia in Egypt or the Jewish Passover Seder, likewise produce the same results since they are local and repetitive, transmitting a fragment of the past to an audience which is more or less obliged to participate at fixed intervals.[31]

Two points are presently in order: First, since the societies in which the above texts were composed are reflected in the texts themselves, their complex relationship with the past comes to the fore within the selfsame narratives. In certain instances, like second century B.C.E. Judaism, if we were to take the different written expressions of a single event in the past and play them as one chord, the result would be dissonance (take, for instance, any episode where 1 and 2 Maccabees have parallel narratives). One thing then is quite clear: the past becomes unimportant in societies of Hellenistic heritage if it does not have some significance and relevance for the present, ideologically or otherwise; this is in itself a fundamental reason for the fragmentation process.

Second, the above has some bearing on the notion of historical time in Antiquity. I cannot deal with this subject here in detail, but I will add that we ought to distinguish between different "kinds" of historical time in the world I am describing. In Polybius' *Histories* we find two notions of time, a cyclical concept with respect to his political science ideas presented in the sixth book (*anakyklosis*), and a linear (or rather spiral) concept, which views past events as *exempla* for the use of present actors in the political arena (*pragmatike historia*).[32] The past as a full linear process that receives an inscribed expression remains the domain of annalistic historians, whereas the past in its fragmented and partial form is what dominated the lives of societies in Antiquity and brought about a chaotic and unstable histori-

---

2002). Another example of localized fragmentation is the selection of biblical scenes in Dura Europus. Cf. for Dura, L. Levine in this volume.

[31] See Mendels, *Memory*, 69–80, concerning the *Ptolemaia*, and in general D. I. Kertzer, *Ritual Politics and Power* (New Haven: Yale University Press, 1988).

[32] For Polybius' concept of *pragmatike historia* see F. W. Walbank, *Polybius* (Berkeley–London: University of California Press, 1972). A. Momigliano (in his *Essays in Ancient and Modern Historiography* [Middletown, Conn.: Wesleyan University Press, 1977], 179–204) appears to confuse the two, just as he confused a ritual memorialization of an event with a cyclical notion of time in his views of the Jewish Passover. For an interesting attempt to deal with biblical notions of time (and recent bibliography concerning this issue) see Diana Lipton, "The Temporal Temple: Was Abraham Standing at Sinai?" forthcoming.

cal perception. This chaotic notion was also expressed in various genres of literature. One should add the various compositions and collections that cited only sections of earlier compositions thus contributing to the fragmentary picture when the original quoted works were subsequently lost.[33] The only processes that stabilized the use of certain fragments of the past were certain rituals.

The books of 1–2 Maccabees present an inscribed form of a fragmented public memory that is far removed from a comprehensive picture of the history of the period (and both were written close to the events themselves, when witnesses to the events who could have provided more testimony were still alive). This notion accords with one found in an early prayer in the *mussaf* for Rosh HaShanah (the *Zichronot*; already mentioned in *m.Roš Haš* 4:5), where God is presented as the only one who remembers everything:

> You remember that which has come to pass from eternity and you are mindful of all that which has been formed in the past. Before you are revealed all secrets and the abundance of hidden things from the world's beginning. For nothing is forgotten before the throne of Your glory, and nothing is hidden from your eyes. You remember all that which has been wrought, and all that which is formed is not concealed from you. All things are revealed and known before you, O God our God; You see and behold until the end of all generations. For you will set an appointed memorial when every spirit and every soul will be considered, when many deeds and an infinite number of creatures will be remembered. You have made this known from the beginning and reveal it from antiquity. This day, the beginning of Your works, is a memorial of the First Day, for there is a statute for Israel; the God of Jacob sits in judgment.[34]

Hence, one can deduce that human beings can remember only fragments. This is perhaps why 1 Maccabees permits itself to record only a very partial picture of the Hasmonean realm: "The rest of the acts of Judah, his battles, the exploits which he performed, and his greatness are not written down; for they were many."[35] The manipulation of the past, its fragmenta-

---

[33] See, for instance, Alexander Polyhistor's composition as well as the Church Fathers Clement of Alexandria and Eusebius who were interested in small pieces of Hellenistic Jewish literature. The collection prepared by Constantinus Porphyrogenitus should be mentioned as well, as a medium that accelerated the process of fragmentation.

[34] See in general for this prayer, J. Heinemann, *Studies in Jewish Liturgy* (Jerusalem: Magnes Press, 1981), 54–73 (in Hebrew). The translation (with slight changes) is from Samson Raphael Hirsch, *The Hirsch Siddur, Translation and Commentary* (Jerusalem and New York: Feldheim, 1978), 636.

[35] 1 Macc 9:22; in 2 Macc 2:14–15 it is stated that "Judah also collected for us all the reports and rumors that had been spread abroad due to the outbreak of the war. We still have them, and if you ever have need of them you may send messengers to us to get them." In 2 Macc 2:25 the target community for the shortened account is both "those who

tion and a complete disregard for the concept of time and the linearity of a total picture of the past is what brought people in Late Antiquity in Cyrene to think that Agamemnon was still their king (Synesius of Cyrene, 148).

This situation also provides clues about why the Jews did not write historiography for so long after the Destruction.[36] In this connection three points can be made: (1) As we have seen, no good linear history had been written since the Bible. The two books of Maccabees cannot be taken into account for they are extremely fragmentary. Josephus writes in the style of Roman and Greek universal history and cannot be considered a typical Jewish historian. (2) As we saw in connection with *Zichronot*, the Rabbis took very seriously the view that God is responsible for the national common memory and its recording as a total history. Thus, writing a "whole history" may be seen as "trespassing" into God's domain of "memory" of "the whole enterprise." (3) The theological reason behind my second point does not contradict the fact that in the Hellenistic period, and in societies descended from it, there prevailed a fragmentary view of the past, both the remote and the more recent.

By posing the question of why the Rabbis did not write a history of the Jews we are in fact misled by our modern conception of the preservation of history. Historiography, namely the formal task of writing and commemorating the past, occupied very few people in Antiquity – indeed a small and isolated group. The masses and most intellectuals who were not particularly interested in historiography, however, were nevertheless surrounded by fragments of their pasts. The Rabbis were no different from their neighbors in this respect and behaved accordingly. Thus a theological reason, combined with the common perceptions of history in the broader Hellenistic environment, deterred the Rabbis from writing a proper history of the Jewish people.

*Theme III: When and by whom?*

At what temporal junctures does the use of the past in Antiquity become more intensified and who initiates such a use of the past? Let us start with *when*. The evidence shows that certain points in time fostered a more intense use than others. There were times when, to judge from the literary

like to read for pastime as well as those who wish to retain facts in their memory." The notion that many other historical details or narratives are "kept" outside the canon appears already in the Old Testament (for instance *sepher hayashar* in Josh 10:13; and perhaps the *midrash sepher hamelachim* in 2 Chr 24:27).

[36] See the rather unsatisfactory attempt by Yerushalmi to find a reason for this silence: Y. H. Yerushalmi, *Zachor: Jewish History and Jewish Memory* (Seattle: University of Washington Press, 1982).

output, Antiquity became more urgent in the life of people in Antiquity and penetrated the thoughts of their intellectuals and politicians. Times of change and revolution bring a sense of insecurity to individuals, groups and leaders alike, which in turn stimulates a symbiosis with one's past. Since many revolutions in history result in a break from the past, the circulating views of the past change accordingly and are manipulated. Pagans had almost no choice and had to look backwards at such times, whereas Jews and Christians had a future at their disposal but, all the same, did not renounce fragments of their past.

The era between the conquests of Alexander the Great, and the final conquest of the Near East by the Roman Empire was an extremely intensive one in terms of such events. Alexander's conquests and the creation of new Hellenistic kingdoms triggered competition among the emerging entities as regards national histories (creating national histories that harkened back to their respective pasts).[37] The rise of Rome to world empire within a hundred years led to the notion that the end of Rome would be like that of the four preceding empires (as reflected in the Book of Daniel).[38] The rise of an independent Jewish kingdom and the appearance of a new Judaism brought about a sharp turn in Jewish perceptions of the past and the uses thereof.[39] Public memory was molded, reshaped and finally inscribed. The rise of Christianity changed the perception of the Jewish past as a result of competing ideas about this very past: Christians in the first century no longer embellished the old past as the Jews had done during a time of a new beginning, but created a narrative of the very recent past. In fact, the first Christians had more "respect" for the old Jewish past than did some of the Jews.

When the Roman Republic was replaced by the Principate of Augustus, the recent past was distorted and altered the prevalent notions of the *mos maiorum*, the old Republican collective memory. The *Res Gestae* of Augustus, revealing an explicitly public expression of this process, records

---

[37] Doron Mendels, *The Rise and Fall of Jewish Nationalism, Jewish and Christian Ethnicity in Ancient Palestine* (2d ed.; Grand Rapids, Mich.: William B. Eerdmans, 1997).

[38] D. Mendels, "The Five Empires: A Note on a Propagandistic *Topos*," in idem, *Identity*, 314–23.

[39] For Alexander and the Hellenistic world, see P. Green, *Alexander to Actium: The Historical Evolution of the Hellenistic Age* (Berkeley and Oxford: University of California Press, 1990). For the concept of empires, Mendels, "Five Empires," 314–23; and for the Hasmoneans see Mendels, *The Land*, and *Rise and Fall of Jewish Nationalism*, in particular part 1.

the recent past chaotically in terms of linearity.[40] The segments of Augustus' past do not keep to the chronological order of this past, and eliminate a great deal of the "history" inscribed. (The author of the Book of Jubilees, aware of the difficulty caused by presenting historical fragments in a disorderly manner, gave his narrative a fictitious chronological framework, i.e. of jubilees). Augustus bestowed a new image on the Republican past and "mixed" it with more recent events, thus imposing on his people a new "collective memory" which is, as it were, distorted in its historical accuracy.[41] In other words, innovation, social and political, revolutions and upheavals were factors that caused societies to manipulate their pasts and define their identities anew.

*Who* were the manipulators of the past? Can we generalize about the identities of those who permitted themselves to alter their histories? The answer is perhaps not too surprising and demonstrates yet again the importance of the individual in the Hellenistic period and beyond. A manipulation of any sort could be done, as we can deduce from the above discussion, by *authority*. The change of the past is not an arbitrary matter that can be performed by anyone, but requires some inherent power to legitimize it. The power or authority behind change and manipulation can be of various kinds and differs from regime to regime. For instance, kings who manipulate the past directly and indirectly through their intellectual circles (Hecataeus, Berossus, the author of Jubilees working for the Hasmoneans, Artaxerxes in the Book of Esther, Eupolemus the son of John, etc.), or kings who do the same directly through their royal inscriptions (the kings of Commagene, the Ptolemies in their *pompe* and the royal inscriptions in their temples, and Augustus in his *Res Gestae*). The public sphere is usually the central *locus* of such manipulation, in the texts and inscriptions that publicize and hence grant authority to the inscribed message (things heard by an audience are especially powerful in societies that are partly oral[42]).

In Jewish circles God is the only one who has overall power over the past, while for Christians God created Christianity at the very beginning of human existence. Those who translated the Bible into Greek apparently believed that they were endowed with divine authority to alter the meaning of the Hebrew text, as the famous story in the Letter of Aristeas shows.

---

[40] For the text and commentary of the *Res Gestae*, the best edition is still P. A. Brunt and J. M. Moore, *Res Gestae Divi Augusti: The Achievements of the Divine Augustus* (Oxford: Oxford University Press, 1979).

[41] Mendels, *Memory,* 37–41.

[42] In general see J. D. Peters, *Speaking into the Air: A History of the Idea of Communication* (Chicago and London: University of Chicago Press, 1999).

The reluctance to harmonize some versions of history can also be explained by God's autocratic authority in such matters. In a democracy, on the verge of collapse, the authority to make changes in the common past (as in Athens of the end of the fifth century B.C.E.) is suddenly split between the parties, each of whom is certain that it is entitled to sole authority in the city-state.[43] And we could go on, not without mentioning that the editors of the Old Testament believed that they had the same authority to change and edit. This brings me to my fourth point.

*Theme IV: The agents are not mere transmitters of the past, but rather significantly impact how antiquity is used in Antiquity.*

Here we include agents such as historiography, theatre, art, coinage as well as other modes of presentation in the public sphere, both inscribed and oral. For example, let us consider historiography, an agent which would have been expected to preserve the past most accurately. Historiography, however, did not live up to expectations; instead, it has destroyed much of our heritage. For instance, many historical writings from Antiquity have disappeared because they were heavily used by later sources; at certain junctures books were banned; summaries and epitomes brought about the elimination of the works they epitomized; when a historian was heavily criticized by others, he was sometimes forgotten; historical curricula may have been formulated in schools, which canonized certain historical books – yet eliminated others. Indeed, canonization processes were often disastrous, resulting in the disappearance of the works of Poseidonius of Apamea, Nicolaus of Damascus, and many others.[44]

Moreover, the canonization of historical works usually produced approaches to the past from a distinctively imperialistic point of view. I would suggest that these and other processes were also at work in the crystallization of a more formal canon, the Bible, whose oral and inscribed sources are no longer extant. When the LXX became a formal text in the western Diaspora the Hebrew manuscripts probably disappeared, only to resurface in the ninth century. Thus, although the Hellenistic period pro-

[43] See my *Memory*, 30–35.

[44] See my *Memory*, chapter 1 for details. Libraries were few and only a few intellectuals used them. They were certainly not known to the masses. But even intellectuals who could be expected to use libraries did not always do so (take Plutarch, for example, whose careless use of the library of Athens is suggested in his biographies, which are problematic due to their exploitative use of sources). For libraries and reading audiences see in general: W. V. Harris, *Ancient Literacy* (Cambridge, Mass. and London: Harvard University Press, 1989), and H. Y. Gamble, *Books and Readers in the Early Church* (New Haven and London: Yale University Press, 1995).

duced a genre of "nationalistic" histories (partly preserved in Diodorus Siculus, but also in Berossus, Manethon, Dionysius Scytobrachion, the Books of Maccabees), very little is monographic. Rather, they express imperialistic view-points, where the reign of Alexander the Great, the Roman Republic, and the Roman Empire frame their historical narratives (likewise, Josephus also wrote a universal history).[45]

Is it only by chance that most of the histories preserved for us are imperialistic in nature? All that we can say for certain is that if individual Greeks and Romans believed in their past, they did very little to safeguard it. If historians and intellectuals mistreated the past, should we expect anything more from ordinary people, native inhabitants, Greeks, Hellenists, and their leaders? Historiography had become seriously confused and distorted, contributing a great deal to the fragmentation and segmentation of the past in contemporary societies.

Other "agents," such as art, coinage, monuments, inscriptions, theatre, etc. did the very same thing: they were created with the intention to fragment past dimensions, localize them, and brand them onto certain segments of society. The Old Testament can be considered as a conglomerate literary "agent," consisting of a corpus of texts expressing views of the past at different periods. The Old Testament, however, differs from the bulk of the material that I have discussed, as its authors' identities and chronologies are far from certain. Moreover, the Old Testament was extensively edited and re-edited.[46] To be sure, this process did not always suppress differences between its sources. Take, for example, the somewhat synoptic view of the past created by the different accounts of David's introduction to Saul in 1 Samuel. In 1 Sam 16 David is chosen by Samuel to become the new king, and Saul invites the young David to play the harp in his presence. Saul, however, did not yet know that David had been chosen by Samuel to succeed him as king. In chapter 17, David and his family are again introduced (1 Sam 17:12); he is also introduced anew

[45] Josephus, who wrote an imperialistic history of the Jews (*Ant.*), is no exception. Most of the sources that he used for history after the Bible have disappeared. The Bible, however, did not disappear, largely because it was considered to be a collection of holy books (which were, perhaps, already canonized).

[46] For instance, the narrator, or editor of 1 Samuel chapter 2 who relates the prophecy of the destruction of the House of Eli knew 1 Kgs 2:27 or vice-versa; in 1 Sam 2:35: "I will build him a faithful house, and he shall go in and out before my anointed one forever" and in 1 Kgs 2:27: "So Solomon banished Ebiathar from being priest to the Lord, thus fulfilling the word of the Lord that he had spoken concerning the house of Eli in Shiloh." 1 Chr 29:22 ignores this altogether, but refers to both passages in 1 Samuel and 1 Kings and says: "They made David's son Solomon king a second time; they anointed him as the Lord's prince, and Zadok as priest." This harmonization is strange and makes little sense.

before his duel with Goliath, yet even Avner does not seem to know David as he walks towards the giant (1 Sam 17:55–56). Chapter 18 harmonizes the images of David as warrior and musician. This is an instance where we can see how readers – starting with the editor himself – manage to cope with different narratives of the same pivotal moment of its own history. Despite these "seams" in the text, the editor's hand is nevertheless very strong and prominent in 1 Samuel. For example, chapter 8, which includes Samuel's negative view of kingship, dictates the whole book's unfavorable attitude towards Saul.[47] In contrast, the body of Hellenistic texts that I have discussed is much more diverse, reflecting a wider array of societies, cultures, and time periods than the heavily-redacted Old Testament.

To conclude: In the Hellenistic period and beyond, we find various strategies for using the past operating alongside each other. If we examine attitudes towards the past in groups within a society at a particular moment, we arrive at a dissonant and chaotic picture. Certain groups considered the mythological past (this includes the Old Testament) as holy and yet at the same time altered it, or parts of it, according to new cultural, political and social circumstances. Others who manipulated the past actually ended up destroying much of it. That is, they did not leave it in its original form for posterity. Therefore one can speak of destructive social currents towards the past in the Hellenistic period and beyond, that is as we in modern times understand historiography and other "agents" who worked to preserve an accurate picture of the past.[48] In short, societies, groups and individuals were imbued with fragments of their past, but did not respect their histories in their totality.

The picture I have drawn here accords with the analysis in my *Memory*, namely that societies in the Hellenistic world lived with memories and inscribed traditions, fragmented, comprehensive, collective and individual, false and true, embodied in temples, art, and literary output as well as in their bureaucracies and regimes. These latter agents were (among other factors) the molders of the past, and thus contributed to the distinction

---

[47] For the book in general and its editorial processes, see P. Kyle McCarter, *I Samuel: A New Translation* (Anchor Bible 8; Garden City, N.Y.: Doubleday, 1980), especially 12–30, passim.

[48] Add to this the impact of the various dating systems that co-existed all over the Hellenistic world. For instance, during Augustus's time, one had to reckon with three dating systems in Macedonia. Until 168 B.C.E., the royal Macedonian system obtained. From 148 B.C.E. onward, the Romans initiated a new dating system, using that year as the new starting point. In 31 B.C.E., after the battle of Actium, an additional dating scheme was added to the previous Roman system. I hope to elaborate on this issue in the near future.

which I have attempted here to demonstrate between history and fragmented pictures and symbols preserved within these ancient societies. From our standpoint we can say that except for a few historians, societies of the Hellenistic world lived quite peacefully with a fragmented, distorted and broken notion of their pasts. The fact that the study of history and its historians in the modern sense of the term was not part of the curriculum of education in the Greek and Roman worlds no doubt contributed to this atmosphere of the fragmentation of the past.[49] To speak of an overall concept of rationalism during this period, as many scholars do, should be regarded as an exaggeration.

[49] Unfortunately there is nothing new or original in Teresa Morgan, *Literate Education in the Hellenistic and Roman Worlds* (Cambridge, U.K.: Cambridge University Press, 1998), making her book superfluous. I fully agree with A. Grafton and M. Williams, in *Christianity and the Transformation of the Book* (Cambridge, Mass. and London: Belknap Press of Harvard University Press, 2006), 304 that "on literary education in the Hellenistic and Roman worlds, Marrou… is still a standard reference." See H. I. Marrou, *Histoire de l' éducation dans L'antiquité, novelle édition* (2d. ed.; Paris: Éditions du Seuil, 1948), especially pages 253–54, 405, 408. On this last page he speaks of "l'histoire au sens moderne".

Part Two

# Jewish, Pagan, and Christian Antiquities in the Greco-Roman World

# Rabbis and Priests, or: How to Do Away with the Glorious Past of the Sons of Aaron

PETER SCHÄFER

The priesthood doubtless belongs to the earliest set of social institutions in ancient Israel, if it is not, in fact, the oldest one. It is definitely older than kingship, which emerged with Saul whom Samuel, quite reluctantly, anointed king over the people. The biblical book of Exodus lets the priesthood begin with Aaron and his sons, when God orders Moses: "You shall bring forward your brother Aaron, with his sons, from among the Israelites, to serve me as priests" (Exod 28:1). The covenant into which God enters with Aaron is "an everlasting covenant of salt before the Lord, for you and for your descendants as well" (Num 18:19). From the moment when King David ordered the priest Zadok, together with the prophet Nathan, to anoint his son Solomon king (1 Kgs 1:32–40), the house of Zadok became the only legitimate priestly family (the Zadokites). Accordingly, the late book of Chronicles finds it appropriate to trace Zadok's genealogy back to Aaron (1 Chr 5:29–34). In the post-exilic period this priestly hierarchy was fully developed: all priests were descendants of Aaron (1 Chr 24:1), and the leading priestly family was the house of Zadok of the tribe of Levi (Ezek 40:46; 44:15; 1 Chr 24:3), which provided the unbroken chain of high priests (1 Kgs 2:27–36).

This, of course, is an ideal picture reflecting the peak of priestly power in the post-exilic period. The reality in ancient Israel (certainly before the erection of the temple in Jerusalem, but even thereafter) was much less clear and much more complicated than such a smooth description conveys. As we will see, it is precisely this still open-ended, unconsolidated situation that the rabbis later exploited for their own benefit. But, before turning to the rabbis let us briefly look at that high point of priestly power and influence as it crystallized in the post-exilic period.

The line of kings from the house of David was broken with the Babylonian exile. True, among those who returned from Babylon was Zerubbabel, the grandson of King Jehoiachin of Judah, who was exiled to Babylon by King Nebuchadnezzar. But already the prophet Zechariah, his contemporary, found it appropriate to emphasize the strong position of the high priest Joshua next to Zerubbabel, the scion of the Davidic dynasty (Zech 4:11–14; 6:10–13). Soon thereafter Zerubbabel disappears from the scene, and with him all hopes for the restoration of Davidic kingship. The high priests took over as the leading political force in the Persian and later Ptolemaic and Seleucid province of Judah. During the Hellenistic period the high priests of the house of Onias (which also traced itself back to Zadok) firmly established themselves.[1]

A snapshot of the power and pride of the high priestly rulers is captured in the non-canonical book of Jesus Sirach (that is, the Wisdom of Ben Sira or Ecclesiasticus), written in Jerusalem during the first quarter of the second century B.C.E, on the eve of the Hellenistic reform. The last part of the book, referred to as the "Praise of the Ancestors" (chs. 44–50), gives an account of the great figures of Israel's past, beginning with the patriarchs and culminating in the high priest Simon II (ruled 219–196 B.C.E.). This historical tour de force is seemingly obsessed with priests.[2] To be sure, Moses appears (Sir 44:23–45:5), but the rather brief praise accorded him is far outshone by that bestowed upon Aaron and his sons (Sir 45:6–25). Similarly, David appears, but he is mainly praised for conducting the service in the "sanctuary" (Sir 47:9–10),[3] although, strictly speaking, the temple was built by his son Solomon. And most conspicuously, the "Praise of the Ancestors" climaxes in a long and enthusiastic homage to the high priest Simon, son of Onias, the leading political figure of the author's own time (Sir ch. 50). This latest scion of Aaron is praised in Messiah-like tones – "like the morning star among the clouds, like the full moon at the festal season, like the sun shining on the temple of the Most High, like the rainbow gleaming in splendid clouds" (Sir 50:6–7). And the Hebrew version of the conclusion of the "Praise of the Ancestors" (which also marks the end of the entire book) reads: "May his [God's] love abide upon Simon, and may he keep in him the covenant of Pinehas; may

[1] For an overview see James C. VanderKam, *From Joshua to Caiaphas: High Priests after the Exile* (Minneapolis, Minn., and Assen: Fortress Press and Van Gorcum, 2004).

[2] See Martha Himmelfarb, "The Wisdom of the Scribe, the Wisdom of the Priest, and the Wisdom of the King according to Ben Sira," in *For a Later Generation: The Transformation of Tradition in Israel, Early Judaism, and Early Christianity* (ed. R. A. Argall, B. A. Bow, and R. A. Werline; Harrisburg, Pa.: Trinity Press International, 2000), 89–99. Himmelfarb convincingly demonstrates Ben Sira's focus on the priests, who are portrayed as kinglike figures, with Aaron wearing a "golden crown upon his turban" (Sir 45:12) and Simon being described in royal language. In contrast, the covenant with David is played down and the institution of kingship depicted as flawed, with emphasis placed on David's and (in particular) Solomon's sins.

[3] All translations of Ben Sira are taken from the *Revised Standard Version with the Apocrypha*. The Greek word used here for "sanctuary" is *to hagiasma*. The Hebrew version has *mishpat* ("law, statute") instead of "sanctuary," which does not make much sense (despite Segal's note, *ad loc.*), and therefore a gloss corrects *mishpat* to *miqdash* ("temple"): see Moshe Z. Segal, ed., *Sefer Ben Sira ha-shalem* (Jerusalem: Bialik Institute, 1958), 326.

one never be cut off from him; and as for his offspring, (may it be) as the days of heaven" (50:24).[4]

This constitutes the peak – and the beginning of the end – of the glory of the Aaronide priests and the high priesthood in general. The Hellenistic reform in Jerusalem broke the chain of the high priests of the house of Zadok: Antiochus IV and his Jerusalem friends installed an illegitimate high priest from another priestly family, the pious Maccabees then revolted against this scandalous intervention – only to install themselves as high priests (with no more legitimacy than their predecessors) and ultimately as kings. Finally, the Idumean Herod, whom Josephus contemptuously calls *hēmiioudaios* and *idiotēs*,[5] after gaining the kingship over Judea, began appointing high priests for either political considerations or completely at whim. The high priesthood effectively came to an end with the Zealots and the destruction of the temple in 70 C.E., a situation that subsequently presented an historic opportunity, *kairos*, for the rabbis.

This is not to say that there were no priests around after 70 C.E. – there definitely were, even some of the rabbis were priests. But the official religious, as well as political, role of the priests and in particular of the high priests was over. They were no longer needed, not until the third temple would be erected. The rabbis took over, or at least so they claim. As I will demonstrate in the following interpretations of some rabbinic passages, they took great pains to eliminate – not the priests (any such attempt would have been foolish and counter-productive), but the role the priests had played in the past. They rewrote biblical and post-biblical history, and in so doing they almost eradicated the priests from the collective memory of their people and replaced them with – themselves, the new heroes of Judaism.

I begin with a rabbinical exegesis that is preserved in two (early) tannaitic midrashim, *Sifra* (on Leviticus) and *Sifre* (on Numbers).[6] There, the biblical verse Num 7:89 is expounded: "When Moses went into the tent of meeting (*ohel mo'ed*) to speak with Him [God], he would hear the voice addressing him from above the cover (*kapporet*) that was on top of the ark of the covenant (*aron ha-'edut*) between the two cherubim; thus He spoke

---

[4] This is a translation of the Hebrew from a note on v. 24. The Greek translation, provided by Ben Sira's grandson after 132 B.C.E. and hence under completely different political circumstances, found it necessary to change this sentence considerably: "May he entrust to us his mercy, and may he deliver us in our days."

[5] *Ant.* 14:403.

[6] *Sifra*, Leviticus 1, ed. Finkelstein, vol. 2, 14; *Sifre Deuteronomy*, ed. Horovitz, #58. On this midrash and the following one from the *Mekilta*, see (with quite a different expanation) Bernard J. Bamberger, "Revelations of Torah after Sinai: An Aggadic Study," *Hebrew Union College Annual* 16 (1941): 97–113.

to him,"[7] followed by a brief statement by R. Yehuda b. Bathyra. We know two rabbis with this name, both Tannaim and both leaving Palestine for Nisibis, one before the destruction of the temple and the other in the early second century C.E.[8] Hence, if there is any value to this attribution (and there is no reason to believe that there is not), we are dealing with a quite early rabbinic statement. According to the *Sifre* version, R. Yehuda b. Bathyra maintains that of all the divine speeches or utterances in the Torah there are 13 cases, in which the Bible deliberately excludes Aaron.[9] The word used for "speeches" is *dibberot* (a technical term for divine speeches or more precisely divine revelations), and the word used for "exclude" is *mi'et* (noun *mi'ut*), a technical term for qualification or limitation. These 13 cases are listed as follows:

(1) When Moses went into the tent of meeting (*ohel mo'ed*) to speak with Him (*le-dabber itto*) (Num 7:89).
(2) He would hear the voice addressing him (*middabber elaw*) (Num 7:89).
(3) Thus He spoke to him (*wa-yedabber elaw*) (Num 7:89).
(4) There I will meet with you (*we-no'adeti lekha*) (Exod 25:22).
(5) And I will speak with you (*we-dibbarti ittekha*) (from above the cover, from between the two cherubim that are on top of the ark of the covenant) (Exod 25:22).
(6) (Place it in front of the curtain that is over the ark of the covenant, in front of the cover that is over the [ark of the] covenant) where I will meet with you (*asher iwwa'ed lekha*) (Exod 30:6).
(7) There I will speak with you (*le-dabber elekha*) (Exod 29:42).
(8) (Which the Lord commanded [*tziwwah*] Moses on Mount Sinai,) when He commanded (*be-yom tzawwoto*) (that the Israelites present their offerings to the Lord, in the wilderness of Sinai) (Lev 7:38).
(9) (And when he [Moses] came out [of the tent of meeting] and told the Israelites) what he had been commanded (*et asher ye-tzuwweh*) Exod 34:34.

---

[7] All translations from the Hebrew Bible follow the JPS translation, with modifications where I find them necessary. All translations from rabbinic literature are my own.

[8] See *Encyclopaedia Judaica*, s.v. Judah ben Bathyra, and Jacob Neusner, *A History of the Jews in Babylonia* (2d ed; Leiden: Brill, 1969), 1:46–49, 122, 130–33.

[9] The *Sifra* version is slightly different: "Thus He spoke to him (Num 7:89): to exclude Aaron (*le-ma'et et Aharon*). R. Yehuda b. Bathyra said: Thirteen speeches (*dibberot*) are directed (lit. said) in the Torah to Moses and Aaron, and corresponding to them there are uttered thirteen exclusions (*mi'utim*) – to teach you that those [latter thirteen] were not directed (lit. said) to Aaron but to Moses, so that he [Moses] might tell [them] to Aaron. And these are they [...]."

(10) (There I will meet with you, and I will speak with you from above the cover, from between the two cherubim that are on top of the ark of the covenant) [and impart to you] all that I will command you (*et kol-asher atzawweh otekha*) concerning the people of Israel (Exod 25:22).
(11) And it came to pass on the day when the Lord spoke (*dibber*) to Moses in the land of Egypt (Exod 6:28).[10]
(12) This is the lineage of Aaron and Moses at the time that the Lord spoke (*dibber*) with Moses on Mount Sinai (Num 3:1).
(13) The Lord called to Moses and spoke (*wa-yedabber*) to him from the tent of meeting, saying (Lev 1:1).

This list is not as chaotic as it seems at first glance. It starts with the biblical verse in question, Num 7:89, and is ordered according to the Hebrew root used for God's communication with Moses:

(1–3) *davar* – "speak", in the Pi'el and Nif'al (Num 7:89);

(4 and 6) *ya'ad* in the Nif'al – "to meet at an appointed place": from this root is *ohel mo'ed*, the term for the tent of meeting (Exod 25:22 and Exod 30:6). This sequence is interrupted by

(5) again *davar* in the Pi'el (because it is included in Exod 25:22) and followed by

(7) *davar* in the Pi'el (Exod 29:42;

(8–10) *tzawah* in the Pi'el – "command" (Lev 7:38, Exod 34:34, Exod 25:22);

(11–13) again *davar* in the Pi'el, moving from Egypt to the Sinai and concluding with the tent of meeting, with which the whole unit started (Exod 6:28, Num 3:1, Lev 1:1).

This is clear enough and indeed beautifully structured – but what is the purpose of the exercise? Why does R. Yehuda b. Bathyra find it necessary to emphasize that in these 13 cases Aaron was excluded? And excluded from what? The answer obviously has to do with the scene of action (the tent of meeting) and with what happens there (God's revelation). Most of the proof texts refer to the tent of meeting. Hence, what our rabbi argues is that the tent of meeting is the place where God meets Moses, Moses alone, and that it is off limits for Aaron. But this is a strange idea. True, this is the place where the ark of the covenant is kept, which serves as God's dwelling place on earth, and where Moses goes to receive exclusive revelations from God. Yet is not the tent of meeting also the mobile tabernacle or

[10] In the last three cases (11–13) the *Sifre* version has simply "and one [exclusion] in Egypt, one on Mount Sinai, and one in the tent of meeting," whereas the *Sifra* version spells the biblical verses out.

sanctuary, modeled according to the image of the (later) Jerusalem temple, with the division between the holy and the holy of holies (where the ark of the covenant is located) and with all the components necessary for proper worship carried out by the priests, such as the burnt offering altar, the table for the Bread of the Presence, and the altar of incense? At least this is the image that we get from the detailed description in Exodus (chs. 25–31, 36–39). So is our rabbi actually saying that Aaron and the priests were excluded from worship in the tent of meeting? This clearly goes too far because the biblical evidence speaks against such a radical conclusion. But I do posit that R. Yehuda plays with this idea and deliberately ignores Aaron and his priestly function at the expense of Moses's function as the recipient of the divine revelation. A closer look at the biblical verses cited by R. Yehuda in their respective contexts will make this claim more transparent.

(1–3) Num 7:89: This verse concludes a chapter that recounts what happened after Moses was finished setting up the tabernacle: he first anoints and consecrates it with all its furnishings (Moses and not Aaron!), and then all the chiefs of the twelve Israelite tribes (the *neśi'im*) bring their offerings to the newly built sanctuary – the Aaronide priests are not even mentioned.

(4–5) Exod 25:22: This verse, similar to Num 7:89, belongs to the chapters that depict the erection of the tabernacle/tent of meeting in all its details, but the emphasis here is put on its function as a meeting place for God and Moses, and not as a temple with offerings.

(6) Exod 30:6: This verse speaks of the altar for burning incense which is to be placed in front of the curtain that divides the holy from the holy of holies in the mobile sanctuary. Hence, the context is clearly the worship conducted by the priests. But our rabbinic author boldly (or shall I say blatantly) ignores the context, a deliberate misreading of the biblical text which becomes even more obvious when we look at the verse following his quotation (Exod 30:7): "On it [the altar] Aaron shall burn aromatic incense: he shall burn it every morning when he tends the lamps." Now it becomes much clearer what R. Yehuda means by excluding Aaron from the divine revelations: the tent of meeting may well have been a place where the priests did their job – but this is not really important. It primarily served, in accordance with its Hebrew term, as the place where God and Moses met and where God spoke to Moses alone.

(7) Exod 29:42: This verse concludes a chapter that describes the consecration of Aaron and his sons as priests. As the beginning of the chapter makes clear, it is Moses who consecrates the first Israelite priests (Exod 29:1). The consecration consists of Moses clothing Aaron with the vestments of the High Priest, anointing him, clothing his sons, and offering a

bull and two rams. Again, it is Moses who slaughters the animals; Aaron and his sons just lay their hands upon their heads. Then follows God's commandment to offer a regular sacrifice twice a day, "a regular burnt offering throughout the generations" (Exod 29:42). This commandment is addressed to Moses, as if Moses – and not Aaron – was supposed to continue the regular offerings in the temple. Of course, neither the Bible nor our rabbinic author claims this – we find ourselves in the mythical grey area before Aaron and his sons were installed as legitimate priests; there must have been someone who made this happen. But why not Aaron? Why wasn't Aaron allowed to offer the first sacrifice after his consecration by Moses? Because Moses, as our rabbinic interpreter reads the biblical text, acted as the first high priest in the sanctuary in the desert. He installed Aaron and transferred the office to him – because he had a much more important office: to communicate directly with God and to receive God's revelations.

(8) Lev: 7:38: Here, too, our rabbi ingeniously plays with a double reading of the biblical text. The full sentence says: "Such are the rituals of the burnt offering, the meal offering, the sin offering, the guilt offering, the offering of ordination, and the sacrifice of well-being, which the Lord commanded Moses on Mount Sinai ..." (Lev 7:37f.). Literally understood, this verse could mean that it was Moses whom God commanded to carry out all the proper sacrifices in the tent of meeting and later on in the temple. But, of course, this is not what the Bible wants to convey. According to the Bible, and also to the rabbinic interpretation, God reveals these commandments to Moses who passes them on to Aaron, informing him what he and his sons are supposed to do. Yet the fact remains that Aaron needs Moses to tell him what his job is all about.

(9) Exod 34:34: Emphasizes the importance of the tent of meeting as the place of revelation as opposed to the place of offering sacrifices.

(10) Exod 25:22: Same.

(11) Exod 6:28: This verse is particularly telling. It says explicitly, in line with R. Yehuda's argument that God spoke to Moses in the land of Egypt (and not to Aaron). But here our rabbi not only ignores the context; he plainly contradicts himself. For immediately preceding the quoted verse, the Bible says: "It is the same Aaron and Moses (in this sequence!) to whom the Lord said: Bring forth the Israelites from the land of Egypt, troop by troop. It was they who spoke to Pharaoh, King of Egypt, to free the Israelites from the Egyptians; these are the same Moses and Aaron" (Exod 6:26f.). So God did speak to Aaron, not just to Moses! Our second rabbinic example from the *Mekilta* will address this problem.

(12) Num 3:1: A much better proof text: Moses and Aaron, both have a family tree, but when it comes to God's communication with human beings, he speaks only with Moses.

(13) Lev 1:1: This verse closes the circle: the tent of meeting is the place where God reveals himself, and only to Moses.

So this is the message of our midrash on Num 7:89: It is only Moses who counts, not Aaron and the priesthood. God's revelation to Moses is much more important than the service of the priests in the temple. And what is God's revelation to Moses? Everything that is contained in the Torah. Hence, the Torah is more important than the worship in the temple. And this is where the rabbis come into play. For the Torah which God revealed to Moses does not stand on its own: it needs constant interpretation and re-interpretation, and the only self-appointed interpreters of the Torah are the rabbis. They alone are the heirs of God's revelations to Moses because the Oral Torah of the rabbis is included in the Written Torah given on Mount Sinai. Just as Moses, as the first high priest, installed Aaron and told him what to do, so now the rabbis have become the real priests and tell the priests what to do (that is to say, if the priestly class is ever needed again).

The second midrash that I would like to discuss goes even a step further. Whereas in the *Sifra/Sifre* midrash Aaron is excluded from the divine revelation without being mentioned in the Bible, this midrash goes as far as to throw him out of the biblical text altogether. It is found in the *Mekilta*, the tannaitic midrash on Exodus. Moreover, it actually serves as the opening sequence of the *Mekilta* and therefore must be regarded as a particularly powerful statement by the editor(s) of this midrashic work. The fact that it is transmitted anonymously clearly adds weight to its significance. I cite from the Lauterbach edition and translation (with slight emendations where necessary):[11]

> (1) And the Lord spoke to Moses and Aaron in the land of Egypt, saying (Exod 12:1).

[11] Jacob Z. Lauterbach ed., *Mekilta de-Rabbi Ishmael: A Critical Edition on the Basis of the Manuscripts and Early Editions with an English Translation, Introduction and Notes* (Philadelphia: The Jewish Publication Society, 1949), 1:1f.; see also H. S. Horovitz and I. A. Rabin, eds., *Mechilta D'Rabbi Ismael, cum variis lectionibus et adnotationibus* (Frankfurt a.M., 1931; repr., Jerusalem: Bamberger & Wahrman, 1960), 1. In the meantime, my student Sarit Kattan Gribetz has provided a brilliant (and much more comprehensive) analysis of this midrash in her Princeton senior thesis "'And God Spoke to Moses and Aaron': Rabbinic Identity and Authority in the *Mekilta* de Rabbi Ishmael" (Princeton University, 2006). I very much hope that the thesis (or a revised version of it) will be published.

> From this I might understand (*shomea' ani*)[12] that the divine word (*dibbur*) was (indeed) addressed to both Moses and Aaron.
>
> When, however, (Scripture) says (*keshe-hu omer*): And it came to pass on the day when the Lord spoke (*dibber*) to Moses in the land of Egypt (Exod 6:28) – (it becomes clear that) the divine word was addressed to Moses (alone) and not to Aaron.
>
> If so, what does Scripture want to teach by saying (*mah talmud lomar*): [And the Lord spoke] to Moses and Aaron (Exod 12:1)?
>
> Rather it teaches (*ela melammed*) that just as Moses was perfectly fit to receive the divine words,[13] so was Aaron perfectly fit to receive the divine words.[14]
>
> And why then did He not speak to him [Aaron]?[15]
>
> Because of Moses' distinction (*kavod*).
>
> Thus you must exclude Aaron (*nimtzeta me-ma'et et Aharon*) from all the divine communications/revelations (*dibberot*) within the Torah, with the exception of three cases because (with regard to these three cases) it is impossible. (*Mekh. Pisha* 1)

This is a perfectly structured classical midrash, using all the appropriate technical language that reveals to the initiated reader where the argument is heading: the *shomea' ani* clause, which makes clear that the suggestion introduced by it will be refuted by another biblical verse, introduced with *keshe-hu omer*.[16] Hence our anonymous author is boldly claiming that, despite the explicit reference to Aaron in Exod 12:1, God spoke only to Moses in the land of Egypt (as becomes evident from another biblical verse, Exod 6:28). We remember that in the *Sifra/Sifre* midrash Exod 6:28 was among the 13 verses in which R. Yehuda wanted to exclude Aaron from the divine speech. The conclusion is the same: God's revelation is addressed solely to Moses, not to Aaron.

But our author continues to ask: why then does Scripture bother to include Aaron in the divine speech? The answer intensifies the outrageous boldness of his argument. Indeed, he maintains, Aaron was as perfectly fit to receive divine revelation as was Moses – but nevertheless poor Aaron

---

[12] Lit.: "I hear."

[13] Following the explicit reading in MS Oxford (*kalul*).

[14] Ibid.

[15] Lit.: "and why was he [Aaron] not spoken to?"

[16] More precisely, the standard terminology is *shomea' ani* and *talmud lomar*; our midrash seems to follow the pattern *shomea' ani – keshe-hu omer – maggid*, which is adopted explicitly in section three (in our section *maggid* is left out). See Wilhelm Bacher, *Die exegetische Terminologie der jüdischen Traditionsliteratur, Erster Teil: Die bibelexegetische Terminologie der Tannaiten* (Leipzig: J.C. Hinrichs, 1899; repr., Darmstadt: Wissenschaftliche Buchgesellschaft, 1965), 189.

wasn't deemed worthy to receive it. Why? Because of Moses' *kavod*, i.e., because Moses was more important than Aaron. And then he tops his impertinence by simply concluding that Aaron must be thrown out of all the biblical references that relate to divine speech, except for three cases in which such a procedure is not possible. He does not even bother to tell us which three cases he has in mind, but a look at the commentaries and the Bible concordance easily reveals the relevant passages. They are Lev 10:8, Num 18:1, and Num 18:8 (to which may be added Num 18:20 which is regarded as a continuation of the preceding verses and not counted separately). In all these three, or rather four, verses the Bible explicitly says: "And the Lord spoke/said[17] to Aaron," making it indeed impossible to throw Aaron out because no-one would be left as the recipient of God's revelation.

The concordance shows that there are a couple more cases which our author does not even bother to mention. First, Exod 4:27, which also begins "The Lord said to Aaron," but since it continues "Go meet Moses in the wilderness," it becomes clear that this is not a revelation but simply the command to get in touch with Moses. The second case is more interesting. There, in Num 12, Miriam and Aaron rebel against Moses and ask the crucial question that threatens Moses' authority: "Has the Lord spoken only through Moses? Has he not spoken through us as well?" (Num 12:2). And God, making an example of Aaron and Miriam, orders them to appear at the entrance of the tent of meeting and teaches them the difference between a (regular) prophet and Moses: to a prophet God makes himself known in a vision and a dream, but it is only with Moses that he speaks "mouth to mouth, plainly and not in riddles," it is only Moses who "beholds the likeness of the Lord" (Num 12:8). Furious with Miriam's and Aaron's doubt about Moses' authority and superiority, God departs, striking Miriam with leprosy.

Our author does not bother to quote this story – which actually supports his claim – because he knows only too well that his interpretation of Exod 12:1 goes against the grain of the biblical text. But he does not care or, rather, he ironically reveals to the reader that his project is a gross and deliberate intervention in the biblical text – for the sole purpose of demonstrating that Aaron never participated in divine revelation.

Yet the editor of our midrash is not satisfied with the first anonymous interpretation or more precisely, he uses his further clarification to drive his point home even more forcefully. He returns to the text in question and

---

[17] Using *wa-yedabber* twice (Lev 10:8 and Num 18:8) and *wa-yomer* twice (Num 18:1 and 18:20).

asks: if this is so, if Aaron is excluded from divine speech, why then does the Bible take the trouble to mention him?

The midrash in the *Mekilta* continues:

> (2) Another interpretation: Why then is it said here: to Moses and Aaron (Exod 12:1)? Because (Scripture) says: And the Lord said to Moses: See, I place you in the role of God (*elohim*) to Pharaoh (Exod 7:1). From this I would know only that Moses was a judge (*dayyan*)[18] over Pharaoh – where do I know from (that also) Aaron (was put by God as a judge over Pharaoh)? (When) Scripture says: to Moses and Aaron (Exod 12:1), it draws an analogy between Aaron and Moses (i.e. it makes Aaron equal to Moses): just as Moses was a judge over Pharaoh, so also was Aaron a judge over Pharaoh; just as Moses would speak his words (to the Pharaoh) fearlessly, so also would Aaron speak his words fearlessly.
>
> (3) Rabbi says:[19] to Moses and Aaron (Exod 12:1). From this I might understand (*shomea' ani*) that the one preceding in the Bible text actually has precedence (over the other). (When, however,) Scripture says (*talmud lomar*): It is the same Aaron and Moses to whom the Lord said (Exod 6:26), it teaches us (*maggid*) that both are equal, one (as important) as the other. (*Mekh. Pisḥa* 1)

These two additional interpretations do just the opposite of what the initial midrash proposed. Instead of eliminating Aaron from the biblical text (where he actually appears), they add him to a text where he actually does not belong. In Exod 7:1, God explicitly addresses Moses as the judge over Pharaoh (and not Aaron), but our midrash declares that God also put Aaron as a judge over Pharaoh, and, with an almost wicked sense of humor, he uses for this procedure of unwarranted addition the very same verse that he (or his anonymous predecessor) had used in the preceding section for Aaron's elimination (Exod 12:1)! So now we learn from precisely this verse that Moses and Aaron were indeed equal. This conclusion is finally supported by Rabbi's (presumably R. Yehuda ha-Naśi, the editor of the Mishnah) exegesis of Exod 12:1: from the sequence in the biblical verse (first Moses and then Aaron) we might understand that Moses is more important than Aaron, but this is wrong. Since Exod 6:26[20] has the reversed sequence of first Aaron and then Moses, we must conclude that the sequence in these verses is arbitrary and cannot be used as an argument for either one's superiority. Hence, again, Moses and Aaron are indeed equal.

---

[18] The midrash interprets the biblical *elohim* as meaning not literally "God" but rather "judge."

[19] Following most manuscripts (the printed editions have "another interpretation"); see the apparatus in ed. Horovitz-Rabin and Lauterbach.

[20] Interestingly enough, Exod 6:26 belongs to the biblical story which the midrash in *Sifra/Sifre* uses to emphasize the superiority of Moses (because in Exod 6:28 God speaks only to Moses).

Now, what shall we conclude from this? That the editor who put these three units together changed his mind and, after first eliminating Aaron from the biblical text and declaring that Aaron and Moses are not equal (unit 1), finally wanted to emphasize the opposite and proclaim that they indeed are equal (units 2 and 3)? This does not make much sense, and I would like to argue that, on the contrary, our editor wants to underline with the last two units his decisive argument in the first unit. The last two units compare Moses and Aaron (and declare them equal) with regard to their relationship to Pharaoh and with regard to their order in a biblical verse: they are both judges over Pharaoh and the biblical verse order does not count. In other words, Moses and Aaron are indeed *always* equal – *except* (and this is the crucial limitation) *for* God's revelation. In the latter situation, Aaron is excluded – only Moses is the recipient of divine revelation. So I suggest that the last two units are purposefully added by our editor in order to emphasize the superiority of Moses as the progenitor of the rabbis over Aaron and the priesthood. The editor of the *Mekilta* opens his midrash on Exodus with the proud "declaration of faith" of the rabbis: we are the new heroes of Judaism; we have superseded the priests.

My third and last example comes from that unique Mishnah tractate *Pirqe Avot* ("Sayings of the Fathers") which usually is regarded as formulating the very essence of rabbinic Judaism. Although a *caveat* is appropriate here (I will come back to this), it is nevertheless useful to include this epitome of rabbinic ideology in our discussion. Its famous chain of tradition in chapters one and two is of particular interest. It begins, as every student of Judaism knows by heart, with the solemn statement:

משה קבל תורה מסיני. ומסרה ליהושע. ויהושע לזקנים. וזקנים לנביאים. ונביאים מסרוה לאנשי כנסת הגדולה

Moses received Torah from [Mount] Sinai and transmitted it to Joshua, Joshua to the Elders, the Elders to the prophets, and the prophets transmitted it to the men of the Great Assembly. (*m. Avot* 1:1)

There are few sentences in the Jewish tradition that have been scrutinized more often and more thoroughly than this one, and I have no intention of dealing with all its problems. I will refer only to those that are relevant for our subject. As to be expected, it centers on the Torah, more precisely on the transmission of the Torah from the moment of its revelation. Moses is the one who received Torah on Mount Sinai, presumably from God, and transmits it to Joshua, the Elders, the prophets, and the men of the Great Assembly. Notably, Moses did not receive "the Torah," but just "Torah," a clear indication of the rabbinic claim to the twofold Torah, the written and oral, both contained in the one Torah given to Moses, a claim which implied, of course, that the rabbis' teaching, i.e. Oral Torah, is part of the Written Torah and goes back to the revelation on Mount Sinai. And, most importantly for our context, the various links in the chain of transmission (Moses – Joshua – the Elders – the prophets – the Great Assembly) constitute quite a peculiar succession: from Moses to his successor Joshua who led the people of Israel into the promised land, to the Elders (the leaders of the tribes), to the prophets, and to the members of the Great Assembly (whatever institution hides behind this expression, presumably a fictitious governing body in the Persian and Hellenistic periods). The common denominator that ties together this group of Moses' successors is some kind of political and spiritual (in the case of the prophets) leadership and not so much the concern for the Torah.

However, the institution that is most conspicuously absent from our chain is indeed the priesthood with Aaron at the top. Again, a very forceful statement which becomes even more telling, if we compare it with what Josephus has to say about Moses' transmission of the law: "all these books he [Moses] transmitted to the priests (*taut' oun ta biblia paradidōsi tois hieroisi*), together with the ark, in which he had deposited the ten commandments written on two tables, and the tabernacle."[21] So for Josephus it is a matter of course that the priests not only received from Moses the tabernacle but also the books of the Torah, whereas the rabbis separate the priests not only from the tabernacle but also from the Torah. That it is the rabbis who are the true heirs of Moses and the Torah becomes obvious from the continuation of the chain of transmission: it continues with Simeon the Righteous, Antigonus of Sokho, the five "pairs" (*zugot*), and climaxes in R. Yehuda ha-Naśi, the Patriarch of the house of Gamliel and editor of the Mishnah (*m. Avot* 2:1).

If we now look at the topics dealt with in the first part of Pirqe Avot (the actual sayings of the fathers), they are quite a hodgepodge of this and that, but a few major themes can be made out. It hardly comes as a surprise, however, that the predominant subject is the Torah. It appears already in the very first saying (of the men of the Great Assembly: "Be deliberate in judgment, raise many disciples, and make a hedge around the Torah") and is addressed in almost all the subsequent sayings: teaching and studying the Torah (the teacher-disciple relationship), continuous learning, honoring the sages – these are virtues that have the highest priority in the rabbinic value system. Most famous among these proverbial sayings that capture the essence of the rabbinic world view is the statement by Hillel: "He who makes (his) name great, loses (his) name; he who does not increase shall cease; he who does not study deserves death; and he who makes use of the crown shall perish" (*m. Avot* 1:13). Most likely, the object of all these activities is the Torah: who makes his name great as a

[21] *Ant.* 4:304.

Torah teacher will be forgotten; who does not increase his study and teaching will vanish; who does not study the Torah at all lives a wasted life; and who makes use of the crown of Torah for his own purpose will disappear. Study of the Torah, in the double sense of learning and teaching, is the ultimate meaning of life – and, naturally, the rabbis are the only ones who determine the study of the Torah (*talmud torah*) in every possible aspect.

No doubt, in this Torah-centered world of the rabbis there can be no place for the priests. To be sure, they appear a few times in Pirqe Avot, however in remarkable disguise. To the same Hillel, who praises the study of Torah, is attributed the following statement: "Be one of the disciples of Aaron, loving peace and pursuing peace, loving the creatures and drawing them close to the Torah" (*m. Avot* 1:12). So at least Aaron does appear in Pirqe Avot – but what kind of Aaron is this: a pious peace-maker and, above all, someone who has made the Torah, of all things, the center of his and his fellows' life.[22] A rabbinized Aaron, deprived of all his priestly attributes and glory, rabbinic Judaism incarnate! Quite a metamorphosis indeed.[23]

There are a few more passages in which the priests and priesthood are mentioned, all with the same bias. R. Shimon bar Yohai, a student of R. Aqiva (first half of the second century C.E.), is quoted with the statement: "There are three crowns: the crown of Torah, the crown of priesthood, and the crown of kingship, but the crown of a good name excels them all" (*m. Avot* 4:13). Here, the pious ending (that the first three crowns are not worth anything without the crown of the good name) should not obscure that fact that the Torah not only has made it into the company of the two ancient crowns of priesthood and kingship, but that it is presented unabashedly as the first of all crowns. The ancient (and competing) institutions of priest-

---

[22] The midrash *Leviticus Rabbah*, presumably alluding to this famous statement, likewise portrays Aaron as an ardent observer of the Torah. Commenting upon Mal 2:5 (here my translation of the biblical verse deviates from the JPS translation, following the structure of the midrash) it declares: "I had with him a covenant of life and peace (Mal 2:5) – because he [Aaron; the biblical text speaks of Levi] was pursuing peace in Israel. And I gave him reverence (mora), and he feared me (*wa-yira'eni*) (Mal ibid.) – because he accepted upon himself the words of Torah with fright, fear, trembling, and shudder." In a wonderful Freudian slip Burt Visotzky translates this passage as "Moses received the words of Torah ...," clearly having in mind *m. Avot* 1:1; see Burton L. Visotzky, *Golden Bells and Pomegranates: Studies in Midrash Leviticus Rabbah* (Tübingen: J.C.B. Mohr [Paul Siebeck], 2003), 79.

[23] See also the passing – but nevertheless very apt – remark by Richard Kalmin (in a completely different context), referring to *m. Avot* 1:12: "and Aaron is a Torah scholar whose priestly activities are deemphasized or ignored altogether: "Christians and Heretics in Rabbinic Literature of Late Antiquity," *Harvard Theological Review* 87 (1994): 160.

hood and kingship are superseded by the new institution set up by the rabbis – the Torah as interpreted and guarded by them. Accordingly, the last and later added sixth chapter[24] of Pirqe Avot declares bluntly: "Greater is the Torah than priesthood and than kingship, for kingship is acquired by thirty stages, priesthood by twenty-four, but the Torah is acquired by forty-eight" (*m. Avot* 6:5).

The self-confident rabbinic bias of Pirqe Avot, which almost completely ignores the priests or, where it addresses them, turns them into pious Torah teachers, is only too obvious. But what about the dating of Pirqe Avot? Günter Stemberger has written a series of articles in which he proposes a rather long literary development of the tractate and casts particular doubt on the chain of transmission at its beginning.[25] His arguments, however, have remained largely unnoticed by English language scholarship. Recently, Daniel Boyarin, referring to the chain of transmission, has emphasized "the late second-century context of the production of this text,"[26] and Amram Tropper has even boldly claimed an *Urtext* for the tractate as a whole which received its final form by the editor of the Mishnah, R. Yehuda ha-Naśi: "Avot emerged from within the circle of the patriarchate during the early third century."[27] Without going into the details of the redaction history of the tractate here, there is one compelling argument for an early dating of the crucial chain of transmission (though not the tractate as a whole!) that even Stemberger concedes:[28] it has long been noticed that

---

[24] This last chapter, known as *Qinyan Torah*, expands the tractate for liturgical use.

[25] His most recent article is "Mischna Avot: Frühe Weisheitsschrift, pharisäisches Erbe oder spätrabbinische Bildung?," *Zeitschrift für die neutestamentliche Wissenschaft und die Kunde der älteren Kirche* 96 (2005): 243–58. Stemberger follows here Alexander Guttmann, "Tractate Abot – Its Place in Rabbinic Literature," *Jewish Quarterly Review* 41 (1950–51): 181–93 = id., *Studies in Rabbinic Judaism* (New York: Ktav, 1976), 102–14, who regards the chain of transmission as a "post-talmudic addition" ("Tractate Abot," 190).

[26] Daniel Boyarin, *Border Lines: The Partition of Judaeo-Christianity* (Philadelphia: University of Philadelphia Press, 2004), 80.

[27] Amram D. Tropper, *Wisdom, Politics, and Historiography: Tractate Avot in the Context of the Graeco-Roman Near East* (Oxford and New York: Oxford University Press, 2004), 88. See also his article "Tractate Avot and Early Christian Succession Lists," in *The Ways that Never Parted: Jews and Christians in Late Antiquity and the Early Middle Ages* (ed. A. Becker and A. Reed; Tübingen: Mohr Siebeck, 2003), 159–61: "Although some modern scholars delay the final editing of the original text to the late third and even the early fourth century C.E., the evidence seems to suggest that the traditionalists were correct to regard Avot as a Mishnaic tractate. Thus, the patriarch R. Yehudah ha-Naśi, or one of his successors, most probably edited Avot in the early to the mid-third century C.E."

[28] Stemberger, "Mischna Avot," 156.

the chain, after some dicta by Hillel and Shammai (the last "pair"), is interrupted by the line of the Gamliel family (*m. Avot* 1:16), culminating in R. Yehuda ha- Naśi and his son Rabban Gamliel III – after which the original sequence is resumed with some more Hillel dicta (*m. Avot* 2:4–7) and then with Rabban Yohanan b. Zakkai as Hillel and Shammai's successor (*m. Avot* 2:8). This insertion of the Gamliel line clearly points to a political agenda, namely to emphasize the power and influence of the patriarchal family. It makes much sense, therefore, to date such an agenda to a time when the office of the patriarch had reached its peak – under Yehuda ha-Naśi. In other words, the insertion of the Gamlielite line speaks strongly in favor of our dating the *chain of transmission* to precisely this peak of rabbinic power, the early third century CE.

To conclude, and to place my argument into a larger historical context: the rabbinic strategy with regard to their priestly predecessors and competitors, as it emerges from the texts discussed, aimed to bolster the rabbis' status and power. This was done not by simply ignoring the priests (although this may also have been the case where appropriate), but by aggressively eliminating and/or recasting them in the rabbis' own image. Clearly, this rabbinic strategy was remarkably successful. True, Bar Kokhba seems to have appointed a priest (Eleazar) as his co-leader – but, as I have argued elsewhere,[29] he certainly did not follow rabbinic advice here (*pace* R. Aqiva's declaration of Bar Kokhba as the Messiah) but deliberately tried to restore ancient, pre-rabbinic institutions. True also, an attempt was made in the fourth century by Emperor Julian, called the Apostate, to rebuild the temple – but the historical circumstances of this event rather support my argument because our rabbinic sources are completely silent about this restorative effort. Equally true, many Palestinian synagogue mosaics recall the lost temple (picturing the menorah, the shofar, the lulav, the ethrog, incense shovels, etc.) – but these synagogue mosaics can hardly be taken as the epitome of *rabbinic* ideas and practices (and we should not forget that all these wonderful sacred utensils often surround the Torah shrine and not the ark of the temple).[30] And indeed, synagogue prayers duly ask for

[29] Peter Schäfer, "Bar Kokhba and the Rabbis," in id. ed., *The Bar Kokhba War Reconsidered: New Perspectives on the Second Jewish Revolt against Rome* (Tübingen: Mohr Siebeck, 2003), 1–22.

[30] More precisely, it is difficult to ascertain whether the façade depicted in some of the synagogue mosaics represents the Torah ark or the temple. A prime example is the Sepphoris nave mosaic where scholars are divided between interpreting the façade as a Torah shrine or the temple; see the excellent volume by Zeev Weiss, *The Sepphoris Synagogue: Deciphering an Ancient Message through its Archaeological and Socio-Historical Contexts* (Jerusalem: Israel Exploration Society, 2005). Weiss opts for a "dual meaning," arguing that the "underlying message of the scenes [the architectural façade,

the rebuilding of the temple, while the synagogue service does give the priests a prominent role: they are the first to be called to the reading of the Torah,[31] and they extend to the community *birkat ha-kohanim*, the priestly blessing. However, the rebuilding of the temple sought in the prayer is definitely not something expected as imminent; rather, it was deferred to the messianic era,[32] whenever this would happen (certainly not too soon, after the disaster of the Bar Kokhba revolt). Moreover, with regard to the role given to the priests in the synagogue service, one could hardly think of a better scheme to domesticate the once powerful priests: *birkat ha-kohanim* is a purely ceremonial act, and the fact that the priests are the first to be called to the reading of the Torah neatly (albeit not so subtly) underlines the rabbinic message – they are subordinate to the Torah and its rabbinic interpretation. The latter is also true for another argument that has often been made to emphasize the ongoing importance of the priests and the temple even under the rabbis: the fact that large parts of the Mishnah deal with customs and laws referring to the temple cult (*Qodashim*) and matters of purity (*Toharot*), both being inherent domains of the priests. Here, too, I propose to turn the argument around. Rather than reading this as an attempt to preserve priestly prerogatives for the time when the temple will be rebuilt (which, to be sure, may be one aspect of their inclusion), I would suggest that these customs and laws, so meticulously detailed in the Mishnah, serve the overarching purpose of advertising the ultimate

---

flanked on both sides with menorot and other Jewish symbols, is followed by two panels depicting Aaron's consecration and images relating to the temple service] is composite, as it attempts to identify the Torah ark with the temple while emphasizing the latter" (ibid., 236). The iconographical program of the Sepphoris mosaic (and related mosaics in other synagogues) clearly reveals a tension or probably even deliberate ambiguity between temple and Torah, and I would suggest that this ambiguity is yet another indication of the rabbinic attempt to occupy the terrain of the priests rather than "expressing the yearning for the rebuilding of the Temple" (ibid., 237). Certainly, the rabbis, like everybody else, wanted the temple to be rebuilt – but rabbinic yearning for this goal still needs to be proven.

[31] *m. Gittin* 5:8: the sequence is priest, Levite, Israelite (and the Mishnah editor was unable to stop himself from adding that this is one of the rules laid down "in the interests of peace" (*mipne darkhe shalom*, lit. "on account of ways of peace").

[32] Conspicuously enough, the Messiah expected by the rabbis was the Davidic and not a priestly Messiah, and this despite the disaster of Hasmonean and Herodian kingship and despite the historical model of the priestly Messiah (starting with Zerubbabel and Joshuah) that was readily available. On the rabbinic Messiah see Jacob Neusner, *Messiah in Context: Israel's History and Destiny in Formative Judaism* (Philadelphia: Fortress Press, 1984). In contrast to the rabbis, the priests could expect to gain something from the restoration of the messianic era: the rebuilding of the temple would automatically restore their power and influence upon the people.

victory and triumph of the rabbis:[33] even the priestly domain has come under our tutelage; we are now the ones who dictate to the priests what it is all about, what they are and are not supposed to do – whenever, God forbid, their time will come again.

---

[33] I am not making any statement here about the historical reality and ultimate success of such a rabbinical claim – that is a completely different matter. For a fresh and illuminating historical interpretation of the complex relationship between rabbis and priests in late antiquity, the tension between both groups, and the re-emergence of the priests in the fifth and sixth centuries C.E., see Oded Irshai, "The Priesthood in Jewish Society of Late Antiquity," in *Continuity and Renewal: Jews and Judaism in Byzantine-Christian Palestine* (ed. L. I. Levine; Jerusalem: Dinur Center, Yad Ben-Zvi, The Jewish Theological Seminary of America, 2004; in Hebrew) 67–106, esp. 82–99. Interestingly enough, Weiss does not regard the priestly elements in the iconography of the Sepphoris mosaic as "proof of any kind for the rise in the status of the priests, who, with the abolition of the Patriarchate and the waning of the rabbinic class, wished to take over the leadership of the community" (Weiss, *Sepphoris Synagogue*, 249).

# “Jewish Christianity” as Counter-history?

## The Apostolic Past in Eusebius’ *Ecclesiastical History* and the Pseudo-Clementine *Homilies*

Annette Yoshiko Reed

The topic of this volume, “Antiquity in Antiquity,” serves as a poignant reminder that the past, as we see it, is always and already a product of a continued process of recollection, interpretation, re-contextualization, and selective preservation.[1] In the centuries following the conquests of Alexander of Macedon, the ancient Greek past became a prime site for dialogue and contestation among the diverse cultures brought into contact by Hellenistic and Roman imperial rule.[2] Jews, and later Christians, numbered among those who defined themselves, both positively and negatively, in terms of their relationship to an idealized antiquity emblematized by Homer and Plato and enshrined in the rhetoric and education of late antique elites.[3]

Of course, for Jews and Christians, this “classical” past was often understood through the lens of another ancient era – a “biblical” past popu-

* Research for this essay was supported by a grant from the Social Science and Humanities Research Council of Canada. Earlier portions were presented at the University of Pennsylvania (February 12, 2007) and University of California, Los Angeles (April 20, 2007); I benefited much from the discussions at both events. Special thanks to Adam H. Becker, Ra‘anan S. Boustan, Benjamin Fleming, Bob Kraft, Claudia Rapp, and Karl Shuve for their questions and suggestions. I am also grateful to Gregg Gardner and Kevin Osterloh for the opportunity to contribute to this wonderful and timely volume.

[1] On the past as “remembered present” see e.g. A. Funkenstein, *Perceptions on Jewish History* (Berkeley: University of California Press, 1993), 3–21.

[2] On the emergence of ideas about the classical past in Alexandrian scholarship, see e.g. R. Pfeiffer, *History of Classical Scholarship: From the Beginnings to the End of the Hellenistic Ages* (Oxford: Clarendon, 1968), 87–279.

[3] E.g. E. Gruen, *Heritage and Hellenism: The Reinvention of Jewish Tradition* (Berkeley: University of California Press, 1998), esp. 246–91; A. J. Droge, *Homer or Moses? Early Christian Interpretations of the History of Culture* (Tübingen: Mohr, 1988); D. Ridings, *The Attic Moses: The Dependency Theme in Some Early Christian Writers* (Göteborg: Almqvist & Wiksell, 1995); A. Cameron, “Remaking the Past,” in *Late Antiquity: A Guide to the Post-Classical World* (ed. G.W. Bowersock, P. Brown, and O. Grabar; Cambridge, Mass.: Harvard University Press, 1999), 1–20.

lated by ancient Israelite patriarchs, kings, priests, and prophets.[4] Jews and Christians appealed to biblical history and heroes for diverse aims, ranging from apologetics and polemics to religious legitimization and ritual and communal etiology.[5] And, arguably, contact with the parallel reflections on the classical past served to intensify the process whereby the biblical past came to be conceptualized as both historical foundation and timeless paradigm for the present.[6]

In this essay, I am interested in the emergence of a third privileged realm in the Christian imagination – namely, the "apostolic" past.[7] Already in the New Testament Book of Acts, the age of Peter, Paul, and the other apostles emerges as a locus for the historiographical articulation of Christian identity. Inasmuch as the apostles were credited with the faithful transmission and mediation of Jesus' message to later generations, these figures were readily redeployed by later authors as emblems of authority and authenticity in debates about theology, epistemology, and ritual practice.[8] Across the full range of our early Christian literature – including

---

[4] For the Jewish conceptualization of the biblical past, the Babylonian Exile and the return under Persian rule are widely viewed as critical precipitants. The process of remembrance, retelling, and reflection seems to have been tightly tied to the practice of reading and writing, such that the intensive idealization of this past seems to have gone hand-in-hand with the elevation of certain texts to the status of "Scripture." For a summary of these developments and their ramifications, see J. Kugel, *Traditions of the Bible: A Guide to the Bible As It Was at the Start of the Common Era* (Cambridge, Mass.: Harvard University Press, 1999), 2–6.

[5] Striking, in this regard, is the quantity of Second Temple Jewish literature which is composed in the name of an ancient biblical figure and/or which interprets or expands older scriptures (esp. Pentateuch); see further A. Y. Reed, "Pseudepigraphy, Authorship and the Reception of 'the Bible' in Late Antiquity," in *The Reception and Interpretation of the Bible in Late Antiquity* (ed. L. DiTommaso and L. Turcescu; Leiden: Brill, forthcoming).

[6] As Glen Bowersock notes, "(i)t can often happen that the partial appropriation of cultural motifs, images, and even ideas from another community or tradition deepens the understanding of one's own heritage"; "The Greek Moses: Confusion of Ethnic and Cultural Components in Later Roman and Early Byzantine Palestine," in *Religious and Ethnic Communities in Later Roman Palestine* (ed. H. Lapin; Bethesda: University Press of Maryland, 1998), 47.

[7] I.e., the first century C.E. The term "apostle" is generally reserved for the twelve disciples whom Jesus chooses to be his apostles and spread his message in the Synoptic Gospels (Matt 10:2; Mark 3:14; Luke 6:13), together with Paul (e.g., Rom 1:1). For a recent discussion of the prehistory and development of the notion of the "apostle" as a link in the chain of tradition from Jesus to the church, see T. Korteweg, "Origin and Early History of the Apostolic Office," in *The Apostolic Age in Patristic Thought* (ed. A. Hilhorst; Leiden: Brill, 2004), 1–10.

[8] This is perhaps most poignantly expressed by the proliferation of apostolic pseudepigrapha, ranging from letters penned in the name of Paul (e.g., Pastoral Epistles), gos-

Patristic writings, so-called New Testament apocrypha, and Nag Hammadi literature – we find evidence of the explanatory and polemical power of the apostles as potently pivotal figures, perched between the life of Jesus and the institutionalization of the church. In texts ranging from Papias' *Logion Kyriakon Exegesis* to the *Apocryphon of James*, the apostles are foci for the expression of anxieties attendant on the loss of the "living voice" of Jesus.[9] In apocryphal acts and Patristic heresiologies alike, stories about the apostles and their followers are used to explore the continuities and discontinuities between the life of Jesus and the norms of those communities that claimed to preserve his memory and message.[10] Appeals to apostles are prominent in arguments about the acceptable range of difference among those who claimed the name "Christian."[11] Likewise, in the first centuries of Christianity, discussions of their written, oral, and institutional legacy played a central role in debates about the nature, scope, and sources of religious authority.[12]

Interestingly, however, it is not until the fourth century that the idealization of apostles becomes explicitly articulated in terms of a periodization

---

pels in the name of other apostles (e.g., Gospel of Philip, Gospel of Thomas), and ritual materials attributed to "the twelve" as a group (e.g., Didache, *Didascalia Apostolorum*). See J.-D. Kaestli, "Mémoire et pseudépigraphie dans le christianisme de l'âge post-apostolique," *Revue de théologie et de philosophie*, 125 (1993): 41–63.

[9] Papias expresses his preference for the "living voice" but nevertheless makes efforts to link written records of Jesus' life and sayings with apostles (Papias *apud* Eusebius, *Hist. eccl.* III 29.4). Also poignant is the image, at the beginning of the *Apocryphon of James*, of the twelve disciples "all sitting together, recalling what the Saviour had said to each one of them, whether in secret or openly, and putting it into books" (*Apoc. James* 2.9–15 [Nag Hammadi codex I,2]). On orality, textuality, and the anxieties surrounding memory in early Christianity, see W. H. Kelber, *The Oral and the Written Gospel: The Hermeneutics of Speaking and Writing in the Synoptic Tradition, Mark, Paul, and Q* (Philadelphia: Fortress, 1983); P. Perkins, "Spirit and Letter: Poking Holes in the Canon," *Journal of Religion* 76 (1996): 307–27; R. A. Horsley, J. A. Draper, and J. M. Foley, eds., *Performing the Gospel: Orality, Memory, and Mark* (Minneapolis: Fortress, 2006).

[10] Note, e.g., the debates about women surrounding the apostle Paul; D. R. MacDonald, *The Legend and the Apostle: The Battle for Paul in Story and Canon* (Philadelphia: Westminster, 1983).

[11] The heresiological appeal to apostolic authority is perhaps most clear in the writings of Irenaeus. As is well known, he constructs "heresy" as the opposite of apostolic truth, depicting the apostles as guarantors of tradition and interpretation, and authenticating Christian writings through association with specific apostles (*adv. Haer.* 1.10.2; 3.1.1; 3.4.1–2; 4.33.8; 5.20.1–2; note also 3.1.1; 3.4.1; 4.33.8). See further G. G. Blum, *Tradition und Sukzession: Studien zum Normbegriff des Apostolischen von Paulus bis Irenäus* (Berlin and Hamburg: Lutherisches Verlagshaus, 1963).

[12] Early examples include *1 Clement* 44.1–2.

of history that elevates the apostolic age to a status akin to the biblical or classical past. Peter van Deun, for instance, points to Eusebius' *Ecclesiastical History* (II 14.3; III 31.6) as the earliest known Christian text to apply the Greek adjective *apostolikos* to a time period.[13] Eusebius here delineates the "apostolic period" (*apostolikôn chronôn*) as encompassing the years from Christ's ascension to the reign of Trajan (III 31.6). Writing from a self-consciously post-apostolic perspective, he describes this era as a bygone age of miracles and wonders (V 7.6) in which the light of truth shone so brightly that even "heresy" posed no real threat (II 14.3). Eusebius also presents the apostolic age as determinative for all that came after: it was then, in his view, that Christianity spread throughout the known world (III 4.1), while Judaism fell to deserved decline (III 5.3).

Studies of Late Antiquity have richly explored the processes by which Christian reflection on the classical and biblical past contributed to the delineation of a Christian collective identity as distinct from so-called "paganism." In this essay, I will ask how the construction and idealization of the apostolic past may have similarly served to articulate the place of Judaism in Christian self-definition. Towards this goal, I will examine two conflicting fourth-century representations of this period: the account of apostolic history in books I–IV of Eusebius' *Ecclesiastical History* and the novelistic narrative about the apostolic past in the Pseudo-Clementine *Homilies*.

The contrast between them, I suggest, sheds light on the role of historiography in the articulation of collective identities in Late Antiquity and, moreover, may further our understanding of the fourth century as a formative age for the conceptualization of "Judaism" and "Christianity" as distinct entities with distinct histories. It may also help to expose some of the prehistory of our modern perspectives on the late antique past, as formed through selective acts of remembering and forgetting, forged in debates over identity and continuity, and indebted to the interplay between histories and counter-histories.

---

[13] P. van Deun, "The Notion *Apostolikos*: A Terminological Survey," in *Apostolic Age*, 49. After Eusebius, we increasingly find a notion of "apostolic times" as the age that saw the birth of the church (e.g. Epiphanius, *Pan.* 73.2.11). On later views of this age, see e.g. B. Dehandschutter, "*Primum enim omnes docebant*: Awareness of discontinuity in the early church: The case of ecclesiastical office," in *Apostolic Age*, 219–27.

## The Pseudo-Clementines and the History of the Apostolic Age

The Pseudo-Clementine *Homilies* and *Recognitions* are famous for presenting a picture of the apostolic age that differs radically from the image in the New Testament Book of Acts. For Luke, the story of the rise of Christianity is framed as the tale of the conversion of Gentiles and the spread of the gospel beyond Judaea.[14] By contrast, the *Homilies* and *Recognitions* offer a different vision: the Jerusalem church of Peter and James here remains central, and ethnic Jews continue to play a leading role in the church. Penned in the name of Clement of Rome, this pair of parallel novels tells of Clement's travels with the apostle Peter. Throughout these two accounts, Peter is depicted as the defender of the true teachings of Jesus, and the criterion for proper belief and practice is coherence with the Jerusalem church and its leader James.[15] Whereas Luke describes the apostolic age as one of harmony between the apostles and downplays any conflict between Peter and Paul (cf. Galatians 2), the Pseudo-Clementines promote Peter and contain traces of anti-Pauline polemics.[16] Affixed to the *Homilies*, moreover, is a letter that purports to be written by Peter himself, wherein he bemoans the popularity of antinomian teachings among Jesus' Gentile followers and counters the misrepresentation of his own teachings as negating the need for Torah-observance (cf. Acts 15).[17]

---

[14] I.e., as outlined in Acts 1:8, the narrative progression of Acts communicates its notion of the Christian community as spreading outwards from Jerusalem (2:1–8:3) to Judea and Samaria (8:4–12:25), then throughout the Eastern Mediterranean, and finally culminating at Rome (13:1–28:31); see G. E. Sterling, *Historiography and Self-Definition: Josephos, Luke-Acts and Apologetic Historiography* (Novum Testamentum Supplements 64; Leiden: Brill, 1992), 348–49.

[15] Note e.g. the instruction in *Hom.* 11.35 to "shun any apostle or teacher or prophet who does not first accurately compare his preaching with that of James, who was called the brother of my lord and to whom was entrusted to administer the church of the Hebrews in Jerusalem" (cf. *Rec.* 4.35). On James as bishop and as appointed leader of the early church, see *Rec.* 1.43, 66, 73, and the preface to the *Epistle of Clement to James*.

[16] G. Lüdemann, *Opposition to Paul in Jewish Christianity* (trans. E. Boring; Minneapolis: Fortress, 1989), 169–94.

[17] Esp. *Epistle of Peter to James* 2.3–4: "Some from among the Gentiles have rejected my legal preaching (*nomimon... kêrugma*), attaching themselves to certain lawless and trifling preaching (*anomon... kai phluarôdê... didaskalian*) of the man who is my enemy (*tou echthrou anthrôpou*). Some have attempted these things while I am still alive, to transform my words by certain intricate interpretations towards the dissolution of the Law (*eis tên tou nomou katalusin*) – as though I myself were also of such a mind but did not freely proclaim it; God forbid!" Most scholars interpret Peter's "enemy" as Paul (cf. Galatians 2) and the one "transforming" Peter's message as Luke (cf. Acts 15).

Could some elements in these accounts reflect historical reality? Might the Pseudo-Clementine literature preserve a lost Petrine perspective that was hostile to Paul, suppressed by Luke, and forgotten by the Gentile Christians who embraced Pauline and Lukan writings as normative? These are the questions that have, until recently, shaped research on the *Homilies* and *Recognitions*. For nearly a century, studies of these late antique texts have been primarily source-critical. Scholars have approached the *Homilies* and *Recognitions* as mines for information about earlier eras, culling them for data about Christian Origins and using them to reconstruct first- and second-century forms of "Jewish Christianity." Accordingly, the popularity of the Pseudo-Clementine literature has risen and fallen with scholarly judgments about their historical value as sources for early traditions about Peter, James, and the Jerusalem church.[18]

In recent years, however, attention has turned to the literary and rhetorical features of the Pseudo-Clementine literature. F. Stanley Jones, for instance, has proposed that the early source preserved in *Rec.* 1.27–71 (ca. 200 C.E.) is best read as a work of competitive historiography.[19] Jones demonstrates that *Rec.* 1.27–71 was dependant on Luke-Acts and framed as a rival account of apostolic history. To Luke's image of the communal apostolic leadership of the primitive church, this source asserts James' preeminence (*Rec.* 1.43.3), depicting him as the bishop appointed by Jesus to lead the church.[20] James is the one credited with successfully spreading the message of Jesus to the Jewish people (*Rec.* 1.69.8; cf. Acts 2:41, 4:4).[21] Moreover, his success is here said to have been thwarted only because of "the enemy"; the Jewish people were persuaded by James' preaching, but their conversion was forestalled by his death, as precipitated by the pernicious efforts of Saul/Paul to undermine the Jerusalem church. Whereas Luke appeals to the Holy Spirit to authorize the mission to the

[18] I discuss this tendency in the history of scholarship in detail in "'Jewish Christianity' after the 'Parting of the Ways': Approaches to Historiography and Self-Definition in the Pseudo-Clementine Literature," in *The Ways that Never Parted: Jews and Christians in Late Antiquity and the Early Middle Ages* (ed. A. H. Becker and A. Y. Reed; Texts and Studies in Ancient Judaism 95; Tübingen: Mohr, 2003), 188–231, building on F. S. Jones' insights in "The Pseudo-Clementines: A History of Research, Part II," *Second Century* 2 (1982): 84–96.

[19] F. S. Jones, "An Ancient Jewish Christian Rejoinder to Luke's Acts of the Apostles: Pseudo-Clementine Recognitions 1.27–71," in *Semeia 80: The Apocryphal Acts of the Apostles in Intertextual Perspectives* (ed. R. Stoops; Atlanta: Scholars Press, 1990), 239–40.

[20] Jones, "Ancient Jewish-Christian Rejoinder," 242.

[21] Jones, "Ancient Jewish-Christian Rejoinder," 242.

Gentiles, *Rec.* 1.27–71 depicts the inclusion of the Gentiles as occasioned by the need to fill the number of the chosen left empty by the Jews.[22]

Elsewhere, Jones has similarly shed light on the literary and rhetorical features of the putative third-century source shared by the *Homilies* and *Recognitions* (i.e., the Pseudo-Clementine *Grundschrift*). Jones' reconstruction of the structure and aims of the *Grundschrift* highlights its points of resonance with debates about fate and astrology in late antique Syria.[23] Likewise, Mark Edwards, Dominique Côté, and others have investigated themes shared by both extant novels, exploring the strategic appropriation of "pagan" literary and philosophical tropes in the Pseudo-Clementine tradition.[24] Other recent studies have focused on the rhetoric of the redacted form of the *Recognitions*: Kate Cooper, William Robins, and Meinolf Vielberg have considered its adoption and subversion of the genre of the Greco-Roman novel,[25] while Nicole Kelley has investigated the dynamics of its discourse about knowledge, situating its concerns with au-

---

[22] Jones, "Ancient Jewish-Christian Rejoinder," 242–43. This contrast is emblematized by the differences between Acts 13:46 and *Rec.* 1.63.2, two parallel statements asserting that the mission to the Jews preceded the mission to the Gentiles. The statement in Acts 13:46 ("It was necessary that the word of God should be spoken first to you (i.e., Jews). Since you reject it and judge yourselves to be unworthy of eternal life, we are now turning to the Gentiles!") is attributed to Paul and Barnabus; it occurs in the context of the rejection of Paul's preaching by a crowd of Jews (Acts 13:47) and is followed by Paul's appeal to Isa 49:6 as prophetic prooftext for the mission to the Gentiles (Acts 13:49). The parallel in *Rec.* 1.63.2 presents the same information with a different spin. The contrast is clearest with the Syriac version, in which Peter says: "Finally, I counseled them that before we should go to the nations to preach the knowledge of the God who is above all, they should reconcile their people to God by receiving Jesus" (trans. Jones). This is followed by polemics, not against the Jews as a people, but rather against the Temple and sacrificial cult.

[23] F. S. Jones, "Eros and astrology in the *Periodoi Petrou*: The sense of the Pseudo-Clementine novel," *Apocrypha* 12 (2001): 53–78.

[24] M. J. Edwards, "The Clementina: A Christian response to the pagan novel," *Classical Quarterly* 42 (1992): 459–74; D. Côté, *Le thème de l'opposition entre Pierre et Simon dans les Pseudo-Clémentines* (Paris: Institut d'Études Augustiniennes, 2001); idem, "La fonction littéraire de Simon le Magicien dans les *Pseudo-Clémentines*," *Laval Théologique et Philosophique* 57 (2001): 513–23.

[25] W. Robins, "Romance and Renunciation at the Turn of the Fifth Century," *Journal of Early Christian Studies* 8 (2000): 531–57; K. Cooper, "Matthidia's Wish: Division, Reunion, and the Early Christian Family in the Pseudo-Clementine *Recognitions*," in *Narrativity in Biblical and Related Texts/La narativité dans la Bible et les textes apparentés*, (ed. G. J. Brooke and J.-D. Kaestli; Leuven: Peeters, 2000), 243–64; M. Vielberg, *Klemens in den pseudoklementischen Rekognitionen: Studien zur literarischen Form des spätankiken Romans* (Berlin: Akademie, 2000).

thority and epistemology in the context of competing claims, both Christian and "pagan," in fourth-century Syria.[26]

In what follows, I will bring a similar perspective to bear on the *Homilies*, the oldest form of the Pseudo-Clementine novel to survive in full. The *Homilies* dates to the first half of the fourth century.[27] Like the hypothetical *Grundschrift* and later *Recognitions*, it probably took form in Syria.[28]

It is likely, in my view, that this text does indeed preserve earlier sources. Whatever the precise scope and character of these sources, however, the authors/redactors of the *Homilies* have clearly reworked their received material in ways that speak to their own time.[29] The language used to describe Jesus, for instance, betrays their engagement with Christo-

---

[26] N. Kelley, *Knowledge and Religious Authority in the Pseudo-Clementines* (Tübingen: Mohr, 2006). Note also her recent conference papers on the fourth-century context of the *Recognitions*, e.g. "Astrological Knowledge and Apostolic Competition: The Pseudo-Clementine *Recognitions* in the Context of Fourth-Century Syria," paper presented at the SBL Annual Meeting, Christian Apocrypha Section, November 2005; "What is the Value of Sense Perception in the Pseudo-Clementine Romance?" paper presented at the 2006 *Colloque sur la littérature apocryphe chrétienne*, Université de Genève and Université de Lausanne; "Pseudo-Clementine Polemics against Sacrifice: A Window onto Religious Life in the Fourth Century?" paper presented at *Christian Apocryphal Texts for the New Millennium*, University of Ottawa, September 2006.

[27] See n. 36 and n. 38 below.

[28] Its Syrian provenance was established by G. Uhlhorn, *Die Homilien und Recognitionen des Clemens Romanus nach ihren Ursprung und Inhalt dargestellt* (Göttingen: Dieterische Buchhandlung, 1854), 381–429; C. Biggs, "The Clementine *Homilies*," *Studia biblica et ecclesiastica* 2 (1890): 191–92. See, more recently, J. N. Bremmer, "Pseudo-Clementines: Texts, Dates, Places, Authors and Magic," in *The Pseudo-Clementines I: Homilies* (ed. J. N. Bremmer; Leuven: Peeters, forthcoming).

[29] The value of situating the *Homilies* in its fourth-century context has been explored in a number of recent conference papers, including various papers presented at the 2006 *Colloque sur la littérature apocryphe chrétienne*, Université de Genève and Université de Lausanne (esp. D. Côté, "Les procédés rhétoriques dans les Pseudo-Clémentines: L'éloge de l'adultère du grammairien Apion"; A. Y. Reed, "From Judaism and Hellenism to Christianity and Paganism: Cultural Identities and Religious Polemics in the Pseudo-Clementine *Homilies*"; K. Shuve, "The Doctrine of the False Pericopes and Other Late Antique Approaches to the Problem of Scripture's Unity"). Note also A.Y. Reed, "Fourth-century Rabbinic Judaism and the redaction of the *Homilies*," paper presented at the SBL Annual Meeting, Christian Apocrypha section, November 2005; eadem, "Rabbis, Jewish Christians and other late antique Jews: Reflections on the fate of Judaism(s) after 70 C.E.," in *The Changing Face of Judaism, Christianity and Other Greco-Roman Religions in Antiquity* (ed. I. Henderson and G. Oegama; Gütersloh: Gütersloher Verlagshaus, 2006), 323–48; D. Côté, "Orphic Theogony and the Context of the Clementines," paper presented at *Christian Apocryphal Texts for the New Millennium*, University of Ottawa, September 2006. These new approaches build on insights in nineteenth-century research on the *Homilies*, on which see n. 36 below.

logical debates of the Nicene age.[30] Moreover, the story of Clement is here framed as an extended defense of apostolic succession and an assertion of the antiquity and necessity of ecclesiastical offices.[31] Throughout this novel, tales about Peter's travels from city to city are punctuated by his ordination of bishops.[32] The *Homilies*' overarching narrative also functions to assert Clement's close relationship with Peter and, by extension, the connections between Rome and Jerusalem.[33] The novel's heresiological concerns, as embodied in its accounts of Peter's debates with Simon Magus (3.30–59; 16.1–21; 18.1–23; 19.24–20.10), similarly reflect its late antique context, as is perhaps most clear from its approach to the genealogy of error as an inverse parallel to apostolic succession.[34]

The *Homilies* has usually been dismissed as a record of a heterodox movement with no influence on the late antique church and/or treated as a relic of an apostolic "Jewish Christianity" rendered irrelevant by the rise of "Gentile Christianity" and Christianity's "Parting of the Ways" with Judaism.[35] When we turn our attention to its final form and fourth-century context, however, this text may emerge as an important piece of evidence for the variety of voices in the late antique Christian discourse about "orthodoxy," Judaism, and the apostolic past.[36]

---

[30] Note the *Homilies*' statement – unparalleled in the *Recognitions* – that Christ the Son is "of the same substance (*tês autês ousias*)" as God the Father (16.15) and the use of the term *homoousios* in *Hom.* 20.5, 7. These references were pivotal for Biggs' initial establishment of a date for the *Homilies* in the decades surrounding the Council of Nicaea ("Clementine *Homilies*," 167, 191–92). Biggs' suggestion of the *Homilies'* affinities with Arianism, however, have never been fully explored.

[31] Esp. *Ep. Clem.* 6–7, 12–18; *Hom.* 3.60–72.

[32] *Hom.* 3.60–73 (Zacchaeus in Caesarea; cf. Luke 19:5; *Hist. eccl.* 4.5.3); 7.5 (unnamed elder in Tyre); 7.8 (unnamed elder in Sidon); 7.12 (unnamed elder in Berytus); 11.36 (Maroones in Tripolis); 20.23 (unnamed elder in Laodicea). It is also notable that the *Epistle of Clement to Rome*, one of the two letters prefaced to the *Homilies*, tells of Clement's ordination by Peter in Rome (esp. 19).

[33] Chapman, "On the date of the Pseudo-Clementines," 155.

[34] On the *Homilies* and late antique heresiology, see A. Y. Reed, "Heresiology and the (Jewish-)Christian Novel: Narrativized Polemics in the Pseudo-Clementines," in *Heresy and Self-Definition in Late Antiquity* (ed. E. Iricinschi and H. Zellentin (Tübingen: Mohr, forthcoming). On the trope of "heretical succession," see A. Ferreiro, "Sexual Depravity, Doctrinal Error, and Character Assassination in the Fourth Century: Jerome against the Priscillianists," *Studia Patristica* 28 (1993): 29–38.

[35] See further Reed, "Jewish Christianity," 188–231.

[36] The final form of the *Homilies* has not been a topic of focused inquiry since the nineteenth century. Especially notable – for our purposes – is the work of Gerhard Uhlhorn, who stressed the unity of the *Homilies* in its present form and the need to consider the aims of its redactors (*Homilien und Recognitionen*, esp. 153); note also A. Schliemann, *Die Clementinen nebst den verwandten Schriften und der Ebionitismus* (Hamburg:

## The *Homilies* and Eusebius' *Ecclesiastical History*

To recover the significance of the *Homilies* for our understanding of the fourth century, comparison with Eusebius' *Ecclesiastical History* proves helpful. Books I–IV of the latter treat many of the same events, themes, and figures that make up the focus of the former: the life of Clement and his contacts with apostles (*Hist. eccl.* III 4.9; 15), the activities of Simon Magus (II 1.11; 13.1–5), Peter's struggles against Simon (II 14.1–15.2), the Alexandrian Apion's slander against the Jews (II 5.3–4; cf. III 38.5; *Hom.* 4–6), and – more broadly – the story of apostolic succession and the spread of Jesus' message beyond the bounds of Judaea.

Moreover, the two texts are temporally and geographically proximate. The first edition of the *Ecclesiastical History* (books I–VII) is typically dated between 290 and 312 C.E.,[37] a few decades before the compilation of the *Homilies*.[38] Whereas Eusebius penned his history in Caesarea, the *Homilies* was most likely compiled in Edessa or Antioch.[39] Eusebius himself attests the transmission of texts and traditions between these cities in

---

F. Berthes, 1844), 130–251; A. Hilgenfeld, *Die clementinischen Recognitionen und Homilien nach ihrem Ursprung und Inhalt dargetellt* (Leipzig, 1848). These studies, however, were penned prior to the establishment of its fourth-century date and thus seek to locate the text in the second century C.E. Some interesting suggestions about the late antique context of the Pseudo-Clementines were made at the turn of the century, when its fourth-century date was established in Biggs, "Clementine *Homilies*," 157–93; J. Chapman, "On the Date of the Clementines," *Zeitschrift für die neutestamentliche Wissenschaft* 9 (1908): 147–59. Until recently, however, these suggestions have been largely ignored, consistent with the source-critical focus of almost all twentieth-century research on the Pseudo-Clementines.

[37] R. M. Grant, *Eusebius as Church Historian* (Oxford: Clarendon, 1980), 13–14; A. Louth, "The date of Eusebius' *Historia ecclesiastica*," *Journal of Theological Studies* 41 (1990): 111–23; R. W. Burgess, "The dates and editions of Eusebius' *Chronici canones* and *Historia ecclesiastica*," *Journal of Theological Studies* 48 (1997): 471–504.

[38] Since Biggs (see n. 36), scholars have concurred that the *Homilies* should be dated to the first half of the fourth century. A topic of continued debate, however, is whether it should be placed before or after the Council of Nicaea. C. Schmidt, O. Cullman, and G. Strecker, for instance, see the *Homilies* as pre-Nicene composition, while H. Waitz and B. Rehm place its composition shortly after 325 C.E. See e.g. H. Waitz, *Die Pseudoklementinen: Homilien und Rekognitionen: Eine quellenkritische Untersuchung* (Leipzig: J. Hinrichs, 1904), 369; G. Strecker, *Das Judenchristentum in den Pseudoklementinen* (2d ed.; Texte und Untersuchungen zur Geschichte der altchristlichen Literatur 70; Berlin: Akademie, 1981), 268; and the summary of the debate in Jones, "Pseudo-Clementines," 73–74.

[39] See n. 28 above. Notably, Caesarea may have also played a part in the pseudepigraphical claims in the Pseudo-Clementine *Grundschrift*, albeit in a manner whose precise significance is now difficult to recover; cf. *Hom.* 1.20.2; *Rec.* 1.17.2.

the fourth century (*Hist. eccl.* I 13).[40] The movement of material between Palestinian and Syrian locales is further evinced by the reception-history of his *Ecclesiastical History*, which was translated into Syriac soon after its composition.[41]

To my knowledge, no study has explored the rhetorical and discursive parallels between these two texts. Rather, research on the Pseudo-Clementines has looked to the *Ecclesiastical History* mainly to test the historical accuracy of the description of figures and events in the *Homilies* and *Recognitions*.[42] In addition, scholars have appealed to Eusebius' references to Petrine and Clementine pseudepigrapha (III 3.2, 38.5) to support source-critical hypotheses concerning the ultimate origins of material now found in the *Homilies*.[43]

Due partly to the power of traditional meta-narratives about "orthodoxy" and "heresy," on the one hand, and "Gentile Christianity" and "Jewish Christianity," on the other, the *Homilies* and *Ecclesiastical History* have been studied in different specialist circles. Moreover, like the *Homilies*, the *Ecclesiastical History* has often been treated as a reservoir of data about earlier times and sources; scholars have too rarely considered its significance as a late antique narrative construction.[44]

In my view, however, there are good reasons to read the *Ecclesiastical History* and the *Homilies* in terms of a shared fourth-century discourse

---

[40] See, however, S. Brock, "Eusebius and Syriac Christianity," in *Eusebius, Christianity, and Judaism* (ed. H.W. Attridge and G. Hata; Studia Post-Biblica 42; Leiden: Brill, 1992), 212–34.

[41] The Syriac translation survives in a manuscript from 461/462 C.E. (Leningrad, Public Library, Cod. Syr. 1, New Series). See W. Wright and N. McLean, *The Ecclesiastical History of Eusebius in Syriac* (Cambridge, U.K.: Cambridge University Press, 1898).

[42] On one level, for instance, H.-J. Schoeps' *Theologie und Geschichte des Judenchristentums* (Tübingen: Mohr Siebeck, 1949) can be read as a comprehensive attempt to fit the evidence of the Pseudo-Clementine *Homilies* and *Recognitions* into the framework of Christian history laid out in Eusebius' *Ecclesiastical History*.

[43] In particular, Eusebius' statements in *Hist. eccl.* III 38.5 have played an important role in scholarly debates about the sources of *Hom.* 4–6. For a summary of the various positions, see Jones, "Pseudo-Clementines," 27–31.

[44] Elizabeth Clark, for instance, notes how the influence of Eusebius' *Ecclesiastical History* has rendered his own assumptions almost invisible. Although the accuracy of his details have often been questioned, not enough has been done to explore how his history "shores up claims for the dominance of the proto-orthodox Church, enhances its leaders' prestige, and justifies particular institutions and teachings"; *History, Theory, Text: Historians and the Linguistic Turn* (Cambridge, Mass.: Harvard University Press, 2004), 169. Important exceptions include Grant, *Eusebius*; A.J. Droge, "The Apologetic Dimensions of the *Ecclesiastical History*," in *Eusebius, Christianity, and Judaism*, 492–509; D. B. Martin, *Inventing Superstition: From Hippocrates to the Christians* (Cambridge, Mass.: Harvard University Press, 2004), 207–25.

about the apostolic past. Not only are two texts contemporaneous, but they exhibit many of the same concerns. Both trace the paths of apostolic succession and assert ecclesiastical authority. They answer "pagan" critiques of Christianity and defend "orthodoxy" against "heresy." Moreover, they seek to map the place of Judaism in apostolic history and late antique Christian identity.

To address these concerns, Eusebius and the authors/redactors of the *Homilies* choose different literary genres.[45] It may be significant, however, that both engage in the large-scale appropriation and subversion of "pagan" literary forms: just as the *Homilies* is our earliest extant example of the Christian use of the genre of the Greco-Roman novel,[46] so Eusebius' *Ecclesiastical History* applies Hellenistic historiographical tropes to the whole of Christian history.[47]

When we look beyond the issue of genre, we also see how the two texts are shaped by many of the same literary practices. Most notable is their integration, consolidation, and reworking of earlier source-materials, including Hellenistic Jewish as well as early Christian writings.[48] To be sure,

[45] To a modern reader, their choice of different genres might seem to preclude their participation in a common discourse. This, however, may say more about the gap between premodern and modern notions of "history" than about literary production in Late Antiquity. That Eusebius and the authors/redactors of the *Homilies* express so many of the same concerns by means of these different genres may, in fact, confirm recent insights into the close connections between history and narrative in Greco-Roman culture. On these connections, see e.g. A. Cameron, ed., *History as Text: The Writing of Ancient History* (Chapel Hill: University of North Carolina Press, 1990), and on the novelistic background of both Greek and Jewish historiography, A. Momigliano, *The Classical Foundations of Modern Historiography* (Sather Classical Lectures 54; Berkeley: University of California Press, 1990), 15–16.

[46] Although novelistic tropes are evident in earlier Jewish and Christian literature (e.g., apocryphal acts), the Pseudo-Clementines are widely acknowledged to be the first full-fledged Christian novel still extant; B. E. Perry, *Ancient Romances: A Literary-Historical Account of their Origins* (Berkeley: University of California Press, 1967), 285–93; T. Hägg, *The Novel in Antiquity* (Berkeley: University of California Press, 1983), 154–65. On the Pseudo-Clementines' subversion of the genre, see the sources cited in n. 25 above.

[47] Cf. *Hist. eccl.* I 1.3–5; Grant, *Eusebius*, 22–32. His debt to the histories of Hellenistic philosophical schools, in particular, is stressed by Momigliano, *Classical Foundations*, 140–41.

[48] For a summary of research on the sources of the Pseudo-Clementines, see Jones, "Pseudo-Clementines," 8–33. On the possibility that *Hom.* 4–6 draws on a Hellenistic Jewish apology, for instance, see W. Heintze, *Der Klemensroman und seine griechischen Quellen* (Leipzig: J. C. Hinrichs, 1914), esp. 48–50, 108–9, 112; C. Schmidt, *Studien zu den Pseudo-Clementinen* (Leipzig: J. C. Hinrichs, 1929), 160–239; W. A. Adler,

Eusebius signals his use of sources in a manner consistent with the conventions of the historical genre,[49] while the authors/redactors of the *Homilies* interweave them without notice.[50] Studies of Eusebius' use of sources, however, have shown how he – no less than the *Homilies* –reworks his received material in the service of his own aims.[51]

In addition, Eusebius and the authors/redactors of the *Homilies* may draw on much the same reservoir of sources, even as they hold different opinions about what constitutes authentic records of the apostolic past. Eusebius, for instance, is familiar with a variety of Petrine and Clementine pseudepigrapha (*Hist. eccl.* III 3.2, 38.5), including a book that circulated in the name of Clement that records Peter's debates with Apion.[52] Although he cites these sources only to reject them, it is striking that he nevertheless felt compelled to mention them.

In turn, the *Homilies* contains hints of awareness of the Pauline epistles so central to Eusebius' understanding of "orthodoxy," even as its authors/redactors seek to purge the apostolic past of any traces of Paul's positive influence.[53] In other words, we find – in both texts – evidence for fourth-century efforts to consolidate certain images of the past by anthologizing, reworking, and reframing earlier sources. In each case, some sources are privileged, while others are subverted or silenced.

Like Eusebius, the authors/redactors of the *Homilies* seem to have drawn selectively on source materials to remodel the apostolic past in the image of their own particular vision of "orthodoxy." In my view, it may not be coincidental that they do so in the middle of the fourth century, concurrent with attempts – by Eusebius and others – to deny the continued place of Judaism in church history and Christian identity. For, as we shall see, they answer the denial of the vitality of "Jewish Christianity" with a radical assertion. According to the *Homilies* Christianity's continuity with

---

"Apion's enconomium of adultery: A Jewish satire of Greek *paideia* in the Pseudo-Clementine *Homilies*," *Hebrew Union College Annual* 64 (1993): 28–30.

[49] On Eusebius' sources, see e.g. Grant, *Eusebius*, 17–19; T. D. Barnes, *Constantine and Eusebius* (Cambridge, Mass.: Harvard University Press, 1981), 130–31.

[50] See below on the possible motivations for this choice.

[51] E.g. G. Hata, "Eusebius and Josephus: The way Eusebius misused and abused Josephus," *Patristica: Proceedings of the Colloquia of the Japanese Society for Patristic Studies*, supp. 1 (2001): 49–66; S. Inowlocki, "Eusebius of Caesarea's *Interpretatio Christiana* of Philo's *De vita contemplativa*," *Harvard Theological Review* 97 (2004): 305–28.

[52] *Hist. eccl.* III 38.5: "And certain men have lately brought forward other wordy and lengthy writings under his (i.e. Clement's) name, containing dialogues of Peter and Apion (*Petrou dê kai Apiônos dialogous periechonta*)." Cf. Clement's debates with Apion in *Hom.* 4–6 and discussion below.

[53] See discussion below.

Judaism is not just inexorable, but the teachings of the two traditions are the same; the true apostolic religion is, in essence, the revelation of Judaism to the Gentiles.

*Apostolic Succession and the Transmission of Truth*

At the beginning of the *Ecclesiastical History*, Eusebius stresses his aim to narrate "the successions of the holy apostles" (*tas tôn hierôn apostolôn diadochas*; I 1.1).[54] As is well known, this aim lies at the heart of his history of the early church and shapes his focus on its teachers and leaders.[55]

Apostolic succession is similarly pivotal for the plot of the *Homilies*, which focuses on a single instantiation. The novel purports to record Clement of Rome's own account of how he came to Christianity, and it establishes his close relationship with the apostle Peter. In its descriptions of Peter's teachings, the theme of proper succession repeatedly arises. Peter presents himself as heir to Jesus, and he stresses that the truth that leads to salvation is known and verified through the lines of succession that run through the Jerusalem church (*Hom.* 2.6–12; 3.15, 19; 11.35). Jesus, as True Prophet, "alone knows the truth; if anyone else knows anything, he has received it from him or from his disciples" (2.12).[56]

The epistemological significance of succession is here matched by its importance for ensuring the legitimacy of leaders and institutions. Central to the *Homilies* are tales about Peter's journeys to preach in different cities, where he founds communities and appoints bishops (*Hom.* 3.72; 7.5, 8, 12; 11.36; 20.23). In the course of Peter's public preaching, he stresses the need for ecclesiastical offices that mirror and maintain proper succession: the sole rule of God over the cosmos is reflected in the bishop's monarchic rule over his community, which is legitimated through the succession from Jesus to Peter and which thus ensures the continued preservation and transmission of true teachings (3.60–71; also *Ep. Clem.* 2–6).

---

[54] English translations of Eusebius' *Ecclesiastical History* are revised from G. A. Williamson, trans., *Eusebius, The History of the Church from Christ to Constantine* (Baltimore, 1965), with reference to G. Bardy, ed. and trans., *Eusèbe de Césarée, Histoire Ecclésiastique, Livres I–IV* (Sources chrétiennes 31; Paris: Cerf, 1952).

[55] Grant, *Eusebius*, 45–83.

[56] English translations of the *Homilies* are revised from *Ante-Nicene Fathers,* eds. A. Roberts and J. Donaldson (repr. ed.; Grand Rapids, Mich.: Eerdmans, 1951), 8.224–52, 324–30, with reference to B. Rehm, *Die Pseudoklementinen*, I: *Homilien* (Berlin: Akademie, 1969) as well as A. Le Boulluec et al., trans., "Roman pseudo-clémentin: *Homélies*," *Écrits apocryphes chrétiens II* (ed. P. Geoltrain and J.-D. Kaestli; Paris: Éditions Gallimard, 2005), 1193–589. On the treatment of proper succession and the transmission of knowledge in the *Recognitions*, see Kelley, *Knowledge*, 135–79.

Whereas Eusebius treats the succession of bishops and Christian teachers as different lines that only sometimes converge,[57] the authors/redactors of the *Homilies* identify apostolic succession with the office of the bishop, and they present this line of succession as the sole conduit for the transmission of Christian truth. Just as the apostles are depicted as Jesus' true and trustworthy heirs, charged with preserving and spreading his teachings (*Hom.* 1.15; 7.11; 17.19), so proper succession vouchsafes the faithful transmission of these teachings and enables the institutional settings for their maintenance in belief and practice.

*Primordial Truth, Jewish Succession, and Apostolic Teaching*

In both the *Homilies* and the *Ecclesiastical History*, however, the importance of the era of the apostles goes well beyond the appeal to apostolic succession to authenticate teachings and to legitimize leaders and communities. This era is granted a special place in human history. In both texts, it is celebrated as a glorious age in which hidden truth shone forth upon the earth (e.g., *Hist. eccl.* II 3.1–2; *Hom.* 1.18–19). In both, moreover, apostolic teaching opens the ways for the restoration of primordial religion (e.g., *Hist. eccl.* I 2.18–19, 4.4, 4.15; *Hom.* 8.10; 10.6).

In the *Ecclesiastical History*, this assertion is explicitly framed as a response to "pagan" polemics against Christianity.[58] Lest anyone "imagine that his teaching is new and strange (*nean... kai ksenên*), framed by a man of recent date no different from other men" (I 4.1; also I 2.1, 3.21, 4.15), Eusebius stresses Christ's status as Logos. Prior to the Incarnation, Christ played a part in creation (I 2.3–5, 8, 14–16) as well as appearing to Abraham, Moses, and other Hebrew patriarchs and prophets (I 2.6–7, 10-13, 21; I 4.8). It was his revelation of the Torah to Moses that first enabled seeds of truth to spread to other nations (I 2.22–23). His role in spreading truth is also, according to Eusebius, evident in the predictions about his Incarnation embedded in the writings of Moses and other Hebrew authors (e.g., I 2.24–3.6), who thus serve as witnesses to the true antiquity of Christ and the Christian faith.

Not only did Christ play an important role in the cosmos before the birth of Jesus, but – Eusebius claims – there were Christians on the earth, long prior to the emergence of the group that now takes that name. Due to the Logos' activities among the Hebrews, some lived as Christians:

---

[57] Grant, *Eusebius*, 45–47.

[58] See further Droge, "Apologetic," 493–98. On the place of anti-"pagan" polemics in Eusebius' work more broadly, see A. Kofsky, *Eusebius of Caesaria against Paganism* (Leiden: Brill, 2000).

> With regard to all these men who have been witnessed as righteous, going back from Abraham himself to the first man, one would not be departing far from the truth in calling them Christians in practice if not in name (*ergô Christianous ei kai mê onomati*). (*Hist. eccl.* I 4.6)[59]

Eusebius stresses that Christianity is the same religion discovered in the age of Abraham, to whom Christ/Logos appeared in the guise of an angel (I 2.7; cf. Gen 18:1):

> It is obviously necessary to regard the religion proclaimed in recent years to all nations through Christ's teaching as none other than the first, most ancient, and most primitive of all religions (*protên... kai pantôn paliotatên te kai archaitatên theosebeias*), discovered by Abraham and his followers... (*Hist. eccl.* I 4.10)

Consequently, he is able to argue that "the practice of religion as communicated to us by Christ's teaching is... not new and strange (*nean kai ksenên*), but – if the truth be told – primary, unique, and true" (*prôtên... kai monên kai alêthê*; I 4.15).

When describing the religion of Abraham, Eusebius takes care to clarify that the pious Hebrews of the distant past did not practice circumcision, kashrut, or Sabbath-observance like later Jews (I 4.8, 11–13). The implications for the lack of continuity in the Jewish transmission of Abrahamic religion are developed in his references of the Mosaic Torah, which he describes as preserving true revelations of Christ/Logos in metaphors and mysteries (I 4.8). Eusebius' assertion of the continuity between Abraham and Christianity is thus predicated on the denial of any inherent connection between the patriarch and his Jewish heirs.[60]

The theme of discontinuity is also determinative in his descriptions of later forms of Judaism. In *Hist. eccl.* I 10.3, Eusebius stresses the lack of continuity in the proper succession of the high priesthood under Roman rule, speculating about the resultant loss of knowledge about purity and ritual practice. Likewise, in III 10.4, he quotes Josephus' assertion that the "accurate succession of prophets" ceased at the time of Artaxerxes (cf. *Ag. Ap.* 1.8). As in his treatment of Christian history, succession is a key theme, and the question of continuity is pivotal. Here, however, the rhetoric of succession is used to convey rupture.

The issue of Jewish succession is also central to Eusebius' explanation of the precise timing of Jesus' earthly sojourn (*Hist. eccl.* I 6.1–8).[61] He

[59] This view of pre-Christian Christians builds, e.g., on Justin, *1 Apol.* 46.

[60] For the many precedents for this use of Abraham, see J. Siker, *Disinheriting the Jews: Abraham in Early Christian Controversy* (Louisville: Westminster/John Knox, 1991).

[61] Strikingly, *diadochê* and related terms occur five times in this single passage, and Eusebius here makes efforts to stress the continuity of royal and priestly succession

stresses that the proper succession of Jewish rulers continued unbroken from the days of Moses to the first century C.E. (I 6.2, 5–6). Citing LXX Gen 49:10, however, he proposes that the Incarnation occurred when the succession was finally broken (I 6.1–8); with the Idumaean Herod, "their rulers and leaders, who had ruled in regular succession from the time of Moses himself (*eks autou Môuseôs kata diadochên*), came to an end" (I 6.4).

Consistent with Eusebius' stated aim of recording apostolic successions together with "the calamities that immediately after their conspiracy (*epiboulês*) against our Saviour overwhelmed the entire Jewish people" (I 1.2), books I–IV of the *Ecclesiastical History* tell the story of Jesus and the apostles in counterpoint to the history of the Jews.[62] For this pattern, LXX Gen 49:10 serves to provide a prophetic explanation. In Eusebius' reading,[63] this verse becomes an ancient prediction of the time when the scepter would fall from Judah, thereby opening the way for the fulfillment of "the expectation of the nations" with the coming of Christ:

> It was without question in his (i.e. Herod's) time that the advent of Christ occurred; and the expected salvation and calling of the Gentiles followed at once, in accordance with the prophecy (i.e. LXX Gen 49:10). As soon as the rulers and leaders of Judah – those from the Jewish people – came to an end, not surprisingly the high priesthood, which had passed in regular succession (*epi tous eggista diadochous*), from generation to generation, was plunged into confusion. (*Hist. eccl.* I 6.8)

Eusebius thus argues that a break in Jewish succession ushered in the birth of Jesus and the establishment of apostolic succession, just as the downfall

between Moses and first-century Judaism – even during the Babylonian Exile, etc. – so as to be able to assert that the breaks in these lines occurred directly prior to the birth of Jesus.

[62] See further *Hist. eccl.* II 5.6–10; III 5.2–7, 7.7–9, where calamities amongst the Jews are direct results of their mistreatment of Jesus and his apostles. For a discussion of the Christian precedents for this approach to Jewish history, see Grant, *Eusebius*, 97–113. On the extension of these views in his *Preparatio Evangelica* and *Demonstratio Evangelica*, see A. Kofsky, "Eusebius of Caesaria and the Christian–Jewish Polemic," in *Contra Iudaeos: Ancient and Medieval Polemics between Jews and Christians* (ed. O. Limor and G. G. Stroumsa; Tübingen: Mohr Siebeck, 1996), 59–84. For a comprehensive survey of Eusebius' references to Jews and Judaism, see J. Ulrich, *Eusebius von Caesarea und die Juden: Studien zur Rolle der Juden in der Theologie des Eusebius von Caesarea* (Berlin: Walter de Gruyter, 1999).

[63] There are precedents for this interpretation, e.g., in Irenaeus, *adv. Haer.* 4.10.2 and Origen, *Princ.* 4.1.3.

of the Jewish nation accompanied the birth of a new nation, namely, the Christians (I 4.2).[64]

In the *Homilies*, the theme of succession similarly serves as a means to answer "pagan" critiques of Christianity. By means of speeches attributed to Peter, the text asserts that monotheistic piety is the natural state of humankind (*Hom.* 8.10; 10.6), to which polytheistic corruptions accrued, due to the weaknesses of humankind, the intervention of demons, and the teachings of false prophets (e.g., 1.18; 2.16–18; 3.23–25; 8.11–20; 9.2–18; 10.7–23). As in the *Ecclesiastical History*, Jesus' Incarnation is presented as ushering in a new era of illumination and salvation for the Gentiles, whereupon the apostles spread the truth of the most ancient religion to those long shackled by idolatry, polytheism, and impiety (e.g., *Hom.* 2.33; 3.19).

Where the texts differ, however, is in their presentation of Judaism. Like Eusebius, the authors/redactors of the *Homilies* stress that Jesus is not a new teacher: he is the ultimate source of all truth in every age. Instead of appealing to the doctrine of the Logos,[65] the *Homilies* presents Jesus as the True Prophet who "has changed his forms and his names from the beginning of the world and so reappeared again and again in the world" (*Hom.* 3.20).[66] He is identified with a series of prophets, including Adam and Moses, who were sent by God to preach the same message of monotheism (2.16–17; 3.17–21). In the *Homilies*, Jesus himself is thus placed in an ancient line of prophetic succession.[67]

Perhaps most notably, this understanding of succession enables the authors/redactors of the *Homilies* to assert the identity of Moses and Jesus. In

---

[64] The view of Christians as an *ethnos* is developed in more detail in his *Preparatio Evangelica*, on which see A. P. Johnson, "Identity, Descent, and Polemic: Ethnic Argumentation in Eusebius' *Praeparatio Evangelica*," *Journal of Early Christian Studies* 12 (2004): 23–56.

[65] This omission is consistent with the *Homilies*' polemic against Hellenistic philosophy, on which see below.

[66] See further L. Cerfaux, "Le vrai prophète des Clémentines," *Recherches de science religieuse* 18 (1928): 143–63; Strecker, *Judenchristentum,* 145–53; H. J. W. Drijvers, "Adam and the True Prophet in the Pseudo-Clementines," in *Loyalitätskonflikte in der Religionsgeschichte: Festschrift für Carsten Colpe* (ed. C. Elsas and H. Kippenberg; Würzburg: Königshausen & Neumann, 1990), 314–23; C. A. Gieschen, "The Seven Pillars of the World: Ideal Figure Lists in the True Prophet Christology of the Pseudo-Clementines," *Journal for the Study of Pseudepigrapha* 12 (1994): 47–82.

[67] Although the identification of Jesus as True Prophet serves primarily to stress his true antiquity and to strengthen the connection between Christianity and the Israelite/Jewish past, it is noted that Jesus is the last of the line and that he will be revealed in the end-times as the *Christos* (*Hom.* 2.17). As such, the salvation of the Gentiles is depicted as a mark of the impending Eschaton.

*Hom.* 8.6–7, for instance, the two are presented as equal sources of the truth:

> ...Jesus is concealed from the Hebrews who have taken Moses as their teacher (*apo men Hebraiôn ton Môusên didaskalon eilêphotôn kaluptetai ho Iêsous*), just as Moses is hidden from those who have believed Jesus (*apo de tôn Iêsou pepisteukotôn ho Môusês apokruptetai*). Since there is a single teaching by both (*mias gar di' amphoterôn didaskalias*), God accepts one who has believed either of these. To believe a teacher is for the sake of doing the things spoken by God.
>
> And our lord himself (i.e. Jesus) says that this is so: "I thank you, Father of heaven and earth, because you have concealed these things from the wise and prudent, and you have revealed them to sucking babes" (cf. Matt 11:25/Luke 10:21). Thus God Himself has concealed a teacher from some (i.e., Jews), who foreknew what they should do (*tois men ekrupsen didaskalon hôs proegnôkosin ha dei prattein*), and He has revealed (him) to others (i.e., "pagans"), who are ignorant about what they should do (*tois de apekalupsen hôs agnoousin ha chrê poiein*). (*Hom.* 8.6.1–5)[68]

In effect, Christianity is here granted an ancient pedigree by means of its equation with Judaism. Whereas Eusebius answers "pagan" critics of Christianity by constructing a Hebrew heritage from broken fragments of Jewish scripture and history, the *Homilies* depicts Jesus' teachings as essentially the revelation of Moses' teachings to the Gentiles.

Accordingly, in the *Homilies*, apostolic succession stands in a close relationship to succession amongst the Jews. Whereas Eusebius stresses the break in the succession of Jewish kings, priests, and prophets, the authors/redactors of the *Homilies* affirm the continued oral transmission of Moses' teachings among the Jews in a line that stretches from the seventy elders of Num 11:16 (*Hom.* 2.38; also *Ep. Pet.* 1.2) to the Pharisees of Jesus' time (*Hom.* 3.18–19; 11.29).[69] Just as the *Homilies* describes Moses and Jesus as two earthly manifestations of the True Prophet (2.16–17), sent by God to teach the same truths to different peoples (8.6–7), so its authors/redactors depict apostolic succession and Pharisaic succession as separate but equal lines for the transmission of true knowledge.

Interestingly, the authors/redactors of the *Homilies* establish the continuance of proper succession among the Jews with appeal to a saying of Jesus. Specifically, they repeatedly cite his assertion that the Pharisees sit

---

[68] For a comparison with the parallel in *Rec.* 4.5, see Reed, "Jewish Christianity," 213–17. God's justice in hiding Jesus from the Jews is addressed in *Hom.* 18.6–7. Inasmuch as the truth was long hidden from the Gentiles, it is deemed fair that the last avatar of the True Prophet is now hidden from the Jews (18.6). The text there affirms that the "way that leads to the kingdom" is still available to them, even though "things of the kingdom" are now hidden from them (18.7).

[69] These statements are unparalleled in the *Recognitions*.

in the "seat of Moses" (*tês kathedras Môuseôs*; cf. Matt 23:2; *Hom.* 3.18–19; 3.70; 11:29; also *Ep. Pet.* 1.2). In *Hom.* 3.18–19, for instance, Jesus' reference to the "seat of Moses" is used to explain how the transmission of Moses' teachings by Jews relates to the transmission of Jesus' teachings by apostles. Peter begins by affirming that the Pharisees, as Moses' heirs, possess the prophetic truth:

> …"Ask your father, and he will tell you; your elders, and they will declare to you" (Deut 32:7). It is necessary to seek this father (i.e. Adam = the True Prophet) and to make further search for these elders (i.e., the Jews)! But you have not sought out concerning the one to whose time belongs the kingdom and to whom belongs the seat of prophecy (*tês prophêteias kathedras*), even though he himself (i.e. Jesus = the True Prophet) points this out himself, saying: "The scribes and the Pharisees sit in the seat of Moses (*tês kathedras Môuseôs*); all things that they say to you, hear them" (cf. Matt 23:2–3). "Hear them," he said, "as entrusted with the key of the kingdom (*tên kleida tês basileias*), which is knowledge (cf. Luke 11:52),[70] which alone can open the gate of life, through which alone is the entrance to eternal life."… (*Hom.* 3.18.1–3)

As in the traditions about the Pharisees in the Gospels of Matthew and Luke (Matt 23:2–3, 13; Luke 11:52), it is here affirmed that these Jews have the knowledge that leads to salvation – and that they have kept it to themselves. In Matthew and Luke, the Pharisees are sharply criticized on these grounds. The authors/redactors of the *Homilies* offer a different interpretation of Jesus' words.[71] Jews are not blamed for keeping Mosaic wisdom from the Gentiles inasmuch as God's plan involves a division of prophetic labor. Consequently, it is the Pharisees' act of concealment that occasions the Incarnation:

> "Truly," he says, "they possess the key, but those wishing to enter they do not suffer to do so" (cf. Matt 23:13). On this account, I say, he himself – rising from his

[70] Note also Matt 16:19, where it is Peter who is said to have "the key of the kingdom of heaven" (*tas kleidas tês basileias tôn ouranôn*).

[71] Elsewhere in the *Homilies*, Peter explains that when Jesus called Pharisees "hypocrites," he was referring only to some of them: "Our teacher, when dealing with certain of the Pharisees and scribes among us – who are separated yet as scribes know the matters of the Law more than others – still reproved them as hypocrites, because they cleansed only the things that appear to men… He spoke the truth with respect to the hypocrites among them, not with respect to all of them (*pros tous hupokritas autôn ou pros pantas*). To some he said that obedience was to be rendered, because they were entrusted with the chair of Moses (cf. Matt 23:2). But, to the hypocrites, he said: 'Woe to you, scribes and Pharisees, hypocrites…' (cf. Matt 23:13)" (*Hom.* 11.28–29). Cf. *Hom.* 3.70: "Therefore, honor the throne of Christ (*thronon oun Christou timêsete*); for you are commanded to honor the seat of Moses (*hoti kai Môuseôs kathedran timan ekeleusthête*), even if those who occupy it are accounted sinners (*kan hoi prokathezomenoi hamartôloi nomizôntai*)."

> seat (*kathedras*) like a father for his children, proclaiming the things which from the beginning were transmitted in secret to the worthy (*ta apo aiônos en kruptô aksiois paradidomena kêrussôn*), extending mercy even to the Gentiles, and having compassion for the souls of all – neglected his own blood (*idiou haimatos êmelei*). (*Hom.* 3.18.3–19.1)

The True Prophet, in other words, took on the form of Jesus precisely to reveal prophetic truths to Gentiles. Just as the *Homilies* here depict the "seat of prophecy" (*tês prophêteias kathedras*) as the source of salvific knowledge and describe the True Prophet as rising from this seat to come to earth, so the reader is assured that his teachings are still transmitted on earth through parallel lines of prophetic succession – with the Pharisees in the "seat of Moses" (*tês kathedras Môuseôs*; 3.18–19; 3.70; 11:29) and Peter's bishops in the "seat of Christ" (*tês Christou kathedras*; 3.60).

As in the *Ecclesiastical History* (I 6.1–8), Jewish succession is thus central to an explanation of the timing and motivation for the Incarnation. Whereas Eusebius focuses on Jewish kingship and asserts a first-century break in the continuity of Jewish royal and priestly lines of succession, the *Homilies* focuses on Jewish learning and affirm the continuity that links Moses to the Pharisees.

Accordingly, the authors/redactors of the *Homilies* use LXX Gen 49:10 in a manner quite different than did Eusebius. In both the *Ecclesiastical History* and the *Homilies*, this verse is interpreted as a Mosaic prediction of Jesus' Incarnation. Whereas Eusebius cites the verse to support his supersessionist approach to Jewish history (*Hist. eccl.* I 6.1–8), the authors/redactors of the *Homilies* present it as a prooftext for Jesus' appointed status as the prophet who points Gentiles to the truths in the Jewish scriptures (*Hom.* 3.49).

Not only do the *Homilies* allow for the Mosaic authority of the Pharisees, but they further propose that proper teaching and leadership are preserved among the Jewish people due to their maintenance of the succession from Moses. In *Hom.* 2.38, Peter asserts that Moses "gave (*paradedôkotos*) the Law with the explanations (*sun tais epilusesin*)" to the seventy elders.[72] This oral tradition is later linked to the continuance of proper leadership among the Jews:

> The Law of God was given, through Moses, without writing (*agraphôs*) to seventy wise men (cf. Num 11:16), to be handed down (*paradidosthai*), so that the government might be carried on by succession (*tê didadochê*). (*Hom.* 3.47.1)

---

[72] This assertion is significant inasmuch as the authors/redactors of the *Homilies* view the written scriptures as corrupted by interpolations; see *Hom.* 2.38–52, 3.4–6, 3.9–11, 3.17–21, 3.37–51, 16.9–14, 18.12–13, 18.18–22. See further Strecker, *Judenchristentum*, 166–86; Shuve, "Doctrine of the False Pericopes."

These assertions prove particularly intriguing in light of the authority claims being made by Rabbis in Palestine, around the same time that the *Homilies* was taking form in nearby Syria. Early Rabbis similarly used the rhetoric of succession to trace their authority to Moses (*m. Avot* 1–5).[73] And, by the fourth century, this assertion of continuity was being articulated in terms of claims to possess, not just the Written Torah, but also the Oral Torah revealed to Moses at Mt. Sinai.[74]

This confluence of ideas has led Al Baumgarten to suggest that the Pseudo-Clementine authors/redactors may have had contact with late antique Rabbis.[75] If so, then it proves all the more significant that the authors/redactors of the *Homilies* appear to accept the Mosaic authority of their Jewish contemporaries. Arguably, their own understanding of succession may even be shaped by an effort to accommodate Rabbinic authority claims into a Christian schema.[76] Whereas Eusebius seems to pattern his understanding of succession on the lineages of Hellenistic philosophical schools,[77] the *Homilies*' model of succession may be indebted instead to Rabbinic models.

---

[73] On the Rabbinic use of succession lists, see e.g. A. Tropper, "Tractate *Avot* and Early Christian Succession Lists," in *Ways that Never Parted*, 159–88.

[74] E.g. *Sifre Deut.* 351; *y. Megillah* 4.1; *y. Pe'ah* 2.6; *Pesikta Rabbati* 14b; *b. Shabbat* 13a; and discussion in M. S. Jaffee, *Torah in the Mouth: Writing and Oral Tradition in Palestinian Judaism, 200 BCE–400 CE* (New York: Oxford University Press, 2001).

[75] The acceptance of Pharisaic claims to possess oral Mosaic traditions is one of several features that leads Baumgarten to suggest that they viewed "the Jewish past in much the same way as the Pharisees and/or their rabbinic heirs did"; "Literary Evidence for Jewish Christianity in the Galilee," in *The Galilee in Late Antiquity* (ed. L. Levine; New York: Jewish Theological Seminary of America, 1992), 43. I discuss other Rabbinic parallels in the above cited articles.

[76] This is made explicit in *Ep. Pet.* 1–2, where proper Jewish succession is held up as a model for proper Christian succession: "I beg and beseech you not to communicate to any of the Gentiles the books of my preachings that I sent to you (*tôn hemôn kêrugmatôn has epempsa soi biblous*) nor to anyone of our own tribe before trial. But if anyone has been proved and found worthy, then to commit them to him, after the manner in which Moses delivered his books to the Seventy who succeeded to his chair (*kath' hên kai tois hebdomêkonta ho Môusês paredôke tois tên kathedran autou pareilêphosin*)… For, his countrymen (i.e., the Jews) keep the same rule of monarchy and polity (*tês monarchias kai politeias phulassousi kanona*) everywhere, being unable in any way to think otherwise or to be led out of the way of the much-indicating scriptures. According to the rule (*kanona*) delivered to them, they endeavor to correct the discordances of the scriptures if anyone, not knowing the traditions (*paradoseis*), is confounded at the various utterances of the prophets. Therefore they charge no one to teach, unless he has first learned how the scriptures must be used. And thus they have amongst them one God, one Law, one hope."

[77] E.g. Momigliano, *Classical Foundations*, 140–41.

At the very least, the views expressed in the *Homilies* represent a striking departure from the supersessionist ideas current in the Christianity of its time. Like Eusebius, the authors/redactors of the *Homilies* answer "pagan" critiques by arguing for an authentic Christian claim to continuity and connection with the biblical past. They, however, also affirm Jewish claims to continuity and connection with the same past. The result is a surprisingly harmonious picture of Judaism and Christianity, conceived in terms of supplementarity rather than supersession.

*The Apostolic Mission*

Despite their very different views of Jews and Judaism, the *Homilies* and *Ecclesiastical History* both characterize Christianity as a primarily Gentile phenomenon. Moreover, in both of these texts, this characterization has important ramifications for the scope and aims of the apostolic mission.

Eusebius describes the apostolic mission to the Jews in much the same manner as he portrays the Jewish people – as important for a delineated period of time but ultimately doomed to failure. When recounting the apostles' missionary activities prior to Saul/Paul, for instance, he notes that the apostles initially preached to Jews. He stresses, however, that they did so solely out of necessity (II 1.8; cf. Acts 11:19).

After describing Saul/Paul's commission by the risen Christ (II 1.14), however, Eusebius evokes a very different situation:

> Thus, with the powerful cooperation of heaven, the whole world was suddenly lit by the sunshine of the saving Logos. At once, in accordance with the Holy Scriptures, the voice of its inspired evangelists and apostles went forth into all the earth, and their words to the ends of the world (cf. Ps 19:4)... Those who, following ancestral tradition and ancient error, were shackled by the old sickness of idolatrous superstition (*hoi te ek progonôn diadochês kai tês anekathen planês palaia nosô deisidaimonias eidôlôn tas psuchas pepedêmenoi*) were freed, as it were – by the power of Christ and through the teachings of his followers and the miracles they wrought – from cruel masters and found liberation from heavy chains. They turned their backs on demonic polytheism in all its forms (*pasês... daimonikês kateptuon polutheias*) and acknowledged that there was one God only, the fashioner of all things... (*Hist. eccl.* II 3.1–2)

Whereas Eusebius celebrates the worldwide spread of Christianity as the long-fated acceptance of Abraham's religion by the Gentiles who are the patriarch's true heirs (I 4.12; cf. Gen 18:18; Gal 3:15–29), the *Homilies* presents the apostolic mission as an attempt by Peter and other "Jewish Christians" to convince "pagans" of truths already known to the Jews. Indeed, by the logic of *Hom.* 8.5–7, no Jewish mission is needed; Jews will be saved through the teachings of Moses, and the appointed task of Jesus and his apostles is solely to save "pagans."[78] Accordingly, the *Homilies* depicts Peter and the other apostles as proselytizing, not their fellow Jews, but only Gentiles like Clement.

The *Homilies* has been so celebrated by modern scholars as a source of "Jewish Christian" traditions that it can be easy to forget that the text's own focus falls on "pagans."[79] Peter here preaches about the dangers of polytheism, idolatry, "magic," philosophy, and astrology (e.g., 1.7; 3.7–8; 7:20; 9.2–18; 10.7–24; 11.6–15; 14.4–5, 11; 15.5; 16.7), and Clement works to expose the impurity and impiety of Greek *paideia* (e.g., 1.11–12; 4.12–21; 6.12–25).[80] Moreover, consistent with the *Homilies'* two-fold model of prophetic succession, Jesus' followers are depicted as joining in the struggle against "paganism" long and still fought by the Jews.[81]

*Peter, Paul, and Clement of Rome*

Given the *Homilies'* focus on the Gentile mission, its omission of Paul is notable. The story of Christianity's spread is here told without any direct reference to the man elsewhere celebrated as "the apostle to the Gentiles" (Rom 11:13; Gal 2:2). When read in light of the extreme prominence of

[78] We also find references elsewhere in the *Homilies* suggesting that Jews are already safe both from demonic influence (e.g., 9.20) and from temptations to polytheism and "heresy": "And with us, who have had handed down from our forefathers the worship of the God who made all things (*kai hêmin men tois ek progonôn pareilêphosin ton ta panta ktisanta sebein theon*) as well as the mystery of the books which are able to deceive, he (i.e. Simon) will not prevail. But with those from among the Gentiles who have been brought up in the polytheistic manner (*tois de apo ethnôn tên polutheon hupolêpsin suntrophon echousin*) and who do not know the falsehoods of the scriptures, he will prevail much" (3.4). Notably, this is one among several passages in which Peter is depicted as contrasting "us" with "Gentiles," thereby communicating his self-identification with the Jewish people.

[79] This focus is consistent with the prominence of Hellenism, flowering of Neoplatonism, and continued survival of "paganism" in fourth-century Syria, on which see e.g. G. W. E. Bowersock, *Hellenism in Late Antiquity* (Ann Arbor: University of Michigan Press, 1990), 29–53; H. J. W. Drijvers, "The Persistence of Pagan Cults and Practices in Christian Syria," in *East of Antioch: Studies in Early Syriac Christianity* (Variorum Reprints; London: Variorum, 1984), XVI; Kelley, *Knowledge*, 194–97.

[80] On Greek *paideia* in fourth-century Antioch, see e.g. A. J. Festugière, *Antioche païenne et chrétienne: Libanius, Chrysostome et les moines de Syrie* (Paris: E. de Boccard, 1959). Interestingly, Clement is credited in *Hom.* 4 with an opinion not unlike that expressed by Ephraim: "Blessed is the one who has never tasted the poison of the wisdom of the Greeks" (*De fide*, *Corpus scriptorum christianorum orientalium* 154.7); see further S. Brock, "From Antagonism to Assimilation: Syrian Attitudes towards Greek Learning," in *Syriac Perspectives on Late Antiquity* (Variorum Reprints; London: Variorum, 1984), V.19.

[81] I explore these dynamics further in "From Judaism and Hellenism."

Paul in other fourth-century Christian writings,[82] the silence seems pointed.

Although the *Homilies* lacks the explicit anti-Pauline polemics found in other Pseudo-Clementine sources (e.g., *Rec.* 1.66–70; *Ep. Pet.* 2.3–7), the text may include an indirect jab at Paul's authority.[83] In the course of a debate about the nature of revelation (17.13–17), Simon Magus accuses Peter as follows:

> You claim that you have learned the things of your teacher exactly, because you have directly seen and heard him, but that it is impossible for another to learn the same thing by means of a dream or vision (*oramati ê optasia*; cf. 2 Cor 12:1). (*Hom.* 17.13.1)

In his response, Peter makes his own position clear:

> Whoever trusts an apparition, vision, or dream is prone to error (*ho de optasia pisteuôn ê horamati kai enupniô episphalês estin*). He does not know whom he is trusting; for it is possible it may be an evil spirit or a deceptive spirit, pretending in his speeches to be what it is not. (*Hom.* 17.14.3–4)

Peter, moreover, goes on to contest any authority rooted in visions and to defend his own apostleship. Interestingly, the words here placed in his mouth resonate both with Paul's defense of his apostleship and with his accusations of Peter (esp. Gal 1:11–2:21; 1 Cor 9:1–5: 15:7–9; 2 Cor 11:4–14):

> If our Jesus appeared to you in a vision (*di' hormatos opstheis*), made himself known to you, and spoke to you, it was as one who is enraged with an adversary – and this is the reason why it was through visions and dreams (*di' horamatôn kai enupniôn*; cf. Acts 18:9) or through revelations that were from without (*di' apokalupseôn eksôthen ousôn*; cf. Gal 1:16) that he spoke to you! Can anyone be ren-

[82] E.g., M. M. Mitchell, *The Heavenly Trumpet: John Chrysostom and the Art of Pauline Interpretation* (Tübingen: Mohr Siebeck, 2000); W. Erdt, *Marius Victorinus Afer, der erste lateinische Pauluskommentar: Studien zu seinen Pauluskommentaren im Zusammenhang der Wiederentdeckung des Paulus in der abendländischen Theologie des 4. Jahrhunderts* (Frankfurt am Main: P.D. Lang, 1980); T. F. Martin, "*Vox Pauli*: Augustine and the Claims to Speak for Paul, an Exploration of Rhetoric at the Service of Exegesis," *Journal of Early Christian Studies* 8 (2000): 238–42; A. S. Jacobs, "A Jew's Jew: Paul and the Early Christian Problem of Jewish Origins," *Journal of Religion* 86 (2006): 258–86. See also, more broadly, M. Wiles, *The Divine Apostle: The Interpretation of St. Paul's Epistles in the Early Church* (Cambridge, U.K.: Cambridge University Press, 1967); W. S. Babcock, ed., *Paul and the Legacies of Paul* (Dallas: Southern Methodist University Press, 1990).

[83] Although some have read the Pseudo-Clementine Simon as merely a stand-in for Paul, I concur with Côté that this equation is too simplistic; see further "La fonction littéraire de Simon le Magicien dans les Pseudo-Clémentines," *Laval Théologique et Philosophique* 37 (2001): 514–16, 19.

dered fit for instruction through apparitions (cf. Gal 1:11–12)?... How are we to believe you, when you tell us that he appeared to you? How is it that he appeared to you, when you entertain opinions contrary to his teaching?[84] If you were seen and taught by him and became his apostle, even for a single hour, then proclaim his utterances, interpret his teaching, love his apostles, and do not contend with me who accompanied with him (*emoi tô suggenomenô autô mê machou*)! For you now stand in direct opposition to me (*pros... enantios anthestêkas moi*) – who am a firm rock, the foundation of the church (cf. Matt 16:18)!... If you say that I am 'condemned' (*kategnôsmenous*; Gal 2:11), you bring an accusation against God, who revealed the Christ to me... (*Hom.* 17.19.1–6)

Ferdinand Christian Baur, Gerd Lüdemann, and others have proposed that this passage was meant to counter Paul's claim to be an apostle by virtue of his vision of the risen Christ (e.g., Gal 1:12; 1 Cor 15:8–10; also Acts 9:3–20).[85] If so, then the association with Simon may prove particularly significant, hinting at a view of Paul's heirs as truly "heretics."[86]

By contrast, Eusebius readily accepts Paul's claims. For him, in fact, it is a mark of Paul's preeminence that he became an apostle "'not of men neither through men, but by the revelation of Jesus Christ himself (*di' apokalupseôs d' autou Iêsou Christou*) and of God the Father who raised him from the dead' (Gal 1:1)... being made worthy of the call by a vision and by a voice which was uttered in a revelation from heaven (*di' optasias kai tês kata tên apokalupsin ouraniou phonês aksiôtheis tês klêseôs*)" (*Hist. eccl.* II 1.14).

In his account of apostolic history, moreover, Eusebius privileges the Pauline version of events, even to the detriment of Peter. In books I–II of the *Ecclesiastical History*, Eusebius follows the New Testament literature

---

[84] Lüdemann further suggests that the false gospel referenced in *Hom.* 2.17 is Paul's gospel (*Opposition*, 185; so too Strecker, *Judenchristentum,* 188–90).

[85] E.g., F. C. Baur, "Die Christuspartei in der korinthischen Gemeide, der Gegensatz des petrinischen and paulischen Christentums in der alten Kirche, der Apostel Petrus in Rom," *Tübinger Zeitschrift für Theologie* 5 (1831): 116; Lüdemann, *Opposition*, 185–88. Inasmuch as Baur followed nineteenth-century Pseudo-Clementine scholarship in dating the *Homilies* to the second century C.E. (see n. 36 above), this passage was central to his famous theory that the early church was split into Petrine and Pauline factions. For the history of research, see Lüdemann, *Opposition*, 1–32, 303; Côté, "Fonction," 515.

[86] Whether or not the tradition, in its present form, is anti-Pauline in any pointed sense, it functions in the *Homilies* as part of the overarching defense of an epistemology rooted in succession directly from Jesus' disciples – a point rightly stressed by Kelley, *Knowledge*, 135–38. Notably, the critique of knowledge gained from dreams and visions also resonates with debates about prophecy in the early fourth century; see P. Athanassiadi, "Dreams, Theurgy and Freelance Divination: The Testimony of Iamblichus," *Journal of Roman Studies* 83 (1993): 115–30. Here, as elsewhere, the authors/redactors of the *Homilies* may take full advantage of the polysemy that the novelistic genre permits, taking aim at multiple enemies.

in granting Peter a central place in the earliest church and a leading role among the other apostles. When he turns to describe the worldwide spread of Christianity in book III, however, it is Paul who looms large. As in Gal 2:7–10, Paul is credited with the mission to the Gentiles, while Peter's activities are almost solely limited to Jews.[87]

Book III opens with a summary account of the apostles' respective roles in spreading Christianity, articulated in explicit contrast to the purported decline of the Jews (III 1.1). Eusebius here celebrates the dispersion of Christ's apostles and disciples "throughout the known world" (*ef' hapasan... tên oikoumenên*): Thomas in Parthia, Andrew in Scythia, John in Asia (III 1.1). Following 1 Pet 1:1, he states that Peter preached to "the Jews of the Diaspora" (*tois (ek) diasporas Ioudaiois*) in Pontus, Galatia, Bithynia, Cappadocia, and Asia (III 1.2).[88] The account, however, culminates with Paul. Following Rom 15:19, Eusebius credits the apostle with "preaching the Gospel of Christ from Jerusalem to Illyricum" (III 1.3).

Also telling are the parallel descriptions of Paul and Peter in *Hist. eccl.* III 4.1–2. Here, Eusebius appeals again to Rom 15:19, together with the witness of Luke, to assert that Paul "preached to the Gentiles and laid the foundations of the churches from Jerusalem even unto Illyricum" (III 4.1). Peter, by contrast, is said to have "preached Christ and taught the doctrine of the new covenant to those of the circumcision (*tous ek peritomês*)," and he is described as writing "to the Hebrews in the Diaspora (*tois ek Hebraiôn ousin en diaspora*) in Pontus, Galatia, Cappadocia, Asia, and Bithynia" (III 4.2).[89] Although the activities of the two are paralleled, Paul is celebrated as the apostle responsible for Christianity's worldwide spread, while Peter is associated with the early mission to the Jews.[90]

In effect, Eusebius repeatedly elevates Paul as the one responsible for the worldwide spread of Christianity, which – in his presentation – is synonymous with its spread among Gentiles outside of Judaea. To this, Peter's preaching pales in significance; his mission is presented as a relic of the pre-Pauline pattern of preaching within Judaea and to Diaspora Jews (II 1.8).

---

[87] The sole exception is *Hist. eccl.* II 3.3, which follows Acts 10–11. Even there, however, Peter's activities remain geographically limited to Judaea.

[88] I.e., inasmuch as 1 Pet 1:1 is addressed to the "exiles of the dispersion" (*parepidêmois diasporas*) in these lands.

[89] Note also *Hist. eccl.* II 7.1 where Peter is said to have met Philo of Alexandria when the two were in Rome.

[90] Contrast Irenaeus, *Adv. haer.* 3.1.1, where Matthew is associated with evangelizing Jews through his Gospel, while "Peter and Paul were preaching at Rome and laying the foundations of the church."

Of course, Peter must be permitted some role in authorizing the succession of bishops in the church of Rome. Even in this role, however, Eusebius consistently pairs him with Paul. Both Peter and Paul are associated with Rome by means of their martyrdoms (II 25.5, 8; III 1.2–3). In *Hist. eccl.* III 2.1, for instance, Eusebius presents Linus' rise to the Roman episcopacy as occurring after the martyrdoms of Paul and Peter. Rather than describing Linus as Peter's successor, however, Eusebius takes the opportunity to note his connection with Paul, associating the bishop with the figure of the same name in 2 Tim 4:21.[91] When he mentions Linus again in III 4.9, it is in the context of a list of Paul's companions; even though Linus is here called Peter's successor, the connection with Paul remains primary. Accordingly, Eusebius refers to later bishops of Rome, not as the successors of Peter, but rather as those "who held the episcopate there after Paul and Peter" (III 11.2; also IV 1.1).[92]

Of special relevance, for our purposes, is Eusebius' approach to Clement of Rome.[93] The first reference to Clement in the *Ecclesiastical History* occurs in the context of his summary of early Christians associated with Paul (III 4.6–11). After discussing Luke, Crescens, and Linus, he adds that "Clement too, who became the third bishop of the church of the Romans, was Paul's co-laborer (*sunergos*) and fellow-soldier (*sunathlêtês*), as he himself testifies" (III 4.9), identifying Clement with the man of the same name mentioned by Paul in Phil 4:3.[94] He repeats this claim in III 15, when recounting the early succession of bishops at Rome. Whereas the *Homilies* purports to preserve Clement's first-person account of his travels with Peter, Eusebius aligns the famous Roman bishop solely with Paul.[95]

### *"Orthodoxy" and "Heresy"*

We also find interesting points of contrast and comparison in their respective accounts of the rivalry between Peter and Simon Magus. This rivalry

[91] I.e. following Irenaeus, *Adv. haer.* 3.3.3.

[92] Cf. *Hist. eccl.* III 36.2, where Ignatius is called the "chosen bishop of Antioch, second in succession to Peter." Note also the precedent of Irenaeus, who describes the Roman church as "founded and organized" by Peter and Paul (*Adv. haer.* 3.3.2). Eusebius seems to resolve the problem of the apparent conflict between Peter and Paul by identifying the "Cephas" of Gal 2:11 with someone other than Peter (*Hist. eccl.* I 12.2); he does not explain Acts 15.

[93] Compare Irenaeus, *Adv. haer.* 3.3.3, in which Clement is associated with the apostles in general, rather than any specific apostle.

[94] In this identification, Eusebius likely follows Origen, *In Joann.* 1.29.

[95] Tertullian, by contrast, describes Clement as Peter's immediate successor as bishop of Rome in *Prescription against Heretics* 32.

is central to the plot of the *Homilies*.[96] Throughout the novel, Peter's missionary travels are occasioned by the need to chase Simon. The apostle scurries from city to city along the eastern coastline of the Mediterranean, seeking to correct the errors spread by the "heretic" and to force him into public debates. Whereas Simon lures his listeners into idolatry and moral corruption, Peter preaches chastity, piety, and ritual purity (e.g., 3.2–4; 7.2–4, 8). Whereas Simon proclaims multiple divinities, Peter defends the unity and goodness of the One God who created the cosmos (e.g., 2.22; 3.38–40; 18.1–4).

In the *Homilies*, this rivalry is presented as part of a broader historical pattern, namely, the rule of syzygies. For every true prophet, we are here told that God sends a false one in advance: Cain came before Abel, Ishmael before Isaac, Esau before Jacob, Aaron before Moses, and John the Baptist before Jesus (2.16–17, 33; 7.2). Likewise for Simon and Peter:

> It is possible, following this order (*tê taxei*), to perceive to which Simon belongs, who came before me to the Gentiles (*ho pro emou eis ta ethnê prôtos elthôn*), and to which I belong – I who have come after him and have come in on him as light on darkness, as knowledge on ignorance, as healing on disease. (*Hom.* 2.17)

When Simon and Peter compete to persuade "pagans," they thus act as agents of true and false prophesy, taking up the perennial battle between the two. Just as Peter learns and transmits the truth, by virtue of his connection to the True Prophet Jesus, so Simon stands in a long line of error. According to the *Homilies*, "heresy" always precedes "orthodoxy."

By comparison, Eusebius' treatment of Simon and Peter is quite brief. Interestingly, however, it integrates many of the same elements found in the *Homilies*: Simon is the "author of all heresy," and his error is marked by the promotion of idolatry, sacrifice, and libations as well as by his own desire to be worshipped (*Hist. eccl.* II 13.6; cf. *Hom.* 2.21). And, even as Eusebius stresses that "heresy" was not yet a real threat in the apostolic age (II 14.2), he nevertheless depicts the conflict between Simon and Peter as a battle between divine and demonic forces:

> At that time, the evil power (*ponêra dunamis*) which hates all that is good and plots against the salvation of humankind raised up Simon… to be a great opponent of great men, our Saviour's inspired apostles. Nevertheless, divine and celestial grace (*hê theia kai huperouranios charis*) worked with its ministers, by their advent and presence speedily extinguishing the flames of the evil one before they could spread… (*Hist. eccl.* II 14.1–2)

As in the *Homilies*, Simon flees, and Peter gives chase:

---

[96] See further Côté, *Thème*, 22–59.

> The sorcerer (*goês*) of whom we have been speaking – having been struck as though his mind's eye by a divine miraculous flash of light when earlier, in Judaea, his evil machinations had been exposed by the apostle Peter – promptly undertook a very long journey overseas from East to West.... (*Hist. eccl.* II 14.4)

These similarities have led Robert Grant to propose that Eusebius here draws on an early version of the Pseudo-Clementine novel.[97] If he is correct, then the points of contrast with the *Homilies* prove all the more significant.

In the *Ecclesiastical History*, the challenge posed by Simon is the impetus for Peter's journey to Rome, whereby he brings the wisdom of the East to the West and establishes Rome as a centre from which Christian truth then radiates (*Hist. eccl.* II 14.5–6; cf. *Hom.* 1.16); Eusebius further claims that Peter's preaching in Rome is preserved in the Gospel of Mark (II 15.1).

In the *Homilies*, Simon's actions similarly motivate Peter's journeys, but Clement is the one who records his preachings (*Hom.* 1.1; also *Ep. Clem.* 19–20), and Rome proves less central. Clement hails from Rome, and his interest in Jesus is piqued when rumors reach Rome and when he sees an unnamed preacher proclaiming the message of eternal life (*Hom.* 1.6–7). To learn the truth, however, Clement must travel to its source in Judaea (1.7). The action of the novel is centered on the port cities of Palestine and Syria: Caesaria, Tyre, Sidon, Berytus, Byblos, Tripolis, Aradus, Laodicea. Consistent with the probable Syrian provenance of the *Homilies*, Peter's journeys are oriented towards – and culminate in – Antioch (11.36; 12.1, 24; 14.12; 16.1; 20.11, 13, 18, 20–21, 23). In the *Homilies*, this is the city where Peter bests Simon and where he has resolved "to remain some length of time" (12.24). Whereas Eusebius refracts the apostolic past through his belief in the centrality of Rome and the Roman Empire for Christian history, the *Homilies* privileges Syria.[98]

In addition, the *Homilies* and *Ecclesiastical History* offer very different assessments of "heresy," its appearance, and its power. Eusebius famously asserts that "orthodoxy" precedes "heresy." He depicts the former as the obvious truth, proclaimed in one voice by the apostles and all their true heirs; "heresies" are derivative, dividing, and ultimately impotent (esp. IV 7.13).[99]

---

[97] Grant, *Eusebius*, 87. I.e. presumably the Pseudo-Clementine *Grundschrift*. Cf. Strecker, *Judenchristentum*, 28, 84, 268.

[98] Eusebius' dismissive approach to Syriac Christianity, both within and beyond the Roman Empire, is noted by Brock, "Eusebius," 212.

[99] On the heresiologial comments in the *Ecclesiastical History*, together with their various sources, see e.g. Grant, *Eusebius*, 84–96; Barnes, *Constantine*, 133–35.

By contrast, the *Homilies* depicts "heresy" as a dire challenge to "orthodoxy": not only does error precede truth, but the two are mirror images of one another.[100] Moreover, it can be difficult to determine the difference between them – not least because "heresy" is often the more popular of the two (*Hom.* 2.18).

Who, then, is here imagined as "heretical"? Consistent with the apostolic narrative setting of the *Homilies*, no reference is made to any specific post-apostolic group. Rather, the nature of "heresy" is sketched solely by means of the conflate character of Simon.[101] In his speeches, he is credited with a number of Marcionite beliefs.[102] At the same time, however, he is also associated with Samaritan anti-Judaism, Alexandrian philosophy, and Greco-Egyptian "magic" (e.g., 2.21–26; 5.2), and chief among his followers are an astrologer, an Alexandrian grammarian, and an Athenian Epicurean (e.g., 4.6). Consequently, as Côté has demonstrated, the *Homilies* departs from earlier traditions to stress Simon's link to Hellenism.[103] Within the *Homilies*, the figure of Simon may thus serve, not just to counter Marcionites, but also to establish the Gentile genealogy of "heresy" and to throw doubt on the "orthodoxy" of all Christians who draw on Hellenistic learning.[104]

### *"Jewish Christianity"*

For the authors/redactors of the *Homilies*, a term such as "Jewish Christianity" would have likely seemed highly redundant. The *Homilies*, as we have seen, depicts the apostolic age as an extension of biblical and Jewish history, marked by the opening of a parallel line of salvation for the Gentiles. Perhaps not surprisingly, then, the terms "Christian" and "Christianity" are never used in the *Homilies*. The text speaks of Jews (and Pharisees in particular) as heirs to the teachings of the prophet Moses. Peter and Barnabus refer to their own Jewish ethnicity and self-identify with Jews and Israel (e.g., 1.13; 3.4; 9.20). Even when referring to Clement and other Gentile followers of Jesus, the text refrains from distinguishing them as "Christians." Most often, they are termed "God-fearers" (*theosebeis*), the

[100] On the parallels between Peter and Simon, see Côté, *Thème*, 23–29.

[101] That the Pseudo-Clementine Simon is a conflate character, not to be identified with any single group or figure, has been convincingly established by D. Côté, "Fonction," 513–23; see also Edwards, "Clementina," 462.

[102] A. Salles, "Simon le magicien ou Marcion?" *Vigiliae christianae* 12 (1958) 197–224.

[103] Côté, *Thème*, 195–96.

[104] I here summarize the results of my more focused inquiries into the issue in "Heresiology" and "From Judaism and Hellenism."

well-known label that we find elsewhere applied to Gentile sympathizers with Judaism.[105]

Moreover, in *Homilies* 11.16, the term "Jew" is redefined so as to include Jewish followers of Moses as well as Gentile followers of Jesus:

> If anyone acts impiously, he is not pious. In the same way, if a foreigner keeps the Law, he is a Jew (*ean ho allophulos ton nomon praksê, Ioudaios estin*), while he who does not is a Greek (*mê praksas de Hellên*). For the Jew, believing in God, keeps the Law (*ho gar Ioudaios pisteuôn theô poiei ton nomon*). (*Hom.* 11.16)

The category of "Jew" here denotes anyone who follows the Law that God laid out for them. As a result, the category of "apostle" is not a subset or paradigm of "Christian"; rather, it serves to mark adherence to the true religion proclaimed by Moses and Jesus, in contrast to polytheistic and idolatrous "pagan" religions and the "heresies" that use Christ's name to promote false beliefs and impure practices.

If Christianity and Judaism appear to be different, the reader of the *Homilies* is assured that this is only because God chose to hide the prophet of one from the followers of the other (8.6). Even as the *Homilies* thus acknowledges that most Jews and Christians are blind to Christianity's true nature as the divine disclosure of Judaism to other nations, it depicts those who understand as specially blessed. Through the mouth of the Jewish apostle Peter, the authors/redactors reveal that no one is richer in wisdom than the few who embrace both Moses and Jesus:

> If anyone has been thought worthy to recognize by himself both (i.e. Moses and Jesus) as preaching one doctrine (*kataksiôtheiê tous amphoterous epignônai hôs mias didaskalias hup' autôn kekrugmenês*), that one has been counted rich in God, understanding both the old things as new in time and the new things as old." (*Hom.* 8.7; cf. *Rec.* 4.5)

Through Peter, they thus propose that there are two paths to salvation, and the two paths are actually one. Jews can be saved as Jews; Christians can be saved as Christians; and "Jewish Christians" are the best of all.

By contrast, Eusebius promotes an image of Christianity as a new/old *ethnos* (e.g., 1.1.9) with a history and religion distinct from those of the Jews. To this effort, Jewish converts to Christianity would seem to pose a problem. Not only does their combination of Christian belief and Jewish ethnicity undermine his claims concerning the historical and spiritual disjunction between Judaism and Abrahamic/Christian religion, but the very fact of their belief in Jesus as messiah might speak against his theory

---

[105] E.g. J. Reynolds and R. Tannebaum, *Jews and God-Fearers at Aphrodisias: Greek Inscriptions with Commentary* (Cambridge, U.K.: Cambridge University Press, 1987), 48–66.

that God brought the destruction of the Temple and other calamities to punish the Jews for rejecting Jesus and his apostles.[106]

Arguably, Eusebius solves such problems through his account of the Jerusalem church, on the one hand, and his description of the Ebionites, on the other. Both accounts echo his treatment of Judaism in poignant ways. And, in each case, issues of succession are emphasized.

We noted above how Eusebius stresses the discontinuity in Jewish history in multiple ways, extricating Abrahamic religion from Judaism and stressing the breaks in the lines of Jewish prophetic, royal, and priestly succession. Similarly, in his description of the Jerusalem church, there is a striking over-determination in the assertion of discontinuity. When discussing the first Jewish revolt against Rome (III 5–8), Eusebius famously claims that the Christians of Jerusalem left the city for Pella prior to the Roman siege of 70 C.E:

> Furthermore, the people of the Jerusalem church (*tou laou tês en Hierosolumois ekklêseias*), by means of a prophesy given by revelation to acceptable persons there, were ordered to leave the city before the war began and settle in a town in Peraea called Pella. When those who believed in Christ from Jerusalem migrated (*tôn eis Christon pepisteukotôn apo tês Hierousalêm metôkismenôn*), it was as if holy men had utterly abandoned the royal metropolis of the Jews and the entire Jewish land, and the judgment of God (*hê ek theo dikê*) at last overtook them for their crimes against Christ and his apostles, completely blotting that wicked generation from among men. (*Hist. eccl.* III 5.3)[107]

Following this passage, we might infer that there was no Christian presence in Jerusalem between the first Jewish War and the city's repopulation by Gentile Christians. Yet, when Eusebius later recounts the succession of bishops at Jerusalem (IV 5.1–4), he lists its "Jewish Christian" bishops up to the time of the Bar Kokhba revolt:

---

[106] That the problem of "Jewish Christianity" was a "live" issue for Eusebius may be confirmed by several instances in which he seems to have changed his mind on related topics; see Grant, *Eusebius*, 15.

[107] The historicity of the tradition has been hotly debated. See e.g. J. Munck, "Jewish Christianity in Post-Apostolic Times," *New Testament Studies* 6 (1959): 103–4; M. Simon, "La migration à Pella: Légende ou réalité?" *Recherches de science religieuse* 60 (1972): 37–54; G. Lüdemann, "The Successors of Pre-70 Jerusalem Christianity: A Critical Evaluation of the Pella Tradition," in *Jewish and Christian Self-Definition*, vol. 1, *The Shaping of Christianity in the Second and Third Centuries* (ed. E. P. Sanders; Philadelphia: Fortress, 1980), 161–73; J. Verheyden, "The Flight of Christians to Pella," *Ephemerides theologicae lovanienses* 66 (1990): 368–84; J. Wehnert, "Die Auswanderung der Jerusalemer Christen nach Pella – historische Faktum oder theologische Konstruktion?" *Zeitschrift für Kirchengeschichte* 102 (1991): 321–55. For our present purposes, its accuracy proves less significant than its function in Eusebius' depiction of the fate of apostolic "Jewish Christianity."

All are said to have been Hebrews (*Hebraious*) in origin, who had received the knowledge of Christ legitimately (*tên gnôsin tou Christou gnêsiôs katadeksasthai*), with the result that those in a position to decide such matters judged them worthy of the episcopal office. For at that time their whole church consisted of Hebrew believers (*eks Hebraiôn pistôn*) who had continued from apostolic times (*apo tôn apostolôn*) down to the later siege in which the Jews, after revolting a second time from the Romans, were overwhelmed in a full-scale war. (*Hist. eccl.* IV 5.2)

In contrast to *Hist. eccl.* III 5.3, this passage assumes a Christian presence in Jerusalem after 70 C.E. Here, Eusebius argues that it was the Bar Kokhba Revolt (IV 6.1–3) that marked the break in the apostolic continuity of the Jerusalem church:

When in this way the city (i.e. Jerusalem) had been emptied of the Jewish nation (*eis erêmian tou Ioudaiôn ethnous*) and had suffered the total destruction of its ancient inhabitants (*pantelê te phthoran tôn palai oikêtorôn*), it was colonized by a different race (*elthousês eks allophulou te genous sunoikistheisês*) and the Roman city which subsequently arose changed its name and was called Aelia, in honor of the emperor Aelius Hadrian. And as the church there was now composed of Gentiles (*tês autothi ekklêsias eks ethnôn sugkrotêtheisês*), the first one to assume the government of it, after the bishops of the circumcision (*meta tous ek peritomês episkopous*), was Marcus. (*Hist. eccl.* IV 6.4).

To make this argument, Eusebius must posit that the life-spans of Jerusalem's first fifteen bishops were all extremely brief (IV 5.1). Nevertheless, he stresses that the "Jewish Christian" succession at Jerusalem was lost in 135 C.E. From that point onwards – according to Eusebius – the bishops at Jerusalem were all Gentiles (see V 12).

Whereas Eusebius' account of the flight to Pella served to extricate the fate of Jerusalem's Christians from the fate of the Jews, the list of Jerusalemite bishops conflates them: not only was the break in their succession caused by the purportedly deserved calamities upon the Jews, but it resulted in the replacement of Jews by Gentiles, simultaneously in the city of Jerusalem and within the Jerusalem church.[108] From a chronological perspective, the details of these two accounts of the Jerusalem church are contradictory. The two accounts, however, work together to make one point

[108] The limitation of the influence of the Jerusalem church may also reflect Eusebius' general tendency, in his early writings, to downplay the sanctity of Jerusalem, associate it with Jewish failure, and deny it any central place in Christian thought – as no doubt spurred, at least in part, by the ecclesiastical rivalry between Jerusalem and Caesarea in his own time. See further P. W. L. Walker, *Holy City, Holy Places? Christian Attitudes to Jerusalem and the Holy Land in the Fourth Century* (Oxford: Clarendon, 1990), 51–92.

very clear: the Jerusalem church was marred by discontinuities, all caused by its geographical and ethnic associations with the Jews.

Furthermore, through his descriptions of the sect of the Ebionites (III 27; V 8.10; VI 17), Eusebius effectively distinguishes the apostolic "Jewish Christianity" of the Jerusalem church from all forms of "Jewish Christianity" that came afterwards.[109] In second-hand sources like the heresiologies of Epiphanius and the sermons of John Chrysostom – as well as in first-hand sources like the *Homilies* – we find hints of continued efforts, by some late antique Christians, to combine Jewish and Christian identities in ways that differed from the combination that later came to be defined as "Christian."[110] For Eusebius, however, the Ebionites emblematize the "heretical" nature of all such efforts.

For Eusebius, "Jewish Christianity" is numbered among the many and diverse "heretical" corruptions of the single and unchanging "orthodoxy" that was established already in the apostolic age – an "orthodoxy" that Eusebius defines with primary appeal to the apostle Paul and to the Gentile Christians who came after him. In Eusebius' schema, Ebionites are actually the heirs, not to the apostolic "Jewish Christianity" of the Jerusalem Church, but rather to the "heresy" of Simon Magus. Unlike the Jews and the Jerusalem church, the Ebionites are granted participation in an unbroken line of succession. This, however, is a line of error, which runs straight back to Simon by means of Menander (III 26–27).

As in the *Homilies*, Simon is thus placed in a genealogy of error that parallels and threatens the "orthodoxy" vouchsafed by apostolic succession. Whereas the *Homilies* uses this trope to associate "heresy" with Hellenism, Eusebius draws the lines of "heretical" succession so to include, amongst Simon's heirs, all Christ-believers who reject Paul and observe the Torah (III 27).

---

[109] The continuity between the Jerusalem church and post-apostolic forms of "Jewish Christianity" remains a topic of debate. For different assessments, see e.g. Schoeps, *Theologie*; J. Munck, "Primitive Jewish Christianity and late Jewish Christianity: Continuation or Rupture?" in *Aspects du Judéo-Christianisme: Colloque de Strasbourg, 23–25 avril 1964* (Paris: Presses Universitaires de France, 1965), 77–94; J. Taylor, "The Phenomenon of Early Jewish-Christianity: Reality or Scholarly Invention?" *Vigiliae christianae* 44 (1990): 313–34.

[110] R. L. Wilken, *John Chrysostom and the Jews: Rhetoric and Reality in the Late Fourth Century* (Berkeley: University of California Press, 1983), 66–94; J. G. Gager, "Jews, Christians, and the Dangerous Ones in Between," in *Interpretation in Religion* (ed. S. Biderman and B. Scharfstein; Leiden: Brill, 1992), 249–57; Reed, "Jewish Christianity," 193, 227–30. With regard to "Jewish Christians," S. G. Wilson concludes that "the evidence seems to point neither to their rapid marginalization nor to their dominance after 70 C.E., but rather to their survival as a significant minority"; *Related Strangers: Jews and Christians, 70–170 C.E.* (Minneapolis: Fortress, 1995), 158.

## History and Counter-history

In modern historiography, it is Eusebius' image of the past that has prevailed. As Arthur Droge notes, the reception of the *Ecclesiastical History* has been largely marked by the embrace of his overall picture of Christian history:

> From the publication of the *Ecclesiastical History* down to the modern era the history of early Christianity has been written and rewritten in the terms established by Eusebius. Not until the publication in 1934 of Walter Bauer's *Rechtgläubigkeit und Ketzerei im ältesten Christentum* was the Eusebian view of church history finally deconstructed and reconfigured. Though Eusebius' accuracy and veracity as a historian had been challenged by numerous scholars, from antiquity to the present, his description of the contours of early Christian history had generally been endorsed.[111]

Of course, modern scholars of early Christianity have had no choice but to depend on Eusebius. For a number of figures, events, and texts, he is our main or only source. Hence, it is perhaps not surprising that many of his opinions have become absorbed, naturalized, and internalized in the scholarly discourse about the development of Christianity. To this day, a number of his overarching categories and concerns are arguably embricated in the field of Patristics – embodied in its disciplinary boundaries and reinforced by the trajectories of training and research.[112]

With regard to "heresy," "paganism," and Judaism, some efforts have been made to move beyond Eusebius' meta-narratives. Just as Walter Bauer shed doubt on the Eusebian view of "heresy" as secondary and derivative,[113] so Marcel Simon challenged the portrayal of post-70 Judaism

[111] Droge, "Apologetic Dimensions," 506. On the late antique, medieval, and early modern reception of the *Ecclesiastical History* – and especially the resurgence of its influence after the Protestant Reformation – see Momigliano, *Classical Foundations*, 141–52; G. F. Chesnut, "Eusebius, Augustine, Orosius, and the Late Patristic and Medieval Christian Historians," in *Eusebius, Christianity, and Judaism*, 687–713; I. Backus, "Calvin's judgment of Eusebius of Caesarea: An analysis," *Sixteenth Century Journal* 22 (1991): 419–37.

[112] Brock notes that "(t)he all pervasive influence of Eusebius has meant that the existence of a third cultural tradition, represented by Syriac Christianity, has consistently been neglected or marginalized by church historians, both ancient and modern" ("Eusebius," 212; so too A. H. Becker, "Beyond the Spatial and Temporal Limes: Questioning the 'Parting of the Ways' Outside the Roman Empire," in *Ways that Never Parted*, esp. 373–74). Arguably, Eusebius' depiction of Judaism has similarly helped to excuse generations of Patristics scholars from the need to study the literature and languages of late antique Judaism.

[113] Bauer's alternative account of "orthodoxy" and "heresy" is arguably founded on his interpretation of the *Ecclesiastical History* as an apologetic account with many

as a religion in decline.[114] The insights of the former have been debated and developed, particularly in the wake of the discoveries at Nag Hammadi,[115] while the insights of the latter are still being refined, not least because of increased interaction between scholars of Judaism and Christianity.[116] Likewise, the continued vitality – and, indeed, resurgence – of late antique "paganism" has been stressed by Peter Brown and others, concurrent with the emergence of "Late Antiquity" as a lively subfield of History.[117]

With respect to "Jewish Christianity," however, Eusebian models still remain regnant. It is perhaps telling, for instance, that when Bauer deconstructed Eusebius' depiction of "orthodoxy" and "heresy," he neglected to consider those who saw Jewish practice as consonant with belief in Christ. Even in the revised edition of *Rechtgläubigkeit und Ketzerei im ältesten Christentum*, "Jewish Christianity" earns only an Appendix.[118] Likewise, even when Simon mounted a concerted challenge to traditional views of Judaism's post-70 decline, he still dismissed "Jewish Christians" as ossified relics of the apostolic past.[119]

Although the bulk of our evidence for "Jewish Christianity" comes from the late third, fourth, and fifth centuries C.E., most scholars persist in characterizing its post-apostolic fate as one of deterioration and/or irrelev-

---

deliberate omissions and misrepresentations; *Rechtgläubigkeit und Ketzerei im ältesten Christentum* (Tübingen: Mohr, 1934; rev. ed. by G. Strecker, 1964), e.g. 135–49.

[114] M. Simon, *Verus Israel: A Study of the Relations between Christians and Jews in the Roman Empire (AD 135–425)* (trans. H. McKeating; London: Littman, 1996).

[115] See e.g. G. Strecker, "The Reception of the Book" (rev. R. A. Kraft), in W. Bauer, *Orthodoxy and Heresy in Earliest Christianity* (trans. and ed. by R. A. Kraft and G. Kroedel with a team from PSCO; Philadelphia: Fortress, 1971), 286–316; D. J. Harrington, "The Reception of Walter Bauer's *Orthodoxy and Heresy in Earliest Christianity* during the Last Decade," *Harvard Theological Review* 73 (1980): 289–98; K. L. King, *What is Gnosticism?* (Cambridge, Mass.: Harvard University Press, 2003), esp. 110–15.

[116] See e.g., A. I. Baumgarten, "Marcel Simon's *Verus Israel* as a Contribution to Jewish History," *Harvard Theological Review* 92 (1999): 465–78, and the essays collected in Limor and Stroumsa, eds., *Contra Iudaeos*, and Becker and Reed, eds., *Ways that Never Parted*.

[117] See e.g., P. Brown, *The World of Late Antiquity, AD 150–750* (London: Thames & Hudson, 1971), 70–95; G. Fowden, "Bishops and Temples in the Eastern Roman Empire 320–425," *Journal of Theological Studies* 29 (1978): 53–78; R. MacMullen, *Paganism in the Roman Empire* (New Haven: Yale University Press, 1981), esp. 62–72; R. Lane Fox, *Pagans and Christians* (New York: Knopf, 1987); P. Chuvin, *A Chronicle of the Last Pagans* (trans. B. A. Archer; Cambridge, Mass.: Harvard University Press, 1990).

[118] I.e., G. Strecker, "The Problem of Jewish Christianity," in *Orthodoxy and Heresy*, 241–85.

[119] Simon, *Verus Israel*, 238–44.

ance.[120] And, just as Eusebius frames the story of "Jewish Christianity" as a tale of a first-century phenomenon that died with the rise of the Gentile church, so research on "Jewish Christians" still remains the domain of specialists in the New Testament and Christian Origins. The phenomenon remains little discussed in research on Late Antiquity.

Somewhat surprisingly, post-modern studies have followed much the same path. In recent years, scholars have increasingly turned our attention to the rhetorical and discursive features of our late antique Christian literature. Inspired by post-structural approaches to language and post-colonialist approaches to power, they have read the writings of Eusebius and other Church Fathers – not as unmediated descriptions of a fully-formed "Christianity" with an ancient and obvious "orthodoxy" – but rather as part of the very process of constructing and promoting these categories and concepts.[121]

Such approaches have had exciting results, which have greatly enriched our understanding of Patristic literature, pushing us to read these texts with new attention to their gaps and silences as well as to the power struggles that their rhetorics can hide. At the same time, however, such approaches have sometimes served to re-inscribe one of the most trenchant biases in the field of Patristics, namely, the privileging of retrospectively "orthodox" writings.[122] If earlier research had accepted Eusebius' own claim to be an objective archivist of the history of Christian "orthodoxy," more recent studies have tended to frame him as one of its architects – those who are ultimately responsible for creating, by means of their powerful rhetorics, "Christianity" as we know it. And, whereas earlier scholarship had naively accepted the negative assessment of "Jewish Christianity" by Eusebius, Epiphanius, and others, such new approaches often relegate "Jewish Christians" to the role of the suppressed, treating our evidence for "Jewish Christianity" merely as an echo of the varied Christian voices that

[120] E.g., J. Carleton Paget, "Jewish Christianity," in *The Cambridge History of Judaism*, vol. 3, *The Early Roman Period* (ed. W. Horbury, W. D. Davies, and J. Sturdy; Cambridge, U.K.: Cambridge University Press, 1999), 750–52; A. J. Saldarini, "The Social World of Christian Jews and Jewish Christians," in *Religious and Ethnic Communities*, 154.

[121] On this important recent shift in the field of Patristics see Clark, *History, Theory, Text*, as well as the essays collected in D. B. Martin and P. C. Miller, eds., *The Cultural Turn in Late Ancient Studies: Gender, Asceticism, and Historiography* (Durham: Duke University Press, 2005).

[122] In this too, the influence of Eusebius is perhaps not irrelevant, inasmuch as his efforts contributed to the elevation of a select group of early Christian authors and philosophers (including, perhaps most strikingly, the much embattled Origen) to the status of "Church Fathers."

were silenced, excluded, and disenfranchised by literate elites in Late Antiquity.

Daniel Boyarin, for instance, often cites the Pseudo-Clementines as evidence for the permeability between "Jewish" and "Christian" traditions "on the ground."[123] For him, however, this evidence forms part of the backdrop for the assertion that "Judaism" and "Christianity" were largely products of hegemonic discourse.[124] As a result, he disembodies second-hand statements about "Jewish Christian" groups, like the Ebionites, from any connection to social reality.[125] Accepting that the religious landscape of Roman Palestine had long been devoid of any actual "Jewish Christians," he reads these figures as a discursive embodiment of the fear of hybridity, produced – as if by thought experiment – by elite efforts to articulate a pure Christianity.[126]

In light of the influence of Eusebius and the *Ecclesiastical History*, it may indeed be tempting to dismiss the *Homilies* as merely a remnant of the variety of lived forms of Christianity disenfranchised by elite discourses of self-definition. Yet, as we have seen, the authors/redactors of the *Homilies* are themselves engaged with the problem of how to construct "orthodoxy." They are hardly passive subjects of this discourse. Rather, they seek to engage as participants.

Moreover, the reception-history of the *Homilies* belies any effort to assert the isolation or marginality of their contribution. The *Homilies* was translated into Syriac soon after its composition.[127] In the East, it circulated

---

[123] E.g., D. Boyarin, *Dying for God: Martyrdom and the Making of Judaism and Christianity* (Stanford: Stanford University Press, 1999), 29–30; idem, *Border Lines: The Partition of Judeo-Christianity* (Philadelphia: University of Pennsylvania Press, 2004), 43.

[124] Boyarin, *Border Lines, passim.*

[125] I do not mean to suggest, of course, that we should take Patristic comments about "Ebionites" simply at face value. More plausibly, Eusebius and others apply the traditional heresiological rubric of "Ebionism" to a range of different groups in their own time, who combined elements of Jewish and Christian identity in ways that jarred with their own understandings of "Christianity"; see A. F. J. Klijn and G. J. Reinink, *Patristic Evidences for Jewish-Christian Sects* (Novum Testamentum Supplements 36; Leiden: Brill, 1973) 43. Accordingly, the relationship between the Pseudo-Clementines and Ebionites is likely indirect.

[126] Boyarin, *Border Lines*, 207–9. For a similar critique of Boyarin's reading of our evidence for "Jewish Christianity," see C. Fonrobert, "Jewish Christians, Judaizers, and Anti-Judaism," in *A People's History of Christianity*, vol. 2, *Late Ancient Christianity* (ed. V. Burrus; Minneapolis: Fortress, 2005), 253–54.

[127] A Syriac translation of portions of the *Homilies* (≈ 10–14) survives, together with portions of the *Recognitions* (1–4), in a manuscript from 411 C.E. (British Museum add. 12150). For the text, see W. Frankenberg, *Die syrischen Clementinen mit griechishem*

in its original Greek as well as in multiple epitomes, which were translated into Arabic and other languages.[128] Quotations from the *Homilies* are also found in the writings of Byzantine chronographers.[129] In addition, the *Homilies* shaped views of the apostolic age in the West, in an indirect fashion, due to the reworking of the Pseudo-Clementine novel in the *Recognitions* and its Latin translation by Rufinus – the same translator responsible for redacting and translating Eusebius' *Ecclesiastical History*.[130]

From the meta-narratives of modern scholarship, we might expect the reception-histories of the *Homilies* and *Ecclesiastical History* to have followed different paths. What is surprising, however, is how comparably little – at least in the early period – they seem to differ. Both texts found early audiences among Syrian Christians; both were used by chronographers in the Greek East; and both circulated in the Latin West in redacted forms, mediated by Rufinus.

It is not yet possible to reconcile all these pieces of evidence. Further analysis of the *Homilies* and *Ecclesiastical History* is needed to determine the precise meaning of the contrasts and connections noted above, and more work will need to be done if we wish to uncover the social realities that may have shaped the late antique creation and reception of these divergent perspectives on the apostolic past.

I suggest, however, that we might best begin by examining the most direct evidence for social practice found in these sources, namely, the evidence for the practice of writing. As noted above, the *Homilies* and *Ecclesiastical History* are significantly shaped by the practices of selecting, collecting, redacting, and reworking earlier sources. More specifically, the *Ecclesiastical History* is a "parade example" of counter-history – the process by which another group's history and sources are appropriated and

---

*Paralleltext: Eine Vorarbeit zu dem literargeschichtlichen Problem der Sammlung* (Texte und Untersuchungen zur Geschichte der altchristlichen Literatur 48.3; Leipzig: J. C. Hinrichs, 1937).

[128] For editions, etc., see references in Jones, "Pseudo-Clementines," 6–7, 80–84.

[129] As noted throughout Rehm, *Homilien*; e.g. 70, 72–73, 77, 85, 133, 277. See also W. A. Adler, "Abraham's Refutation of Astrology: An Excerpt for Pseudo-Clement in the Chronicon of George the Monk," in *Things Revealed: Studies in Jewish and Christian Literature in Honor of Michael E. Stone* (ed. E. G. Chazon, D. Satran, and R. A. Clements; Supplements to the Journal for the Study of Judaism 89; Leiden: Brill, 2004), 227–42.

[130] Rufinus' Latin translation of the *Recognitions* is dated to 406/7 C.E. and survives in over a hundred manuscripts; see B. Rehm, *Die Pseudoklementinen*, vol. 2, *Rekognitionen in Rufinus Übersetzung* (Die griechische christliche Schriftsteller der ersten [drei] Jahrhunderte 51; Berlin: Akademie, 1969). On his translation of Eusebius' *Ecclesiastical History*, see F. Thelamon, *Païens et Chrétiens au IV^e^ siècle: L'apport de l'Histoire ecclésiastique de Rufin d'Aquilée* (Paris: Études Augustiniennes, 1981).

reworked in the service of contrasting aims.[131] To tell the story of Judaism's demise, Eusebius quotes heavily from Josephus and Philo. Likewise, to tell the tale of the decline of "Jewish Christianity," he draws heavily on Hegesippus, whose own account of the apostolic age appears to have lionized James and the Jerusalem church; the possibility that Hegesippus himself may have been a "Jewish Christian" makes Eusebius' appropriation of his writings all the more striking.[132] Moreover, Eusebius seems to know of some sources in the Pseudo-Clementine tradition and perhaps even makes use of them.[133]

Intriguing, in my view, is the possibility that the *Homilies* was compiled, at least in part, to counter this counter-history.[134] No less than Eusebius, the authors/redactors of the *Homilies* engage in the fourth-century discourse about "orthodoxy," using the apostolic past to promote models of authenticity and authority in the present. Here too, the practices of collection, redaction, and reinterpretation are central, and they serve a means of enshrining certain memories while negating others. In the service of their own vision of an authentically apostolic Christianity in radical continuity with Judaism, they invoke the sayings of Jesus, and they evoke the image, not only of the apostle Peter, but also of the Gentile bishop Clement. They allude to Paul in order to exclude him. Much like the *Ecclesiastical History*, the *Homilies* opens a window onto one picture of the late antique church, constructed by means of the preservation and reinterpretation of a carefully selected slice of its literary heritage and history. But, whereas Eusebius self-consciously pens a history cobbled from written documents derived from archives, the authors/redactors of the *Homilies* marshal their sources towards a different aim: they claim to preserve Cle-

[131] I use this category in the sense outlined in Funkenstein, *Perceptions*, 36–49; S. Heschel, *Abraham Geiger and the Jewish Jesus* (Chicago: University of Chicago Press, 1998), esp. 14–16.

[132] For a recent discussion of Hegesippus' identity see F. S. Jones, "Hegesippus as a Source for the History of Jewish Christianity," in *Le Judéo-Christianisme dans tous ses états* (ed. S. C. Mimouni with F. S. Jones; Paris: Cerf, 2001), 201–12. For our present purposes, the question of whether Hegisippus was a Jewish convert to Christianity proves less significant than the fact that Eusebius perceives and presents him as such because of his knowledge of Hebrew or Aramaic and because of his familiarity with "other matters as if taken from the Jewish unwritten tradition (*eks Ioudaikês agraphou paradoseôs*)" (*Hist. eccl.* IV 22.9).

[133] See discussion above.

[134] I.e., whereas the early third-century source preserved in *Rec.* 1.27–71 may counter Luke-Acts (see above), the redacted form of the *Homilies* may counter late antique accounts that develop Luke-Acts. If so, then it proves particularly fitting that both Pseudo-Clementine novels so readily served – many centuries later – as a basis for F. C. Baur's modern counter-history of apostolic times.

ment's own first-hand account of his life and his eye-witness testimony to the mission and teachings of the apostle Peter.

If I am correct to interpret the contrasts between the two accounts in terms of active competition, we might further ask: is it possible to situate this discursive contestation in its social context? At present, of course, we can only speculate. It may be significant, however, that so many elements of Eusebius' understanding of Christianity are maligned as "heretically" Hellenistic by the *Homilies*. Eusebius, as a self-styled heir to Origen and Pamphilus, embraces allegorical interpretation and philosophical learning.[135] The *Homilies*, however, denounces all Greek *paideia* as "pagan" error, and its authors/redactors dismiss allegory and philosophy as merely a smoke-screen for the polytheism and impiety to which "pagans" and "heretics" are demonically addicted (e.g., 2.22, 25; 4.12–20; 6.17–23).[136] Whereas Eusebius expands apostolic succession to include Alexandrian Christian philosophers and depicts the Egyptian city as an ancient center of Christian philosophical wisdom,[137] the *Homilies* presents Alexandria as a nexus of all things pernicious – including philosophy and allegory as well as sorcery, polytheism, astrology, "heresy," and anti-Judaism (*Hom.* 1.8–14; 2.22; 4–6 esp. 4.4).[138]

Such contrasts may point us to the possibility that the discursive contestation over the apostolic past in these two texts may speak to another struggle, coming in the wake of the importation of Alexandrian forms of Christianity into Syro-Palestine due to the influence of Origen, Pamphilus, and Eusebius in Caesaria. It is possible, for instance, that the literary activity that shaped the *Homilies* may represent the response of other forms of Christianity, perhaps native to the area.[139] If some Syrian and Palestinian Christians were claiming continuity with the Jerusalem church, it might help us to understand why Eusebius might make such efforts to disenfran-

[135] Barnes, *Constantine*, 81–105.

[136] Note esp. Clement's assertion in *Hom.* 4.12.1: "Therefore I say that the entire *paideia* of the Greeks is a most dreadful fabrication of a wicked demon (*autika goun egô tên pasan Hellênôn paideian kakou daimonos chalepôtatên hupothesin einai legô*)." On the critique of *paideia* in the *Homilies*, see Adler, "Apion's enconomium"; Reed, "From Hellenism and Judaism." On the polemic against allegory, see Shuve, "Doctrine of the False Pericopes."

[137] Grant, *Eusebius*, 46–47, 72–76.

[138] See also *Hom.* 6.23; 9.6; 10.16–18 on Egyptian religion as paradigmatic of false worship.

[139] I here build on Pierluigi Piovanelli's suggestion about the social and cultural context that shaped the anti-Pauline traditions in the Ethiopian *Book of the Cock*; see "The *Book of the Cock* and the Rediscovery of Ancient Jewish-Christian traditions in Fifth-Century Palestine," in *Changing Face*, 308–22.

chise "Jewish Christianity" in the first place. In turn, if there were some Christians in the area who viewed themselves as heirs to the Jerusalem church of James and Peter, they might well be alarmed at the growing dominance of strikingly different views of Judaism, Hellenism, and Christianity.

Of course, further research is needed to determine the precise socio-historical setting and literary aims of the *Homilies*. Nevertheless, it is my hope that the above inquiry has helped to expose the significance of this text for our understanding of the place of "Jewish Christianity" in late antique Christian history and modern historiography.

When we consider the *Homilies* and our other evidence for "Jewish Christianity" on their own terms – without trying to fit them into the historical narratives outlined by Eusebius and others – what emerges is a richer picture of on-going debates about Judaism, often waged on the stage of the apostolic past. In many of our late antique sources, the age of the apostles is depicted as a pivot between Judaism and Christianity: it is presented as the era in which the truth of the church's supersession of Judaism was actualized, as Christians multiplied and spread while Jews fell victim to war and destruction. This supersessionist narrative, however, was clearly not the only option. A very different version of events seems to have remained vital and viable, in the fourth century and beyond.

If Boyarin and others are correct to see the fourth century as a critical era for the setting of the boundaries between "Judaism" and "Christianity" in the Roman Empire,[140] then the *Homilies* also provides us with neglected evidence for the resistance that these efforts faced. Such resistance surely resonated in rich ways with the Syrian cultural context of the Pseudo-Clementine tradition.[141] The wide reception of the Pseudo-Clementine

[140] E.g. Boyarin, *Dying*, 18; G. Stemberger, *Jews and Christians in the Holy Land: Palestine in the Fourth Century* (trans. R. Tuschling; Edinburgh: T & T Clark, 2000), 1–2.

[141] E.g. R. Kimelman, "Identifying Jews and Christians in Roman Syria-Palestine," in *Galilee through the Centuries: Confluence of Cultures* (ed. E. M. Meyers; Winona Lake: Eisenbrauns, 1999), 301–333; R. M. Grant, "Jewish Christianity at Antioch in the Second Century," in *Judéo-Christianisme: Recherches historiques et théologiques offertes en homage au Cardinal Jean Daniélou* (Paris: Beauchesne, 1972), 93–108; A. F. J. Klijn, "The Study of Jewish Christianity," *New Testament Studies* 20 (1973–74): 428–31; Strecker, *Judenchristentum*, esp. 260; idem, "Problem," 244–71; C. Fonrobert, "The *Didascalia Apostolorum*: A Mishnah for the Disciples of Jesus," *Journal of Early Christian Studies* 9 (2001): 483–509; Wilken, *John Chrysostom*; H. J. W. Drijvers, "Edessa und das jüdische Christentum," *Vigiliae Christianae* 24 (1970): 3–33; idem, "Syrian Christianity and Judaism," in *The Jews Among Pagans and Christians* (ed. J. Lieu, J. North, and T. Rajak; London: Routledge, 1992), 124–46, esp. 142–43 on the fourth century; Kelley, *Knowledge*, 197–200.

literature, however, cautions us against dismissing its message as relevant only for a certain locale.

The example of the *Homilies* might also serve to remind us – as modern historians – of the dangers of depending too heavily on retrospectively "orthodox" accounts. Eusebius makes efforts to extricate Judaism from Christian history, but his own use of sources hints at the enduring place of both Judaism and "Jewish Christianity" in that history. Moreover, even in his own time, Eusebius' vision of the apostolic past appears to have been contested. In the *Homilies*, we may hear the answers of voices now forgotten, who resisted the efforts of those who sought to inscribe, in apostolic history, the decline of the Jews, the irrelevance of "Jewish Christianity," and the parting of the church from its connections to a living Judaism.

# Jewish Collective Memory in Late Antiquity

## Issues in the Interpretation of Jewish Art

LEE I. LEVINE

Jewish art underwent a major revolution in Late Antiquity. For some 1500 years, Jews had a fairly limited artistic repertoire, consisting primarily of a selection of motifs drawn from surrounding cultures. Only on rare occasions, for instance under the Hasmoneans, was a unique policy introduced that diametrically opposed the regnant practice.

Before Late Antiquity, specifically Jewish depictions or symbols were virtually nonexistent. The menorah, for example, which was to become the most ubiquitous Jewish symbol, made its first appearance only in late Second Temple Jerusalem, and even then only in four known instances.[1] Since these early examples were all found in priestly contexts, it seems that the menorah, at times together with the Showbread Table, may have been intended at this juncture as depictions of Temple appurtenances with no particular symbolic dimension. Only in Late Antiquity (fourth–seventh centuries C.E.) did its symbolic dimension emerge on a massive scale in Roman and Christian contexts, as well as among Jews.[2]

The dramatic, heretofore unimagined, appearance of Jewish art in Late Antiquity was quite a different phenomenon from that described by R. R. R. Smith with regard to Greco-Roman art generally:

> After the visual revolution of the fifth century BC, changing styles were part of a single broad visual language that lasted through late antiquity, in which new expressive forms were constantly being added *without any of the old ones being thrown away—whether metaphorically or literally* (my emphasis). The cities and

---

[1] These include the coinage of the last Hasmonean king, Antigonus; the walls of Jason's tomb in Jerusalem's Rehavia neighborhood; a plastered wall in the excavations of the Upper City in today's Jewish Quarter; and a sundial from the Temple Mount excavations. Current excavations in Beit Loya, in the vicinity of Maresha in the Judean Shephelah (2006, directed by Oren Gutfeld), have yielded a menorah incised on the wall of a cave containing an olive press from the late Second Temple period (personal communication).

[2] See Lee I. Levine, "The History and Significance of the Menorah in Antiquity," in *From Dura to Sepphoris: Studies in Jewish Art and Society in Late Antiquity* (ed. L. I. Levine and Z. Weiss; Ann Arbor: Journal of Roman Archaeology, 2000), 131–53.

> sanctuaries of antiquity became like huge open-air museums with a prodigal millennium-long acquisition policy.[3]

Unlike this linear model, which accreted additional layers of expression over time, Jewish society and culture throughout antiquity was in a state of flux, with dramatic changes affecting every aspect of society, including its art. The transition from the Biblical to Second Temple periods, the encounter with Hellenism, the creation of a sovereign state under the Hasmoneans, the emergence of a far-flung Diaspora, incorporation into the Roman Empire, and the fall of Jerusalem and the Temple in 70 C.E. all had a powerful – and often unsettling – impact on Jewish society.

As will be argued below, Late Antiquity was far from being merely an appendage to the previous Roman era,[4] but rather constituted a unique and distinct period in ancient Jewish history.[5] The status of this period is similar to that which Roman historians now accord Late Antique society generally, i.e., not as a period of decline as Edward Gibbon had claimed, but as one of economic expansion as well as cultural and religious creativity as Peter Brown contends.[6] Besides developments that affected all of Byzantine society, the main factor that makes this era most challenging for the Jews is the emergence of Christianity, whose triumph created an entirely new political, social, and religious reality for the Jews throughout the length and breadth of the Roman Empire. They were now faced not only with an inimical ecclesiastical leadership, ranging from leading church figures down to local bishops and monks, but also with the increasingly hostile legislation of the imperial government.[7]

Parallel to the radically new external circumstances, i.e., the transition from a tolerant pagan context to a zealous monotheistic one, Jewish society also witnessed far-reaching internal changes. Existent political and religious leadership groups, such as the rabbis, may have retreated from histo-

---

[3] R.R.R. Smith, "The Use of Images: Visual History and Ancient History," in *Classics in Progress: Essays on Ancient Greece and Rome* (ed. T. P. Wiseman; Oxford: Oxford University Press, 2002), 96–97.

[4] Often referred to in Jewish historiography as the Mishnaic and Talmudic era.

[5] See Lee I. Levine, *Visual Judaism: History, Art, and Identity in Late Antiquity* (New Haven: Yale University Press, in preparation).

[6] Edward Gibbon, *The History of the Decline and Fall of the Roman Empire* (3 vols.; New York: Heritage, 1946), originally published in 1776–82; Peter Brown, *The World of Late Antiquity: From Marcus Aurelius to Muhammad* (London: Thames & Hudson, 1971).

[7] James Parkes, *The Conflict of the Church and Synagogue* (Cleveland: World Publishing Company, 1961), 151ff.; Marcel Simon, *Verus Israel: A Study of the Relations between Christians and Jews in the Roman Empire AD 135–425* (London: Littman Library by Oxford University Press, 1996), 135–233.

ry's stage toward the end of the fourth century C.E.; neither the names of sages nor the existence of Talmudic academies are known after ca. 380.[8] The Patriarchate disappeared in the early fifth century and was only a memory after ca. 425. We have no clear idea of who, if anyone, replaced these earlier constellations. It would seem that, despite the fragmentary literary evidence at hand, circles of *paytanim*, *meturgemanim*, Hekhalot mystics, priestly groups, and undoubtedly others (rabbis, too?) played some sort of role alongside the traditional synagogue and urban leadership that functioned as the primary leaders on the local level, as they had beforehand.

The Jews responded to the new Byzantine-Christian historical setting in a variety of ways: largely, though not totally, ignoring the new reality (rabbinic literature); escaping this reality (Hekhalot mystics); passivity, memory, and resignation while nurturing hopes for the future (*piyyut*); conversion; physical attacks on Christians and Christian symbols (Theodosian Code 16.8.18[9]; mocking Christian beliefs and narratives (*Toledot Yeshu*), continued acceptance (encouragement?) of Judaizers and their integration in one form or another into the Jewish community structure (the Aphrodisias inscriptions); imminent messianic expectations (*Book of Zerubbabel*); an enhanced prominence of Jewish institutions (i.e., the Patriarchate through the first quarter of the fifth century and the synagogue during this entire period); and, finally, adopting and adapting regnant cultural and religious models as well as modes of expression and behavior of the surrounding Byzantine-Christian world (e.g., epigraphy, asceticism, magic).

Second to none in this last-noted category of cultural activity is the emergence, as noted, of a vibrant Jewish artistic expression, recognized over the last century owing to the discovery of scores of Late Antique synagogues and cemeteries with their wide range of artistic remains.[10] On the one hand, this art was heavily indebted to regnant modes of expression in Late Antiquity generally, yet, on the other, it reflects unique symbols

---

[8] The single exception, and an historically problematic one at that, is Mar Zutra, who supposedly came from Babylonia to Palestine in the early sixth century and assumed some sort of authority. Our only source for this is the ninth-century Babylonian work, *Seder 'Olam Zuta*, which is of dubious historical value.

[9] Amnon Linder, *The Jews in Roman Imperial Legislation* (Detroit: Wayne State University Press, 1987), 236–37, no. 36.

[10] See, e.g., Erwin R. Goodenough, *Jewish Symbols in the Greco-Roman Period* (13 vols.; New York: Pantheon, 1953–68); Rachel Hachlili, *Ancient Jewish Art and Archaeology in the Land of Israel* (Leiden: Brill, 1988); eadem, *Ancient Jewish Art and Archaeology in the Diaspora* (Leiden: Brill, 1998); eadem, *The Menorah, the Ancient Seven-Armed Candelabrum: Origin, Form, and Significance* (Leiden: Brill, 2001).

and its own particular set of forms and patterns. The enormous amount of scholarly and popular interest in this subject has generated a number of questions, including the following: Why was there such a proliferation of Jewish art at this particular time? Why were certain biblical scenes and motifs chosen (and not others), and what do they signify? Why was there now a manifestation of Jewish symbols on a universal scale? What does all this tell us about the nature of Jewish social, cultural, and religious life toward the close of antiquity?

Recognizing the visual dimension in Jewish life is just one component of a general reassessment of Jewish society in Late Antiquity, one that argues against the older conception that this was an era of decline and retreat. With all the difficulties and hostilities endured by the Jews under Christianity, we have become acutely aware of the fact that Late Antiquity was also a time of communal, religious, and intellectual creativity.[11] The flourishing of a vibrant Jewish art, continuing for some three centuries, should be viewed in this context.[12]

## The Use of the Past

One of the salient aspects of Late Antique Jewish art is its use of the past, particularly through images, scenes, and symbols drawn from the Hebrew Bible. Generally speaking, the dominance of Scripture in shaping Jewish ethnic, cultural, and religious identity is reflected in a variety of expressions from the Persian through Byzantine eras (and, of course, later on in the Middle Ages): the retelling of biblical stories (Josephus, Jubilees, *Liber Antiquitatum Biblicarum*); the interpretation of biblical narratives, laws, and prophesies (Philo, the Qumran *pesharim*); the composition of plays, poems, and novels based on biblical accounts (Eupolemus, Artapanus, Ezekiel the Tragedian, and others); and the regular recitation of scriptural

---

[11] The primary, though not exclusive, catalysts in this reassessment are twofold: archaeological finds from Byzantine Palestine and the Diaspora, and the discovery of many Genizah documents relating to this period and to the region of Palestine in particular.

[12] As ironic as it may seem, we will exclude the art of Dura Europos from our discussion for three reasons: (1) The Dura remains are from the mid-third century and thus are somewhat earlier than the period we are addressing; (2) The remains there are so extensive and have generated such a rich bibliography with little agreement among scholars regarding the basic issues of overall intention and programmatic design, that it would be foolhardy to try and include this material in our discussion; and (3) The art of the Dura synagogue is so unique and isolated a case that, in my opinion, it should be considered a local phenomenon, and not the tip of the proverbial iceberg with respect to ancient Jewish art elsewhere. On the art in the Dura synagogue, see Levine, *Visual Judaism*.

*Illustration 1:* Jewish symbols depicted in the Ḥammat Tiberias synagogue floor.

readings and their exposition in synagogue liturgy, and more.[13] Talmudic discussions in the Yerushalmi, and especially in the Bavli, often focus on, or refer back to, biblical stories, and the creation of a myriad of aggadic midrashim in Palestine revolves almost exclusively around the Bible. *Piyyut* often had a similar focus on the weekly Torah readings and the holidays, while the foundations of the mystical Hekhalot experience were based on the visions of Isaiah and Ezekiel, and apocalyptic visions drew their inspiration from biblical sources as well.

Late Antique artistic representations and memories of the Jewish past can be divided into three rubrics:

[13] See, *inter alia*, the following collections of sources, studies, and summaries: James Charlesworth, ed., *The Old Testament Pseudepigrapha* (2 vols.; Garden City: Doubleday, 1983–85); Michael Stone, ed., *Jewish Writings of the Second Temple Period: Apocrypha, Pseudepigrapha, Qumran Sectarian Writings, Philo, Josephus* (Assen: Van Gorcum, 1984); Robert A. Kraft and George W. E. Nickelsburg, eds., *Early Judaism and Its Modern Interpreters* (Atlanta: Scholars, 1986); Martin J. Mulder, ed., *Mikra: Text, Translation, Reading and Interpretation of the Hebrew Bible in Ancient Judaism and Early Christianity* (Assen: Van Gorcum, 1988).

*1. Jewish Symbols*

Jewish collective memory is expressed most extensively through Jewish symbols appearing at the overwhelming majority of Jewish archaeological sites. The menorah is the most ubiquitous symbol, but the shofar, *lulav*, *ethrog*, and incense shovel (the latter appearing only in Israel) are also widely represented. These symbols are at times depicted together with a façade (that has been interpreted in several ways; see below). While these symbols often appear individually, they are also found clustered together in one combination or another (Ill. 1).[14] Their meaning and significance have been long debated. One popular theory maintains that they were primarily intended to recall the Jerusalem Temple (or possibly the Wilderness Tabernacle), with the façade representing the Temple, and the menorah, shofar, *lulav*, *ethrog*, and incense shovel symbolizing the cultic rituals once performed in that setting. If this interpretation is granted, then the clear implication is that remembering the Temple was of paramount importance to many Byzantine Jewish communities. The appearance of this motif in a synagogue, then, might be viewed as triggering a memory of the Temple and hopes for its restoration, and perhaps also reflecting a desire that the synagogue itself be considered a continuation of the Temple in terms of sanctity and religious significance.

A second approach regards these religious symbols as representative of the synagogue itself. The façade is thus interpreted as depicting the synagogue's Torah shrine while the other symbols indicate the various objects found in this setting or used in its liturgy.[15] By Late Antiquity, the shofar and *lulav* had become integral parts of synagogue worship, and the gold glass remains from the Roman catacombs incontrovertibly indicate that the façade could represent a Torah shrine. With the doors flung open, one can see shelves containing scrolls.

However, each of the above interpretations has its weaknesses. To interpret the façade as a depiction of the Temple's exterior is problematic. It rarely resembles either what we know of the Temple façade from literary sources (Josephus or Mishnah *Middot*) or the Temple façade as depicted in second- and third-century Jewish art (i.e., on the Bar-Kokhba coins and Dura Europos frescoes). Thus, it has been suggested that these depictions refer to an inner portal of the Temple – and not its façade; such claims,

---

[14] Hachlili, *Menorah*, 211–49.

[15] On representations of the Torah shrine, see Eric M. Meyers, "The Torah Shrine in the Ancient Synagogue: Another Look at the Evidence," *Jewish Studies Quarterly* 4 (1997): 303–38; Rachel Hachlili, "Torah Shrine and Ark in Ancient Synagogues: A Re-evaluation," *Zeitschrift des deutschen Palästina-Vereins* 116 (2000): 146–83. On the problematics of the incense shovel in a synagogue setting, see below, n. 16.

however, are entirely speculative. The incense shovel and menorah are certainly appropriate for the Temple context, but one wonders why the shofar, *lulav*, and *ethrog* were so emphasized since they seem to have been peripheral to official Temple worship. Only in the synagogue setting of the post-70 era did these symbols play a central role in Jewish religious consciousness. Moreover, a Temple setting would not explain the reason for two menorot to be displayed, as is usually the case in synagogue and funerary art. Finally, if the Temple were indeed intended to be the focus, one could readily suggest other items that would have been even more closely identified with its ritual, such as an altar, the Showbread Table, priestly garments, etc.

While the symbols depicted in much of Jewish art seem to fit a synagogue context rather nicely, the major problematic element in this regard is the incense shovel, as it patently does not apply to the synagogue or its liturgy – at least on the basis of what we know to date.[16]

Finally, a more modest, yet perhaps more compelling, argument regarding the façade is that the alternatives noted above are, in fact, not mutually exclusive and that either the Temple or the synagogue context might have been intended, with each community choosing the symbol most meaningful to it. When all is said and done, some depictions are clearly Torah shrines (Beit She'arim, Beit Alpha, and Rome) or look very much like a Torah *aedicula*, as at Dura Europos (e.g., Ḥammat Tiberias), while others appear to be building façades and were likely to have been representations of the Temple (Sepphoris, Beit Shean).[17]

Turning now to the symbols accompanying the façade and *menorot*, one might interpret them as components referring to the High Holiday season

---

[16] At least some Jews may have used incense in tombs, as reported by the sixth-century Christian pilgrim Antoninus Martyr regarding the Cave of Machpelah in Hebron; see Titus Tobler and Auguste Molinier, eds., *Itinera hierosolymitana et descriptiones terrae sanctae* (Geneva: Fick, 1880), 1/2:374; Aubrey Stewart, trans., *Of the Holy Places Visited by Antoninus Martyr* (London: Palestine Pilgrims' Text Society, 1896), 24. See, however, Richard A. Freund who argues for some usage of incense, even in the synagogues of Late Antiquity ("The Incense Shovel of Bethsaida and Synagogue Iconography in Late Antiquity," in *Bethsaida: A City by the North Shore of the Sea of Galilee* [ed. R. Arav and R. A. Freund; Kirksville, Miss.: Truman State University Press, 1999], 413–57, and especially 445–49).

[17] Another approach views these symbols as representing two basic concepts in Judaism – temple and Torah. Certain symbols are associated with the temple setting, and others seem to indicate the sanctity of the Torah shrine. As these two dimensions are often interrelated in Jewish tradition – starting with placing the two tablets of stone bearing the Ten Commandments together with Moses' Torah in the wilderness tabernacle (Deut 31:9, 26) and later in the First Temple – this combination may have found expression in Late Antique Jewish art as well.

in the month of Tishri, when three major Jewish festivals occur in rapid succession – Rosh Hashanah (the New Year), Yom Kippur (the Day of Atonement), and Sukkot.[18] Thus, the smaller symbols noted above can easily be associated with each of these holidays: the shofar – Rosh Hashanah; the incense shovel – Yom Kippur;[19] the *lulav* and *ethrog* – Sukkot.

In this vein, John Chrysostom, preaching in Antioch in the late fourth century C.E., chose to inveigh against these holidays and their observance in one of his homilies against the Judaizing Christians in his congregation:

> What is this sickness? The festivals of the wretched and miserable Jews which follow one after another in succession – Trumpets, Booths, the Fasts – are about to take place. And many who belong to us and say that they believe in our teaching, attend their festivals, and even share in their celebrations and join their fasts. It is this evil practice I now wish to drive from the church.[20]

Elsewhere, Chrysostom rails against those Christians who are drawn to the sound of the shofar (Rosh Hashanah), dancing (*sic!*), fasting (Yom Kippur), and building booths (Sukkot).[21] Thus, it is indeed conceivable that synagogues featured these particular symbols, which were associated with the holidays of Tishri and recognized for their centrality by non-Jews as well. These very symbols are also depicted on fragments of gold glass found in the Jewish catacombs of Rome.[22]

Whichever of the above options are preferred, it is quite clear that ritual objects having roots deep in the Jewish past were first mobilized at this time to serve the religious, cultural, and psychological needs of the community. Undoubtedly, the use of art for symbolic purposes, made universal by the church in the fourth century and thereafter, facilitated or perhaps even stimulated such a development among the Jews as well. Just as the

---

[18] This concept was first suggested by Y. Braslawski ("Symbols and Mythological Figures in Ancient Galilean Synagogues," in *All the Land of Naphtali* [ed. H. Hirschberg; Jerusalem: Israel Exploration Society, 1969], 115–18, [Hebrew]) and was later espoused by a number of other scholars.

[19] On the importance of the incense shovel for the Yom Kippur ceremony, see Jacob Z. Lauterbach, *Rabbinic Essays* (Cincinnati: Hebrew Union College Press, 1951), 51–83; Freund, "Incense Shovel," 413–57.

[20] *Adversus Judaeos*, 1.1.844 (also in Wayne A. Meeks and Robert L. Wilken, *Jews and Christians in Antioch in the First Four Centuries of the Common Era* [Missoula: Scholars, 1978], 86).

[21] See *Adversus Judaeos*, 1.5.851; 1.2.846; 7.1.915; and Robert L. Wilken, *John Chrysostom and the Jews: Rhetoric and Reality in the Late Fourth Century* (Berkeley: University of California Press, 1983), 75.

[22] Goodenough, *Jewish Symbols*, 2:108–19; Harry J. Leon, *The Jews of Ancient Rome* (Philadelphia: Jewish Publication Society, 1960), 218–24.

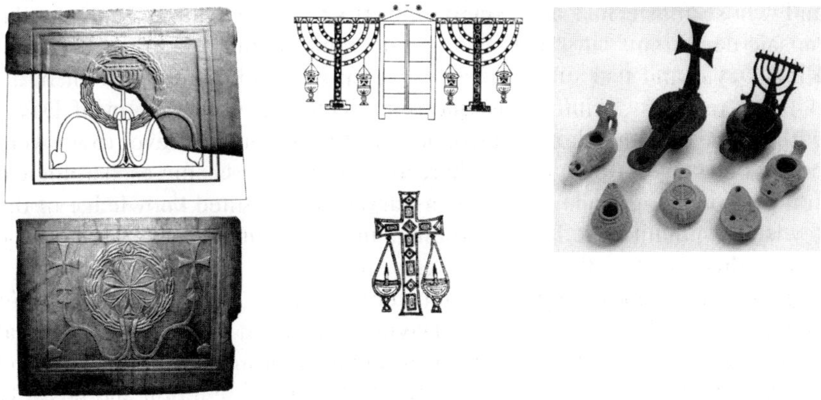

1 2 3

*Illustration 2:* Similar use of crosses and menorot in Late Antique art: on balustrades (1), hanging lamps (2), and oil lamps (3). (2.2 [above] reprinted by permission of Oxford University Press, Inc.)

cross became the Christian symbol par excellence, so, too, the menorah became the predominant symbol in Jewish art (Ill. 2).[23]

### 2. Biblical Figures

Within Late Antique art we often find depicted of a series of biblical figures, most of which appear in the context of a biblical scene (see below). However, in a few instances, and only in Byzantine Palestine, we find a biblical figure appearing alone, in no specific narrative context.

One such depiction is that of David at the western end of the nave in the Gaza synagogue, which dates to 508–509 C.E (Ill. 3). Identified by the Hebrew name David (*dwyd*), the figure exhibits the combined traits of royal personage and musician. On the one hand, he sits on a throne with an accompanying footstool and cushion, dons what appears to be a crown, and wears Byzantine imperial robes; on the other, he plays a harp and is portrayed *en face* before a series of animals, including a lion cub with a bowed head, a coiled snake, and a giraffe.[24] Given the garb, the animals and the lyre, David is clearly likened to Orpheus, who tamed the beasts

[23] See Levine, "Menorah," 145–53.

[24] Asher Ovadiah, "Excavations in the Area of the Ancient Synagogue at Gaza (Preliminary Report)," *IEJ* 19 (1969): 193–98; Hachlili, *Art and Archaeology – Israel*, 297.

and whose music had a mesmerizing effect on the animals.[25] Thus, the mosaic depiction synthesizes two iconographic traditions, that of the royal King David and that of Orpheus.[26] The crown halo would fit both traditions. It remains an intriguing question whether the association of David with Orpheus in the Gaza synagogue was on a superficial level (both were poets and singers) or whether there is a deeper messianic-eschatological comparison being made here. Given our severely limited knowledge of the Jewish community and its surroundings in sixth-century Gaza, little can be said in this regard without being overly speculative.[27]

It is worthwhile noting at this juncture a somewhat similar depiction of David in the Dura synagogue.[28] David is depicted in the lower central panel above the Torah shrine as a musician wearing a Phrygian cap and Persian royal garb while playing a lyre. Before him are a lion and possibly several other animals (birds, a duck, and a monkey) while an eagle is perched on his right shoulder. There is little question that here, as well, the model of Orpheus was employed to represent David.[29] In contrast to Gaza, however, the Dura representation bears no trace of an imperial motif.

---

[25] On the depictions of Orpheus in the Byzantine era (including Palestine), see the articles of Asher Ovadiah, "Orpheus from Jerusalem – Pagan or Christian Image?" and "Orpheus Mosaics in the Roman and Early Byzantine Periods," in *Art and Archaeology in Israel and Neighbouring Countries: Antiquity and Late Antiquity* (ed. Asher Ovadiah, London: Pindar Press, 2002), 427–46 and 528–46, respectively. See also Josef Strzygowski, "Das neugefundene Orpheus Mosaik in Jerusalem," *Zeitschrift des deutschen Palästina-Vereins* 24 (1901): 139–71.

[26] Moshé Barash, "The David Mosaic of Gaza," *Assaph: Studies in Art History* 1 (1980): 1–42. See also Henri Stern, "Un nouvel Orphée-David dans une mosaïque du 6$^{e}$ siècle," *Académie des Inscriptions et Belles-Lettres: Comptes Rendus* (July 1970), 63–82.

[27] See, however, Barash's attempt to map out such a context (ibid.). On Gaza as a religious and cultural center in the fourth–sixth centuries, see the illuminating collection of studies in *Christian Gaza in Late Antiquity* (ed. B. Bitton-Ashkelony and A. Kofsky; Leiden: Brill, 2004).

[28] Carl H. Kraeling, *The Synagogue* (vol. 8, part 1 of *The Excavations at Dura-Europos*; New Haven: Yale University Press, 1956; repr., New York: KTAV, 1979), 223–25. See also Henri Stern, "The Orpheus in the Synagogue of Dura-Europos," *Journal of the Warburg and Courtauld Institutes* 21 (1958): 1–6. Kraeling (op. cit., n. 885), and in greater detail Goodenough (*Jewish Symbols*, 2:19–20 and 3: no. 752), noting, *inter alia*, Robert Eisler's claim to have seen the depiction of a man, a lyre, and an animal in the Roman catacomb on the Via Appia (also referred to as Vigna Randanini). Whether or not this is related to our discussion is unclear; in any case the depiction has since disappeared.

[29] On the appearance of Orpheus in earlier Jewish writings from the Diaspora, see Goodenough, *Jewish Symbols*, 9:89–104; Barash, "David Mosaic," 14–15.

*Illustration 3:* Depiction of David in Gaza synagogue mosaic.

Another figure often identified as David was discovered in the Merot synagogue located in the Upper Galilee, some seven kilometers northeastof Safed (Ill. 4). The figure appears on a fragmentary panel of a mosaic floor measuring 1.70 x 2.15 meters and dating to the mid fifth century.[30] The mosaic depicts a young redheaded man wearing a short white tunic with long sleeves; a red cloak (*sagum*) covers his left shoulder and is fastened above his right shoulder with a pin (*fibula*). The man is surrounded by a

[30] Zvi Ilan, "The Synagogue and Study House at Meroth," in *Ancient Synagogues: Historical Analysis and Archaeological Discovery* (ed. D. Urman and P. V. M. Flesher; Leiden: Brill, 1995), 1:256–88. See also Hachlili, *Art and Archaeology – Israel*, 299.

*Illustration 4:* David (?) in Merot synagogue mosaic.

number of large-sized objects including an elliptical shield, a helmet, and a long sword (*spatha*). To the left of the figure is a short Aramaic inscription reading: "Yudan bar Shimon *menei*."

The inscription is unclear on a number of counts. First of all, was Yudan the artist, the figure depicted, or the donor? Secondly, is the word *menei* an abbreviated form of a personal name (Menaḥem?), a family name, the title of a functionary? Does it simply mean "appointee," or might it refer to a sum of money presumably contributed to the synagogue? Depending on which of the above options is chosen, there may or may not be a direct connection with the figure depicted.

The most accepted identification of the figure is that of David, owing both to his red hair, his arguable military garb, and the large-sized military equipment surrounding him (perhaps that of Goliath after having been slain – 1 Sam 17:4–7, 45–54). Moreover, it has been suggested that the

*Illustration 5:* Daniel (?) on ‘Ein Semsem stone relief.

remains of an elliptical design in front of the figure be identified as a harp or some other stringed instrument; if accepted, it would connect the figure with David, as would the fact that he may be wearing a crown. A connection with Orpheus may also be drawn from the figure's seated posture.[31]

Daniel is another biblical figure appearing in as many as three synagogues in ancient Palestine although in an extremely fragmentary fashion in two of them. He is clearly represented in the sixth-century synagogue of Na‘aran and most probably in the late fourth- or early fifth-century Susiya synagogue as well.[32] In the former, the figure of Daniel with arms in an *orans* position stands between two animals (probably lions) in a panel basically devoted to religious objects, nearest the *bima* and next to the zodiac. An accompanying inscription, "Danie[l] Shalom," clinches the identification.[33] However, in the western panel of the Susiya synagogue only the last two letters of the name "[Dani]el" have been preserved; together with the very partial remains of a hand and two animals (lions?), this depiction, too, has been identified as representing the biblical Daniel in the lions' den. The third instance is, unfortunately, more problematic. A well-preserved stone relief from ‘Ein Semsem in the Golan (identified as

[31] Other suggestions for identifying this figure include an ordinary soldier or a person of high status whose weapons are displayed. Although somewhat implausible, it has also been suggested that the scene be understood in light of the messianic verse from Isa 65:25 that appears together with a depiction in another part of the synagogue. The scene could then be explained as the messianic hope for redemption; see Sonia Mucznik et al., "The Meroth Mosaic Reconsidered," *Journal of Jewish Studies* 47 (1996): 286–90.

[32] Hachlili, *Art and Archaeology – Israel*, 294–95; Ephraim Stern, ed., *The New Encyclopedia of Archaeological Excavations in the Holy Land* (Jerusalem: Israel Exploration Society, 1993), 4:1419.

[33] Steven Fine has interpreted the position of this Daniel figure in the *orans* posture before the ark as reflecting a Jewish prayer position that was being assumed by the prayer leader who probably stood nearby (*Art and Judaism in the Greco-Roman World: Toward New Jewish Archaeology* (Cambridge, U.K. and New York: Cambridge University Press, 2005), 193.

*Illustration 6: ʻAqedah* mosaic depiction in Beit Alpha synagogue.

one of the bases of a Torah shrine) depicts a figure standing frontally, with raised hands of exaggerated size, between two lions (sometimes interpreted as a lion and lioness suckling her cub) and beside two eagles (Ill. 5).[34] This, too, may be a rendition of Daniel in the lions' den, although some of the details (the lioness suckling and the eagles) do not fit the Daniel narrative.[35]

The Daniel depictions are similar to those found in Christian contexts from the third through sixth centuries. Often portrayed as nude and beardless, the Christian Daniel stands in a similar *orans* pose, with his arms raised in prayer. Lions, often in a heraldic posture, flank him on either side. The figure of Daniel was significant to Christians for a number of reasons: owing to his prophetic-messianic predictions (i.e., the coming of Jesus or the end of the Roman Empire); his brave defiance of the command to defile his faith (i.e., a prototype of the Christian martyr); as one who escaped death to be resurrected, i.e., a prototype of a newly baptized Christian or even of Jesus himself.[36] The implications of the Daniel depictions in a Jewish context are less certain.

---

[34] Ibid., 95, figs. 37–38. This suggestion was made decades earlier, though with some reservations, by Zvi Maʻoz, "The Art and Architecture of the Synagogues of the Golan," in *Ancient Synagogues Revealed* (ed. L. I. Levine; Jerusalem: Israel Exploration Society, 1981), 111–12.

[35] Hachlili, *Art and Archaeology – Israel,* 321–23.

[36] Robin M. Jensen, *Understanding Early Christian Art* (London: Routledge, 2000), 174–75, 177–78. On the *orans* figure in early Christian art, see ibid., 35–37.

### 3. Biblical Scenes

The more impressive type of artistic remains referring to the past are the representations of scenes from the Hebrew Bible. Dura, of course, stands alone with regard to the richness and variety of such depictions.[37] Remarkably, and disappointingly, no other Diaspora synagogue, with but one exception, bears any type of biblical representation.[38]

The single exception is Gerasa in Jordan, where a scene from the Noah narrative is depicted. Excavated in 1929, the synagogue is situated on the city's acropolis, west of the temple of Artemis.[39] Remains of the synagogue's mosaic floor were found about fifteen centimeters beneath the

---

[37] A description of this rich array of Biblical panels would be both cumbersome and extraneous for our present purposes. Detailed summaries of the Dura synagogue art can be found, *inter alia*, in Kraeling, *The Synagogue*; Goodenough, Vols. 9–11; Joseph Gutmann, "Early Synagogue and Jewish Catacomb Art and Its Relation to Christian Art," *Aufstieg und Niedergang der römischen Welt*, II, 21.2 (ed. H. Temporini and W. Haase; Berlin and New York: de Gruyter, 1984), 1315–1322; Hachlili, *Art and Archaeology – Diaspora*, 96–197.

[38] It is very doubtful whether the Hammam Lif (Naro) mosaic from North Africa was intended as a creation scene, as has been suggested; see Franklin M. Biebel, "The Mosaics of Hammam Lif," *Art Bulletin* 18 (1936): 541–51; Goodenough, *Jewish Symbols*, 2:89–100; Hachlili, *Art and Archaeology – Diaspora*, 207-9; Edward Bleiberg, *Tree of Paradise: Jewish Mosaics from the Roman Empire* (Brooklyn: Brooklyn Museum, 2005), 24–35. Similar marine scenes were a familiar phenomenon in North African mosaics at the time; see Katherine M. D. Dunbabin. *The Mosaics of Roman North Africa: Studies in Iconography and Patronage* (Oxford: Clarendon, 1978), s.v. "marine scenes," and comment on p. 195: "Here too there is an adaptation of the stock current motifs, with the addition only of the indispensable sacred symbols, rather than the invention of something new."

Mention should be made of the intriguing appearance of Noah and his wife on coins from Apamea in Phrygia from the late second and early third centuries; see Emil Schürer, *The History of the Jewish People in the Age of Jesus Christ (175 B.C.–A.D. 135)*, (rev. ed., 3 vols.; Edinburgh: T&T Clark, 1973–87), 3:28–30; William M. Ramsay, *The Cities and Bishoprics of Phrygia* (2 vols.; Oxford: Clarendon Press, 1895–97), 2:667–72; Andre Grabar, "Images bibliques d'Apamée et fresques de la synagogue de Doura," in *No Graven Images: Studies in Art and the Hebrew Bible* (ed. J. Gutmann; New York: KTAV, 1971), 114–19.

Finally, a mosaic floor in Mopsuestia (in Cilicia, Asia Minor) depicts Noah's ark (identified as such by an inscription) surrounded by two rows of animals. Nearby, the story of Samson is portrayed in nine sequential scenes. However, the issue here of whether this building was a synagogue or church remains unresolved; see Ernst Kitzinger, "Observations on the Samson Floor at Mopsuestia," *Dumbarton Oaks Papers* 27 (1973): 133–44; Michael Avi-Yonah, "The Mosaics of Mopsuestia – Church or Synagogue?" in Levine, *Ancient Synagogues Revealed*, 186–90.

[39] Lee I. Levine, *The Ancient Synagogue: The First Thousand Years* (2d ed.; New Haven: Yale University Press, 2005), 257–58.

floor of the church that replaced it in the sixth century. The floor of the synagogue's vestibule was completely covered with a mosaic pavement containing the familiar cluster of Jewish symbols (menorah, shofar, incense shovel, *lulav*, and *ethrog*), a Greek inscription flanking the menorah that reads: "To the most holy place, Amen, Selah. Peace upon the congregation," and a scene from the Noah story.[40] The latter includes a depiction of animals exiting the ark; to its left are the heads of two young men, Noah's sons Shem and Yaphet (whose names appear in Greek), as well as a dove carrying an olive branch in its beak.

The first discovery of a biblical scene in Byzantine Palestine was in 1928–29 at Beit Alpha in the Jezreel Valley. The narrative of the *'Aqedah* (the Binding of Isaac; Gen 22:1–19) is depicted in the first panel one encounters upon entering the synagogue hall (Ill. 6). Beyond this panel are two others exhibiting the zodiac signs and Helios, followed by a representation of a Torah shrine flanked by a series of religious objects, as discussed above. The *'Aqedah* panel shows the two servants and their ass standing to the left, while to the right is Abraham holding Isaac (actually almost flinging him) with one hand and a knife in the other. Isaac is depicted here, as in other such scenes and contrary to most rabbinic traditions, as a little boy. Both Abraham and Isaac are identified by a Hebrew inscription, as is the hand representing God that emerges from above accompanied by a quote from Gen 22:12: "Do not raise your hand." In an intriguing break with the biblical account, the ram is depicted tied to a tree in the middle of the panel, and not to the far right as the chronological sequence would dictate. Moreover, the ram, which is also identified by a Hebrew caption, stands vertically and not horizontally.[41]

The richest remains of biblical scenes are found in Sepphoris. Discovered in 1993, the synagogue has preserved two very distinct and different types of biblical scenes.[42] When entering the hall from the southeast, the first two registers of the mosaic floor, regrettably the most poorly preserved ones, depict scenes from the life of Abraham (Ill. 7). In the first panel, only the top of the head of a woman standing in a doorway on the left is visible; the remainder of this register is destroyed. On the basis of a

[40] Lea Roth-Gerson, *The Greek Inscriptions from the Synagogues in Eretz-Israel* (Jerusalem: Yad Izhak Ben-Zvi, 1987), 46–50 (Hebrew).

[41] For an interesting explanation of this unusual depiction, see Marc Bregman, "The Riddle of the Ram in Genesis Chapter 22: Jewish-Christian Contacts in Late Antiquity," in *The Sacrifice of Isaac in the Three Monotheistic Religions* (ed. F. Manns; Jerusalem: Franciscan Printing Press, 1995), 127–45.

[42] For a detailed discussion of these registers, see Zeev Weiss, *The Sepphoris Synagogue: Deciphering an Ancient Message through Its Archaeological and Socio-Historical Contexts* (Jerusalem: Israel Exploration Society, 2005).

1
2

*Illustration 7:* Partially preserved Genesis scenes in the Sepphoris synagogue mosaic: (1) Sarah standing in tent entrance (Ch. 18); (2) two servants with an ass at the foot of Mount Moriah (Ch. 22).

depiction in the sixth-century church of San Vitale in Ravenna, Italy, Weiss has suggested identifying this panel as the visit of the three angels (Gen 18), with Sarah appearing at the entrance to her tent. The next register depicts the narrative account of the *'Aqedah*, similar to Beit Alpha although, from what remains, clearly more elaborate and sophisticated. In contradistinction to Beit Alpha, the register devoted to the *'Aqedah* is divided into two: The left side is well preserved and shows the two servants and an ass; the right side, however, is almost totally obliterated, with only the head of a ram tied to a tree alongside two pairs of shoes remaining.

Beyond the *'Aqedah* scene is a large panel containing the zodiac signs, a depiction of the sun (not Helios!) in a chariot, and the four seasons. The

*Illustration 8:* Tabernacle and Temple appurtenances in the Sepphoris synagogue

next two registers revolve around the theme of the Wilderness Tabernacle, featuring Aaron officiating at the altar surrounded by a series of cultic objects.[43] Many of these components are drawn from Exod 28–29, where they are associated with the Tabernacle's consecration (Ill. 8).

The first of these two registers displays an elaborate water basin on the right. According to the biblical description, the laver stood between the tabernacle and the outer altar (Exod 30:18), and was used regularly for the washing of hands and feet. In the consecration ceremony described in Exod 29 it is not mentioned, perhaps because purification of the entire body was required in that instance (verse 4).

[43] Another *'Aqedah* depiction, though quite different, is found in a Dura fresco (Kraeling, *Synagogue*, 125–33). Located above the Torah shrine and occupying a relatively small space, it shows Abraham holding a knife in his right hand, Isaac lying on an elaborate altar, the ram standing tied to a tree in the foreground and in the distance a figure (alternatively identified as Abraham, Isaac, or Sarah) standing at the entrance to a tent. Abraham demonstratively stands with his back to the viewer, as do the other two, smaller, figures.

Left of the laver, in the center of the register, stands a very partially preserved altar (identified by a horn-shaped corner) together with the almost totally obliterated depiction of Aaron, who is identified by an inscription bearing his name and bells on the fringes of his cloak (Exod 28:33–35). To the left of this panel are two animals – a bull and a lamb – the latter accompanied by the biblical phrase "one lamb" (Exod 29:39; Num 28:4). Directly below these depictions, in the next register, are four other objects that were also part of the Tabernacle (and later Temple) ritual. Each is labeled by a Hebrew word: a lamb ("and the second lamb" – Exod 29:41; Num 28:4), a black jug or amphora with the word "oil," a container with the word "flour," and two trumpets identified as such. To the right of these is the Showbread Table with twelve loaves of bread, and next to it, on the far right, a wicker basket containing fruit that apparently represents the "first fruits" (*bikkurim*) offering.

### *4. From Depiction to Interpretation*

Having reviewed the above artistic remains, what are we to make of these biblical scenes? Their identification is generally not an issue; such scenes are readily recognizable, either by the depictions themselves (the *'Aqedah*) or with the help of an identifying inscription. If this is what we mean by "antiquity in antiquity," then our job would be quite simple. The greater challenge is trying to understand what the artisan/donors/congregation intended to convey by using a particular scene or a combination thereof? Thus, some scholars assumed that the depictions were for decorative purposes only and simply reflected the tastes of those who determined their placement.[44] Others assumed that such representations indeed bore a Jewish religious message, but they differ as to its precise content. The scores of attempts to decipher the Dura paintings around one or more central ideas or purposes is a case in point.[45]

---

[44] So, for example, Heinrich Strauss, "Jüdische Quellen frühchristlicher Kunst: Optische oder literarische Anregung?" *Zeitschrift für die neutestamentliche Wissenschaft und die Kunde der älteren Kirche* 57 (1966): 114–36 (repr. in Gutmann, *No Graven Images*, 362–84); Asher Ovadiah, "Art of the Ancient Synagogues in Israel," in Urman and Flesher, *Ancient Synagogues*, 2:301–18.

[45] See a summary of the various approaches by Joseph Gutmann, "Programmatic Painting in the Dura synagogue," in *The Dura-Europos Synagogue: A Re-Evaluation (1932–72)* (ed. J. Gutmann; Missoula: American Academy of Religion Society of Biblical Literature, 1973), 137–54; idem, "Early Synagogue and Jewish Catacomb Art and Its Relation to Christian Art," *Aufstieg und Niedergang der römischen Welt: Geschichte und Kultur Roms im Spiegel der neueren Forschung* 2, 21.2 (ed. H. Temporini and W. Haase; Berlin and New York: de Gruyter, 1984), 1313–28.

Some scholars have suggested that certain representations may have resulted from historical exigencies. So, for example, it has been opined that the appearance of Daniel in the Na'aran synagogue may have been a reaction to the distress felt by the Jewish community in the sixth century C.E. The depiction of Daniel praying for salvation, the destruction of figural representation in that synagogue (attributed by some to the Byzantine authorities), and the generally acknowledged difficulties for Jews at that time all led to this interpretation.[46] A similarly motivated explanation has been accorded the zodiac arrangement in the Beit Alpha synagogue, likewise dated to this same century. The zodiac signs were shifted (and thus misaligned with the seasons) in order to place Scorpio at the top of the panel, nearest the *bima* and Torah shrine, with the lion next to it but somewhat below. This has been interpreted as an indication of the community's messianic longings and expectations, which are expressed by placing Scorpio, considered a symbol of Israel, above the lion, the personification of Rome.[47] As for the David figure in Gaza and perhaps Merot, no serious suggestion has been made as to why this motif was chosen at these places.[48]

Regarding Beit Alpha with its three decorative panels, a number of scholars have suggested an overall programmatic conception behind this mosaic floor. Rachel Wischnitzer, for one, understood the mosaic as representing the holiday of Sukkot and the related themes of harvest, fertility, rainfall, abundance, and even messianic expectations.[49] John Wilkinson interpreted the panels as representing the various sacred areas of the Jerusalem Temple, with the *'Aqedah* symbolizing the altar and the other two panels, the *heikhal* and *devir* (Holy of Holies), respectively. Progression into the synagogue thus led the worshipper into ever-greater holiness.[50]

On a different plane, Erwin R. Goodenough posited that the various Beit Alpha panels represent the ascent of the soul from a state of earthly purifi-

---

[46] See, for example, Ovadiah, "Art," 310.

[47] Isaiah Sonne, "The Zodiac Theme in Ancient Synagogues and in Hebrew Printed Books," *Studies in Bibliography and Booklore* 1 (1953): 11.

[48] Only Moshé Barash, focusing on the similarities between the David figure and Orpheus, has ventured an explanation that this identification stemmed from the vibrant Hellenized culture in Gaza in Late Antiquity and from the fact that "the thoroughly Hellenized Jews of Gaza were particularly deeply influenced by the beliefs of their neighbors..." ("David Mosaic," 29).

[49] Rachel Wischnitzer, "The Beth Alpha Mosaic: A New Interpretation," *Jewish Social Studies* 17 (1955): 133–44.

[50] John Wilkinson, "The Beit Alpha Synagogue Mosaic: Towards an Interpretation," *JJA* 5 (1978): 16–28, and especially 26–28.

cation to the heavenly and then to the mystical worlds beyond. In the *'Aqedah* scene, he focused on the hand of God with its appended seven rays, and the heavenly sphere from which the hand emerges, arguing that the beginnings of the mystical experience are represented here.[51] Bernard Goldman, following Goodenough's overall mystical thrust but with some variation, understood the sequence of panels as symbolizing the human-earthly tradition of sacrifice (the *'Aqedah*), the movement to the heavenly astronomical-astrological sphere "where the destinies of nations and men were ordered," and, finally, the Temple façade of the third panel, which represents the sacred heavenly portal, "the ubiquitous symbol of transformation."[52]

The Beit Alpha pavement encapsulates the problematics in attempting to interpret Jewish artistic remains. This sixth-century synagogue stands in splendid isolation. We know nothing of its local context – who its leaders and members were, what issues and problems they confronted, or what traditions they preserved. Even the ancient name of the village is unknown; the name Beit Alpha is taken from the modern-day kibbutz.[53] Thus, the door is wide open for competing interpretations; everything depends on which detail(s) one chooses to emphasize, which source(s) or model(s) one invokes, and at times one's own scholarly agenda.

Over the past decade or so, and especially following the discovery of the Sepphoris synagogue in 1993, but not limited to it, two very different approaches have come to dominate scholarly discussions. One is the possible liturgical factor behind this art and the other is its arguable polemical message.[54]

---

[51] Goodenough, *Jewish Symbols*, 1:246–47. See also p. 253: "Mystics who follow the Perennial Philosophy have always tended to see three stages in mystical ascent, stages which have most generally been called purgation, illumination, and unification. The three stages here might well be given the names purgation, ascent, and arrival."

[52] Bernard M. Goldman, *The Sacred Portal: A Primary Symbol in Ancient Judaic Art* (Detroit: Wayne State University Press, 1966), 21, 56–68. Goldman also notes approvingly the three-part mosaic as representing priesthood, kingdom, and Torah (p. 67).

[53] Ironically, even here, the problem of identification continues. As it turns out, the synagogue is located in Kibbutz Ḥefzibah, next to Kibbutz Beit Alpha!

[54] With regard to the Sepphoris synagogue specifically, another approach has been suggested by Joseph Yahalom and this author, namely, viewing the mosaic as reflecting the interests and orientation of a priestly group that may have been especially prominent and influential in the city, or at least in that particular congregation. See Joseph Yahalom, *Poetry and Society in Jewish Galilee of Late Antiquity* (Tel Aviv: Hakibbutz Hameuchad, 1999), 107–10 (Hebrew); idem, "The Sepphoris Synagogue Mosaic and Its Story," in Levine and Weiss, *From Dura to Sepphoris*, 89–90; Lee I. Levine, "Contextualizing Jewish Art: The Synagogues at Hammat Tiberias and Sepphoris," in *Jewish Cul-*

## Liturgy and Art[55]

Basing himself on the studies of a number of scholars of Christian art (*inter alia* Thomas F. Mathews, Peter Brown, and Staale Sinding-Larsen), Steven Fine assumes that the art of the Sepphoris mosaic was closely related to synagogue liturgy, just as art was often in close sync with ritual in Christian settings:

> The approach that I am suggesting has, in fact, been used with considerable results by scholars of Christian art. A number of scholars... have interpreted the late antique church building as the backdrop for the liturgical life of a community.... While synagogue remains in Palestine are not nearly as rich as the churches of Rome, Ravenna, and Constantinople, many of the insights of scholars of Christian art are applicable to the Sepphoris mosaic.[56]

And elsewhere:

> That all of this imagery appears in the Sepphoris floor is no accident. These themes were central to Jewish liturgical life during this period.... The art and the liturgy of the synagogue are cut from a single cloth, reflecting differing but always interwoven aspects of the synagogue religiosity in Byzantine Palestine.
>
> To conclude: the Sepphoris floor, like all synagogue appurtenances, is preeminently a liturgical object.[57]

At about the same time, Seth Schwartz chose a similar path. Although repeatedly disclaiming one's ability to really understand the art of the synagogue ("The art of the ancient synagogue is not a code to be broken... the intentions of its patrons are unrecoverable and its reception was exceptionally complex..."[58]), he, too, associates the themes articulated in several *piyyutim* (the menorah, heavenly spheres, divine chariot, and zodiac signs) with those displayed on the Sepphoris floor. However, Schwartz adds a twist, i.e., these artistic depictions were, in fact, subverted by the *paytan*:

---

*ture and Society under the Christian Roman Empire* (ed. R. Kalmin and S. Schwartz; Leuven: Peeters, 2003), 115–30.

[55] A number of scholars in the past have suggested a relationship between *piyyut* and synagogue art, but usually on specific motifs. See, for example, Aaron Mirsky, *The Piyyut: The Development of Post-Biblical Poetry in Eretz Israel and the Diaspora* (Jerusalem: Magnes, 1990), 93–101 (Hebrew); Joseph Yahalom, "Zodiac Signs in the Palestinian Piyyut," *Jerusalem Studies in Hebrew Literature* 9 (1986): 313–22 (Hebrew).

[56] Steven Fine, "Art and the Liturgical Context of the Sepphoris Synagogue Mosaic," in *Galilee Through the Centuries: Confluence of Cultures, Proceedings of the Second International Conference in Galilee* (ed. E. M. Meyers et al.; Winona Lake: Eisenbrauns, 1999), 229–30.

[57] Idem, *Art and Judaism*, 189.

[58] Seth Schwartz, "On the Program and Reception of the Synagogue Mosaics," in Levine and Weiss, *From Dura to Sepphoris*, 181.

> Although some of the *piyyutim*, like those just discussed, retain the idea that earthly ritual mirrors cosmic ritual, they relentlessly incorporate synagogue decoration into a Rabbinic-style reading of Pentateuchal narrative and prophetic oracle that prefigures the great cycle of Israel's past glory, presents punishment as recompense for its sins, and heralds future messianic restoration. In this way, they constitute an attempt to subvert any notion of the service as an adequate substitution for the temple cult, or as a reflection of some cosmic worship of God.[59]

Despite the seeming plausibility of this line of argument, i.e., that synagogue liturgy and synagogue art are interrelated, especially on the basis of Christian parallels, the problems inherent in the above approach are not inconsequential. Comparing *piyyutim* with the repertoire of themes in the Sepphoris mosaic floor is an almost fool-proof exercise. There are bound to be similarities, as there would be with any analogous corpus of religious sources, such as rabbinic literature or Philo. In fact, besides the *piyyutim*, other contemporary literary genres such as midrash and *targum* also contain most, if not all, of the artistic themes. Thus, the fact that many common themes appear in both *piyyut* and art is no proof of a connection between the two.[60] These are merely two among a number of possible cultural media in which these themes and ideas found expression in Late Antiquity.

Moreover, assuming that *piyyutim* were recited in (some? most? all?) synagogues is certainly a weighty consideration in making such comparisons. The fact remains, however, that we have no idea how widespread the practice of reciting *piyyutim* was in Late Antiquity. In fact, it may well not have been a universal practice. *Piyyut* was a new genre in early Byzantine Palestine, only now first being created and then eventually introduced into the synagogue setting; even then, it was almost certainly not a dominant component of the liturgy, certainly not in its initial stages. *Piyyut*, with few exceptions, is a sophisticated and difficult literary genre to understand. Most *piyyutim* are in Hebrew, ranked as a distant third spoken language (after Aramaic and Greek) among Jews in Byzantine Palestine. Epigraphic evidence, especially of donors and in funerary contexts comprising the overwhelming majority of such evidence, points to the dominance of the latter two languages.

The chronological factor is also of some importance here, and it does not make such a connection any more likely. The examples cited above are usually drawn from the poet Yannai, who lived in the mid to late sixth

[59] Ibid.

[60] Contra Avigdor Shinan, "Synagogues in the Land of Israel: The Literature of the Ancient Synagogue and Synagogue Archaeology," in *Sacred Realm: The Emergence of the Synagogue in the Ancient World* (ed. S. Fine; New York: Oxford University Press, 1996), 151–52.

century, some 150 years after the Sepphoris synagogue was built. In this light, the cogency of basing a claim on the confluence of these two genres becomes somewhat tenuous.[61] Moreover, Schwartz's suggested "subversion" depends upon a particular interpretation of both the *piyyut* and the "message" or intention of the iconography, both of which are far from certain.

Finally, any comparison of the usage of art in a Christian liturgical context with that of the Jews in this period is fraught with questionable assumptions. Much of the concern of church art historians in relating artistic material to liturgical ritual is often explained by the need to illustrate and concretize highly complex theological issues. The didactic function of art in the church setting is assumed to be of great importance. For example, in discussing apsidal imagery, Hellemo remarks:

> During the liturgical introductory invocation (*Sursum corda*), the congregation's attention is called upon and mental concentration is requested. As the celebration of the Eucharist involves complicated chains of thought, the participants need all the help they can get in order to understand the depths of meaning contained in the act. To the overall synthesis of the various chains of thought which contribute to the meaning of the Eucharist, the visible pictorial programs are of the greatest value. Imagery's most important quality is to recapitulate in synthesis that which words and ritual acts take much time to present. Thus, all additional elements entering the liturgy as it progresses can be retained by the congregation. In our opinion, apsidal imagery unifies and summarizes the central content of the eucharistic prayer. By doing this it furnishes a certain support for members of the congregation in their participation and understanding of the ritual celebration itself.[62]

One must be extremely cautious in assuming the same need for visual elucidation in Judaism as in Christianity. Given the striking differences in the nature of the liturgy of each, one would be hard pressed to make a case for comparable complex liturgical doctrines among Jews that might have required the assistance of narrative or symbolic art. Any comparison between Christian and Jewish practice thus demands careful scrutiny and a rigorous rationale as to why symbolic art would have been deemed necessary in a synagogue context. Christianity and Judaism were indeed far different in this respect. For example, in contrast to Christian liturgy that gave expression to the mysteries of that faith, as spelled out clearly in the

---

[61] See the problematic assertions regarding the connection between *piyyut* and the Dura paintings in S. Laderman, "A New Look at the Second Register of the West Wall in Dura Europos," *Cahiers Archéologiques* 45 (1997): 5–18.

[62] Geir Hellemo, *Adventus Domini: Eschatological Thought in Fourth-Century Apses and Catecheses* (Leiden: Brill, 1989), 281. See also Robin M. Jensen, "The Offering of Isaac in Jewish and Christian Tradition: Image and Text," *Biblical Interpretation* 2 (1994): 108.

above quotation, Jewish liturgy was comparatively straightforward. The prayers and scriptural readings were either self-explanatory or, by the fifth century, their elucidation had already developed and crystallized in Aramaic or Greek translations, scriptural explanations (*targums*), and homiletical explications (sermons).

On a more modest plane, it has been suggested that synagogue art was simply meant to illustrate one or another theme in *piyyut* (e.g., the zodiac, the *'Aqedah* narrative, or an eschatological theme). Even if one wished to entertain such a claim, it would be of an entirely different order than the situation envisioned for the contemporary Christian context. Moreover, since some, if not many, of these themes arise only occasionally in the Jewish liturgical cycle, one may ask why these themes, and not others, appeared.

The above comments are not intended to categorically preclude *piyyut* as shedding light on synagogue art. The overlap of these two realms in the synagogue is certainly conducive to exploring such ties. However, given the current stage of the research, the evidence presented is simply not persuasive.

## Polemics and Art

A second approach in contemporary studies of synagogue art aims to position it in the context of the Jewish-Christian polemic of Late Antiquity. We are well informed concerning this controversy although, admittedly, the evidence from the Christian side far outweighs that which is available from Jewish sources. Christian attacks on Jews and Judaism can be divided between theoretical, abstract constructs geared primarily for internal Christian polemical purposes (where the terms Jews and Judaism are invoked negatively to tar opponents), and those statements intended to counter Jewish claims against Christianity and thwart the influence of Judaism on the local Christian population (often referred to as "conflict theory").[63] From the Jewish side, however, the sum total of such material is not very large, nor does it constitute much more than a collection of passing comments, criticisms, and barbs at Christian beliefs.

---

[63] See, for example, Parkes, *Conflict of the Church*, 121–95; Simon, *Verus Israel*, 135–233; Meeks and Wilken, *Jews and Christians in Antioch*, 13–52; Wilken, *John Chrysostom*, 66–127; Miriam S. Taylor, *Anti-Judaism and Early Christian Identity* (Leiden: Brill, 1995); Paula Fredrickson and Oded Irshai, "Christian Anti-Judaism: Polemics and Policies," *Cambridge History of Judaism*, IV (ed. S. T. Katz; Cambridge, U.K.: Cambridge University Press, 2006), 977–1034.

But how seriously should such claims of a Jewish-Christian polemic be entertained? What are the criteria by which to judge such assertions? Were all Jews and Christians throughout the empire "plugged into" these polemics or are we dealing here, as elsewhere, with a local and varied phenomenon, at best? Should the historical context of Alexandria automatically be equated with that of Antioch or, conversely, either of the above with that of the Galilee or Dura? Even were we to conclude that a particular polemic of a specific church father was indeed directed against the Jews, how much impact might his tirades have had on the local population, and how far reaching, geographically, was its ripple effect – if at all? There is no blanket answer to these questions; perhaps each Christian polemic had its own dynamic that was the product of a particular local context or a particular church father. Thus, every instance must be judged on its own merits.

This is not always easy, or even possible, to do. The case of Melito of Sardis is instructive in this regard. His vituperative and disparaging fulminations against Jews (including the charge of deicide) are well documented, but was this a purely theoretical Christological statement intended for internal Christian purposes, or was he targeting a powerful local Jewish community in the city? Theories abound in both directions.[64]

Yet, certain polemics are readily discernible when directed against the contemporary Jewish community. When John Chrysostom attacks the synagogue and specific Jewish customs and practices in a series of tirades against the Judaizing members of his own church, we can be sure that serious tensions existed in late fourth-century Antioch, at least in his eyes.[65] Yet, the Antiochan social and religious realities cannot automatically be assigned to each and every Christian attack against the Jews. Indeed, there is not always a correlation between the intensity of a polemic and local social tensions. As David Satran has pointed out, neither Origen nor Eusebius is particularly vindictive regarding the local Jewish community, although we are well aware that Christians and Jews – and even Samari-

[64] Andrew R. Seager and A. Thomas Kraabel, "The Synagogue and the Jewish Community," in *Sardis from Prehistory to Roman Times* (ed. G. M. A. Hanfmann; Cambridge: Harvard University Press, 1983), 171–73; Marianne P. Bonz, "The Jewish Community of Ancient Sardis: A Reassessment of Its Rise to Prominence," *Harvard Studies in Classical Philology* 93 (1990): 343–59; David Satran, "Anti-Jewish Polemic in the *Peri-Pascha* of Melito of Sardis: The Problem of Social Context," in *Contra Iudaeos: Ancient and Medieval Polemics between Christians and Jews* (ed. O. Limor and G. G. Stroumsa; Tübingen: Mohr-Siebeck, 1996), 49–58; Lynn H. Cohick, "Melito's *Peri Pascha*: Its Relationship to Judaism and Sardis in Recent Scholarly Discussion," in *Evolution of the Synagogue: Problems and Progress* (ed. H. C. Kee and L. H. Cohick; Harrisburg: Trinity International, 1999), 123–40.

[65] Wilken, *John Chrysostom*, 66–127.

tans and pagans – often rubbed shoulders in Caesarea and argued with one another over the truth and authenticity of their respective religions. On the other hand, in North Africa, where the diatribes of Tertullian or Cyprian were often quite harsh, there exists little evidence of Jewish-Christian encounters.[66]

While a number of scholars have raised the possibility that both Christian and Jewish art served polemical purposes,[67] it was only in 1990 that Herbert Kessler argued this case extensively with regard to Dura, and again, a decade later, with respect to the Sepphoris mosaic floor.[68] He is joined in this assessment by a slew of Israeli archaeologists and art historians.[69] This approach to explaining the Sepphoris mosaic has become so widespread of late that we can rightfully deem it, at least in Israeli circles, the *communis opinio*.

What is required to make a serious and credible claim that behind the art of a particular synagogue lay a polemical intent? Maximally, it should be located in a place where both Christians and Jews lived and where a local figure (Christian or Jewish) had articulated explicit polemical statements. Moreover, the evidence for such a local polemic would have to be persuasive and clear-cut; to appeal to other sources centuries apart and geographically distant does not make for a compelling argument. Thus, as has often been the case, invoking a seventh- or eighth-century midrash in order to support a suggested polemic that supposedly transpired in fourth-century Galilee or third-century Dura, is unacceptable, nor should Chrysostom, Ephrem, or even Jerome be utilized as background for an alleged Tiberian or Sepphorean polemic. In this light, then, there is little justification for claiming that the Dura synagogue paintings reflect an anti-Christian polemic, given the fact that we know of no such exchanges either in early third-century Dura or contemporary Mesopotamia for that matter. Even Dura's local church offers no evidence for such a pointed polemic.

[66] Satran, "Anti-Jewish Polemic," 57–58.

[67] See, for example, Marcel Simon, *Recherches d'histoire judéo-chrétienne* (Paris: Mouton, 1962), 188–208.

[68] Herbert L. Kessler, in *The Frescoes of the Dura Synagogue and Christian Art*, Part II (ed. K. Weitzmann and H. L. Kessler; Washington, D.C.: Dumbarton Oaks, 1990), 153–83; idem, "The Sepphoris Mosaic and Christian Art," in Levine and Weiss, *From Dura to Sepphoris*, 65–72.

[69] See, *inter alia*, Bianca Kühnel, "The Synagogue Mosaic Floor in Sepphoris: Between Paganism and Christianity," in Levine and Weiss, *From Dura to Sepphoris*, 31–43; Weiss, *Sepphoris Synagogue*, 249–56; Elisabeth Revel-Neher, "From Dream to Reality: Evaluation and Continuity in Jewish Art," in Levine and Weiss, *From Dura to Sepphoris*, 53–63.

When it comes to Sepphoris, however, the issue is far more intriguing, straddling the improbabilities of a Jewish-Christian polemic in Dura and the certainty of such activity in Antioch. Rabbinic literature attests to disputes and exchanges with sectarians in the Galilee (who, in many cases, can be identified as Christians) during the second to fourth centuries. However, not only is the veracity of some of these traditions problematic, but there is no way of determining the extent of such exchanges. In any case, such material is wholly inadequate for attempting to reconstruct a fifth-century Galilean polemic.

The issue, however, is not primarily an overall Galilean one but, more specifically, what was transpiring in and around Sepphoris in the early fifth century, when this particular synagogue was constructed. Fortunately, we are not entirely bereft of evidence in this regard, as several church sources offer some information about later fourth-century Sepphoris. Theodoret, in his *Ecclesiastical History* (4.19), reports, albeit tendentiously, about the persecution of the Catholic leadership in Alexandria during the reign of the Arian emperor Valens (364–378 C.E.).[70] Having described the cruelties promulgated by the newly appointed Arian bishop Lucius, Theodoret notes the following:

> In all, after many fruitless efforts, they drove into exile to Diocaesarea, a city inhabited by Jews, murderers of the Lord, eleven of the bishops of Egypt,[71] all of them men who from childhood to old age had lived an ascetic life in the desert, had subdued their inclinations to pleasure by reason and by discipline, had fearlessly preached the true faith of piety, had imbibed the pious doctrines, had again and again won victory against demons, were ever putting the adversary out of countenance by their virtue, and publicly posting the Arian heresy by wise argument.[72]

This exile took place soon after the death of Athanasius in 373.[73] That these bishops were indeed regarded by some as important figures in Catholic circles is reflected in a number of communications with them by several eastern church figures: Apollinaris of Laodicea, eight leaders of the Marcellian community (?) in Ancyra,[74] and Basil of Caesarea in Cappadocia.[75]

---

[70] On Valens's religious policy generally, see André Piganiol, *L'empire chrétien (325–395)* (Paris: Presses universitaires de France, 1947), 161–65.

[71] Writing a few years later, Epiphanius lists their names (*Panarion* 72.11.1).

[72] Piganiol, *L'empire chrétien*, 162–63.

[73] Hans Lietzmann, *Apollinaris von Laodicea und seine Schule* (Tübingen: Mohr [Siebeck], 1904), 60–61; Piganiol, *L'empire chrétien*, 162–63; Michael Avi-Yonah, *The Jews of Palestine: A Political History from the Bar Kokhba War to the Arab Conquest* (New York: Schocken, 1976), 209.

[74] Epiphanius, *Panarion* 72.11.1. On this community generally, see ibid., 72.

[75] Basil of Caesarea, *Letter* 265.

What the first may have wanted to convey is unknown; the communication may have been primarily of a personal nature though, based on other communications with these exiles, it appears likely that the subjects discussed were related to Christological issues.[76]

The inclusion of Apollinaris is of especial significance. He was a respected,[77] though controversial, figure in orthodox circles owing to his beliefs regarding the humanity of Jesus as well as his millenarianist ideas, which included the restoration of the Jewish Temple and sacrifices, as well as the observance of Jewish customs as part of his projected eschatological scenario.[78] In fact, we know almost nothing of these latter doctrines, undoubtedly owing to Apollinaris's condemnation by his Catholic colleagues on such matters, with the resultant erasure of his writings that have survived only fragmentarily, if at all.[79] While some of his theological disputes

[76] Lietzmann, *Apollinaris von Laodicea*, 22–24.

[77] See Epiphanius, *Panarion* 66.21.3; 77.2.1.

[78] Basil of Caesarea, *Letter* 263, 4: "And the theological works of Apollinaris are founded on scriptural proof, but are based on a human origin. He has written about the resurrection, from a mythical, or rather Jewish, point of view; urging that we shall return again to the worship of the Law, be circumcised, keep the Sabbath, abstain from meats, offer sacrifices to God, worship in the temple at Jerusalem, and be altogether turned from Christians to Jews." See also idem, *Letter* 265, 2: "But where have the promises of the Gospel been blunted and destroyed by his figments? So meanly and poorly has he dared to explain the blessed hope laid up for all who live according to the gospel of Christ, as to reduce it to mere old wives' fables and doctrines of the Jews. He proclaims the renewal of the temple, the observance of the worship of the Law, a typical high priest over again after the real High Priest, and a sacrifice for sins after the Lamb of God who taketh away the sin of the world He preaches partial baptisms after the one baptism, and the ashes of a heifer sprinkling the Church which, through its faith in Christ, has not spot or wrinkle, or any such thing; cleansing of leprosy after the painless state of the resurrection; an offering of jealousy when they neither marry nor are given in marriage; Showbread after the Bread from heaven; burning lamps after the Light. In a word, if the law of the Commandments has been done away with by dogmas, it is plain that under these circumstances the dogmas of Christ will be nullified by the injunctions of the law." For further references to Apollinaris's millenarianist doctrines, see Gregory of Nazianzus, *Letter* 102, 114; Jerome, *De viris illustriabus* 18; Epiphanius, *Panarion* 77, 36, 5–6; 38, 1.

[79] Lietzmann, *Apollinaris von Laodicea,* 43–78. Gregory of Nyssa in his *Epistle* 3, 24 cites many statements ostensibly from Apollinaris's work, *Apodeixis*. Frances M. Young (*From Nicaea to Chalcedon: A Guide to the Literature and Its Background* [London: SCM Press, 1983], 183–84) remarks that although many fragments are preserved in anti-Apollinarian works, such as Gregory of Nyssa's refutation of the *Apodeixis*, it is difficult to decide whether these are direct quotes or whether they have been altered to fit the orthodox position. The reconstruction of Apollinaris's works is further complicated because his followers published his writings under false names.

are at times treated caustically and critically,[80] others merited a good deal more respect.[81] At one point, Basil attempted to dissuade the bishops in Sepphoris from following Apollinaris's Christological doctrines (theological? millenarianist? both?), pleading instead for their assistance in bringing Apollinaris around to see the true light and return to accepted Catholic dogma.[82] Thus, the possibility exists – though, admittedly, it is indeed remote – that these exiles were exposed to (sympathized with?) Jewishly oriented messianic hopes.

Unfortunately, for all their importance, these sources leave many issues unanswered. For one, the exile of bishops to Sepphoris clearly points to the fact that the city referred to specifically as a Jewish one was considered to be a setting bereft of any significant Christian population. Thus, the teachings of these "heretics" would not harm the Arian cause. It is of interest to note that the Marcellians' letter to exiles in Diocaesarea refers to a recent visit with them. However, we have no way of knowing whether this visit took place in Alexandria or Sepphoris. If the latter, then it might be a sign that these bishops remained active in promoting their brand of Christianity while residing in the city. Moreover, if Apollinaris's letter to them addressed, *inter alia*, his millenarianist ideas, including outright Jewish components, then we might further assume that these ideas were part of Christian discourse in the city that could have become known to the Jews as well. Or, if we are to take Basil's letter seriously, then we might conclude that the exiled bishops were espousing the eschatological views of Apollinaris and this could have provoked or stimulated the local Jewish community into some sort of response, including, perhaps, a message transmitted through one synagogue's mosaic floor. All the above possibilities, however, remain mere speculation.

Moreover, the extent to which the local Jews had contact with these exiles at all, or whether they were even aware of these Christian theological discussions, is unclear. Thus, the degree of impact that these Egyptian bishops may have wielded on the local Jewish population in Sepphoris, in the short or long run, is an open question.[83]

---

[80] See Gregory of Nazianzus, *Epistle* 102, 14.

[81] As, for example, Gregory of Nyssa, *Epistle* 3, 24, written some time in the 380s.

[82] Basil, *Letter* 265. Marcellus, too, focused on Christological issues in his correspondence with the exiled bishops living in Diocaesarea (see Epiphanius, *Panarion* 72.11–12).

[83] A letter sent from a Jerusalem synod to Theophilus, bishop of Alexandria, around 400 C.E. may be relevant in this regard; therein it was announced that a series of heresies, including that of Apollinarius, had been eradicated from Palestine. Did this include Sepphoris as well? See Jerome, *Letter* 93; Lietzmann, *Apollinaris von Laodicea*, 36–37.

Finally, there is also a chronological issue. From all appearances, these bishops remained in the city for a relatively short time. It can readily be assumed that they returned to Egypt upon Valens's death in 378, following the ascent of the orthodox Theodosius I to the throne and his reinstatement of Catholic doctrines as normative and official policy.[84] The question, then, is how much of an impact their sojourn in Sepphoris for some four or five years had on the local Jewish community. Was it significant enough to have influenced Jewish thinking when constructing a synagogue some forty-or-so years later? Would this earlier exposure to Christian doctrine have been so powerful and challenging that a local synagogue community might have felt compelled to respond with a full-blown programmatic artistic composition that attempted to combat such Christian claims? There are, of course, no clear-cut answers to these questions, but – at least in the case of Sepphoris – there is some basis, however tenuous, for entertaining the suggestion that some Jews in the city were once exposed (seriously?) to Christian doctrine which, at least in part, might have stimulated them to respond through the medium of their synagogue's mosaic floor.

Returning to the Sepphoris mosaic, the proposed interpretation of its polemical nature has to be assessed, first and foremost, on its own merit. Is its polemical intent compelling? Are the sources cited to support this claim persuasive (for, in the end, such assertions can be seriously grounded only with the aid of literary material)?

Whatever the case, a possible polemical dimension of Jewish art should not be considered separately from the wider historical context relating to this phenomenon generally in Late Antiquity. As noted above, one of the enigmatic phenomena in this regard is the absence of any developed Jewish anti-Christian polemic at this time.[85] What does exist can be summed up in isolated statements relating to Christians and Christianity (rabbinic literature, *piyyut*), parodies of New Testament accounts about Jesus (especially *Toledot Yeshu*),[86] and a number of instances in which Christian literary motifs have been reworked while presenting a Jewish counter-narrative, often referred to as "counter-history" or "dialogue" (*The Apocalypse of Zerubbabel*, *The Legend of the Ten Martyrs*, and perhaps certain

[84] *Theodosian Code* 16.1.2; 16.5.6.

[85] Robert Chazan, *Fashioning Jewish Identity in Medieval Western Christendom* (Cambridge, U.K. and New York: Cambridge University Press, 2004), 67–76.

[86] Hugh J. Schonfield, *According to the Hebrews* (London: Duckworth, 1937); Hillel Newman, "The Death of Jesus in the 'Toledot Yeshu' Literature," *JTS* 50 (1999): 59–79; Yaakov Deutsch, "New Evidence of Early Versions of *Toldot Yeshu*," *Tarbiz* 69 (2000): 177–97 (Hebrew).

*midrashim*).[87] Nowhere in Jewish writings is there any crafted or developed argument that either attacks Christianity or defends Judaism's beliefs and practices in the face of Christian assaults. Such systematic polemics first appear only in the ninth century under Islam,[88] and begin to flourish in early twelfth-century Ashkenaz and thereafter.[89]

Given this wider context, it is not impossible that a particular Sepphorean congregation attempted to do something that no other group or individual we know of from this period did, i.e., to construct a well thought-out, sustained, and detailed polemic against Christianity on its mosaic floor. However, given the notable absence of such efforts in Late Antiquity, the likelihood of such a polemic coalescing in early fifth-century Sepphoris requires stretching credulity beyond its limits. It would be as amazing as it is unlikely.[90]

---

[87] See, for example, David Biale, "Counter-History and Jewish Polemics against Christianity: The *Sefer Toldot Yeshu* and the *Sefer Zerubavel*," *Journal of Social Studies* 6 (1999), 130–45; Martha Himmelfarb, "The Mother of the Messiah in the Talmud Yerushalmi and Sefer Zerubbabel," in *The Talmud Yerushalmi and Greco-Roman Culture* (ed. P. Schäfer; Tübingen: Mohr Siebeck, 2002), 3:369–89; Ra'anan Abusch, "Rabbi Ishmael's Miraculous Conception: Jewish Redemption History in Anti-Christian Polemic," in *The Ways that Never Parted: Jews and Christians in Late Antiquity and the Early Middle Ages* (ed. A. H. Becker and A. Y. Reed; Tübingen: Mohr Siebeck, 2003), 307–43.

[88] Daniel Lasker and Sarah Stroumsa, eds., *The Polemic of Nestor the Priest: Qiṣṣat mujādalat al-usquf and Sefer Nestor ha-Komer* (2 vols.; Jerusalem: Yad Izhak Ben-Zvi, 1996).

[89] See David Berger, *The Jewish-Christian Debate in the High Middle Ages* (Philadelphia: Jewish Publication Society, 1979), 7–8; Daniel Lasker, "Jewish-Christian Polemics at the Turning Point: Jewish Evidence from the Twelfth Century," *HTR* 89 (1996): 161–73; Chazan, *Fashioning Jewish Identity*, 67–87.

[90] The reasons why such a polemical response was not forthcoming from the Jewish side deserve a separate treatment. However, in the meantime, it might be pointed out that this aversion to constructing a more comprehensive, logical, and systematic synthesis is not only absent from the field of polemics but is true of other areas as well. For example, the rabbinic corpus of post-tannaitic Late Antiquity (this would include the two talmuds and the myriad aggadic *midrashim*) show little interest in systematizing their contents, either in terms of law, thought, or even with regard to any specific topic. Ephraim E. Urbach, in his introduction to *The Sages: Their Concepts and Beliefs* (2 vols.; Jerusalem: Magnes, 1979), 4, has the following to say in this regard: "Common to all the sources is the fact that none of them provides systematic treatment of the subject of beliefs and conceptions, and there are almost no continuous discourses dealing with a single theme. In most instances we have to integrate and arrange the scattered material into one unit of thought… The signification of these concepts is not defined or discussed in detail in the sources, and no attempt has been made to relate them or to reveal their common elements. Such attempts on our part are likely to show contradictions between the conclusions drawn for one set of ideas and those derived from another. It is just this lack of consistency and system that provided subsequent generations with a great measure of

## The Elusive Quest for Interpretation

The above two approaches have one thing in common, namely, they are dependent in varying degrees on Christian models and sources. As noted, part of the *piyyut*'s relevance to synagogue art is related to the connection between art and liturgy often made in Christian literary sources and modern scholarship, while the phenomenon of a Jewish-Christian polemic rests almost entirely on Christian sources. Thus, it may be remiss to suggest a particular interpretation from a literary tradition with respect to an artistic representation, as is done in similar Christian contexts. Here the differences between the Christian and Jewish enterprises become chasmic, with a main issue being the vast quantitative and qualitative differences between Christian evidence on the one hand and Jewish data on the other.

Owing to the wealth of Christian art that had accumulated by the fifth to seventh centuries, internal artistic comparisons and their relationship to well-documented current customs and to the ideology articulated by contemporary church fathers is a promising exercise. It allows for a detailed examination of the liturgical context and the utilization of art in explicating its message. Moreover, in addition to the art itself, there are a number of Christian literary sources from these centuries that describe and interpret contemporary church artistic decoration. Both Paulinus of Nola and Prudentius discuss scenes depicted in the churches of Italy, as does Choricius of Gaza with regard to the mosaics of this city's church.[91] Thus, when Mathews suggests that the "processional convergence on an axially organized core image provided a formula for the program of the Early Christian church,"[92] he is relying upon the following:

> A confluence of figures toward Christ is prominent in the art of the catacombs and sarcophagi, and this composition governs a surprising number of church programs of the widest diversity in size, shape, and function. Over sixty percent of the apse compositions catalogued by Ihm include centripetal processions. All of the mosaicked churches of Ravenna fall in this class, including basilicas, baptisteries, and the octagon of Saint Vitale.[93]

---

freedom in defining the principles of faith.... The philosophers of the Middle Ages, the Cabbalists, and the Hasidim all based themselves on Rabbinic dicta in expounding their systems." In short, any kind of systematic anti-Christian polemic by Jews awaits the Middle Ages.

[91] Caecilia Davis-Meyer, ed., *Early Medieval Art, 300–1150: Sources and Documents* (Toronto: University of Toronto, 1986), 17–23 (Paulinus), 25–33 (Prudentius).

[92] Thomas F. Mathews, *Clash of Gods: A Reinterpretation of Early Christian Art* (Princeton: Princeton University Press, 1993), 176

[93] Ibid., 150.

The remains of Jewish art known to us today are negligible by comparison. There is no Jewish equivalent to the Ravenna churches. Besides the Dura synagogue, no other Diaspora building (with the modest exception of Gerasa) has biblical themes. The six synagogues with the zodiac design from Byzantine Palestine, in addition to about the same number featuring a biblical figure (Gaza, Susiya, Na'aran, Sepphoris, and perhaps Merot and 'Ein Semsem) or a biblical scene (Beit Alpha and Sepphoris), are a distinct minority among the country's synagogue remains. Most synagogues appear to have had minimal or very modest ornamentation, featuring mostly floral and geometric designs of greater or lesser sophistication. Thus, in the majority of synagogues from Late Antiquity, the possible functions of art – to stimulate historical memory; to highlight ritual symbols and, through them, certain religious observances; to complement the instruction that took place in religious institutions; and to instill messianic hopes – can be realized only very partially.

On another front, the lack of contextual material is compounded by the realization of the diversity among ancient synagogues. No two synagogue buildings are identical; their plans, architecture, art, and inscriptions exhibit a remarkable diversity. In the Diaspora, for example, Sardis is a far cry from Dura, as is Ostia from Stobi, while in Byzantine Palestine, despite geographical propinquity, Capernaum is worlds apart from Ḥammat Tiberias, as is Reḥov from Beit Alpha and Jericho from Na'aran. In the realm of artistic interpretation, an urban setting may well have given rise to interpretations that would have been unknown or unacceptable for a rural congregation, and vice versa. The same potential for diversity holds true for a Galilean setting as against a Judean one, of a Palestinian community as against a Diaspora one, or a Greek-speaking environment as opposed to an Aramaic or even Latin one. Thus, the depiction of Helios in Tiberias in all probability reflects a set of beliefs and associations different from those evoked in rural Na'aran or Beit Alpha. It can quite readily be assumed that the façade of the Temple or Torah shrine or various Jewish symbols did not necessarily have the same meaning in third-century Dura as they did in fourth-century Tiberias, fifth-century Sepphoris, or sixth-century Beit Alpha.

In noting what he calls the polyvalent dimension in Roman and Byzantine art, Jaś Elsner claims: "People relate to works of art in different ways, depending upon different contexts and at different times,"[94] and while

---

[94] Jaś Elsner, *Art and the Roman Viewer: The Transformation of Art from the Pagan World to Christianity* (Cambridge, U.K. and New York: Cambridge University Press,

discussing portrayals of flora and fauna in Byzantine Christian contexts, Henry Maguire has articulated a similar view:

> Most of the images from natural history that appear in early Byzantine art were not like modern traffic signs, with necessarily fixed and invariable messages, but... were more akin to metaphors. The meanings of any given image, an eagle, for example, or a fish, could be nuanced or even completely altered according to the context provided by a given work of art, just as works in a language can change their meanings in different situations. Also like words in a language, the images employed by artists could change their meanings over the course of time.[95]

The above-noted diversity in Jewish life of Late Antiquity has much to do with an extensive and pervasive communal autonomy. Thus, local needs and tastes were crucial variables in determining local synagogue policies. If one wishes to discover why certain motifs were used and what they were intended to signify, at least originally, the answer inevitably lies in decisions made by a particular artisan, patron, communal leader, or local community when embarking on such a project. Unfortunately, the reality is that most synagogue art stands alone (e.g., Dura Europos and Beit Alpha), unaccompanied by contemporaneous literary sources that might illuminate the immediate social, communal, and cultural contexts of this art.

We are thus left with several considerations that should be brought into play when trying to explain Jewish art. First, there can be no all-inclusive explanation that will hold true for all remains from the third to seventh centuries, either in the Byzantine Diaspora or Palestine. The interpretation of Jewish art by art historians over the last half century has often been characterized by the assumption of universal meanings. They have, as a matter of course, attempted to define the precise meaning of a depiction and then apply this interpretation to all representations appearing in synagogues from different times and places. According to this systematic and

---

1995), 1. Nevertheless, one must remember that similarities did exist, not only in the representations themselves but undoubtedly also in their interpretations. However, unless some evidence exists in this regard, and in light of the fact that the representations themselves vary from place to place (as, for instance, with respect to the zodiac), it is unjustified to assume *a priori* identical meanings and significance from place to place.

[95] Henry Maguire, *The Earth and Ocean: the Terrestrial World in Early Byzantine Art* (University Park: Published for the College Art Association of America by the Pennsylvania State University Press, 1987), 8.

restrictive approach, artisans, patrons, or communities at large invariably invoked the same message when using a particular motif.[96]

We are suggesting that such an approach is not only a-historical but also lacks a degree of sophistication in terms of contextualizing the material within specific social, cultural, and religious settings. It is only this local context that can best account for the many differences between the various Jewish communities, be it in their architecture, liturgy (Torah reading, *piyyutim*, and prayers), epigraphy, and, of course, art. This is certainly true for the Diaspora, and the scattered remains of a score and more of Late Antique Diaspora synagogues indicate the degree to which each was influenced, often quite heavily, by the immediate surroundings. It is as evident in Dura, Sardis, and Apamea as it is in Ostia, Naro (Ḥammam Lif) and Elche (Spain).[97]

Finally, as is argued elsewhere,[98] there can be no question that the emergence of a vigorous Jewish art in Late Antiquity, in so many places and so many varieties, was in no small measure a product of the Byzantine-Christian historical orbit. Whether it be the large-scale use of figural art, the incorporation of pagan motifs, Christian models, or Jewish symbols, it was the challenge/threat of Christianity that in large measure stood behind these developments. For a brief 300-or-so-year period in Late Antiquity, art became an important medium of cultural and religious expression for Jewish communities throughout the Byzantine world. On one level, this art served a social function, enhancing the importance of the synagogue hall, stirring religious sentiment, and offering prestige and stature to its donors and patrons.

On a deeper level, however, reference to the Jewish past through symbols and biblical scenes was a means of transmitting a cultural reality that

[96] In this regard, see Schwartz, "On the Program and Reception," 165–81, contra Fine, *Art and Judaism*, 195.

[97] Levine, *Ancient Synagogue*, 250–309. In Byzantine Palestine, the influential role played by immediate contexts also finds expression on the regional level. Given the concentration of synagogues in a number of geographical areas, regional characteristics are often quite evident and had a hand in shaping of the synagogue, including its art. This phenomenon has always been well recognized regarding the Galilee, but over recent decades it has become apparent for the Golan and southern Judea as well. See Heinrich Kohl and Carl Watzinger, *Antike Synagogen in Galilaea* (Leipzig: Heinrichs, 1916); Zvi U. Ma'oz, "The Art and Architecture of the Synagogues of the Golan," in Levine, *Ancient Synagogues Revealed*, 98–115; Rachel Hachlili, "Late Antique Jewish Art from the Golan," in *The Roman and Byzantine Near East: Some Recent Archaeological Research* (ed. J. Humphrey; Ann Arbor: Cushing-Malloy, 1995), 183–212; David Amit, "Architectural Plans of Synagogues in the Southern Judean Hills and the 'Halakah'," in Urman and Flesher, *Ancient Synagogues*, 1:129–56.

[98] See my forthcoming *Visual Judaism*.

served the needs of many congregations, sharpening their collective memories. The resultant sense of continuity is what Danièle Hervieu-Leger calls *anamnesis*, a recollection of the past. It "is affirmed and manifested in the essentially religious act of recalling a past which gives meaning to the present and contains the future."[99] There was a lineage of belief as well as a belief in the lineage of the people, and both of these goals were achieved by placing aspects of Jewish antiquity at center stage. Together with the art, the Jews had already forged a wide variety of other triggers for this purpose, ranging from the regular recourse to the Bible in their liturgy to the cyclical observance of the holidays with their varied historical foci. The new circumstances of Christian domination served to stimulate many Jewish communities to search for additional avenues of expression and reinforcement of their identity.

Deciphering meaning in art is not a simple task and must be undertaken with caution and circumspection. Reshaping one's identity in the light of historical circumstances was (and remains) a never-ending challenge. It requires the utilization of existing modes and themes, be they of Jewish or non-Jewish origin, as well as the creation of new ones. The Byzantine-Christian orbit of Late Antiquity was a historical context that in some ways threatened the very core of Jewish identity; the visual medium, reflecting a communal imprint, was utilized as never before in meeting this challenge.

*Photo Credits*

Ill. 1, 3, 4, 5, 6 are published with the permission of the Institute of Archaeology, The Hebrew University of Jerusalem.

Ill. 2 (1) Chancel screens decorated with a menorah and a cross from the synagogue at Hammat Gader (above) and the church at Massuot Yiyzhaq (below). Byzantine period, 6th century C.E. Marble. W 100 cm; 118 cm. Israel Antiquities Authority Collection. Photo © The Israel Museum, Jerusalem.

Ill. 2 (2; above) Drawing of the mosaic floor depicting two menorahs with hanging lamps from the synagogue at Naaran; Steven Fine, *Sacred Realm: The Emergence of the Synagogue in the Ancient World* (New York and Oxford: Oxford University Press and Yeshiva University Museum, 1996), p. 112, Fig. 5.11 (a). By permission of Oxford University Press, Inc.

Ill. 2 (2; below) Cross with hanging lamps from a baptistery mosaic in Skira, Tunisia; Mohamed Fendri. *Basiliques chrétiennes de la Skhira* (Paris: Presses Universitaires de France, 1961), Plate K, no. 3. By permission of, and copyright © Presses Universitaires de France.

Ill. 2 (3) Oil lamps decorated with Jewish and Christian symbols. Byzantine period, 5th-6th century C.E. L 8.8–21.5 cm. Institute of Archaeology, The Hebrew University of

---

[99] Danièle Hervieu-Leger, *Religion as a Chain of Memory* (New Brunswick: Rutgers University Press, 2000), 125.

Jerusalem, the Schloessinger Collection; Reifenberg Collection; Israel Museum Collection, Carmen and Louis Warschaw Collection. Photo © The Israel Museum, Jerusalem.

Ill. 7, 8 Courtesy of the Sepphoris Expedition, The Hebrew University of Jerusalem. Drawing by P. Arad.

# Tradition and Transmission

## Hermes Kourotrophos in Nea Paphos, Cyprus

ELIZABETH KESSLER-DIMIN

## Introduction

A multi-paneled mosaic gracing the triclinium floor of a luxurious home in Nea Paphos, Cyprus employs particularly creative iconography to promote Dionysos (Figure 1). The long iconographic tradition of Hermes Kourotrophos beautifully culminates in the fourth-century C.E. mosaic in the House of Aion in a magnificent representation of the Epiphany of Dionysos (Figure 2).[1] This image of the infant Dionysos in the care of Hermes visually substantiates the notion of "Antiquity in Antiquity" by both attesting to the respect held for traditional ancient iconography by pagans in Late Antique Cyprus and by revealing the significance of the antiquity of pagan art in the development of Christian iconography.

The House of Aion lies in the vicinity of several other homes richly decorated with mosaics of pagan subject matter.[2] An imposing pagan presence is documented on Cyprus throughout the first centuries of the common era not only by mosaics and other works of art, but also by the continued use of pagan sanctuaries.[3] There was also a Christian presence.[4]

---

[1] Wiktor A. Daszewski, *Dionysos der Erlöser: griechische Mythen im spätantiken Cypern* (Mainz: P. von Zabern, 1985).

[2] Six habitation levels, dating from the late Classical period to the late fourth century/early fifth century C.E., have been discovered beneath it. A coin of Licinius I, Roman Emperor in the east from 313 through 324 C.E., was found just under the tesserae that compose the mosaic, establishing a terminus post quem for its creation that is also consistent stylistically. This date places the mosaic into the timeframe when the age of Constantine as sole emperor was imminent. These dates are corroborated by pottery evidence, as well as by utilitarian objects, such as lamps (Ellen Herscher, "Archaeology in Cyprus," *American Journal of Archaeology* 102 [1998]: 342). In addition to the numismatic and other material evidence, epigraphic evidence is also useful in the dating of the mosaic. The forms of the letters are late, particularly the C-shaped *sigma* and fully extended *pi*.

[3] There is evidence for the use of an underground pagan sanctuary in Nea Paphos through the end of the fourth century C.E./beginning of the fifth century C.E. See Her-

The Acts of the Apostles records the evangelization of the island by the Apostles Paul and Barnabas and Mark the Evangelist. The city of Paphos itself is mentioned: "When they had traveled through the whole island, even as far as Paphos."[5] Three Cypriot bishops participated in the Council of Nicaea; clearly there was a secure Christian presence in Paphos at the time of the House of Aion mosaic's creation and subsequent utilization.[6] A number of factors contributed to the obliteration of artistic and architectural data for early Christianity on Cyprus including the remodeling of many early basilicas over the centuries, intentional destruction committed during iconoclastic movements and natural devastation caused by earthquakes.[7] It is not until the fifth and sixth centuries C.E. that archaeological and literary evidence indicates that Christianity had gained dominance over the island.[8]

A mosaic in a fourth-century C.E. church, the Basilica of Chrysopolitissa, located in Nea Paphos, bears a depiction of a ram and a grapevine with an inscription from John 15:1: "I am the true vine."[9] A second inscription reveals that the mosaic was made on behalf of a vow by a man named Hesychios. Figural mosaics are rare amongst the abundant geometric work that survives from the early Christian period. As one of only a few figural

---

scher, "Archaeology," 347. Literary evidence, such as that provided by the Christian Epiphanius, also illuminates the commanding pagan presence on Cyprus in the fourth century C.E.

[4] The fourth century C.E. was a tumultuous period, with many emperors favoring Christians and passing laws against pagans, while a select few other emperors, notably Julian the Apostate, attempted to boost the practice of paganism throughout the empire; see Glen W. Bowersock, *Julian the Apostate* (Ann Arbor: University of Michigan Press, 1978).

[5] Acts 13:4–12; They converted the city's Roman Governor, Sergius Paulus, to Christianity; see John Hackett, *A History of the Orthodox Church of Cyprus* (London: Methuen & Co., 1901).

[6] Demetrios Michaelides, "The Early Christian Mosaics of Cyprus," *Biblical Archaeologist* 52, 4 (1989): 194. See also Doros Alastos, *Cyprus in History* (London: Zeno Publishers, 1955), 112.

[7] Michaelides, "Early Christian Mosaics," 195. There were several major earthquakes in the fourth century C.E. which may have destroyed early Christian monuments on Cyprus. It is unknown how the House of Aion was affected by the earthquakes. It was probably built before the earthquake of 332 C.E. and only miraculously suffered minimal damage; the mosaic does show slight repairs.

[8] See Athansios Papageorghiou, *Masterpieces of the Byzantine Art of Cyprus* (Nicosia: Nicosia Printing Works, 1965) and Demetrios Michaelides, "Mosaic Pavements from Early Christian Cult Buildings in Cyprus," in *Mosaic Floors in Cyprus* (ed. W. A. Daszewski; Ravenna: M. Lapucci-Edizioni del Girasole, 1988), 81–152, for studies of the archaeological evidence of Christianity on Cyprus.

[9] Michaelides, "Early Christian Mosaics," 194.

*Figure 1:* Drawing of the Mosaic in the House of Aion, 4th century C.E., Nea Paphos, Cyprus.

mosaics in the basilica, the choice of subject and inscription is extremely telling for the religious atmosphere in Nea Paphos during the fourth century C.E. The "true vine" allegory is particularly apt when considered in conjunction with the concurrent promotion of Dionysos, pagan god of the vine, in the House of Aion and other homes located only a few hundred meters away.

Marielouise Cremer discusses the appropriation of the symbol of the vine in relation to her work in Asia Minor, but it is applicable throughout the ancient world: "wie die Traube den Gott Dionysos verkörperte, sah die christliche Kirche seit dem 4. Jh. in ihr ein Abbild Christi."[10] The coexistence of two substantial works of art, permanent mosaic floors, promoting

[10] Marielouise Cremer, *Hellenistisch-römische Grabstellen im nordwestlichen Kleinasien,* v. 2 – *Bithynien* (Bonn: R. Habelt, 1992), 44.

the religious significance of the vine intimates that there was a lively religious dialogue between different communities in Nea Paphos. The Eustolios House located in Kourion, near Nea Paphos, dating to the end of the fourth century/early fifth century C.E., reveals an intriguing blend of religious influences.[11] One inscription declares that the building was erected in the spirit of the symbols of Christ, while another links the homecoming of the owner, a former resident of Kourion, with Apollo.[12] A Sanctuary of Apollo Hylates, only several kilometers away, was in use throughout the late fourth century C.E. The coexistence and commingling of religions, as confirmed in Kourion, reveals that divisions between religious ideas and the iconography that reflects them were not always clearly delineated in this period.

## The House of Aion

The House of Aion has only been partially excavated.[13] In addition to the triclinium with the figural mosaic, two small rooms with geometric floor mosaics have been found. The identification of the triclinium is revealed by the three-sided pattern around the mosaic. The function of the room is reflected in this design as couches were placed atop the delineated area. The owners of the House of Aion and their guests can be imagined discussing and debating the artistic, religious, and philosophical manifestations of the mosaic. The character of the room is gleaned from several other features in the room. A semicircular niche was built into the west wall of the triclinium, directly behind the mosaic, most likely to house a statue. Figural paintings adorned the walls of the triclinium; iconographically and stylistically, the paintings seem to belong to the same time period as the mosaic itself.[14]

---

[11] Daszewski, *Mosaic Floors*, 194.

[12] Department of Antiquities, Cyprus, *A Guide to Kourion* (Nicosia: Filokipros, 1996), 30.

[13] The triclinium measures 9 x 7.6 meters. The name given to the house is somewhat of a misnomer since Dionysos is the key figure in the mosaic. However, a nearby house, excavated in the 1960s had already been named the House of Dionysos. See Wiktor A. Daszewski and Demetrios Michaelides, *Guide to the Paphos Mosaics* (Nicosia: Bank of Cyprus Cultural Foundation, 1988), 52–62. It will be interesting to see whether there are any other figural mosaics in the House of Aion and, if so, whether they continue to follow a Dionysian theme.

[14] The fragmentary paintings now hang in the Paphos Museum.

*Figure 2:* Epiphany of Dionysos, 4th century C.E., panel from the House of Aion mosaic, Nea Paphos, Cyprus.

Important scenes of Dionysos' life appear to mark the beginning and end of the multi-paneled mosaic in the House of Aion with the top right panel displaying the Epiphany of Dionysos and the illustration of his Triumph on the bottom left. The mosaic was excavated by Wiktor A. Daszewski who, in his publication, *Dionysos der Erlöser,* recognized in the image: "eine spezielle Art des Monotheismus."[15] Whereas Daszewski advocates that the mosaic promotes a monotheizing Dionysian message, other scholars, such as Johannes Deckers fervently disagree. Deckers published a counter-attack to Daszewski's publication provocatively called, "Dionysos der Erlöser?" in which Deckers argued that the iconography of the mosaic is purely neutral: "Das Mosaikbild im "Haus des Aion" ist keine heidnische Ikone!"[16] While Glen Bowersock asserts that Dionysos was an important god in Late Antiquity, he nevertheless maintains that the

[15] Daszewski, *Dionysos,* 45.

[16] Johannes G. Deckers, "Dionysos der Erlöser: Bemerkungen zur Deutung der Bodenmosaiken im "Haus des Aion" in Nea-Paphos auf Cypern durch W. A. Daszewski," *Römische Quartalschrift für christliche Altertumskunde und Kirchengeschichte* 81 (1986): 161.

owners of the House of Aion were Christian, interpreting the pagan images there as constituting "traditions [that] held meaning for them by evoking cultural roots that they shared with the pagans."[17] Bowersock contends that the Christians of the House of Aion "transform[ed] Hermes into a Madonna."[18]

Scholars are often inclined to discredit any visual evidence for the flourishing of pagan religions in late antiquity. In the case of the House of Aion, they prefer to bury it within the norms of contemporaneous Christianity rather than attempt an exploration of the complex makeup of this brand of paganism, which for lack of a better term, I am here describing as a monotheizing Dionysian religion. An exploration into the meaning and impact of the mosaic's iconography reveals a vibrant pictorial religious discourse at work in Late Antique Cyprus. This paper exposes the iconography of *kourotrophos* in the House of Aion mosaic as part of a visual language of antiquity that ultimately reveals how the success of the Christian icon of the Virgin and Child is firmly embedded within this pagan iconographic tradition of Hermes Kourotrophos.

## The Epiphany Panel

Returning to the first panel, there are several variations to the myth of Dionysos' birth, but Semele, a mortal, is usually credited as his mother.[19] After Semele was impregnated by Zeus, she was deceived by a jealous Hera into asking to see Zeus reveal himself in his full form. The resulting thunderbolt caused Semele to burst into flames. Because Dionysos was not yet ready to be born, Zeus found the fetus amongst the ashes and sewed it into his thigh, giving birth to him some time later. Like Athena, Dionysos was born into the world from his father's body. This allotted him an indisputable pedigree as the son of the most superior of the gods on Mount Olympus. Dionysos also functioned as king of the Orphic theogony, in

[17] Glen W. Bowersock, *Hellenism in Late Antiquity* (Ann Arbor: University of Michigan Press, 1990), 41; "Recapturing the Past in Late Antiquity," *Mediterraneo antico. Economie, società, culture* 4, 1 (2001): 7.

[18] Bowersock, "Recapturing the Past," 14.

[19] Homer identifies Semele as the mother of Dionysos (*Il.* 14.323–35). Hesiod explains that although she is mortal, Semele gives birth to Dionysos, an immortal, thus securing immortality for herself (*Th.* 940–42). In *Homeric Hymn* 1, the author first lists various locations which have been suggested as the location where Semele gave birth to Dionysos. The author then discredits all of these with the statement that Mount Nysa was the scene where Zeus brought Dionysos into the world. Herodotus (2.146.2) confirms the story.

which Persephone is his mother. In the latter account, Persephone is depicted as a virgin who is said to have conceived Dionysos via Zeus disguised as a serpent.[20] The Titans, the fathers of the Olympian gods, tore the infant Dionysos to pieces.[21] Zeus was able to save Dionysos' heart and he recreated his son either by implanting the heart into the womb of Persephone or sewing the heart into his own thigh. Thus, whether conceived in the womb of Semele or Persephone, Dionysos, the son of the king of the gods, was reborn.

In the House of Aion mosaic Zeus, who brought Dionysos into the world, is nowhere present thus indicating that Dionysos has already been born. After Dionysos' birth, Zeus entrusted him to Hermes as *kourotrophos*, or one in charge of his care, instructing Hermes to take the infant to Mount Nysa where he could be safely raised away from the wrath of the jealous Hera. The mosaic represents the moment when Hermes presents Dionysos to those responsible for his upbringing. Wings attached to Hermes' head and feet secure his identity in addition to the inscription of his name.[22] Dionysos sits poised on Hermes' lap, naked except for the golden fillet and wreath of green leaves he wears in his hair. In addition, a silver-blue nimbus surrounds his head, highlighting his significance in the mosaic. The powerful presence of Dionysos indicates his central importance to the entire mosaic. Enthroned, the infant god raises his hands. The implications of this gesture prompted Daszewski to identify Dionysos as the "Erlöser."[23] The action implies that he is conferring his blessings upon those in the mosaic holding their hands out towards him, and also upon those very people in the House of Aion who may have done the same when looking upon his image.[24] Hermes' hands are veiled by the cloth of his silver-blue cape in a purposeful gesture of reverence towards Dionysos. This deliberate symbol, *manuum velatio*, denotes the importance of whomever or whatever lies atop the veil.

---

[20] This tradition comes from an Orphic theogony dating to the latter fifth century B.C.E.

[21] Diodorus Siculus, 5.75.4. After the Titans were subsequently defeated, the human race is said to have sprung from the ashes of their bodies.

[22] The names of almost all of the figures in the mosaic are identified by inscriptions.

[23] Friedrich Wilhelm Hamdorf remarks that "Bacchus hat in der späten Kaiserzeit neben anderen Erlöser-Göttern spürbar an Bedeutung gewonnen" in *Dionysos Bacchus: Kult und Wandlungen des Weingottes* (Munich: Callwey, 1986), 38.

[24] Maria Teresa Marabini Moevs, "Dionysos at the Altar of Rhea: A Myth of Darkness and Rebirth in Ptolemaic Alexandria," in *Terra Marique: Studies in Art History and Marine Archaeology in Honor of Anna Marguerite McCann on the Receipt of the Gold Medal of the Archaeological Institute of America*. (ed. J. Pollini; London: Oxbow Books, 2005), 83.

A personification of Nysa stands at the left of the scene holding one hand out towards Dionysos with the other hand wrapped in a golden garment, exhibiting *manuum velatio*. The women in the scene are all crowned with wreaths of purple flowers and green leaves and most wear gold diadems. A gray rectangular box in which one purple flower grows is situated in the left corner of the panel. Flowers are frequently associated with Dionysos and are particularly appropriate here in a celebration of his epiphany.[25] Next to Nysa appears a nurse, Anatrophe, who displays an identical pose of *manuum velatio*. Three nymphs dressed in colorful garments prepare a bath for Dionysos in the left corner. One fills a gold or bronze tub with water, while another kneels before it and lets the water run through her fingers. The third nymph stands behind them, looking away from Dionysos, as she exhibits the sheet in which Dionysos will be wrapped after his bath. Both of her hands are enclosed within the fabric in a gesture of *manuum velatio*.

Tropheus, the silenus who will serve as Dionysos' teacher, stands directly before his charge with both hands held forward.[26] Ambrosia and Nektar, the divine foods, stand behind Hermes on his left and right respectively. Theogonia, the personification of divine birth, appears at the right end of the panel with her right hand raised. She is dressed in a luxurious white and gold dress and is specially adorned with a nimbus around her head; in this panel, only Theogonia and Dionysos feature a nimbus. Her chief status in the panel is certainly logical. Most of the figures look towards Dionysos with their hands held out in what could be interpreted as merely a gesture of welcoming, but more likely as a sign of veneration.

Images of the infant Dionysos are relatively popular in Greek and Roman art from the fifth century B.C.E. onward. When the representation of the panel of the Epiphany of Dionysos in the House of Aion is considered in its local Late Antique eastern Mediterranean context, the manner in which Hermes holds Dionysos coupled with the personifications accompanying the god, can be taken to convey a significant religious idea.[27] The mosaic's proclamation of the divinity of Dionysos suggests that the Cy-

---

[25] Orphic Hymn, 30; Pindar Fr. 75.

[26] Sileni is a term often used to describe older satyrs, male followers of Dionysos who are distinguished by their human and animal features. Silenus himself is typically accredited as the father of the chorus of satyrs in satyr-plays, and ancient literary tradition treats him as the tutor of Dionysos, the one with whom Hermes leaves the infant to be nurtured when he departs Mount Nysa. "[Dionysos] was accompanied... by a personal attendant and caretaker, Seilenos, who was his adviser and instructor in the most excellent pursuits and contributed greatly to the high achievements and fame of Dionysos." (Diodorus Siculus, 4.4.3)

[27] Daszewski and Michaelides, *Guide*, 64–71.

priot owner of the House of Aion was a pagan who believed that Dionysos was the new supreme god, a pagan savior as opposed to the Christian savior, Jesus Christ.[28]

## The Other Panels

The top left scene of the mosaic features the mythological story of Leda and Zeus.[29] Leda, Queen of Sparta, is a mortal woman whose beauty interests Zeus. Although somewhat damaged, Zeus is discernable, disguised as a swan. Leda reveals her nude body to him as the three other women with whom she was bathing look on. The one at left rests her elbow upon an altar behind which stands a male figure and the middle woman carries a pitcher. A bearded personification of the Eurotas River is seated at the right of the scene accompanied by a personification of Lakedaemonia.

A rare scene is illustrated in the center panel of the mosaic: the beauty contest between Cassiopeia and the Nereids. Cassiopeia is the wife of either Cepheus, ruler of Ethiopia, and mother of their daughter, Andromeda, or Phoenix, king of Sidon or Tyre.[30] The most common myth revolves around the audacity of Cassiopeia, a mere mortal; after she proclaimed that she was more beautiful than the Nereids, Poseidon sent a sea monster which could only be stopped from ravaging the entire land by the sacrifice of Andromeda.[31] The mosaic in the House of Aion displays a different version in which Cassiopeia is victorious and presumably presents Cassiopeia as the wife of Phoenix. The eastern tradition behind the story is revealed by the fact that two other mosaics in Syria are the only other visual representations showing this outcome, while there is no literary evidence to support it.[32] The scene in Nea Paphos is divided, with the left

---

[28] Arthur Evans explores the concept of Dionysian religion as a salvation religion in *The God of Ecstasy: Sex-Roles and the Madness of Dionysos*, New York: St. Martin's Press, 1988, 158.

[29] See Timothy G. Gantz, *Early Greek Myth: A Guide to Literary and Artistic Sources* (Baltimore: The Johns Hopkins University Press, 1993), 318–21, for the Leda and Zeus myth.

[30] Hesiod, *Ehoiai,* 20.

[31] See Jean-Charles Balty, "Kassiepeia," in *Lexicon Iconographicum Mythologiae Classicae Supplementum.* (Zurich: Artemis Verlag, 1997), 666–70. Sophocles and Euripides both wrote tragedies about Andromeda which are now lost.

[32] Jean-Charles Balty, "Une version orientale mécunnue du myth de Cassiopée" in *Mythologie gréco-romaine, mythologies périphériques: études d'iconographie* (ed. L. Kahil and C. Augé; Paris: Editions du centre national de la recherché scientifique, 1981), 95–106; W. A. Daszewski, "Cassiopeia in Paphos: A Levantine Going West," in *Acts of*

side depicting the scene on land and the right side illustrating the one at sea. Aion, the personification of eternity, sits as the judge in the middle of the picture, wearing a golden crown and grasping a golden scepter. His partially preserved right hand points to Cassiopeia, declaring her the victor of the contest. The Cypriot mosaic differs from the Syrian works in a significant way in that Aion replaces Poseidon as the judge.

The left panel with Cassiopeia has sustained some damage. Cassiopeia presents her nude body in a manner reminiscent of Aphrodite Anadyomene, arisen from the sea. Her pose is nearly identical to the one Leda models in the panel above. A winged personification of judgment, Krisis, adorned with a nimbus, stands to Cassiopeia's right and crowns her with one hand, while holding a palm branch in her other hand. Two other crowns lie on a table positioned behind her. Perhaps three crowns would have been in order had the Nereids been victorious, as only three of Nereus' reputed fifty daughters appear on the right panel. However, Cassiopeia's crown is crafted of gold and features a jewel in its center, while the others look as though they were fashioned from inferior materials. Behind Cassiopeia appears a small female servant, mostly destroyed, whom an inscription names [Ther]apaine. A small nude boy, identified as Kairos, the personification of good fortune, presents a small round object to Cassiopeia, perhaps a golden coin which he has drawn from the vase to his right. Helios reaches down from the top register of the panel to congratulate Cassiopeia. A line beneath his torso creates a clear separation, an indication that he was perched in the clouds high above, looking down at the scene from Mount Olympos. He displays his characteristic whip in hand and a nimbus surrounds his head. Selene may have appeared with him, hovering above the left side of the scene.[33] On the right panel appear Doris, Thetis, and Galatea, the three representative Nereids whose heads are each adorned with a nimbus.[34] They depart into the sea aided by Bythos and Pontos; the former is a sea centaur who personifies the depths of the sea by the crab pincers atop his head, while the latter is a triton who embodies the surface of the sea by the rudder he holds in his hand. Zeus and Athena gaze at Cassiopeia with approval and hold their hands out towards

---

*the International Archaeological Symposium, "Cyprus Between the Orient and the Occident"* (ed. V. Karageorghis; Nicosia: Published for the Republic of Cyprus by the Dept. of Antiquities, 1986), 454–71.

[33] Daszewski and Michaelides, *Guide*, 69.

[34] The distribution of the nimbus in the House of Aion mosaic seems to have been carefully planned. It is striking that only Dionysos and Theogonia display one in the Epiphany panel, where it may allude to a heightened religiosity. In other panels, it serves to highlight the importance of certain figures, such as Krisis, the three Nereids and the Olympian divinities.

her from above. Two *erotes* create an appropriate atmosphere for a beauty contest.[35]

The musical contest between the silenus, Marsyas, and the god, Apollo is represented in the bottom right panel.[36] Apollo sits at the right of the panel, leaning upon his beloved lyre, the instrument of Marsyas' demise. The god holds a symbol of his victory, a laurel branch in which a chain of red and white beads has been intertwined. These beads also hang from the crown of laurel leaves he wears in his hair. Apollo points at Marsyas with his right hand, condemning the silenus to death. Marsyas had committed a fatal mistake by daring the god to compete in a musical contest. Marsyas had intended to use his double-flutes, which now lie useless at Apollo's feet, in the challenge against the divine music produced by Apollo's lyre. Two Scythians, identified as such by an inscription above their heads, constrain Marsyas. They lead him towards the tree on the left of the panel from which they will presently hang him, their hands clutching his hair and crown of reeds. Marsyas' hands and eyes reach towards Apollo in supplication, while Olympos, a student of Marsyas, has thrown himself before the god's feet. An inscription identifies the woman observing the scene next to Apollo as Plane, personification of the errant mind. She leans against a column and holds up her right hand.

The final panel, on the bottom left, depicts the triumphal procession of Dionysos. A male and a female centaur lead the golden chariot on which the god was brought in. Unfortunately, this panel is quite damaged and a few fragments of a blue cloak are all that remain of Dionysos. Tropheus appears at the left of the scene, seated upon a donkey. His mostly bald head crowned with flowers, Tropheus clutches a long staff in his right hand. Below his feet sits a flowerbox, similar in formation to the one in the Epiphany of Dionysos panel, from which spring two purple flowers. A small satyr boy identified as Skirtos offers a tray of fruit to the god in his chariot. His face is directed towards the god with full awe. The remaining figures in this panel are discussed later.

---

[35] Eros, the Greek god of love, frequently appears in multiple forms [erotes] throughout ancient art.

[36] Ovid, *Metamorphoses*, 6.380–390.

## Monotheizing Dionysos

Literary evidence for a possible monotheizing trend in Dionysian religion is provided by Macrobius.[37] In his work, *Saturnalia,* written in the early fifth century C.E., he addresses the notion of monotheizing tendencies in which there is one supreme pagan god who embodies all of the other gods. He specifically cites evidence illustrating how Apollo and Dionysos are worshipped as the same god. Of particular note is his declaration that "likewise the Boeotians, although they speak of Mount Parnassus as sacred to Apollo, nevertheless pay honor there both to the Delphic oracle and to the caves of Bacchus as dedicated to a single god."[38] In Nea Paphos, then, the mythological scene of Apollo and Marsyas would have likely been understood as a direct reference to Dionysos.[39]

The inclusion of Plane in this panel may have been striking at first in a pagan context, but within the constructs of a new monotheizing Dionysian religion influenced by Christianity, Orphism, and Neoplatonism, such a figure is indeed appropriate. In an exploration of the Christian conception of Plane, George MacRae describes the relationship between the Sophia myth and the figure of Plane using the *Gospel of Truth* from the Nag Hammadi Library.[40]

> Indeed the all went about searching for the one from whom he had come forth, and the all was inside him, the incomprehensible, inconceivable one, who is superior to every thought. Ignorance of the Father brought about anguish and terror. And anguish grew solid like a fog so that no one was able to see. For this reason Plane became powerful; she fashioned her own matter, not having known the truth. She set about making a creature, virtually preparing, in beauty, a substitute for truth.[41]

This Gospel is a Gnostic document that reveals the intellectual atmosphere which led to the development of such religious figures as Plane. It is "the projection of the human predicament onto a 'pleromatic' scale," that led to her creation and the Marsyas story can also be understood in such a context.[42]

---

[37] See Alan Cameron, "The Date and Identity of Macrobius," *Journal of Roman Studies* 56 (1966): 25–38.

[38] Macrobius, *Saturnalia,* I. 18. 2.

[39] Bowersock, *Hellenism*, 52.

[40] George W. MacRae, "The Jewish Background of the Gnostic Myth of Sophia," *Novum Testamentum* 12, 2 (1970): 96.

[41] Opening lines of the *Gospel of Truth*, as quoted in MacRae, "Jewish Background," 96.

[42] MacRae, "Jewish Background," 97.

Marsyas himself is often chosen as a traditional symbol of the uncivilized barbaric world. Representative of the savage tendencies of humankind, Marsyas and his impulsive action perhaps can be understood as standing in opposition to all that a monotheizing Dionysian religion symbolizes.[43] The gesture of Plane's raised hand may signify objection or disbelief, but it more fittingly represents a combination of farewell and an acknowledgment that Marsyas had to pay the ultimate sacrifice for committing error.[44] Writing in the fifth century C.E. as well, was Nonnos of Panopolis who composed a great epic entitled *Dionysiaca*.[45] Emphasizing the singularity of Dionysos and promoting him to a level worthy of the subject of an epic, Nonnos attests to the popularity of Dionysos in Late Antiquity. Nonnos' religious persuasion is somewhat uncertain, though, as he also composed a hexameter version of St. John's Gospel. Nonetheless, Nonnos' sentiments are so charged with religious fervor for Dionysos that it is difficult to dismiss him as simply a Christian who wrote "classicizing verse."[46]

The story of Leda and Zeus alludes also to Dionysos, as their encounter symbolizes the immense consequences of Zeus' sexual escapades with mortals.[47] Dionysos' status as the son of the king of the gods is expressly stressed by their inclusion. The satyr figure draped in a panther's skin and crowned with a wreath of green leaves standing in the upper left hand corner of this panel, although much damaged, adds a distinctive Dionysian element to the scene. He may have been included exclusively to ensure the presence of Dionysos in the panel.[48]

The central image of the Beauty Contest between Cassiopeia and the Nereids fits well into a reading of the mosaic as part of a Dionysian monotheizing trend. There is a clear influence of Neoplatonist thought on the panel. One of the major preoccupations of Neoplatonism was with the

---

[43] Greek philosophers commonly refer to Marsyas. Plato, *Symposium*, 216d, f.; *Republic*, 3.399e. Daszewski and Michaelides, *Guide*, 70.

[44] As the personification of the concept of error, the presence of Plane here could represent the embodiment of the defined path of rectitude that one who embraced the Dionysos could attain.

[45] See Paul Collart, *Nonnos de Panopolis: Études sur la Composition et le Texte des Dionysiaques* (Paris: L'Institut Français D'Archéologie Orientale, 1930).

[46] Simon Hornblower and Antony Spawforth, eds. *The Oxford Classical Dictionary* (3d ed.; Oxford and New York: Oxford University Press, 1996), s.v. "Nonnos". See Evans, *The God of Ecstasy*, 153f. for further discussion of Nonnos. Bowersock has suggested that Nonnos' version of St. John was perhaps written by an imitator because of the stylistic differences in his *Dionysiaca* (Bowersock, *Hellenism*, 43).

[47] Daszewski, *Dionysos*, 33–35.

[48] Daszewski and Michaelides, *Guide*, 65.

notion of beauty and its embodiment of order.[49] Cassiopeia presents a visual manifestation of the philosophical message of Neoplatonism as the mortal embodiment of its tenets.[50] Her supreme beauty signifies peace as opposed to the violence and negativity embodied by the less beautiful Nereids and their tumultuous home in the sea, a philosophical idea that can be extended to a division between the gods of the heavens and those of the sea; Cassiopeia's cosmic character extends beyond her death as she was transformed into a constellation. The correlation between Aion and Dionysos is clarified later, but presumably in this period and location, Dionysos was seen as the ultimate cosmic god and Cassiopeia's story was understood as a means to denote his power.

One of the two Syrian mosaics showing Cassiopeia's victory was discovered in what Jean-Charles Balty has suggested was a philosophical school.[51] Such an image as Cassiopeia's victory in Nea Paphos reflects the education and influences behind the religious and philosophical beliefs of the owners of the House of Aion. Additionally, the last panel, illustrating the Triumph of Dionysos, features several items associated with the Dionysian mysteries. The initiatory manner of the cult of Dionysos is made known from archaic and classical Greek imagery and literature down to the famous Latin inscription, the senatus consultum of Bacchanalibus of 186 B.C.E.[52] The niche behind the great figural mosaic was presumably home to a statue in antiquity. The statue may have been the object of cult worship, but this cannot be substantiated beyond its consideration in combination with the iconographical and other evidence from the home. The imagination quickly conjures images of a Dionysian ritual enacted before this very niche, the feet of his followers moving about the colorful mosaic

---

[49] Suidas III, p. 39, n. 455 (A. Adler edition) Suidas defines Cassiopeia as an *onoma kurion* which has connotations of beauty, power, and authority.

[50] Such pagan emperors as Licinius and Julian the Apostate were educated in Neoplatonism. See Richard T. Wallis, *Neoplatonism* (Cambridge: Hackett Publishing Company, 1995) and Dominic J. O'Meara, *Neoplatonism and Christian Thought* (Albany: State University of New York Press,. 1982) for the intersections of Neoplatonism, paganism, and Christianity. Daszewski provides a detailed discussion of this issue (Daszewski, "Cassiopeia," 461–67).

[51] Jean-Charles Balty, "Cassiopée," 95–106. There is a famous mosaic depicting Socrates and his disciples in Apamea, Syria which has been interpreted as a visual statement made by Neoplatonists on the development of Christian art, particularly the motif of mother and child, under Julian the Apostate. It has even been suggested that the image of Socrates in the likes of Jesus Christ is supposed to reference Julian himself. See Bowersock, *Julian*, 19.

[52] See Thomas H. Carpenter, *Dionysian Imagery in Archaic Greek Art* (Oxford: Clarendon Press, 1986) and Martin Persson Nilsson, *The Dionysian Mysteries of the Hellenistic and Roman Ages* (Salem: Ayer, 1957).

boasting of his birth and life. Perhaps they also conducted a ritual centered on a bath in the triclinium or a nearby room as remarkably, a small oval basin with mosaic flooring was discovered in the wall of one of the small rooms.[53] In his effort to deny the holiness of the mosaic, Deckers raises the important issue that the mosaic is featured on the floor of a dining room and not a cultic room. The triclinium, however, is a sensible room for worship of the god Dionysos, particularly within the unique religious context of the House of Aion in Nea Paphos. The recognition of the function of the room as a place in which men ate and drank by no means devalues the religious interpretation of the mosaic, as Deckers attempts to do by claiming that the mosaic stood simply as a message for "ein daseinsfreudiges Lebensideal."[54] Merrymaking and drinking were activities strongly associated with Dionysos and they certainly could have been enjoyed in a triclinium decorated with what can be deemed religious art.

The figure at left in the Triumph of Dionysos panel carries a *liknos*, a type of ritual basket, on her head, while the lead maenad holds a strange object which is decorated with a fillet and set on a low base. On a mosaic in the House of Dionysos, only a few hundred meters away from the House of Aion, a maenad carrying a similar object leads another procession.[55] The similarities between the two suggest the survival of some semblance of the traditional Dionysian mysteries into the fourth century C.E. in Nea Paphos. The Triumph scene in the House of Aion has a notably solemn character, distinctly unlike typical representations of the event, and its message may be clarified by a small detail noted by Daszewski. He observed that Tropheus' ears appear as those of the typical silenus in the panel of the Epiphany, however after adhering to the path set forth by Dionysos his ears were transformed by the Triumph into a distinctive anthropomorphic form.[56] The appearance of flowers both in the Epiphany and Triumph panels can be compared to the growth of flowers on the bottom edge of the Christian mosaics in the Sant'Apollinare Nuovo in Ravenna. Both pagan and Christian examples attest to the ushering in of a new religious era in which flowers can be understood to didactically symbolize the flourishing brought by each respective god.[57] A scene such as a triumph certainly has the connotations of power and victory appropriate to a new monotheizing

[53] It measured 54 x 30 cm. Daszewski, *Dionysos*, 18.

[54] Deckers, "Dionysos," 166.

[55] See Christine Kondoleion, *Domestic and Divine: Roman Mosaics in the House of Dionysos* (London: Cornell University Press, 1994).

[56] Daszewski, *Dionysos,* 44.

[57] See Natalya Sidorova, *Corpus Vasorum Antiquorum*, Pushkin State Museum of Fine Arts. Russia. Fasc. IV, Rome: L'Erma, 2001, Plate 22; see Figure 4 below.

conception of a god in a competitive religious environment, while also serving as an emphatic conclusion to the series of panels in the House of Aion mosaic.

## Pagan Past

Cyprus, located in the eastern Mediterranean at the crossroads of East and West, was the locus of an interesting combination of religious and philosophical influences that created a particularly ripe environment for the production of unique imagery by both pagan and Christian communities. In the scene of the Epiphany of Dionysos, several iconographic motifs appear strikingly similar to Christian scenes of the Virgin Mary holding the infant Christ. The action of the scene itself, the preparation of a bath for a new god, is a popular Christian subject. Another bath scene on a mosaic is extant from Nea Paphos. In the Villa of Theseus, a fifth-century C.E. representation of Achilles' first bath decorated the floor of a triclinium.[58] Daszewski describes how "this representation sets the pattern for later depictions of the Nativity and the first bath of Jesus Christ as depicted in mosaics and murals of Byzantine and Medieval churches."[59] In the mosaic, Anatrophe, the nurse who appears also in the panel of the Epiphany of Dionysos in the House of Aion mosaic, kneels down before a bath, carefully holding the infant Achilles with her intentionally covered hands. A strong connection can be established between the two mosaics, as in each one the main subject is an infant, treated with deliberate care in the form of *manuum velatio*, who appears on the lap of an important figure before a bath. The unearthing of an actual basin in the House of Aion is particularly intriguing given the significance of these bath scenes. Both the infants Dionysos and Achilles raise their hands in the mosaics, conjuring up images of the raised hands of Christ as the Redeemer.[60] Although the mosaics are separated by a number of years, the parallels between such specific motifs are too great to dismiss.

---

[58] Daszewski proposes that the Imperial governor of Nea Paphos officiated in the room in which the mosaic of the Bath of Achilles was discovered (Daszewski and Michaelides, *Guide*), 60, fig. 44.

[59] Daszewski and Michaelides, *Guide*, 62–63.

[60] A silver vial for oil, dating to c. 600 C.E., bears a rather early representation of the Virgin and Child with Christ depicted raising one of his hands. Wolfgang Fritz Volbach, *Early Christian Art* (New York: Harry N. Abrams, 1962), fig. 254.

When *manuum velatio* appears in Late Antique art, the motif is historically associated with Roman imperial iconography.[61] In an article entitled, "Der Ritus der verhüllten Hände," Albrecht Dieterich traces the use of *manuum velatio* from the fourth century C.E. through the Renaissance period.[62] In his review of Dieterich's work, Clifford Moore relates Dieterich's theory of the history of *manuum velatio* as a "custom, originally Persian...made known to the West by the campaigns of Alexander the Great...taken into the ritual of Isis...and gradually spread over the Roman world."[63] Dieterich explores how Constantinus Porphyrogenitus, writing in the tenth century C.E., specified that Diocletian featured the gesture as a part of his ceremonial court program by the third century C.E. and that *manuum velatio* was used in the church throughout the Byzantine period.[64] As Cyprus was under the authority of the Diocese of the East, this plausibly could have been one route for the spread of iconographical motifs.[65] However, *manuum velatio* was indeed used as a gesture of respect across the empire, as it appears in a painting from a chamber tomb at Durostorum on the Danube. Dating to the mid fourth century C.E., servants are shown approaching the deceased couple for whom the tomb was built.[66] A belt associated with the master's official uniform of state office is treated with special care; one servant passes it to another whose covered hands wait to receive it.

*Manuum velatio* appears in Christian scenes often when the Magi present gifts to Christ or when Christ blesses objects. In several mosaics from the Sant'Apollinare Nuovo in Ravenna, dating to the late fifth and early sixth centuries C.E., *manuum velatio* emphasizes the solemn religious significance of the scenes. In an image of the Adoration of the Magi,

---

[61] See Andreas Alföldi, *Die monarchische Repra□sentation im ro□mischen Kaiserreiche* (Darmstadt: Wissenschaftliche Buchgesellschaft, 1970), 33–35; Deckers, "Dionysos," 159–160.

[62] Albrecht Dieterich, "Der Ritus der verhüllten Hände," *Kleine Schriften* (Leipzig: B.G. Teubner, 1911), 440–49.

[63] Clifford H. Moore, "Review of *Kleine Schriften mit einem Bildniss und zwei Tafeln*," *Classical Philology* 9, 1 (1914): 103–7. Richard Wünsch worked on preparing Dieterich's *Kleine Schriften* for publication after the latter's death and Wünsch himself added to the evidence that *manuum velatio* was "native to the Roman worship of Fides." Moore, "Review," 105. Elfriede Regina Knauer investigates the eastern evidence in, "Toward the History of the Sleeved Coat: A Study of the Impact of an Ancient Eastern Garment on the West," *Expedition* 21, 1 (1978): 21–23.

[64] Dieterich, "Ritus," 445–46.

[65] See Glainville Downey, "The Claim of Antioch to Ecclesiastical Jurisdiction over Cyprus," *Proceedings of the American Philosophical Society* 102, 3 (1958): 224–28.

[66] Katherine M. Dunbabin, "The Waiting Servant in Later Roman Art," *American Journal of Philology* 124, 3 (2003): 461.

*Figure 3:* Three Magi before the Virgin and Child enthroned with Angels, 6th century C.E., S. Apollinare Nuovo, Ravenna

two of the kings' hands are conspicuously draped with elaborately decorated fabric (Figure 3).[67] Melichior, the young beardless king, perhaps confirms his youth by his failure to cover his hands. Another example shows fabric covering the figures' hands as Christ blesses loaves and fish.[68] Particularly intriguing scenes of the Baptism of Christ decorated both apexes of the Arian and Orthodox Baptisteries, dating to the first half of the sixth century C.E. and 458 C.E. respectively. Around the circular scene of each baptism, apostles hold crowns out for Christ with distinctly veiled hands.[69] In the present day, Catholic churches still use the gesture in various capacities.

Although *manuum velatio* is historically associated with Imperial and Christian art, the scene of the Epiphany of Dionysos in the House of Aion is steeped in an iconographic tradition that is distinctly pagan. An examination of older representations of the Epiphany of Dionysos reveals the Greek convention of *manuum velatio*. Hermes consistently uses some sort of cloth to hold the infant Dionysos which in the case of a mid-fifth century B.C.E. red-figured *pelike* even covers his hands.[70] It is a natural protective inclination to envelop infants in soft material in an effort to provide a safe haven and thus it is sometimes difficult to distinguish *manuum velatio* from an image of a mother or guardian, divine or mortal, simply swaddling a child as expected. On a white-ground calyx-krater, also of the mid-fifth century B.C.E., Hermes soberly hands the infant Dionysos, wrapped

[67] Volbach, *Early Christian Art*, fig. 152–53.

[68] Ibid. fig. 150.

[69] T. F. Mathews, *The Clash of the Gods* (Princeton: Princeton University Press, 1999), fig. 102 and 128.

[70] See *Lexicon iconographicum mythologiae classica* III, 1986, 683.

*Figure 4:* Hermes and Dionysos, 5th century B.C.E.; detail of an Attic calyx-krater by the Villa Giulia Painter.

in red fabric, to a seated silenus.[71] The iconographic tradition of the enthroned infant son of a god can be identified on a fifth-century B.C.E. red-figured calyx-krater on which a seated Hermes holds out the infant Dionysos as he stretches his hands towards a nymph standing before him (Figure 4).[72]

A herm discovered in the Athenian agora acts as a support for a statue of Hermes holding the infant Dionysos.[73] Only partially preserved, the shaft and head of the herm are complete. Atop the head lies a heavily draped arm in the gesture of *manuum velatio*, holding the nude bottom of an infant. This work is identified as a Roman copy of a work originally created by the fourth-century B.C.E. sculptor, Kephisodotos.[74] He also

[71] Calyx-krater, Vatican, 559. Beth Cohen, *The Colors of Clay: Special Techniques in Athenian Vases (*Los Angeles: J. Paul Getty Museum, 2006), 334–36.

[72] Pushkin State Museum of Fine Arts, Moscow. Inv. II 1b 732 (Inv. 31749 / 95). See *Corpus Vasorum Antiquorum* Russia 4, Pushkin 4, pl. 22. Deckers, "Dionysos," 156, fig. 7.

[73] Evelyn B. Harrison, *Archaic and Archaistic Sculpture* (Athenian Agora 11; Princeton: American School of Classical Studies at Athens, 1965), 162–65, pl. 56.

[74] Pliny, *Natural History*, XXXIV, 87. Pliny provides evidence for the existence of two sculptors named Kephisodotos. One was the son of Praxiteles, named Kephisodotos presumably, as Greek tradition required, after his grandfather. Praxiteles' father is never

crafted a famous sculpture of Eirene, or Peace, with her infant son, Ploutos, or Wealth, known only from Roman copies. Pausanias records that the statue of Eirene and Ploutos stood in the Athenian Agora, between the Tholos and the Temple of Ares.[75] Eirene, heavily draped, carries Ploutos in her left arm. The infant's lower body is wrapped in a garment that separates his skin from that of his mother. Pausanias describes a sculpture of Hermes holding the infant Dionysos made by Praxiteles, a son of Kephisodotos; a sculpture of Hermes and Dionysos discovered in the late nineteenth century is believed by most scholars to be a copy of the Praxitelean masterpiece.[76] Praxiteles employed a composition similar to that used by his father for the groups of Hermes holding Dionysos and Eirene carrying Ploutos. The infant sits perched on Hermes' left forearm, resting upon drapery arranged specifically to cover the skin where Dionysos makes contact with Hermes. Although it is now missing, Dionysos once reached for something, probably a bunch of grapes, held by Hermes in his right hand. Kephisodotos' sculpture of Eirene holding Ploutos and Praxiteles' work of Hermes carrying Dionysos each feature *manuum velatio* and stand as significant hallmarks of Greek sculpture whose fame persisted through the Roman period due to the frequent copies made of both images.[77]

A Roman wall-painting, dating to the first-century B.C.E., bears a depiction of a seated nymph, probably Nysa, holding the infant Dionysos on her lap. Crowned with ivy leaves, Dionysos is wrapped tenderly in her skirts.[78] Two heavily draped women observe them from the left of the scene. The seated position of the female figure and Dionysos echoes the enthroned motif of Hermes and Dionysos on earlier Greek vases and anticipates its portrayal in the later House of Aion mosaic. Hermes carries Dionysos with his cloak positioned intentionally over his arm, in the form of a second-century C.E. Corinthian table support and also on a mosaic from Antioch, dated to the second half of the fourth-century C.E.[79] In the

---

named explicitly, but the other Kephisodotos known to Pliny had a floruit of the hundred and second Olympiad, 371–368 B.C.E., which would correspond to the time of Praxiteles' father.

[75] Pausanias, 1.8.3 and 9.16.2.

[76] Pausanias describes the location of the Praxitelean Hermes and Dionysos in the Temple of Hera, 5.17.3. The Olympia Museum identifies the work as the original sculpture of Praxiteles.

[77] The utilization of manuum velatio in Greek art is explicit in these scenes, securing a date for its use before the time of Alexander the Great.

[78] Hamdorf, *Dionysos Bacchus*, 99. The painting was unearthed in a home beneath the Villa Farnesia in Rome.

[79] Aileen Ajootian, "A Roman Table Support at Ancient Corinth," *Hesperia* 69 (2000): 487–507. Lawrence Becker and Christine Kondoleon, *The Arts of Antioch, Art*

latter example, Dionysos' head is surrounded by a nimbus and Hermes' cloak is carefully draped around his hands in a gesture of *manuum velatio*. The mosaic is dated between 350 and 400 C.E. and thus was essentially contemporaneous with the House of Aion mosaic.

Another fragment from the Antioch mosaic shows the head of a nymph and so the mosaic may have featured a scene at Mount Nysa similar to the one in Nea Paphos. The relationship between the two mosaics is particularly intriguing given the tension that existed between the two cities in the early Christian era. Since the late third century C.E, the Church of Cyprus had been administered by Antioch and controversies between the two finally erupted in the early fifth century C.E.[80] A connection between the two cities' pagan communities, at least on an artistic level, may be suggested. The Syrian influence on the Cassiopeia panel in the House of Aion is apparent and the Hermes and Dionysos connection in Antioch strengthens the evidence for shared iconography between Cyprus and the East.

Beyond the realm of iconography, the Classical period produced various cultural artifacts in many forms that would be later studied and appropriated by future generations in the development of their religious ideologies. Arthur Evans wrote a revealing study of Euripides' *Bacchae* as a source for much of Christian mythology in which he says "in the 4$^{th}$ century…Christian theologians rediscovered the play and, struck by parallels between it and the gospels, came to the conclusion that God had providentially used Euripides to help prepare the way for Christian belief."[81] Gregory Nazianzos' *The Passion of Christ*, written in the fourth century C.E., even uses direct quotations from Euripides.

The motif of mother and child is not a purely Christian iconographic image nor does it originate in fifth-century B.C.E. art, rather it extends back to a time before the third millennium B.C.E. The concept of a goddess and divine child is already seen with the Sumerian Dumuzi (Tammuz) and Inanna (Ishtar).[82] Imagery of *kourotrophoi* as all-encompassing Mother goddesses are found all over the ancient world.[83] The *kourotrophos*,

---

*Historical and Scientific Approaches to Roman Mosaics and a Catalogue of the Worcester Art Museum Antioch Collection* (Worcester: Worcester Art Museum, 2005), 190–95.

[80] Michaelides, "Early Christian Mosaics," 195.

[81] See Evans, *The God of Ecstasy*, 145–73, for the chapter, "Dionysos and Christ"; Heinz Noetzel, *Christus und Dionysos: Bermerkungen zum religionsgeschichtlichen Hintergrund von Johannes 2, 1–11* (Stuttgart: Calwer Verlag, 1960); Robert M. Price, *Deconstructing Jesus* (Amherst: Prometheus Books, 2000).

[82] Sir Arthur Evans, *The Palace of Minos at Knossos* (London: Macmillan & Co., 1930), III, 468.

[83] Frazer has argued that this concept is universal in ancient religion. A great goddess is typically attended by a male attendant who is born, dies, and is resurrected and thus

then, is a "multi-faced deity" whose image persists throughout ancient art and continues into the Christian repertoire of icons to become the standardized Virgin and infant Christ.[84] In Egyptian art, mother and child imagery existed also in the iconography of the boy-god, Horus or Harpokrates, son of Isis and Osiris. Images of Horus seated on the lap of his mother begin in the second millennium B.C.E. and continue through the Common Era.[85] The motif appears also in images of Neferure, the daughter of the Pharaoh Hatshepsut, and her tutor, Senenmut dating to the mid-second millennium B.C.E.[86] His pride in serving as the child's protector is apparent in the way he encloses her within his cloak. In addition to sharing similar iconographical motifs, Dionysos and Osiris had similar experiences as Osiris was dismembered by his brother Seth and then reassembled and brought back to life by Isis. In the first century B.C.E., Diodorus declares that Dionysos and Osiris are "the same."[87]

## Christian Future

Arnold Toynbee referred to the patent connections between the Egyptian and Christian motifs when he stated, "The parallel with the Madonna and Child of Christian iconography is too obvious to need comment and in fact such paintings may well have influenced Early Christian art."[88] Such a statement recognizes that connections exist, but fails to investigate the cultural atmosphere responsible for the development of such parallels. Jaś Elsner appears more open to such an investigation when he says, "It is by no means impossible that Christianity borrowed the Virgin and Child

symbolizes the cycle of agriculture (*Lectures on the Early History of Kingship,* London: Macmillan, 1905), 128f. See also Lucy Goodison and Christine Morris, *Ancient Goddesses: The Myths and the Evidence* (London: British Museum Press, 1998), 113. Theodora Hadzisteliou Price, *Kourotrophos: Cults and Representations of the Greek Nursing Deities* (Leiden: E. J. Brill, 1978) is a comprehensive study of the iconography of the nursing goddess.

[84] Price, *Kourotrophos*, 2. Goddesses as diverse as Demeter, Hera, and Hestia could take on the role of a *kourotrophos*.

[85] See Hans Wolfgang Müller, "Isis mit dem Horuskinde," *Münchner Jahrbuch der bildenden Kunst* 14 (1963): 7–38.

[86] Catherine H. Roehrig, *Hatshepsut: From Queen to Pharaoh* (New Haven: Yale University Press, 2005), 112–19.

[87] Diodorus Siculus, *Library,* 1.15.6

[88] Arnold Joseph Toynbee, *The Crucible of Christianity: Judaism, Hellenism, and the Historical Background to the Christian Faith* (New York: World Publishing Company, 1969), 237.

theme from such images of Isis."[89] Bowersock upholds that "the polytheist past and its antiquities, both physical and conceptual, were absorbed into the new order and became arguably the most fundamental part of it...The Christian empire was a place in which the past was redeployed with new meaning and new fervor. The antique was not something distant or alien. It stood on the front lines of social and religious confrontation."[90] It is here that the specific iconography of Hermes Kourotrophos serves to exemplify this acculturation through which specific pagan imagery is incorporated and manipulated into the iconographical repertoire of a new religion. Scholars, however, often shy away from broadening the spectrum of influence to include specifically Dionysian influence on Christian iconography, rather typically insisting that the opposite was true. The iconographical motif of mother and child and the specific gesture of *manuum velatio* demonstrate how geographical and temporal distances did not hinder the adaptation necessary for the continuation of traditions.

The discourse between pagan and Christian iconography is expressed particularly well on the Projecta casket; found in Rome and dating to the mid-fourth century C.E., this object is distinctly Christian as the inscription "SECUNDE ET PROIECTA VIVATIS IN CHRISTO" attests. A scene of Venus at her toilette, however, accompanied by *erotes*, Nereids, and other sea creatures appears as one decorative motif. The Venus scene had presumably lost any religious value when it was incorporated on such an object, particularly as the alignment of the images suggests that Venus is intended to be understood as a reflection of Projecta herself. Scholars often cite such an object and other silver plates as evidence for the complete appropriation of pagan imagery by Christians. It is important to recognize, though, that the secular nature of the Venus imagery on the Projecta Casket should be treated as markedly different from objects like the House of Aion mosaic. The creation of such images as appear on these luxury silver objects, particularly in the Western Empire, confirm the gradual supremacy of Christianity over paganism. However, scenes of a pagan toilette are not particularly representative of pagan religious scenes. In the Archaic and Classical Greek periods and onward, Aphrodite's toilette was a popular subject for the decoration of vessels made especially for women. Characteristically associated with daily life and religious ritual in the context of weddings, such scenes acted for Athenian women as the

[89] Jaś Elsner, *Imperial Rome and Christian Triumph: The Art of the Roman Empire AD 100–450* (Oxford: Oxford University Press, 1998), 220.

[90] Bowersock, "Recapturing the Past," 3.

same "flattering visual analogy" as Kathleen Shelton suggests it does here for Projecta.[91]

Three painted images in the Catacomb of Priscilla in Rome are among the candidates for the earliest visual representations of the Virgin and Child. The poorly preserved, third-century C.E. paintings appear in three settings. In one of the images, it is possible to make out the form of a seated woman with an infant at her breast. A man, perhaps the prophet Balaam, stands nearby pointing to a star above their heads.[92] Another image depicts three stages from the life of a deceased woman, one of which shows the woman cradling her child. The room in which this painting was discovered is named the "Cubiculum of the Velatio" because one of the stages of the woman's life shows her praying with a veil over her head. The third painting is an illustration of the Adoration of the Magi story in which it is possible to recognize a seated infant on a female's lap.[93] Jarl Fossum, though, contends that images of the Virgin and Child are not created until after the Council of Ephesus in 431 C.E. in which Mary was proclaimed "God-Bearer."[94] A painting from the Catacombs of Saints Mark and Marcellian of the fourth century C.E. displays an image similar to the later canonical Virgin and Child. [95] Although the quality is somewhat poor, the correspondences in composition between the relatively contemporaneous images of this Christian scene and the House of Aion mosaic are still conspicuous. The sarcophagus of Adelphia, dating to c. 340 C.E., is a sculptural example of an early Virgin and Child. It features a scene of the Adoration of the Magi with the Virgin and Child enthroned in a nearly identical pose as Hermes Kourotrophos in the House of Aion.[96]

Although it existed in some form, it is not until the fifth and sixth centuries C.E. that the icon of the Virgin and Child became standardized and widespread. The personifications of the divine food, Nektar, and the birth of the gods, Theogonia, stand behind Hermes and Dionysos in the House of Aion mosaic in a nearly identical manner to the two archangels who typically attend the Virgin and Child. The well-known encaustic painting

[91] Kathleen J. Shelton in *Age of Spirituality* (ed. K. Weitzmann; New York: Metropolitan Museum of Art, 1979), 330.

[92] Numbers 24:17. See Leonard Victor Rutgers, *Subterranean Rome: In Search of the Roots of Christianity in the Catacombs of the Eternal City* (Leuven: Peeters, 2000); and André Grabar, *The Beginnings of Christian Art* (London: Thames and Hudson, 1967), 116, pl. 115.

[93] Mathews, *Clash*, 81–83.

[94] Jarl Fossum, "The Myth of the Eternal Rebirth: Critical Notes on G. W. Bowersock, *Hellenism in Late Antiquity*," *Vigliae Christianae* 53 (1999): 313–14.

[95] Mathews, *Clash*, fig. 61.

[96] Volbach, *Early Christian Art,* 1962, fig. 37.

from the Monastery of St. Catherine, Sinai, dating to the sixth-seventh centuries C.E., makes a dramatic comparison with the House of Aion mosaic.[97] Nektar and Theogonia possess similar characteristics to the two archangels in the Christian work, such as their upward glances, designating them as distinctive figures who invoke the greater religious sense of the scene.[98]

Representations of the Adoration of the Magi correspond to pagan scenes, as already mentioned in regards to their frequent utilization of *manuum velatio*. The manner in which the three Magi line up before Christ draws a parallel with the way the nymphs and other figures surround Hermes and Dionysos in the House of Aion mosaic. A further correlation in iconography can be discerned between the sarcophagus of Adelphia and a Roman sarcophagus on which nymphs wait to receive Dionysos from the seated personification of Mount Nysa.[99] Beyond the iconographic connections between the Adoration of the Magi and the Epiphany of Dionysos panel in the House of Aion mosaic is the similarity between the very narratives. In the Christian version, three kings or wise men bear gifts for Christ on the twelfth day after his birth. Although in the pagan scene in the House of Aion, the nymphs and personifications do not bear tangible gifts, they provide representative gifts; the nymphs prepare a bath, Tropheus represents the future education of Dionysos, and Nektar and Ambrosia provide divine nourishment. Thus, as Bowersock has explored, conceptually, the motives behind the gatherings are not altogether that different.[100]

## Conclusion

The mosaic in the House of Aion attests to the "unparalleled war of images" waged in the fourth century C.E. which Tom Mathews explores in his work, *The Clash of the Gods*.[101] Demetrios Michaelides writes of the period that "there is, if anything, a new forcefulness in the re-statement of pagan values, probably considered to be threatened by the rise of Chris-

[97] Kurt Weitzmann, *The Monastery of Catherine at Mount Sinai* (Princeton: Princeton University Press, 1976), pl. XLIII.

[98] Susan A. Boyd, *Age of Spirituality*, 533.

[99] Villa Albani, 624. See *Lexicon iconographicum mythologiae classicae* III, Dionysos / Bacchus, 150.

[100] Bowersock, *Hellenism*, 52. An opposing view supported by Deckers interprets the mosaic's extraordinary display of iconography in a superficial manner, explaining that "ihre adaption bei der Illustration neuer christlicher – oder auch alter heidnischer – Themes unterlag keinen ideologischen Beschränkungen," Deckers, "Dionysos," 167.

[101] Mathews, *Clash*, 4.

tianity, a phenomenon best illustrated by the mosaics in the House of Aion at Nea Paphos…this age-long tradition…was steadily losing ground to the art of the rising new religion, that finally triumphed in the $6^{th}$ century A.D."[102] The motifs of *manuum velatio* and *kourotrophos* in the House of Aion mosaic present unique glimpses into the way antiquity in antiquity functioned locally in a Cypriot village of the fourth century C.E. Tradition functioned as both a means to sustain the past, and to spur on the creation of new 'pasts' more amenable to contemporary concerns. Before addressing the mosaic in one of his many publications on it, Bowersock explains: "This is late antiquity. What Gibbon and others had seen as a time of decline and decay has been reconceptualized as an era of innovation, creativity, and heightened spirituality…its vigor depended significantly upon a dramatic reappropriation of the legacy of its past."[103]"

Finally it is essential to address why Aion would have been bestowed with such great significance by his central position in the mosaic. His religious significance and Dionysian connections are accentuated by the nimbus around his head and the wreath of golden leaves atop it. Some insight is provided by Epiphanius, a bishop in Salamis, Cyprus who wrote the text *Panarion* in the fourth century C.E. He discusses the pagan festival of Saturnalia and describes its institution on January sixth as a deliberate move to rival the Christian feast of Epiphany. In his mention of the pagan celebrations, Epiphanius states, "if anyone asks them what manner of mysteries these might be, they reply, saying: 'Today at this hour Kore [Persephone], that is the virgin, has given birth to Aion.'"[104] Epiphanius states at another point in his work that January sixth is the birthday of Dionysos. As the celebration of Saturnalia took place in late December Epiphanius is most likely describing the feast of Sol Invictus of December twenty-fifth.[105]

Epiphanius' words as a Christian, Cypriot bishop in the very century in which the House of Aion flourished aid in piecing together the significance behind the House of Aion mosaic and could support a reading of a monotheizing Dionysian message that encompasses Aion, the Sun, and the other gods. Macrobius also considers Dionysos and the Sun one and the same god; quoting Orpheus, he proclaims: "The sun, which men also call by the

[102] Michaelides, *Cypriot Mosaics,* 4.

[103] Bowersock, "Recapturing the Past," 1.

[104] Epiphanius, *Panarion*, 51, 30. Kore (Persephone) is typically attributed as Aion's mother.

[105] See Hugo Rahner, *Greek Myths and Christian Mystery* (London: Burns and Oates, 1957), 137–40, for detailed discussion of this issue.

name Dionysos."[106] Citing an early Orphic verse, Macrobius states, "One Zeus, one Hades, one Sun, one Dionysos."[107] Sir James George Frazer cites Proclus, who was writing in the fifth century C.E., as saying "Dionysos was the last king of the gods appointed by Zeus. For his father set him on the kingly throne, and placed in his hand the scepter, and made him king of all the gods of the world."[108] The House of Aion mosaic dates to an earlier period, but it presents a powerful visual message of a monotheizing Dionysian religion although on the surface it may seem to feature merely a conglomeration of common mythological themes. The many subsidiary figures in the mosaic only increase Dionysos' power, emphasizing the new image of Dionysos. The iconography demonstrates that the transformation of Hermes into Madonna was a conversion which had not yet been completed. This mosaic thus reveals not only the way in which pagans in late antiquity reconstituted their own past, but it also provides a clear pagan history for a major icon of Christianity.

## *Photo Credits*

Fig. 1: Wiktor A. Daszewski and D. Michaelides, *Guide to the Paphos Mosaics* (Nicosia: Bank of Cyprus Cultural Foundation, 1988), Fig. 45. Reproduced with permission of the Department of Antiquities of Cyprus.

Fig. 2: Daszewski and Michaelides, *Guide to the Paphos Mosaics*, Fig. 46. Reproduced with permission of the Department of Antiquities of Cyprus.

Fig. 3: Photo courtesy of Robert Dimin.

Fig. 4: Photo courtesy of the Pushkin State Museum of Fine Arts, Moscow.

[106] Macrobius, *Saturnalia*, I. 18. 18.

[107] Ibid.

[108] Sir James George Frazer, *The Golden Bough* (New York: Macmillan, 1922), 451.

Part Three

# Antiquities of Late Antiquity and Today

# The Bavli's Discussion of Genealogy in *Qiddushin* IV

MOULIE VIDAS

Rabbinic law divides the Jewish people into marital castes or genealogical classes.[1] The Mishnah, in *m. Qidd* 4:1, lists these classes and details the permissible unions among them. In order to prevent the unions proscribed by rabbinic law, the rabbis were concerned with keeping genealogical records and with developing procedures to ensure that each individual was assigned to the correct class. This concern with genealogical knowledge was particularly urgent since this knowledge, given its consequences for personal lives and social status, was likely to be manipulated and abused.

The Babylonian Talmud dedicates a series of *sugyot*, appended to *m. Qidd* 4:1, to a general discussion of this genealogical division. The Talmud's discussion shares with previous rabbinic texts a concern with genealogical knowledge. Surprisingly, though, its authors choose to focus on the instability of this knowledge and its contingent nature. Again and again, these *sugyot* address the gap between innate and socially ascribed genealogical identities.

While earlier rabbinic texts were certainly aware of this gap, the Talmud's discussion departs from those texts in important ways. First, the Bavli presents a special interest in the social processes which lead to the production or manipulation of genealogical identities. It links this production with personal interest and political power. Furthermore, in contrast with its predecessors, the Talmud does not perceive socially ascribed identities as mere errors to be reversed by divine action or rabbinic procedure. In one passage, the Talmud goes so far so as to say that God approves the human processes which lead to the creation of these identities.

More importantly, rabbinic procedure itself is portrayed here as the origin of the perversion and abuse of genealogical knowledge. That is to say, the Talmud does not present us with a reasoned rabbinic discourse which salvages innate, fixed genealogical information from social deception or misperception. Rather, the rabbis are represented as the most authoritative participants in the dynamic processes which produce genealogical know-

[1] I would like to thank Peter Schäfer, Martha Himmelfarb, Vered Noam, Gregg Gardner, Kevin Osterloh, Holger Zellentin, Yair Lipshitz, Elana Messer and Carey Seal for reading earlier versions of this paper and offering helpful advice and comments.

ledge. Rabbinic decisions are shown to be motivated by personal passions, collective interests and power struggles. This focus on the contingent processes behind rabbinic decisions gives rabbinic knowledge a historical dimension.

The historical aspect of genealogical knowledge plays a central role in the first *sugya* on *m. Qidd.* 4:1. The Talmud discusses the historical significance of the mishnah for understanding the biblical Ezra. It contrasts an earlier interpretation of this significance, which is also documented elsewhere in the Talmud, with a new one concerned with the history of genealogical knowledge. In the same opening *sugya,* the Talmud challenges the ideas of genealogical homogeneity and geographical homogeneity, both of which are associated with Ezra, the biblical hero who established Israel as a holy seed and led the restoration of national life in Palestine.

The image of genealogical knowledge presented by the Talmud is realized not only through explicit statements but also through the Talmudic authors' subversive treatment of their literary sources. The Talmud does reproduce earlier teachings which perceive genealogical identity as fixed and innate, but through the reconfiguration and arrangement of these teachings the Talmud either reinterprets them or undermines them.

Genealogy has received much attention in recent scholarship as an important aspect of Ancient Judaism in general and of Babylonian Talmudic culture in particular. It has been studied in the context of the Babylonian community's self-perception,[2] relations between rabbis and non-rabbis,[3] religious and public life,[4] academic leadership,[5] relations between Jews

---

[2] Isaiah Gafni, *The Jews of Babylonia in the Talmudic Era* (Jerusalem: Zalman Shazar Center, 1990; in Hebrew). See also idem, *Land, Center and Diaspora* (Journal for the Study of the Pseudepigrapha: Supplement Series 21; Sheffield: Sheffield Academic Press, 1997), 54–55.

[3] Richard Kalmin, "Genealogy and Polemics in Literature of Late Antiquity," *Hebrew Union College Annual* 67 (1996): 77–94, and idem, *The Sage in Jewish Society in Late Antiquity* (London: Routledge 1999), 51–60.

[4] Aharon Oppenheimer, "Purity of Lineage in Talmudic Babylonia," in *Sexuality and Family in History* (ed. I. Gafni and I. Bartal; Jerusalem: Zalman Shazar Center, 1998; in Hebrew), 71–82.

[5] Jeffrey Rubenstein, *Talmudic Stories: Narrative Art, Composition and Culture* (Baltimore: Johns Hopkins University Press, 1999), 201–6. Rubenstein also dedicates a whole chapter to genealogy in his reconstruction of "talmudic culture"; idem, *Culture of the Babylonian Talmud* (Baltimore: The Johns Hopkins University Press, 2003), 80–101. Both of these studies build upon the arguments in Geoffrey Herman, "*Hakohanim bebavel bitqufat hatalmud*" (Master's Thesis, Hebrew University, 1998), especially those about the place of priestly lineage as a criterion for leadership, 85–90.

and gentiles,[6] and, naturally, marriage.[7] Scholars have also noted that the importance accorded to lineage in Jewish Babylonian culture corresponds to Iranian attitudes towards lineage.[8]

While the Bavli's discussion of *m. Qidd.* 4:1 has played a central role in most of these studies, it has functioned more as evidence for cultural and historical reconstruction than as an object of study in itself. This paper seeks to explore the editorial choices made by the Bavli's creators in the coordination of their sources and to reveal what message – rather than evidence – these choices of composition seek to convey.

The *gemara* to our mishnah presents neither a tightly-redacted line of argument nor a unified literary structure; rather it is composed of a series of literary units which are tied to one another to varying degrees.[9] There-

---

[6] Christine Hayes, *Gentile Impurities and Jewish Identities* (Oxford: Oxford University Press, 2002). For texts discussed in this paper, see pages 171 and 185–87, as well as the general statement on intermarriage and impurity in rabbinic literature, 191–92.

[7] Michael Satlow, *Jewish Marriage in Antiquity* (Princeton: Princeton University Press, 2001), 133–61 (see especially the discussion on 147–56 about the ideological developments in the rabbinic period, and 151–56 on the Babylonian peculiarities); and Adiel Schremer, *Male and Female He Created Them* (Jerusalem: Zalman Shazar Center, 2004; in Hebrew), 147–58 (see especially his comparison between Palestinian and Babylonian traditions, 148–52).

[8] Kalmin, *Sage in Jewish Society*, 8–10 and 58–59; Rubenstein, *Talmudic Stories*, 205–6; and Satlow, *Jewish Marriage*, 152. In an article that appeared after these studies, Maria Macuch argues that the role of descent in Iranian culture was even more central than previously recognized; see her "Zoroastrian Principles and the Structure of Kinship in Sasanian Iran," in *Religious Themes and Texts of Pre-Islamic Iran and Central Asia* (ed. C. Cereti et al.; Beiträge zur Iranistik 24; Wiesbaden: Reichet, 2003), 231–46. On page 232, she writes: "The organization of Zoroastrian kinship seems to be far more important for our understanding of the social and political history of Sasanian Iran than hitherto realized, especially, if we bear in mind that this was a completely different society from our own, in which descent groups were the basic political, religious and economic units."

[9] The *gemara* is composed of the following units: (1) a discussion of the implications of the Mishnah's words, "came up from Babylonia"; (2) identification of biblical verses which support the Mishnah's claim, that specific classes came up from Babylonia; (3) a discussion, taking one of these verses as its point of departure, of marrying genealogically unfit women, which includes a long narrative on Rav Yehuda and sayings in praise of genealogical purity (see more on the structure of this part in n. 44 below); (4) a discussion of the purification of *mamzerim*; (5) a discussion of the Babylonian claim to superiority and the borders of Jewish Babylonia (see below, n. 26 on the interweaving of units 4 and 5); the last three units are each brief and may not have been redacted with the other units; (6) retracts the Babylonian claim to superior genealogy by attributing the Mishnah to a minority view; (7) discusses a *baraita* on the purification of *mamzerim*; (8) discusses the legal situation of the male convert (see below, n. 39 on the relation of units 6–8 to the previous units).

fore, I will focus here on three literary units which are relatively well-defined. The first part of this paper explores the Talmud's attitude to genealogical knowledge in the sequence on the purification of *mamzerim* (*b. Qidd.* 70b–71a) and in the story about Rav Yehuda's trial (70a–b) along with other passages. The second part analyzes the opening *sugya*, which addresses the historical significance of our mishnah (69a–b).

## I. The Situation of Genealogical Knowledge

### *1. The purification of Israel (70b–71a)*

The genealogical division described by our mishnah prohibits some of the classes to come into union with most Jews. The most prominent of these "prohibited" classes is the class of *mamzerim* ("bastards" or offspring of illegitimate unions). The first text which I want to offer for analysis addresses some of the problems which stem from the existence of these prohibited classes.

This text is interesting not just because of its content but also because we are able to trace its fascinating literary development by comparing it with an earlier version of the same discussion recorded in the Palestinian Talmud.[10] The parallels between the Talmuds can be seen in the following synopsis:

---

[10] The parallels themselves have been already noted by Noah Aminoah, *The Redaction of the Tractate Qiddushin in the Babylonian Talmud* (Tel Aviv: Rosenberg School, 1977), 322, without analysis. See also Shamma Friedman, *Talmud Arukh: BT Bava Mezi'a VI: Text Volume* (New York and Jerusalem: Jewish Theological Seminary of America, 1996), 10 and n. 24.

It is beyond the scope of this study to determine whether these similarities between the Talmuds should be explained by a hypothetical "early Talmud" upon which both were built or by direct literary dependency of the Babylonian Talmud on the Palestinian Talmud. Scholars have posited the existence of an "early Talmud," an arrangement of rabbinic material already redacted in the Amoraic period, in order to explain structural parallels between the Talmuds and other phenomena in Talmudic composition (see e.g., Friedman, ibid.). Gray has recently criticized this hypothesis and argued that at least in the case of tractate Avodah Zarah, the evidence suggests direct literary dependency of the Bavli on the Yerushalmi. See Alyssa Gray, *A Talmud in Exile: The Influence of Yerushalmi Avodah Zarah on the Formation of Bavli Avodah Zarah* (Providence: Brown Judaic Studies, 2005), 15–33.

While Gray's general dismissal of the "early Talmud" hypothesis may be premature, there are reasons to think her conclusions about the relationship between the Talmud in *Avodah Zarah* should be applied to our *sugya* in *Qiddushin* as well. The Bavli's discussion takes two discrete sections whose juxtaposition makes better sense in the context of the Yerushalmi's general discussion, and by changing their function the Talmud makes

| Palestinian Talmud, *Qidd.* 4:1 65c | Babylonian Talmud, *Qidd.* 70b–71a |
|---|---|
| R. Yohanan: Midrash on the beginning of Mal 3:3. God will purify only Levites in the future to come. | R. Hama: Midrash on the beginning of Mal 3:3. When God will purify the tribes, he will begin with the Levites. |
| R. Zeira: As a person who drinks from a clean cup. | |
| | R. Yehoshua b. Levi: Midrash on Mal 3:3. Money purifies *mamzerim.* |
| R. Hoshaya: And we shall lose out since we are Levites? | |
| R. Hanina: Midrash on the other half of Mal 3:3. God will show grace to them.<br><br>R. Yohanan: We do not inquire after families in which a disqualified person was mixed. | *stam:* Question about the other half of Mal. 3:3<br><br>R. Yitzhak: Midrash on Mal 3:3. God showed grace to Israel. "A family which was intermingled remains intermingled. |
| | "*Gufa*": All lands are dough to Palestine... |
| | A story about Rabbi Yehuda and his students. |
| | A story about Rabbi Pinehas and his students. |
| | Rabbi Yohanan: "By the Temple! It is in our hands, but what can I do, that the greatest men of the generation were intermingled in it." |
| | He was of the same opinion as R. Yitzhak:<br><br>"A family which was intermingled remains intermingled." |
| R. Shimeon: The Mishnah instructs this as well:<br><br>*m. Eduyyot 8:7* 'The family of Beit Ṣerifa was on the right bank of the Jordan..." | Abaye: we have learned this in the Mishnah as well:<br><br>*m. Eduyyot* 8:7: "The family of Beit Ṣerifa was on the right bank of the Jordan... ...like these Elijah comes to render pure or impure..." |
| | 'Like these' – which are known. |

them one (see more below). It is possible therefore that the Bavli received an already redacted Yerushalmi *sugya.* If indeed the Babylonian discussion depends directly on the Palestinian discussion as we have it, the case for viewing the differences between the two *sugyot* as evidence for the Bavli's particular approach becomes even stronger.

| Palestinian Talmud, *Qidd.* 4:1 65c | Babylonian Talmud, *Qidd.* 70b–71a |
|---|---|
| And still there was another one there, and the sages did not want to publicize it, but they do transmit it to their sons and their students two times every seven years (cf. *t. Eduyyot* 3:4). | *Tana*: And still there was another one there... and the sages did not want to reveal it. But they do transmit it to their sons and their students once every seven years (cf. *t. Eduyyot* 3:4). |
| R. Yohanan, "By the Temple service! I know them, but what can I do, that the greatest men of the generation were mixed in them." | |

Let us begin with a brief description of the version in the Yerushalmi and then proceed to see how the Bavli completely transforms it in a few powerful acts of redaction.

1. a. R. Issa in the name of R. Yohanan: Even in the future to come the Holy One, blessed be he, only deals with the tribe of Levi. What is the proof [for this]? "And he shall sit as a refiner and purifier of silver and he shall purify the sons of Levi" (Mal 3:3).

   b. Said R. Zeira: As a person who drinks from a clean glass.

   c. Said R. Hoshaya, And because we are[11] Levites, we shall lose out?

   d. Said R. Hanina b. R. Abbahu: Even in the future to come the Holy One, blessed be he, will show them grace. What is the proof? "and they shall offer unto the Lord *minḥa* offerings in righteousness" (Mal 3:3).

2. a. Said R. Yohanan: We do not meticulously inquire after a family in which a disqualified person was mixed.

   b. Said R. Shimon ben Lakish: The Mishnah [already] said so: "The family of Beit Ṣerifa was across the Jordan, and Ben Zion distanced it [i.e., rendered it prohibited] using force. And there was another one there which Ben Zion brought closer [i.e., rendered it permitted] using force (*m. Eduyyot* 8:7). And the sages did not wish to reveal them. But the sages transmit them to their sons and students twice every seven years."

   c. Said R. Yohanan: [I swear by the Temple] service! I know them, and what can I do, that the greatest of the generation were intermingled with them. (*y. Qidd.* 4:1 65c)

This passage comes after a discussion which describes how God purges society of members of one of the prohibited classes, the *mamzerim*. God kills *mamzerim* every sixty or seventy years, lest they be intermingled with families of the permitted classes. The Yerushalmi goes on to point out that

[11] Both MS Leiden and the printed edition read "because we are not Levites," possibly under the influence of the Bavli. My translation omits the word "not" based on the parallel in *y. Yebam.* 8:3 9d as well as on interpretive considerations; see below.

along with these *mamzerim* God kills some members of the permitted classes in order not to expose the identity of the *mamzerim*. It then concludes that this purging only affects *mamzerim* whose status is unknown (since there is no danger that members of the permitted classes will marry known *mamzerim*). Known *mamzerim* are therefore unaffected by the purge. The significance of God's actions is that we human beings cannot, and should not, concern ourselves with the presence of hidden *mamzerim* among us. God will purge them, but in a discreet way which does not make their identity public.

It is in this context that the Yerushalmi adduces R. Yohanan's midrashic comment on Malachi 3:3 (§1a). Even in the Messianic era, God will continue this discreet treatment of intermingled disqualified persons. Since, however, the Levites will be called once again to serve in the Temple, God will expose the status of those Levites who are genealogically blemished and therefore disqualified from service, setting them apart from the rest of the tribe. We learn this in Mal 3:3, a verse which describes an eschatological purification but mentions only the Levites. R. Zeira's teaching (§1b) compares God's unwillingness to tolerate disqualified Levites and Priests in the Temple to the unwillingness of a person to drink from a contaminated glass. R. Hoshaya objects to this discrimination against the Levites (§1c),[12] but R. Hanina uses the second half of Malachi 3:3 as evidence that God had actually shown them grace (§1d).

The second part of the Yerushalmi's discussion begins with R. Yohanan's teaching, "we do not meticulously inquire after any family in which a disqualified person was mixed" (§2a). This saying builds on the general conclusions of the Yerushalmi's discussion. Since God purges the *mamzerim*, and since even God takes care not to make prohibited genealogical identities public, we should not be particular about families in which a disqualified person was intermingled.

R. Shimon comments that this lenient policy toward intermingled families could already be seen in a Tannaitic source or a *baraita* which comments on a mishnah from tractate *Eduyyot* (§2a). This mishnah tells of two families whose genealogical identities had been violently changed. The

[12] The version transmitted in *y. Qidd.* (as opposed to *y. Yebam.*; see n. 11) which has R. Hoshaya say, "because we are *not* Levites" (בגין דלית אנן לויים), might be due to a positive understanding of the purification, perhaps influenced by the Bavli; but the Yerushalmi seems to perceive the purification as a negative necessity. The version in *y. Yebam.* is even more probable if our R. Hoshaya is not R. Hoshaya of the first generation but R. Hoshaya the third; the latter was known to be a priest (see Albeck, *Introduction*, 241 *s.v.* Rav Hanina) and therefore could only make the utterance as it appears in *y. Yebam.* Finally, R. Hoshaya's exclamation is about the irony and injustice of punishing the most selected, dedicated tribe.

*baraita* observes that the Mishnah only identifies the family which was originally permitted and is now considered disqualified. The family which benefited from the violent manipulation remains anonymous, though the *baraita* assures us that the sages transmit its name discreetly.[13] We may therefore conclude that the Mishnah wished to limit investigation of intermingled disqualified families. This part of the discussion concludes with R. Yohanan, who exclaims that he knows the identity of the originally prohibited family and laments that it has intermingled with prominent members of society (§2c).

We may now turn to the version of this discussion in the Babylonian Talmud. Unlike the discussion in the Yerushalmi, the Bavli's version does not proceed from a discussion on the purging of *mamzerim*.[14] Rather, it opens a new discussion of the eschatological purification:

1. a. Said Rabbi Hama b. Hanina, "When the Holy One, blessed be he, purifies the tribes, he will first purify the tribe of Levi, for it was said, "And he shall sit as a refiner and purifier of silver, and he shall purify the sons of Levi" (Mal 3:3).

   b. R. Yehoshua b. Levi said: Money purifies *mamzerim*, as it was said, "and money shall sit as a refiner and purifier" (ibid.).[15]

   c. What is [meant by the end of that verse] "and they shall offer unto the Lord *minḥa* offerings by grace [*ṣedāqâ*, צדקה]"?

   d. R. Yitzhak said: The Holy One, blessed be he, showed grace to Israel: a family which was intermingled – [remains] intermingled.

2. a–c. [These units will be reproduced below.]

---

[13] Satlow writes that "R. Shimeon ben Lakish's dictum deliberately blurs the boundaries of the mishnah he cites, thus implying greater authority to his assertion" (Satlow, *Jewish Marriage*, 151). It seems, though, that R. Shimeon's dictum, like Abaye's in the Bavli parallel, is not just citing the mishnah but also a *baraita* (which itself treats the mishnah as a "lemma"). The "intermingling" of baraita and mishnah in this manner is not uncommon, especially in the Yerushalmi. See Jacob Epstein, *Introduction to the Mishnaic Text* (2 vols.; 2d ed.; Tel Aviv: Dvir, 1974; in Hebrew), 2:799–801, with reference to our text on 2:801. See also Chanoch Albeck, *Studies in the Baraita and the Tosefta and their Relationship to the Talmud* (2d ed.; Jerusalem: Mossad Ha-Rav, 1969), 3, for the general lack of citation terms for *baraitot* in the Yerushalmi, and ibid., 53, on the meaning of *tana* as a citation term for *baraitot* which present commentary on other Tannaitic materials, just as it is found in the Bavli parallel of R. Shimeon's teaching (attributed there to Abaye).

[14] The idea that God purges *mamzerim* does appear in the Bavli, in *b. Yebam.* 78b, but the discussion here, in *b. Qidd*, is not connected with it and indeed seems to contradict it.

[15] In its original context, this part of the verse reads: "And he [the angel of God] shall sit as a refiner and purifier of silver [*kesep*, כסף] and he shall purify the sons of Levi." This midrashic comment, however, takes "*kesep*" to be the subject of the sentence and to mean "money."

d. Said R. Yohanan: "[I swear by] the Temple! It is in our power. But what can I do, that the greatest men of the generation were intermingled in it."

e. He was of Rabbi Yitzhak's opinion, for R. Yitzhak said, "A family which was intermingled – [remains] intermingled."

f. Said Abaye: We have also learned so in the Mishnah:

g. The family of Beit Ṣerifa, was across the Jordan, and Ben Zion distanced [i.e., rendered prohibited] it using force. And there was another one there which Ben Zion brought close [i.e., rendered permitted] using force. [Families] like these Elijah comes to purify or declare impure, to distance or bring closer' (*m. Eduyyot* 8:7)."

h. "Like these" – which are known, but a family that was intermingled – [remains] intermingled.

i. "It was taught on Tannaitic authority [*tana*]: '"And there was another one there [which Ben Zion brought closer by force' (*m. Eduyyot* 8:7)], and the sages did not want to reveal it. But they do tell it to their sons[16] and students once every seven years." And some say, "twice every seven years."

j–m. [These units will be reproduced below.] (70b–71a)[17]

The most important difference between the Talmuds in the first part of the discussion concerns the nature of the purification. In the Yerushalmi, God purifies the Levites by setting apart the disqualified members of the tribe. In the Bavli we learn, with R. Yehoshua b. Levi (§1b), of a very different purification. The target of that purification is *mamzerim* whose wealth was sufficiently enticing to members of the permitted classes that they married them, and who thus became intermingled with these permitted classes and came to be perceived as pure. This socially-ascribed, pure genealogical status prevails over the original impure status with which they were born.[18]

The Talmud's question regarding the second half of Mal 3:3, and R. Yitzhak's answer (§1c–d), extend this process of purification to all sorts of intermingling, not just that motivated by wealth. A family that was intermingled will remain intermingled, its prohibited status written off by God as part of the grace he has shown Israel.

The idea that in the Messianic era God will render the members of the prohibited classes permissible or pure has its precedents in earlier rabbinic

[16] "Their sons" is missing in both MS Munich 95 and MS Vatican 111.

[17] All citations in this paper are from *b. Qidd.* unless otherwise noted. All line numbers refer to the Vilna edition of the Babylonian Talmud.

[18] Following Rashi, ad loc. See Hayes, *Gentile Impurities*, 186: "This is a remarkable and counterintuitive reading of Mal 3:3, which on the face of it suggests purification by means of *purging* rather than by means of dilution, absorption, and ultimate assimilation" (emphasis original).

literature,[19] but the way this purification is understood here is surprising. Essential to the Bavli's discussion is the idea that often there is a difference between people's innate or natural identity, on the one hand, and the identity society ascribes to them, on the other. The passage argues that God would approve the transformation of the former into the latter, even if the latter identity was created under dubious conditions (and R. Yehoshua's statement hints at one example of such conditions).

Two significant editorial actions contribute to the reinterpretation of the Palestinian discussion in the Bavli. First is the addition of Rabbi Yehoshua b. Levi's interpretation of the word "silver" as pertaining to the wealth of the *mamzerim*. This statement, which is the only one the Bavli adds (rather than modifies) in this part of the discussion, suggests a human motivation behind the formation of genealogical identities.[20]

The second act of redaction is more intriguing. R. Yohanan's teaching in the Yerushalmi (§2a) and R. Yitzhak's teaching in the Bavli (§1d) are two versions of the same fundamental teaching or tradition.[21] In its original essence, this teaching is a halakhic instruction which aims to limit the inquiry into genealogical blemishes through legitimizing the status quo attained by each family or person (because of the clear moral and social difficulties inherent in such an inquiry). The variations in terms and attribution between these versions are typical of such inter-Talmudic parallels and do little, in themselves, to change the meaning of the instruction.

---

[19] The earliest recorded manifestation of this idea in rabbinic literature is in the following *baraita*, which appears in the Tosefta and both Talmuds:
"*Netînim* and *mamzerim* become pure in the future to come" – the words of R. Yosi. R. Meir says, "They do not become pure." R. Yosi said to him, "But has it not been said, 'And I will sprinkle clean water upon you'" (Ezek 36:25). R. Meir said to him, "'From all your impurities, and from all your idols' (ibid.). R. Yosi said to him, "What does [scripture's] teaching say [with the words], 'I will cleanse you (ibid.) – even from the *netînut* and from the *mamzerut*." (*t. Qidd.* 5:4, 294–5.22–26)

See Saul Lieberman, *Tosefta Kifshutah VIII: Seder Nashim* (New York: Jewish Theological Seminary, 1973), 971–72, and Hayes, *Gentile Impurities*, 185–86 and 191. Both Talmudic passages under study (i.e., *b. Qidd* 70b–71a and *y. Qidd* 4:1) contradict R. Yosi (in their own way), even though elsewhere in both Talmuds his opinion is cited positively, without referring to any contradictory opinion but that of R. Meir (*b. Qidd.* 72b and *y. Qidd.* 3:13, 64d following Lieberman's famous emendation, for which see *Tosefta Kifshutah*, ibid.). See also n. 39 below.

[20] This is emphasized by the parallel placement of R. Yehoshua b. Levi's tradition in the Bavli and R. Zera's tradition in the Yerushalmi (see synopsis). If the former speaks of human motives, the latter speaks of God's motives (though with human imagery which reminds one of the famous discussion in *b. Git.* 90a–b on husbands' attitudes to their wives).

[21] See Friedman, *Bava Mezi'a VI: Text*, 10.

This tradition, however, receives different meanings in the two Talmuds. The Bavli unifies what in the Yerushalmi were two different, unrelated, sources and points, creating one teaching. R. Yitzhak's teaching parallels not only R. Yohanan's teaching (§2a), but also the midrash which precedes it (§1c). The Bavli sets up the two traditions as an argument ("an intermingled family remains intermingled") and its proof (Mal 3:3). The midrash in the Yerushalmi answers R. Hoshaya's question about the mistreatment of Levites; the midrash in the Bavli buttresses R. Yitzhak's point on intermingled families. The midrash in the Yerushalmi is applied only to Levites and the "future to come"; the midrash in the Bavli applies to the present and to all of Israel (God *has shown* grace to *Israel*).[22]

The result of this literary manipulation is that R. Yitzhak's teaching is no longer simply a halakhic instruction, but also a factual statement about the transformation of genealogical identities: a person's intermingling, that is, the achievement of legitimization by society, affects the genealogical identity which will be given by God in the process of purification. R. Yohanan's parallel teaching is never understood as being anything but a halakhic instruction; the principle behind it does not affect the reality of genealogical identities.[23] The facts which in the Yerushalmi are assumed to be natural or divine in origin are represented by the Bavli as being determined by human processes and conditions.[24]

The next three units in the Bavli differ from the trajectory common to the two Talmuds to such an extent (see the synopsis) that it would be best to defer full treatment of them until later in this section and discuss them here only briefly. Using the Talmudic term *gufa* (the "body" of the matter), the first of these units indicates that the discussion is returning to a statement which was cited earlier in passing. In our case, this is Shmuel's genealogical hierarchy (all lands are considered genealogically mixed,

---

[22] In his brief comment, Friedman (ibid.) does not discuss these differences, and therefore it is not clear whether he sees the midrashic part of the teaching in the Bavli as original or not. In my opinion, since the *stam* asks the midrashic question, the teaching before Talmudic redaction did not include reference to Mal 3:3.

[23] While R. Yohanan's dictum in the Yerushalmi is clearly a description of rabbinic policy ("we do not inquire"), R. Yitzhak's words in the Bavli, "a family which was intermingled – remains intermingled" lend themselves to being understood as a description of reality rather than a normative instruction. This difference in wording may have occurred in the process of transmission before the "Stammaitic" redaction. Still the formulation alone does not demand the meaning ascribed to it by the Bavli (even if the Bavli's creators had it before them as it is, and it is not unlikely that they would have changed a teaching's wordings to better fit its new context), and that meaning remains evidence primarily of the Bavli's own agenda.

[24] The interpretation of the Yerushalmi offered here follows, roughly, the *Pnei Moshe* to *y. Yebam.* 8:3.

'dough,' compared to Palestine, and Palestine is considered 'dough' compared to Babylonia).[25] The interpretive effect of this *gufa* statement is significant, especially in terms of the differences between the Talmuds. It applies all subsequent sources in the Bavli to a matter which is not mentioned in this part of the Yerushalmi at all.[26] The two stories which follow tell how Palestinian sages tried to reverse this genealogical hierarchy to no avail.

The Bavli then cites a statement by R. Yohanan: "[I swear by] the Temple! It is in our power. But what can I do, that the greatest men of the generation were intermingled in it" (§2d). In this context, the saying means that Palestinian sages have the ability to reverse the genealogical hie-

---

[25] The term "dough" (*'isâ*; עיסה) may also be rendered "admixture." The hierarchical teaching argues that in all lands, the genealogical classes are mixed with one another (i.e. through intermarriage) more than in Palestine; in Palestine, the classes are more mixed with one another than in Babylonia. The more genealogically suspicious the place one comes from, the more inquiry is needed before marriage is allowed. For the history of the term *'isâ*, see Satlow, *Jewish Marriage*, 155–56 and Hayes, *Gentile Impurities*, 191–92. See also below, n. 61.

[26] The *gufa* statement seems to fit better in unit 5 than its current placement in unit 4 (using the division proposed above, n. 9). Unit 5 begins on 71a, line 43 with Shmuel's instruction that "Babylonia is considered [genealogically] permitted... all other lands are considered prohibited... Palestine is considered prohibited." That instruction clearly bears on the genealogical hierarchy statement to which the *gufa* relates. The sources placed between the two stories which follow the *gufa* statement and Shmuel's instruction not only are thematically unrelated to the hierarchy teaching, as they continue a discussion which began before the *gufa* statement with the midrashim on Mal 3:3, but also, as we have seen, belong to a pre-redaction arrangement shared by the Talmuds, an arrangement which contains sources that appear before the *gufa*.

Here is what I suggest happened: the *sugya* which begins in 71a.43 (unit 5) with Shmuel's teaching originally began with the stories about Rabbi Yehuda and Rabbi Pinehas. Following these stories appeared R. Yohanan's exclamation ("By the Temple!"), and the *stam*'s remark tying this statement with R. Yitzhak's teaching ("an intermingled family remains intermingled"). R. Yitzhak's teaching also appeared in the version of the Yerushalmi's discussion available to the Bavli's creators (unit 4), where it was followed by Abaye's comment citing the *baraita* on the secret transmission of genealogical knowledge (just like R. Yohanan's teaching on avoiding inquiry, paralleling R. Yitzhak's, is followed in the Yerushalmi by Reish Lakish's comment, which parallels Abaye's; see synopsis above).

The Bavli's authors simply spliced in that portion of unit 5 which ended with R. Yitzhak's teaching (i.e.: the two stories on the Palestinian coup attempt, R. Yohanan's exclamation, the *stam*'s comment tying this exclamation to R. Yitzhak's teaching), immediately after this very teaching was cited in unit 4. They then placed the continuation of unit 5 after unit 4's end. It seems likely to me that the *gufa* statement was originally part of unit 5's redaction, and was moved with its beginning into unit 4, but it might have been an even later addition.

rarchy, subordinating Babylonia to Palestine in genealogical reputation. Unfortunately, however, "the greatest men of the generation" were already intermingled in it (in the mixed "dough" which is Palestine) through marriage with originally prohibited families. An inquiry into the genealogical identities of all Jews in Palestine, one which aims to identify the genealogical ingredients of the Palestinian Jewish community and makes sure the classes do not mix, should be avoided because it will expose the blemished identity of prominent members of that community.

This statement by R. Yohanan, it may be recalled, appears in the Yerushalmi as well (§2c). There are two differences in the role it plays in the two Talmuds; one is readily apparent, while the other is both more obscure and significant. The first and more obvious difference is that in the Yerushalmi the statement is not connected to the hierarchy between Palestine and Babylonia, but rather to the issue of hidden prohibited families.

The second and more important difference is in the nature of the statement. In the Yerushalmi, the function of the statement is not to suggest R. Yohanan's reason for not exposing or inquiring into these families. That reason has already been supplied by R. Yohanan himself, in the earlier mention of his principle which is also exemplified by the mishnah (§2a–b). The Bavli, however, suggests that the fact that the "greatest of the generation" were intermingled is itself the reason for R. Yohanan's non-action. Unlike the Yerushalmi, the Bavli uses the word "but" to link the first part, "it is in our power," to the second, "the greatest generations have intermingled," suggesting that Rabbi Yohanan would have acted differently if it were not for this intermingling. In order to justify R. Yohanan's decision not to act, the Bavli speculates that "he was of R. Yitzhak's opinion, for R. Yitzhak said, 'A family which was intermingled – [remains] intermingled.'"

The Talmud's interpretation of R. Yohanan's motive emphasizes again that genealogical identity is affected by social factors: earlier in the discussion it was wealth, now it is a more general kind of prominence, most probably rabbinic prominence.[27] Still, this source adds an important ele-

---

[27] Cf. Kalmin, *Sage in Jewish Society*, 55. Kalmin's thesis that rabbinic policies of genealogical knowledge are connected with the rabbis' attitude to prominent non-rabbis is very persuasive, but he frequently marginalizes the possibility that these policies also reflect inner rabbinic tensions (while the number of sources in which it is likely or possible that the tension is with rabbis – such as Rabbi Yohanan's saying, or groups that include rabbis – such as whole towns and villages – seems larger than the sources in which the tension is explicitly between rabbis and non-rabbis; see more below). In any event, while Kalmin is interested in the reconstruction of rabbinic policies in the Amoraic period, my interest here is in the Babylonian *sugya*, which seems to be more concerned with the problems stemming from *rabbinic* control of genealogical knowledge.

ment to the picture. By having a rabbi approve, even reluctantly, the situation, the Talmud implicates the rabbinic establishment itself in the production and manipulation of genealogical information.

Rabbinic control of genealogical information is also the topic of the next step in the Talmud's discussion. It may be recalled that in the Yerushalmi, R. Shimeon cites a mishnah about families whose class identity was altered violently (§2b). This mishnah is adduced to support R. Yohanan's policy of leniency towards intermingled families. In the Yerushalmi, the support for that policy is found in the Mishnah's discretion concerning the intermingled family's name, and in the Tannaitic teaching about the confidential transmission of that name. In the Babylonian version, the same mishnah is adduced by Abaye to support the same policy (which in the Bavli is attributed to R. Yitzhak).[28] The Bavli's addition of an interpretive comment on the mishnah, however, significantly changes this part of the discussion.

After it tells us of the two families, this mishnah goes on to promise that the original identities of families "like these" would be restored by Elijah at the end of times (§2g; this clause is not cited in the Yerushalmi). That is to say, Elijah will remedy the corrupt state of affairs in which families are assigned to a class not originally theirs, but one which was forced upon them.[29] The Bavli draws our attention to this clause and adds an interpretive comment on the words "like these," stating that Elijah will only restore identities which "are known, but a family which was intermingled – remains intermingled."[30]

[28] The fact that Abaye's teaching is part of a complete discussion adapted from Palestinian source qualifies, I think, the extent of particular agency Kalmin ascribes to Abaye when he states that "the fact that Abaye asserts that this Palestinian view [i.e., R. Yitzhak's/R. Yohanan's; M.V.] is 'also taught in a mishnah' suggests strongly that he agrees with it; further support for my characterization of later Babylonian attitudes" (Kalmin, *Sage in Jewish Society*, 56). Kalmin's more recent description of a wide-ranging Palestinian influence on later Babylonian sages which includes straightforward textual reception does much more to illustrate our text; see his *Jewish Babylonia between Persia and Roman Palestine* (Oxford: Oxford University Press, 2006).

[29] As it explicitly says before Ben Zion is first mentioned: "R. Yehoshua said: I have received a tradition from R. Yohanan b. Zakkai [...] that Elijah will not come to pronounce impure or pure, to put distance or to bring near, but to distance those who were brought close by force and to bring near those who were distanced by force." This mishnah seems to contradict other views on the eschatological purification (see n. 19).

[30] My reading of this comment as an addition made by the Bavli, rather than part of Abaye's saying, is based on the following considerations: first, R. Shimeon's parallel teaching in the Yerushalmi, similar to Abaye's in every way, does not include the comment; the comment may be easily excised; the gloss interrupts the continuity between the mishnah and the *baraita* which interprets it.

This comment is puzzling, almost outrageous: Elijah was summoned by the Mishnah to dispel genealogical uncertainty and misperception, not to preserve it! The task of genealogical restoration is assigned to the prophet Elijah precisely because he can see beyond the intermingling and recognize true genealogical identities. When the Talmud limits Elijah's mission to families which are known, surely it does not imply that there are families which are not known to him. To whose knowledge, then, does the Talmud refer?

The answer lies in the conclusion of the Tannaitic teachings cited by the Talmuds (§2i in the Bavli), which tell us that that even though the name of the family is not mentioned in the mishnah, it is secretly transmitted by the sages. This reference to rabbinic transmission explains the Talmud's comment on the Mishnah: by "those who are known," the *stam* means those who are known to the rabbis. This is also a reinterpretation of the term "intermingled." Since one of the families is known only to the rabbis, who do not publicize its name, the term now signifies families whose names have not been transmitted by the rabbis.

Rabbinic transmission, then, is the final catalyst and criterion by which genealogical identity will be determined. Elijah will come to change the genealogical identities only in those cases in which the rabbis chose to transmit names. This move also solves for the Bavli the contradiction between its interpretation of R. Yitzhak's assertion, "a family which was intermingled remains intermingled," and the mishnah's promise of genealogical restoration.

The Bavli thus departs from the tradition recorded in the Mishnah, the *baraita* and the Yerushalmi.[31] For the Mishnah, as we have seen, the important distinction was between those families whose genealogical status was violently manipulated and those families who were not victims of such action. Elijah will restore the status of the former. By not stating the name of the family whose original status was prohibited, the Mishnah also makes

[31] Satlow, *Jewish Marriage*, 151, similarly observes that this is an "assertion that the rabbis controlled genealogical knowledge." While Satlow's comment refers to the Yerushalmi, I think it is more applicable to the Bavli and less to the Yerushalmi or the *baraita*. In the latter sources, it seems more of a reassurance: do not worry, even though the name is not mentioned, we transmit it. It is only in the Bavli – where the transmission actually affects genealogical identities by determining Elijah's list of clients – that the argument is made for absolute rabbinic control of genealogical knowledge. See also Satlow's important observation that Kalmin (*Sage in Jewish Society*, 54), who reads in this source only an expression of rabbinic discretion in genealogical matters, "neglects to take into account the implicit power of secret knowledge, the mere mention of which serves notice that it can, if needed, be instantly deployed" (Satlow, *Jewish Marriage*, 327 n. 143).

an implicit distinction between families whose situation would be made worse by having their status made public, and those families whose situation would be ameliorated. This implicit distinction is acknowledged by the *baraita*.

In the Yerushalmi there are also two operative distinctions. The first distinction is between families whose original status is known to the public and families whose status is unknown. The second distinction, as in the Mishnah, is between families who were originally prohibited and families who were originally permitted. Thus, R. Shimeon uses the mishnah and the *baraita* to show that the sages avoided exposing families whose original status, now unknown to the public, is prohibited.

The Bavli's emphasis on the rabbinic aspect of the demarcation of genealogical identities is most evident in those passages in which it significantly diverges from the Yerushalmi (or from the source common to both Talmuds) The Bavli's addition (see synopsis) begins with a discursive reference and continues with two stories very similar in form:

2. a. *Gufa*: Said Rav Yehuda said Shmuel: All lands are dough to Palestine, and Palestine is dough to Babylonia.

   b. In the days of Rabbi they [Palestinian students] sought to make Babylonia dough to Palestine. He said to them, "Thorns you are putting in my eyes! If you wish, R. Hanina b. Hama will join [issue] with you." R. Hanina b. Hama joined [issue] with them and told them: "This I have in tradition from R. Ishmael son of R. Yosi who stated on his father's authority: 'All lands are dough to Palestine and Palestine is dough to Babylonia.'"

   c. In the days of R. Pinehas they [Palestinian students] sought to make Babylonia dough to Palestine. He said to his slaves: "the moment I have said two things in the beit-midrash, take me in my chair and run!" When he entered [the beit-midrash] he told them [the scholars]: "Slaughter of fowl has no basis in Scripture." As they were seated and [were preoccupied] studying this [teaching], he told them: "All lands are dough to Palestine, and Palestine is dough to Babylonia." They [his slaves] took him in the cradle and ran, and they [the scholars] ran after him but did not reach him. They sat and examined [matters genealogical], until they encountered danger, and quit [investigating]. (71a)

Both of these stories tell us of attempts by Palestinian scholars to overturn the genealogical hierarchy of the Jewish world so as to favor their own Palestinian community.[32] While both stories have similar structure and

[32] These stories at first seem to be nothing but Babylonian propaganda. But is it possible that they originated in Palestine? Kalmin seems to presuppose as much when he takes them as reliable evidence for the Palestinian position (*Sage in Jewish Society*, 55). I find it improbable that the stories as they now appear in the Bavli came from Palestine; but it is possible that they were not originally concerned with the genealogical hierarchy between the two communities. Just as R. Yohanan's exclamation ("it is in our hands"

probably bear a similar message, the second story expresses the Talmud's point more clearly. R. Pinehas devises a plan to evade his students' demand for thorough genealogical investigation of Palestine. He will distract them with an unrelated, difficult subject; as they struggle with it he will utter Shmuel's teaching of genealogical hierarchy and make a hasty exit with the help of his slaves (the irony of having Rabbi Pinehas use slaves, one of the low genealogical classes, to help him evade the consequences of his opinion on this matter is surely intended).

While at first it seems that the Talmud portrays R. Pinehas as a comical coward with his clumsy diversion tactics and evasive maneuvers, his students end up backing down after encountering danger, presumably political. Once again, the Talmud represents genealogical knowledge as arbitrary and contingent upon the politics of Jewish society.

In fact, the story does more than that: it suggests that rabbinic discourse is itself politicized and arbitrary. From the very beginning, the students' motivation is self-serving: they want their community to be in a better position than Babylonia. R. Pinchas's behavior, though justified by the story, is in any event not a good example of reasoned discourse. He never justifies his support for the genealogical hierarchy. The topic he chooses as a diversion is not accidental: just like the slaughter of fowl, so too the issue of genealogy is based not on scriptural reasoning but on rabbinic authority.[33]

---

etc.) appears in the Bavli in direct relation to the regional hierarchy while in the Yerushalmi it is a general statement about genealogical inquiry, so also these stories might have at first dealt with a general discussion about exposing disqualified families, without any connection to the hierarchy.

[33] The story about Rabbi Yehuda is less clear, though Rashi (ad loc.) suggests an interpretation with which my interpretation of the *sugya* coheres. Rashi explains Rabbi Yehuda's reaction as personally motivated. The Patriarch's family, as was well known, went back to Hillel, who famously emigrated from Babylonia; an inquiry which would undermine Babylonia's claims to purest descent would also undermine the Patriarchal family's genealogical status. R. Hanina is appointed to block the new effort. At first, his answer seems to be a mere re-assertion of the situation the students wanted to revise. If we stick to the logic of Rashi's explanation, though, we may be able to make good sense of it. If Rabbi Yehuda's reaction had to do with his personal Babylonian interest, R. Hanina's answer might have aimed to assure the students that this kind of Babylonian interest was not behind the genealogical hierarchy by attributing it to a Palestinian tradition (R. Ishmael b. Rabbi Yosi, from his father). A problem with this explanation is posed by Rashi himself, who suggests elsewhere in his interpretation of the Talmud that R. Yosi was also known to be of Babylonian pedigree (*b. Yoma* 66b). Rashi's interpretation there was criticized by I. Helevy, *Dorot Ha-Rishonim* (Frankfurt: Jüdische Literarische Gesellschaft, 1906), 120. At any event, even if there is some sort of implied and vague association between R. Yosi and Babylonian descent, it is not prominent in rabbin-

These two stories are then followed by R. Yohanan's statement (§2d), discussed above, that the inquiry required to overturn the hierarchy is undesirable because prominent members of society are in danger of being downgraded in status. Read together, the two stories and R. Yohanan's statement (§2b–d) expose the motivations that affect rabbinic decisions.

The personal motivation behind rabbinic decisions on genealogical matters is more explicitly presented in two statements which are cited later in the Bavli. These statements appear in the long discussion which seeks to determine which settlements are included in the superior pedigree zone of Babylonia. In the case of two such settlements, suspicion arises about a certain rabbi's reason to include or exclude the settlement:

> Hanan ben Pinehas says: "[The district of] Ḥavel Yama is the blue [i.e., the best] of Babylonia; Šunya, Guvya and Ṣiṣura are the splendor of Ḥavel Yama." Rav Papa said: "But now foreigners [lit. Cutheans] have intermingled in these [places]"; and this is not [so – rather,] he [Rav Papa] wanted [to marry] a woman from them [the people of these places], and they did not let him [and he has been resentful ever since.] (72a.9–12)

> Said Rav Iqa bar Abin in Rav Hananel's name, citing Rav: "Ḥelwan Nihawand is like 'Exile' [i.e., Babylonia] with respect to genealogy." Abaye said to them: "Do not heed him! a *yebama* [his dead brother's widow, which he should according to law either marry or release] has fallen for him [Rav Iqa] there [and he wanted to marry her]." He [Rav Iqa] said: "is this [teaching] mine?! It is Rav Hananel's!" They went and asked Rav Hananel who told them, "Thus said Rav – Ḥelwan Nihawand is like 'Exile' with respect to genealogy" (72a.17–21).[34]

In both instances we are exposed (either by the Talmud itself or by a tradition the Talmud adduces) to the possibility that rabbinic instruction itself may be used to manipulate genealogical information and that this manipulation is motivated by the personal interests of individual rabbis. The Talmud thus chooses to draw our attention to the problems inherent in rabbinic control of genealogical information.[35]

In the discussion in which these comments are cited, though, genealogical inquiry serves collective rather than personal interests as it fortifies the privileged genealogical status of Babylonian communities. The Talmud

---

ic literature and should not be presupposed as even a fictive biographical fact of his literary character.

[34] The names of places are reproduced here as they are transliterated in Aharon Oppenheimer, *Babylonia Judaica in the Talmudic Period* (Wiesbaden: Ludwig Reichert Verlag, 1983). See also Aharon Oppenheimer and Michael Lecker, "The Borders of Bavel with Respect to Lineage," *Zion* 50 (1985; in Hebrew): 173–87 for an attempt to reconstruct the borders of Babylonia according to the Bavli's discussion.

[35] The tradition about Ḥavel Yama is also brought in *y. Qidd.* 4:1 without the addition of Rav Papa's reservation and the *stam*'s comment.

does not explicitly call our attention to its own collective interest as it does to the collective interests of the Palestinian rabbis (in §2b–c) or the personal interests mentioned above.

I think that at one point, however, the Talmud might invite its readers to notice that collective Babylonian interest. In the middle of its discussion on the boundaries of Babylonia, the Bavli cites a statement made by Rabbi (Yehuda the Prince) on his deathbed in which he names several places in pure Babylonia which are genealogically contaminated. Rabbi goes on to point out that in another Babylonian location, on that day in which he was speaking, a certain scholar died; he proceeds to say that this day also marks Rav Yehuda's birth. The Talmud then reproduces the following source:

> A master said: When R. Akiva died Rabbi [Yehuda] was born. When Rabbi [Yehuda] died Rav Yehuda was born. When Rav Yehuda died Rava was born. When Rava died, Rav Ashi was born. [This] teaches you that a righteous [man] will not die until an equally righteous [man] is created, as it is said: "the sun riseth and the sun goeth down" (Eccl 1:5) (72b)

The ostensible function of this source is to expand on the previous one. Rabbi associated the death of one scholar with the birth of Rav Yehuda, and the comment which dates Rabbi's words to the day of his death implied the coincidence of his death with Rav Yehuda's birth. This source describes a general principle which makes intergenerational connections between the deaths and births of prominent rabbis.

The teaching may have an additional function, however. The chain it describes does not include any Palestinian rabbi after the Tannaitic period. Rabbinic merit, we are thus told, emigrated from Palestine to Babylonia.[36] This supercessionist comment is placed in the middle of the discussion of the genealogical purity of Babylonia, which is premised on Babylonia's superior status over Palestine. Is the Talmud inviting us to think that like the history of rabbinic instruction, genealogy too is written by the winners?

This supercessionist claim brings us back to the discussion in *b. Qidd.* 71a, which also makes a supercessionist claim, albeit a different one. It may be recalled that in §2i, we were offered two accounts of how frequently the sages transmit the name of intermingled families: "'they tell it to their sons and students once every seven years.' And some say, 'twice every seven years.'" The Bavli proceeds to discuss this difference:

---

[36] Significantly, the same midrash is cited in the name of Rabbi Yohanan, the prominent Palestinian Amora, in *b. Yoma* 38b, without the chain leading from Rabbi Yehuda to Babylonia.

j. Rav Nahman b. Yitzhak said: "he who says 'once every seven years' is of the more probable opinion, as we have learned in a Tannaitic source: [when someone takes a vow saying] 'I shall be a Nazirite if I shall not reveal [the genealogical identities of] families – he should be a Nazirite rather than revealing [the genealogical identities of] families'."

k. Rabbah b. b. Hana said in the name of R. Yohanan: "the [divine] name of four letters is transmitted by the Rabbis to their students once every seven years" and some say: "twice every seven years." Rav Nahman b. Yizhak said: "he who says once every seven years is of the more probable opinion..." (71a)

Rav Nahman supports the version which would have the transmission occurring less frequently. He demonstrates that publicizing names of genealogically blemished families is treated elsewhere with utmost severity. The Talmud then goes on to cite a similar discussion. Then we hear again of a tradition about esoteric transmission of a name, though this time it is the divine name (or names) rather than family names; this tradition also has two versions.

The discussion then concludes with passages that at first seem to come in by mere "free association" from the discussion of divine names and have no bearing on the discussion of genealogical identity:

l. It was taught on Tannaitic authority: "At first, the name of twelve letters was transmitted to every person. But when the morally corrupted had become many it was transmitted only to the most pious of the priesthood, and the most pious of the priesthood would silence it in the singing of their brethren the priests." It was taught on Tannaitic authority: "R. Tarfon said: 'I once climbed up after my mother's brother to the stand, and I tuned my ear to the high priest, and I heard him silence the name in the singing of his brethren the priests'."

m. Rav Yehuda said in Rav's name: "the name of forty-two letters is not transmitted but to he who is pious and humble, and is in his middle age, and does not get angry nor drunk, and does not insist on his rights. And he who knows it and uses it carefully and preserves it with purity, is beloved in the heavens and beloved on earth, and is feared by people and has a part in both worlds – this world and the world to come." (71a)

Read one after the other the passages place the two divine names in a clear hierarchy: the first is shorter than the second; the first used to be common knowledge; the second bestows upon its knower all sorts of rewards which are not mentioned regarding the first. The first is transmitted by priests (or, more correctly, was transmitted by priests, as the transmission is set in a Temple ritual), but the transmission of the second name, the more important one, does not necessitate priestly status. In other words, it stipulates no genealogical merit. Everyone – a *mamzer*, convert, slave – may know it and transmit it, if he is pious and humble and of the right age, conduct and character. In this sense, this passage expresses one side of the Talmud's ambiguous relationship with hierarchies based on heredity.

This passage, however, is also a statement about the authority to transmit knowledge. We learn that rabbinic tradition has replaced priestly tradition in the transmission of *theological* knowledge. The priestly tradition is reduced to a nostalgic anecdote about R. Tarfon's uncle in the Temple. The rabbis, in contrast, continue to transmit better, more rewarding theological knowledge. This passage is placed at the end of a discussion which conferred on the rabbis the absolute control of *genealogical* knowledge. The implied message with which the Bavli concludes the discussion, then, is that the rabbis replaced the priesthood in genealogical matters, a field of knowledge more closely associated with the priests, just as they replaced it in theological matters.[37]

The Talmudic discussion we analyzed invoked the conditions under which genealogical knowledge is produced and transmitted. The Talmud drew our attention to these conditions, showed us how they may change halakhic reality, and even argued that the human processes which modify or manipulate this knowledge are approved by God.

The Talmud's attention to the context of genealogical knowledge is persistent throughout our *sugyot*. This attention, however, is not necessarily connected to the notion that the context of knowledge is constitutive of reality or to the idea that God takes genealogy's contingent nature into consideration. A story about Rava may demonstrate this point.

The story is cited at the end of a discussion in which the status of converts is examined. The male convert emerges from a scriptural inquiry as a unique borderline case between the permitted classes and prohibited ones: on the one hand, he may marry a female *mamzer* (*mamzeret*), which is prohibited to the permitted classes; on the other, he may come in union with a woman of priestly stock, which is prohibited to the prohibited classes.[38] The story describes the communication of this law in the Jewish suburb of the Persian capital:

> Rabbi Zera lectured in Mahoza, "A convert may take a *mamzeret* for a wife!" Everyone pelted him with their citrons. Said Rava, "Is it possible to lecture this way in

---

[37] The Yerushalmi *sugya* also concludes with a polemic against the priesthood, though one of a different nature: "Said R. Joshua b. Levi, 'Pašḥur ben Immer had five thousand slaves, and all of them were mixed up with the high priesthood; indeed they are the arrogant among the priesthood.' Said R. Eleazar, 'Complaint is inherent in them – "for with you is my contention, O Priest" (Hos 4:4)'" (*y. Qidd* 4:1 65c as well as *y. Yebam* 8:3 9d). Note, however, that while the Bavli's polemic focuses on the transmission of knowledge, the Yerushalmi focuses on exposing the "natural" prohibited genealogical identities. The Pašḥur comment is also found in the Bavli; see below, n. 41 and the conclusion of the story about Rav Yehuda).

[38] On the halakhic discussion itself, see Hayes, *Gentile Impurities*, 168–71, with citation of the story on 171.

a place full of converts?!" Rava lectured in Mahoza, "a convert may take a woman of priestly stock for a wife!" Everyone loaded him with silk garments. He then said: "A convert may take a *mamzeret* for a wife." They told him, "You have spoiled the first [teaching]." He replied, "I have done what is best for you. If he wants, he can marry from this [stock]; if he wants, he can marry from that [stock]!" (73a)

Rava is astonished that in the presence of so many converts R. Zera should emphasize the aspect in the convert's legal status which is similar to that of the prohibited classes. He then gives a more balanced presentation which opens with the more crowd-pleasing law. While the Talmudic story does focus, then, on the way context affects the transmission of knowledge, this context is shown to affect only the way halakhah is presented, not halakhic status or genealogical reality.[39]

### *2. Rav Yehuda's trial (70a–b)*

The story of Rav Yehuda's trial, introduced about halfway through our series of *sugyot*, can be read as a long meditation on the problems inherent in rabbinic authority over genealogical demarcation.

The Talmud introduces the story with a brilliant sequencing which changes the course of the *sugya*. The sequence is found after several admonitions against marrying into the prohibited classes, the last of which reads:

*Tana*: "Elijah writes everyone, and the Holy One, blessed be he, puts his signature: woe to him, who disqualifies his semen and taints his family; that is, to him who marries a woman who is not genealogically fit for him. Elijah binds him and

[39] This story's more modest expression of the contingent nature of genealogy maybe connected to the possibility that it was composed separately from the other parts of our Talmudic discussion. The story and the deliberation about the convert's status (unit 8 according to the numbering suggested above, n. 9), as well as the two units that precede them (units 6 and 7), appear to depart from the rest of the *sugyot*. These units are not connected to one another, nor are they connected to what precedes them, whereas all the previous units are interwoven one way or another (see above, nn. 9 and 26 above and n. 44 below). Two of them also contradict statements found in the earlier parts of the Bavli's discussion. In unit 6 (72b.31–35), the Talmud attributes a tradition to Shmuel which argues that *m. Qidd* 4:1, with its implication of Babylonian genealogical superiority, presents only the opinion of Rabbi Meir, rather than the majority of the sages. The sages then do not accept R. Meir's position that Babylonia is of superior genealogy (since that is what is implied in the Mishnah) and say that "all lands should be considered fit." This explicitly contradicts Shmuel himself who is cited on 71a saying "all lands should be considered unfit." In unit 7, the Talmud cites the *baraita* about the purification of *mamzerim*, which contradicts the discussion in 70b–71a (see n. 19 above). Whether or not these differences point to a different provenance or different redaction for 72b.29–73a.26 than the rest of the Bavli's discussion is uncertain.

> the Holy One, blessed be he, whips him. And whoever disqualifies is [himself] disqualified, and he never speaks in praise [of others]." And Shmuel said: "[He, who disqualifies,] disqualifies [with] his [own] defect." (70a)

This teaching, introduced as Tannaitic,[40] addresses one of the moral problems of the Jewish genealogical system. Jewish law practically excommunicates whole families for generations because of their ancestors' sins. This source is a clear and harsh admonition against such a sinful ancestor who disqualifies his family by entering into a prohibited union. We are promised that God will punish him for the ruin he has brought upon his descendants.

The next clause, "and whoever disqualifies is [himself] disqualified," is less clear. If we maintain the terminology used in the previous lines, the subject of this assertion is the person who disqualifies his own family through a prohibited union. The meaning of the assertion, then, is that this person himself, and not only his descendants, should be viewed as disqualified. This meaning fits well with the source's attempt to punish the one responsible for genealogical disqualification.

This interpretation of the clause, however, does not sit well with the concluding statements of the passage. What is the connection between a person who disqualifies his own family and the statement that he "never speaks praise"? Furthermore, how can Shmuel's interpretive addition, "he disqualifies [with] his [own] defect" be applied to someone who is not himself already disqualified, but rather disqualifies his descendants?

The use of the teaching in the story about Rav Yehuda's trial, which follows our passage, provides an answer to these questions. In the story, the disqualifier is not someone who married an unfit woman and thus disqualified his own descendants, but rather someone who *says* a certain person is of the prohibited, disqualified classes. Our teaching thus asserts that whoever disqualifies in that way must himself already be disqualified. This instruction is rooted in the intuitive psychological observation that someone who goes around ascribing genealogical blemishes to other people

---

[40] Based on the citation term, *tana*, Schremer suggests that this is a "Babylonian *baraita*" (*Male and Female*, 150). Additional support for Schremer's argument is that the *tana* here comes immediately after an Amoraic saying: "Said Rav Himnona in Rav's name: anyone who marries a woman unfit for him, Elijah binds him and the Holy One, blessed be he, whips him, *Tana:* Elijah writes everyone" etc. Schremer also notes (ibid., n. 107) that the citation term used in a version recorded in Genizah fragment TS-NS 329.843 is *tania nami haki* (תניא נמי הכי). It seems to me, however, that TS-NS 329.843 is a fragment of *sefer ha-she'iltot* (*va'era*, §41) rather than of the Talmud; the version seems to be *tania nami hakhi* in the printed editions of *ha-she'iltot* as well. The difference in the citation term may be because the *baraita* there comes after an interpretive gloss from the author.

might have some blemishes of his own to hide (an observation shared by other Talmudic sources dealing with genealogy[41]). Shmuel comments on this principle, adding that a person disqualifies using his own defect: a *mamzer* is likely to call others *mamzerim*, a slave is likely to call others slaves, and so forth.

When this observation is given halakhic significance and codified in a rabbinic teaching, it makes negative genealogical judgment impossible: if I say so and so is a slave, *mamzer* or convert I will be seen as a slave, *mamzer* or convert myself.[42] Indeed, it seems that this teaching was originally conceived for the purpose of limiting genealogical slander. The term "disqualifier," then, seems to have changed its meaning in the middle of this passage.

I would like to suggest that this passage includes two originally unrelated teachings which were unified by the Talmud's redactors. The first teaching concerned physical disqualification of one's own family and a description of the horrible punishment it incurs ("woe to him, who disqualifies his semen..."); the second concerned genealogical speech ("and whoever disqualifies is disqualified...").

The Bavli, however, has blurred the distinction between these two teachings by putting them one right after the other without separation,

---

[41] Similar is the association of silence and peacefulness with good pedigree cited in 72b: Ulla's advice to Rav Yehuda in selecting a bride of prime stock for his son is "Follow the silence. Just like the Palestinians examine: if two are fighting with each other, they see who becomes quiet first, and they say: 'he is of better pedigree'"; Rav's saying, "Silence, in Babylonia, means good genealogy"; and two very similar traditions from Babylonia and Palestine: "Said Rav Yehuda in Rav's name, 'If you see two persons quarreling with each other, there must be some [genealogical] defect in one of them'"; "Said R. Yehoshua b. Levi, 'If you see two families quarreling with each other there must be some defect in one of them'" (all from 72b). See also the saying that Pašḥur ben Immer's slaves, now intermingled into the priesthood, account for those priests who are belligerent (70b). Some of these sources are cited by Schremer, *Male and Female*, 156. Kalmin (*Sage in Jewish Society*, 60–61) takes the dialogue between Ulla and Rav Yehuda to represent precisely the difference between the Palestinian and Babylonian societies for which he argues: Rav Yehuda, the Babylonian, is obsessed with genealogy whereas Ulla, the Palestinian, urges him to view silence and self-restraint as evidence of superior lineage. Kalmin concludes that even if the story was written by a Babylonian it is the exception. This position, however, is also cited by Rav Yehuda himself and is attributed to Rav.

[42] The problems in legal application of the general psychological observation are apparent in what seems to be a later addition to the statement: "and he never speaks praise"; that is, since this behavior (of disqualifying people) now has consequences, it has to be more severe, otherwise anyone could be suspect.

taking advantage of the ambiguity in the term "disqualifier."[43] The blurring of this distinction between the two manners of disqualification, the first through a prohibited union and the second through the attribution of prohibited status to another, parallels the blurring of the distinction between ascribed and natural genealogical identities seen in the previous section. Genealogical identity is as much the result of human speech as it is of procreation.

More importantly, this almost covert rhetorical jump has a dramatic effect on the course of the *sugya*. As noted above, our passage comes after harsh admonitions aimed at the first, "physical" disqualifier; it is immediately followed by the story about Rav Yehuda, after which the Talmud cites sayings which stress the importance of genealogical purity.[44] By equating the two disqualifiers and adding the story about Rav Yehuda, which revolves around the second type of disqualifier (and is cited because of the rule concerning that disqualifier), the Talmud shifts the entire focus of this section of the discussion. The harsh criticism leveled against the

---

[43] The account of the redactors' work here as the mere placement of sources one after the other is admittedly "conservative" in that it assumes that both sources were similar in the first place and that the Bavli's creators simply exploited this similarity. It is certainly possible, especially considering the recent work done on *baraitot* in the Talmud, that the shared terminology employed by the sources (i.e. terming both different actors as "disqualifiers") is itself already due to some editing process (see for example Shamma Friedman, "Uncovering Literary Dependencies in the Talmudic Corpus," in *The Synoptic Problem in Rabbinic Literature* [ed. S. J. D. Cohen; Brown Judaic Studies 326; Providence: Brown University Press 2000], 35–57).

[44] After the discussion regarding the words "came up from Babylonia," the *gemara* goes on to specify, using verses from Ezra and Nehemia, how we know each of the classes was part of the immigration to Palestine. The Bavli identifies the *mamzerim,* hush-children and foundlings in Neh 7:61 ("The following were those who came up from Tel-melah, Tel-harsha, Cherub, Addon, and Immer, but they could not prove their ancestral houses or their descent, whether they belonged to Israel"), through interpretations of the place names. The verse is also used by both Rabbi Abbahu and Rabbah b. b. Hana to state the importance and holiness of genealogical purity.

The latter's teaching ("Everyone who marries a woman unfit for him, Scripture says of him that he plowed (*ḥarash*) the entire world and sowed it with salt (*melaḥ*), as it was written: 'and the following were those who came up from Tel-melah, Tel-harsha'") is of special importance because in association with it the Talmud presents three more teachings which exhort against marrying an unfit woman. The discussions appended to each of these exhortations stretch the citation over almost two full talmudic pages, most of which are taken up by our story and the appended declarations. After the declarations, the Talmud returns to one more exhortation against he who marries an unfit woman, then goes on to remark that God's *shekhina* only resides among families of good pedigree. It continues with two negative sayings about converts, before proceeding to the discussion on the purification of *mamzerim*.

first disqualifier is thus shifted to the disqualifier by speech, who is assigned an equal share of the responsibility for genealogical impurity.

The story itself is no less interesting than the manner in which it is introduced. It begins as a person from Nehardea asks for a piece of meat in a butcher shop during a visit to Pumbedita. He is told that he will have to wait until one of Rav Yehuda's servants comes to pick up the prominent rabbi's order. The Nehardean customer is outraged and curses Rav Yehuda. Upon hearing this, the rabbi is himself infuriated and decides to excommunicate the Nehardean. Moreover, after hearing that this Nehardean frequently calls people "slaves," the rabbi declares him to be of slave stock. In response, the Nehardean sues Rav Yehuda, who is then summoned to Rav Nahman's court in Nehardea. After some deliberation, the trial begins.

Throughout the story, legal and genealogical knowledge is represented as context-dependent in various ways.[45] This representation is really pushed into the foreground in the dialogue between the Nehardean, Rav Yehuda and Rav Nahman. The Nehardean, i.e. the complainant, uses a strange argument to prove that contrary to the claims made by the defendant, Rav Yehuda, he is not of inferior, but rather excellent stock:

> Said that complainant to Rav Yehuda: "You call me a slave, I, who descend from the royal house of the Hasmoneans!?" He [Rav Yehuda] replied: "So said Shmuel: 'Whoever says, "I come from the house of the Hasmoneans" is a slave'." He [Rav Nahman, the arbiter] said to him [Rav Yehuda]: "[But] do you not agree with that [teaching] that Rav Abba said in Rav Huna's name who said in Rav's name: 'Any

---

[45] In fact, the very existence of the trial is contingent on politics. Twice the trial is almost avoided: once because Rav Yehuda is not legally obliged to appear in a court of an equal, Rav Nahman, and then because Rav Nahman himself (who first forgets about the subpoena) is reluctant to judge Rav Yehuda. In both instances, the reason for continuing with the trial is political.

First, Rav Yehuda is advised by Rav Huna to attend the court "because of the honor of the Exilarch" (with whom Rav Nahman is presumably associated). That does not suggest that he was a functionary of the exilarch. See Catharine Heszer, "The Slave of a Scholar is Like a Scholar" in *Creation and Composition* (ed. J. Rubenstein; Texts and Studies in Ancient Judaism 114; Tübingen: Mohr Siebeck, 2005), 181–200, esp. 192 n. 35. There is another way to interpret Rav Huna's advice without resorting to Rav Nahman's personal connections. If the question here is whether a rabbi is answerable to rabbinic courts other than the one he manages, then at stake might be the honor of the Jewish community and its political coherency, as personified by the Exilarch.

Second, after Rav Yehuda shows the subpoena to Rav Nahman, the latter notes that they should go on with the trial lest it be said that the Rabbis are going easy with one another. I see the story's expression of tension between rabbis and prominent non-rabbis, to which Kalmin draws attention (*The Sage in Jewish Society*, 51), as well as between two Babylonian Jewish communities (Nehardea and Pumbedita), as part of the overall tendency to implicate the discourse of genealogy with politics.

scholar who issues a ruling: if he had said it before the event [to which he wishes to apply the ruling] he is heeded, but if [he did not] he is not heeded [because we suspect he invented the principle for the purpose of the case]'?" (70b)

Rav's rule, cited at the end of this passage, seems to express a concern with rabbinic partiality: it is suspicious of rabbis who issue rulings after the fact and is concerned about potential ad-hoc inventions of tradition. This suspicion itself stems from the perception of rabbinic decisions as being intrinsically connected to the situation in which they are made. As the dialogue continues, the extremely detailed mode of literary description draws the reader's attention to this matter:

He [Rav Yehuda] said to him, "Rav Mattena is here; may it stand according to him." Rav Mattena had not seen Nehardea in thirteen years, but came that day. [Rav Yehuda] said to him, "Does his mastership remember what Shmuel said as he was standing with one leg on the bank [of the river], and one foot on the ferry boat?" [Rav Mattena] said, "So said Shmuel: 'Whoever says, "I come from the house of the Hasmoneans" is a slave.'" (70b)

Rav Yehuda and the Talmudic narrator present details concerning the situation of legal procedure and instruction. These details aim to stabilize what is understood to be unstable knowledge; to prove that Rav Yehuda's teaching was a reliable tradition; and to meet the requirements set up by Rav's rule. Rav Mattena cannot have been affected by the event because he had not been in Nehardea for thirteen years, and Rav Yehuda's question is phrased indirectly, without mentioning the subject matter, lest he be accused of begging the answer. These details, especially as they are specified in Rav Yehuda's question – down to the location and bodily posture of its instructor – also illustrate the localized context of halakhic information.

Rav's procedural rule represents an explicit thematization of the Bavli's intensified concern with the conditions in which knowledge is produced. It therefore presents an opportunity for us to discuss, briefly, whether this concern is intensified with respect to genealogical matters in particular or whether it applies to the production of knowledge in general. While both options might be true to a certain extent, the first finds support in the fact that of the four times that the Talmud cites Rav's teaching, three are connected with genealogical matters.[46]

Rav Yehuda uses two rabbinic traditions to justify his declaration that the person from Nehardea is genealogically a slave; we have encountered both. The first tradition is the circular principle, "whoever disqualifies is [himself] disqualified," with Shmuel's addition, "he disqualifies using his

[46] In addition to the citation here, see *b. Yebam.* 77a and *b. Yebam.* 88b. In, *b. Bek.* 38b, it appears in a different though not entirely unrelated context – namely, in a discussion on disqualifying mutilations.

own defect." Since the Nehardean "regularly declares" that certain people are of slave stock, he is, according to Shmuel's interpretation of the Tannaitic teaching, of that stock himself. That is the original justification given by the story for Rav Yehuda's declaration that the Nehardean is a slave. The second tradition is that any person claiming to have Hasmonean descent is genealogically a slave. As we have seen, the Nehardean claimed at Rav Nahman's court to be a descendant of that house.

Rav Yehuda's original reasoning is rejected by Rav Nahman, who understands the circular principle discussed above to be a good reason to *suspect* that someone is disqualified, but not to declare him disqualified. He is compelled, though, to declare the complainant a slave after the latter claims to be a Hasmonean and after Rav Matenna confirms Rav Yehuda's tradition that the descendants of the Hasmoneans are slaves. Rav Yehuda is victorious.

From the beginning, however, the story invites us to think about Rav Yehuda's motives. We know that he wanted to punish the Nehardean for insulting him. At first it seems to us that the punishment, at least, follows rabbinic protocol: when Rav Yehuda was told (by his own circle) that the Nehardean calls other people slaves, the rabbi applied the circular principle and declared him to be a slave. This declaration, however, loses its original reasoning in the trial: first, Rav Nahman refuses to accept the application of the circular principle, and second, the declaration is only validated by a fact which Rav Yehuda had not known at the time. Rav Yehuda's original decision, then, is reduced to simple revenge.

I would like to suggest that both of the traditions Rav Yehuda uses, along with a third one, constitute an effort by Shmuel to remove genealogical stratification from daily interaction. Adiel Schremer has already suggested that the intention behind Shmuel's hierarchical teaching, "All lands are dough to Palestine, and Palestine is dough to Babylonia," was to create in Shmuel's immediate social environment a space free of genealogical suspicion.[47] The two traditions used here by Rav Yehuda seem to have a similar intention. We have already seen how the circular principle, "whoever disqualifies is disqualified," can operate to limit genealogical slander. The instruction concerning Hasmonean descent should probably be read not just in terms of a rabbinic assertion regarding the historical house of the Maccabees (though it was certainly understood to be so later[48]), but also as targeting genealogical boasting by honor-seeking or

[47] Schremer, *Male and Female*, 155. He interprets other statements, some ascribed to Shmuel and some to other sages, in the same vein, on 155–57.

[48] In the printed edition, the Talmud supports Shmuel's teaching with a historical anecdote about the last of the Hasmoneans proclaiming, on the verge of suicide, that her

match-seeking Jews who affiliated themselves with the Jewish royal house in order to boost their genealogical status.[49]

If these two traditions seek to preempt the abuse of genealogical language for the personal advantage of the speaker and to prevent further social stratification, Rav Yehuda uses them for precisely the opposite purpose.[50] He abuses genealogical discourse, subordinating it to his own vengeful agenda. Whatever problem he may have had with the Nehardean, it had nothing to do with the man's genealogical status. Rabbinic decision-making is represented as being arbitrary.

The conclusion of the story invites a comparison with the story about Rava in Mahoza, already discussed at the end of the previous section. .

> He [Rav Nahman, after Rav Mattena approved Rav Yehuda's teaching] declared [the Nehardean] to be a slave. On that day, several marital contracts were torn up in Nehardea. As he [Rav Yehuda] went out [of the court, citizens of the town] came out after him to throw stones at him. He said to them, "If you will be silent, I will be silent, but if not, I reveal upon you that which Shmuel said, 'two lineages are in Nehardea. One is called the House of the Dove and one the House of the Crow, and the mark [through which one is to know their different natures] is that the impure is impure, and the pure is pure." They threw away those stones from their hands, and a great levee rose in the Royal River. (70b)

The tale about Rava celebrates his rhetorical use of the flexibility inherent in the law to adapt legal presentation to social circumstance. In contrast, Rav Yehuda uses his authority to create turmoil and stratification rather than peace. Rava avoided the "fruity stoning" mentioned above through an

---

house is of slave stock (found also in *b. B. Batra*). This story is absent, however, from both MS Munich 95 and MS Vatican 111.

[49] This understanding of Shmuel's intention, with Schremer, undermines the case for Kalmin's reconstruction of Amoraic attitudes towards genealogical discretion. Kalmin argues that whereas Palestinian rabbis supported discretion in genealogical matters, Babylonian rabbis had no qualms about publicly exposing blemished genealogies, and that they directed this discourse against non-rabbis (*Sage in Jewish Society*, 52–58). Kalmin himself writes that Shmuel's comment, "he disqualifies with his own defect," means that he "knows and comments on the Palestinian view" (ibid., 57; Shmuel not only knows of this view, but accepts it as a halakhic policy). Kalmin's statement, it seems to me, is applicable to what the story as a whole does with Shmuel's teaching, but less to the teaching itself. Kalmin's study might have drawn too sharp a line between Palestinian and Babylonian Amoraim on this matter (see also n. 41 above). One story in the Yerushalmi, not cited by Kalmin, seems to present precisely the opposite picture: "When R. Zera came up here [= Palestine], he heard people calling [this person] a *mamzer*," [that one] a female *mamzer*." He told them, 'What is this? But R. Huna said [...], 'A *mamzer* does not live more than thirty days'" (*y. Qidd.* 4:1 65c).

[50] This discussion concerns Rav Yehuda's character in this story, not the historical Rav Yehuda.

instruction of the law; Rav Yehuda stops the "rocky stoning" by concealing the law.[51] He is forced to compromise the genealogical zeal that brought him to this situation in the first place, revealing that he pursues genealogical purity only when he can use it as a punitive instrument to defend his honor, abandoning it when his well-being is in danger.

The Talmud's best joke at the expense of rabbis who abuse genealogical knowledge extends beyond the literary boundaries of the story to the next literary unit, which includes teachings by Rav Yehuda, Rava, and other rabbis:

> Rav Yehuda announces in Pumbedita: "Ada and Yonatan – slaves; Yehuda bar Papa – *mamzer*; Bati bar Tuvia – in haughty spirit did not take a *get* of manumission." Rava announces in Mahoza: "The Belans, Denans, Telans, Melans and Zegans are all disqualified." Said Rav Yehuda: "The people of Guvai – Givonites; Durnunita – a town of *netînim*" [*gûbā'ê – gîb'ônā'ê; dûrnûnîtā' – dûra' denetînā'ê*[52]]. Said Rav Yosef: "That [settlement in] Kube of Pumbedita – all of them are slaves." Said Rav Yehuda in Shmuel's name: "Pašḥur ben Immer had four hundred slaves" – and some say four thousand slaves – "and they all intermingled into the priesthood. And any priest who displays impudence is descended from them." (70b)

The Talmud adduces these declarations in connection with the public declaration of the Nehardean (and with him any self-proclaimed Maccabee) as a slave. They appear immediately after a story which showed us how an unsuspecting person entered a butcher shop, and, because he angered a rabbi, wound up being branded a slave, unworthy of marriage. By reproducing the above statements after this story, the Talmud is urging us to be suspicious of these declarations. Each of these declarations might be a product of a similar blend of emotions, politics, personal interest and truth. The punning used in Rav Yehuda's penultimate declaration, "The people of Guvai – Givonites; Durnunita – a town of *netînim*," seems in this context to be a parody of the arbitrariness of the production of genealogical stratification. To use Robert Cover's terms, "Narrative" here undermines, rather than supports, "Nomos."[53]

---

[51] The comparison between the two rabbis is made more explicit in MS Vatican 111. In that MS's version of the story about Rava in Mahoza, the "insensitive" rabbi is not R. Zera but Rav Yehuda. Rabbi Zera makes more sense chronologically, though.

[52] According to all manuscripts; printed editions have the version "*dara'ei netînā'ê*" ("pedigrees of *netînim*) which maintains the pun.

[53] Robert Cover, "Nomos and Narrative" in *Narrative, Violence and the Law: The Essays of Robert Cover* (ed. M. Minow et al.; Ann Arbor: University of Michigan Press, 1992), 95–172. See Barry Wimpfheimer, "Legal Narratives in the Babylonian Talmud" (Ph.D. diss., Columbia University, 2005) for an application of Cover's ideas to the analysis of Talmudic narratives.

The story about Rav Yehuda was introduced by blurring the distinction between the person who disqualifies by prohibited union and the one who disqualifies by speech. I suggested that the purpose of this blurring was to assign an equal share of responsibility for genealogical stratification to the latter. Now that I have presented the story, I can be more precise about who bears most of the responsibility. The Talmud moves from the admonitions against prohibited unions to disqualification by speech and finally to the dynamics of rabbinic decisions. The production of prohibited families is still the problem; however, it occurs not in the bedroom but in the rabbinic courtroom. If the rabbis, as we have seen, have the authority and ability to dictate genealogical reality, which is perceived as ascribed rather than natural, then the extent of genealogical purity – and the subsequent personal welfare of their communities – is up to them. If they disqualify, they are themselves disqualified.

Let me conclude this part of the paper with some general comments. The rabbis inherited a rich tradition of genealogical terms which they not only continued to use but also expanded with great interpretive and legal sophistication. Already in Tannaitic sources, though, genealogical matters are treated with a reservation that attests to the rabbis' break with the ancestry-centered culture evident in the Second Temple period. Some Tannaitic sources clearly present a replacement of lineage with scholarly or moral merit as a hierarchy-determining factor.[54] A famous mishnah in *Horayot* 3:8 presents a hierarchy of the Jewish people based on descent, only to conclude with the general principle, "a *mamzer*, who is a scholar, and a high priest, who is an ignoramus: the *mamzer* scholar takes precedence over the ignorant high priest."

A development of particular importance for understanding our text's discussion is the configuration of genealogical demarcation not as a fixed biological condition but rather as a legal condition, subject to change. The Mishnah presents this approach as an innovative, though controversial possibility: "Rabbi Tarfon says: '*mamzerim* could be purified. How so? A male *mamzer* that has married a female slave, [according to the law] their offspring is [genealogically] a slave'" (*m. Qidd.* 3:13).[55]

---

[54] Himmelfarb has recently offered a cautious evaluation of this process. See Martha Himmelfarb, *A Kingdom of Priests: Ancestry and Merit in Ancient Judaism* (Philadelphia: University of Pennsylvania Press, 2006).

[55] Hayes, *Gentile Impurities*, 278 n. 51, notes that "the use of the verb 'to purify' to refer to legal mechanism or process whereby one illegitimate and unfit for marriage is declared legitimate and fit for marriage is anticipated in *T. Levi* 14:6." It should be noted though, that this is a process to which *Testament of Levi* objects (as Hayes makes clear ibid., 247 n. 67).

The Bavli's discussion is indebted to these developments in rabbinic thought, but it goes in a different direction. If previous rabbinic texts invested more prestige in ascribed status than innate status, the Bavli blurs the distinction between them. If some earlier sources bestowed some power upon man to change birth-determined conditions, the Bavli is concerned with the problems, advantages and responsibilities associated with this power.

The Talmud's moves here are, as in other cases, at once "conservative" and "critical" in our terms. On the one hand, it avoids explicit criticism of the manipulation and use of genealogical information as vehicles of personal gain. It preserves and justifies the corrupted order of things. On the other hand, it acknowledges the contingency of this genealogical information and draws our attention to the conditions under which it is produced.

Finally, the Bavli is critical of the connection between genealogy and society not despite the prominence of genealogical concerns in the culture in which it was written, but because of that prominence. Its critique targets its own Babylonian rabbinic culture, a culture obsessed with genealogical stratification.[56] The way in which Babylonian Jewish society implicated genealogy with power is precisely what enables the Bavli to expose the social processes and structures of authority that construct genealogical identities.

## II. The Beginning of Genealogy

We can now turn to the Talmud's opening moves in its discussion of *m. Qidd.* 4:1, which address our mishnah's historical implications. In the first

---

[56] See nn. 2–8 above. One interesting witness to the importance of genealogical purity in late antique Judaism is found in the hymns opening *Hekhalot Rabbati*, which describe one aspect of the mystic's power: "Greatest of all is that all people would be before him like silver before a silversmith who knows which silver is adulterated and which silver is pure. He will be able to see in a family how many *mamzerim* are in it... how many descendants from slaves, how many descendants from gentiles" (*Hekhalot Rabbati* §86). This passage is similar to the Bavli in that it views genealogical knowledge as a problem and breaks with earlier rabbinic traditions that felt that this knowledge could be attained by normal legal or scholastic procedures. Its solution is just as radical as the Bavli's, but in the complete opposite direction: if for the Bavli perception was everything, *Hekhalot Rabbati* insists that behind it there exists truth which is accessible only to particular individuals, which that text indeed claims to possess. This text is particularly interesting in the context of the Talmud's treatment of the matter since some scholars have suggested that parts of the Hekhalot corpus originated in Babylonia (see most recently Ra'anan Boustan, *From Martyr to Mystic* [Texts and Studies in Ancient Judaism 112; Tübingen: Mohr Siebeck, 2005], 277–78 and the references there).

section below, I demonstrate that through its discussion of Ezra's purification of Babylonia the Talmud offers an innovative approach to genealogical inquiry, an approach consistent with the Talmud's focus on the situation in which genealogical knowledge is produced. In the second section, which concludes this paper, I argue that we can read in these opening moves a certain reversal of the hierarchies underlying two of the most memorable of Ezra's actions: the Return to Zion and the prohibition on intermarriage. Confronting these two central aspects of Jewish nationality, the land and the people, the opening passage of the *gemara* can be read as an ambitious introduction to the entire discussion.

### *1. The Purification of Babylonia*

Our mishnah, which lists the genealogical classes, opens with informing us that the "ten genealogical classes came up from Babylonia." The Talmud proceeds by analyzing this expression:

> a. What distinction is made by saying: "Came up from Babylonia"? Let it say: "Went to Palestine!" It teaches us something along the way, as we were taught on Tannaitic authority: "'Then you shall arise and go up to the place which the Lord your God will choose' (Deut 17:8), [this verse] teaches that the temple is higher than Palestine, and Palestine is higher than all lands." [...]
>
> b. [to be reproduced below]
>
> c. What distinction is made by saying: "Came up from Babylonia?" Let it say, "Came up to Palestine!" [This Mishnaic expression] supports Rabbi Eleazar, as R. Eleazar said: "Ezra did not go up from Babylonia before he made it like pure sifted flour and [then] went up."
>
> d. It was said: Abaye said, "we read [in the Mishnah] 'they came up,' by themselves,"[57] and Rava said, "we read 'they were brought up'."
>
> e. And they are in dispute over R. Eleazar's [dictum], that R. Eleazar said, Ezra did not come up from Babylonia until he made it like pure sifted flour, and came up." For Abaye, R. Eleazar's [dictum] is not true; for Rava, R. Eleazar's [dictum] is true.
>
> f. Or you may say that for everyone R. Eleazar's [dictum] is true, and here they are in dispute over this: one says that they were set apart and [then] came up by themselves, and one says that they were brought up against their will (69a–b).

The Bavli first suggests that what should be learned from the expression "came up" is that Palestine is higher than all lands (§a); after a short exegetical discussion of this topographical claim, to be discussed below, the

[57] "By themselves" is lacking in MS Vatican 111 and MS Munich 95; it might be a secondary interpretive addition.

Talmud expresses dissatisfaction with this solution: had the Mishnah's subject of implicit teaching been only the Land of Israel it would have mentioned only the Land of Israel; since the Mishnah specifically refers to Babylonia, the Talmud reasons, it must also teach us something about Babylonia (§c).[58]

It is then offered that this Mishnaic reference to Babylonia supports R. Eleazar's opinion, that Ezra did not leave Babylonia before he attended to matters of genealogical purity there.[59] How, precisely, our mishnah sup-

[58] The type of inquiry pursued by the Talmud in §§a–c, with its special terminology ("What distinction is made… let it say… it teaches us something along the way" – "מאי איריא...ליתני... מילתא אגב אורחא קמשמע לן"), appears in sugyot which modern scholarship, following traditional rabbinic historiography, attribute to the Saboraic, i.e., post-Talmudic, period (the most prominent of which is the opening sugya of tractate *Qiddushin*); see already Nehemia Brüll, *Jahrbücher für Jüdische Geschichte und Literature* II (Frankfurt: Wilhelm Erras, 1876), 46–47 n. 64. See also Avinoam Cohen, "The Problem of Identifying Saboraic Passages in the Bavli," in *Sefer Ya'akov Lesloy* (ed. Yitzhak Alfasi; Tel Aviv 1985; in Hebrew), 83–96 (91, n. 27) and most recently Moshe Benovitz, *BT Berakhot: Chapter I* (Talmud Ha-Igud; Jerusalem: The Society for the Interpretation of the Talmud, 2006; in Hebrew), 20. The nature of Saboraic literary activity and the extent to which it should be distinguished from previous redactional activity are still insufficiently defined. It is clear, however, that our *sugya* in 69a–b is from a late stage, since it incorporates an already redacted discussion (§d–f); see more infra.

[59] R. Eleazar's teaching itself should be read in two contexts. First, other sayings by *amoraim* seek to identify what Ezra was doing before he came up to Palestine. One by Rav or Rav Shmuel b. Martha, "As long as Baruch ben Nerya was alive, Ezra did not leave him to come up" (*b. Meg.* 16b), the other, again by Rav, through Rav Yehuda, "Ezra did not come up from Babylonia until he wrote his own genealogy [in the Book of Chronicles] and came up" (*b. B. Bat.* 15a). Though each of these sayings, including R. Eleazar's, has its own point, they all seem to also try to justify the delay between Cyrus' permission to immigrate to Palestine and Zerubabbel's immigration, on the one hand, and Ezra's immigration on the other (the shared purpose is evident, among other things, in the similarities of wording, especially between the saying in *Qiddushin*, לא עלה עזרא מבבל עד שעשאה כסולת נקיה ועלה and the one in *Baba Batra*, לא עלה עזרא מבבל עד שיחס עצמו ועלה, but also in *Megillah*,שכל זמן שברוך בן נריה קיים לא הניחו עזרא ועלה. This apologetic dimension of R. Eleazar's saying is not emphasized in the current context (see further in the last section of this paper). On the saying in *Megillah*, see Kalmin, *Sage in Jewish Society*, 16.

In addition, R. Eleazar's dictum provides a biblical and historical context for the Babylonian claim to genealogical superiority, which is its main function in the Bavli. R. Eleazar (b. Pedat) himself certainly had an interest in buttressing that Babylonian claim of excellent descent: though he is remembered as one of the Palestinian *amoraim* (being the notorious student of R. Yohanan), he was born in Babylonia and thus had a stake in fortifying the reputation of his own descent (for R. Eleazar's Babylonian origin and subsequent immigration to Palestine, see *y. Ber.* 2:1 and other places in the Talmuds; see also Chanoch Albeck, *Introduction to the Talmud, Babli and Yerushalmi* [Tel-Aviv: Dvir, 1969; in Hebrew], 224–27). R. Eleazar's Babylonian descent seems to undermine Kal-

ports this account is not explained at this stage, but it is certainly suggested that the mishnah's juxtaposition of the Babylonian emigration with the list of genealogical classes implies some causal association between the emigration of the classes and an act of purification made by Ezra.

The Talmud then proceeds to cite a disagreement between Abaye and Rava regarding the form which the verb "come up" takes in the mishnah; while Abaye reads "came up," Rava reads "brought up" (§d).[60] The Bavli supplies two interpretations of the nature of this disagreement (§e–f). First it speculates that the two rabbis differ with respect to R. Eleazar's assertion mentioned above: agreeing with R. Eleazar, Rava imagines an organized, forced emigration that constituted a purification of Babylonian Jewry; disagreeing with R. Eleazar, Abaye insists that it was a voluntary emigration undertaken by whoever wished to emigrate, which therefore could not even have practically functioned as an absolute purification of Babylonia (§e).

In the second interpretation, the Talmud attempts to interpret the disagreement based on the conjecture that both Rava and Abaye agree with R. Eleazar (§f). Their dispute is limited to the nature of Ezra's purifying project, but both, under this second interpretation, do agree that it took place. Rava's version, as under the first interpretation, is interpreted to imply that Ezra's act was one of purification through forced emigration. Abaye, it is now speculated, believes that Ezra's purification was an action distinct from the emigration itself: Ezra has "set aside" the forbidden classes, marking their identities as such.

It is with this suggestion, namely that Abaye's understanding of the mishnah may be in agreement with R. Eleazar's account of the purification of Babylonia, that the Talmud offers its readers a thorough revision of genealogical inquiry.

Let us look more closely at the difference between the two narratives which the Bavli associates with each of the Amoraim. The act of purification presented to support Rava's version consists of a physical removal of population from a certain community; the impure, prohibited classes were "brought up" to Palestine, leaving Babylonia with only the permitted

---

min's argument that "the Babylonian authors or editors most likely attribute a Babylonian sentiment to an important Palestinian rabbi, producing effective pro-Babylonian propaganda" (ibid., 17). R. Eleazar is an unlikely choice for such a move, since his genealogical identity was Babylonian. On R. Eleazar's teaching, see below.

[60] Epstein, *Introduction to the Mishnaic Text*, 1:379, lists our text as an instance of a widespread phenomenon, in which the dispute is not in the Mishnaic text itself but rather in its interpretation, even though the Bavli uses terms which are usually connected with text-criticism. In my discussion of the dispute, I follow the Bavli's terminology, usually using the terms "version" rather than "interpretation" or "understanding."

classes. The purifying activity presented to support Abaye's version consists of the distinction, made by Ezra, between the different genealogical classes, a demarcation which prevents illegal unions and genealogical intermingling.

These two narratives present not only different accounts of Ezra's activities, but different foci of genealogical inquiry. The main concern of the Jewish genealogical project, according to Rava's narrative, is homogeneity. In this respect, it parallels the view of genealogical purification which may be detected in R. Eleazar's language (cited in §c). R. Eleazar uses a metaphor of a pure substance, flour, which is separated from contaminating, extraneous substances by means of physical removal, so as to create "pure sifted flour." The idealized community is one without the extraneous prohibited classes. Similarly, Rava's narrative imagines the physical removal of the prohibited classes from Babylonia. In contrast, Abaye's narrative is concerned with genealogical knowledge: the purpose of the purifying action is not, as it is in Rava's narrative, to achieve homogeneity, but rather to separate the different classes and to prevent unlawful unions by making genealogical identities public.[61]

The first narrative, Rava's, imagines a purifying project that uses, and centers on, a dichotomy between "permitted" and "prohibited" genealogical classes: the object of purification is the permitted classes and purification is accomplished by the removal of the prohibited classes. In Abaye's version, Ezra makes multiple distinctions between several sets of classes and is concerned with the prohibition of illegitimate unions.

[61] If Rava's narrative and its conception of the genealogical project may be paralleled with the language used by R. Eleazar, Abaye's may be paralleled with the language used in Shmuel's hierarchical teaching. Shmuel's teaching imagines a genealogical scale on which different communities are placed with respect to the extent that they are mixed – the more intermingled a community is, the worse it is genealogically. The non-mixed communities which are at the better end of the scale may well *contain* different genealogical classes, but they are kept *apart*. The mixed communities are like a chemical solution in which different genealogical classes blend and, in permanently modifying one another, become indistinguishable. Again, with R. Eleazar's metaphor, the desired society is homogeneous: it idealizes a community without the extraneous classes; for the second metaphor, Shmuel's, the concern is genealogical knowledge: it places on the better side of the genealogical scale the unmixed society and the situation it wishes to avoid is a community in which genealogical identities are unmarked and unknown. Of course, each of these teachings has a different purpose and none of them try to define the genealogical project: R. Eleazar's teaching is historical (describing Ezra's action), Shmuel's is contemporary, halakhic and practical (setting the level of suspicion or trust one should exercise towards the specified communities regarding marriage eligibility). Still in their different terminology we may read two different ways to perceive the nature of purity to which a Jewish community should strive.

The Bavli's discussion is at this point premised on the claim that the mishnah implies the purification act. While the discussion of Abaye and Rava's positions (§d–f) seems to have been composed independently of the literary unit in which that claim is made (§c),[62] and taken by itself does not necessarily hold that claim,[63] in its current placement the Talmud's reconstruction of the two different narratives should also entail different understandings of the way the mishnah implies Ezra's purification of Babylonia. It is clear how Rava's purification is implied in the mishnah, since he identifies it with the emigration of the classes which the mishnah describes. But how can Abaye's purification be implied in the mishnah (which tells us only of the emigration) if it is not identified with the emigration?

In answering this question, let me build on the characterization offered above of Abaye's narrative. Since the important moment here is not the physical departure of the classes but rather their demarcation, the fact that the mishnah tells us that the emigrating population was *already classified* when it left Babylonia is taken as evidence that the classification itself originated in Babylonia, in an act of demarcation by Ezra. Our mishnah is taken, then, to describe the moment in which genealogical identities, as we know them, were assigned; it describes a development in the history of Jewish knowledge. This conjecture admittedly goes further than the explicit statements in the Talmud allow, but at the very least it highlights the direction towards which, I believe, the *sugya* aims.

The focus on physical purification and homogeneity is evident not only in the narrative associated with Rava but also in a different instance in which our mishnah is connected with Ezra's purification of Babylonia and Babylonian genealogical superiority. A few pages after our *sugya* but still within the Talmud's discussion of *m. Qidd* 4:1, we read:

> Zeiri was avoiding R. Yohanan who was urging him, "Marry my daughter." One day they were walking together on a road and arrived at a pool of water. He [Zeiri, expressing reverence] mounted R. Yohanan on his shoulders and carried him. He [R. Yohanan] told him, "Our Torah is fit, our daughters are unfit? What makes you think so? If it is our mishnah, 'Ten genealogical classes came up from Baby-

---

[62] While this cannot be demonstrated with definitive philological evidence, it is supported by the Talmud's argumentation: when it first associates the mishnah with R. Eleazar's saying, the Bavli assumes that the form "come up" can be used to support R. Eleazar's words by implying the purification of Babylonia, while in the discussion about Amoraic versions, Abaye's support of this very version is taken to mean that he objects to R. Eleazar's account, and the possibility that this form can accord with that account is suggested only later.

[63] Thus, the *stam* understands the dispute to be about whether the Amoraim subscribe to R. Eleazar's teaching or not, and not about the mishnah's support of that teaching.

> lonia: priests, Levites [and Israelites…]' – did priests, Levites and Israelites come up [from Babylonia] in their entirety? Just like some of these [permitted classes] remained [there], some of those [prohibited classes] remained." It escaped him [R. Yohanan] that which was said by Rabbi Eleazar, that Ezra did not go up from Babylonia before he made it like pure sifted flour and then went up." (71b)

R. Yohanan understands that Zeiri's refusal to marry his daughter has to do with the Babylonian claim to supreme genealogical purity, and grapples with what he believes to be the source of this claim. If the argument is that we know from the mishnah in *Qiddushin* that Ezra made Babylonia genealogically pure because it tells us of the emigration of prohibited classes from there to Palestine, we have to note, says R. Yohanan, that the Mishnah also tells us of the emigration of permitted classes – priests, Levites and Israelites. Just like the Babylonian community takes for granted that many members of these classes stayed and did not emigrate to Palestine (and in fact traces its origin to these people), it should also concede that members of the prohibited classes remained. There is nothing in the Mishnah that tells us that certain genealogical classes emigrated to Palestine in their entirety while others did not; therefore, there is nothing which makes Babylonia genealogically purer than Palestine, and there is no reason that Zeiri should refuse to marry his daughter.

The Talmud now comments that R. Yohanan must have forgotten R. Eleazar's tradition about Ezra's purification.[64] Unlike the *stam* in our *sugya*, the discussion of Rava's and Abaye's dispute, the *stam* here concedes that our mishnah does not tell the story of Babylonia's purification and sees in R. Eleazar's teaching, which it understands as not supported by the mishnah, the only support for Babylonia's superior genealogy. This difference in the *stam*'s treatment of the mishnah appears to indicate that the two *sugyot* are independent of each other.

In the historical narrative which the Talmud constructs to match Abaye's understanding of the mishnah, we can read an answer to R. Yohanan's objection: Ezra distinguished, rather than removed, the prohibited classes. The population remaining in Babylonia was genealogically marked and prohibited marriages were thus avoided, and it is that which supports Babylonian genealogical superiority.

Both *sugyot*, then, are independent responses to what must have been an established *aetia* to Babylonian genealogical supremacy. But in our *sugya*

---

[64] See Kalmin, "Genealogy and Polemics," 91–92, who observes that this editorial comment is curious, "since Eleazar is a younger, inferior contemporary of Yohanan whom Yohanan certainly has authority to contradict. Far from an effective refutation of Yohanan's view, the editorial comment illustrates the lengths to which the editors are willing to go to refute Palestinian claims, and the strength of the editors' desire to promote Babylonian supremacy."

the Talmud re-imagines that *aetia* thoroughly, offering a challenge to its underlying assumption of what constitutes purification and implying a new approach to genealogy, which is concerned less with physical separation and more with control through information.

The composition of our *sugya* creates a dialectical effect which builds on the reader's expectations. The *sugya* first implicates, without explanation, the mishnah with Ezra's purification act (§c). This implication is then explained through the controversy about the mishnah's meaning (§d–f): the student is first led to believe that it only makes sense by imagining an act of forced physical mobilization of the prohibited classes (§e); the assertion that only Rava, who reads in the Mishnah "brought up," supports R. Eleazar's teaching means that the Mishnah implies Ezra's purification only if it is understood to describe the forced mobilization. Even if the Babylonian reader was not previously familiar with the narrative of purification – a source of pride for his community – he is now led by the Bavli to believe one version of that narrative, the same version to which R. Yohanan responds. But with the suggestion that Abaye's version may also agree with R. Eleazar's account the Talmud offers its student-reader an alternative way altogether to think not only about that narrative but about genealogical purification in general.

The Talmud never chooses between the two narratives, Abaye's or Rava's, and the discussion is not concluded with any prevailing argument about genealogical inquiry and the way it should be conducted. The Bavli's moves, however, do restructure our sets of concerns and interests, replacing one perspective with another. This is particularly evident in the final part of our discussion, in which Rava's narrative successfully sustains two objections:

> g. It accords well for him who says "came up," that which Rav Yehuda said in Shmuel's name, "All lands are dough [i.e., "blended," inferior genealogically] to Palestine, and Palestine is dough to Babylonia." But for him who says "brought up," they must have been known [i.e., their genealogical identity was already marked as impure when they arrived to Palestine; why then is Palestine considered "blended"]? They were known to that generation, but to other generations they were not known.

> h. It accords well for him who says "came up," that which is written, "I gathered them by the river that runs to Ahava, and there we camped for three days. As I reviewed the people and the priests, I found there none of the descendants of Levi" (Ezra 8:15). But for him who says "brought up," he must have been mindful [of the genealogical identities of the emigrants, since the emigration was part of a purification effort; how come was he taken by surprise when he reviewed the people]? He was certainly mindful of the unfit, but of the fit he was not (69b).

The Talmud presents two instances in which Rava's position seems to contradict what we know to be true; first it is pitted against Shmuel's instruction of Babylonia's genealogical superiority, then against the biblical narrative itself. But while Rava's narrative is eventually maintained, the examination itself is already carried through under the knowledge-centered genealogical paradigm: the question is not whether the prohibited classes were transferred in their entirety or not, as we would have expected if the purification was associated with the physical removal (and as we have seen in R. Yohanan's story); rather, the discussion focuses on Ezra's knowledge of the émigrés' genealogical identity, with appropriate vocabulary (the first objection utilizes the root ידע, the second has both בין from the biblical verse and זהר in the Talmud's comment).

The Talmud's opening moves reflect, then, the same patterns of attention that we have seen in operation throughout the *gemara* on our mishnah in the first section of this paper. It focuses on the production of genealogical knowledge and the situation and manner in which it occurs.

This is, however, not the only way the opening *sugya* is tied with the rest of the Bali's discussion; rather, the historical discussion with which the Bavli opens these discourses can be seen as an introduction which sets the tone of the following literary units, denoting that this is a discussion confronting the basic components of Jewish nationhood.

### 2. *The Land and the People*

Among the endeavors made in Ezra's generation to restore the national life of Israel in the sixth-fifth centuries B.C.E., two especially – the return to Palestine, on the one hand, and the establishment of the Jewish people as a "holy seed" with ethnic genealogical homogeneity (by the prohibition on intermarriage), on the other – have become the hallmarks of Jewish nationhood. For many, these elements define the Jewish nation to this very day.

The Mishnah rarely refers in explicit fashion to the "return to Zion" or to the establishment of the "holy seed," and, as far as I know, never ties the two together. Our mishnah, however, does allude to these two issues in conjunction by referring to the immigration to Palestine from Babylonia of the "ten genealogical classes." Again, the organized return to Palestine led by Ezra is by no means the subject of the mishnah, but the emigration from Babylonia is referred to; Ezra's prohibition of intermarriage is not mentioned, but the subject of the mishnah is the genealogical project.

The authors of the Bavli chose to engage these nationally charged materials, marginal in our mishnah but central to their own agenda: the land and the people. We have already seen how the first part of our discussion deals with the people. In its discussion of Ezra's action, the Talmud restructures genealogical inquiry, which transforms from an enterprise defined in terms of homogeneity to one concerned with preventing illegal unions through the accumulation of genealogical knowledge; this restructuring is a long way from Ezra's establishment of a homogeneous "holy seed."[65]

Let us now discuss its treatment of the land. The geographical theme is taken up in the very first teaching of the *gemara*, which seeks to learn from the expression "came up" the topographical fact that Palestine is higher than all other lands:

> a. What distinction is made by saying: "Came up from Babylonia"? Let it say: "Went to Palestine!" It teaches us something by the way, as we were taught on Tannaitic authority: "'Then you shall arise and go up to the place which the Lord your God will choose' (Deut 17:8), it teaches that the temple is higher than Palestine, and Palestine is higher than all lands."
>
> b. It accords well, that the Temple is higher than Palestine, that which is written, "[should there be] any such matters of dispute in your towns – then you shall immediately go up [to the place that the Lord your God will choose]" (Deut 17:8). But how do we know that Palestine is higher than all other lands? It is written, "Therefore, the days are surely coming, says the Lord, when it shall no longer be said, 'As the Lord lives who brought the people of Israel up out of the land of Egypt', but 'As the Lord lives who brought out and led the offspring of the house of Israel out of the land of the north and out of all the lands where he had driven them.'" (Jer 23:7–8) (69a–b)

The classic commentators have already noticed the problematic scope of the comparison: the mishnah only mentions Babylonia and Palestine, so how can the conclusion be that Palestine is higher than *all other lands*? In my view, to run the risk of tautology, the Bavli puts Palestine and all other lands in opposition because it wants to put Palestine and all other lands in opposition. While for the Babylonian Jewish community, as our *sugyot* clearly attest, the relevant opposition has mostly been that of Babylonia with Palestine as the two competing Jewish centers, in some contexts, such as Ezra's return, that community might have felt the need to argue for the Diaspora as a whole.

To prove that Palestine is higher than all lands, the Bavli quotes two scriptural verses which, in addition to describing the relative height of Jerusalem and Palestine (which is the given reason for the citation of these verses), evoke two of Palestine's most distinctive features: it *was* the site of the Temple (Deut 17:8), and it *will be* the site of the people of Israel who will be brought there at the time of redemption (Jer 23:7–8). The

[65] Satlow demonstrated that the very idea of genealogical division, innovated by the rabbis, already presents a break with pre-rabbinic authors, including Ezra, who assume the unity of Israel (*Jewish Marriage*, 148–50). The Talmud then only accentuates (or further polarizes) a difference which is already there.

importance of the Land of Israel is thus restricted to anytime but the present.[66]

The Bavli shifts the historical focus from Palestine, the place of arrival, to Mesopotamia, the place of departure; the immigration has become an emigration. With Rava's view, it conceives of the entire project of immigration as an act centered on the maintenance of genealogical purity in the Babylonian community.[67] The Talmud's underlying assumption is that there is nothing inevitable or requisite in the immigration to the Promised Land. Even in the second interpretation of the Rava-Abaye dispute, we learn that one makes *aliyah* when there is no other, or no better choice: the prohibited classes have emigrated to Palestine either because they were forced to ("Rava") or because having been marked as prohibited by their community's leadership they could not marry ("Abaye"). Immigration to Palestine becomes unnecessary as the Talmud legitimizes exile; the hegemony of the Land of Israel as the ultimate destination for Jews becomes irrelevant. The action the Bavli takes with respect to geographical matters is similar to the one it took with respect to ethnic matters: it decentralizes the Jewish world not only genealogically but geographically by allowing multiple communities. The extensive discussion regarding the borders of Babylonia (71b–72b) echoes the other tradition of rabbinic territorial mapping, the mapping of the Land of Israel.

In order to realize a different image of the nation, replacing the images of its elements and of the space in which it exists, the Bavli turns to the moment with which those images are most associated. It offers a reinterpretation of that moment and presents an image of the Jewish people very much at variance with that which Ezra epitomizes: it is a dispersed, heterogeneous people whose genealogical identity is contested and flexible and, to return to the topic of this volume, historically contingent.

---

[66] While Deut 17:8 is used in this way already in Tannaitic literature (see, e.g., *Sifre Deut* §37), its conjunction with Jer 23:7–8 and their appearance together is unique to the Bavli (in *Sifre*, the verse appears after a series of verses adduced to teach the merit of Palestine, and its interpretation emphasizes that "everything which is higher than the something, is better than something"; ibid.). Aside from our passage, this appears only in *b. San.* 87a, which is comparable to *Sifre Deut* §152, but ends with the comment on Jer 23 that appears in our *stam*.

[67] This is perhaps Rashi's intention when he explains the first association between R. Eleazar's dictum and the Mishnah: "Ezra's lone intention was to cleanse Babylonia."

# The Spoils of the Jerusalem Temple at Rome and Constantinople

## Jewish Counter-Geography in a Christianizing Empire

RA'ANAN S. BOUSTAN

## I. Introduction[1]

The *Apocalypse of Baruch* (*2 Baruch*), set during the destruction of the First Temple by the Babylonians in 586/7 B.C.E. but written in response to the destruction of the Second Temple by the Romans more than 600 years later, addresses quite candidly the anxieties of its grieving audience.[2]

[1] Preliminary work on this project was undertaken during a Fellowship at University of Pennsylvania's Center for Advanced Judaic Studies (2003–2004), whose support I gratefully acknowledge. Portions of this essay were delivered at the Association for Jewish Studies, December 18, 2005; at Princeton University, January 22, 2006; at University of Minnesota, February 6, 2006; and at University of California, Los Angeles, November 5, 2006. I would like to thank all those who offered insightful comments and mid-course corrections on those occasions, many of which have significantly enhanced the final product. I am especially grateful to Andrea Schatz for opening up my thinking on travel literature and Jewish culture, to Peter Brown, Gregg Gardner, Ron Mellor, David Myers, Kevin Osterloh, and Claudia Rapp for their valuable advice as the paper came to fruition, and to Leah Platt Boustan for passing her skilled editorial eye over the near-finished version. Needless to say, I alone am to blame for any remaining errors, imperfections, and infelicities.

[2] On the basis for dating *2 Baruch* to the period between the fall of Jerusalem (70 C.E.) and the Bar Kokhba revolt (132–135/6 C.E.) and, more specifically, between 100–130 C.E., see A. F. J. Klijn, "2 (Syriac Apocalypse of) Baruch," in *The Old Testament Pseudepigrapha, vol. 1: Apocalyptic Literature and Testaments* (ed. J. H. Charlesworth; New York: Doubleday, 1983–1985), 615–52, esp. 616–17. Rivka Nir, *The Destruction of Jerusalem and the Idea of Redemption in the Syriac Apocalypse of Baruch* (Early Judaism and its Literature 20; Leiden: Brill, 2003), has recently argued that *2 Baruch* was penned by a Christian author. However, Nir's dichotomy between Judaism and Christianity, her highly selective conception of what constitutes Judaism, and her assumption that rabbinic literature reflects "earlier" Jewish tradition are all methodologically unsound. For a detailed refutation of Nir's thesis, see James R. Davila, *The Provenance of the Pseudepigrapha: Jewish, Christian, or Other?* (Supplements to the Journal for the Study of Judaism 105; Leiden: Brill, 2005), esp. 126–31, which affirms that *2 Baruch* was most likely written "by a Torah-observant author with a Jewish ethnic identity" (131). While I generally agree with Davila's assessment, I would place more stress on the unsuitability

Foremost among these concerns are the fate of the Temple vessels and the bearing of their fate on the shrine's eventual restoration. Will these mobile repositories of sanctity fall into enemy hands? And will God permit these artifacts to serve as material testimony to the superiority of the conqueror?

As the earthly army surrounds the city, the seer has a vision of four angels stationed at the four corners of the besieged city holding the torches they will use to set it ablaze. But their hands are momentarily stayed by a fifth angel, who will first collect from the Holy of Holies the cult objects stored there. The angel then invokes the earth to guard them for a future time:

> "Earth, earth, earth, hear the word of the mighty God, and receive the things which I commit to you, and guard them until the last times, so that you may restore them when you are ordered, so that strangers may not get possession of them. For the time has arrived when Jerusalem will also be delivered up for a time, until the moment that it will be said that it will be restored forever." And the earth opened its mouth and swallowed them up.[3]

This evocative image of the sacred vessels from the Jerusalem Temple secreted away in or near the land of Israel in preparation for the future renewal of the cult echoes a long-standing literary tradition from the Second Temple period. According to its earliest extant formulation, found in 2 Maccabees, the prophet Jeremiah is said to have sealed the Tent of Meeting and the Ark of the Covenant from the First Temple in a cave on the mountain in trans-Jordan from which Moses had surveyed the Promised Land at the end of Israel's wanderings in the wilderness.[4] In resistance to the centrifugal forces of exile that had scattered the Judean population, the vessels are saved from the sacrilege of falling into the impure hands of the enemy. Their hidden presence – in both sacred earth and sacred narra-

---

of applying to many pseudepigrapha – including *2 Baruch* – the categories of "Christian" or "Jewish" as mutually exclusive labels. See David Frankfurter, "Beyond 'Jewish Christianity': Continuous Religious Sub-Cultures of the Second and Third Centuries and their Documents," in *The Ways That Never Parted: Jews and Christians in Late Antiquity and the Middle Ages* (ed. A. H. Becker and A.Y. Reed; Texts and Studies in Ancient Judaism 95; Tübingen: Mohr Siebeck, 2003), 131–43.

[3] *2 Baruch* 6:8 (Klijn, "2 Baruch," 623).

[4] 2 Macc 2:1–8. Close parallels also appear in *4 Baruch* (*Paraleipomena Jeremiou*) 3:7–20; *Vit. Proph.* 2:11–14. In all versions, except *2 Baruch*, it is the prophet Jeremiah – and not an angel – who acts as the agent. On the interrelationship of these sources and their relationship to 2 Maccabees, see George W. E. Nickelsburg, "Narrative Traditions in the *Paralipomena of Jeremiah* and *2 Baruch*," *Catholic Biblical Quarterly* 35 (1973): 60–68. For general discussion of this theme, see Isaac Kalimi and James D. Purvis, "The Hiding of the Temple Vessels in Jewish and Samaritan Literature," *Catholic Biblical Quarterly* 56 (1994): 679–85.

tive – stands as a promise of the auspicious restoration of the Jerusalem cult.[5]

The author of *2 Baruch* seems to refuse to acknowledge the fact that Titus and his victorious armies had in very recent memory paraded the sacred implements of the Jerusalem cult through the streets of Rome in triumphal procession, enshrined this celebration in monumental public art on the Arch of Titus, and even placed some of these items on display in the newly built Temple of Peace (*Templum Pacis*).[6] Perhaps this reality was simply too troubling. But Steven Weitzman has convincingly argued in his rich study of the various tactics and strategies that made possible the persistence of Jewish cultural identity in antiquity that, by side-stepping its own present reality, *2 Baruch* offers its reader the hope, however attenuated, that the "real" Temple vessels – those from the First Temple – remain ready at hand in the soil of the Land of Israel.[7] According to Weitzman, this impulse to transform the temple vessels imaginatively into a kind of hidden treasure was not unique to *2 Baruch*, but represented a broader cultural pattern. Thus, he argues that texts such as the *Copper Scroll* literally veiled the temple artifacts in language and symbol in the hopes that, in this cryptic form, they might transcend the vagaries of political circumstance.[8]

---

[5] It is worth noting, however, that this tradition is in considerable tension with the explicit discussion in various biblical texts of the removal of the temple vessels to Babylon by Nebuchadnezzar (esp. 2 Kgs 24:13–17, 25:12–17; Jer 52:17–23; 2 Chron 36:18–19; Dan 1:2), their pollution by the Babylonians and the subsequent need for their purification (Dan 5:2–4, 22–23), and their eventual return from Babylon to Jerusalem (Ezra 1:6–11; Neh 13:5–9).

[6] On the public display of the vessels during the triumph and, later, in the *Templum Pacis*, see Section II below.

[7] Steven Weitzman, *Surviving Sacrilege: Cultural Persistence in Jewish Antiquity* (Cambridge, Mass.: Harvard University Press, 2005), 108, suggests that the tactic employed in *2 Baruch* "was to wait the enemy out – to surrender control over the real contents of the Second Temple and cling to the hope that the lost contents of the First Temple will, with God's help, be recovered one day."

[8] Weitzman, *Surviving Sacrilege*, 96–117; also idem, "Myth, History, and Mystery in the Copper Scroll," in *The Idea of Biblical Interpretation: Essays in Honor of James L. Kugel* (ed. H. Najman and J. H. Newman; Leiden: Brill, 2004), 239–55. Weitzman here builds upon and nuances the pioneering "mythologizing" interpretation of the scroll formulated by Jósef Milik in M. Baillet, J. T. Milik, and R. de Vaux, *Les 'petites grottes' de Qumrân* (Discoveries in the Judaean Desert III; Oxford: Clarendon Press, 1962), 198–302, esp. 282–83. For a polar opposite analysis of the text, which views it not as "legend" but as an abstract of a longer catalogue of actual valuables and their hiding places, see especially Judah K. Lefkovits, *The Copper Scroll–3Q15: A Reevaluation: A New Reading, Translation, and Commentary* (Studies on the Texts of the Desert of Judah 25; Leiden: Brill, 2000); also the studies of Lefkovits, Hanan Eshel, Meir Bar Ilan, Ruth

The present paper builds upon the important work that has been done by Weitzman and others on how this "continuity theme" operates within Second Temple Jewish sources.[9] I analyze the subsequent transformations in the theme of the Temple implements as it evolved within Jewish literary culture immediately following the destruction of the Second Temple by the Romans (70 C.E.) and subsequently throughout Late Antiquity (c. 200–750 C.E.). Indeed, Second Temple literature represents only one moment in a larger history of the "styles of continuity" that characterize Jewish culture, to borrow a phrase from Benedict Anderson.[10] Like Anderson, I take as my fundamental premise that change happens where it is said to happen, and also where it is not. As we shall see, the often self-appointed guardians of continuity within the "native tradition" of the colonized – in our case, drawn from the various groups of Jewish elites or sub-elites who produced late antique Jewish writings – are, ironically, as much agents of rupture as were the imperial conquerors themselves.

The history of Jewish approaches to the problem of destruction and restoration, as seen through the particular theme of the Temple vessels, discloses a dialectical tension between "centrifugal" and "centripetal" conceptions of space in Jewish culture – with both tendencies deployed in the service of "continuity."[11] Thus, we find that biblical sources from the Persian and early Hellenistic periods carefully stage-manage the ideological implications of the historical fact that the Babylonians had carried off the Temple treasure from Jerusalem not by asserting that these objects had in fact never been displaced, but instead by emphasizing the inherent invi-

---

Fidler, Israel Knohl, and Piotr Muchowski in *Copper Scroll Studies* (ed. G. J. Brooke and P. R. Davies; Journal for the Study of the Pseudepigrapha: Supplement Series 40; London: Sheffield Academic Press, 2002), although it must be stressed that these scholars are not of one mind concerning whether the valuables belonged to the Qumran community, the Jerusalem Temple, a rival priestly group, or another constituency entirely.

[9] The phrase "a continuity theme" was coined by P. R. Ackroyd over 30 years ago to characterize the palpable effort exerted by the biblical authors, following the destruction of the First Temple, to develop narrative traditions – and an ideological framework – that would help safeguard the future validity and viability of Israel's sacrificial cult ("The Temple Vessels: A Continuity Theme," in *Studies in the Religion of Ancient Israel* [Supplements to Vetus Testamentum 23; Leiden: Brill, 1972], 166–81).

[10] *Imagined Communities: Reflections on the Origin and Spread of Nationalism* (rev. ed.; London: Verso, 1991), 11.

[11] I plan to pursue in a future essay the general insights outlined here. On the important recent contributions of the new "critical geography" to the study of Jewish history and culture, see Charlotte E. Fonrobert and Vered Shemtov, "Introduction: Jewish Conceptions and Practices of Space," *Jewish Social Studies* 11 (2005): 1–8, and the essays contained in this special issue of the journal.

olability of these moveable objects.[12] By contrast, Jewish texts produced in the Hasmonean and early Roman periods – from 2 Maccabees to *2 Baruch* (c. 150 B.C.E.–100 C.E.) – came to insist that the cult vessels had, in fact, always remained hidden near the center of the nation's devotional life. And, after 70 C.E., we observe precisely the opposite trend, as the initial emphasis on the fundamental immovability of the sacred vessels in texts like *2 Baruch* gives way to a rich and multifaceted tradition concerning the historical and religious meanings of their dislocated presence in the imperial capital of Rome. In fact, over time, Jewish sources not only accepted that the relics of the Second Temple were now in exile, but increasingly embraced the paradoxical symbolic potential of this notion. As we shall see, by the end of Late Antiquity, the image of the Temple vessels stockpiled at Rome would be absorbed into a robust eschatological discourse that might have puzzled the author of *2 Baruch*, but would also surely have made him proud.

It will thus be my contention in this paper that the trajectory of Jewish traditions concerning the vessels of the destroyed Second Temple can be mapped against broader developments in the Jewish response to the changing nature of Roman imperial discourse and practice. I trace the shifting functions of the motif of the Temple vessels in contemporaneous Jewish and Roman (and later Roman-Christian) sources. I show that this potent literary theme, as it was deployed over the course of Late Antiquity in these rival discursive traditions, indexes broader patterns in the politico-theological contest between Jews and Romans concerning the meaning of imperial conquest and power. Moreover, I locate a major shift in the way that Jewish sources deploy the theme of the Temple implements in the particular context of the emergent interest in sacred relics in the Byzantine world during the fifth- and especially sixth-centuries. Perhaps not surprisingly, included among those relics are the vessels from the Jerusalem Temple, which reappear in this period in Greek and Latin historiography after a more than 400 year absence. It is precisely at this historical juncture that the Temple vessels came to serve as a highly charged theme within a novel Jewish messianic discourse – now directed against a specifically Christian Roman Empire.

Central to the argument of this paper is the claim that the Roman-Christian remapping of Palestine as the Christian Holy Land, which already began during the lifetime of the Emperor Constantine,[13] finds a direct counterpart in a group of contemporaneous Jewish texts that imagi-

---

[12] Ackroyd, "Temple Vessels," 166–81.

[13] Jaś Elsner, "The *Itinerarium Burdigalense*: Politics and Salvation in the Geography of Constantine's Empire," *Journal of Roman Studies* 90 (2000): 181–95.

natively inverts this process of travel, discovery, and ideological appropriation. These texts explore the fate of a wide variety objects from the biblical or Jewish past – not only the Temple implements, but also the clothing of the First Man, the throne of King Solomon, and even relics of Jewish martyrs. Although these sources locate Jewish artifacts from earlier Roman persecutions or conquests in the heart of the Empire – the city of Rome itself – they resoundingly reject the notion that the Roman capture and possession of objects from Israel's glorious past constitute numinous physical proof of the legitimacy of Christian imperial power. Rather, the Jewish sources situate these physical artifacts within an alternative narrative of Jewish triumph and redemption, which treats the dominant Roman-Christian interpretation of the current religious and political order as deceptive and transitory. By imagining late antique Jews – rabbis among them – in the act of discovering the remains of the Jewish past at Rome, in the heart of the Empire, these texts reverse the direction of travel and exploration, turning Christian sacred space inside-out. They thereby map out what I will call a "counter-geography" within which a resistant Jewish identity could be fashioned.

My notion of "counter-geography" draws especially from David Biale's concept of "counter-history," which he has applied to the particular mode of oppositional discourse that was generated by Jews within the Christianizing cultural of the late Roman Empire.[14] In Biale's usage, "counter-history" refers to the ways that Jewish literary artifacts such as the seventh-century Hebrew apocalypse *Sefer Zerubavel* and the Jewish anti-gospels, the *Toldot Yeshu* tradition, which present Jesus as a demonic miracle-worker, simultaneously draw from and invert the dominant historical paradigm articulated by Christian writers and theologians. This strategy resists the dominant narrative of Christian triumphalism by manipulating elements of Christian salvation history for its own ends. In the resulting cultural artifacts, polemical and apologetic aims jostle against each other precariously. My exploration of a Jewish "counter-geography" aims to contribute to our understanding of the precise idioms through which the shared discourses and practices of Jews and Christians were fashioned into rival cultural forms.

---

[14] David Biale, "Counter-History and Jewish Polemics against Christianity: The *Sefer Toldot Yeshu* and the *Sefer Zerubavel*," *Jewish Social Studies* n.s. 6 (1999): 130–45. On the notion of "counter-history," see also Amos Funkenstein, "History, Counter-History and Memory," in *Probing the Limits of Representation* (ed. S. Friedlander; Cambridge, Mass.: Harvard University Press, 1992), 66–81; idem, *Perceptions of Jewish History* (Berkeley: University of California Press, 1993), esp. 169–201.

A number of recent studies, especially those of Jaś Elsner, Blake Leyerle, and Andrew Jacobs, have explored the role that Christian pilgrimage to Palestine and the literature that grew up around it had begun, already by the late fourth century, to play in the transformation of the "Holy Land" from a locus of biblical and Jewish history into a site for the construction of Christian imperial ideology.[15] And, over the subsequent two centuries (400–600 C.E.), the Roman-Christian state – assisted by a host of Christian writers, travelers, and ecclesiastical authorities – gradually consolidated its hold over both the conceptual and the concrete geography of Palestine. This scholarship reflects a renewed interest in the political dimensions of religious discourse and practice in general and in the role of imperialism and colonialism in the formation of early Christianity in particular. Moreover, this work has increasingly drawn on the theoretical framework of postcolonial studies, in which the colonial encounter is understood to generate common, if highly asymmetrical, cultural domains within which both colonizer and colonized are constrained to speak and act.[16]

For this reason, scholars working in this mode have speculated about and even posited the existence of Jewish cultural products that contested the hegemonic claims of the emergent Christian discourse of empire. But the challenge of locating and analyzing these voices has fallen outside the scope of these studies, which principally focus on Greek and Latin Patristic sources. Nor have scholars yet systematically addressed the evolution of late antique Jewish conceptions of imperial geography in response to the process of Christianization.[17] Thus, while a great deal of scholarly atten-

---

[15] Andrew S. Jacobs, *Remains of the Jews: The Holy Land and Christian Empire in Late Antiquity* (Stanford: Stanford University Press, 2004), esp. 174–99; Elsner, "*Itinerarium Burdigalense*," 181–95; Blake Leyerle, "Pilgrims to the Land: Early Christian Perceptions of the Galilee," in *Galilee through the Centuries: Confluence of Cultures* (ed. E. M. Meyers; Winona Lake, Ind.: Eisenbrauns, 1999), 345–57; idem, "Landscape as Cartography in Early Christian Pilgrimage Narratives," *Journal of the American Academy of Religion* 64 (1996): 119–43. On pilgrimage to the "Holy Land" in the early Christian period more generally, see Edward David Hunt, *Holy Land Pilgrimage in the Late Roman Empire, AD 312–460* (Oxford: Oxford University Press, 1982); also the important recent study of Brouria Bitton-Ashkelony, *Encountering the Sacred: The Debate on Christian Pilgrimage in Late Antiquity* (Transformation of the Classical Heritage 38; Berkeley: University of California Press, 2005).

[16] See especially the influential foundational formulations in Edward W. Said, *Culture and Imperialism* (New York: Vintage Books, 1994), esp. 191–281; Homi Bhabha, *The Location of Culture* (New York: Routledge, 1994).

[17] But see the discussion of Jewish–Christian competition over the "Holy Land" at Oded Irshai, "Confronting a Christian Empire: Jewish Culture in the World of Byzantium," in *Cultures of the Jews: A New History* (ed. D. Biale; New York: Schocken Books,

tion has been paid to the efforts of Christian writers to conceptualize and legitimate Christian imperial power, Jewish resistance to and accommodation of the new political dispensation have not received comparable attention. This paper seeks to redress this significant lacuna.

## II. The Limits of Positivism: The Temple Vessels at Rome, 71–192 C.E.

It is a widely attested historical fact that the Roman army under the command of Titus transported a variety of cultic implements from the Jerusalem Temple to Rome following the protracted, but ultimately successful siege of the city. Whether or not the Romans had initially intended to destroy the temple complex and take its sacred vessels as war-spoils,[18] these symbolically potent items were readily incorporated into the joint triumph celebrated by Vespasian and Titus at Rome circa June 71 C.E. for their victory in the (first) Jewish War.[19] This dramatic scene of the conquering Roman army parading the temple vessels through the streets of Rome would subsequently be etched in stone for all time on the triumphal

---

2002), 187. Irshai's observations build on the path-breaking analysis of the sacralization by Jews of the Galilean landscape in the early and especially high Middle Ages in Elchanan Reiner, "From Joshua to Jesus: The Transformation of Biblical Story to a Local Myth–A Chapter in the Religious Life of the Galilean Jew," in *Sharing the Sacred: Religious Contacts and Conflicts in the Holy Land* (ed. A. Kofsky and G. G. Stroumsa; Jerusalem: Yad Izhak Ben-Zvi, 1998), 223–71. On the impact of Christian imperialism on late antique Judaism more generally, see Daniel Boyarin, *Border Lines: The Partition of Judaeo-Christianity* (Divinations; Philadelphia: University of Pennsylvania Press, 2004), and Seth Schwartz, *Imperialism and Jewish Society, 200 BCE to 640 CE* (Princeton: Princeton University Press, 2001).

[18] Josephus, *BJ* 6.387–388, famously maintains that Titus did not wish the Temple to be burned; the cultic vessels were not so much plundered as handed over to the Romans for safe-keeping. See, however, James Rives, "Flavian Religious Policy and the Destruction of the Jerusalem Temple," in *Flavius Josephus and Flavian Rome* (ed. J. Edmondson, S. Mason, and J. Rives; Oxford: Oxford University Press, 2005), 145–66, which argues that the destruction of the Jerusalem cult by the Romans was in fact an intentional strategy for dispiriting and thus subduing the rebellious population of Judea. Rives situates the removal of the cult vessels within the context of the Roman practice of *evocatio*, "whereby the Roman general would summon deities away from the enemy city and offer them a home among the Romans" (149).

[19] The fullest source on the triumphal procession is Josephus, *BJ* 7.118–162. For comparative assessment of the triumph within the broader Roman tradition, see Michael McCormick, *Eternal Victory: Triumphal Rulership in Late Antiquity, Byzantium, and the Early Medieval West* (Cambridge, U.K.: Cambridge University Press, 1986), 14–17.

arch erected soon after the death of Titus in 81 C.E.[20] Moreover, ancient sources report that Vespasian vowed – perhaps already during the triumphal ceremonies – to construct a temple to Peace in which the vessels would be placed on permanent public display alongside a wide range of other works of art collected at Rome.[21] This grand architectural project, intended to reinforce the emperor's claim that he had established peace throughout the entire empire, was dedicated in 75 C.E.[22] Fergus Millar has recently emphasized how significant this series of commemorative gestures, which quite literally enshrined the Roman conquest of Judea within the public space of the imperial capital, were in legitimating the political aspirations of the new Flavian dynasty.[23]

By far our most detailed ancient source for this series of events is, of course, the Jewish historian and polemicist Flavius Josephus, himself resident at Rome under Flavian sponsorship and supervision in the decades after the war (died c. 100 C.E.).[24] Josephus discusses the multi-step process of the transfer of the Temple vessels to Rome in a variety of literary contexts within the *Jewish War*, published circa 75 C.E. soon after the events it describes.[25] But, for the purposes of tracing the subsequent fate of the Temple implements at Rome, no passage is more informative than

---

[20] I follow the date for the erection of the arch given in Michael Pfanner, *Der Titusbogen* (Mainz: Philip von Zabern, 1983), 91–92. For the most comprehensive discussion of the spoils panel of the arch, see Leon Yarden, *The Spoils of Jerusalem on the Arch of Titus: A Re-investigation* (Stockholm: Svenska Institutet i Rom, 1991).

[21] Suetonius, *Ves.* 9.1; Josephus, *BJ* 7.158.

[22] Cassius Dio 65.15.1; Aurelius Victor, *Caes.* 9.7 and *Epit. de Caes.* 9.8. For the phases of the construction of the *Templum Pacis*, its shifting relationship to the wider topography of various imperial fora, and the numerous artistic treasures that it held, I am dependent upon: James C. Anderson, Jr., *The Historical Topography of the Imperial Fora* (Brussels: Latomus, 1984), 101–18; idem, "Domitian, the Argiletum and the Temple of Peace," *American Journal of Archaeology* 86 (1982), 101–10; Eva Margareta Steinby, ed., *Lexicon Topographicum Urbis Romae* (6 vols.; Rome: Quasar, 1993–2000), 4:67–70; Lawrence Richardson, Jr., *A New Topographical Dictionary of Ancient Rome* (Baltimore: Johns Hopkins University Press, 1992), 286–87.

[23] Fergus Millar, "Last Year in Jerusalem: Monuments of the Jewish War in Rome," in *Flavius Josephus and Flavian Rome* (ed. J. Edmondson, S. Mason, and J. Rives; Oxford: Oxford University Press, 2005), 101–28.

[24] On Josephus' evolution as a historian and the historical reliability of his various works, see the (sometimes opposing) assessments in Tessa Rajak, *Josephus: The Historian and His Society* (London: Duckworth, 1983), and Shaye J. D. Cohen, *Josephus in Galilee and Rome: His* Vita *and Development as a Historian* (Leiden: Brill, 1979).

[25] See especially Josephus' account of the delivery of the vessels to the Romans by the personnel of the Jerusalem Temple (*BJ* 6.387–391) and of the display of the vessels during the triumphal procession (*BJ* 7.148–152).

Josephus' detailed report concerning the division of the spoils between the newly constructed Temple of Peace and the imperial palace:

> The triumphal ceremonies being concluded and the empire of the Romans established on the firmest foundations, Vespasian decided to erect a Temple of Peace (*temenos Eirênês*). This was very speedily completed and in a style surpassing all human conception. For, besides having prodigious resources of wealth on which to draw he also embellished it with ancient masterpieces of painting and sculpture; indeed, into that shrine were accumulated and stored all objects for the sight of which man had once wandered over the whole world, eager to see them severally while they lay in various countries. Here, too, he laid up the vessels of gold from the temple of the Jews, on which he prided himself; but their Law (*ton de nomon autôn*) and the purple hangings of the sanctuary (*ta porphura tou sêkou katapetasmata*) he ordered to be deposited and kept in the Palace (*en tois basileiois*).[26]

At least according to Josephus, only those Temple implements made from metal were displayed by Vespasian in the Temple of Peace, apparently preferring to place the sacred fabrics and scrolls in his official – and almost-equally public – imperial residence at Rome.[27]

Other contemporary Greek and Latin writers certainly shared Josephus' wide-eyed estimation of this architectural monument and its spectacular artistic contents.[28] But it is Josephus alone who catalogues the specific vessels on display and offers precise details concerning their distribution in multiple locations. No other source accords pride of place to the vessels from the Jewish Temple among this impressive exhibition of imperial largess – and most do not so much as give them a passing mention. It would seem that the attention Josephus lavishes on the Temple spoils likely reflects his own distinctive historiographic and ideological interests. Indeed, without Josephus and the Arch of Titus to remind us of the distinc-

[26] *B.J.* 7.158–162. All citations of Josephus refer to the edition and translation in the Loeb Classical Library, Henry St. John Thackeray, Ralph Marcus, Allen Wikgren, and Louis H. Feldman, ed. and trans., *Josephus Flavius: The Complete Works* (Cambridge, Mass.: Harvard University Press, 1926–65).

[27] The passage likely refers to what later became the *Templum Gentis Flaviae*, which Domitian built on the site of the house of his father Vespasian and his brother Titus (i.e. the *Domus Titi imperatoris*). According to Pliny, *Natural History* 36.37, the famous Laocoon and other works of art were on public display here – and so perhaps also the temple veil and Torah scroll. On possible public access to items displayed in private imperial residences, see Fergus Millar, *The Emperor in the Roman World, 31 BC–AD 337* (2d ed.; London: Duckworth, 1992), 144–46.

[28] On the impressive architectural quality of the *Templum Pacis*, see Pliny, *Natural History* 36.102. More than a century later, various authors could offer equally glowing reports: Herodian 1.14.2–3; Ammianus Marcellinus 16.10.14; *Scriptores Historiae Augustae, Trig. tyr.* 31.10. For a succinct list of the ancient sources that identify the works of art held in the temple, see Anderson, *Historical Topography*, 106 n. 14.

tive ceremonial role that the Temple vessels played in legitimating the dramatic rise of the Flavian dynasty, we might easily come to the conclusion that these seemingly symbolically-laden artifacts simply slipped through the cracks of Roman consciousness.

Indeed, in the century following the reign of Domitian (81–96 C.E.), Greek and Latin sources are surprisingly silent concerning the Temple vessels. There are only three extant references to the *Templum Pacis* found in works produced in the second century. The traveler and geographer Pausanias (c. 115–180 C.E.) briefly comments that a statue of the Olympic victor Cheimon was on display there.[29] The two other brief notices are both found in the *Attic Nights* of Aulus Gellius (c. 125–192 C.E.), an eclectic collection of learned notes on grammar, law, history, philosophy, and numerous other disciplines.[30] What is most notable for our purposes is that, in his comments on the *Templum Pacis*, this Roman gentleman praises the vast contents of the public library (*bibliotheca Pacis*) that had been incorporated into the complex, but passes over the artistic works that had so impressed Pliny and Josephus in total silence. He makes no mention of the Jewish patrimony installed at Rome.

More significant still, not a single one of the sources that describe the massive fire that devastated the Temple of Peace and its surroundings in 192 C.E., during the waning days of the emperor Commodus, remarks upon the fate of the Temple implements.[31] And when the temple complex was subsequently restored – most likely under Septimius Severus in the early third century – and once again merited the heated praise of Roman

[29] Pausanias 2.9.3. For Pausanias' dates, I follow Christian Habicht, *Pausanias' Guide to Ancient Greece* (Berkeley: University of California Press, 1985), 8–12.

[30] Aulus Gellius 5.21.9; 16.8.2. The dates for Aulus Gellius are highly speculative. I here follow the relatively generous range suggested in Leofranc Holford-Strevens, *Aulus Gellius: An Antonine Scholar and his Achievement* (rev. ed.; New York: Oxford University Press, 2005), 11–21.

[31] Cassius Dio 72(73).24.1, emphasizes the destruction of State records. By contrast, Herodian 1.14, after commenting on the almost total destruction of both public property and private wealth deposited in the temple, chooses to highlight the damage caused to the neighboring Temple of Vesta and the scandalous exposure of the statue of Pallas. The medical writer Galen (*De comp. med.* 1.1; Kühn 13.362), bemoans the destruction of the library, which contained copies of his own works. Historical information concerning the fire also entered the Christian chronographic tradition through the notice in Eusebius, *Chronicon* 2.174, repeated with some changes by his transmitters and translators (e.g., Jerome's *Chronicle* places the event under the year 191 A.D.). None of these sources so much as mentions either the destruction or the survival of the Temple vessels. Modern scholarly assertions concerning the survival of the vessels (e.g., Yarden, *Spoils of Jerusalem*, 64) are entirely speculative.

authors,[32] the physical remains of the Jerusalem cult never come back into view. As we shall presently see, the spoils taken by Titus from Jerusalem are not mentioned again in either Roman or Christian-Roman historiographic writings until the time of Justinian in the sixth century, approximately 200 years after the death of Constantine.[33]

How might we explain the fact that, although the defeat of the Jews by the founders of the Flavian dynasty had quite literally become enshrined at the heart of imperial Rome through commemorative monumental architecture, surviving Roman sources show so little interest in the Temple vessels? A well-known dedicatory inscription from the Colosseum, recently reconstructed by Géza Alföldy, strongly suggests that the creation of this most ambitious of Flavian building-projects was funded by booty from the Jewish war.[34] Might we, then, explain the disappearance of the Temple vessels from Roman sources by positing that the Flavians simply melted down the Temple implements for their metallic value? It is, of course,

---

[32] See especially Ammianus 16.10.14; also the more oblique comments in *Scriptores Historiae Augustae*, *Trig. tyr.* 31.10. For consideration of the sources for the dating of the fire, its disastrous impact on the affected part of the city, and the restoration of the temple complex under Severus, see Anderson, *Historical Topography*, 113–18.

[33] On the total silence of Greek and Latin sources written between 100 and 475 C.E. concerning the fate of the actual vessels from the Jerusalem Temple, see Martin Harrison, "From Jerusalem and Back Again: The Fate of the Treasures of Solomon," in *Churches Built in Ancient Times* (London: Society of Antiquaries of London; Accordia Research Centre, University of London, 1994), 239–48; also Yohanan (Hans) Lewy, "The Fate of the Temple Implements after the Destruction of the Second Temple" (Hebrew), in *Studies in Jewish Hellenism* (Jerusalem: Mosad Bialik, 1960), 255–58. For both practical and methodological reasons, I have exempted from the present consideration Christian exegetical treatments of biblical passages concerning the vessels found in the wilderness Tabernacle (e.g., Exod 25–34) or in the Temple of Solomon (e.g., 1 Kgs 7–8; 2 Chron 2–4). This vast exegetical corpus primarily reflects the ongoing interest among Christian writers in the appurtenances of the Temple cult as strictly textual objects from Scripture rather than as actual historical artifacts – and much care is needed in order to discern the difference between the two. Still, these exegetical sources may contain still unexplored sources that might further illuminate Christian knowledge of and interest in the Temple vessels prior to the sixth century and may very well repay further exploration. It is interesting to note, however, that no extended *verse-by-verse* commentary on the sacred architecture described in the Hebrew Bible was produced by a Christian exegete until Venerable Bede in the eighth century. For discussion of Bede's place in the Christian exegetical tradition, see Arthur G. Holder, trans., *Bede: On the Tabernacle* (Texts Translated for Historians 18; Liverpool: Liverpool University Press, 1994), esp. xv–xvii.

[34] For Alföldy's original reconstruction of the inscription, see "Eine Bauinschrift aus dem Colosseum," *Zeitschrift für Papyrologie und Epigraphik* 109 (1995): 195–226. For further discussion, see Millar, "Last Year in Jerusalem," 117–19; Louis H. Feldman, "Financing the Colosseum," *Biblical Archaeology Review* 27.4 (2001): 20–31, 60–61. I would like to thank Ron Mellor for discussing the inscription with me.

theoretically conceivable that the phrase used in the inscription, "from the spoils of war" (*ex manubi[i]s*), is meant to encompass *all* of the spoils from the Jewish War, including the specific sacred objects from the Jerusalem Temple that had been displayed before the Roman populace. At the same time, nothing in the inscription itself or in our other sources necessitates such an inference; there may well have been sufficient spoils from the war without the Flavians' resorting to the "liquidation" of what they clearly viewed as the most impressive symbols of their victory. In the absence of further evidence, I think it is safer to assume that the Temple vessels remained at Rome for some time, but simply fascinated second-century Roman writers far less than they did their later Byzantine counterparts – or than they do us moderns. It would seem that, despite their continuing presence in stone on the Arch of Titus and their enduring significance for Jewish authors throughout Late Antiquity, the Temple vessels failed to lodge themselves firmly within the Roman historiographic tradition.

In the face of this deafening silence on the Roman side, historians of ancient Judaism have frequently turned to Jewish sources to establish positive information concerning the fate of the Temple vessels. Thus, for example, David Noy has recently argued that a series of rabbinic narratives concerning the visit of rabbis to Rome suggest that the Temple vessels on display in the *Templum Pacis* served as a "pilgrimage" destination for Jewish travelers.[35] Like all rabbinic literature, these sources, to which I will presently return, were crystallized as written traditions well after the second-century events they narrate. In the hopes of counteracting the regnant skepticism among rabbinicists concerning the historical value of such traditions, Noy advances the following claim: "There are various references in rabbinic texts to some of the objects from Jerusalem being seen, but always with reference to one visitor, R. Eleazar ben Jose. There is no obvious reason why he is *the only one mentioned*."[36] This assertion, on which Noy bases his subsequent historical reconstruction of this pilgrimage practice, is not in fact correct. Parallel rabbinic traditions – similar in both form and function – exist concerning R. Eleazar (sometimes Eliezer or Leazar)[37] ben (R.) Yose's near contemporary, R. Simeon ben Yoḥai,

[35] David Noy, "Rabbi Aqiba Comes to Rome: A Jewish Pilgrimage in Reverse?" in *Pilgrimage in Graeco-Roman and Early Christian Antiquity: Seeing the Gods* (ed. J. Elsner and I. Rutherford; Oxford: Oxford University Press, 2005), 373–85.

[36] Noy, "Rabbi Aqiba Comes to Rome," 382. The italics are mine.

[37] I refer to this figure as R. Eleazar ben Yose throughout my exposition, although my translations of specific passages follow the orthography of the best editions or manuscripts available.

who likewise is reported to have visited Rome and seen the Temple vessels there.[38]

In a similar – though considerably more careful – spirit, Steven Fine has pointed to some general similarities between the Temple implements listed or described in the rabbinic sources, on the one hand, and those mentioned in Josephus and depicted on the Arch of Titus, on the other. Fine suggests that these similarities be taken as an indication of the relative historical reliability of the rabbinic sources.[39] Yet Fine himself acknowledges that the correlation between the two sets of data is far from perfect: rabbinic sources discuss items that find no echo in the first-century evidence. And even more fundamental questions must be asked. Did the rabbis in these sources see the Temple vessels themselves or merely their likeness on the triumphal arch? Or perhaps the later composers or codifiers of rabbinic literature simply integrated first- or second-hand knowledge of this monument into these narrative creations. Here, too, the historian runs up against insurmountable epistemological challenges in using these sources as positive evidence for Jewish reactions to the public display of the Temple vessels.

Of course, it is hardly implausible that, over the course of the second century, Jews from the Roman east – perhaps Palestinian "rabbis" among them – had occasion to travel to Rome and view the actual Temple implements on display in the Temple of Peace. The new and very tangible monuments of Flavian Rome surely had an impact on both residents of and visitors to the capital. Indeed, in a provocative article, Ellen Bradshaw Aitken has argued that the New Testament Epistle to the Hebrews, with its theologically potent image of an inviolable heavenly shrine as the locus of the eternal cult of Christ, represents an attempt on the part of a Christian community in Rome to subvert the triumphalism of the Flavian propaganda with which they were surrounded.[40] In this reading, the spiritualization of

[38] E.g., *t.Kippurim* 2:16; *Yoma* 57a. I analyze these sources in depth below in the next section of the paper.

[39] Steven Fine, "When I Went to Rome… There I Saw the Menorah...": The Jerusalem Temple Implements During the Second Century CE," in *The Archaeology of Difference: Gender, Ethnicity, Class and the "Other" in Antiquity, Studies in Honor of Eric M. Meyers* (ed. D. R. Edwards and C. T. McCullough; Winona Lake, Ind.: Eisenbrauns, 2007). I would like to thank Steven Fine for sharing his paper with me in advance of its publication.

[40] Ellen Bradshaw Aitken, "Portraying the Temple in Stone and Text: The Arch of Titus and the Epistle to the Hebrews," in *Religious Texts and Material Contexts* (ed. J. Neusner and J. F. Strange; Lanham, Md.: University Press of America, 2001), 73–88; reprinted in *Sewanee Theological Review* 45 (2002): 135–51; and in *Hebrews: Contem-*

the biblical cult and especially its implements (Heb 9:1–10) that is so characteristic of Hebrews is at least as much a response to imperial domination as it is a general critique of now-superseded Jewish cultic practices.

Yet, while I do not wish to deny the very real power of the Flavian architectural program, I would caution against reading third-, fourth-, and early fifth-century rabbinic sources as transparent travelogues that record the actual experiences of second-century rabbis in the capital. We are certainly not well served by trying to harmonize these strikingly similar episodes in the biographies of R. Eleazar and R. Simeon – and, in any case, later rabbinic tradition would see to that (see my discussion of *Bavli Me'ilah* 17a–b below). Instead, rabbinic traditions concerning the fate of the Temple implements should be read both within their immediate *literary* contexts as well as against the sweeping changes that reconfigured the landscape of Jewish cultural memory over the course of Late Antiquity.

## III. The Fate of the Temple Implements in Rabbinic Literature, c. 200–450 C.E.

I have already remarked on the total silence of Greek and Latin sources written between 100 and 500 C.E. concerning the fate of the implements from the Jerusalem Temple. By contrast, the vast corpus of rabbinic writings produced during this same period includes a variety of traditions that not only acknowledge that the Temple vessels are in Rome, but explore in considerable detail their precise location and physical form. Rabbinic texts of the third, fourth, and early fifth centuries do not yet thematize the discovery of the Temple vessels in the imperial storehouses of Rome and their repatriation to Jerusalem as a decisive stage in the salvation of Israel, as will subsequent Jewish writings from the Byzantine world. Rather, these sources typically embed "eye-witness" testimonies concerning the cultic vessels within the legal-exegetical discourse characteristic of rabbinic literature, employing these reports as a narrative validation of specific points of *halakhah*. In this way, the rabbis drew the vessels within the domain of rabbinic authority and expertise.

At the same time, however, I would like to suggest that these sources are not pursuing what is often taken as the relatively straightforward rabbinic agenda of supplanting the physical cult with an edifice of learned

*porary Methods – New Insights* (ed. G. Gelardini; Biblical Interpretation Series 75; Leiden: Brill, 2005), 131–48.

discourse and pious prayer.[41] Rather, these texts are marked by a palpable tension between appropriation of the Temple cult, on the one hand, and its preservation as a privileged site of religious meaning and experience, on the other. They explicitly juxtapose scripturally-derived knowledge with experientially-derived knowledge, often preferring visual confirmation to exegesis. These sources thus forge a powerful link between rabbinic expertise concerning the Temple vessels and the act of visualization itself. I will argue that this linkage builds upon widespread traditions concerning the public viewing of the Temple vessels by the laity during pilgrimage festivals. While these rabbinic "memories" of the Jerusalem cult likely do not reflect historical practice *per se*, they shaped rabbinic speculation concerning the fate of the Temple vessels. In this respect, these rabbinic traditions betray an abiding fascination with the unique and inimitable power embodied in the concrete remains of a ritual system over which the rabbis are not quite able – or willing – to assert complete control.

In this portion of the paper, I analyze the attitudes expressed specifically in early rabbinic literature toward the presence of the Temple vessels in Rome. I restrict my discussion here to material found in rabbinic compilations dating from approximately 200–450 C.E. (Mishnah, Tosefta, the so-called halakhic midrashim, the Palestinian Talmud, and the earliest exegetical and homiletical midrashim).[42] In a number of cases, I include material whose dating is uncertain but which seems to belong to this earlier cultural context or sheds light upon its subsequent reception in rabbinic literature. I reserve discussion of material found in later Palestinian midrashim until the final portions of the paper, where I describe what I believe is a significant shift in the attitudes of Jewish authors in the Byzantine world toward physical relics in general and toward the Temple vessels in particular.

---

[41] For a classic description of this project and its importance for understanding rabbinic Judaism as a whole, see Jacob Neusner, *Judaism: The Evidence of the Mishnah* (Chicago: University of Chicago Press, 1981), esp. 25–44; also Baruch M. Bokser, "Approaching Sacred Space," *Harvard Theological Review* 78 (1985): 279–99. Compare, however, Jonathan Klawans, *Purity, Sacrifice, and the Temple: Symbolism and Supersessionism in the Study of Ancient Judaism* (New York: Oxford University Press, 2006), 175–212, which offers a thorough-going critique of this traditionalist account of the role of the rabbis in fashioning post-sacrificial Judaism as well as a more nuanced and gradualist analysis of this process that situates it within the larger context of developments across the ancient Mediterranean world.

[42] Except where otherwise indicated, I follow the dating and provenance of specific rabbinic compilations as expressed in H. L. Strack and Günther Stemberger, *Introduction to the Talmud and Midrash* (trans. and ed. M. Bockmuehl; Minneapolis: Fortress Press, 1996).

It should perhaps also be stressed up front that rabbinic writings are hardly alone in their ongoing interest in the Temple implements. Jewish material culture – coins, architectural elements, synagogue mosaics, and other artifacts of daily Jewish life – likewise attests to the potent religio-nationalist valence these objects continued to carry in the Jewish imagination after the destruction of the Temple and throughout Late Antiquity.[43] Implements associated with the Jerusalem cult constituted one of the most pervasive figural motifs in late antique Jewish art; these symbolically-laden images appear not only on synagogue mosaics but also in a variety of other media, such as coins, lead coffins, tombstones, and glass "pilgrim" vessels.[44] The precise meaning of this cultic imagery, however, remains hotly debated among historians and archaeologists. Thus, scholars do not agree on whether, at what historical point, and in precisely which contexts the figure of the *menorah* might have carried explicit messianic resonances.[45] Similarly, while some have argued that the images of the Jerusalem Temple and its cultic paraphernalia decorating various late antique synagogue mosaics are central components of a larger message of eschato-

[43] The bibliography on representations of the Jerusalem Temple and its vessels in late antique Jewish art is vast. For synthetic consideration and bibliography, see Steven Fine, *Art and Judaism in the Greco-Roman World: Toward a New Jewish Archaeology* (New York: Cambridge University Press, 2005), 146–63; Lee I. Levine, *The Ancient Synagogue: The First Thousand Years* (2d ed.; New Haven: Yale University Press, 2005), 230–36, 602–8. See also Herbert L. Kessler, "Through the Temple Veil: The Holy Image in Judaism and Christianity," *Kairos* 32–33 (1990/91): 53–77.

[44] For a systematic catalogue of figural uses of the *menorah* and other Temple vessels in the full range of media (except coins), see Rachel Hachlili, *The Menorah, The Ancient Seven-Armed Candelabrum: Origin, Form, and Significance* (Supplements to the Journal for the Study of Judaism 68; Leiden: Brill, 2001), 285–480. For interpretation of the Jewish coins minted during the Bar-Kokhba revolt, which are stamped with images of the façade of the Jerusalem Temple, the showbread table, and other cultic items such as the *lulav* and *etrog*, as an expression of Jewish aspirations for renewal of the cult, see Dan Barag, "The Table of the Showbread and the Façade of the Temple on Coins of the Bar-Kokhba Revolt," in *Ancient Jerusalem Revealed* (ed. H. Geva; Jerusalem: Israel Exploration Society, 1994), 272–76; also appears as idem, "The Table of the Showbread and the Temple on the Bar-Kokhba Coins" (Hebrew), *Qadmoniot* 20 (1987): 59–62. On the "afterlife" of the Temple vessels in medieval Byzantium, see Elisabeth Revel-Neher, *Le témoignage de l'absence: Les objets du sanctuaire à Byzance et dans l'art juif du XI^e au XV^e siècles* (Paris: De Boccard, 1998).

[45] Unlike scholars who offer one or another interpretation of the *menorah*, Rachel Hachlili suggests that it ought to be viewed as a multivalent symbol: while in some cases it could specifically signify Jewish yearning for religious or national restoration, it often functioned as an emblem of Jewish (in contradistinction to Christian or pagan) identity (*Menorah*, 204–9, and scholarship cited there).

logical "promise and redemption,"[46] others have raised important questions – both empirical and methodological – about the very possibility of reconstructing a single, fixed interpretation of these compositions in stone, either as a unified group or as independent compositions.[47]

It is not my aim in this paper to resolve all of these quite fundamental interpretative questions concerning the meaning(s) of late antique Jewish iconography at various points in time, in various locations, and in various media. Rather, I hope to add to this discussion by focusing primarily on the textual tradition, which will enable me to trace the literary processes through which the shifting Jewish discourse concerning the Temple implements was fashioned. Where I find it productive, I use material artifacts to illuminate specific texts. But I leave for subsequent research the ultimate task of drawing the literary and material data together into a unified account of the cultural significance of the Temple and its vessels for late antique Jews.

The motif of the presence of the Temple vessels in Rome already makes its appearance in the earliest strata of rabbinic literature. These sources present rabbinic visual testimonials concerning the physical form of a variety of Temple vessels, including the seven-branch candelabrum (*menorah*), the Temple veil (*parokhet*), and various vestments of the High Priest. In the earliest of these sources, these reports stand as isolated rabbinic dicta without a larger narrative, exegetical, or dialectical context. But, relatively quickly, these statements came to be used as definitive evidence to resolve debates over cultic practice. Thus, for example, we read in the Tosefta that R. Eleazar ben R. Yose saw the Temple veil during a visit to Rome:[48]

---

[46] See especially the interpretation of the Sepphoris mosaic in Zeev Weiss and Ehud Netzer, *Promise and Redemption: The Synagogue Mosaic of Sepphoris* (Jerusalem: Israel Museum, 1996), from which I take the phrase.

[47] See Seth Schwartz's assessment of the reading offered by Weiss and Netzer in his *Imperialism and Jewish Society*, 248–59. Schwartz's "minimalist" interpretation, which he believes allows for more fluidity of meaning, downplays the eschatological dimension of the Sepphoris mosaic, arguing instead that it should be read in cosmological and hieratic terms as a reflection of the increasing sacralization of the space, liturgy, and community of the synagogue in the fifth and sixth centuries.

[48] The transfer of the Temple veil to Rome at the time of the destruction is reported in a wide variety of rabbinic sources. Most famously, the veil plays a central role in lurid rabbinic narratives concerning Titus' desecration of the Holy of Holies at the time of the destruction (*LevR* 22:3; *b.Git* 56b; *NumR* 18:22; shorter and probably early forms of the narrative appear in *SifreiDeut* §328; *PRK* 26; *LevR* 20:5; *GenR* 10:7; *DeutR* 21 (Lieberman); *Tan, aḥare mot* 4; *TanB, aḥare mot* 5; *EcclR* 5:8; brief allusions to the narrative appear in *PRE* 49; *MidrPs* 121:3). For a reading of this narrative within the Roman culture of spectacle, see Joshua Levinson, "Tragedies Naturally Performed: Fatal Cha-

> And thus did he (the High Priest) count (when sprinkling the sacrificial blood during the expiatory ritual on the Day of Atonement): "One, one and one, one and two, one and three, one and four, one and five, one and six, one and seven." R. Judah said in the name of R. Eliezer: "One, one and one, two and one, three and one, four and one, five and one, six and one, seven and one." He went out to his left, along the veil (*parokhet*). And he did not touch the veil. But if he touched it, he touched it. R. Eleazar b. R. Yose said: "I myself saw it (i.e. the veil) in Rome and there were drops of blood on it (אני ראיתיה ברומי והיו עליה טיפי דמים). And they told me:[49] These (drops) are from the blood of the Day of Atonement (ואמ׳ לי אילו מדמים של יום הכפורים)."[50]

R. Eleazar's testimony is here appended to a series of relatively disconnected rabbinic dicta concerning the precise dynamics of the Yom Kippur ritual: mention of the *parokhet* seems to have prompted the redactor to include the R. Eleazar tradition, which does not otherwise substantiate or refute an argument.[51]

By contrast, when R. Eleazar's testimony is found in both the Palestinian and the Babylonian Talmuds, it is used explicitly as evidence to settle a matter of ritual law.[52] As we might expect, the Babylonian Talmud is particularly aggressive in its modification and application of R. Eleazar's dictum. In order to demonstrate the later fate of this unit of tradition, I analyze its elaboration in the Bavli. I have broken down this complex passage into its two main building-blocks, both of which are further divided into a series of parallel sub-units:

---

rades, *Parodia Sacra*, and the Death of Titus," in *Jewish Culture and Society under the Christian Roman Empire* (ed. R. Kalmin and S. Schwartz; Leuven: Peeters, 2003), 349–82. On the narrative as an anti-Christian polemic concerning the destruction of the Temple, especially in response to New Testament traditions concerning the rending of the Temple veil at Jesus' death (Mark 15:38; Matt 27:51), see Israel Yuval, "The Lord Will Take Vengeance, Vengeance for His Temple" (Hebrew), *Zion* 59 (1994): 362–73. But see Menahem Kister's critical assessment of Yuval's argument in "Legends of the Destruction of the Temple in *Avot de-Rabbi Natan*" (Hebrew), *Tarbiz* 67 (1998): 483–529, esp. 508.

[49] The version in *y.Yoma* 5,5 (42d) offers a slightly different version of this phrase, in which it is R. Eleazar who is the speaker: "I said: These (drops) are from the blood that they would sprinkle upon it on the Day of Atonement" (אמרתי אילו מןהדמים שהיו מזין עליה ביום הכיפורים).

[50] *t.Kippurim* 2:16 (Lieberman). My translation.

[51] R. Eleazar's testimony is absent in the Mishnah's parallel description of the sacrificial ritual carried out by the high priest on the Day of Atonement.

[52] *y.Yoma* 5,5 (42d); *b.Yoma* 57a.

UNIT A

A1: It was taught (תנא): When he (the High Priest) sprinkled (the blood), he did not sprinkle directly upon the veil (על הפרוכת), but rather toward the veil ( כנגד הפרוכת).

A2: R. Eleazar b. R. Yose said: "I saw it in Rome (אני ראיתיה ברומי), and there were upon it many drops of blood of the bullock and of the goat of the Day of Atonement (והיו עליה כמה טיפי דמים של פר ושעיר של יום הכפורים)."

A3: Perhaps (the drops) were those of the bullock offered up for an error of the community (דפר העלם דבר של צבור) or of the goats (offered as expiation) for idolatry (שעירי עבודה זרה)?

A4: He saw that they were made in their regular pattern (דעבידי כסדרן).

UNIT B

B1: Also we have learned (ותנן) in connection with the bullock offered up for an error of the community: When he (the High Priest) sprinkled (the blood), the drops were not to reach the veil, but if they did, they just did (i.e. the ritual was not thereby annulled).

B2: And R. Eleazar b. R. Yose said: "I saw it in Rome and there were upon it many drops of blood of the bullock offered up for an error of the congregation and of the goats offered up for idolatry ( והיו עליה כמה טיפי דמים של פר העלם דבר של צבור ושעירי עבודה זרה)."

B3: But perhaps they came from the bullock and goat of the Day of Atonement?

B4: He saw that they were *not* made in their regular pattern ( דעבידי שלא כסדרן).[53]

R. Eleazar's testimony appears in two different forms in the two structurally parallel sections of the passage. And, in both cases, the testimony differs from its previous formulations, which do not specify the particular species of sacrificial animal from which the blood has come. I have underlined this added element in the citations above. The creators of this passage clearly realized that, in order for R. Eleazar's testimony to carry binding force in determining how the priest actually carried out the ritual dispersal of the blood, his statement must specifically refer to the spatter-pattern created by a particular type of sacrificial practice – *either* the Yom Kippur offerings *or* the various purification offerings for communal sins.[54] The passage plays out both possibilities: not only do the authors amend R. Eleazar's

[53] *b.Yoma* 57a. I have slightly adapted the Soncino translation.

[54] The biblical laws concerning purification offerings for errors of the congregation differ between Lev 4:13–21 and Num 15:22–26. For rabbinic attempts to sort out these sources, see, e.g., *b.Hor* 8a, 13b. On the nature of these sacrifices, see Jacob Milgrom, *Leviticus 1–16* (Anchor Bible 3; Garden City, N.Y.: Doubleday, 1991), 253–69.

statement to suit the logical need of the immediate argument, but also append an Aramaic addendum to each of the two main units that correspondingly states whether the blood was or was not in the standardized spatter-pattern of the Yom Kippur sacrifice.[55] The alleged historical event is now quite firmly ensconced in legal dialectic.

But traditions concerning R. Eleazar's sighting of the Temple vessels in Rome were not only expanded and reframed *over* time with developments in rabbinic literary culture – from the Tosefta to the Palestinian Talmud and eventually to the Babylonian Talmud. We also find significant variation in the basic content of this tradition *across* the rabbinic corpora of the third and fourth centuries. Thus, R. Eleazar elsewhere testifies that, while in Rome, he saw the head-plate (*tzitz*) of the High Priest – and not the Temple veil. More significantly, this tradition, which is found twice in the Jerusalem Talmud, likewise situates R. Eleazar's testimony within the context of halakhic debate regarding the precise appearance of the sacred object:

> On the head-plate (ציץ) was written "Holy unto the Lord" (קודש ליי׳). "Holy unto" (was written) below, while the Divine Name was above. Just as a king sits on his throne (קתדרין), so one (part of the phrase) is below and the Divine Name is above. But R. Eleazar b. R. Yose said: "I myself saw it in the city of Rome (אני ראיתיו ברומי), and it was actually engraved upon it on one line, "Holy unto the Lord" (ולא היה כתוב עליו אלא שיטה אחת קודש ליי׳).[56]

The anonymous authority cited in this passage is apparently in possession of a tradition that asserts that the words "Holy unto the Lord" were engraved upon the head-plate on two separate rows, with the Divine Name on top. This anonymous tradition does not rest on either an exegetical or an experiential rationale, but instead appeals to the obvious iconic function of the phrase: the vertical configuration not only embodies the elevated position of God, but also signifies the logical relationship between the priestly head-plate and God's divine kingship. By contrast, R. Eleazar grounds his conflicting position that the entire phrase was written on a single line in eye-witness testimony, which, while perhaps less graphically apt, carries with it the authority of experience. I would suggest that this debate concerning the proper configuration of the inscription – to the exclusion of all other features of the head-plate – dramatizes what is implicit in the text,

[55] What exactly this pattern was is uncertain. Rashi, loc. cit. (s.v. כסדרן), probably basing himself directly on the description of the motion used by the High Priest in *m.Yoma* 5:3, suggests that the pattern was a vertical series of spots – "from above to below" (מלמעלה למטה) – as would be formed by the flicking of a "whip" (כמצליף).

[56] *y.Yoma* 4,1 (41c); cf. *y.Meg* 1,9 (71d); *b.Shab* 63b. My translation.

namely, the assertion that verbal testimony and debate displace the very *sancta* that are here the explicit objects of rabbinic discourse.

How shall we square the existence of these various alternative traditions concerning R. Eleazar reviewed above? Of course, we might wish to speculate that the historical R. Eleazar either saw both the veil and the headplate during a single trip to Rome. Or that he saw each object on two separate occasions. I would suggest instead that the motif of the sighting of the Temple vessels remained quite flexible and could be adapted to new textual settings. It is, I believe, impossible to determine the original form of the statement – and foolish to try. What is important is that the figure of R. Eleazar functions like a magnet, attracting more than one Temple vessel.

Indeed, other *tannaitic* figures could similarly attract various cultic objects to their names. We find in the fragmentarily preserved halakhic midrash *Sifrei Zuta* a statement attributed to R. Simeon ben Yoḥai concerning the form of the *menorah* from the Jerusalem Temple, which he claims to have spent a good, long time inspecting while in Rome. But, unlike what is probably the earliest form of the R. Eleazar statement found in the *Tosefta*, R. Simeon's report is here already embedded in a *halakhic* context and juxtaposed to an exegetical argument:

> From where [in Scripture do we know] that all the lamps [of the *menorah*] must be turned inward toward the middle lamp (ומניין שיהיו כל הנרות מוסטרין כנגד נר האמצעי). Thus Scripture teaches: (*When you set up the lamps, let the seven lamps give light*) *toward the front of the lampstand* (אל מול פני המנורה; Num 8:2). And [elsewhere] it says: (*There is a people that came out of Egypt; it hides the earth from view*) *and it is settled next to me* (והוא יושב ממולי; Num 22:5). R. Simeon said: "When I went to Rome and saw there the *menorah* (כשהלכתי לרומי וראיתי שם את המנורה), all of its lamps were turned inward toward the middle lamp (היו כל הנרות מוסטרין כנגד נר האמצעי)."[57]

It is worth noting that the specific form of the *menorah* described here as well as in a number of other rabbinic texts,[58] with the six outer flames oriented inward toward the central one, bears a striking resemblance to a number – though certainly not all or even most – of the artistic representations of the *menorah* on mosaic floors of synagogues from late antique

[57] *Sifrei Zuta, be-ha'alotekha*, 8:2 (Horovitz, 255). My translation.

[58] The view that the middle flame serves as the focal point of the arrangement is associated with the name of R. Nathan in *SifreiNum* 59 (Horovitz, 57), *b.Meg* 21b, and *b.Men* 98b, where he comments: "This shows that the middle one is especially prized." In the tannaitic source cited in both of the *Bavli* passages, an anonymous sage teaches instead that all seven of the lamps faced in a single direction toward the western-most lamp and thus in the direction of the *Shekhinah*.

Palestine.[59] This shared iconographic tradition suggests that rabbinic literature participated in the creation or preservation of a relatively wide-spread artistic idiom common to other late antique Jews.

Perhaps not surprisingly, however, the discussion in *Sifrei Zuta* does not appeal to the authority of contemporary synagogue iconography. Instead, it substantiates its claim that the outer six lamps of the *menorah* were oriented toward the central lamp through midrashic exegesis. The passage notes the echo of the verbal element מול ("in front of") in two unrelated verses from the Pentateuch – one stipulating how Aaron should arrange the lamps of the *menorah* and the other relating how the Moabite king Balak feared he was being encircled by the people of Israel. The physical arrangement conjured up in the former verse is not, however, self-evident. The midrashist reasons that, just as in the Balak story, this element of the prepositional phrase implies encirclement, so should it be understood in the description of the *menorah*. The passage thus determines that the three candles on each side of the *menorah* were oriented inwards toward the central flame. Unlike R. Eleazar's report concerning the head-plate, R. Simeon's testimony confirms, rather than contravenes the received tradition cited anonymously by the text.

In addition to the direct testimonials attributed to R. Eleazar and R. Simeon, the motif of the Temple vessels can also appear in another type of rabbinic text, the "canonical" inventory or list.[60] We find such examples of *Listenwissenschaft* in the relatively late rabbinic tractate *Avot de-Rabbi Natan* in a passage that juxtaposes a variety of originally independent traditions concerning the hidden or lost patrimony of the Jewish people:

> There are five things that were made and later hidden away: the Tent of Meeting and the vessels contained therein (אהל מועד וכלים שבו), the ark and the broken tablets, the jar of manna, the staff [of Moses], the flask of anointing oil, Aaron's rod with its almonds and blossoms, the robes of the priesthood, the robes of the anointed [High] Priest; but the mortar (*makhteshet*) of the House of Avtinas, the table (*shulḥan*), the lampstand (*menorah*), the veil (*parokhet*), and the [High

---

[59] Most notably, the two *menorot* on the upper panel of the mosaic floor from the Hammath Tiberias synagogue (reproduced in Hachlili, *Menorah*, 53*); also the left-hand *menorah* on the Ḥuseifa mosaic (reproduced in Rachel Hachlili, *Ancient Jewish Art and Archaeology in the Land of Israel* [Leiden: Brill, 1988], pl. 56a). On the relationship between the depictions in the synagogue mosaics and in rabbinic literature, see Zeev Weiss, *The Sepphoris Synagogue: Deciphering an Ancient Message in Its Archaeological and Socio-Historical Contexts* (Jerusalem: Israel Exploration Society; Institute of Archaeology, Hebrew University of Jerusalem, 2005), 74–75.

[60] On numerical lists as an organizing principle within rabbinic literature, see Wayne Sibley Towner, *The Rabbinic Enumeration of Scriptural Examples* (Leiden: Brill, 1973), although here primarily with reference to the rabbinic penchant for collecting a series of scriptural examples of various phenomena.

Priest's] head-plate (*tzitz*) remain deposited in Rome (אבל מכתשת של בית אבטינס שלחן ומנורה ופרוכת וציץ עדיין מונחין ברומי).[61]

The list of four or five objects "that were made and later hidden away" appears in a variety of other rabbinic sources, although, in no other case, is it paired with the list of the vessels from the Second Temple that were taken to Rome.[62] This passage expands the inventory of Temple implements kept at Rome to five: along with the three vessels mentioned in the "eye-witness" reports of R. Eleazar and R. Simeon – variously the veil, the *menorah*, and the head-plate – it also mentions the mortar used by the priestly Avtinas family to crush the incense-offering and the golden table upon which the bread-offering was laid out. While it is interesting to note, as does Fine,[63] that the veil, *menorah*, and showbread table likewise appear in either the spoils-panel of the Arch of Titus or in Josephus or in both, the relative independence of the rabbinic tradition is equally apparent. There are no extra-rabbinic sources that mention either the High-priest's head-plate found in some R. Eleazar traditions or the incense mortar included in the list in *Avot de-Rabbi Natan*.

In sum, the "eye-witness" testimonies concerning the Temple vessels form a tiny sub-genre of their own. In each example, a rabbinic authority – either Rabbi Eleazar ben Yose or Rabbi Shimon ben Yoḥai, both of whom lived in the second century C.E. – reports having seen one or another of the Temple implement during a visit to Rome. The formulation of the tradition is almost identical for both rabbis: the only difference is that, while R. Eleazar merely reports what he "saw" in Rome, R. Simeon adds a verb of motion ("When I went...") at the front of his report. The motif of the "eye-witness" testimony generally functions within its immediate literary setting to resolve a legal (*halakhic*) dispute concerning either the precise design of one of the Temple implements or some sacrificial practice that would have left a physical mark upon one of these vessels.[64]

---

[61] *Avot de-Rabbi Natan A* 41 (ed. S. Schechter, *Avot de-Rabbi Nathan: Edited from Manuscripts with an Introduction, Notes, and Appendices* [3rd ed.; New York: Feldheim, 1967], 67). The translation is from Judah Goldin, trans., *The Fathers according to Rabbi Nathan* (New Haven: Yale University Press, 1955), 173. On the dating of the text and its various versions, see Menahem Kister, *Studies in Avot de-Rabbi Nathan: Text, Redaction, and Interpretation* (Hebrew) (Jerusalem: Yad Izhak Ben-Zvi, 1998), 214–19; M. B. Lerner, "The External Tractates," in *The Literature of the Sages I* (ed. S. Safrai; Philadelphia: Fortress Press, 1987), 367–409, esp. 378.

[62] See the parallels at *b.Hor* 12a; *b.Ker* 5b; *b.Yoma* 52b.

[63] Fine, "When I Went to Rome."

[64] On the legal function of such eye-witness testimonials in rabbinic discourse, see Dina Stein, "Believing is Seeing: *Baba Batra* 73a–75b" (Hebrew), *Jerusalem Studies in Hebrew Literature* 17 (1999), 9–32.

But beyond their immediate halakhic aims, I believe that these "eye-witness" testimonies participate in what seems to be a broader cultural tradition – common in both early Judaism and early Christianity – that acknowledges how contentious visual access to the Temple vessels was. To report that one has laid eyes on the sacred objects from the Temple cult was no insignificant claim. Thus, for example, an otherwise unknown non-canonical gospel (P. Oxyrhynchus 840), likely composed before the end of the second century C.E. not long before the motif will emerge in the *Tosefta*, relates that the High Priest rebuked Jesus and his disciples for having entered the Temple sanctuary and gazed upon the Temple vessels in an impure state:

> And having taken them, he (Jesus) brought them (the disciples) into the place of purification (*eis auto to hagneutêrion*) and was walking in the temple. And having approached, a certain Pharisee, a chief priest, whose name was Levi, joined them and said to the Savior: "Who gave you permission to enter this place of purification and to see these holy vessels (*tauta ta hagia skeuê*) when you have not washed yourself, nor have your disciples surely washed their feet? But you, in a defiled state, you have entered this temple, which is a pure place that no one enters nor dares to view these holy vessels without first having washed themselves and changed their clothes."[65]

Much about this passage remains obscure, not least of which the question of whether the author of this gospel was familiar with the actual functioning of the by-then defunct Jerusalem cult. Daniel Schwartz has rightly noted that, in its equal emphasis on prohibitions against both visual and physical violation of the cult, the passage is perfectly consistent with other Second Temple sources that likewise proscribe the improper *viewing* of the Temple utensils.[66] Here, of course, the author understands the actions of Jesus and his disciples as an out-and-out rejection of the exclusivist posture of the Jerusalem priesthood. Schwartz suggests that the anti-priestly

[65] P. Ox. 840, 2:1–3. I have followed the text and translation in François Bovon, "Fragment Oxyrhynchus 840, Fragment of a Lost Gospel, Witness of an Early Christian Controversy over Purity," *Journal of Biblical Literature* 119 (2000): 705–28, esp. 714–15. Compare the old-fashioned translation in Wilhelm Schneemelcher, ed., *New Testament Apocrypha* (trans. R. McL. Wilson; 2 vols.; rev. ed.; Louisville: Westminster/John Knox Press, 1991), 1:94–95. The fragment was originally published in Bernard P. Grenfell and Arthur S. Hunt, *The Oxyrhynchus Papyri*, vol. 5 (London/Oxford: Oxford University Press, 1908), no. 840.

[66] Daniel R. Schwartz, "Viewing the Holy Utensils (P Ox V,840)," *New Testament Studies* 32 (1986): 153–59. For example, Schwartz cites Josephus' report that, when Pompey and his men entered the Temple and saw various cultic vessels, they "saw what it was unlawful for any but the high priest to see" (*A.J.* 14.71–72).

impulse in this text was also shared by both the pharisaic and rabbinic movements.

François Bovon has recently raised questions concerning Schwartz's mutually reinforcing assumptions that (1) the gospel fragment reflects, however obliquely, the *realia* of ancient Judaism, that (2) rabbinic traditions concerning the Pharisees can readily be used to reconstruct Pharisaic practice, that (3) there is a fundamental continuity between pharisaic and rabbinic Judaism, and that (4) both movements embraced "liberalizing" views concerning access to the Jerusalem cult. Bovon thus points out that Schwartz's reading depends on the contradictory assertions that, on the one hand, the designation of the High Priest as a "Pharisee" likely reflects later Christian criticism of Pharisaism rather than an accurate historical memory of the priest's identity, while, on the other, the document provides reliable insight into actual Pharisaic practice.

Bovon instead argues, convincingly to my mind, that the gospel fragment should be read in the context of second-century Christian controversies concerning the need for purification during water baptism rather than as evidence for first-century Judaism or the historical Jesus.[67] He points out that the expression "the holy vessels" (*ta hagia skeuê*) is precisely the same language used by early Christians to describe the liturgical utensils employed in the ritual of the Eucharist. On this reading, the lost gospel tells us not about the history or fate of the actual Temple vessels, but about how their memory could be appropriated in early Christian culture.

Unlike Second Temple Jewish sources – but very much in the spirit of P. Oxyrhynchus 840 – rabbinic literature nowhere places restrictions on the viewing of the Temple vessels.[68] In a fascinating article, Israel Knohl has analyzed a variety of rabbinic sources that represent the act of viewing the Temple vessels by the laity during the Second Temple period as a sacred rite, one almost akin to a theophany.[69] Knohl's argument largely hinges on later rabbinic reports concerning sectarian controversy surrounding the display of the showbread table and the *menorah* on pilgrimage

---

[67] For his assessment of Schwartz's argument, see Bovon, "Christian Controversy over Purity," 711–12.

[68] This fact was already stressed by Abraham Sulzbach, "Zum Oxyrhynchus-Fragment," *Zeitschrift für die neutestamentliche Wissenschaft und die Kunde der älteren Kirche* 9 (1908): 175–76.

[69] Israel Knohl, "Post-Biblical Sectarianism and Priestly Schools of the Pentateuch: The Issue of Popular Participation in the Temple Cult on Festivals," *The Madrid Qumran Congress* (ed. J. T. Barrera and L. Vegas Montaner; 2 vols.; Leiden: Brill, 1992), 2:601–9; also published as "Participation of the People in the Temple Worship – Second Temple Sectarian Conflict and the Biblical Tradition" (Hebrew), *Tarbiz* 60 (1991): 139–46.

festivals outside the inner-sanctuary of the Temple.[70] While I am myself not persuaded by Knohl that these rabbinic sources can be used to reconstruct the history of actual cultic practice in the Jerusalem Temple in so straightforward a fashion,[71] I do think he is fundamentally correct in identifying a strong "democratizing" or "popularizing" impulse within rabbinic literature itself. Quite clearly, the rabbinic authors of these texts wished to present the Temple vessels as the patrimony of all Israel – and not just the priesthood.

Yet, paradoxically, these diverse rabbinic traditions, including the "eyewitness" testimonies that I have analyzed at length above, are marked by a provocative emphasis on the visual power of the Temple vessels. They carry within them a powerful interest in the very materiality of the cult. Of course, unlike early Christianity, late antique Judaism was relatively slow to develop liturgical practices and personnel that could be understood, however provisionally, to replace the Jerusalem cult; indeed, it was most likely not until the Byzantine period that the synagogue was gradually transformed, under considerable Christian influence, into a kind of surrogate temple.[72] But, while third- and fourth-century rabbinic sources do not

---

[70] This material is found in increasingly expansive forms at *m.Hag* 3:8; *t.Hag* 3:35; *y.Hag* 3,8 (79d); *b.Hag* 26b. Knohl finds echoes of the debate between the Pharisees and Sadducees described in these sources with an ordinance found in the Qumran *Temple Scroll* column 3, lines 10–12. Knohl's view is in keeping with the interpretation of the rabbinic sources in Ya'akov Sussman, "The History of the Halakhah and the Dead Sea Scrolls: Preliminary Talmudic Observations on *Miqsat Ma'ase ha-Torah*," Appendix 1 in Elisha Qimron and John Strugnell, *Qumran Cave 4*, vol. 5: *Miqsat Ma'ase ha-Torah* (Discoveries in the Judaean Desert 10; Oxford: Clarendon Press, 1994), 199; Saul Lieberman, *Tosefta Kifshutah* (10 vols; New York: Jewish Theological Seminary of America, 1973), 5:1336. But for a contradictory interpretation, see Joseph M. Baumgarten, "Immunity to Impurity and the Menorah," *Jewish Studies Internet Journal* 5 (2006): 141–45, which attributes Sadducean ridicule of the Pharisaic practice of purifying the menorah not to their rejection of Pharisaic liberalism (i.e. allowing the public to come into contact with the vessel) but to their conviction that the menorah was itself immune to impurity because of "the purifying power of its radiance" (145).

[71] For a principled critique of (1) the tendency in secondary scholarship to treat *all* of halakhic texts found at Qumran (even the *Temple Scroll*) as belonging to a single sectarian halakhic system and (2) overly facile attempts to harmonize the halakhic traditions found in the Qumran documents with rabbinic traditions concerning Second Temple sectarian halakhah, see Yaakov Elman, "Some Remarks on 4QMMT and the Rabbinic Tradition: or, When Is a Parallel Not a Parallel?" in *Reading 4QMMT: New Perspectives on Qumran Law and History* (ed. J. Kampen and M. J. Bernstein; Atlanta: Scholars Press, 1996), 99–128.

[72] Levine, *Ancient Synagogue*, esp. 236–49, 630–32. But a higher degree of continuity with earlier periods is emphasized in Steven Fine, *This Holy Place: On the Sanctity of the*

provide the lost Temple implements with a tangible new referent comparable to the Christian Eucharist, rabbinic claims of special knowledge about their appearance and function paradoxically reaffirms their continuing cultural, religious, and political significance. In this small regard, while the attitude toward the Temple vessels in early rabbinic literature is still a long way from their integration into the emerging Jewish messianic discourse of the Byzantine period, the rabbis have gone far toward establishing them yet again as a major "continuity theme" in late antique Judaism.

As an aside, it is worth observing that later rabbinic authors likewise took note of the replication of this motif in earlier rabbinic literature. An elaborate literary complex found in the Babylonian Talmud at *Me'ilah* 17a–b, but not elsewhere in classical rabbinic literature, develops these atomized traditions concerning R. Eleazar b. Yose and R. Simeon b. Yoḥai into a highly imaginative and integrated travel narrative.[73] This unique composition bears many of the literary features characteristic of the extended narratives found in the Babylonian Talmud – most notably, its harmonization of disparate earlier traditions, distinctive shift from Hebrew core to Araṃaic addendum, elaborate length, and use of vocabulary not found in Palestinian sources – and is thus likely the product of this document's anonymous redactors (the *stammaim*).[74]

According to the story, the two sages, after having been selected by their fellow sages for the task of petitioning the imperial government to annul its harsh decrees (apparently during the Hadrianic persecutions), set off together on their embassy to Rome. On the way, while debating fine points of *halakhah*, they encounter a demon named Ben Temalion,[75] who has been sent by God to help them deliver the Jewish people from persecu-

---

*Synagogue during the Greco-Roman Period* (Christianity and Judaism in Antiquity Series 11; Notre Dame, Ind.: University of Notre Dame Press, 1997).

[73] Versions of this tradition also appear in a number of later sources: the apocalyptic composition "The Prayer of R. Simon b. Yoḥai" (Adolf Jellinek, ed., *Beit ha-Midrash*, [6 vols.; Leipzig: Fridrikh Nies, 1853–1877; repr., Jerusalem: Wahrmann Books, 1967], 4:117–18); the medieval compilation *Yalqut Shim'oni* (to the *Pentateuch* §537). A closely related narrative, although with different protagonists and historical setting, is found in Benjamin Klar, ed., *Megillat Aḥima'ats* (Jerusalem: Tarshish, 1974), 18–20. For discussion of the relationship of this story to its talmudic precursor and its development within the Byzantine context, see Stephen Benin, "*Megillat Aḥima'ats* and its Place within Byzantine Literature" (Hebrew), *Jerusalem Studies in Jewish Thought* 4 (1985): 237–50.

[74] On the formal, textual, and linguistic features that characterize the aggadic compositions of the *stammaim*, see Jeffrey L. Rubenstein, "Criteria of Stammaitic Intervention in Aggada," in *Creation and Composition: The Contribution of the Bavli Redactors (Stammaim) to the Aggada* (ed. J. L. Rubenstein; Texts and Studies in Ancient Judaism 114; Tübingen: Mohr Siebeck, 2005), 417–40, as well as the other studies in this volume.

[75] The demonic name Ben Temalion is not otherwise attested in rabbinic literature.

tion. Ben Temalion explains that he will take possession of the Roman Emperor's daughter, so that she will require the "miraculous" intervention of the visiting rabbis. When the rabbis call out Ben Temalion's "personal" name, which he has taught them, he will be compelled to leave the girl.[76] The indebted Emperor will then reward them for their services by granting any request they make. Although Simeon would prefer to have merited the help of an angel, as did even Abraham's maid-servant Hagar, he nonetheless accedes to the demon's offer of assistance. Ben Temalion proceeds to Rome ahead of the sages, takes possession of the Emperor's daughter, and awaits their arrival. R. Simeon succeeds in exorcising the demon by whispering the demon's name in the girl's ear. The story then arrives at its denouement:

> [The Emperor] said to them: "(In return for having healed my daughter) request whatever you desire." They were led into his treasure house (לגנזיה) to take whatever they wished. They found the document (announcing the decree) (אשכחו ההיא איגרתא), took it and tore it to pieces (שקלוה וקרעוה). It is in reference to this that R. Eleazar bar R. Yose related: "I saw it in the city [of Rome] (אני ראיתיה בעיר [רומי]),[77] and on it were several drops of blood (והוו עליה כמה טיפי דמים)."[78]

Although the narrative explicitly authenticates only R. Eleazar's testimony, it offers a plausible "historical" context in which the two sages might have traveled together to Rome and visited the Temple vessels. R. Simeon, who emerges as the hero of the tale, may in part have been chosen because of his wide renown as a miracle-working sage: the passage attributes his selection to his status as "learned in miracles" (מלומד בנסים).[79] Yet, the juxtaposition of these two figures, both known to have seen the Temple vessels in Rome, cannot be a coincidence. The narrative harmonizes and, thereby, authorizes these seemingly repetitive or even contradictory sources.

More significantly, the creators of this story embedded R. Eleazar's viewing of the Temple implements within a narrative that thematizes the role played by the imperial storehouse at Rome in the deliverance of the

---

[76] The use of angelic or demonic names in exorcism was widespread in antiquity in general and in Jewish and rabbinic sources in particular. On the centrality of names in the rabbinic conception of exorcism, see especially Meir Bar-Ilan, "Exorcism by the Rabbis: Talmudic Sages and Magic" (Hebrew), *Da'at* 34 (1995): 17–31.

[77] The deletion of the word "Rome" is due to either internal or external censorship.

[78] I have slightly modified the Soncino translation.

[79] On R. Simeon ben Yoḥai as a "wonder-worker" or "magician" in rabbinic literature, see Ben-Zion Rosenfeld, "Simeon b. Yohai – Wonder Worker and Magician Scholar, *Saddiq* and *Hasid*," *Revue des études juives* 158 (1999): 349–84, esp. 362–64 for treatment of this story.

Jewish people from Roman oppression. Of course, the motif of the Temple implements is an addendum; it does not directly advance the plot. Indeed, the linkage between divine intervention on behalf of the Jewish people and travel to the imperial capital is relatively undeveloped in this narrative produced in the Sasanian east. Yet, as we shall presently see, more-or-less contemporary Jewish sources from the Byzantine west developed the theme of the hidden contents of the Roman treasury into an absolutely pivotal theme in their anti-imperial discourse – and they did so in a future-oriented, eschatological key.

## IV. The *Inventio*(n) of the Temple Vessels in the Byzantine Period

We will presently see that various types of Jewish texts produced under Christian Rome after around the year 500 C.E. – midrashic as well as apocalyptic – situated the theme of the Temple implements within a highly-developed eschatological discourse, which found increasingly vibrant expression during this period. But this renewed interest in the Temple vessels was hardly an isolated Jewish phenomenon. Rather, this impulse belongs to a much broader cultural development in the Byzantine west, where sacred relics from the biblical, Jewish, and Christian pasts came to play an increasingly important role in conferring authority, legitimacy, and power on specific people, practices, places, and institutions. Indeed, Roman-Christian sources from the late fifth century onwards attest to a similar, if not even more powerful, fascination with imagery from the Jerusalem Temple in general and with the fate of the Temple vessels in particular.

It would, of course, be impracticable for me to review in any substantial detail the well-known story of the rise of the cult of relics – and, somewhat later, icons – over the course of the fourth, fifth, and sixth centuries.[80] Nor

[80] The scholarly literature on the rise and function of relics in late antique Christian culture is vast, but see especially Patricia Cox Miller, "'Differential Networks': Relics and Other Fragments in Late Antiquity," *Journal of Early Christian Studies* 6 (1998): 113–38; Peter Brown, *The Cult of the Saints: Its Rise and Function in Latin Christianity* (Chicago: University of Chicago Press, 1981), esp. 78–81. See also the following classic considerations of the rise of icons: Hans Belting, *Likeness and Presence: A History of the Image before the Era of Art* (trans. E. Jephcott; Chicago: University of Chicago Press, 1994); Averil Cameron, "Images of Authority: Elites and Icons in Late Sixth-Century Byzantium," *Past and Present* 84 (1979): 3–35; repr. in Averil Cameron, *Continuity and Change in Sixth-Century Byzantium* (London: Variorum, 1981), XVIII; Peter Brown, "A Dark-Age Crisis: Aspects of the Iconoclastic Controversy," *English Historical Review* 88

can I do justice to the central role that the translation of sacred objects to the city of Constantinople played in its formation as a specifically Christian imperial capital.[81] But, as we approach the Byzantine textual traditions concerning the Temple vessels, we must bear in mind just how significant an impact the image of Jerusalem, both earthly and heavenly, had on the urban landscape and architecture of Constantinople. Indeed, Martin Harrison has shown that, already in the generation before the Emperor Justinian (527–565 C.E.) began the ambitious building projects that would famously be compared to those of King Solomon, Byzantine architects and their imperial patrons were making self-conscious use of the imagery and scale of Solomon's legendary Temple in designing the new monumental churches of Constantinople.[82] It is within this cultural and religious framework that we must place the unexpected resurfacing of the vessels from the Jerusalem Temple in sixth-century Christian sources.

In a now classic article that has been cited approvingly by Jewish historians ever since, Yohanan Lewy called attention to the claim found in a number of places in the histories of Procopius of Caesarea (c. 500 565 C.E.) that the Byzantine general Belisarius recaptured the Temple implements from the Vandal tribes in North Africa and subsequently relocated them to Constantinople, where they were paraded through the streets on the occasion of the Vandalic triumph in 534.[83] Procopius then reports that, on the advice of a Jew, Justinian elected to deprive his capital of these powerful objects, lest they cause him and his regime harm, returning them instead to the Holy Land for safe keeping in a church. Although this act of repatriation is rather uncharacteristic for Byzantine emperors, who were otherwise busy importing sacred relics from throughout the Empire, Lewy seems to have been eager for whatever scant information regarding the vessels he could find. Thus, he accorded this account positive historical

(1973): 1–34; Ernst Kitzinger, "The Cult of Images in the Age before Iconoclasm," *Dumbarton Oaks Papers* 8 (1954): 85–150.

[81] See Bernard Flusin, "Construire une nouvelle Jérusalem: Constantinople et les reliques," in *Orient dans l'histoire religieuse de l'Europe: l'invention des origins* (ed. M. A. Amir-Moezzi and J. Scheid; Turnhout: Brepols, 2000), 51–70; Cyril Mango, "Constantine's Mausoleum and the Translation of Relics," *Byzantinische Zeitschrift* 83 (1990): 51–62. Compare Sarah Bassett, *The Urban Image of Late Antique Constantinople* (New York: Cambridge University Press, 2004), which in my view accords relics too minor a role in the development of Constantinople's urban identity, only mentioning them in passing at the very end (135–36).

[82] Martin Harrison, *A Temple for Byzantium: The Discovery and Excavation of Anicia Juliana's Palace-Church in Istanbul* (London: Harvey Miller Publishers, 1989); idem, "From Jerusalem and Back Again," 239–48.

[83] Lewy, "Fate of the Temple Implements," 255–58.

value and used it as a basic reference point for tracking the faint traces of the Temple *sancta* in subsequent Jewish and Christian sources. Indeed, in order to trace the history of the Temple vessels beyond Procopius' sixth-century sighting, Lewy even tries to determine which church in Jerusalem might have been the lucky recipient of this valuable horde.[84]

In what follows, I argue, *contra* Lewy, that the narrative of rediscovery presented by Procopius has no factual basis in reality whatsoever. I show, rather, that the various passages in the Procopius' histories that discuss the Temple vessels are mutually contradictory. Moreover, Procopius' reconstruction of how various barbarian groups came to possess the Temple vessels in the first place is not corroborated by a number of late fifth-century sources that are far closer to the events in question. Instead, I argue that the supposed transfer of the Temple vessels to Constantinople seems to have been motivated by Procopius' larger objective of modeling the Vandalic triumph on the triumph celebrated by Vespasian and Titus almost 500 years earlier. But I believe that, beyond this immediate rhetorical aim, the re-emergence of the Temple vessels reflects the much broader conjunction between the prestige of Solomon and the fascination with sacred relics that is so characteristic of mid-sixth-century Byzantine culture. As we will see, Byzantine Jewish writers also participated in many of these same highly distinctive cultural impulses.

Before proceeding, I cite at considerable length Procopius' account of Belisarius' triumphant return to Constantinople after his defeat of Gelimer and his Vandal army:

> Belisarius, upon reaching Byzantium with Gelimer and the Vandals, was counted worthy to receive such honors as in former times were assigned to those generals of the Romans who had won the greatest and most noteworthy victories. And a period of about 600 years had now passed since anyone had attained these honors, except, indeed, Titus and Trajan, and such other emperors as had led armies against some barbarian nation and had been victorious. For he displayed the spoils and slaves from the war in the midst of the city and led a procession which the Romans call a "triumph" (*thriambon*), not, however, in the ancient manner, but going on foot from his own house to the hippodrome and then again from the barriers until he reached the place where the imperial throne is. And there was booty – first of all, whatever articles were wont to be set apart for the royal service – thrones of gold and carriages in which it is customary for a king's consort to ride, and much jewelry made of precious stones, and golden drinking cups, and all the other things which are useful for the royal table. And there was also silver weighing many thousands of talents and all the royal treasure amounting to an excee-

[84] Lewy, "Fate of the Temple Implements," 256–57, speculates that the church that served as the repository was the "New" Church that Justinian dedicated to Mary in 543 C.E. Lewy provides no concrete evidence for his "educated guess" (השערה) other than Justinian's sponsorship of the project.

> dingly great sum (for Geiseric had despoiled the Palatium in Rome, as has been said in the preceding narrative). And among these were the treasures of the Jews (*ta Ioudaiôn keimêlia*), which Titus the son of Vespasian, together with certain others, had brought to Rome after the capture of Jerusalem. And one of the Jews, seeing these things, approached one of those known to the Emperor and said: "These treasures I think it inexpedient to carry into the palace in Byzantium. Indeed, it is not possible for them to be elsewhere than in the place where Solomon, the king of the Jews, formerly placed them. For it is because of these that Geiseric captured the palace of the Romans, and that now the Roman army has captured that of the Vandals." When this had been brought to the attention of the Emperor, he became afraid and quickly sent everything to the sanctuaries of the Christians in Jerusalem (*es tôn Xristianôn ta en Hierosolumois hiera*).[85]

It is perhaps worth stressing that no independent confirmation of this remarkable account exists in contemporaneous sixth-century sources. And, while we can certainly find the same or similar accounts in the later Byzantine historical and chronographic tradition, it seems that all of these sources – without obvious exception – are dependent on Procopius himself, either directly or indirectly. Thus, for example, Theophanes' account of the events of 533/4 is embedded in what amounts to nothing other than "a lengthy précis of the whole of the two books of the *Vandal Wars*," in the words of his English translators.[86]

But, in the absence of corroborating witnesses, how shall we assess the historical value of this passage? The account of the Vandal triumph is a well-known crux in historians' attempts to parse Procopius' enormously complex relationship to the imperial household, especially with respect to his view of the obvious tensions between the Emperor Justinian and his general Belisarius.[87] The scene of Belisarius walking "on foot" to the hippodrome and there paying obeisance to Justinian is often understood in light of Procopius' pointed, if not entirely consistent, attempt to contrast

---

[85] Procopius, *History of the Wars* 4.9.1–9. Citations of Procopius refer to the edition and translation in H. B. Dewing, trans., *Procopius* (7 vols.; Cambridge, Mass.: Harvard University Press, 1914–1940).

[86] Cyril Mango and Roger Scott, trans., *The Chronicle of Theophanes the Confessor: Byzantine and Near Eastern History, AD 284–813* (Oxford: Clarendon Press, 1997), xciii; the relevant passage is found on page 295.

[87] For the most important general assessments of Procopius' political allegiances and how these shaped his writings, see the differing accounts in Anthony Kaldellis, *Procopius of Caesarea: Tyranny, History, and Philosophy and the End of Antiquity* (Philadelphia: University of Pennsylvania Press, 2004), and Averil Cameron, *Procopius and the Sixth Century* (Transformation of the Classical Heritage 10; Berkeley: University of California Press, 1985).

the general's humility with the Emperor's despotic tendencies.[88] At the same time, despite his intricate negotiation of competing allegiances, this "engaged" historian also clearly wished to cast the celebration of the victory over the Vandals in the most glorious terms he could muster.

Averil Cameron has pointed out the palpable artificiality of Justinian's celebration, which "took the form of an archaizing revival of the old Roman triumph."[89] I would go a step further and argue that this self-conscious "archaizing" impulse did not only shape the triumph itself as an actual public event, but also informed Procopius' ideologically potent representation of it. Indeed, his account of the supposed "reappearance" of the Temple vessels and their almost immediate "repatriation" to a church in the Holy Land where they are secreted away is suspiciously convenient. It offers Procopius an effective rhetorical strategy for linking the triumph to the glorious victories of the Flavians over an earlier "internal enemy" – in their case, the Jews rather than the Vandals – but without actually having to contend with the inconvenient traces that the vessels might have left behind in the capital.

Similarly striking is Procopius' curious deployment of the figure of an anonymous Jew, who succeeds in persuading the Emperor to rid himself of these enormously powerful objects because their sanctity is dangerously "out of place" everywhere except "the place where Solomon, the king of the Jews, formerly placed them." Cameron's own more recent work, which emphasizes the complex way that Jews and Judaism are used as rhetorical tropes in Byzantine literature, might be productively applied to this passage in order to raise the possibility, at least, that we are dealing here with literary representation rather than with positive history.[90] Indeed, this passage is reminiscent of the ways that earlier Christian accounts of the discovery and authentication of relics make particular use of Jews as authorizing devices, as Ora Limor has so compellingly shown.[91]

---

[88] Cameron, *Procopius and the Sixth Century*, 137–42. Contrast Kaldellis, *Procopius of Caesarea*, 141–42, which places almost exclusive emphasis on the polemical quality of the passage.

[89] Cameron, "Images of Authority," 8–9. See also the important analysis of the ceremony in Michael McCormick, *Eternal Victory: Triumphal Rulership in Late Antiquity, Byzantium, and the Early Medieval West* (Cambridge: Cambridge University Press, 1986), 125–29.

[90] See especially Averil Cameron, "Byzantines and Jews: Some Recent Work on Early Byzantium," *Byzantine and Modern Greek Studies* 20 (1996): 249–74.

[91] Ora Limor, "Christian Sacred Space and the Jew," in *From Witness to Witchcraft: Jews and Judaism in Medieval Christian Thought* (ed. J. Cohen; Wiesbaden: Harrassowitz, 1996), 55–77; see also Jacobs, *Remains of the Jews*, 174–91.

But beyond these internal literary considerations, I believe that a range of external evidence also supports my skeptical reading of this account. Most significantly, Procopius' other discussions of the Temple vessels elsewhere in the *History of the Wars* provide no corroborating evidence for his account here – and is at times even at odds with it. Thus, when Procopius recounts Geiseric's original sack of Rome, he discusses the "great amount of gold and other imperial treasures" taken and even the fact that he plundered the temple of Jupiter Capitolinus, but nowhere does he mention the Temple vessels.[92] More curious still, Procopius also reports in his *History of the Wars* that the Temple vessels had, in fact, been taken from Rome to southern Gaul (Gallia Narbonensis = modern Carcassonne) by Alaric in 410, rather than to Carthage by the Vandal Geiseric in 455.[93] This claim stands in marked contrast to Procopius' earlier account of Alaric's sack of Rome, where he makes no mention of the Temple implements.[94] Nor do we ever again hear about the fate of those vessels that supposedly found their way to France. Lewy, of course, makes sense of this seeming contradiction by positing that the Temple treasure must have been divided up into a number of separate hoards – in a manner akin to the multiplication of the fragments of the True Cross.[95] This image of multiple stashes of Temple implements circulating in barbarian hands throughout the fifth and sixth centuries offers Lewy a foolproof, though wholly unverifiable, strategy for harmonizing the various strands of Procopius.

Yet, when we turn to our other contemporary historical sources for the Gothic wars, we find something fascinating: none mentions the Temple implements! Jordanes, author of the *Gothic History* written around 551, describes Geiseric as "very well known" for his sack of Rome, but does not mention that he took the Temple vessels.[96] Later in the work, Jordanes discusses the Vandalic triumph of 534, but again – no mention of the vessels.[97] Similarly, Victor of Vita, the pious author of a late-fifth-century chronicle of the Vandalic persecution of the North African Christian community, offers a highly unsympathetic account of Geiseric's plunder of Rome. But, although he is writing only decades after these events and has an obvious motivation to have included this detail in his otherwise damning portrait of Geiseric, he, too, says nothing of the Temple vessels. As for

[92] *History of the Wars*, 3.5.1–7.

[93] *History of the Wars*, 5.12.41–42.

[94] *History of the Wars* 3.2.1–7.

[95] Lewy, "Fate of the Temple Implements," 257–58.

[96] Jordanes, *Gothic History* §168. Translated in Charles Christopher Mierow, *The Gothic History of Jordanes* (Cambridge, U.K.: Speculum Historiale; New York: Barnes & Noble, 1960), 98.

[97] Jordanes, *Gothic History* §307 (Mierow, *Gothic History*, 139–40).

the nature of the plunder, Victor reports merely that, when Geiseric seized Rome "he took into captivity the wealth of many kings, as well as people."[98]

It seems to me, then, that the lack of independent corroboration from earlier, contemporary, or later sources – in combination with my assessment of Procopius' rhetorical aims and inner-contradictions – speaks strongly against the historical "reappearance" of the Temple vessels at Constantinople in the middle of the sixth century. Rather, I would suggest that the *sancta* from the Jerusalem Temple presented Procopius with a highly appealing motif through which he might heighten the drama of Byzantine ascendance during the age of Justinian. This relatively minor authorial decision would be of a piece with the much larger processes that were then giving shape to the city of Constantinople. Like the Justinianic building projects and the intensive acquisition of relics, the Temple implements would have served to embed the new power, wealth, and sanctity that were flowing into the imperial capital within long-standing biblical and Roman narratives. Indeed, the vessels from the Jerusalem Temple were in many respects unique in their ability to embody simultaneously the glories of both the Solomonic and Roman pasts.

## V. Jewish Relics at "Rome" in the Jewish Messianic Discourse of the Byzantine Period

Before I address the function of the Temple vessels in the Jewish messianic discourse of the early Byzantine period (the fifth to seventh centuries), a few general words about the central role that the capital of the Roman Empire played in Jewish anti-Roman rhetoric are in order. First, it is essential that we bear in mind that late antique Jewish sources – both rabbinic and non-rabbinic – do not appear to draw a clear distinction between the cities of Rome and Constantinople, stubbornly adhering to an anti-Roman vocabulary of opposition first developed in an earlier age.[99] Thus, well into the fifth, sixth, and seventh centuries, Jewish sources speak about the Roman Empire in timeless terms, as if its emperors were still "pagan" and

[98] Victor of Vita, *History of the Vandal Persecution*, 24. Translated in John Moorhead, trans., *Victor of Vita: History of the Vandal Persecution* (Liverpool: Liverpool University Press, 1992), 139–40.

[99] On the symbolism of Edom/Esau as Rome in Jewish culture, see the classic study of Gerson D. Cohen, "Esau as Symbol in Early Medieval Thought," in *Jewish Medieval and Renaissance Studies* (ed. A. Altmann; Cambridge, Mass.: Harvard University Press, 1967), 19–48; see also Yuval, *Two Nations*, 16–33.

continued to be housed at old Rome. We can, however, sometimes detect, beneath this insistent rhetorical continuity, changing conceptions of the emperor or his imperial capital within Jewish sources.[100] Indeed, I will argue below that the transformation in the uses and meaning of the motif of the Temple vessels provides us with a parade example of how processes of Christianization shaped the ways that Jews imaginatively remapped their salvation history against the shifting geography of empire. I, therefore, bracket the question of which of the two capital cities serves as the precise referent in any given text in favor of a more general assessment of the changing nature of the Jewish anti-imperial rhetoric.

A number of sources from the later Roman/Byzantine period absorbed aspects of the motif of the Temple vessels from its earlier, oblique legal contexts into increasingly elaborate narrative structures. And, among these sources, those that come from later Roman or Byzantine Palestine consistently place the Temple implements within an eschatological framework. Within this messianic discourse, the physical movement of these artifacts traces the historical trajectory of divine favor, from Israel's glorious past to Roman ascendancy and, finally, to Israel's future vindication. I would suggest that this distinctive emphasis on "sacred relics" within this discourse was shaped in large measure as part of a dialogue with Byzantine Christian culture.

A passage in the midrashic commentary on the book of Esther from Byzantine Palestine traces the fate of the throne of Solomon.[101] According to the text, the fate of Solomon's throne indexes the political fortunes of the numerous great empires that have shaped the history of Israel from its earliest beginnings; it embodies divine favor itself, as it is passed from Egypt to Ethiopia to Babylonia to Persia to Greece to Rome.

> It is related that when Solomon died, Shishak, king of Egypt came up and took it [the throne] from them. R. Samuel b. Naḥman said: "Shishak is the same as Pharaoh." And why was he called Shishak? Because he came impelled by greed (*sheqiqut*) against Israel, saying, "I am taking it in lieu of my daughter's marriage settlement." He made war with Zeraḥ the Ethiopian, who took it from him. Then Asa made war with Zeraḥ the Ethiopian and he conquered him and took it from him; it has been taught that Asa and all the kings of Judah sat upon it. And when Nebuchadnezzar came up and sacked Jerusalem he carried it off to Babylon. From Babylon it was taken to Media and from Media to Greece and from Greece to

[100] See my preliminary observations on this matter in *From Martyr to Mystic: Rabbinic Martyrology and the Making of Merkavah Mysticism* (Texts and Studies in Ancient Judaism 112; Tübingen: Mohr Siebeck, 2005), 82–84, esp. fn. 110.

[101] This passage comes from the first part of *Esther Rabbah* (sections 1–6), which may date as early as the sixth century (Strack and Stemberger, *Introduction*, 318–19).

Edom. R. Eleazar b. Yose said: I saw its fragments in Rome (א״ר אלעזר ברי יוסי אני ראיתי שבריו ברומי).[102]

Perhaps most interesting for our purposes is the direct transposition of R. Eleazar ben Yose's eye-witness testimony from its original referent, one of the Temple implements, to a novel literary context. The object he reports having seen in Rome, Solomon's throne, belongs to a far more distant past. Here the conflict between Israel and Rome is not depicted as a family drama, the story of the fraternal conflict between Jacob and Esau, as in other texts we have examined. Rather, the motif of the sacred relic has been assimilated to a variant on the eschatological four-empire scheme of Daniel.[103] In this branch of Jewish anti-Roman rhetoric, Rome is just the next manifestation of God's punishing rod with which he chastises His unruly people.

The incorporation of the theme of the Temple vessels at Rome into Jewish messianic discourse reaches its fullest realization in a work known as *'Otot ha-Mashiaḥ* (*The Portents of the Messiah*). This text is not a single, coherent composition. Rather, this loose cluster of early medieval Hebrew apocalypses is organized as a catalogue of the ten "signs" that will herald the coming of the Jewish Messiah.[104] The dating of *'Otot ha-Mashiaḥ* or its component parts is extraordinarily difficult to determine: several versions of this "ten portents" literature exist and their textual history has not yet been satisfactorily studied. But whatever the precise literary history of the various forms of this work, the section with which I am concerned here does not bear clear markings of the fully distinct Islamic cultural context that crystallized only gradually over the course of the late seventh and eighth centuries, such as explicit references to Muslim rulers or the use of the figure of Ishmael as a symbol for Islamic rule.[105] I think it quite likely that this textual complex derives from the penumbral period of the late sixth and seventh centuries when apocalyptic forms and eschatological expectations served as a common idiom for various – and, in some cases, overlapping – groups of Jews, Christians, and Muslims.[106]

---

[102] *EsthR* 1:12. I use Mirkin's edition of the text. The translation follows M. Simon, trans., *Midrash Rabbah: Esther and Song of Songs* (London: Soncino Press, 1983), 28.

[103] On the use and adaptation of the "four empires" scheme in rabbinic literature, see Rivka Raviv, "The Talmudic Formulation of the Prophecies of the Four Kingdoms in the Book of Daniel" (Hebrew), *Jewish Studies Internet Journal* 5 (2006): 1–20.

[104] John C. Reeves, *Trajectories in Near Eastern Apocalypses: A Postrabbinic Jewish Apocalypse Reader* (Atlanta: Society of Biblical Literature, 2005), 106–10.

[105] Reeves, *Trajectories*, 106–10.

[106] For discussion of early Islamic apocalyptic sources within the context of late antique Jewish and Christian sources, see the path-breaking study of David Cook, *Studies in Muslim Apocalyptic* (Princeton: Darwin Press, 2002).

In the "sixth portent" of one version of *'Otot ha-Mashiaḥ*, we find an elaborate eschatological scenario that narrates the ascendance and subsequent fall of Rome. The discovery of the Temple vessels in the heart of the Empire and their transfer back to the Holy Land play central roles in this narrative of messianic redemption. It should be noted, however, that, unlike the passage from *Esther Rabbah*, this text does not explicitly link the motif of the Temple vessels to a rabbinic figure like R. Eleazar and need not be understood as a direct adaptation of earlier rabbinic literary traditions. Simply put, this is not an overtly "rabbinized" form of discourse. Nevertheless, the pervasive interweaving of scriptural citation in this work separates it from earlier Jewish apocalyptic writings from the Second Temple period and marks it as a distinctively post-rabbinic form of Jewish apocalyptic literature.[107] I cite the passage at length:

> The sixth sign: The Holy One, blessed be He, establishes evil Edom (i.e., Rome) as ruler of the entire world. And a king shall arise in Rome and rule the entire world for nine months. He will devastate numerous lands. He shall become enraged with Israel and levy a heavy tax upon them. Israel shall be in great distress at that time because of the numerous decrees and depredations, which shall be renewed each day against them. And, at that time, Israel shall become weak and feeble and shall have no helper. It is concerning that time that Isaiah prophesied, saying, *He saw that there was no man, and he gazed long*, etc. (Isa 59:16). At the end of nine months, the Messiah son of Joseph will be revealed; his name is Nehemiah son of Hushiel from the tribes of Ephraim, Menasheh, Benjamin, and – for a small part – from the sons of Gad. And Israel shall hear that, in every province into which the Messiah of God comes, only very few people gather to him from each province and each city, as it is written in Jeremiah, *Turn back, rebellious children – declares the Lord. Since I have espoused you, I will take you, one from a town and two from a clan, and bring you to Zion* (Jer 3:14). And the Messiah son of Joseph shall come and wage war against the king of Edom and he shall defeat Edom, and he shall slaughter heaps and mounds of them (ויהרוג מהם תילי תילים) and he shall kill the king of Edom. And he shall destroy the province of Rome and take some of the implements of the Temple, which are hidden in the household of Julius Caesar[108] (ויוציא קצת כלי בית המקדש שהם גנוזים בבית

[107] On the uses of Scripture in later Jewish apocalyptic literature – in contrast to Second Temple apocalyptic – see Reeves, *Trajectories*, 5–7.

[108] I have translated the Emperor's name (יוליינוס קיסר) as "Julius Caesar" because I believe it is used here as a generic designation for the Roman Emperor. It is, however, conceivable that the name should be identified with a more recent figure, such as the fourth-century Emperor Julian (the Apostate); the passage could then be understood to provide positive evidence for Jewish knowledge of Julian's plans for the restoration of the Temple in Jerusalem during his short reign (361–363 C.E.), which might help explain its deployment in Jewish messianic discourse. But, as David Levenson has so convincingly documented, Julian does not make an appearance in Jewish sources until the early modern period ("Julian's Attempt to Rebuild the Temple: An Inventory of Ancient and Medieval Source," in *Of Scribes and Scrolls: Studies on the Hebrew Bible, Intertesta-*

יוליינוס קיסר) and he will come to Jerusalem. And Israel shall hear [of his deeds] and gather to him.[109]

This tableau of divine vengeance is quite familiar from numerous other Jewish messianic sources from Late Antiquity: Rome identified as wicked Edom; the idiom of holy war applied to the final battle between Israel and its foes; the figure of Nehemiah the Messiah son of Joseph.[110] Even the notion that some of the *sancta* were stored (*genuzim*) in the "household of Julius Caesar" may perhaps be explained as a faint reflex of Josephus' account of the division of the spoils between the *Templum Pacis* and the imperial palace in Rome.[111]

What is distinctive in this passage, however, is the integration of the Temple vessels into an eschatological scenario. The Romans misrecognize their possession of these relics as physical confirmation of their divine election. Despite having been swallowed up into the maw of the Empire, the Temple vessels remain fundamentally inviolable. Indeed, this passage celebrates the very condition of dispersal that serves as the precondition for the construction of restoration, in spatialized terms, as triumphant return.

Not every Jewish source that situates the Temple vessels within a messianic framework links this theme *explicitly* to anti-Roman sentiment. A notable exception is the elusive medieval text known as *Massekhet Kelim*, which presents a catalogue of cultic vessels hidden before the destruction of the First Temple whose locations will be kept secret until the King Messiah "David son of David" will redeem Israel.[112] The author of this

---

*mental Judaism, and Christian Origins, Presented to John Strugnell on the Occasion of his Sixtieth Birthday* [ed. H. W. Attridge, J. J. Collins and T. H. Tobin; Lanham, Md.: University Press of America, 1990], 261–79).

[109] Yehudah Even Shmuel, ed., *Midreshei Ge'ulah* (2nd ed.; Jerusalem: Mosad Bialik, 1954), 320. Translation mine. Compare the text in Eisenstein, *Otzar ha-Midrashim*, 202. This passage is translated by Reeves in his *Trajectories*, 124–25.

[110] For a useful survey of messianic themes in rabbinic and non-rabbinic Jewish sources, see Jacob Neusner, "Messianic Themes in Formative Judaism," *Journal of the American Academy of Religion* 52 (1984): 357–74. On the Messiah son of Joseph, see David Berger, "Three Typological Themes in Early Jewish Messianism: Messiah Son of Joseph, Rabbinic Calculations, and the Figure of Armilus," *AJS Review* 10 (1985): 141–64; cf. Joseph Heinemann, "The Messiah Son of Joseph," *Harvard Theological Review* 68 (1975): 1–15.

[111] Compare *B.J.* 7.162.

[112] Jellinek, *Beit ha-Midrash*, 2:88–91, here 91. In addition to the medieval version printed by Jellinek, in the mid-twentieth century Jean Starcky discovered a variant of this text in Beirut inscribed on two marble plaques. For a critical edition and French translation of this text, see Jósef Milik, "Notes d'épigraphie et de topographie palestiniennes," *Revue Biblique* 66 (1959): 567–75, esp. 567–68. Milik here argues that *Massekhet Kelim*

composition does not relate its cryptic geography to the space of the Roman Empire, but rather quite logically maps the hiding places of the sacred treasure onto the world of the First Temple during Babylonian ascendancy. It is uncertain whether we are entitled to understand its references to Babylon as a cryptic critique of Rome or if it should be read in an entirely different context. Indeed, *Massekhet Kelim* remains a puzzle; it, too, deserves further attention. Still, it is certainly significant that this text emphasizes the dispersal of the vessels and their spatial restoration: "At that time, a great river will flow out from within the Holy of Holies – the name of which is the Gihon (Tigris?). It will wash across the great and terrible desert and mix with the River Perat (Euphrates?). And immediately the vessels will rise and be revealed."[113] With this vision of the Temple implements being reassembled in Jerusalem from the heart of the ruling Empire, *Massekhet Kelim* is in line with the late antique Jewish source we have surveyed here, but departs fundamentally from earlier apocalyptic sources like *2 Baruch* and their insistence on the immovability of the *sancta*.

The incorporation of the motif of the Temple vessels in Rome into Jewish messianic discourse belongs to the much broader resurgence of messianic elements in the Jewish literature of the early Byzantine period.[114] As I have elsewhere argued, the notion that redemption is to begin in the heart of empire, which is so central to the texts just discussed, is likewise formulated in the graphic and concrete idiom of sacred relics in the Byzantine-period rabbinic martyrological anthology *The Story of the Ten Martyrs*.[115] This work relates that Jewish martyr-relics remained in Roman hands after the supposed Roman persecutions of the Jews during the first half of the second century. This rich and complicated narrative reports that, following the death of one of the rabbinic martyrs, R. Ishmael ben Elisha, the re-

provides the missing link for understanding the *Copper Scroll* as a "legend" rather than "history." But see the critical assessment of this connection in Weitzman, *Surviving Sacrilege*, 103.

[113] Jellinek, *Beit ha-Midrash*, 2:91.

[114] For general discussion of this phenomenon, see Moshe Idel, "Jewish Apocalypticism: 670–1670," in *The Encyclopedia of Apocalypticism* (ed. J. J. Collins, B. McGinn, and S. J. Stein; 3 vols.; New York: Continuum, 1998), 2:204-37; Robert L. Wilken, "The Restoration of Israel in Biblical Prophecy: Christian and Jewish Responses in the Early Byzantine Period," in *"To See Ourselves as Others See Us": Christians, Jews, and "Others" in Late Antiquity* (ed. J. Neusner and E. S. Frerichs; Chico, Calif.: Scholars Press, 1985), 443–71, esp. 453–61. For a thorough discussion of the corpus of Hebrew apocalypses from the Byzantine period, see Philip S. Alexander, "Late Hebrew Apocalyptic: A Preliminary Survey," *Apocrypha* 1 (1990) 197–217.

[115] *From Martyr to Mystic*, 125–30. On the provenance of the martyrology, see ch. 2.

mains of his face were preserved in the imperial treasury at Rome in defiance of the forces of decay. According to the narrative, the Romans themselves make use of this relic in a public ritual performed in the capital every seventy years.[116]

I have suggested that this passage playfully parodies the way that the relics of a "vanishing" biblical and Jewish past in the Holy Land were pressed into service within Christian supersessionist discourse. Within the context of the martyrology, the Jewish "discovery" of the physical remains of the rabbinic martyr R. Ishmael in the treasury at Rome mimics the Christian cult of relics. Just as local Jews figure heavily in narratives that authenticate Christian holy sites and sacred relics, here, too, Roman spectacles performed in the heart of the metropolis are appropriated for the articulation of a competing history of salvation. The creators of this scene reversed the spatial directionality of conquest and travel. Indeed, the passage insists that the present structure of power relations is not theologically meaningful, since history will only disclose its true, divinely-sanctioned meaning at a future time. The narrative thus neatly destabilizes and subverts Roman-Christian triumphalism.

Perhaps better known is that rich vein of rabbinic traditions that describes the Jewish Messiah as a despised and leprous beggar who dwells at the gates of Rome biding his time until God summons him to action.[117] Much like Christian messianic discourse, sources such as the Byzantine-period Hebrew apocalypse *Sefer Zerubavel* imagine the Messiah as a downtrodden figure destined to rise from the bottom of the Roman social order and take command of God's kingdom.[118] In this text, the pseudonymous visionary Zerubbabel is instructed by God to travel to Rome, where he finds the Messiah:

> Then He (God) said to me, "Go to the house of disgrace, to the house of merriment." I went as He commanded. "Turn yourself this way," He said. When I turned, He touched me and I saw a man, despised and wounded, lowly and in pain. Now that despised man said to me, "Zerubbabel, what is your business here? Who brought you here?" "The spirit of the Lord lifted me up," I answered, "and depo-

---

[116] Gottfried Reeg, ed., *Die Geschichte von den Zehn Märtyrern* (Texts and Studies in Ancient Judaism 10; Tübingen: Mohr Siebeck, 1985), 22.65–73; 54.1–6 (the passage appears in a number of different forms in the various recensions); cf. *b.AZ* 11b.

[117] See Abraham Berger, "Captive at the Gate of Rome: The Story of a Messianic Motif," *Proceedings of the American Academy for Jewish Research* 44 (1977): 1–17.

[118] The *locus classicus* for this motif in rabbinic literature is in the Babylonian Talmud, *b.San* 98a. But the redactors of the *Bavli* have placed this passage in a context that subtly criticizes the notion that the messianic age is imminent and instead emphasizes the individual Jew's ethical and *halakhic* responsibility in the pre-messianic age. For this reason I cite the version in the eschatological context of *Sefer Zerubavel*.

sited me in this place." "Fear not," he said, "for you have been brought here in order to show you." When I heard his words, I took comfort, and my mind was at rest. "My lord," I asked, "what is the name of this place?" "This is Rome the Great, in which I am imprisoned," he said. My Lord, who are you," I asked, "and what is your name? What do you seek here? What are you doing in this place?" "I am the Lord's anointed, the son of Hezekiah," he answered, "and I am imprisoned until the time of the end."[119]

The image of the Jewish Messiah as a captive of the imperial capital reverses the spatial trajectory of Christian salvation-history found in such classic texts as Luke-Acts, in which the narrative movement traces the path of the Holy Spirit from Jerusalem to Rome. By contrast, the Jewish Messiah of *Sefer Zerubavel* will begin his itinerary in the heart of the Empire rather than in provincial Palestine.

More provocatively, just as Christians incorporated into their theology the notion that the Christian Messiah had issued forth from Israel, late antique Jews speculated about the possibility that the Jewish Messiah would be reared among the Romans as a Roman. Thus, we find in the medieval homiletical midrash *Exodus Rabbah* the following interpretation of Exodus 2:10, *She* (Miriam) *brought him* (Moses) *to Pharaoh's daughter*:

Pharaoh's daughter used to kiss and hug him (Moses), loved him as if he were her own son, and would not allow him out of the royal palace. Because he was so handsome, everyone was eager to see him, and whoever saw him could not tear himself away from him. Pharaoh also used to kiss and hug him, and he (Moses) used to take the crown of Pharaoh and place it upon his own head, as he was destined to do when he became great. It was this which God said to Hiram (king of Tyre): *So I made a fire issue from you*, etc. (Ezek 28:18), and even so did the daughter of Pharaoh bring up him who was destined to exact retribution from her father. The Messianic king, too, who will one day exact retribution from Edom (שעתיד ליפרע מאדום), dwells among them in that province (יושב עמהם במדינה), as it is said, (*For the fortified city* [i.e. Rome] *is solitary*); *there shall the calf feed, and there shall he lie down* (Isa 27:10).[120]

The typological idiom of this passage establishes the figure of Moses as the archetype for the Jewish Messiah. This particular text does not specify the precise nature of the familial or ethnic relationship between the Jewish

[119] The translation is from Martha Himmelfarb, "Sefer Zerubbabel," in *Rabbinic Fantasies* (ed. D. Stern and M. J. Mirsky; New Haven: Yale University Press, 1990), 71–72. Himmelfarb follows the edition in Israel Lévi, "L'apocalypse de Zorobabel et le roi de Perse Siroès," *Revue des études juives* 68 (1914): 129–60; compare Levi's French translation in *Revue des études juives* 69 (1919): 108–21. The text is also printed in Even Shmuel, *Midreshei Ge'ulah*, 55–88; Jellinek, *Beit ha-Midrash*, 2:54–47.

[120] *ExodR* 1.26. I have slightly modified the translation in S. M. Lehrman, trans., *Midrash Rabbah: Exodus* (London: Soncino Press, 1983), 33.

Messiah and his Roman overlords. But it does express nicely the following double paradox: the Messiah will not only usher in a profound historical reversal in Israel and Rome's political fortunes, but will initiate that process from within the ranks of the Romans. Its skillful juxtaposition of intimacy and antagonism, so appropriate to family-relations, adds yet another dimension to the general pattern of Jewish political speculation in this period, which takes the sibling rivalry of Jacob and Esau as its primary image of Israel and Rome competing with each other over the tokens of divine favor.

With texts like *'Otot ha-Mashiaḥ*, *The Story of the Ten Martyrs*, and Byzantine midrashim like *Esther Rabbah*, we have come full circle to the forms of eschatological discourse employed to such dramatic effect in apocalypses like *2 Baruch*, albeit with a significant difference. Unlike the Second Temple fixation on fixity, these later texts stress the possibility of continuity in the face of spatial dislocation. Indeed, it is through the process of their textualization that the scattered remains of the Jewish past – the vessels from the Jerusalem Temple in some sources, the shards of Solomon's throne in others, and the royal and temple treasures of ancient Israel in yet others – are transfigured into mobile and thus endlessly resistant repositories of the sacred.

## Conclusion

The Jerusalem Temple, in the wake of its destruction, became a site for articulating a particular Jewish account of the historical conflict between Israel and Rome, past, present, and future. In my view, the production of Jewish "collective memories" of the Temple should not be read as an attempt either to reconstitute a ruptured Jewish past or to transmit seamlessly a fixed body of traditions. Rather, this process belonged to the shifting circumstances of Roman imperial domination. In particular, those sources that were composed in the post-Constantinian period constitute part of the broader ideological response of late antique Jews to the emergent Christian discourse of empire.

I have argued in this paper that the late antique Jewish writers we have been reading both mocked and mirrored Roman imperial ideology and the narratives that underwrote it. The memorialization of the Temple vessels and other relics of the Jewish past functioned as a targeted strategy aimed at critiquing Roman (and later Roman-Christian) political power. But this process did not entail the out-and-out rejection of the Christian discourse of sacred relics, which emerged as a dominant mode of Christian religious piety in the fifth and sixth centuries. I have argued instead that Jewish writers and story-tellers – bound in complex relations of power with their Christian rulers and neighbors – appropriated the idioms associated with the cult of relics for their own ends, simultaneously contesting and replicating Christian forms of religious discourse and practice.

After reviewing the information found in Greek and Latin authors, including Josephus, concerning the transfer of the vessels from the Jerusalem Temple to the city of Rome and their potent symbolic role within Flavian imperial ideology, I considered the variety of functions that the image of the captured Temple vessels serves within early rabbinic literature (c. 200–450 C.E.). In these early rabbinic writings, the Temple vessels are generally embedded within the eternal present of rabbinic legal discourse, safely outside the flow of a Jewish salvation history that leads inevitably from a ruptured past to future redemption. Yet, while these sources clearly wish to assert rabbinic authority over the remains of the Jerusalem cult, they also acknowledge the status of these objects as fundamentally irreplaceable embodiments of divine presence.

The Temple vessels only return to view in Roman imperial sources in the sixth century, at a time when Christians throughout the Byzantine east were developing a deepening fascination with the production and dissemination of physical repositories of the sacred in the form of saints' relics and later icons. Jewish literature from this period likewise reflects this interest in the power of physical objects to intervene in human affairs. These "literary relics" served as an idiom through which Jewish writers could articulate an alternative to the triumphalism of Christian imperial discourse.

Perhaps most importantly, I have suggested that the mode of cultural dialogue in which these Jewish sources are engaged cannot be properly understood within an analytical framework governed by notions of passive cultural influence.[121] Nor, I think, is it even sufficient to explain this Jewish counter-discourse of sacred relics as an example of active cultural borrowing or imitation in which Jews both replicated the cultural practices of the Christian majority and internalized them as their own. Rather, we must recognize in this discourse those ambivalent and often ironic forms of mimicry that post-colonial critics have identified as a hallmark of colonial

---

[121] For recent discussion of the serious methodological pitfalls inherent in "influence-based" models of cultural change in Jewish history, see David N. Myers, *Resisting History: Historicism and Its Discontents in German-Jewish Thought* (Princeton: Princeton University Press, 2003), 157–72; Peter Schäfer, *Mirror of His Beauty: Feminine Images of God from the Bible to the Early Kabbalah* (Princeton: Princeton University Press, 2002), 229–35.

situations.[122] Through such gestures, Jews in the Byzantine world of the fifth, sixth, and seventh centuries deployed what had, by then, become distinctively Christian idioms of pilgrimage and sacred space to comment sardonically on the dynamics of imperial power, simultaneously drawing themselves into and distancing themselves from a whole universe of discursive practices that they shared with their Christian neighbors.

But we must bear in mind that this fusion of apologetic and polemical aims was as precarious as it was productive. By formulating Jewish religious and political aspirations in diametrical opposition to the discursive figure of "Rome," these writers in many ways permanently enshrined a particular understanding of Judaism's relationship with the emergent Christian empire. Jewish fortunes would forever be yoked within the Jewish imagination in counter-cyclical fashion to the historical rise and fall of Western Christendom.

[122] On the notions of "mimicry" and "ambivalence" as applied to the colonial context, see Bhabha, *Location of Culture*, esp. 121–31, and the helpful discussion of Bhabha's distinctive critical vocabulary within the broader field of postcolonial and subaltern studies in Robert J. C. Young, *Colonial Desire: Hybridity in Theory, Culture and Race* (London: Routledge, 1995), 159–66. But see also the important refinements to Bhabha's theoretical framework offered in Anne McClintock, *Imperial Leather: Race, Gender, and Sexuality in the Colonial Contest* (London: Routledge, 1995), 61–71.

# A Debate about the Rebuilding of the Temple in Sixth-Century Byzantium

YANNIS PAPADOYANNAKIS

> Because both the Jews and the majority of Christians claim this, that their city [i.e. Jerusalem] can be rebuilt and their temple can be erected and that they can celebrate the law and that 'had God not wanted to accept their sacrifices, He would not have enjoined Abraham to sacrifice' and [because] they say that 'Romans conquered us by force, they wished to put an end to our feasts and by taking away our city and everything'. We however keep everything to do with the Law and we [keep] the feasts and we sacrifice. Both the city and the temple must be restored and returned to us'. Because they boast these [things] and [because] the majority of our church agree with them, we beseech you to refute them extensively, and put them to shame by using a plethora of scriptural testimonies since in no way do they want to refrain from this hope. (*Dial.* IV 218, 1–11)[1]

Surprisingly, this text has escaped the notice of almost all scholars,[2] despite the considerable amount of work and attention devoted to the discussions among Christian thinkers about the potential, dangerous resumption of Jewish power in the late sixth-century Byzantine world.[3] The request outlined in the above excerpt may in fact preserve an original inquiry (or so the author wants us to believe) from the second half of the sixth century,

---

[1] The edition is by Rudolf Riedinger, ed., *Caesarii Dialogi quatuor. Die Erotapokriseis / pseudo-Kaisarios* (Berlin: Akademie-Verlag, 1989). All references will be to this edition.

[2] Absent from Heinz Schreckenberg, *Die christlichen Adversus-Judaeos-Texte und ihr literarisches und historisches Umfeld (1.–11. Jh.)* (Frankfurt am Main: P. Lang, 1990) and Andreas Külzer, *Disputationes graecae contra Iudaeos: Untersuchungen zur byzantinischen antijüdischen Dialogliteratur und ihrem Judenbild* (Stuttgart: B.G. Teubner, 1999). A passing mention in Vincent Déroche, "Iudaizantes," *Reallexikon für Antike und Christentum* 19:130–42, esp. 139.

[3] See Vincent Déroche, "La polémique anti-judaïque au VI$^e$ et au VII$^e$ siècle: un mémento inédit, les Képhalaia," *Travaux et Mémoires* 11 (1991): 275–311. For a review of the literature see Averil Cameron "Byzantines and Jews: Some Recent Work on Early Byzantium," *Byzantine and Modern Greek Studies* 20 (1996): 249–74. Also Vincent Déroche, "À propos des sources byzantines sur les Juifs," *Byzantinorossica* 3 (2005): 75–84.

which prompts the author, known to us as pseudo-Kaisarios,[4] to offer in turn a lengthy reply that requires him to delve into the past. The question posed by the inquirer, however, requires an answer that is not simply historical.

For both Jews and Christians, it is the past then that must be relied upon to provide not only a justification and legitimacy for the present but for the future as well.

To a significant degree the debate is: in what way and how much (or which aspects) of the past would be allowed to affect the present and, by implication, the future. Paradoxically, from the Christian point of view, when the issue is framed in this way, it is the Christians who must defend the old (in terms of what has already happened – the *status quo*), and the Jews who look for signs of the coming of a new age. For both (Jews and Christians), the city of Jerusalem and the Temple as both physical and textual entities, provided the central locus of a coherent religious, geographical, political and cultural thought world.

## The *Erotapokriseis* of pseudo-Kaisarios

But first a few words about the nature of the work from which this inquiry stems are in order. The *erotapokriseis*, otherwise known as dialogues, of pseudo-Kaisarios, is a collection of 218 questions and answers on the most diverse topics attributed pseudonymously to the brother of Gregory Nazianzen, Kaisarios in the fourth century. This collection of inquiries belongs to the question and answer literature (*erotapokriseis*).[5] As a literary form, *erotapokriseis* were particularly well-suited for instruction and refutation and this collection is no exception combining as it does both aims.[6]

---

[4] Rather than *Caesarius*, throughout the paper I have opted for the transliteration *Kaisarios* which is more faithful to the way that the author has transliterated the name in the Greek text.

[5] See Gustave Bardy, "La littérature patristique des 'Quaestiones et responsiones' sur l'Ecriture Sainte," *Revue biblique* 41 (1932): 210–36; 341–69; 515–37; 42, (1933): 14–30; 211–29; 328–52. Also Lorrenzo Perrone, "Il genere delle 'Quaestiones et responsiones' nella letteratura cristiana antica fino ad Agostino," in *"De diversis quaestionibus octoginta tribus", "De diversis quaestionibus ad simplicianum", di Agostino D'Ippona* (Rome, 1996), 11–44. For the most recent approach to this literature, see Annelie Volgers and Claudio Zamagni, eds., *Erotapokriseis: Early Christian Question- and- Answer Literature in Context* (Louvain: Peeters, 2004).

[6] See Averil Cameron, "Dispute Poems and Dialogues in the Ancient and Mediaeval Near East," in *Dispute Poems and Dialogues in the Ancient and Mediaeval Near East: Forms and Types of Literary Debates in Semitic and Related Literatures* (ed. G. J. Rei-

According to the preface, these questions were asked by seven persons and answered by Kaisarios in conversations over four consecutive days while he was teaching in Constantinople. The individual inquiries are not always ascribed to each of the seven persons mentioned in the title.

The painstaking scholarship of the editor of the work Rudolf Riedinger has shown that the text is an ambitious compilation composed perhaps in the monastery of the sleepless monks in Constantinople in the second half of the sixth century A.D.[7] The work is a text consciously constructed out of earlier texts, a compilation that draws on a large number of authors.[8]

Apart from the specific questions that the interlocutors are made to pose, they remain otherwise undeveloped *dramatis personae*. In fact, it is fair to assume that the anonymous author has blended his own concerns – but also other contemporary inquiries which were put to him – with those of the *dramatis personae* of his dialogues. As a result of this, the collection is a mixture of contemporary realities[9] and commonplaces combining polemic, didactic and apologetic purposes.

nink and H. L. J. Vanstiphout; Leuven: Peeters 1991), 91–108; eadem, "Texts as Weapons: Polemic in the Byzantine Dark Ages," in *Literacy and Power in the Ancient World* (ed. A. K. Bowman, G. Woolf; Cambridge, U.K.: Cambridge University Press, 1994), 198–215. For the didacticism and the catechetical dimension of these collections, see Yannis Papadoyannakis, "Instruction by Question and Answer in Late Antiquity: The Case of Late Antique and Byzantine Erotapokriseis," in *Greek Literature in Late Antiquity: Dynamism, Didacticism, Classicism* (ed. S. Johnson; Aldershot: Ashgate 2006), 91–105.

[7] Rudolf Riedinger, "Akoimeten," in *Theologische Realenzyklopädie* (ed. G. Krause and G. Müller; Berlin: de Gruyter, 1977–), 2:148–53.

[8] Almost exhaustively indexed by Rudolf Riedinger, *Pseudo-Kaisarios: Überlieferungsgeschichte und Verfasserfrage* (München: Beck, 1969) and in his edition *Caesarii Dialogi quatuor. Die Erotapokriseis / pseudo-Kaisarios* (Berlin: Akademie-Verlag, 1989).

[9] For the existence of reliable historical information on the Slavs in this collection see for example Florin Curta, *The Making of the Slavs: History and Archaeology of the Lower Danube Region, c. 500–700* (Cambridge, U.K. and New York: Cambridge University Press, 2001), 43–45, 85, 326, 348. The usefulness of such anti-Jewish literature as a historical source is also acknowledged by Averil Cameron who, when speaking of a text from the early seventh century, notes that: "Even so dry a literary genre as Christian/Jewish polemic may have a specific historical context, and even a few hints in literary sources are enough to suggest the ideological rivalries and religious questioning which centred round the Jewish Temple and the Temple Mount in Jerusalem in the early seventh century and the early Umayyad period," Averil Cameron, "The Trophies of Damascus: The Church, the Temple and Sacred Space," in *Le Temple lieu de conflit: actes du colloque de Cartigny 1991* (Université de Genève.; Centre d'étude du Proche-Orient ancien; Leuven: Editions Peeters, 1995), 203–12, esp. 212. On the historical value of the collections of *erotapokriseis* see also Déroche, "À propos des sources byzantines sur les Juifs," 78.

All four dialogues are punctuated by the interaction between a teacher and disciples (or more generally stated: between a person with authority to instruct and a circle of students). From the very beginning of the work the inquirers ask the teacher to provide them with sound instruction in various (disputed) topics of the Bible lest they are misled by fools (*mataiophrosin*). The inquirers seek both edification and a correlative strengthening of their belief.

In one of the longest responses to any inquiry in the text,[10] pseudo-Kaisarios, in response to the inquiry which opens this essay, is at pains to prove that prophets foretold the destruction of the Temple and Jerusalem with startling accuracy. At the same time he refers in some detail to the historical events which, when interpreted in the light of the situation he faced, proved that the Temple was not going to be rebuilt. In doing so he draws heavily on Chrysostom, particularly his homilies against the Jews.[11] The reader is steered through a carefully-compiled series of arguments, from prophecy as well as historical episodes such as the captivity in Egypt, the second captivity in Babylonia, the conquest by Antiochus Epiphanes and his desecration of the Temple, the destruction of Jerusalem by Titus, the Hadrianic ban on entering Jerusalem and the renaming of Jerusalem as Aelia Capitolina, and finally Julian's failed attempt to rebuild the Temple.[12] In short, the author gives a brief panorama of Jewish history focusing on the plight of the Jews. Throughout the response, he interjects mordant and vitriolic comments (and even poems) as the response changes its features mid-way, and turns from a response to an inquiry into a vehement attack in the form of a diatribe against the Jews.[13]

Previous scholarship has shown the existence of a steady stream of eschatological expectation among the Jews in the fourth and fifth centuries[14] and certainly after the time of pseudo-Kaisarios, at the beginning of

[10] *Dial.* IV 218, 12-907.

[11] John Chrysostom, *Discourses Against Judaizing Christians* (trans. P. W. Harkins; Washington, D.C.: Catholic University of America Press, 1979). For further remarks and revisions on the order of the manuscripts see Rudolf Brändle, Wendy Pradels, and Martin Heimgartner, "The Sequence and Dating of the Series of John Chrysostom's Eight Discourses Adversus Iudaeos," *Journal of Ancient Christianity* 6 (2002): 90–116.

[12] For the historical circumstances surrounding Chrysostom's homilies see Robert Louis Wilken, *John Chrysostom and the Jews: Rhetoric and Reality in the Late 4th Century* (Berkeley: University of California Press, 1983).

[13] *Dial.* IV 218, 729–907.

[14] For the eschatological expectations see Robert Louis Wilken, *The Land Called Holy: Palestine in Christian History and Thought* (New Haven: Yale University Press, 1992). Wolfram Kinzig, "Jewish and Judaizing Eschatologies in Jerome," in *Jewish Culture and Society Under the Christian Roman Empire* (ed. R. Kalmin and S. Schwartz; Leuven: Peeters, 2003), 409–29.

the seventh century.[15] During that time the capture of Jerusalem by the Persians and later by the Arabs provided the impetus for the Jews to reclaim the Temple Mount as the focus of their religious identity.[16] Earlier, in the middle of the sixth century, scholars have pointed out that it may have been Persian invasions which led to a feeling that Byzantium was losing its grip on the area. This fact, in combination with a general worsening of the state's oppression of the Jews,[17] may have in turn led to a rise in eschatological expectations at least in some Jewish quarters.[18]

Pseudo-Kaisarios knew all too well that "if appeal to historical events could validate religious claims, new events could invalidate those same claims."[19] Whatever the historical reality, what is at issue here is what it meant for the author to have Christian claims of dominance over Judaism challenged, and more importantly, how he sought to counter this challenge. Therefore, we cannot separate the "reality" of these Jewish claims about Jerusalem and the Temple from the views of the Christian authors: for this was a construct, in which for many generations, there had been a considerable investment.[20]

The Temple was significant not only because of what once happened there, but as a symbol of the Jewish observance of the Law even in those matters that had no relation to the Temple cult. To illustrate the centrality of the Temple for the Jewish cult throughout the centuries and to show how definitive a defeat for the Jewish people and their way of life its destruction would be, pseudo-Kaisarios employs the following image:

---

[15] Wout Jac Van Bekkum, "Jewish Messianic Expectations in the Age of Heraclius," in *The Reign of Heraclius (610-641): Crisis and Confrontation* (ed. G. J. Reinink and B. H. Stolte; Leuven: Peeters, 2002), 95–112.

[16] Cyril Mango, "The Temple Mount, A.D. 614–638," in *Bayt al-Maqdis: 'Abd al-Malik's Jerusalem* (ed. J. Raby and J. Johns; Oxford: Oxford University Press 1992), 1:1–16. Cameron, "The Trophies of Damascus," 203–12.

[17] See Nicholas de Lange, "Jews in the Age of Justinian," in *The Cambridge Companion to the Age of Justinian* (ed. M. Maas; Cambridge, U.K. and New York: Cambridge University Press, 2005), 401–26, esp. 418–20. Cameron, "The Trophies of Damascus," 206.

[18] Van Bekkum, "Jewish Messianic Expectations in the Age of Heraclius," 95–112. See also Mischa Meier, *Das andere Zeitalter Justinians: Kontingenzerfahrung und Kontingenzbewältigung im 6. Jahrhundert n. Chr.* (Göttingen: Vandenhoeck & Ruprecht, 2003), for the unrest 209–15, 668.

[19] Wilken, *John Chrysostom and the Jews*, 143.

[20] Francis E. Peters, *Jerusalem: The Holy City in the Eyes of Chroniclers, Visitors, Pilgrims, and Prophets from the Days of Abraham to the Beginnings of Modern Times* (Princeton: Princeton University Press, 1985). Yaron Z. Eliav, *God's Mountain: the Temple Mount in Time, Place, and Memory* (Baltimore: Johns Hopkins University Press, 2005), esp. 83–188.

> Just as a builder who has laid the foundations and has erected the walls [of an edifice] and has built a vaulted roof which is held together by a stone which the builders call keystone [*sphēn*],[21] once/when this stone is removed the whole edifice collapses, so did God provide the city [Jerusalem] as a link [keystone] of the cult, and He shook the foundation, putting an end to the entire religion, never to be restored again in the future by anybody. (*Dial.* IV 218, 183–188)

It is clear that the main point of the argument was that any observance of the Law was now illegitimate. Pseudo-Kaisarios proceeds to align what he interprets as God's will to punish the Jews in the Old Testament and the prophecies about the destruction of the Temple with Jesus's prophecy about the destruction of the Temple.[22] In the centuries prior to Pseudo-Kaisarios, this point had been of crucial importance since it was taken to be one of the signs of Jesus's prophetic charisma and, by implication, divinity.[23] Julian's failed attempt to rebuild the Temple in 363 C.E. had reinforced the historical application and interpretation of this prophecy in contrast to its original eschatological meaning.[24]

Thus, in the eyes of Christians, God appeared to continue to punish the Jews through Jesus's prophetic agency. This is why one of Julian's incentives for rebuilding the Temple was presumably his desire to disprove Jesus's prophecy about the definitive destruction of the Temple and thus to expose his lack of divinity.[25] For many Christians, then, it would seem that the ruined remains of the Temple served as a powerful theological argument from history against Judaism, as the very fulfillment of Jesus's prophecy. Indeed, it was the final act in a dramatic set of episodes which had consistently shown God's will to punish the Jews.[26] This is why many Christian authors before pseudo-Kaisarios had repeatedly sought to emphasize in their rhetoric the devastating defeat highlighted by the largely empty space that marked the remains of the Jewish Temple.

---

[21] Utto Riedinger, "ΣΦΗΝ = Gewölbeschlusstein. Ein Hapaxlegomenon in den Erotapokriseis des Pseudo-Kaisarios," in *Polychronion. Festschrift Franz Dölger zum 75. Geburtstag* (ed. P. Wirth; Heidelberg: C. Winter, 1966), 441–49.

[22] Matt 24:1–2.

[23] Martin Parmentier, "No Stone Upon Another? Reactions of Church Fathers Against the Emperor Julian's Attempt to Rebuild the Temple," in *The Centrality of Jerusalem: Historical Perspectives* (ed. M. Poorthuis, Ch. Safrai; Kampen: Kok Pharos, 1996), 143–59.

[24] ibid., 143–59.

[25] On this as well as a review of the different explanations that have been offered for Julian's motives see Robert J. Penella, "Emperor Julian, the Temple of Jerusalem and the God of the Jews," *Koinonia* 23 (1999), 15–31, esp. 24.

[26] Heinz-Martin Döpp, *Die Deutung der Zerstörung Jerusalems und des Zweiten Tempels im Jahre 70 in den ersten drei Jahrhunderten n. Chr.* (Tübingen: Francke, 1998).

Throughout his response, pseudo-Kaisarios presses into service a number of prophets (Isaiah, Jeremiah, Malachi, Daniel) as well as Jesus's prediction of the destruction of the Temple. As a result, there is a dense clustering of prophecies. These are intertwined with the report of the historical events which they are said to have predicted and foretold.

By marshalling and carefully interlacing prophetic verses about tribulation and suffering with historical events, pseudo-Kaisarios is able to portray the defeat and humiliation of the Jews throughout their history, from the Egyptian and Babylonian captivity to the most recent events such as their defeats at the hands of the Romans as well as Julian's later failed attempt to rebuild the Temple.

For pseudo-Kaisarios it was not enough to show that this pattern of repeated defeats had recurred in the past and was therefore limited only to the past. "To prove this, I am not going to refer either to Isaiah or Jeremiah's prophecies," he says, "lest you think that I am using prophets whose prophecies have already been fulfilled."[27] All the miserable prophecies of destruction, pseudo-Kaisarios insists, continue for the Jews to this day. They apply to the Jews for now and always. To back this latter claim he presses into service Malachi:

> I will not accept an offering from your hands. For from the rising of the sun to its setting my name is great among the nations, and in every place incense is offered to my name, and a pure offering, for my name is great among the nations, says the Lord of hosts. But you profane it. (Mal 1:11)[28]

This prophecy has been fulfilled and applies to the present, says pseudo-Kaisarios.[29] The debate then is as much about the past meaning of these prophecies as it is about elucidating their meaning for the present.

## Julian

The latest historical episode, with the most lasting impact which – according to pseudo-Kaisarios – sealed the fate of any attempt to rebuild the Temple, was Julian's failed effort.[30] Pseudo-Kaisarios dwells on this epi-

---

[27] *Dial.* IV 218, 651–654.

[28] *Dial.* IV, 218, 657-661. Translation from New Revised Standard Edition of the Oxford Bible.

[29] *Dial.* IV 218, 659–662.

[30] On this see Johannes Hahn, "Kaiser Julian und ein dritter Tempel? Idee, Wirklichkeit und Wirkung eines gescheiterten Projektes," in *Zerstörungen des Jerusalemer Tempels: Geschehen –Wahrnehmung- Bewältigung* (ed. J. Hahn; Tübingen: Mohr Siebeck, 2002), 237–62. For a collection of the testimonies and a discussion of the

sode and is keen to flesh out the theological and historical implications so as to get his message across unambiguously.

As in other parts of his reply, here too pseudo-Kaisarios's interpretation of the event relies on Chrysostom's version, which he excerpts heavily,[31] supplementing it with twists and emphases of his own. He presents it as the most "recent" development whose impact continued into his own lifetime. As with the rest of his account, here too pseudo-Kaisarios seeks to establish a recurring pattern whereby the history of destruction and punishment repeats itself in every stage of Jewish history. To make things worse, pseudo-Kaisarios adds the accusation of deicide (also in Chrysostom) in order to claim that any prophetic charisma left among the Jews was extinguished on account of this act.[32]

Yet this emphasis on the constant defeat of the Jews, their divine punishment, and their tribulations disguised very thinly, perhaps, a Christian fear of Jewish resurgence or at least of a (Jewish) past that was not yet fully transcended. Beneath the alluring confidence with which pseudo-Kaisarios stakes out his claims, there remained a deep concern with the Temple and the city of Jerusalem.

"In the Christian capital of Jerusalem, there would always be something foreign (or alien) about the past. There would always (so the Christian feared) be Jews lurking in the shadows, waiting to sneak in and reassert their treacherous hold on the city."[33] The full weight and force of this perception was to become apparent a few decades later in the Christian accounts of the allegedly treacherous role of the Jews in the fall of Jerusalem to the Persians (614) and then to the Arabs (634).[34] It has been stressed

evidence see David B. Levenson, "Julian's Attempt to Rebuild the Temple: An Inventory of Ancient and Medieval Sources," in *Of Scribes and Scrolls: Studies on the Hebrew Bible, Intertestamental Judaism, and Christian Origins* (ed. H. W. Attridge, J. J. Collins, T. H. Tobin; New York: University Press of America, 1990), 261–79; idem, "The Ancient and Medieval Sources for the Emperor Julian's Attempt to Rebuild the Jerusalem Temple," *Journal for the Study of Judaism in the Persian, Hellenistic, and Roman Periods* 35 (2004): 409–60. See also Fergus Millar, "Rebuilding the Jerusalem Temple: Pagan, Jewish and Christian Conceptions," *Viestnik Drevnei Istorii (Journal of Ancient History)* 1 (264) (2008): 19–37.

[31] See also Adolf Martin Ritter "Erwägungen zum Antisemitismus in der alten Kirche. Joannes [sic] Chrysostomos, 'Acht Reden wider die Juden'," in *Bleibendes im Wandel der Kirchengeschichte: kirchenhistorische Studien* (ed. B. Moeller, G. Ruhbach; Tübingen: Mohr, 1973), 71–91.

[32] *Dial.* IV 218, 601.

[33] Andrew S. Jacobs, *Remains of the Jews: The Holy Land and Christian Empire in Late Antiquity* (Stanford, Calif.: Stanford University Press, 2004), 158.

[34] Averil Cameron, "Blaming the Jews: The Seventh-Century Invasions of Palestine in Context," in *Mélanges Gilbert Dagron* (ed. V. Déroche; Travaux et Mémoires 14; 2002),

that it was "the awareness and fear of this resistance that run through Christian attempts to reconstruct the Jew as eternally conquered and defeated."[35]

In the period between Constantine and Justinian, both the city of Jerusalem (and the Temple) became focal points for the creation of a transformed religious and cultural identity.[36] As Christianity sought to articulate its own identity, fifth- and sixth-century Christians "continued to invest the site (and the city) primarily with a sense of Jewish failure and resistance to Christian truth"[37] which went hand in hand with an appropriation of Jerusalem by the Christians and its transformation into a Christian city.

We should therefore not underestimate how reassuring a psychological effect for sixth-century Christians it was, that Jews were seen to be reconquered, and re-mastered. For this reason the Jews are conjured up by pseudo-Kaisarios to suffer defeat and humiliation over and over again.

Pseudo-Kaisarios's approach to the Jewish and Christian past then is conditioned by the need to refute an alleged challenge and provide scriptural testimonies for that refutation. This involved engagement with and interpretive rearrangement of the older Christian exegetical and apologetic traditions, and a sustained rethinking of the Christian past in the light of the present. In this he was not alone. The bulk of anti-Jewish literature that grew significantly during the sixth and seventh centuries is an indication of an intensification of the debates among Christians regarding the position of Judaism in a Christian empire.[38]

---

57–78; eadem, "The Trophies of Damascus," 203–12. Günter Stemberger, "Jerusalem in the Early Seventh Century: Hopes and Aspirations of Christians and Jews," in *Jerusalem: Its Sanctity and Centrality to Judaism, Christianity, and Islam* (ed. L. I. Levine; New York: Continuum, 1999), 260–72.

[35] Jacobs, *Remains of the Jews*, 192.

[36] This continuous hold of the Temple on Christian imagination emerges forcefully in the case of the building of Hagia Sophia. As presented in the sources, the building of the Hagia Sophia is cast as a competition between the emperor Justinian and Solomon. On this see Johannes Koder, "Justinians Sieg über Salomon," in *Thymiama: stē mnēmē tēs Laskarinas Boura* (Athēna: Mouseio Benakē, 1994), 1:135–42. (I thank Manolis Papoutsakis for this reference). While the Temple had become an object of emulation early in Christian tradition (see Robert Osterhout, "The Temple, the Sepulchre and the *Martyrion* of the Savior," *Gesta* 29 [1990]: 44–53) it seems to have acquired a significant weight during the sixth and seventh centuries. On this see Jonathan Bardill, "A New Temple for Byzantium: Anicia Juliana, King Solomon and the Gilded Ceiling in the Church of St Polyeuktos in Constantinople," in *Social and Political Life in Late Antiquity* (ed. W. Bowden, A. Gutteridge and C. Machado; Leiden: Brill, 2006), 339–70.

[37] Jacobs, *Remains of the Jews*, 141.

[38] Déroche, "La polémique anti-judaïque au VIe et au VIIe siècle," 275–311. Pieter van der Horst, "Twenty-Five Questions to Corner the Jews: A Byzantine Anti-Jewish

## Conclusion

The Temple and Jerusalem were not static entities consigned to the distant past, but persistently active and heavily charged symbols in the Christian present of the sixth century. What the case of pseudo-Kaisarios illustrates is the complex relationship between physical place, text and the past in the formation of religious opinion. It highlights not only the ways in which Christians attempted to come to terms with and incorporate an alien past into their (own) present, but also the ways in which they attempted to make it work for them.[39] Pseudo-Kaisarios's treatment is important for what it can tell us about the notion of tradition as well. By drawing on Christian apologetic traditions (most notably Chrysostom) on the importance of the Temple and Jerusalem, and by adjusting and adapting pre-existing arguments to his own time and fashioning them into paradigmatic proofs in the debate about the validity of Jewish cult, the restoration of the Temple and Jerusalem, Pseudo-Kaisarios re-shapes tradition. It is through the reworking of older identity-affirming Christian traditions that pseudo-Kaisarios sought to meet new needs and challenges as they emerged from an untranscended past in antiquity.

---

Document From the Seventh Century," in *Things Revealed: Studies in Early Jewish and Christian Literature in Honor of Michael E. Stone* (ed. E. G. Chazon, D. Satran and R. A. Clements; Leiden and Boston: Brill, 2004), 289–301. See the also the comments in the review article Cameron, "Byzantines and Jews," 249–74.

[39] On this process see Averil Cameron, "Remaking the Past," in *Late Antiquity: A Guide to the Postclassical World* (ed. G. W. Bowersock et al.; Cambridge, Mass.: Belknap Press of Harvard University Press, 1999), 1–20.

# Helena's Bridle and the Chariot of Ethiopia

G. W. BOWERSOCK

The Kingdom of Ethiopia became a Christian nation in the fourth century of our era. If the precise date of its conversion from polytheism cannot be determined, there can be little doubt that the reign of Constantius II in the middle of the century provides the correct time-frame. Athanasius reported in his apology to Constantius that the emperor had sent Frumentius to Aksum to establish Christian churches. Ezana (Greek Aezanas),[1] the Ethiopian king at this time, can be observed, on his inscriptions and coins, as both pagan and Christian – first as son of the invincible Ares (the Greek equivalent of the Ethiopic god Maḥrem), and subsequently as the humble servant of Christ. The conversion is played out before our eyes on magnificent steles with texts in two languages, Greek and Ge'ez, inscribed in three scripts – Greek, Ethiopic, and Sabaic (South Arabian).[2] Sumptuous gold coins similarly proclaim Ezana both as a pagan *negus*, as the Ethiopian king was called, and later as a Christian one.[3] Like his inscriptions, his coins display two languages, although only unvocalized Ethiopic conveys the Ge'ez.

[1] Athanasius, *Apologia ad Constantium* 31.

[2] For Ezana before his conversion, see E. Bernand, A. J. Drewes, and R. Schneider, eds., *Recueil des Inscriptions de l'Éthiopie des périodes pré-axoumite et axoumite*, (Paris: Diffusion de Boccard, 1991), vol. 1 "Les Documents," no. 185, pp. 241–45 with Ge'ez (unvocalized) and Sabaic texts; for the Greek text on the other side of the same stele see no. 270, pp. 363–67; [images in vol. 2 "Les Planches," plates 99–101 (for no. 185) and plate 179 (for no. 270)]. Similarly, no. 185bis, pp. 246–50, inscribed on the two faces as well as one side, with Ge'ez (unvocalized) and Sabaic, plus Greek on the same stele, which is no. 270bis, pp. 367–70. Nos. 187 and 188 are written in vocalized Ethiopic letters from the time of Ezana's paganism (Maḥrem is mentioned), and no. 189 is a vocalized text of the Christian Ezana. For the bilingual of Ezana as a Christian, see no. 190, pp. 268–71, a text in Ge'ez written in a form of Sabaic script from right-to-left (unlike Ethiopic). The Greek text on the same stele is no. 271, pp. 370–72 [images on plates 124–28 (for no. 190) and 181 (for no. 271)].

[3] Stuart Munro-Hay, *Catalogue of the Aksumite Coins in the British Museum* (London: British Museum Press, 1999), 31–32.

No one now believes that the Ezana documents represent two or more people of the same name.[4] With what is now available, such an idea is completely untenable. The Greek numismatic legend, *bisi Alene* (βισι Αλενε), gives the tribal affiliation of the pagan Ezana – a man of Ḥalen. (βισι is a transliteration of *be'sī*, the Ge'ez word for man.) The Greek coin legend reproduces the designation *be'eseya ḥalen* in the vocalized Ge'ez inscriptions of both the pagan and Christian Ezana, and it turns up again in Greek as βισι Αληνε on the Greek-Ge'ez bilingual inscription of the Christian Ezana. There can be no doubt that we are dealing with one and the same *negus*.

Frumentius' mission to Aksum was a reflection of the increasing power of Ethiopia after the collapse and conquest of the Nubian kingdom of Kush centered at Meroë. The end of Nubian power came towards the end of the third century. It clearly coincided with increasingly aggressive and imperialistic conduct on the part of the Ethiopians to the south. Their ambitions not only extended northwards into Kush but eastwards across the strait at the southern end of the Red Sea into South Arabia and the territory of the Himyarites. It was just as the Meroitic kingdom was coming to an end that the first Ethiopian coins were struck. These were handsome pieces, designed for export and propaganda, in gold and silver as well as bronze,[5] and the Aksumite coinage, which continued from that time until the mid seventh century, constituted an anomaly in ancient sub-Saharan Africa. It was clearly meant to put Ethiopia into the main stream of late antiquity. The more than twenty holders of the title *negus* maintained Greek along with Ge'ez on their coins.

This was a Christian monarchy that took itself seriously. Accordingly, when the Himyarite Arabs, who had been converted to Judaism, undertook a persecution of Christians in Najran, it was the Ethiopian *negus*, Ella Asbeha known as Kālēb, who, with the support of Justin I in Constanti-

[4] For an excellent discussion of the issues before 1981, when inscriptions nos. 185bis and 270bis were discovered (cf. n. 2 above), see Albrecht Dihle, "Frumentios und Ezana" in his *Umstrittene Daten* (Cologne: Westdeutscher Verlag, 1965), 36–64.

[5] Munro-Hay, *Catalogue*, 27–30. Textual sources are admirably assembled in T. Eide, et al., eds., *Fontes Historiae Nubiorum III: From the First to the Sixth century AD* (Bergen: University of Bergen, 1998). For the collapse of the Meroitic kingdom in Nubia, see William Y. Adams, *Nubia. Corridor to Africa* (Princeton: Penguin and Princeton, 1977, repr. 1984), 382–90. For the rise of Ethiopia, A. H. M. Jones and Elizabeth Monroe, *A History of Ethiopia* (Oxford: Clarendon Press, 1935; original title *A History of Abyssinia*) is still serviceable, as is Edward Ullendorff, *Ethiopia and the Bible*, The Schweich Lectures of the British Academy (London: Press, 1968).

nople, went to war against the Jewish Arabs.[6] Like his great predecessor, Ezana, Kālēb left behind an impressive epigraphical and numismatic record of his achievements, which included eloquent professions of his Christian faith. He even left a memorial of his victory in South Arabia in a surviving inscription at Marib that can be seen today in the Museum at Sana'a. In that text, beautifully inscribed in the vocalized Ethiopic alphabet, Kālēb recounted what God had done for him, and he invoked the glory of David (*kebra dāwit*).[7]

The reference to the House of David provides contemporary testimony for what is undoubtedly the most important item in the ancient history of Christian Ethiopia. That, somewhat paradoxically, is its claim to direct descent from the Jews through the Queen of Sheba. Ethiopian tradition identified the Queen of Sheba with the queen Kandake mentioned in a famous encounter of St. Philip in the Acts of the Apostles, and the tradition maintained that King Solomon had a son with this composite queen. That son, Menelik, was the founder of the Ethiopian dynasty. His story is told, along with much else, in the Holy Book of Ethiopia, the *Kebra Nagast* ("The Glory of Kings").[8]

This extraordinary book survives in a classical Ge'ez text from the fourteenth century, but a colophon at the end states that it had been translated from an Arabic version that was itself a translation from Coptic. No one knows whether there was an original Ethiopic text in Ge'ez, but there can be little doubt that the *Kebra Nagast* conserves much authentic material from late antiquity. Already thirty years ago Irfan Shahid insisted on a sixth-century date for at least some of the historical information in the work, in particular the account of Kālēb's war against the Jewish Arabs as

[6] See the exhaustive review of current documentation in Christian-Julien Robin, "Himyar et Israël," *Comptes-Rendus de l'Académie des Inscriptions et Belles-Lettres* (2004): 831–906. Cf. G. W. Bowersock, "The Ḥaḍramawt between Persia and Byzantium," in *La Persia e Bisanzio* (Rome: Accademia dei Lincei, 2004), 263–73.

[7] Bernand et al., *Recueil des Inscriptions de l'Éthiopie*, vol. 1., no. 195, with the words cited from stone 2, line 24. For images see plates 143–44 in vol. 2.

[8] For the meeting of Philip with Kandake's eunuch, see Acts of the Apostles 8:27. The Ethiopic text of the *Kebra Nagast* may be found in Carl Bezold, *Kebra Nagast. Die Herrlichkeit der Könige*, Abhandlungen der I Kl. der Kön. Akad. d. Wissensch. 23, Bd. I (Munich: G. Franz, 1905). This remains the only edition of the original text. It is accompanied by a scrupulous German translation. Cf. translations by E. A. Wallis Budge, *The Queen of Sheba and Her Only Son Menyelek* (London: M. Hopkinson, 1922) – a version that is often cited with greater confidence than it deserves – and by Gérard Colin, *La Gloire des Rois (Kebra Nagast), Épopée nationale de l'Éthiopie* (Geneva, 2002). Colin's is a straightforward translation with minimal annotation, but the references to biblical allusions are helpful in the absence of any publication of D. A. Hubbard, "The Literary Sources of the Kebra Nagast," (Ph.D. diss., St. Andrews University, 1956).

well as the assignment of Chalcedonianism to the reign of Marcian.[9] Overall the book is designed to establish the Solomonic origins of Ethiopian kingship and the rightness of those monophysite doctrines that put the *negus* in direct competition with the king of Rum, in other words the king of the Greeks who resided in Constantinople. Since the opposition of the *negus* to the Byzantine emperor is so important in the *Kebra Nagast*, it is all the more significant that the author was well aware that the two rulers made common cause together for a brief moment, in the 520s, in the action against their common enemy, the Jews of South Arabia.[10]

The symbolic centerpiece of Ethiopian identity was nothing less than the ark of the covenant, which the *Kebra Nagast* reported to have been removed from Jerusalem in the days of Solomon by means of a magic chariot that flew through the air at supersonic speed. The ark itself formed, and still forms, a central part of the Ethiopian liturgy, and the chariot remained in Aksum. But in the final pages of the *Kebra Nagast*, Gregory Thaumaturgus, who functions as an interlocutor with the Ethiopian bishops, addresses apocalyptic matters. For it was said that the ark would be returned to Jerusalem when Christ reappeared there, and every Ethiopian Christian knew that the psalmist had foretold, in Psalm 68:31, "Ethiopia shall stretch out her hands unto God."

In this context, two of the last chapters of the *Kebra Nagast* (113 and 116) consider the prospects of two holy objects at the time of Christ's return and the dissolution of the earthly empire. One of these objects is something called the "subduer of the enemy of the king of Rum."[11] It is kept in Rome, that is – Constantinople, and possesses a supernatural power that evidently keeps the Persians at bay. It is a horse's bridle,[12] which Constantine's Helena is alleged to have had made out of the nails from the crucifixion. She had the nails melted down and made into a mystic bridle which would be taken away from the Byzantine kings when they perverted their faith. The Persians would then make war on Rum. Marcian is named as the one who would start the perversion. This is clearly a reference on the part of the Ethiopian monophysite writer to the Chalcedonians in Constantinople. In his *vaticinium ex eventu* Gregory Thaumaturgus predicts that the Persian king will take away the bridle with its horse, but the horse

[9] Irfân Shahîd, "The *Kebra Nagast* in the Light of Recent Research," *Le Muséon* 89 (1976), 133–78. Alessandro Bausi has recently criticized Shahîd's argument as unnecessary because the historical details in the *Kebra Nagast* ultimately derived from the Ethiopic version of the Martyrium of Arethas: A. Bausi, A. Gorsi eds., *Tradizioni orientali del Martirio di Areta* (Florence: University of Florence, 2006), 106 with n. 35.

[10] *Kebra Nagast* 117.

[11] *magrarē ḍar la-negūsa rōm*.

[12] *leguām*.

will go into the sea and die. The nails on the bridle will glitter in the water until Christ comes in glory.

Many scholars have supposed reasonably that the bridle story here is connected somehow with the legend of the True Cross. Jerome acknowledges that Helena was reported to have discovered the nails from the crucifixion, but he is disinclined to credit a story he had heard – that Constantine had made a bridle for his own horse out of one nail and a diadem out of another. Nevertheless, Ambrose had not hesitated to proclaim this story in his speech on the death of Theodosius, and it was repeated in essentially the same form by all the main Byzantine ecclesiastical historians.[13]

That traditional legend of a bridle for Constantine's horse is utterly different from the *Kebra Nagast* version, which has a character all its own. Here it was Helena herself who caused the nails she brought back (not just one of them) to be melted down and fashioned into a bridle. The object was made not for Constantine's horse, but rather to serve as a mystic indicator of the beginning of the end, with the onslaught of the enemy and the coming of Christ.

The other holy object has a similar apocalyptic role. The bishops in the *Kebra Nagast* say to Gregory in chapter 116, "You have spoken to us about the subduer of the enemy of Rum. Now tell us about the chariot of Ethiopia. Will it remain down to the coming of Christ, as you said Sion (i.e. the ark) and the Ethiopian faith would?" The ark, which was known in Ethiopia as Sion, would go back to Jerusalem, and Ethiopian faith would remain unshaken to that moment. But, the bishops want to know, will the chariot stay once the world begins to come apart?

Wallis Budge, in his often cited translation of the *Kebra Nagast*, rendered what follows at this point as, "It shall assuredly not disappear." But Bezold, who had already published the still standard edition of the Ethiopic text, translated, quite correctly, "Nein, er wird verschwinden!", and the new French version of Colin reads, "Non, il est destiné à disparaître."[14] It is precisely at this point that Gregory brings up the Jews in Najran and foretells, in the next chapter (117), the ultimate annihilation of the entire Jewish people. Budge misunderstood what was going on here, as well as the actual meaning of the Ge'ez: *'albô halawô yesawwar*. The chariot, like

---

[13] See Jerome, *Commentary on Zachariah* 14.20: (Migne) PL 25.1540, where Jerome mocks the story of Constantine's making a bridle for his horse out of one of the nails. The story is repeated in Ambrose, *De Obitu Theodosii* 47, ed. O. Faller, CSEL 73 (Vienna: Hölder-Pichler-Tempsky, 1955), 396, and in the *HE* of Rufinus (2.8), Socrates (1.17.9), Sozomen (2.1.9), and Theodoret (1.18.5).

[14] For the renderings of Bezold, Budge, and Colin, see the references in n. 8 above.

Helena's bridle, will go when the end is at hand. It will not remain after Christ appears and the psalmist's Ethiopian stretches out his hands to God. Those two objects serve to give signs of what is to come.

The apocalyptic of the *Kebra Nagast* turns out to have an important parallel in west Syrian apocalyptic of the seventh century, for which David's verse in Psalm 68 had no less importance than for the Ethiopians. When the west Syrian and Ethiopic traditions are brought into conjunction the prophecies of Gregory Thaumaturgus in the *Kebra Nagast* suddenly acquire unexpected clarity. A *vaticinium ex eventu*, falsely ascribed to the fourth-century Bishop Methodius from Patara or Lycian Olympus, evokes the cross of Christ's crucifixion as "the sign which will be seen prior to the Advent of our Lord". At the end of time it will appear on Golgotha and be raised up to heaven from there. And at that moment, according to this text, an Ethiopian will hand over all power to God in accordance with the psalm.[15] Sebastian Brock has plausibly dated the apocalypse of Pseudo-Methodius to the late seventh century (ca. 691) on the basis of its references to the Arab presence in the region for some seventy years.[16] The apocalypse anticipates the removal of all sovereignty and power as the King of the Greeks gives up his soul to his creator.[17] This is obviously the Byzantine emperor, or, as he is sometimes called, the King of the Romans.

The treatise of Pseudo-Methodius is a confection that draws upon Mesopotamian literature such as the Alexander Legend, the Julian Romance, and the so-called Syrian Treasure Cave. It displays a curious preoccupation with the Ethiopic royal family and, in a bizarre genealogical excursus, demonstrates that the mother of Alexander the Great was the daughter of the King of Ethiopia, and that she subsequently married Buz, the eponym of Byzantium. One of their offspring married Romulus.[18] All this is evidently designed to explain why Ethiopia should be involved at the end of days after the imagined defeat of the Arabs. The Byzantine Empire, which

[15] G. J. Reinink, *Die syrische Apokalypse des Pseudo-Methodius*, an edition of the Syriac text with German translation in two volumes: CSCO, vols. 540–541, Scriptores Syri 220–221 (Louvain: E. Peeters, 1993), 14.4–5, (p. 44 in the Syriac, p. 73 in the German translation). Cf. Sebastian Brock, Robert Hoyland and Andrew Palmer, eds., *The Seventh Century in the West-Syrian Chronicles* (Liverpool: Liverpool University Press, 1993). On pp. 222–42, Sebastian Brock has provided translation, notes, and bibliography for an extract from Pseudo-Methodius.

[16] For Brock's comments, see Brock, Hoyland and Palmer, eds., *Seventh Century*, 225. See also the unpublished dissertation of F. J. Martinez, *Eastern Christian Apocalyptic in the Early Muslim Period: Pseudo-Methodius and Pseudo-Athanasius* (Ph.D. Diss., Catholic University of America, 1985), 30–31, for a date of 688/9.

[17] Pseudo-Methodius 14.6.

[18] Pseudo-Methodius 9 (note the mention of Romulus in 9.4 and 9.6).

was known at the time as the empire of the Romans as well as of the Greeks, thus had Ethiopian roots.

In elaborating on the Ethiopian connection Pseudo-Methodius explicitly refers to Christians who had believed that the reference in the Psalms referred to a role for the king of Ethiopia. They were wrong, according to the writer, but it is of the greatest importance that they existed at all.[19] Pseudo-Methodius gives us a glimpse into a much more central role for the *negus* than mere genealogical fabrication would allow. A hint of this role may be seen in Pseudo-Methodius' own prophecy that the King of the Greeks (*malkā d-yawnāyē*, ܡܠܟܐ ܕܝܘܢܝܐ) would rise up against the sons of Ishmael in anger and "would set forth from the Sea of the Kushites (the Ethiopians) and bring the sword and destruction into the desert of Yathrib (the name for Medina)".[20] Here the King of the Greeks, though clearly the leader of the Byzantine Empire, can only be the *negus*, launching a campaign from Aksum across the Red Sea.

The Ethiopic allusions in Pseudo-Methodius are dramatically enhanced in a remarkable fragment of a treatise written in Edessa very soon afterwards – within a year or two, it seems – as a revision of the apocalypse of Pseudo-Methodius.[21] The author of this fragment clearly distinguishes the Byzantines, whom he calls Romans (*rhūmāyē*, ܪܗܘܡܝܐ), from the Greeks (*yawnāyē*, ܝܘܢܝܐ), whose king will hand over his kingdom to God. And here at last we find the full story of Helena's bridle. It is said to have been forged not only from the nails that were in the hands of Jesus but also from the nails in the hands of one of the thieves – clearly the one whom Jesus said he would see in paradise. The text goes on to say, "They cast [the nails] in the fire all together and forged a bridle-bit (*pgūdā*, ܦܓܘܕܐ), that is – a bridle (*lgāmā*, ܠܓܡܐ), which they hung in a church. When a horse that has never been ridden and never even been fitted with a bridle puts its head on its own into that bridle, then the Romans [the Byzantines] will know that the kingdom of the Christians has come."[22]

The final moment in Jerusalem is similar to Pseudo-Methodius but a little more detailed: "Then the king of the Greeks will enter Jerusalem, climb up to Golgotha, where our Savior was crucified...This king of the Greeks shall be descended from Kushyat, daughter of Kushyat, of the kings of

[19] Pseudo-Methodius 9.7.

[20] Pseudo-Methodius 13.11.

[21] G. J. Reinink, "Der edessenische 'Pseudo-Methodius'", *Byzantinische Zeitschrift* 83 (1990), 31–45. The fragment is translated by Brock *apud* Brock, Hoyland and Palmer, eds., *Seventh Century*, and is re-edited in Martinez, *Eastern Christian Apocalyptic*.

[22] *Edessene fragment* folio 99r, Martinez, *Eastern Christian Apocalyptic*, 223. Cf. the Syriac *lgāmā* here with Ethiopic *leguām* in the *Kebra Nagast* (n. 12 above).

Kush [Ethiopia]."[23] Here we have the conjunction of an Ethiopian king of the Greeks with a much fuller explanation of the bridle, one that coheres perfectly with the account in the *Kebra Nagast*. Contact between Edessa and Aksum is unavoidable. By this period the Ethiopian monarchy appears to have come to an end, at least in the grandiose form of past centuries. The coinage stops completely about 640,[24] but presumably the Ethiopian claim, as mentioned by Pseudo-Methodius and documented in the Edessa fragment, continued in Mesopotamia for decades afterwards. So we must now ask why an Edessene Christian in the late seventh century would have not only have had access to this Ethiopian tradition but why he might have accepted it.

The answer, in a word, is monophysitism. The sources of the *Kebra Nagast* explicitly trace the perversion of the faith in Constantinople to Chalcedon in the fifth century and the emperor Marcian. From that time onwards the *negus* could lay claim to being the defender of the true faith. It may be suggested that this is exactly what he did. He and the Ethiopians expected that he would assume the leadership of Christianity and thus become the king of the Greeks, and his claims must have been disseminated throughout monophysite communities in Mesopotamia and Syria. In Aksum, the Ethiopians had the ark of the covenant which they could place in opposition to the True Cross at Constantinople. In the apocalyptic moment of dissolution when the ark would return to Jerusalem the *negus* could have confidence in the psalm of David that put him at the forefront stretching out his hands to God.

The Ethiopian claim to the kingship of monophysite Greeks from the days of Marcian, who is explicitly named as a perverter of the faith in the *Kebra Nagast*,[25] can be confirmed by Aksumite coins of the mid-fifth century, when the fateful council was held at Chalcedon. A *negus*, unknown to any surviving literary texts, coined in gold, silver, and bronze, with the epithet "victor" attached to his name in Ge'ez (*mawāʾī*) and a legend, again in Ge'ez, "In this cross (*masqal*) you will conquer (*temawe'*)," or on other specimens "In this cross conquer."[26] There cannot be the slightest doubt, as the late Stuart Munro-Hay recognized in his catalogue of the Aksumite coinage, that this is an evocation of the famous phrase attached to the revelation of Constantine at the Milvian Bridge (ἐν τούτῳ νικᾷς, *in hoc signo vinces*). The vocalization of the king's name is

---

[23] *Edessene fragment* folio 103r (*ad fin.*) – folio 103v (*ad init.*), Martinez, *Eastern Christian Apocalyptic*, 226.

[24] See Munro-Hay, *Catalogue*, 41.

[25] *Kebra Nagast* 113: *marqeyānōs 'elwa hāymānōt.*

[26] Munro-Hay, *Catalogue*, 36.

uncertain since it is found on the coins only in unvocalized letters (MḤDYS). The claim of MḤDYS to being an Ethiopian Constantine is incontestible.

A newly published gold coin of this king adds to the previously published dossier of his claim.[27] It is a most unusual piece, with a full-length portrait of the *negus* on the obverse and a full-length figure of Nike/Victoria, holding a long processional cross, on the reverse. The Ge'ez legends of "victor" and "In this cross you will conquer" both appear along with the king's name. Munro-Hay, who published the coin, observed that there are close parallels to the Victory figure in fifth-century imperial coinage, and the closest from the reign of Marcian.[28] He therefore proposed to date MḤDYS to about 450. Since the *Kebra Nagast* is explicit about the perversion of the faith at Constantinople under Marcian (or, in another chapter, 130 years after Constantine[29]), the claim of MḤDYS to be another Constantine would seem manifestly designed to assert the leadership of the "orthodox," who are, in both Ge'ez and Syriac, the monophysites.

The Constantinian character of MḤDYS' coinage is reinforced in other ways too. The epithet "victor" is attached to his name as unvocalized MW', but, as indicated, it clearly represents *mawā'ī*. This too evokes Constantine, whose titulature is well documented on inscriptions as *maximus victor*, or in some instances *victoriosissimus*.[30] Beyond this we should look to the royal name itself. Since no tribal affiliation is given for MḤDYS, we might suspect that he has added a significant name to his given name, much as Ella Asbeha a century later took the biblical name Kālēb. The root of MḤDYS' name is ḥ-d-s, which means "to restore" or "to renew." The Ethiopic adjective for new is ḥadīs, and hence the royal name would mean "the restorer." It was as *restitutor* that Constantine was hailed in his lifetime: *restitutor libertatis* and even *restitutor generis humani*.[31] The Ethiopian monarchy in the mid-fifth century knew exactly what it was doing in laying claim to restoration of the true faith after the supposed betrayal at Chalcedon.

---

[27] Stuart Munro-Hay, "A New Gold Coin of King MḤDYS of Aksum," *Numismatic Chronicle* 155 (1995), 275–77.

[28] Cf. R. A. G. Carson, C. H. V. Sutherland, eds., *The Roman Imperial Coinage*, vol. 10 (London: Spink and Son, 1994), 386–87, 505 (Marcian).

[29] *Kebra Nagast* 93.

[30] For the titulature of Constantine, see the convenient register in *Inscriptiones Latinae Selectae* (*ILS*) 3.1, 307–9. For *victoriosissimus*, *ILS* 723. On Constantinian victory titles, Timothy D. Barnes, *The New Empire of Diocletian and Constantine* (Cambridge Mass.: Harvard University Press, 1982), 27.

[31] *ILS* 691–692.

The role for the *negus* of Ethiopia among the monophysites fits perfectly with possession of the ark of the covenant ("Sion") as a relic of the kingdom's ancient origins in Jerusalem. The ark was Aksum's answer to the True Cross in Constantinople, and the Edessa fragment explicitly says that the Cross will be taken away before the King of the Greeks stretches out his hands to God. It also says explicitly that the King is none other than an Ethiopian. Pseudo-Methodius recognized, as we have seen, that Christians had made this identification, even though he insisted that the King of the Greeks had to be the Byzantine emperor. But the Edessa fragment gives us an apocalyptic grounded in Ethiopian antiquity precisely as it is presented in the *Kebra Nagast*. It documents, as never before, the close link between Mesopotamia and Ethiopia, or – put more generally – the link that united monophysite Christianity.

The reality of the Kingdom of Ethiopia was, of course, quite different at the end of the seventh century, and some monophysites at that time would not have shared Pseudo-Methodius' hostility to the Arabs, whom they saw as potential liberators from the Chalcedonians. The author of the Edessa fragment is no less fierce in his condemnation of the oppression of those he calls the sons of Hagar.[32] But what is conspicuously conserved in this text, and, through Alexander's alleged Ethiopian mother in Pseudo-Methodius, is an earlier tradition of monophysite support for the claim of the Ethiopian *negus* to be a post-Chalcedonian Constantine. The biblical past had been compounded with the more recent past. If monophysites had looked favorably upon Muhammad, not all necessarily approved of those who succeeded him. In 692 or 693 a western Syrian could still dream of an Ethiopian king of the Greeks in Jerusalem at the end of the world. By contrast, the Jews of Mesopotamia, who would have known through the Christians the apocalyptic role of the *negus*, could draw from Ethiopia's mythical origins in Israel and its possession of the ark some hope that the Arab invaders, as fellow Semites, might protect them.[33]

---

[32] *Edessene fragment* folio 98r, Martinez, *Eastern Christian Apocalyptic*, 222 (ܒܢܝ ܗܓܪ).

[33] My colleague Patricia Crone pointed out to me that in the period between the end of the Ethiopian coinage in the seventh century and the Syriac apocalyptics discussed here a Shi'ite fanatic in Kufa, al-Mukhtār (died 687), who presented himself as the Mahdi's vizier, took to parading a new ark of the covenant (تابوت) around town (Patricia Crone, *Medieval Islamic Political Thought* [Edinburgh: Edinburgh University Press, 2004] 78). This would certainly suggest some contamination with traditions of Ethiopic Christianity, and possibly a wild effort to take over its leadership in the eyes of South Arabian Jews, with whom al-Mukhtār appears to have cultivated relations. The Armenian history by Sebeos mentions (ch. 30) that a group of Jews from precisely Edessa tried to enlist the support of Arabs across the desert against the Byzantines under Heraclius. As Peter

Helena's miraculous bridle, forged from the nails of two crosses at Golgotha, was suspended in a church at Constantinople, called Rome in the Edessa fragment, to await the untamed horse that would voluntarily put its head into it on the last day. This object, with the ark, comprised Ethiopia's answer to the True Cross and just as the Cross was to disappear before the coming of Christ the bridle would fall into the sea and gleam beneath the waters. According to the *Kebra Nagast*, the Chariot of Ethiopia that brought the ark so long ago from Jerusalem would disappear as well. The ark would be returned from Aksum and with it an Ethiopian king would come as the king of the Greeks to stretch forth his hands, as the psalmist had sung, unto God.

This was the monophysite vision of the end, created from Ethiopia's tradition of its own distant past and, at the same time, proclaiming Ethiopian claims to leadership in late antiquity. The *negus*, as a new Constantine, kept the faith and guarded the ark. It should be said, parenthetically, that it is inconceivable that the *negus* actually stood, nearly naked, on top of the ark to receive a Byzantine ambassador in about 530, as Irfan Shahîd once suggested on the basis of a misunderstood passage in Malalas.[34] The presence of Ethiopia's magic chariot in Aksum was visible and numinous proof of the kingdom's origins, and as such it, and its surrogates, played (and still play) an important part in the Ethiopian liturgy.

Helena's magic bridle, hanging in a church in Constantinople, played a similar role in Ethiopian belief. The Persians took away the True Cross for a time, but the Byzantines eventually recovered it. So it was clear, to Ethiopian eyes, that the Persian theft had not introduced the end of the world. Of course it had not, because no horse had submitted to the far more potent trophy that Helena had fashioned from the nails she had brought from Jerusalem. In this tradition the *negus* continued victorious.[35]

---

Brown suggested to me, this too could be a response to Ethiopic claims as they were known in Edessa in the seventh century.

[34] Shahîd, "The Kebra Nagast," 156, with reference to Malalas, pp. 457–58 (Bonn). For the scene described there, see L. Oeconomos, "Remarques sur trois passages de trois historiens grecs du Moyen Age," *Byzantion* 20 (1950), 177–83, with an explanation of that passage in Malalas, on the *negus*' reception of the Byzantine ambassador, ca. 530.

[35] I am deeply indebted to Peter Brown, Patricia Crone, and Christopher Jones for comment on this paper.

# The Ancient Near East in the Late Antique Near East

## Syriac Christian Appropriation of the Biblical East

ADAM H. BECKER

In the summer of 2005 I had a friendly but persistent disagreement, while staying in south eastern Turkey at Deyr-ul-Zafaran, the Syrian Orthodox monastery just outside the city of Mardin, which also serves as the see for the archbishop of the Mardin diocese, a region which is both a literal and a spiritual homeland for many of the Syrian Orthodox (or West Syrians, as they are also known).[1] For several days I had spoken only a pigeon English-Turkish and it was a great pleasure when someone with a familiar – Boston! – accent approached me and started speaking. My interlocutor turned out to be a scholar like myself, but one of Syriac Christian descent, in fact, the author of two books on Assyrians, that is, East Syrians or "Nestorian" Christians, in America.[2] Appropriate to the interests of this essay, his name was Sargon, a third generation Assyrian American whose family comes in part from Kharput, near modern Elaziğ in south eastern Turkey. Our disagreement was over an issue that understandably angers some Syriac Christians.[3]

---

[1] They are also known inaccurately as "Monophysites." For a discussion of the numerous names used for the various churches that identify with the Syriac tradition, see John Joseph, *The Modern Assyrians of the Middle East: Encounters with Western Christian Missions, Archaeologists, and Colonial Powers* (Leiden: Brill, 2000), 1–32. I would like to thank the editors for their work on both the colloquium and this volume. Sargon Donabed was kind and patient enough to read the manuscript and provide numerous useful comments. I dedicate this article to Bridget M. Purcell as a small recompense for the inspiration she has provided in other, more significant matters.

[2] Sargon Donabed, *Remnants of Heroes: The Assyrian Experience: The Continuity of the Assyrian Heritage from Kharput to New England* (Skokie, Ill.: Assyrian Academic Society Press, 2004). See also Sargon Donabed and Ninos Donabed, *Assyrians of Eastern Massachusetts* (Portsmouth, N.H.: Arcadia, 2006).

[3] I use the term "Syriac Christian" here for Christians from all the churches that identify with the Syriac linguistic, cultural, and ecclesiastical traditions. It serves as a form of short hand and I do not use it as a definitive appellation somehow essential to the identity of the communities addressed here. In other words, I am aware of the political definitional problems that arise from using such a term, especially one that has been employed as an outsider term until recently.

It is a commonplace to find in books and articles on the history of Syriac Christianity, especially those published by either ecclesiastical or nationalist-ethnic organizations, claims about the ancient pedigree of the Syriac peoples. Related to these claims is an easy slippage in contemporary discussions between the use of diverse ethnic terms, such as Syriac, Aramaic, Assyrian, and Syrian.[4] For example, the website of the Assyrian International News Agency divides the long history of the "Assyrian people" in the following manner.[5]

1. Emergence: beginnings to 2400 B.C.
2. First Golden Age: 2400 B.C. to 612 B.C.
3. First Dark Age: 612 B.C. to 33 A.D.
4. Second Golden Age: 33 A.D. to 1300 A.D.
5. Second Dark Age: 1300 A.D. to 1918 A.D.
6. Diaspora: 1918 A.D. to the present

The website provides a detailed explanation of what constitutes each of these periods. The "First Golden Age" is the period of the *floruit* of ancient Assyrian culture. "This period would see 1800 years of Assyrian hegemony over Mesopotamia, beginning with Sargon of Akkad in 2371 B.C. and ending with the tragic fall of Nineveh in 612 B.C."[6] The "First Dark Age" ends with the crucifixion and resurrection of Christ, traditionally placed at 33 C.E. The "Second Golden Age" includes the period of the growth of the Syriac Christian communities as well as the centuries of their greatest literary production. This period came to an end, according to this account, due to the ongoing economic oppression of Christians by Arabs as well as the Mongol invasion of the late thirteenth century. This led to the "Second Dark Age" which itself ended with the nadir of the Assyrian genocide, concomitant with the more well known Armenian Genocide, and the subsequent Assyrian global diaspora. Strikingly, according to this account, the different Assyrian communities only in the later period began to define themselves by church affiliation. Before this they were rather an ethnic community.

The continuity between ancient Assyria and the Christian communities from Mesopotamia known as Assyrian is constituted in a number of ways. For example, Assyrians today celebrate the Akitu festival, the ancient

---

[4] On the development of the term "Assyrian," see Wolfhart Heinrichs, "The Modern Assyrians – Name and Nation," in *Semitica: Serta philologica Constantino Tseretli dicata*, (ed. R. Contini, Fabrizio Pennacchietti and Mauro Tosco; Torino: Silvio Zamorani, 1993), 99–114.

[5] "Brief History of Assyrians," [cited 13 August 2006]. Online: http://www.aina.org/aol/peter/brief.htm.

[6] Ibid.

Assyrian new year celebration, in the same way that Kurds, Iranians, and some central asian Turkic peoples continue to celebrate Norouz, the ancient Persian new year festival. Some modern celebrants of the Akitu infuse the event with contemporary notions of ancient Assyria, wearing toga-like costumes in imitation of modern reconstructions of ancient dress. Similarly, some modern Assyrian church architecture specifically imitates modern reconstructions of ancient Assyrian architecture,[7] while ancient Assyrian iconography has been reproduced in nationalist literature and webpages, often with the Assyrian national flag superimposed on it. Furthermore, academic articles are published making arguments for racial and cultural continuity.[8] The most significant connector between the past and the present is the name "Assyrian" itself, which facilitates these socio-historical conflations.

My immediate response to many of these claims of continuity is: hogwash. As others have pointed out, Western missionaries to the region in the nineteenth century introduced the idea that the indigenous Christians were an ancient race, or the remains of Nineveh, to steal from the title of A. H. Layard's book on the archeology of the region which also makes such suggestions.[9] Syriac Christians were equated by European travelers, missionaries, and diplomats, with the lost tribes of Israel, the last of the ancient Assyrians, and, since they used the same language as Jesus, the oldest Christian churches in the world.[10] These modern ideas about the special continuity between the Syriac present and the ancient world were then taken up by Syriac Christians and must be understood as a modern invention worthy of the study of a Benedict Anderson or an Eric Hobsbawm rather than an ancient historian.[11]

---

[7] See Alison Salvesen, "The Legacy of Babylon and Nineveh in Aramaic Sources," in *The Legacy of Mesopotamia* (ed. S. Dalley, et al.; Oxford: Oxford University Press, 1998), 157 for a similar comment.

[8] See, for example, the paper of the Assyriologist Simo Parpola, "Assyrian Identity in Ancient Times and Today," n.p. [cited Oct. 19, 2006]. Online: www.aina.org/articles/assyrianidentity.pdf.

[9] Austen Henry Layard, *Nineveh and its Remains: With an Account of a Visit to the Chaldæan Christians of Kurdistan, and the Yezidis, or Devil Worshippers; and an Inquiry into the Manners and Arts of the Ancient Assyrians* (2 vols.; London: J. Murray, 1848–1849).

[10] See for example Asahel Grant, *The Nestorians or The Lost Tribes* (New York: Harper, 1841); Henry Holme, *The Oldest Christian Church, Supplying the Missing Link of Centuries. A Historic Revelation from the Assyrian Mountains of Adiabene, the Gozan of Scripture* (London: Marshall Brothers, 1896[?]); and W. A. Wigram, *The Assyrians and Their Neighbours* (London: G. Bell, 1929).

[11] For the development of modern Assyrian identity and nationalism, see H. L. Murre-van den Berg, "A Syrian Awakening: Alqosh and Urmia as Centres of Neo-Syriac Writ-

At one point in my conversation with Sargon he referred me to the Episcopalian missionary Horatio Southgate's "Narrative of a Visit to the Syrian (Jacobite) Church of Mesopotamia" from 1844.

> I observed that the Armenians did not know them under the name which I used, *Syriani*; but called them ASSOURI, which struck me the more at the moment from its resemblance to our English name *Assyrians*, from whom they claim their origin, being sons, as they say, of Assour, (Asshur,) who 'out of the land of Shinar went forth, and builded [*sic.*] Nineveh, and the city Rehoboth, and Calah, and Resin between Nineveh and Calah: the same is a great city.'[12]

This passage appears on a website that lists references to the Assyrians as a continuously existing people up to the present.[13] Clearly some modern Assyrians feel threatened and are publishing testimonia lists online. The point we are supposed to take from the Southgate evidence is this: the Assyrians were called Assyrians before the Europeans came – thus the claims about ancient origins are true and the Assyrians have always been Assyrians. There are other instances of this and the issue is in part one of semantics: "Assyrian" was a term that Aramaic-speaking Christians employed to refer to themselves for centuries, but does this make them Assyrian? I would like to present a compromise position, one lying between the radical discontinuities I tend to focus on as a historian and the continuities my interlocutor Sargon was arguing for.

This compromise position would not please some Assyrian nationalists – such as the author of the timeline I cited above – and it in fact maintains the position that a large part of Assyrian self-understanding is dependent on Western sources. However, the difference is that this positioning vis-à-

---

ing," in *Symposium Syriacum VII*, (ed. René Lavenant; Orientalia Christiana Analecta 256; Rome, 1998), 499–515; idem, "The Church of the East in the Sixteenth to the Eighteenth Century: World Church or Ethnic Community?" in *Redefining Christian Identity: Cultural Interaction in the Middle East since the Rise of Islam* (ed. J.J. van Ginkel, H.L. Murre-van den Berg and T.M. van Lint; Leuven: Peeters, 2005), 301–320; Robert William De Kelaita, "On the Road to Nineveh: A Brief History of Assyrian Nationalism 1892-1990," *Journal of the Assyrian Academic Society* 8.1 (1994): 6–30.

[12] Horatio Southgate, *Narrative of a Visit to the Syrian (Jacobite) Church of Mesopotamia: With Statements and Reflections upon the Present State of Christianity in Turkey, and the Character and Prospects of the Eastern Churches* (New York: Dana and Company, 1856; repr., Piscataway, N.J.: Georgias Press, 2003), 80.

[13] "Assyrians from the Fall of Nineveh to the Present," [cited 19 August 2006]. Online: http://www.christiansofiraq.com/facts.html. We also find at this site among other references a passage from the *Chronicle* of Michael the Syrian, the West-Syrian Patriarch (1126–1199), in which he comments on the connections between ancient Near Eastern kings and Syriac Christians. For this text, see J. B. Chabot, ed., *Chronique de Michel le Syrien, Patriarche Jacobite d'Antioche, 1166–1199* (Paris: Leroux, 1899–1904), appendix II, 748–51 (p. 750 is quoted on this webpage).

vis an Occidental Other does not find its origin in the nineteenth century, but rather in the sixth century and even before. Syriac Christians lived on the margins of the noisy and prolific Christian cultures of the Roman Empire and, despite the aspersions they often cast on things Greek, commonly took their self-understanding from texts and ideas coming from the West. Moreover, those Syriac Christians who lived in the Sasanian Empire further identified with the East as they found a place for themselves within that realm. Elsewhere, I have addressed what has been referred to as the "Egyptianization" of Syriac Christianity.[14] This entailed the disappearance of the indigenous pre-monastic tradition of celibacy, while the "influx of western monasticism, and more specifically western monastic texts, effected a rewriting of monastic history, thus obfuscating the origins of Syriac Christianity and early Syriac monasticism."[15] This "Egyptianization" of East-Syrian monasticism from the sixth century onward culminates in the very late Mar Awgen (St. Eugenios) tradition, which holds that monasticism was brought to Mesopotamia by an Egyptian monk.[16] A similar process can be seen in the appropriation of the works of Evagrius of Pontus (d. 399) and the later Alexandrian Neoplatonic commentary tradition on Aristotle's logical works to articulate in a more technical manner ideas that can be found in the works of the fourth-century Syriac poet Ephrem the Syrian.[17]

I would suggest that, to a much lesser degree and in a different manner, there was also an "Assyrianization" of Syriac culture particularly from the sixth century onwards. By "Assyrianization" I mean the process whereby Syriac-speaking Christians in Mesopotamia employed the Assyria they found in the Bible as well as in Greek sources translated into Syriac as a model for understanding themselves and their place in the world.[18] I emphasize that this was only a tendency, one that showed itself at certain times in response to specific conditions. The biblical Assyria shows up in a number of Syriac sources and serves as a paradigm for understanding

[14] Adam H. Becker, *Fear of God and the Beginning of Wisdom: The School of Nisibis and the Development of Scholastic Culture in Late Antique Mesopotamia* (Philadelphia: University of Pennsylvania Press, 2006), 172–75.

[15] Ibid., 173.

[16] J.-M. Fiey, "Aones, Awun et Awgin (Eugène). Aux origines du monachisme mésopotamien," *Analecta Bollandiana* 80 (1962): 52–81.

[17] Becker, *Fear of God*, 150–53.

[18] See comments at Sebastian P. Brock, "Christians in the Sasanian Empire: A Case of Divided Loyalties," *Studies in Church History* 18 (1982): 18–19 (repr. as ch. VI in *Syriac Perspectives on Late Antiquity* [London: Variorum, 1984]). A similar argument may be found in John Joseph, "The Bible and the Assyrians: It Kept Their Memory Alive," *Journal of the Assyrian Academic Society* 12.1 (1998): 70–76.

events as diverse as saints' lives and the Arab conquest.[19] A tendency to auto-orientalize appears in some of the earliest of eastern Christian sources: for example, the second century Tatian's strong self-identification as a *barbaros* Assyrian vis-à-vis the Greek tradition.[20] (With this it is worth noting Drijvers' elevation of Tatian to central but forgotten importance in earliest Syriac Christianity.[21]) This process was facilitated by the continuing use of the geographical name Assyria or Asorestan in Middle Persian in the Sasanian era. This issue of auto-orientalizing is perhaps best exemplified in a pre-Christian mosaic from Edessa: it is not clear if the figure in a mosaic from c. 200 simply reflects Orpheus as he was often depicted in classical art with his Phrygian cap or whether his turban-like headwear in this context may have been read as simply local flavor.[22] This seems to be an instance of easterners depicting something as eastern.

The process I am addressing can be divided into two parts: One, the spatial, temporal, and cultural localizing of their church and its history within an East described within scripture and, two, a tendency to treat Christians within that space-time-culture complex as a people or a nation, especially one descended from the scriptural nation of Assyrians. A corollary to this ethno-geographic localization via the biblical text is the appropriation of Biblical Israelite "people" language, something commonly done by Jews and Christians at different points in history.[23] This corollary finds it fullest development in the much later tradition of the "lost tribe." Also related to these tendencies is the notion that Syriac is the original language, the one God spoke when he created the world.[24]

---

[19] For the latter see Amir Harrak, "*Ah! The Assyrian is the Rod of My Hand!*: Syriac View of History after the Advent of Islam," in *Redefining Christian Identity: Cultural Interaction in the Middle East since the Rise of Islam* (ed. J. J. Van Ginkel, H. L. Murre-Van den Berg, T. M. Van Lint; Orientalia Lovaniensia Analecta 134; Louvain: Peeters, 2005), 45–65.

[20] Tatian, *Oratio ad Graecos and Fragments* (ed. and trans. M. Whittaker; Oxford: Clarendon Press, 1982), 1.1–2.17.

[21] E.g., Han J. W. Drijvers, "East of Antioch. Forces and Structures in the Development of Early Syriac Theology," in *East of Antioch: Studies in Early Syriac Christianity* (London: Variorum Reprints, 1984), ch. I.

[22] J. F. Healey, "A New Syriac Mosaic Inscription," *Journal of Semitic Studies* 51 (2006): 313–27. Note what looks like a phrygian cap in mosaics depicting locals, H. J. W. Drijvers and J. F. Healey, eds., *The Old Syriac Inscriptions of Edessa and Osrhoene: Texts, Translations, and Commentary* (Leiden: Brill, 1999), Am 2 and 4a.

[23] E.g., Anthony D. Smith, *Chosen Peoples: Sacred Sources of National Identity* (New York: Oxford University Press, 2003), esp. 66–94.

[24] Milka Rubin, "The Language of Creation or the Primordial Language: A Case of Cultural Polemics in Antiquity," *Journal of Jewish Studies* 49 (1998): 306–33, esp. 322–28.

In addressing "Assyrianization" I am not referring to the actual reception of ancient near eastern culture, such as vocabulary, dialogue and dispute poems, and wisdom traditions such as those of Ahiqar.[25] I am interested, rather, in evidence that is more difficult to interpret. For example, the references to ancient near eastern Gods in some of the Syriac sources, especially those in the transitional period of the fourth through sixth centuries, reflect both the remnants of extremely old cults but also a Christian re-imagining of these cults. With regard to pre-Christian religion in the sources it is difficult to draw a line between the reflection of reality and the plain fantasy of idolatry.[26]

One Eastern Syriac text that exemplifies a number of these issues is the *History of Karkha d-Beth Slokh and the Martyrs therein.*[27] Karkha d-Beth Slokh was the capital of the ancient province of Beth Garmai and is today the modern city of Kirkuk, which since the American invasion of Iraq in 2003 has become a center of violent contestation between Sunni Arabs and Kurds. The *History* attests to a striking local Christian civic pride. We find something similar earlier in the Syriac sources in an effort on the part of Christians in Edessa to link their city to Jesus and the apostles. Such an effort is apparent in the Abgar tradition,[28] the related story of the *mandylion*,[29] the Thomas tradition of the city, which included the maintenance of the apostle's supposed remains in an eponymous church,[30] and in literary texts, such as Jacob of Sarug's homily on Edessa and Jerusalem.[31] The *History* consists of three parts: [32] the ancient history of the city, the origins of Christianity and the persecution under Shapur II in the fourth century, and more recent persecutions under Yazdegard II in 445. The ancient history of the city includes the story of its foundation by "Sardana," son of

[25] E.g., Salvesen, "Legacy of Babylon," 139–61. However, pp. 157–58 briefly address "Syriac Views of the Assyrians".

[26] An example of this problem can be found in Jacob of Serug's *Memra on the Fall of the Idols*, Jacob of Sarug, *Homiliae selectae* (ed. P. Bedjan; Paris and Leipzig: O. Harrassowitz, 1905–1910) III.795–823.

[27] *Acta martyrum et sanctorum syriace* (ed. P. Bedjan; 7 vols.; Paris and Leipzig, 1890–1897; repr. Hildesheim, Germany: O. Harrassowitz, 1968), II:507–35.

[28] E.g., Sebastian P. Brock, "Eusebius and Syriac Christianity," in *Eusebius, Christianity and Judaism* (ed. H. W. Attridge and G. Hata; New York: Brill, 1992), 212–34.

[29] Han J. W. Drijvers, "The Image of Edessa in the Syriac Tradition," and Averil Cameron, "The Mandylion and Byzantine Iconoclasm," both in *The Holy Face and the Paradox of Representation* (ed. H. L. Kessler and G. Wolf; Bologna: Nuova Alfa 1998), 13–31 and 33–54 respectively.

[30] J. B. Segal, *Edessa, "The Blessed City"* (Oxford: Clarendon Press, 1970), 175–76.

[31] Jacob of Sarug, *Homiliae selectae*, V.731–47

[32] The text is fully summarized in J.-M. Fiey, "Vers la réhabilitation de l'Histoire de Karka d'Bét Slōh," *Analecta Bollandiana* 82 (1964): 189–222.

"Sanherib," its enlargement under the Achaemenid ruler Darius I, and its transformation under the Hellenistic king, Seleucus I. The text begins:

> The king of Assyria, whose name in Syriac was Sardana, established the foundations of this great city. This king was great and feared in the whole world and his kingdom was one of the three of the inhabited (earth). This Sardana was the son of Sanherib, who was the thirty-second in line to (or: of the thirty-two kings since) Balos, the first king of the Assyrians. In the days of this Sardana Jonah was sent by God to Nineveh, this man who by his prophecy and preaching moved the Ninevites. Sardana submitted to the preaching of the prophet and proclaimed a fast for the Ninevites. They put on sackcloth. God saw their penitence, as it is written, and he turned the heat of his wrath from them and he did not destroy them. In the fifteenth year of that son of Nimrod, Arbak, the king of Media, showed forth rebellion against the kingdom of the Assyrians, to which he was subject.[33]

The name "Balos" suggests that this text ultimately relies on a Greek source, since it reflects the Greek "Belos," cognate with the Hebrew "Ba'al," "Belos" being commonly referred to euhemeristically as the first king of Assyria, even as Dido's father in the *Aeneid*.[34]

Sardana, son of Sanherib, seems to be the seventh century B.C.E. Esarhaddon, son of Sennacherib.[35] The name may come from the Greek "Asordan." However, Sardana is also reminiscent of "Sardanapalus," the Assyrian monarch described in the *Persica* of Ctesias of Cnidos as a sybarite who died when he set his court on fire after a two-year siege by the Medes.[36] This figure was taken up as exemplary of Oriental decadence in the eponymous play by Byron and Delacroix's *Death of Sardanapalus*. There is confusion in the manuscript of the *History* in that this Sardana is also referred to as Sargon. This is Sargon II, the father of Sennacherib, who destroyed the northern kingdom of Samaria. The Peshitta version of this name is attested as in use from the seventh century onward among Christians. For example, the father of John of Damascus was named Sargon.[37] Furthermore, Sardanapalus is often equated with Ashurbanipal, the son of Esarhaddon. In any case, the Sardana described here is neither a sacker of cities nor a slave to a life of luxury. Rather, this eastern king is described as a pious ruler who built the city of Karkha d-Beth Slokh as a

[33] *Acta martyrum et sanctorum syriace* (ed. P. Bedjan), II:507.

[34] Virgil, *Aeneid* I.621, 729.

[35] 2 Kgs 19:37; Isa 37:38. His father laid siege to Jerusalem in 701 B.C.E., while he ruled 681–669.

[36] Felix Jacoby, ed., *Die Fragmente der griechischen Historiker* (Leiden: Brill, 1995), III.C.F 1.23–28.

[37] Isa 20:1. Frederick A. Aprim, *Assyrians: The Continuous Saga* (Philadelphia: XLibris, 2004), 210–12 and the plaque reproduced on p. 213.

defense against Arbak the Mede.[38] Their struggle is covered in the East-Syrian commentary tradition, but Karkha d-Beth Slokh is never mentioned by the commentators.

After a relatively detailed description of the building projects of Darius and Seleucus in the city, the text describes how the city was converted to Christianity by Mar Addai and Mar Mari, two mythical apostles who are responsible in Syriac tradition, especially in the later period, for the conversion of Mesopotamia.[39] The first person they convert is a Joseph, after whom, according to the text, the Monastery of the Followers (or, House) of Joseph (*dayrā d-bēyt Yawseph*) is named (although the modern site is associated with Joseph the husband of Mary).[40] Christianity flourishes in the city until the heresy of Mani begins to spread under Shapur I (d. 272).[41] Much of the rest of the text consists of descriptions of the various persecutions against the Christian community orchestrated by Manichean heretics and especially by the Sasanian authorities, and the development of cult sites around the locations of persecution under the guidance of the city's various bishops. There is often an extremely local feel in these descriptions: the author refers to places that the audience must have known, for example, "the church which Tuqrete built is the one which John the diligent pastor and distinguished priest rebuilt there."[42] There is the "place of the fig tree" where a series of martyrdoms occurred and now special devo-

[38] This story appears elsewhere, e.g., Išo'dad of Merv, *Commentaire sur l'Ancient Testament* (ed. J.-M. Vosté et C. van den Eynde; Corpus Scriptorum Christianorum Orientalium 126–186 [passim]; Louvain: L. Durbecq, 1950–1981), IV: Isaiah and the Twelve, 94 (120). For Sardanapalus as the last king and Belus as the first, see, e.g., in the *Chronicle to 724* (ed. E. W. Brooks; *Chronica Minora II* (Corpus Scriptorum Christianorum Orientalium 3/3: Louvain: Secrétariat du CorpusSCO, 1904), 84 (versio: Corpus Scriptorum Christianorum Orientalium 4/4, 68). This tradition derives from Greek sources.

[39] See the two main texts concerning these figures: George Howard, trans., *The Teaching of Addai* (Chico, Calif.: Scholars Press, 1981) and Amir Harrak, trans., *The Acts of Mār Mārī the Apostle* (Atlanta: Society of Biblical Literature, 2005). The liturgy is also attributed to them.

[40] J.-M. Fiey, *L'Assyrie Chrétienne: Contribution a l'etude de histoire et de la géographie ecclésiastiques et monastiques du nord de l'Iraq* (3 vols.; Beirut: Imprimerie Catholique, 1967–1969), III.49–50.

[41] The chronology of the text is clearly confused. It seems to set the second-century Roman Emperor Hadrian and a persecution of Christians which occurred under him after the time of third-century heresiarch, Mani (*Acta martyrum et sanctorum syriace* [ed. P. Bedjan], II:512).

[42] *Acta martyrum et sanctorum syriace* (ed. P. Bedjan), II:513.

tions are offered.[43] And we are told that bishop Isaac "was stoned on a hill which is above the Kenar village, which is by the Neqator inn."[44]

In this text, the bishops of the city are like the rulers of the past, Sardana, Darius, and Seleucus, and just as its ancient structures were founded by these rulers, so its bishops laid the foundations for its holy places after

[43] "There was persecution in the city not only by murder but also robbery of possessions, imprisonments, and bitter tortures, with the result that even women, female covenanters, who were known for their virginity, who had come from the capital city (lit. city of the kingdom) due to the persecution which had begun against the church and were abiding in our city – they were slandered before the Paygān Salār (Sasanian official) by some Manicheans who were in the city. That accursed beast ordered that they be killed outside the city in that place called 'The White Poplar.' After the crowning of these holy (or: consecrated) women, in the place where they were crowned a fig tree sprouted up from their blood. It was as a remedy for whoever fled to it for succour. But the Manicheans when they saw the miracle which was done cut down that fig tree and burned that spot with fire. Then God, who does not allow those who love him to be spurned by enemies, gave power over them to the pain of the lion which torments them until they came to an end and were done away with from the city. That spot in which the holy women proved glorious is named the place of the figtree until today. Now a place of refuge is made there for all believers and from year to year whenever they complete the remembrance of the great day of crucifixion and go up to the great place of the martyrs (or: martyrion), as is the custom of the city, the whole ecclesiastical crowd, the pastor and the flock in all its orders, a cross at the front and before them, they turn off to the place of the figtree in a great pomp with praises and holy songs (?) of thanksgiving, which are fit for God, the Lord of all, as a shame to the infidels (lit. deniers) and a pride for the believers, and upon us sinners mercy, pity, and salvation, amen." *Acta martyrum et sanctorum syriace* (ed. P. Bedjan), II:513–14; translation from Sebastian P. Brock and Susan Ashbrook Harvey, eds., *Holy Women of the Syrian Orient* [Berkeley: University of California Press, 1998], 77–78). "Tahmizgard went up to the place which is called the place of the figtree, there where the martyrs were killed in the days of King Shapur, and he sat on the seat of judgment and he arranged before the crowds all vessels of torture of every sort and he said to them, 'Yazdgard the king commands thus: if you do not listen to his kingship and his commands and you do not do his will and you do not worship the great God, the sun, and you do not honor fire and water, the children of Hormizd, your lives will be finished on account of this (lit. in these things).' Along with tortures there were with them also sixteen elephants which they brought that they might crush all of those who would not deny the Messiah. The blessed Isaac then took the torture implements and kissed them. He placed them upon his eyes and said, 'Greetings (lit. peace) to these irons by which we will enter that palace of the lofty kingdom and enjoy the habitations (lit: huts, booths) of light which were prepared for us by our Lord the Messiah from before the foundations of the world.'" *Acta martyrum et sanctorum syriace* (ed. P. Bedjan), II:522–23. The text describes "the place of figtree" as: "the second holy Mt. Sinai, the place of the divine presence (*škīntā*), the habitation of light which celebrates the treasure of the bones of the holy ones." *Acta martyrum et sanctorum syriace* (ed. P. Bedjan), II:532

[44] The name "Neqator," derives from Nicator, which was the epithet of Seleucus I.

each persecution. In contrast, the Sasanians are distant kings whose only involvement in civic life is their occasional persecution of Christians.[45]

An important link between the hoary antiquity of the city and its more recent Christian history is the figure of Jonah, who appears at the beginning of the text. While the original biblical book of Jonah attests a tendency toward universalism inasmuch as the God of the whole world enjoins the hero to prophesy to "pagan" Gentiles, in this context Jonah functions as a link to a particular, local past. Furthermore, Jonah links the story to other developments in the same region in the sixth and seventh century. As Alison Salvesen has pointed out, it is probably not a coincidence that it was the bishop of Karkha d-Beth Slokh who introduced the so-called Fast of the Ninevites into the East-Syrian liturgy in the late sixth century.[46] Sabrisho', the bishop of the city who instituted this fast was acting like the righteous king Sardana who listened to the prophet Jonah.[47] The Fast of the Ninevites entails special portions within both the West and East Syrian liturgies, including the *Ba'utha d'Ninewe*, rhythmical prayers attributed to St. Ephrem. In Nineveh itself there was a monastery of Jonah which later became the Mosque of Nabi Yunis in Mosul.[48] It is important to emphasize that Nineveh was called *Nineveh* by Syriac Christians in Late Antiquity. In fact, the city was the main Sasanian settlement in the area and became more significant in the late Sasanian period, under Khusraw II (d. 628).[49] Its bishops are attested for the sixth and seventh centuries, but it continued to be occupied until much later.[50] Now it is simply part of the larger city of Mosul, an Arab garrison town on the other side of the Tigris in an area that

---

[45] Patricia Crone and Michael Cook, *Hagarism: The Making of the Islamic World* (New York: Cambridge University Press, 1977), 57 sees this focus on Assyria as "a chauvinist assertion of a provincial identity"; however, this is fit into a larger argument about provincial contrariness, an argument which seems to reflect contemporary European speculation about colonial subjects rather than the historical subjectivity of Christians in Mesopotamia.

[46] Fiey, *L'Assyrie Chrétienne* II:20; II:498. See the Rogation of the Ninevites in Arthur John MacLean, trans., *East Syrian Daily Offices* (London: Rivington, Percival & Co., 1894), 226–28, or S. Y. H. Jammo, *The Rogation of Nineveh: A Compilation of Penitential Texts, Translated to Modern Chaldean* (Troy, Mich.: St. Joseph Chaldean Church, 1992). See, for example, the discussion of this liturgical innovation during the time of plague in *Histoire Nestorienne (Chronique de Séert)* ed. A. Scher, *Patrologia Orientalis* 13:4 (1907–1918):II 633 (313).

[47] See Jonah 3:5: "And the people of Nineveh believed God; they proclaimed a fast, and everyone, great and small, put on sackcloth." Cf. Jonah 3:5–10.

[48] Fiey, *L'Assyrie Chrétienne* II:493.

[49] Chase Robinson, *Empire and Elites after the Muslim Conquest: The Transformation of Northern Mesopotamia* (Cambridge, U.K.: Cambridge University Press, 2000), 66–70.

[50] Ibid. 72.

was previously semi-occupied but which only became a full city in the late seventh century.[51]

Along with that of Jonah there are a number of holy sites associated with biblical figures in upper Mesopotamia. Like the Mosque of Nabi Yunis, these sites have historically been visited by Muslims, Christians, and Jews, but often go back to Christian origins. The biblical prophet Nahum of the seventh century B.C.E, according to the prophetic text which bears his name, prophesied among the Ninevites and was, "of Elqosh."[52] Elqosh is a disputed site, but the town of Alqosh, north of Mosul, has been posited by locals as this city (and some modern scholars have accepted the authenticity of this assertion). There was a monastery and a shrine of the Prophet Nahum there from at least the tenth century C.E.[53] This localizing was reinforced by texts such as the *Lives of the Prophets*, which, among a number of other languages, was translated into Syriac.[54] The eastern traditions around Esther and her tomb, which remains a holy place for Jews in contemporary Iran, could provide another perspective on this eastern reception of biblical figures depicted as from the east.

Daniel is another eastern scriptural figure who takes on special significance in the Church of the East. References to Daniel and his companions are commonly found in early Christian martyr acts. However, when used in texts composed in the Persian Empire these figures have a more precise significance. For example, in the *Martyrdom of Simeon bar Sabba'e*, which describes the mid-fourth-century martyrdom of the Catholicos (i.e., Patriarch) as well as others, Guhishtazad,[55] a Christian martyr at the Shah's court is specifically compared to Daniel.

> This is the believer, son of Daniel the believer, to whom he was similar in all things. The former served Darius, the latter Shapur. The former the King of Media and Persia, the latter the king of Persia and Media. The former did not fear the lions, the latter was not moved nor agitated by the sword.[56]

---

[51] For the foundation of Mosul, see ibid. 63–89.

[52] Nah 1:1.

[53] Fiey, *L'Assyrie Chrétienne* II:396–400; on Jews and Christian contesting the site, see 398–99.

[54] On this text and its Christian provenance, see David Satran, *Biblical Prophets in Byzantine Palestine: Reassessing the Lives of the Prophets* (Leiden: E.J. Brill, 1995).

[55] J.-M. Fiey, *Saints syriaques* (ed. L. I Conrad; Princeton, N.J.: Darwin Press, 2004), 87–88. This may be the same as another Guhishtazad identified in the sources, ibid., 88.

[56] *Acta martyrum et sanctorum syriace* (ed. P. Bedjan), II:177.

This local "Danielic" awareness appears in several places in this text as well as other Syriac martyr texts.[57] We also find it in the Mesopotamian apocalypticism of the seventh century, such as the *Syriac Apocalypse of Daniel*, in which Sennacherib also plays an important role.[58]

Parallel to this modeling of persecution on that of eastern kings in the Danielic tradition, so also the good relations between Christians and the government could also be put in scriptural terms. In the canons of the Synod of Mar Aba of 544, Khusraw I is said to be a second Cyrus.[59] The significance of being from the East, particularly Persia, can also be seen in how Syriac Christians addressed Christianity's place vis-à-vis Zoroastrianism.[60] For example, both West- and East-Syrian sources place a particular focus on how it was that the Magi knew that Jesus was going to be born.[61] This speculation could at times become extensive. For example, the East Syrian Theodore Bar Konai (d. after 792) quotes a supposed dialogue between Zardosht (Zoroaster) and his disciples in which Zardosht tells them about the coming of the Messiah.[62]

---

[57] On the prior page when the confessor prays: "Introduce me to the number of your heavenly sheep, that I may be a son to the apostles and a brother to the martyrs who have been crowned in the West and a good model for your people in the East." *Acta martyrum et sanctorum syriace* (ed. P. Bedjan), II:176.7–9. At one point the texts states: "This is the true martyr of the land of the East who through Simeon who was bishop and martyr of the East was ensnared to life." *Acta martyrum et sanctorum syriace* (ed. P. Bedjan), II:178.1–3; see also II:183.10–11. This tendency can be found in other texts, e.g., in the Pethion-Adurhormizd-Anahid cycle we find the prayer: "Show also now, Lord, your great power, as you showed it to Hananyah, Mishael, and his holy companions" (i.e., Shadrach, Meshach, and Abednego for Hananiah, Mishael, and Azariah). *Acta martyrum et sanctorum syriace* (ed. P. Bedjan), II:616.18–19. See also Barḥadbĕšabbā 'Arbaya, *La second partie de l'histoire ecclésiastique*, ed. and trans. F. Nau, *Patrologia Orientalis* 9:5 (Paris, 1913), 595.

[58] Matthias Henze, ed., *Syriac Apocalypse of Daniel* (Tübingen: Mohr Siebeck, 2001), 68–69. See pp. 2–11 for a discussion of apocalypses attributed to Daniel.

[59] J.-B. Chabot, trans., *Synodicon Orientale ou recueil des Synodes Nestoriens publié, traduit et annoté* (Notices et extraits de la Bibliothèque Nationale, Tome 37; Paris: Imprimerie Nationale 1902), 307–8; O. Braun, trans., *Das Buch der Synhados oder Synodicon Orientale* (Stuttgart: J. Roth, 1900; repr. Amsterdam: Philo, 1975), 99.

[60] One question that needs resolving is the degree to which material from Greek and Latin authors affected Syriac Christian perceptions of Zoroastrianism; cf. Albert de Jong, *Traditions of the Magi: Zoroastrianism in Greek and Latin Literature* (Leiden: E.J. Brill, 1997).

[61] The Chronicle of Pseudo-Dionysius of Tel-Mahre, written 775/6, preserves a possibly sixth- or seventh-century document, "The Story of the Magi," which provides details about the names of all twelve. Witold Witakowski, "The Magi in Syriac Tradition," paper read at the Syriac Studies conference in Washington, D.C. in August, 1995 (I thank Prof. Witakowski for sharing his unpublished work with me).

[62] Ibid.

The manuscript tradition of the pseudepigraphic 2 Baruch seems to depend partly on the tendencies I have been discussing. This text was composed by Jews in the period after the destruction of the Second Temple in 70 C.E. The text was preserved fully intact only in one Syriac manuscript.[63] However, part of the text has been copied repeatedly and become part of the West-Syrian liturgical tradition. This is the so-called Epistle of Baruch, which presents itself as a letter from the pseudepigraphic scribe of Jeremiah to the nine and a half tribes of the dispersion (78:1–87:1).[64] The interest in this particular portion of the text appears to derive from a self-conscious connection to the group of people referred to in it. The West-Syrian preservation of 2 Baruch and especially the Epistle of Baruch is perhaps a case where Christians who understood themselves as eastern in some way had a special identification with a particular text because it was marked as eastern in orientation.[65]

Joel Walker, in his recent book as well as in an article in the journal *ARAM*, suggests that, however "reinterpreted through the prisms of exegesis and folklore", there were "memories of ancient Assyria" within the Christian community of the later Sasanian Empire.[66] Walker's work focuses on the *Legend of Mar Qardagh*, a perhaps early seventh century martyr text whose cult site at Melqi, an unknown site outside of Arbela, seems to have been the important Neo-Assyrian site of Milqia, where the akitu temple of the goddess, Ishtar of Arbela, stood. Based on the suggestion of Paul Peeters, Walker argues that "the Qardagh legend must have developed

---

[63] Bibliotheca Ambrosiana B. 21 Inf., fols. 257a–265b in Milan, from the sixth or seventh century. Some short portions exist in West-Syrian lectionaries. There is also an Arabic version which follows the Syriac, but shows some Muslim adaptations, as well as a Greek fragment. See A.F.J. Klijn, "2 (Syriac Apocalypse of ) Baruch," in *The Old Testament Pseudepigrapha* (ed. J. H. Charlesworth; Garden City, N.Y.: Doubleday, 1983–1985), I:615–16.

[64] Thirty six copies of the letter are extant, cf. Mark F. Whitters, *The Epistle of Second Baruch: A Study in Form and Message* (London: Sheffield Academic Press, 2003), 12–14.

[65] Whitters, *Epistle of Second Baruch*, 21 argues that the ms. 7a1 in which we find the one full Syriac version of 2 Baruch may derive originally from a Jewish collection aimed at responding to the destruction of the temple, since the manuscript also contains 4 Ezra and an excerpt from book 6 of Josephus's *Jewish War*. However, I think it is more likely that the compilation is a later collection and, closer to Whitters second suggestion, that, if anything, the compiler's interests reflect sixth and especially seventh century Christian concerns about Jerusalem.

[66] Joel Thomas Walker, "The Legacy of Mesopotamia in Late Antique Iraq: The Christian Martyr Shrine at Melqi," *ARAM* 18–19 (2006–2007): 501. See also idem, *The Legend of Mar Qardagh: Narrative and Christian Heroism in Late Antique Iraq* (Berkeley: University of California Press, 2006), 249–54 and passim.

as a narrative that explained, for a Christian audience, how the tell at Melqi became a center for trade and religious observance."[67] Corresponding to the spatial continuity of the Milqia/Melqi site is the connections the *Legend of Mar Qardagh* draws between its hero and the ancient Near East. In typical classical biographical style the text describes Qardagh's lineage:

> Now holy Mar Qardagh was from a great people (*gensā*) from the stock of the kingdom of the Assyrians (*'ātūrāyē*). His father was descended from the renowned lineage of the house of Nimrod, and his mother from the renowned lineage of the house of Sennacherib. And he was born of pagan parents lost in the error of Magianism.[68]

Walker astutely goes through the place of Nimrod and Sennacherib in late antique, particularly Syriac, exegesis.

Beyond this it is worth noting the popularity within the region as a whole of Nimrod, the primordial king of Genesis transformed in later tradition into a giant who persecuted Abraham. The *Acts of Mar Mari*, a text that purports to describe the origins of Christianity in the East but in fact derives from perhaps the early Islamic period, praises Jesus specifically for the transformative power of his name in the East:

> Glory to you, Jesus, power that cannot be overpowered, for it was through simple and uneducated people that you filled the earth with the knowledge of the truth! Who could say to the East, mother of magic and astrology (*kaldāyūtā*), that it would bend its knees in worship of the Living and True God? Who could say to the sons of powerful Nimrod, that instead of an adversary tower that they built against God, they would offer him the fruits of love and thanksgiving, acknowledging him as the true Creator?[69]

Modern Urfa, that is, ancient Edessa, a key center for early Syriac Christianity, maintains to the present day a tradition that Nimrod resided in the city. On the rock acropolis that forms a natural fortress in the middle of the city, the two columns remaining from an earlier structure, one of which bears one of the oldest extant Syriac inscriptions, are commonly known as the throne of Nimrod.[70] The most popular tourist destination in south eastern Turkey, Nemrut Dag, or Nimrod Mountain, where the famous massive heads of the kings of Comagene remain, also attests to the continuous tradition in the region of a special identification with Nimrod.

---

[67] Walker, "Legacy of Mesopotamia," 498.

[68] *Acta martyrum et sanctorum syriace* (ed. P. Bedjan),:II:443, text also in J.-B. Abbeloos, "Acta Mar Ḳardaghi," *Analecta Bollandiana* 9 (1890): 5–105 (paragraph 3), translation from Walker, *Legend of Mar Qardagh*, 20.

[69] *Acta martyrum et sanctorum syriace* (ed. P. Bedjan), I:90; translation from Harrak, *The Acts of Mār Mārī the Apostle*, 74–75.

[70] Drijvers and Healey, *Old Syriac Inscriptions*, As1 (D27).

Walker's work is brilliant in its fine balance of textual and concrete archeological analysis. However, I wonder if he is correct in positing a folkloric continuity between the Neo-Assyrians and the late Sasanian period. He fully brings together the little evidence we have for the "dark ages" running from the Median sack of Nineveh in 612 B.C.E. through the centuries that follow. To be sure, we know that local beliefs and practices persisted for a long time, in fact even later than the last datable cuneiform tablet of 75 C.E. Although transformed or Hellenized, the local gods continued to receive worship in Late Antiquity. But as Walker himself acknowledges we have no evidence for Milqia/Melqi itself from 600 B.C.E. to 600 C.E. Melqi then continued to be a Christian center through the Middle Ages; as Walker points out, "the monastery at Melqi had become the burial chapel for the metropolitan bishops of Arbela."[71] He then sums up the relationship to the Assyrian past: "The only trace of its pre-Christian heritage were the garbled memories of 'Assyria' embedded in the *History of Mar Qardagh*."[72] I would question this.

I doubt any near eastern connections can be found that are not also attested in scripture or post-scriptural exegetical tradition. Perhaps it is not a coincidence that the positive focus on the ancient Near East which we find in this text and in others only appears in the sixth century, at the same time that the Church of the East was coming into its own. Furthermore, the antagonists in the *Legend of Mar Qardagh* are Zoroastrians and the site at Melqi seems to have been a Zoroastrian fire temple. Thus, we have to look at the synchronic function of such myths and at how the ancient past is being employed to address contemporary communal issues.

Another text that engages in the kind of "Assyrianizing" I am addressing is the *Life of Mar Behnam*, where Sennacherib, the Zoroastrian (!) king of Assyria, as well as his children convert to Christianity after miraculous healings.[73] This is not unlike the story behind the "prayer of Nabonidus" and other tales of pagan kings converting after a divine cure, such as the story of St. Nino and the conversion of the royal family of Georgia to Christianity. This focus on Assyria, particularly the depiction of it as a space open to Christianization, also may help to explain the passage in the *Liber Scholiorum* of Theodore Bar Konai in which Zoroaster is described

---

[71] Walker, "Legacy of Mesopotamia," 500.

[72] Ibid.

[73] *Acta martyrum et sanctorum syriace* (ed. P. Bedjan), II:97–441. For a discussion of this text, see Helen Younansardaroud, "Die Legende von Mār Behnām," in *Syriaca: Zur Geschichte, Theologie, Liturgie, und Gegenswartslage der syrischen Kirche: 2. Deutsches Syrologen-Symposium (Juli 2000, Wittenberg)* (ed. M. Tamcke; Münster, Hamburg, and London: LIT Verlag, 2002), 185–96.

as a captive brought from Samaria to Assyria who flees Nineveh for "Sagastan" in order to fulfill his desire for women.[74] Apparently, according to this anti-Zoroastrian anecdote, the moral standards of the Assyrian women were higher than those in Sagastan.[75]

I suspect that parallels to the kind of scriptural self-localization that I have been discussing can also be found in Rabbinic sources, however, with one significant difference. In the opposite way, the Rabbis – no matter how many centuries Jews lived in Mesopotamia and however much the relationship between Palestine and Babylonia was renegotiated – understood themselves as in *Galuta*, exile. As we know, exile became a central metaphor for Judaism until the metaphor was concretized with the rise of Jewish nationalism. Scripture as well as Jewish and Christian traditions carry with them a certain geography and it is natural for Jews and Christians to employ this geography when they reside in those regions it describes (as some of the contemporary American evangelical Christian support for the invasion of Iraq shows for Christians who do not even reside in Mesopotamia). We find a similar phenomenon in the spread of the Thomas tradition among the Christians of India. Once this story reached India, the exotic India of the *Acts of Thomas*, a c. 200 C.E. text composed in Syria, possibly Edessa, became local and indigenous.

A catalyst to this imaginative localization in the East may have been the method of exegesis of the Church of the East. Although the distinction between Alexandrian and Anthiochene exegesis is no longer as clear as scholars once thought, there is a strong tendency in Antiochene – and therefore Syriac – exegesis, especially in the Church of the East, to look at texts on the historical level.[76] Here I do not mean "history" in our modern sense of the word, but rather "history" as it is practiced in patristic exegesis, such as Theodore of Mopsuestia's commentaries, where there is a focus on God's interest in humans' wellbeing from generation to generation and the diversity of scripture is not simply allegorized away.[77] Such

---

[74] Sagastan may be the contemporary province of Sistan in eastern Iran. However, it may be used in general to refer to any land associated with the Sakas, an ancient Iranian people, who lived in Central Asia and were possibly related to the Scythians.

[75] Theodore Bar Konai, *Liber Scholiorum* (ed. A. Scher; (Corpus Scriptorum Christianorum Orientalium, Scrip. Syri, ser. II, t. 66; Paris: Carolus Poussielgue, 1912), 295.24–27.

[76] For a general discussion on the relationship between Alexandrian and Antiochene exegesis, see Frances M. Young, *Biblical Exegesis and the Formation of Christian Culture* (Cambridge, U.K.: Cambridge University Press, 1997), 161–213.

[77] See, e.g., D. S. Wallace-Hadrill, *Christian Antioch: A Study of Early Christian Thought in the East* (Cambridge, U.K.: Cambridge University Press, 1982), 61. On Theodore's influence on the Church of the East, see Becker, *Fear of God*, 113–25.

exegetical work would have had a particular effect on readers who lived in those lands described by scripture, although the tendency shows up more often in hagiography, perhaps due to the popular interest of such texts.

Another factor that may help us to understand this tendency is the political dynamic of the Christian community of the Sasanian and later Arab empires. Christians in the East never had a Constantine. Communal differences would have increased after the Arab conquest: increasing arabicization would have sharpened their awareness of cultural difference and increased a sense of "Assyrian" peoplehood. Arabs had been settling on the margins and even within the cities of Aramaic speakers for several centuries, but with the Arab conquest in the seventh century Syriac Christians became aware of a new people. In fact, as scholars have pointed out, for some time the early Muslims were simply understood by Syriac Christians in ethnic terms as descendents of Hagar and not as introducing any particularly new theology or religious practice.[78]

Instead of the older historiographical model, which simply posits a progressive hellenization of Syriac Christianity and a move away from an indigenous form of Christianity, I am imagining a development of indigenous Christianity via the negotiation of received traditions from the West. Ephrem of Nisibis (d. 373), an author who has in the past been represented as a pure Semite, has been re-characterized in more recent scholarship as a Nicene Christian, more in tune with Roman church developments than he was previously imagined.[79] In contrast, it is especially by the early sixth century that we begin to see Christians in the East imagining themselves as easterners, not coincidentally at the time when the separate church hierarchies were developing for both the West and the East Syrians.[80] This de-

[78] See, e.g., Sebastian P. Brock, "Syriac Views of Emergent Islam," in *Studies on the First Century of Islamic Society* (ed. G. H. A. Juynboll; Carbondale-Edwardsville: Southern Illinois University Press, 1982), 9–21, 199–203; repr. in Sebastian P. Brock, *Syriac Perspectives on Late Antiquity* (London: Variorum, 1984), ch. 8, and G. J. Reinink, "The Beginnings of Syriac Apologetic Literature in Response to Islam," *Oriens Christianus* 77 (1993): 165–87.

[79] E.g., Sidney Griffith, "Setting Right the Church of Syria: Saint Ephraem's Hymns against Heresies," in *The Limits of Ancient Christianity: Essays on Late Antique Thought and Culture in Honor of R. A. Markus* (ed. W. E. Klingshirn and M. Vessey; Ann Arbor: University of Michigan Press, 1999), 97–114

[80] E.g., Becker, *Fear of God*, 12, or Wilhelm Baum and Dietmar W. Winkler, *The Church of the East: A Concise History* (London: Routledge, 2003; first published *Die Apostolische Kirche des Ostens*. Klagenfurt: Verlag Kitab, 2000), 7–41. For the West Syrians, see Ernest Honigmann, *Évêques et Évêchés Monophysites d'Asie Antérieure au VIe Siècle* (Corpus Scriptorum Christianorum Orientalium Subsidia 2; Louvain, 1951) and now Volker-Lorenz Menze, *The Making of a Church: The Syrian Orthodox in the Shadow of Byzantium and the Papacy* (Ph.D. diss., Princeton University, 2004).

velopment of self-consciousness is closely tied to the influx of Greek texts, ideas, and monastic practices into the East.

Aside from the historiographical interest it may have, this material may help us to think about the complex relationship between ethnicity and religion.[81] Scholars have noted a shift in Late Antiquity from a focus on ethnic identity to one on religious community.[82] Christianity (and its opposite in a sense, Judaism) had come into being, where previously the opposite of Jew was Greek. Religion began to take on the characteristics associated in the West with "religion," such as the centralization of scripture, an emphasis on monotheism (or rather, henotheism), and a concern for communal boundaries. Daniel Boyarin states "Christianity's new notion of self-definition via 'religious' alliance was gradually replacing self-definition via kinship and land." [83] This fits with much of Boyarin's earlier work and the distinctions he draws between Paul and other Jews,[84] and is further played out, according to him, with imperial Christianity in the fourth and fifth centuries.[85]

My interest in this is not one of either/or-ness: is it religion, or peoplehood, or sometimes both? But how do these categories relate to one another? Is it that while in our (post-)nationalist setting religious arguments raise the stakes and make social conflict more intractable and the barriers of ethnic difference greater,[86] while in Late Antiquity it was ethnic arguments that could raise the stakes since in the end the religious world was one that was shared? Religion and ethnicity are complexly related in our own world, each often serving to shore up the claims of the other. In a sense, Boyarin's view of Late Antiquity is a mirror image of Durkheim's reading of modernity: while the latter saw a shift from religion to nationalism in the modern period, the former finds a shift from ethnicity to religion

---

[81] This conversation has been invigorated of late for the pre-Constantinian period with the publication of Denise Kimber Buell, *Why This New Race: Ethnic Reasoning in Early Christianity* (New York: Columbia University Press, 2005). Also see Aaron Johnson's *Ethnicity and Argument in Eusebius'* Praeparatio Evangelica (Oxford: Oxford University Press, 2006).

[82] See, for example, Shaye J. D. Cohen, *The Beginnings of Jewishness: Boundaries, Varieties, Uncertainties* (Berkeley: University of California Press, 1999), 109–39.

[83] Daniel Boyarin, *Borderlines: The Partition of Judeo-Christianity* (Philadelphia: University of Pennsylvania Press, 2004), 202.

[84] For example, see his discussion in Daniel Boyarin, *A Radical Jew: Paul and the Politics of Identity* (Berkeley: University of California Press, 1994).

[85] Daniel Boyarin, *Dying for God: Martyrdom and the Making of Christianity and Judaism* (Stanford: Stanford University Press, 1999), 18.

[86] Janet Jakobsen, "Is Secularism Less Violent than Religion?" in *Interventions: Activists and Academics Respond to Violence* (ed. E. A. Castelli and J. Jakobsen; New York: Palgrave Macmillan, 2004), 53–67.

in Late Antiquity.[87] However, the rise of religion as a category in Late Antiquity is not as simple as this seems to suggest.

Yes, for many, Christians were a people from all the peoples, the only land that Christians belonged to was the metaphorical one in heaven, and the only Jerusalem was the one above. Land and genealogy were metaphorized away and language was often treated as an interchangeable system of conventional equivalencies, ultimately based upon a notion of semiotics found in Greek philosophical literature, such as Aristotle's *De Interpretatione*. However, there were exceptions to this: the rise of the cult of the saints and the very beginnings of pilgrimage to the holy land that we see in this period point to a counter trend of localization and particularism.[88]

Furthermore, I am not suggesting that Syriac Christians did not engage in Christian universalism as well. For example, the Syriac *deḥltā* ("fear") as opposed to the more specific *deḥlat alāhā*, equivalent to the Greek *theosebeia*, and its opposite, *deḥlat ptakrē* ("idolatry"), developed into a term not unlike *religio* or the Arabic *dīn*. For example, in the preface to the c. 600 Syriac collection of prophecies aimed at converting the pagan community of Harran "fear" is employed in this way as a general abstract category.[89] Similarly, from Bardaiṣan of Edessa (d. c. 222) onward we find references in Syriac literature to the special, that is, metaphorical, peoplehood of Christians.[90] They are a people, like the Arabs, the Gauls, and the Brittani, but since they are everywhere they transcend the local.

Elsewhere I have commented on the tendency in the Syriac version of Eusebius's *Ecclesiastical History*, probably translated from Greek in the late fourth century, to employ pedagogical terms.[91] This tendency, however, must also be understood as a downplaying of Eusebius's habit of using racial language in his discussion of Christianity. For example, the Greek *to*

---

[87] Cf. "The greatest work ever written in the sociology of religions, Émile Durkheim's *Elementary Forms of Religious Life* (1912), is, at its core, a discussion of how nationalism becomes the chief religion of a putatively secular, but only nontheist modernity." Bruce Lincoln, *Holy Terror: Thinking about Religion after September 11* (Chicago: University of Chicago Press, 2003), 63.

[88] For example, see comments at Peter Brown, *The Cult of the Saints: Its Rise and Function in Latin Christianity* (Chicago: University of Chicago Press, 1981), 86 and 124.

[89] Sebastian P. Brock, "A Syriac Collection of Prophecies of the Pagan Philosophers," *Orientalia Lovaniensia Periodica* 14 (1983): 214 (Syriac) 227 (English); repr. in Sebastian P. Brock, *Studies in Syriac Christianity* (Aldershot, Hampshire: Ashgate, 1992), ch. 7.

[90] H. J. W. Drijvers, *Bardaiṣan of Edessa* (Studia Semitica Neerlandica 6; Assen 1966), 46 (pp. 58–61).

[91] Becker, *Fear of God*, 27–28.

*genos* ("race") is rendered *tulmādā* ("instruction").[92] In fact, the Syriac tendency to understand Christianity in pedagogical terms may be understood as a form of universalism, especially since conversion to Christianity is often set in pedagogical terms in Syriac sources.[93]

Despite some intriguing and unique examples of the tendency toward universalism within Syriac texts, the material I have discussed in this essay shows a strong emphasis on peoplehood, land, and language among Syriac Christians and much of this derives from scripture. The recent project in Leiden led by Bas Ter Haar Romeny has looked at a tendency toward ethnic communal notions among the West Syrians and the development of the church into an ethnic community during the Middle Ages.[94] However, it is not always clear in which direction the tendency goes. In fact, some texts use categories that simply confuse our own and further analysis is required. For example, in the very late *History of Mar Awgen*, a text which intriguingly describes Jacob of Nisibis, the fourth century bishop who became a representative in the later tradition for Nicene orthodoxy, as a descendent of the family of James, the brother of the Lord,[95] we find a passage that exemplifies the ethno-religious complex which needs to be unraveled in the Syriac sources. At one point, the text describes a Marcionite "heretic" in the following manner:

> There was a certain man from the confession (*tawdītēh*) of the accursed Marcion, this man who crucified the people (*'ammā*) of the Christians, and he belonged to the race (*gensā*) from the land of Pontus and was an important person in the kingdom (*malkūtā*) of the Romans.[96]

"Confession," "people," "race," and "kingdom" are terms that often overlap and share multiple valences. Most noteworthy in this passage is the tension between "people" and "race." Both are ethnic terms, but the latter has no religious valence, while the former, also used at times in Syriac literature as a shorthand for the Jews, that is, the "people" par excellence, has a more biblical sense and is less genealogical. In future work one might attempt to untangle the complex semantic and categorical relations between religion and ethnicity as employed within the Syriac Christian

[92] Eusebius, *Ecclesiastical History* 2.17.67; W. Wright and N. McLean, eds., *The Ecclesiastical History of Eusebius in Syriac* (Cambridge, U.K.: Cambridge University Press, 1898), 88.

[93] See the discussion in Becker, *Fear of God*, 22–40.

[94] Bas Ter Haar Romeny, "From Religious Association to Ethnic Community: a Research Project on Identity Formation among the Syrian Orthodox under Muslim Rule," *Islam and Christian-Muslim Relations* 16 (2005): 377–99.

[95] *Acta martyrum et sanctorum syriace* (ed. P. Bedjan), III:397

[96] Ibid., III:402–3.

communities, both historically and in the present.[97] Ironically, while I would question the historical accuracy of linking contemporary Assyrians with those of the ancient Near East, the term "Syriac" itself is a modern, Western term only taken up of late by some parts of the "Syriac" community.

[97] Note Aaron P. Johnson's point at the end of his review of Buell's *Why This New Race* for the Bryn Mawr Classical Review, n.p. [cited 16 Oct. 2006]. Online: http://ccat.sas.upenn.edu/bmcr/2006/2006-02-31.html.

# List of Contributors

ADAM H. BECKER is an Assistant Professor in the Religious Studies Program and the Classics Department at New York University. He received his PhD from the Religion Department at Princeton University in 2004. His publications include several articles on both Syriac Christian sources and Jewish-Christian relations in antiquity. His book, *The Fear of God and the Beginning of Wisdom: The School of Nisibis and the Development of Christian Scholastic Culture in Late Antique Mesopotamia* (2006), is an intellectual and institutional history of the foremost Syriac Christian center of learning in late antiquity. He also co-edited *The Ways That Never Parted: Jews and Christians in Late Antiquity and the Early Middle Ages* (2003; repr. 2007).

RA'ANAN S. BOUSTAN is an Assistant Professor in the Departments of History and Near Eastern Languages and Cultures at the University of California, Los Angeles. His research focuses on early Jewish mysticism, Jewish–Christian relations in Late Antiquity, and Jewish society and culture in Roman-Byzantine Palestine. His publications include *From Martyr to Mystic: Rabbinic Martyrology and the Making of Merkavah Mysticism* (2005) and *Heavenly Realms and Earthly Realities in Late Antique Religions* (co-edited with A.Y. Reed; 2004).

GLEN W. BOWERSOCK is Professor Emeritus of Ancient History at the Institute for Advanced Study. Before joining the Institute's School of Historical Studies in 1980, he was professor of classics and ancient history at Harvard University. Prof. Bowersock, who has been awarded a number of honorary doctorates, has published over 300 articles and books on the ancient world, including *Roman Arabia* (1983), *Hellenism in Late Antiquity* (1990), and *Martyrdom and Rome* (1995). His most recent books are *Mosaics as History: The Near East from Late Antiquity to Islam* (2006), *Lorenzo Valla: The Donation of Constantine* (2007), and *Saggi sulla tradizione classica dal settecento al novecento* (2007).

HARRIET I. FLOWER is Professor of Classics at Princeton University. She teaches and writes about Roman social and cultural history, with a special emphasis on material culture. Her research has focused on various facets of the study of memory and of spectacle in Roman culture, notably during the Republic. She has published *Ancestor Masks and Aristocratic Power in Roman Culture* (1996) and *The Art of Forgetting: Disgrace and Oblivion in Roman Political Culture* (2006), as well as many articles. In addition, she is the editor of the *Cambridge Companion to the Roman Republic* (2004). Her current research is a book on the city of Rome during the republican period.

GREGG GARDNER is a doctoral candidate in Religion at Princeton University, specializing in religions of late antiquity. He holds an M.A. in the History of the Jewish People from Hebrew University. His research interests include rabbinic and Hellenistic Jewish literature, as well as the archaeology of Palestine in the Greco-Roman era. His dissertation examines early rabbinic texts on charity and social justice, and his publications include "Jewish Leadership and Hellenistic Civic Benefaction in the Second Century B.C.E." (2007) and "Astrology in the Talmud: An Analysis of Bavli Shabbat 156" (2008).

ELIZABETH KESSLER-DIMIN is a doctoral candidate in Classical Archaeology at Princeton University. She has a B.A. in Classics from New York University and a M.A. in Classical Archaeology from Princeton. Elizabeth is writing her dissertation on the religious iconography of pagans and Christians in Late Antiquity and its origins in ancient Greco-Roman art.

LEE I. LEVINE is professor of Jewish History and Archaeology at the Hebrew University of Jerusalem. His research interests include the ancient synagogue, Jewish art in antiquity, the history and archaeology of Jerusalem, Judaism and Hellenism, as well as the rabbinic class and the Patriarchate in late Roman Palestine. He is currently working on a monograph entitled *Visual Judaism: Art, History, and Identity in Late Antiquity*, which attempts to explain the dramatic and extensive appearance of Jewish art in many Jewish communities of Late Antiquity (third–seventh centuries C.E.), in light of the new historical reality then crystallizing in the Byzantine-Christian era. His recent publications include: *The Ancient Synagogue: The First Thousand Years*, (revised and expanded paperback edition, 2005), "Bet Še'arim in Its Patriarchal Context" (2005), "Figurative Art in Jewish Society" (2005), "The First-Century Synagogue: Critical Reassessments and Assessments of the Critical" (2004), "Jewish Archaeology in Late Antiquity: Art Architecture, and Inscriptions" (2006).

STEVE MASON is Canada Research Chair in Greco-Roman Cultural Interaction and Professor of History at York University. Among his many publications are *Flavius Josephus on the Pharisees* (1991; paperback edition, 2003) and *Josephus and the New Testament* (2nd edition, 2003). He is the general editor of the twelve-volume project, *Flavius Josephus: Translation and Commentary*, published by Brill, for which he has also prepared the volumes on Josephus's *Life* and *War 2*. He is currently writing *The Judean-Roman War of 66–73 CE* and *Flavius Josephus: An Introduction*.

DORON MENDELS is the Max and Sophie Mydans Professor of the Humanities at the Hebrew University of Jerusalem. His research projects include Hellenistic historiography in the ancient Near East during the fourth century B.C.E. to the fourth century C.E., nationalism in the Hellenistic Near East, Jewish political thought in the Graeco-Roman era, as well as communication and media issues concerning the ancient world. Among his books are: *Identity, Religion and Historiography: Studies in Hellenistic History* (1998); *The Media Revolution of Early Christianity* (1999); *Memory in Jewish, Pagan and Christian Societies of the Graeco-Roman World* (2004). He is currently preparing a commentary on the Book of First Maccabees for the *Hermeneia* series.

KEVIN L. OSTERLOH is an Assistant Professor of Ancient History in the Department of History at Miami University. He received his Ph.D. in the Department of Religion and the Program in the Ancient World at Princeton University in 2007. His dissertation, "The Reinvention of Judean Collective Identity in a Hellenistic World Contending with Rome," demonstrates how Judean elites of the second-century B.C.E. reinvented their communal identity through the appropriation and subversion of Greekness in conscious emulation of contemporary Roman attitudes with respect to Greek culture and communities.

YANNIS PAPADOYANNAKIS is Lecturer in Greek patristics at Wolfson College, at the University of Oxford. His research focuses on the Christianization of the Roman Empire, apologetics, and late antique and Byzantine religious life and literature. He is currently preparing a monograph on the apologetics of Theodoret of Cyrrhus against the Greeks.

ANNETTE YOSHIKO REED is an Assistant Professor in the Department of Religious Studies at the University of Pennsylvania. Her publications include *Fallen Angels and the History of Judaism and Christianity* (2005), *Heavenly Realms and Earthly Realities in Late Antique Religions* (co-edited with R.S. Boustan; 2004); and *The Ways that Never Parted: Jews and Christians in Late Antiquity and the Early Middle Ages* (co-edited with Adam H. Becker; 2003). She is presently working on a book about "Jewish-Christianity."

PETER SCHÄFER is the Ronald O. Perelman Professor of Judaic Studies and Professor of Religion at Princeton University. His teaching and research interests include Jewish History in Late Antiquity, the religion and literature of Rabbinic Judaism, Jewish Mysticism, 19th and 20th century *Wissenschaft des Judentums*, and Jewish Magic. In 1994 he was awarded the German Leibniz Prize and in 2006 the Mellon Distinguished Achievement Award. His latest books are: *Jesus in the Talmud* (Princeton University Press, 2007) and *Mirror of His Beauty: Feminine Images of God from the Bible to the Early Kabbalah*, (Princeton University Press, 2002). Co-editor of *Jewish Studies Quarterly* since 1993, Schäfer currently serves as the Director of the Program in Judaic Studies at Princeton. During the 2007–08 academic year, he is a fellow at the Wissenschaftskolleg/Institute for Advanced Study, Berlin, Germany.

MOULIE VIDAS entered the Religion program at Princeton after studies in the universities of Tel Aviv and Jerusalem and the Hartman Institute of Advanced Judaic Studies. He is interested in the history of religion in late antiquity and various disciplinarily traditional questions of modern Talmudic scholarship.

HOLGER ZELLENTIN is an Assistant Professor of Rabbinics at the Richard S. Dinner Center for Jewish Studies at the Graduate Theological Union in Berkeley. His dissertation, in the Department of Religion at Princeton University, was titled *Late Antiquity Upside Down – Rabbinic Parodies of Christian and Jewish Literature* (2007). He is the editor, together with Eduard Iricinschi, of *Heresy and Identity in Late Antiquity* (Mohr Siebeck, 2008).

# Index of Sources

## Hebrew Bible/Septuagint

## Dead Sea Scrolls



## Pseudepigrapha



## Rabbinic Literature

## Nag Hammadi

## Christian Pseudepigrapha



## Pseudo-Clementine Literature

## Church Fathers and Histories

## Medieval Christian Literature



## Greco-Roman Literature

## Other Greco-Roman Sources

## Byzantine and Syriac Literature

# Index of Names and Subjects

# Texts and Studies in Ancient Judaism
Alphabetical Index

*Hezser, Catherine:* Form, Function, and Historical Significance of the Rabbinic Story in Yerushalmi Neziqin. 1993. *Vol. 37.*
– Jewish Literacy in Roman Palestine. 2001. *Vol. 81.*
– see *Schäfer, Peter*
– The Social Structure of the Rabbinic Movement in Roman Palestine. 1997. *Vol. 66.*
*Hezser, Catherine* (Ed.): Rabbinic Law in its Roman and Near Eastern Context. 2003. *Vol. 97.*
*Hirschfelder, Ulrike:* see *Schäfer, Peter*
*Horbury, W.:* see *Krauss, Samuel*
*Houtman, Alberdina:* Mishnah und Tosefta. 1996. *Vol. 59.*
*Ilan, Tal:* Jewish Women in Greco-Roman Palestine. 1995. *Vol. 44.*
– Integrating Woman into Second Temple History. 1999. *Vol. 76.*
– Lexicon of Jewish Names in Late Antiquity. 2002. *Vol. 91.*
– Silencing the Queen. 2006. *Vol. 115.*
*Instone Brewer, David:* Techniques and Assumptions in Jewish Exegesis before 70 CE. 1992. V*ol. 30.*
*Ipta, Kerstin:* see *Schäfer, Peter*
*Iricinschi, Eduard* and *Holger M. Zellentin* (Ed.): Heresy and Identity in Late Antiquity. 2008. *Vol. 119.*
*Jacobs, Martin:* Die Institution des jüdischen Patriarchen. 1995. *Vol. 52.*
*Kasher, Aryeh:* The Jews in Hellenistic and Roman Egypt. 1985. *Vol. 7.*
– Jews, Idumaeans, and Ancient Arabs. 1988. *Vol. 18.*
– Jews and Hellenistic Cities in Eretz-Israel. 1990. *Vol. 21.*
*Knittel, Thomas:* Das griechische ‚Leben Adams und Evas'. 2002. *Vol. 88.*
*Krauss, Samuel:* The Jewish-Christian Controversy from the earliest times to 1789. Vol. I. Ed. by *W. Horbury.* 1996. *Vol. 56.*
*Kuhn, Peter:* Offenbarungsstimmen im Antiken Judentum. 1989. *Vol. 20.*
*Kuyt, Annelies:* The ‚Descent' to the Chariot. 1995. *Vol. 45.*
*Lange, A.:* see *Albani, M.*
*Lange, Nicholas de:* Greek Jewish Texts from the Cairo Genizah. 1996. *Vol. 51.*
*Lapin, Hayim:* Economy, Geography, and Provincial History in Later Roman Galilee. 2001. *Vol. 85.*
*Lehnardt, Andreas:* Qaddish. 2002. *Vol. 87.*
*Leonhardt, Jutta:* Jewish Worship in Philo of Alexandria. 2001. *Vol. 84.*
*Lohmann, Uta:* see *Schäfer, Peter*
*Loopik, M. van* (Transl. a. comm.): The Ways of the Sages and the Way of the World. 1991. *Vol. 26.*
*Luttikhuizen, Gerard P.:* The Revelation of Elchasai. 1985. *Vol. 8.*
*Mach, Michael:* Entwicklungsstadien des jüdischen Engelglaubens in vorrabbinischer Zeit. 1992. *Vol. 34.*
*Mendels, Doron:* The Land of Israel as a Political Concept in Hasmonean Literature. 1987. *Vol. 15.*
*Miller, Stuart S.:* Sages and Commoners in Late Antique *'Erez* Israel. 2006. *Vol. 111.*
*Moscovitz, Leib:* Talmudic Reasoning. 2002. *Vol. 89.*
*Mutius, Georg von:* see *Schäfer, Peter*
*Necker, Gerold:* see *Schäfer, Peter*
*Netzer, Ehud:* The Architecture of Herod, the Great Builder. 2006. *Vol. 117.*
*Niehoff, Maren:* Philo on Jewish Identity and Culture. 2001. *Vol. 86.*
*Noy, David, Alexander Panayotov,* and *Hanswulf Bloedhorn* (Ed.): Inscriptiones Judaicae Orientis.
Vol. 1: Eastern Europe. 2004. *Vol. 101.*

–, and *Hanswulf Bloedhorn* (Ed.): Inscriptiones Judaicae Orientis. Vol. 3: Syria and Cyprus. 2004. *Vol. 102.*
*Olyan, Saul M.:* A Thousand Thousands Served Him. 1993. *Vol. 36.*
*Oppenheimer, Aharon:* Between Rome and Babylon. 2005. *Vol. 108.*
*Orlov, Andrei A.:* The Enoch-Metatron Tradition. 2005. *Vol. 107.*
*Osterloh, Kevin L.:* see *Gardner, Gregg*
*Otterbach, Rina:* see *Schäfer, Peter*
*Panayotov, Alexander:* see *Noy, David*
*Prigent, Pierre:* Le Judaisme et l'image. 1990. *Vol. 24.*
*Pucci Ben Zeev, Miriam:* Jewish Rights in the Roman World. 1998. *Vol. 74.*
*Pummer, Reinhard:* Early Christian Authors on Samaritans and Samaritanism. 2002. *Vol. 92.*
*Reed, A. Y.:* see *Becker, A. H.*
*Reeg, Gottfried* (Ed.): Die Geschichte von den Zehn Märtyrern. 1985. *Vol. 10.*
– see *Schäfer, Peter*
*Reichman, Ronen:* Abduktives Denken und talmudische Argumentation. 2005. *Vol. 113.*
–: Sifra und Mishna. 1998. *Vol. 68.*
*Renner, Lucie:* see *Schäfer, Peter*
*Rocca, Samuel:* Herod's Judaea. 2008. *Vol. 122.*
*Rohrbacher-Sticker, Claudia:* see *Schäfer, Peter*
*Rubenstein, Jeffrey L. (Ed.):* Creation and Composition. 2005. *Vol. 114.*
*Salvesen, A.* (Ed.): Origen's Hexapla and Fragments.1998. *Vol. 58.*
*Samely, Alexander:* The Interpretation of Speech in the Pentateuch Targums. 1992. *Vol. 27.*
*Schäfer, Peter:* Der Bar-Kokhba-Aufstand. 1981. *Vol. 1.*
– Hekhalot-Studien. 1988. *Vol. 19.*
*Schäfer, Peter* (Ed.): Geniza-Fragmente zur Hekhalot-Literatur. 1984. *Vol. 6.*
– The Bar Kokhba War Reconsidered. 2003. *Vol. 100.*
– see *Goldberg, Arnold*
– in cooperation with *Klaus Herrmann, Rina Otterbach, Gottfried Reeg, Claudia Rohrbacher-Sticker, Guido Weyer:* Konkordanz zur Hekhalot-Literatur. Band 1: 1986. *Vol. 12.*
– Band 2: 1988. *Vol. 13.*
*Schäfer, Peter, Margarete Schlüter, and Hans Georg von Mutius* (Ed.): Synopse zur Hekhalot-Literatur. 1981. *Vol. 2.*
*Schäfer, Peter* (Ed.) in cooperation with *Hans-Jürgen Becker, Klaus Herrmann, Ulrike Hirschfelder, Gerold Necker, Lucie Renner, Claudia Rohrbacher-Sticker, Stefan Siebers:* Übersetzung der Hekhalot-Literatur. Band 1: §§ 1–80. 1995. *Vol. 46.*
– Band 2: §§ 81–334. 1987. *Vol. 17.*
– Band 3: §§ 335–597. 1989. *Vol. 22.*
– Band 4: §§ 598–985. 1991. *Vol. 29.*
*Schäfer, Peter,* and *Hans-Jürgen Becker* (Ed.) in cooperation with *Anja Engel, Kerstin Ipta, Gerold Necker, Uta Lohmann, Martina Urban, Gert Wildensee:* Synopse zum Talmud Yerushalmi. Band I/1–2: 1991. *Vol. 31.*
– Band I/3–5: 1992. *Vol. 33.*
– Band I/6–11: 1992. *Vol. 35.*
– Band II/1–4: 2001. *Vol. 82.*
– Band II/5–12: 2001. *Vol. 83.*
– Band III: 1998. *Vol. 67.*
– Band IV: 1995. *Vol. 47.*

*Schäfer, Peter,* and *Shaul Shaked* (Ed.): Magische Texte aus der Kairoer Geniza. Band 1: 1994. *Vol. 42*
– Band 2: 1997. *Vol. 64.*
– Band 3: 1999. *Vol. 72.*
*Schäfer, Peter* (Ed.): The Talmud Yerushalmi and Graeco-Roman Culture I. 1998. *Vol. 71.*
*Schäfer, Peter,* and *Catherine Hezser* (Ed.): The Talmud Yerushalmi and Graeco-Roman Culture II. 2000. *Vol. 79.*
*Schäfer, Peter* (Ed.): The Talmud Yerushalmi and Graeco-Roman Culture III. 2003. *Vol. 93.*
*Schlüter, Margarete:* see *Goldberg, Arnold*
– see *Schäfer, Peter*
*Schmidt, Francis:* Le Testament Grec d'Abraham. 1986. *Vol. 11.*
*Schröder, Bernd:* Die ‚väterlichen Gesetze'. 1996. *Vol. 53.*
*Schwartz, Daniel R.:* Agrippa I. 1990. *Vol. 23.*
*Schwemer, Anna Maria:* Studien zu den frühjüdischen Prophetenlegenden. Vitae Prophetarum. Band I: 1995. *Vol. 49.*
– Band II (mit Beiheft: Synopse zu den Vitae Prophetarum): 1996. *Vol. 50.*
*Shahar, Yuval:* Josephus Geographicus. 2004. *Vol. 98.*
*Shaked, Shaul:* see *Gruenwald, I.*
– see *Schäfer, Peter*
*Shatzman, Israel:* The Armies of the Hasmonaeans and Herod. 1991. *Vol. 25.*
*Siebers, Stefan:* see *Schäfer, Peter*
*Sivertsev, Alexei:* Private Households and Public Politics in 3rd – 5th Century Jewish Palestine. 2002. *Vol. 90.*
*Spilsbury, Paul:* The Image of the Jew in Flavius Josephus' Paraphrase of the Bible. 1998. *Vol. 69.*
*Stroumsa, G.G.:* see *Gruenwald, I.*
*Stuckenbruck, Loren T.:* The Book of Giants from Qumran. 1997. *Vol. 63.*
*Swartz, Michael D.:* Mystical Prayer in Ancient Judaism. 1992. *Vol. 28.*
*Sysling, Harry:* Tehiyyat Ha-Metim. 1996. *Vol. 57.*
*Teppler, Yaakov Y.:* Birkat haMinim. 2007. *Vol. 120.*
*Tov, Emanuel:* Hebrew Bible, Greek Bible, and Qumran. 2008. *Vol. 121.*
*Urban, Martina:* see *Schäfer, Peter*
*Veltri, Giuseppe:* Eine Tora für den König Talmai. 1994. *Vol. 41.*
– Magie und Halakha. 1997. *Vol. 62.*
*Visotzky, Burton L.:* Golden Bells and Pomegranates. 2003. *Vol. 94.*
*Wandrey, Irina:* „Das Buch des Gewandes" und „Das Buch des Aufrechten". 2004. *Vol. 96.*
*Weyer, Guido:* see *Schäfer, Peter*
*Wewers, Gerd A.:* Probleme der Bavot-Traktate. 1984. *Vol. 5.*
*Wildensee, Gert:* see *Schäfer, Peter*
*Wilson, Walter T.:* The Mysteries of Rigtheousness. 1994. *Vol. 40.*
*Zellentin, Holger M.* see *Iricinschi, Eduard*

*For a complete catalogue please write to the publisher*
*Mohr Siebeck • P.O. Box 2030 • D-72010 Tübingen/Germany*
*Up-to-date information on the internet at www.mohr.de*